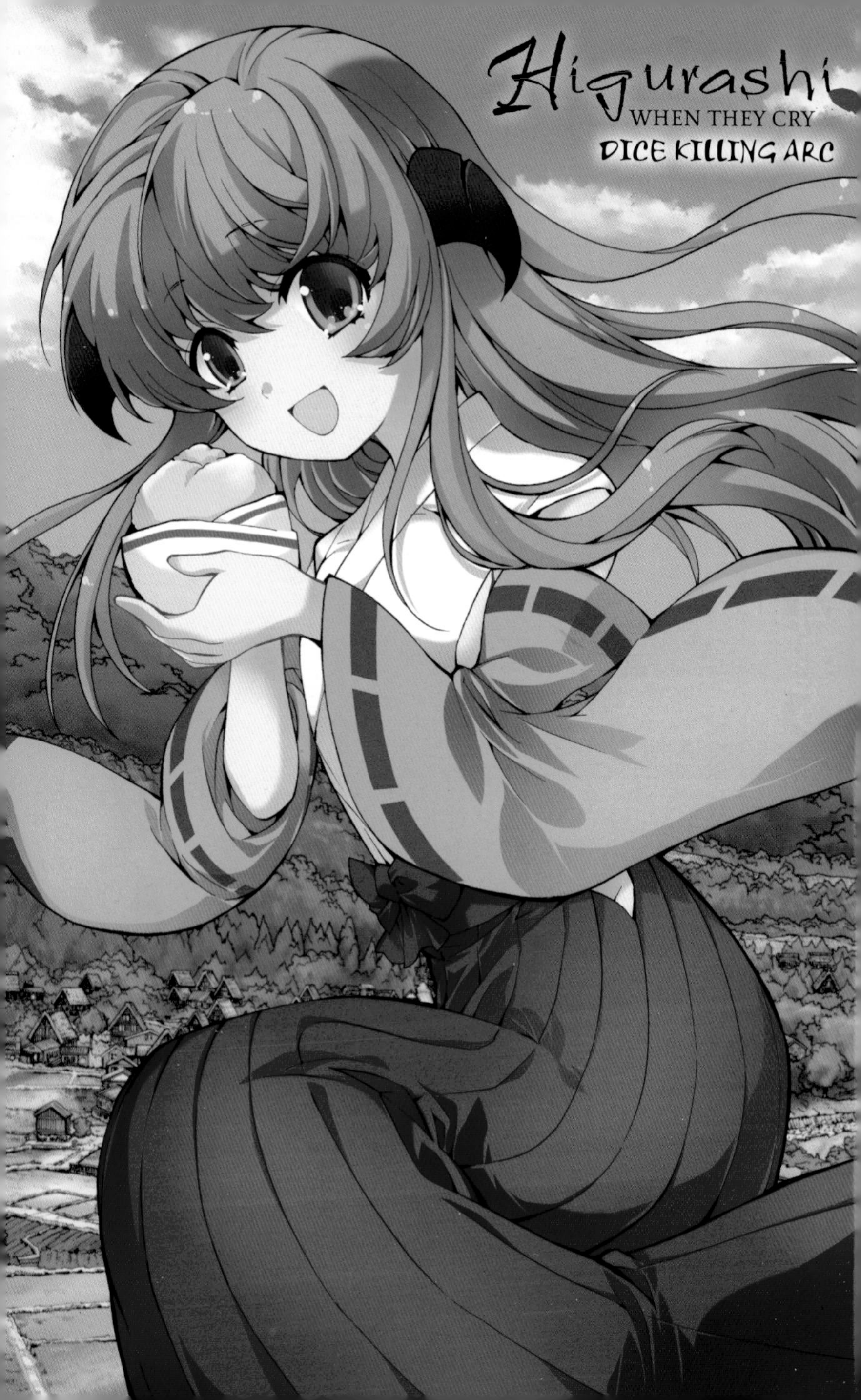
Higurashi
WHEN THEY CRY
DICE KILLING ARC

Higurashi
WHEN THEY CRY
DICE KILLING ARC

CONTENTS

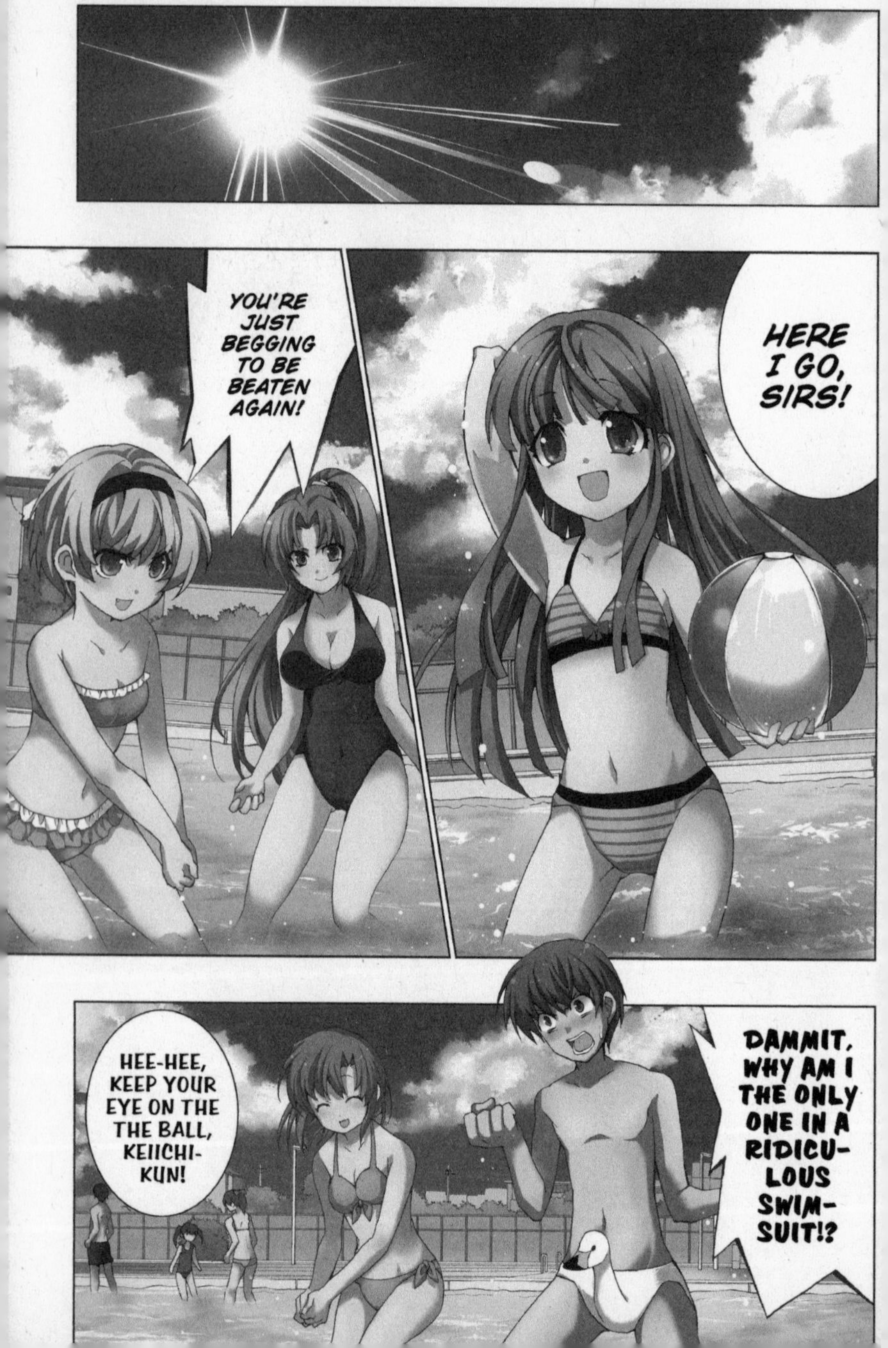
HERE I GO, SIRS!
YOU'RE JUST BEGGING TO BE BEATEN AGAIN!
DAMMIT, WHY AM I THE ONLY ONE IN A RIDICU-LOUS SWIM-SUIT!?
HEE-HEE, KEEP YOUR EYE ON THE THE BALL, KEIICHI-KUN!

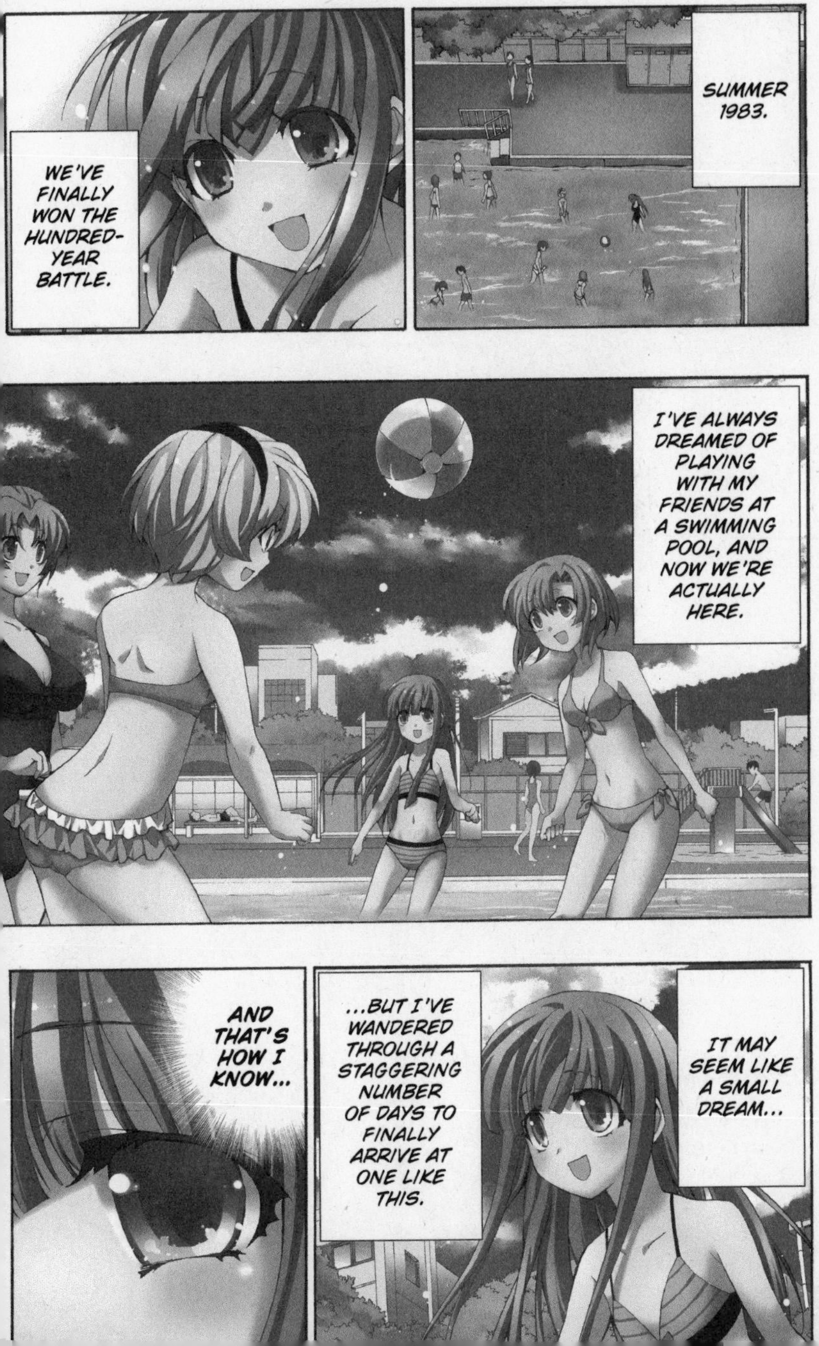
SUMMER 1983.
WE'VE FINALLY WON THE HUNDRED-YEAR BATTLE.
I'VE ALWAYS DREAMED OF PLAYING WITH MY FRIENDS AT A SWIMMING POOL, AND NOW WE'RE ACTUALLY HERE.
IT MAY SEEM LIKE A SMALL DREAM...
...BUT I'VE WANDERED THROUGH A STAGGERING NUMBER OF DAYS TO FINALLY ARRIVE AT ONE LIKE THIS.
AND THAT'S HOW I KNOW...

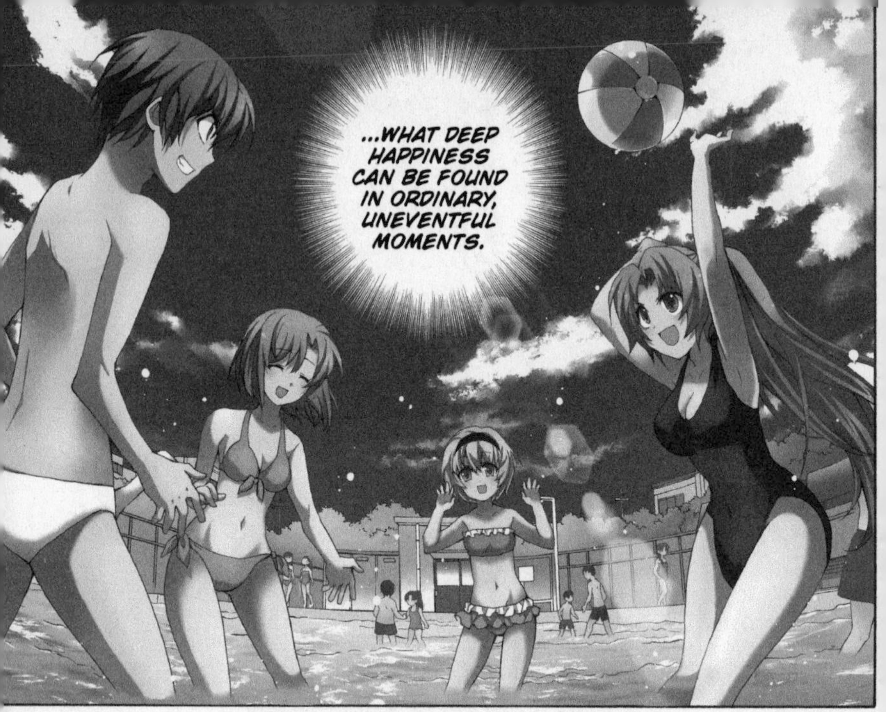
...WHAT DEEP HAPPINESS CAN BE FOUND IN ORDINARY, UNEVENTFUL MOMENTS.
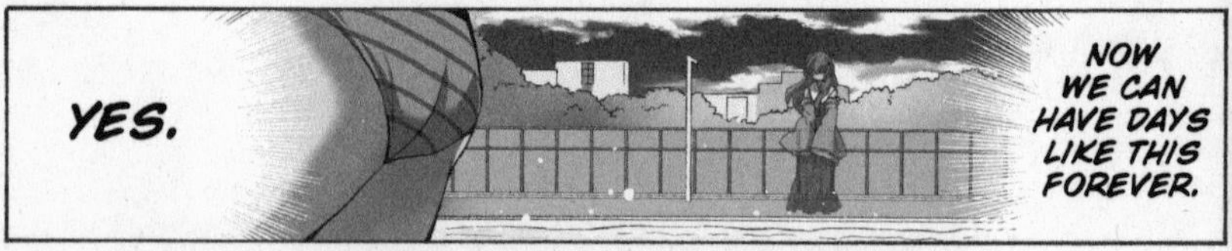
NOW WE CAN HAVE DAYS LIKE THIS FOREVER.
YES.
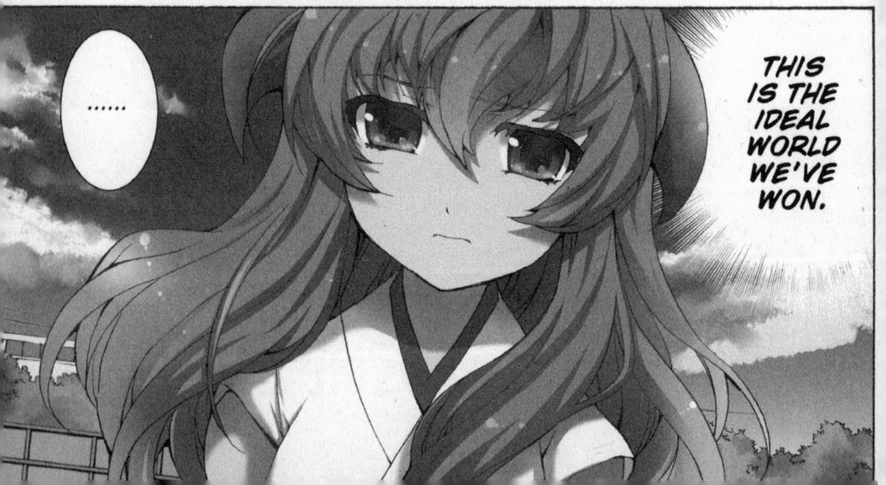
THIS IS THE IDEAL WORLD WE'VE WON.
......

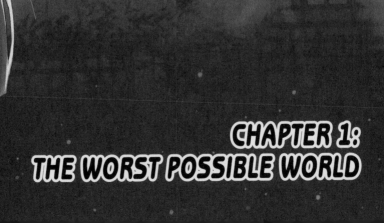

CHAPTER 1:
THE WORST POSSIBLE WORLD

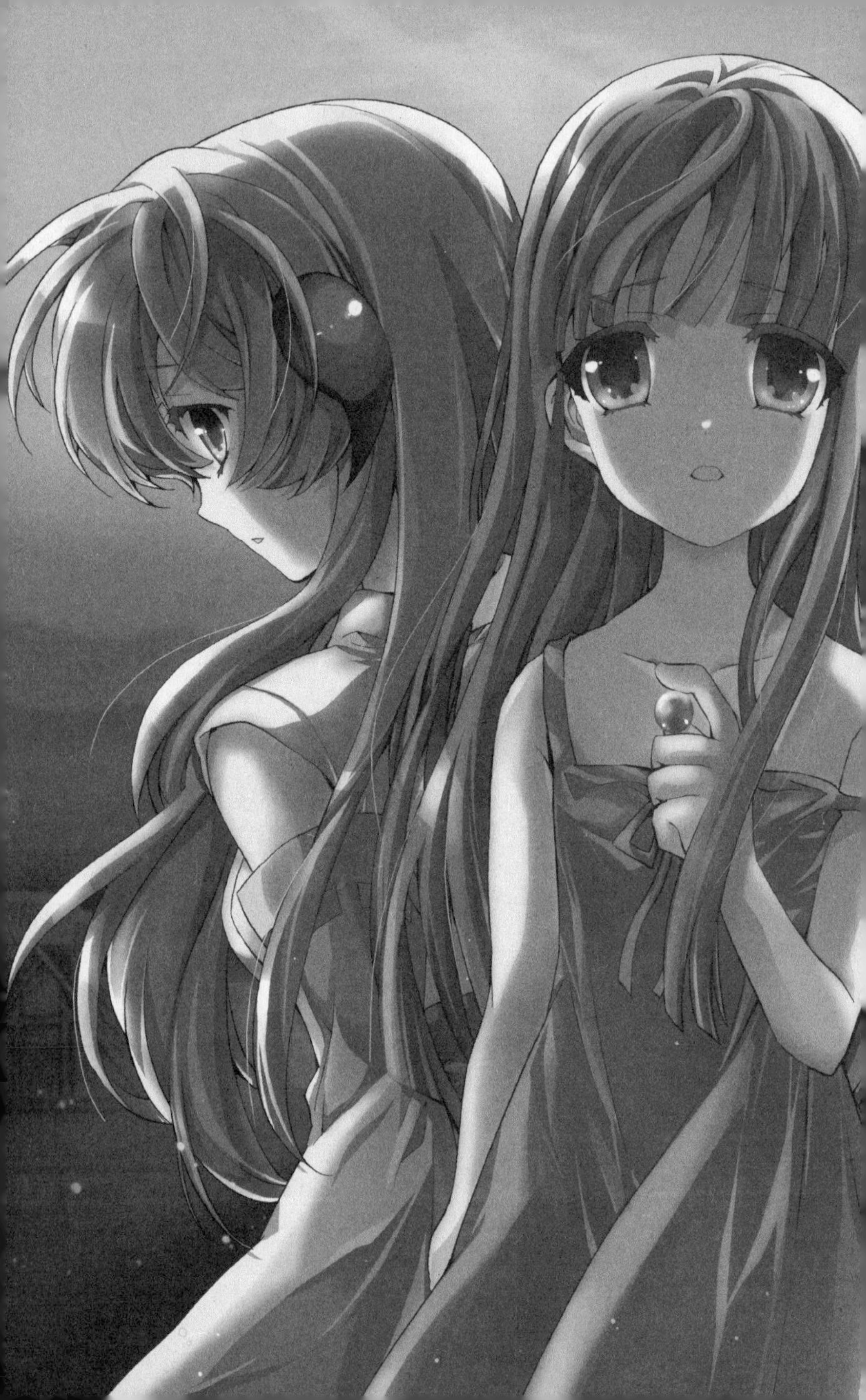

Bread fell down from heaven.
Some lamented loudly that the bread was not meat.

Meat fell down from heaven.
Some lamented loudly that they preferred the bread.

God came down from heaven.
He will make water fall down for a time
until everyone knows what will make them happy.

Frederica Bernkastel

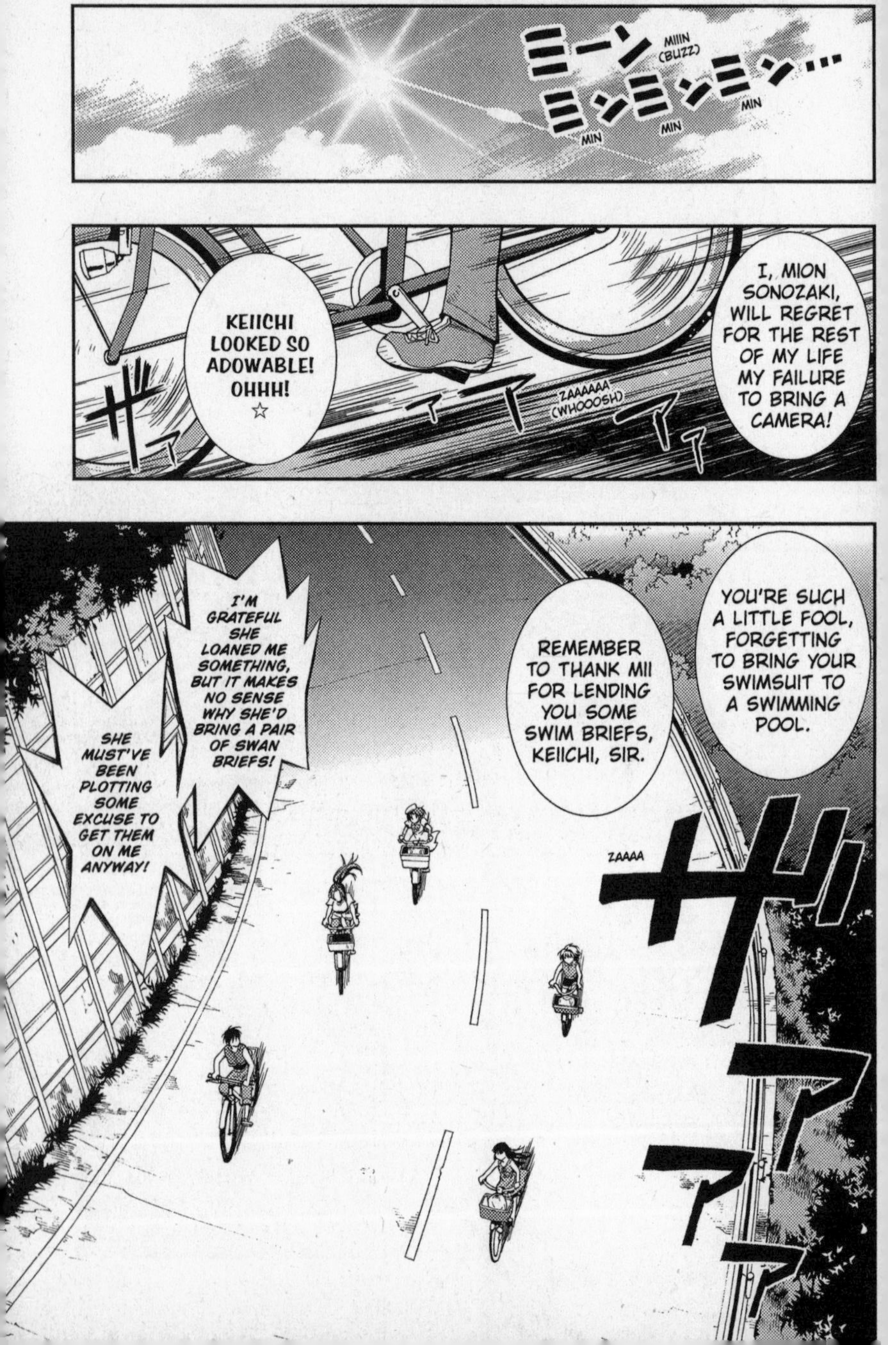
ミーン
MIIIN (BUZZ)
ミンミンミン…
MIN
MIN
MIN
I, MION SONOZAKI, WILL REGRET FOR THE REST OF MY LIFE MY FAILURE TO BRING A CAMERA!
ZAAAAAA (WHOOOSH)
KEIICHI LOOKED SO ADOWABLE! OHHH! ☆
YOU'RE SUCH A LITTLE FOOL, FORGETTING TO BRING YOUR SWIMSUIT TO A SWIMMING POOL.
REMEMBER TO THANK MII FOR LENDING YOU SOME SWIM BRIEFS, KEIICHI, SIR.
I'M GRATEFUL SHE LOANED ME SOMETHING, BUT IT MAKES NO SENSE WHY SHE'D BRING A PAIR OF SWAN BRIEFS!
SHE MUST'VE BEEN PLOTTING SOME EXCUSE TO GET THEM ON ME ANYWAY!
ZAAAA

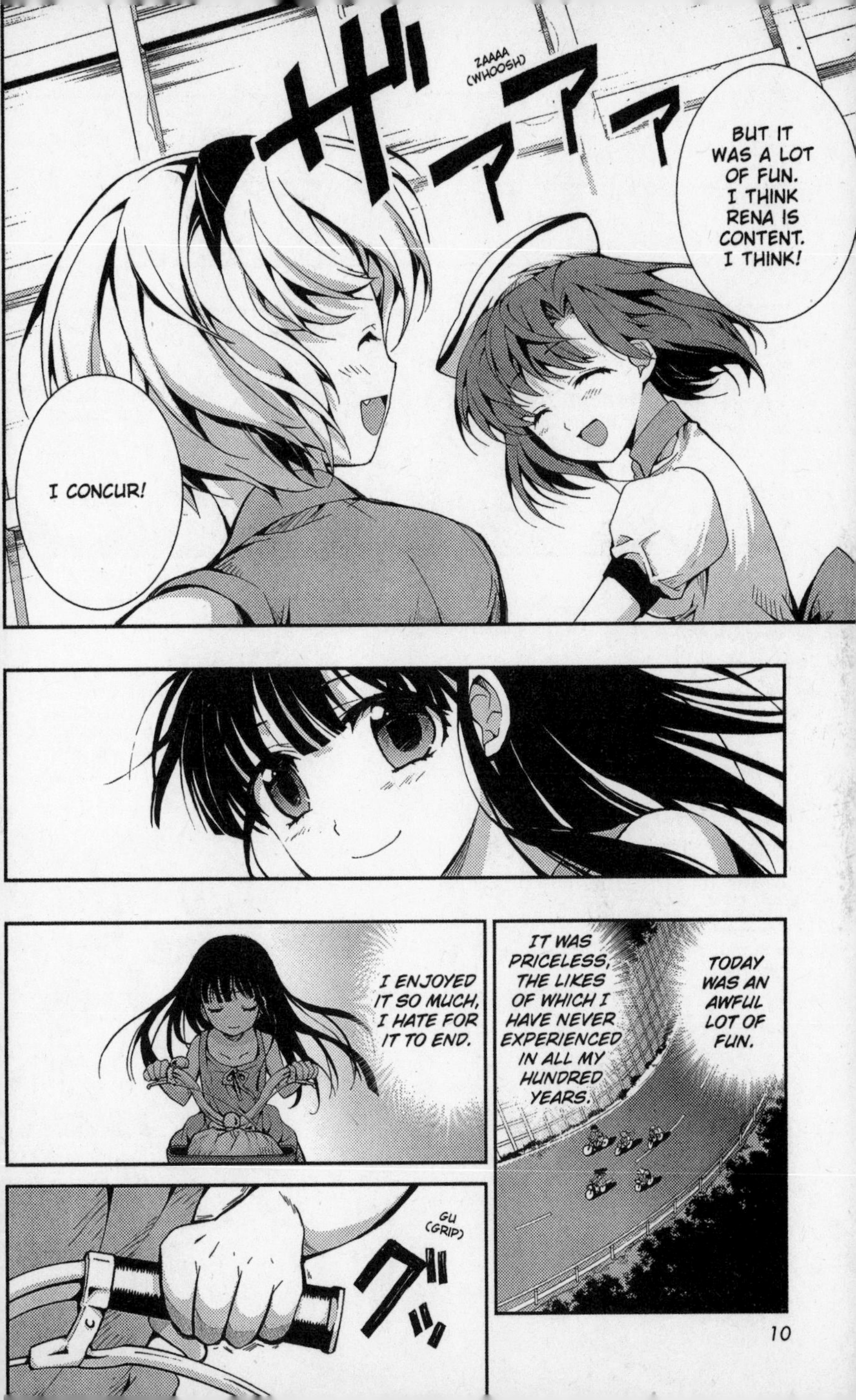
BUT IT WAS A LOT OF FUN. I THINK RENA IS CONTENT. I THINK!
ZAAAA (WHOOSH)
I CONCUR!
TODAY WAS AN AWFUL LOT OF FUN.
IT WAS PRICELESS, THE LIKES OF WHICH I HAVE NEVER EXPERIENCED IN ALL MY HUNDRED YEARS.
I ENJOYED IT SO MUCH, I HATE FOR IT TO END.
GU (GRIP)

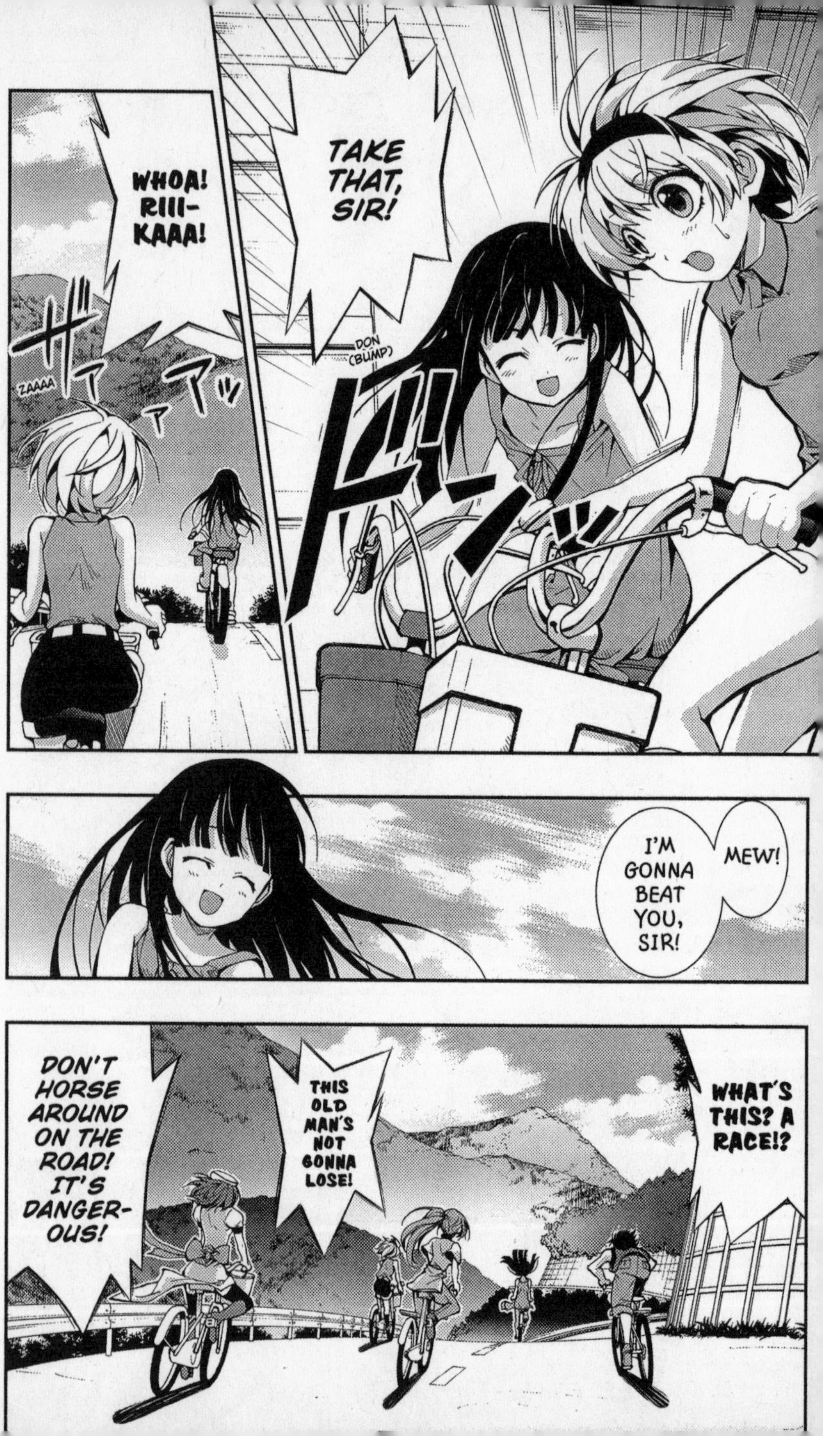
TAKE THAT, SIR!
DON (BUMP)
WHOA! RIII-KAAA!
ZAAAA
MEW!
I'M GONNA BEAT YOU, SIR!
WHAT'S THIS? A RACE!?
THIS OLD MAN'S NOT GONNA LOSE!
DON'T HORSE AROUND ON THE ROAD! IT'S DANGER-OUS!

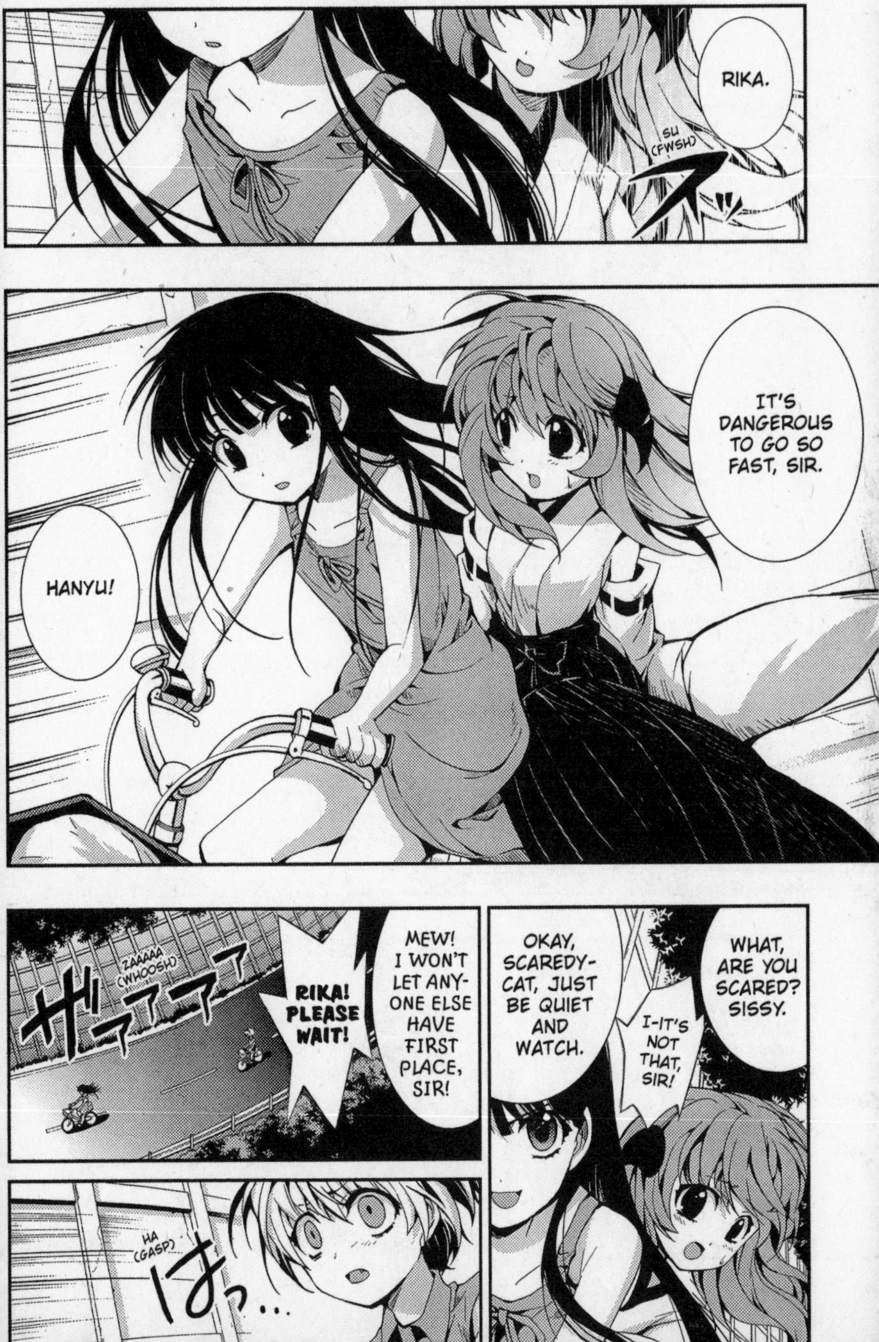
RIKA.
SU (FWSH)
IT'S DANGEROUS TO GO SO FAST, SIR.
HANYU!
WHAT, ARE YOU SCARED? SISSY.
I-IT'S NOT THAT, SIR!
OKAY, SCAREDY-CAT, JUST BE QUIET AND WATCH.
MEW! I WON'T LET ANY-ONE ELSE HAVE FIRST PLACE, SIR!
RIKA! PLEASE WAIT!
ZAAAAA (WHOOSH)
HA (GASP)

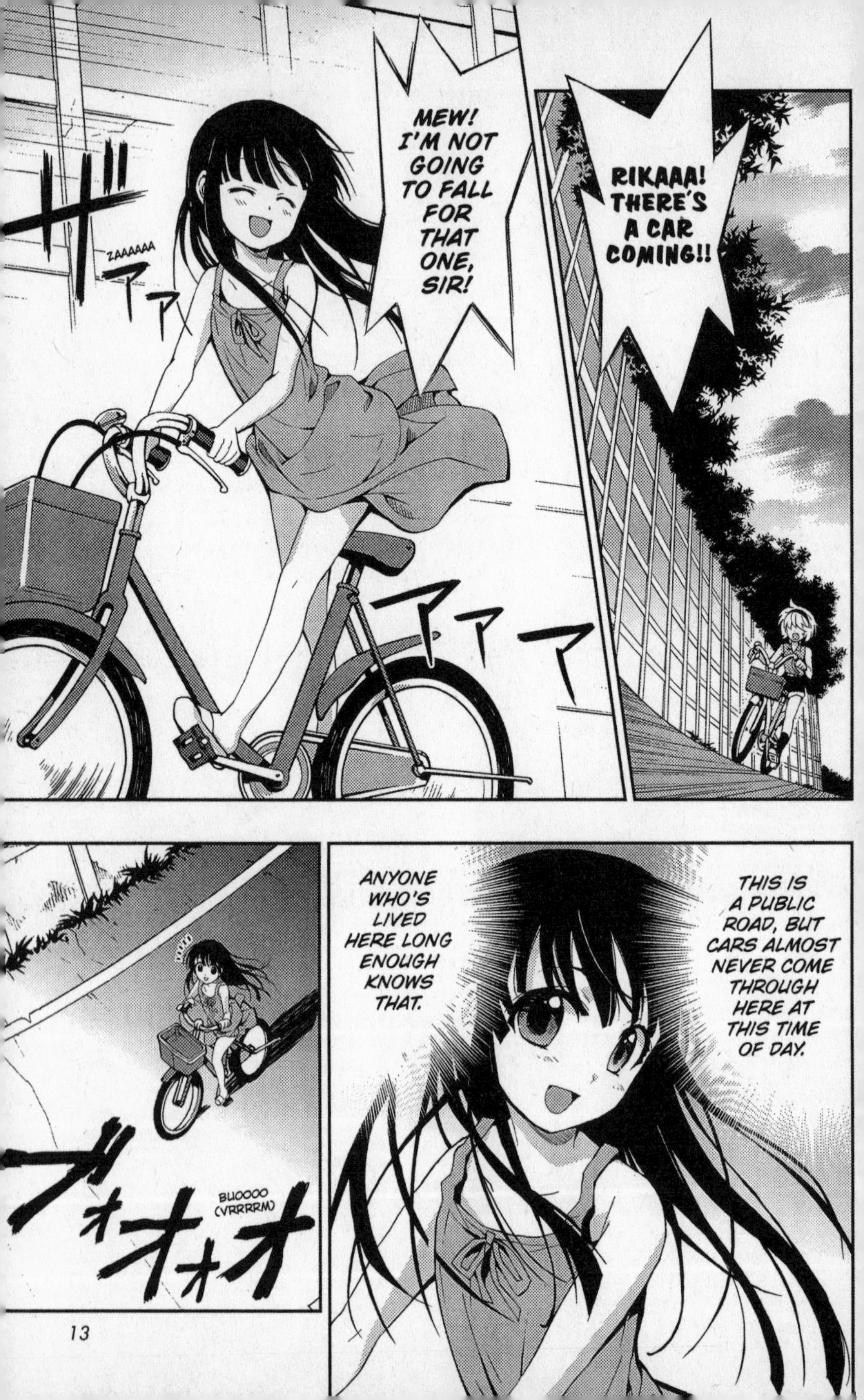
RIKAAA! THERE'S A CAR COMING!!
MEW! I'M NOT GOING TO FALL FOR THAT ONE, SIR!
ZAAAAAA
THIS IS A PUBLIC ROAD, BUT CARS ALMOST NEVER COME THROUGH HERE AT THIS TIME OF DAY.
ANYONE WHO'S LIVED HERE LONG ENOUGH KNOWS THAT.
BUOOOO (VRRRRM)

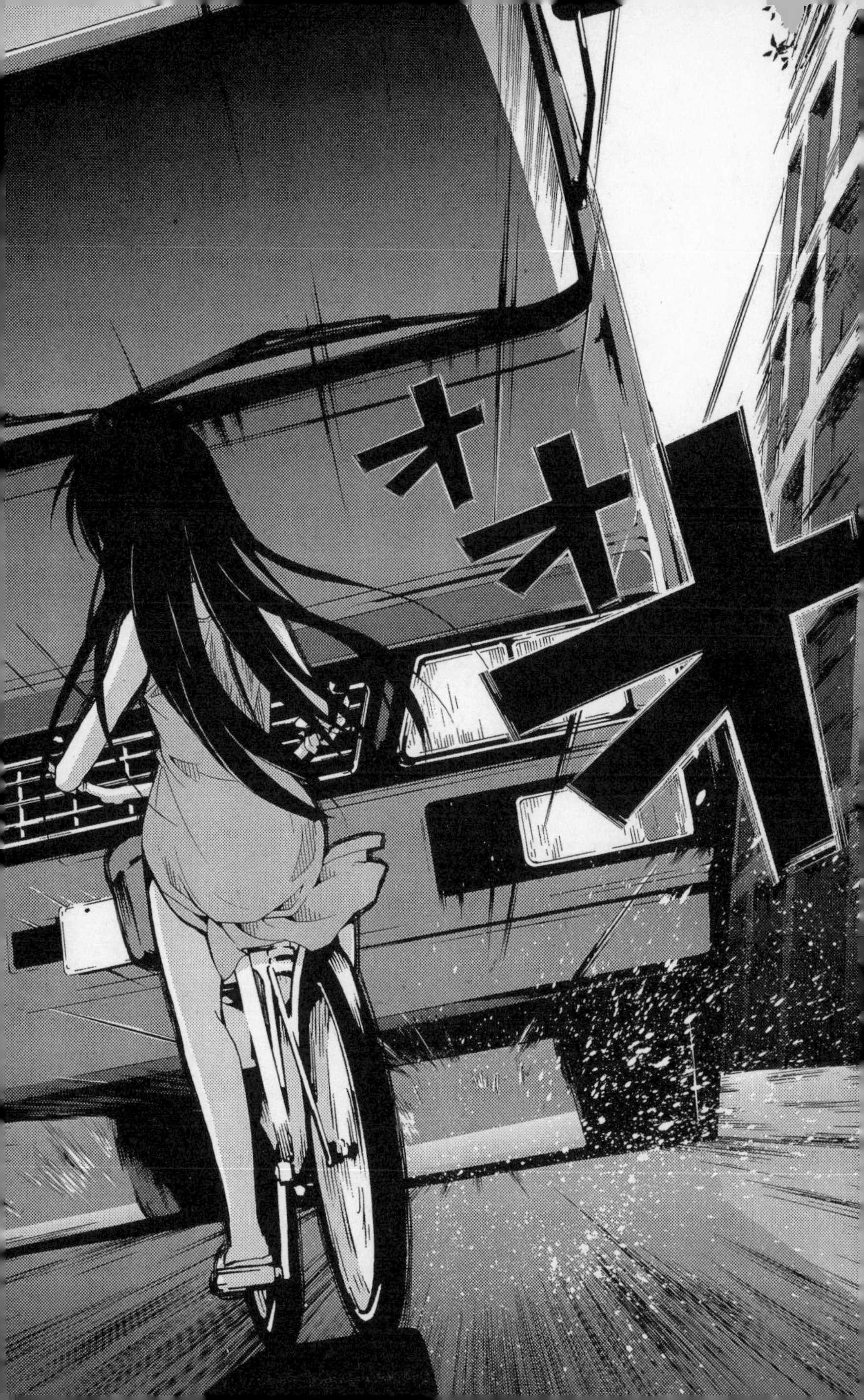
オオオ

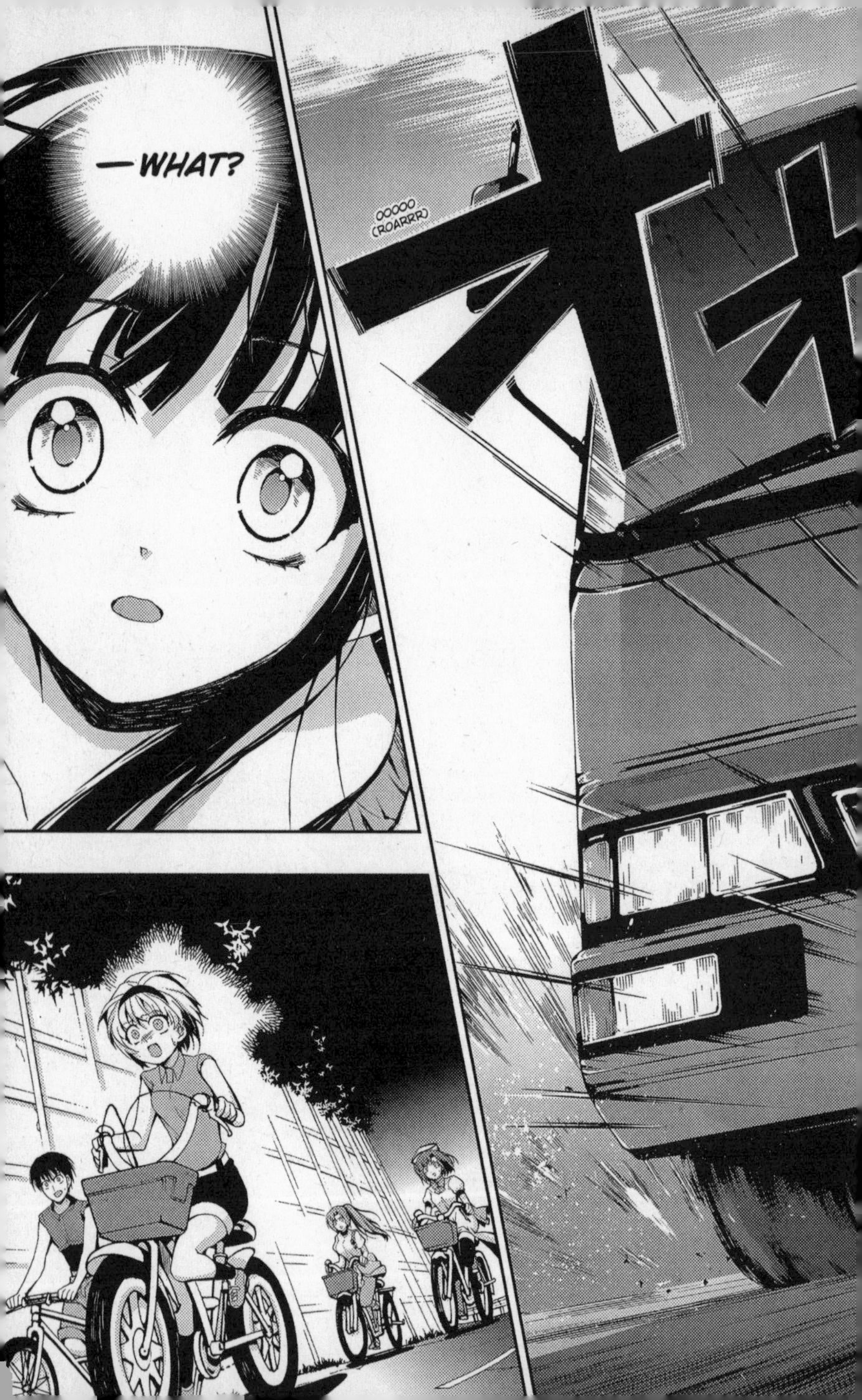
OOOOO (ROARRR)
—WHAT?

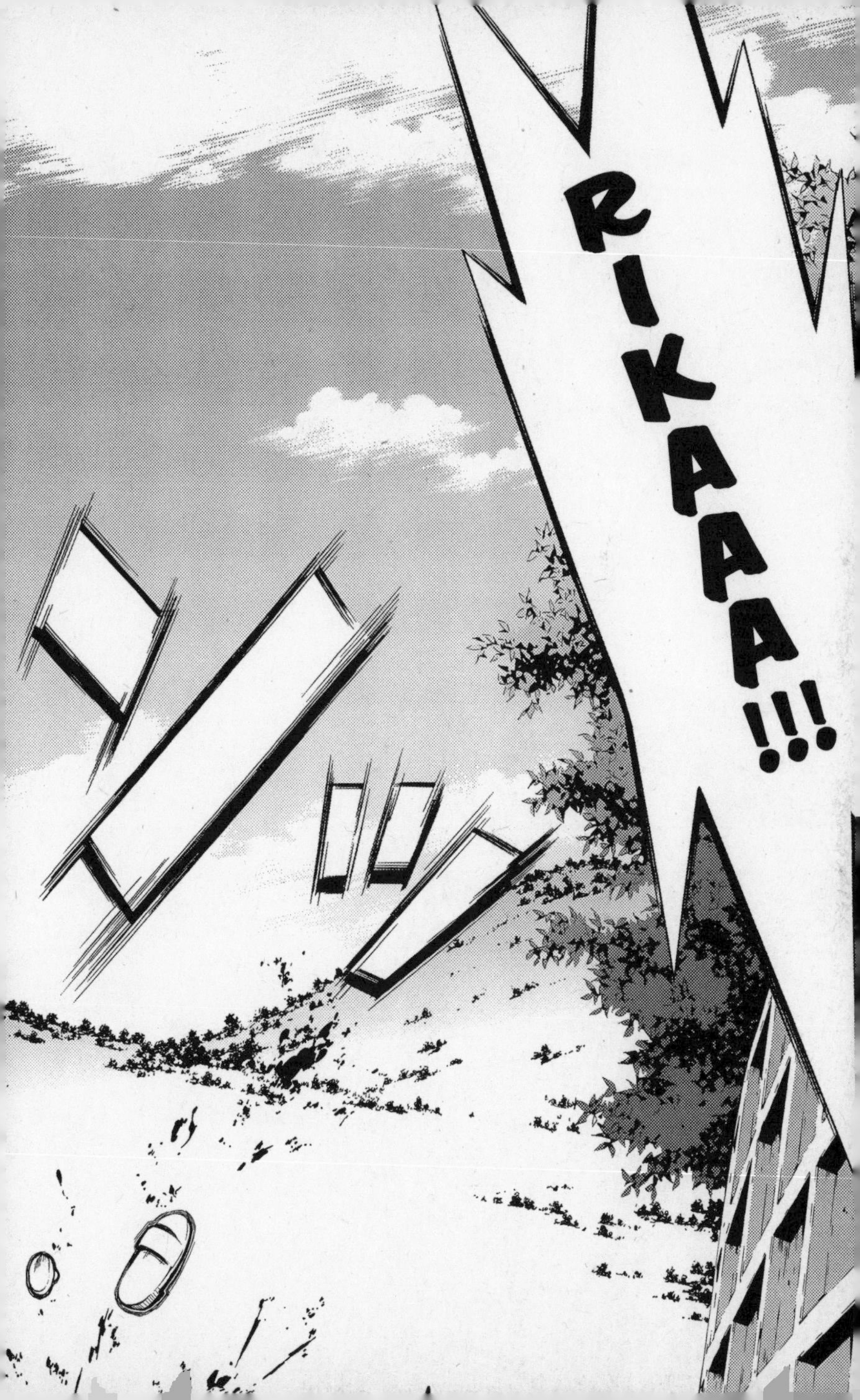
RIKAAA!!!

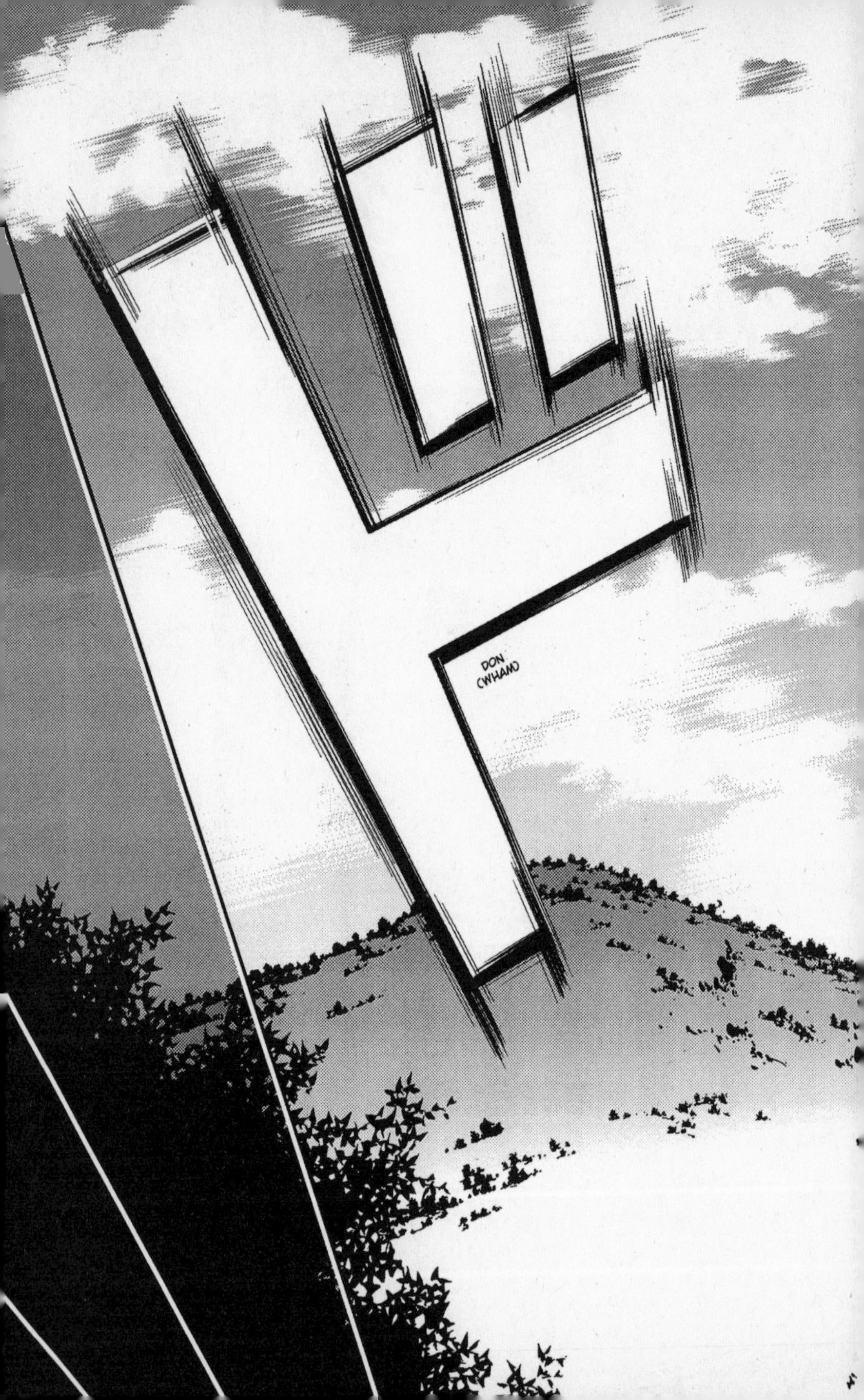
DON
(WHAM)

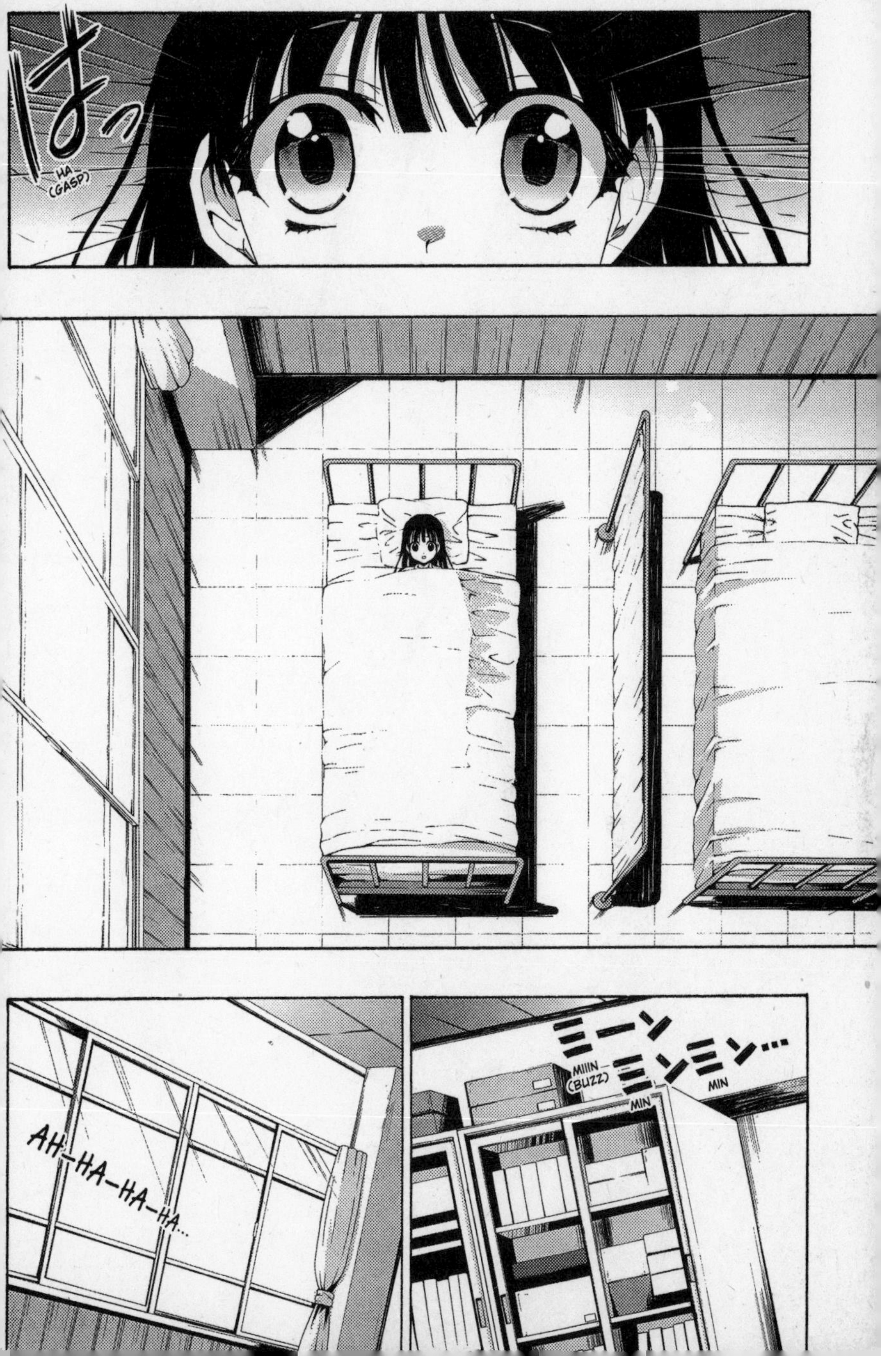
はっ
HA (GASP)
ミーン
MIIIN (BUZZ)
ミンミン…
MIN
MIN
AH-HA-HA-HA...

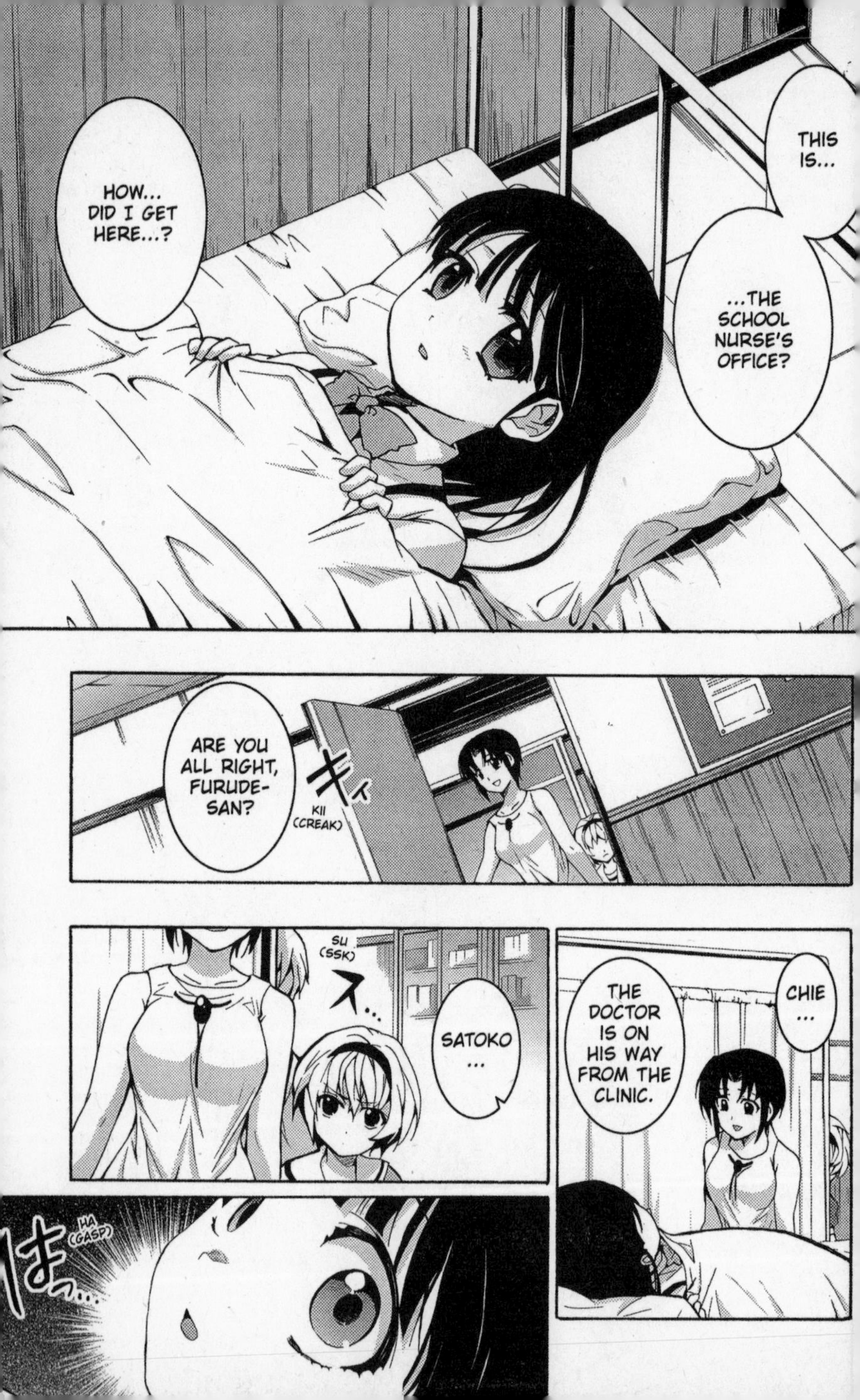
THIS IS...
...THE SCHOOL NURSE'S OFFICE?
HOW... DID I GET HERE...?
ARE YOU ALL RIGHT, FURUDE-SAN?
KII (CREAK)
CHIE ...
THE DOCTOR IS ON HIS WAY FROM THE CLINIC.
SATOKO ...
SU (SSK)
HA (GASP)

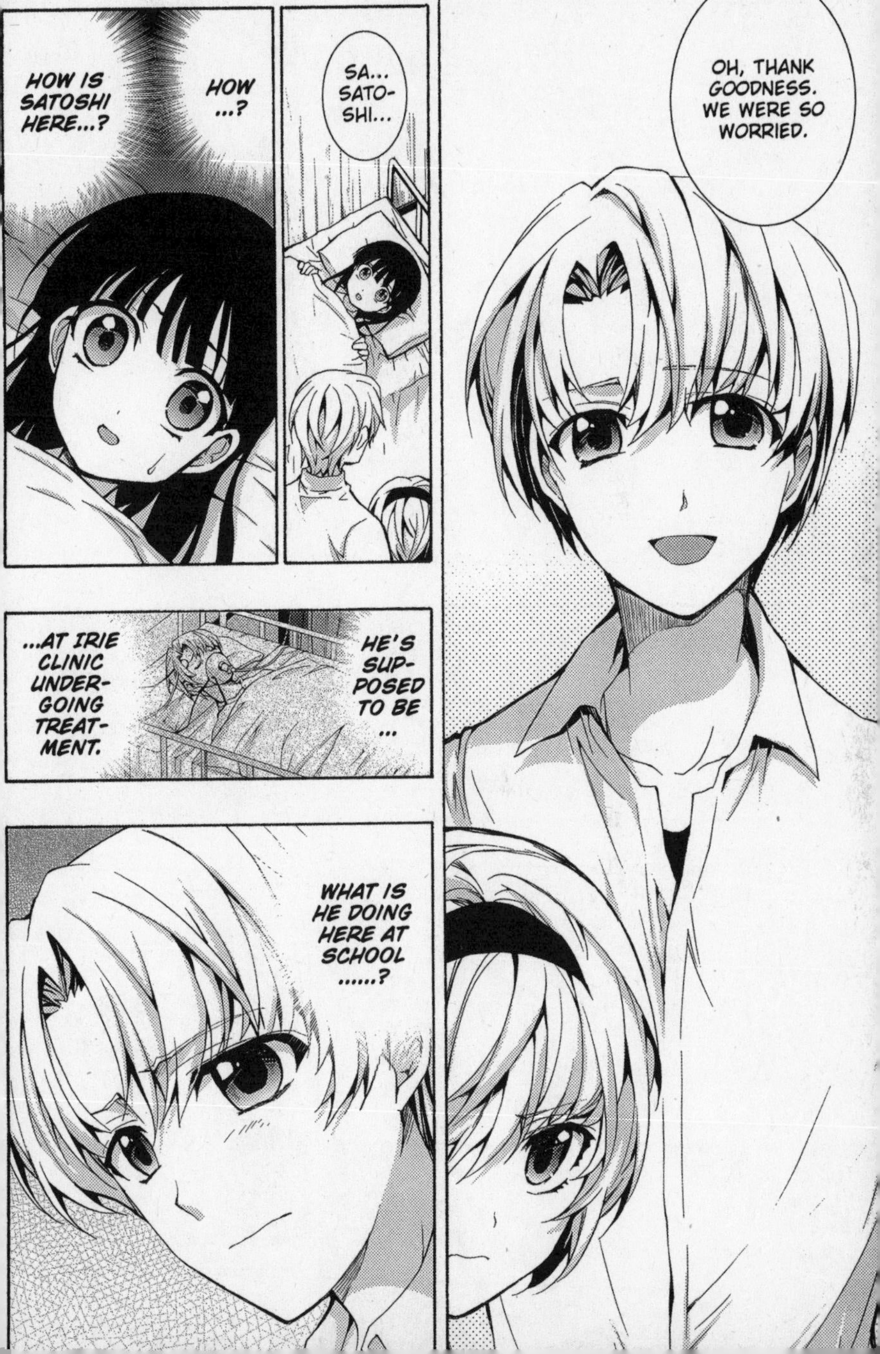
OH, THANK GOODNESS. WE WERE SO WORRIED.
SA... SATO-SHI...
HOW ...?
HOW IS SATOSHI HERE...?
HE'S SUP-POSED TO BE ...
...AT IRIE CLINIC UNDER-GOING TREAT-MENT.
WHAT IS HE DOING HERE AT SCHOOL ......?

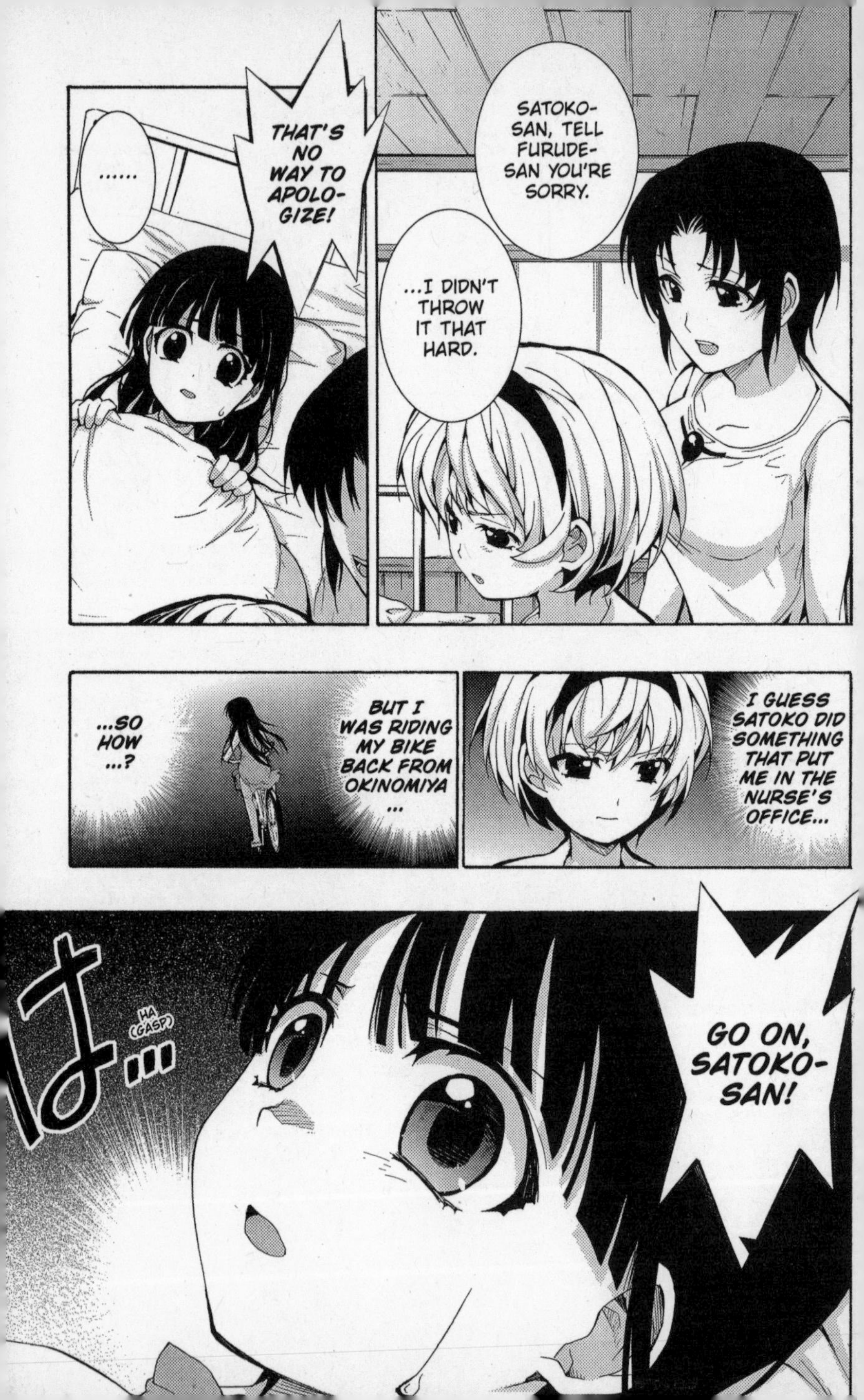
SATOKO-SAN, TELL FURUDE-SAN YOU'RE SORRY.
...I DIDN'T THROW IT THAT HARD.
THAT'S NO WAY TO APOLO-GIZE!
......
I GUESS SATOKO DID SOMETHING THAT PUT ME IN THE NURSE'S OFFICE...
BUT I WAS RIDING MY BIKE BACK FROM OKINOMIYA ...
...SO HOW ...?
GO ON, SATOKO-SAN!
HA (GASP)

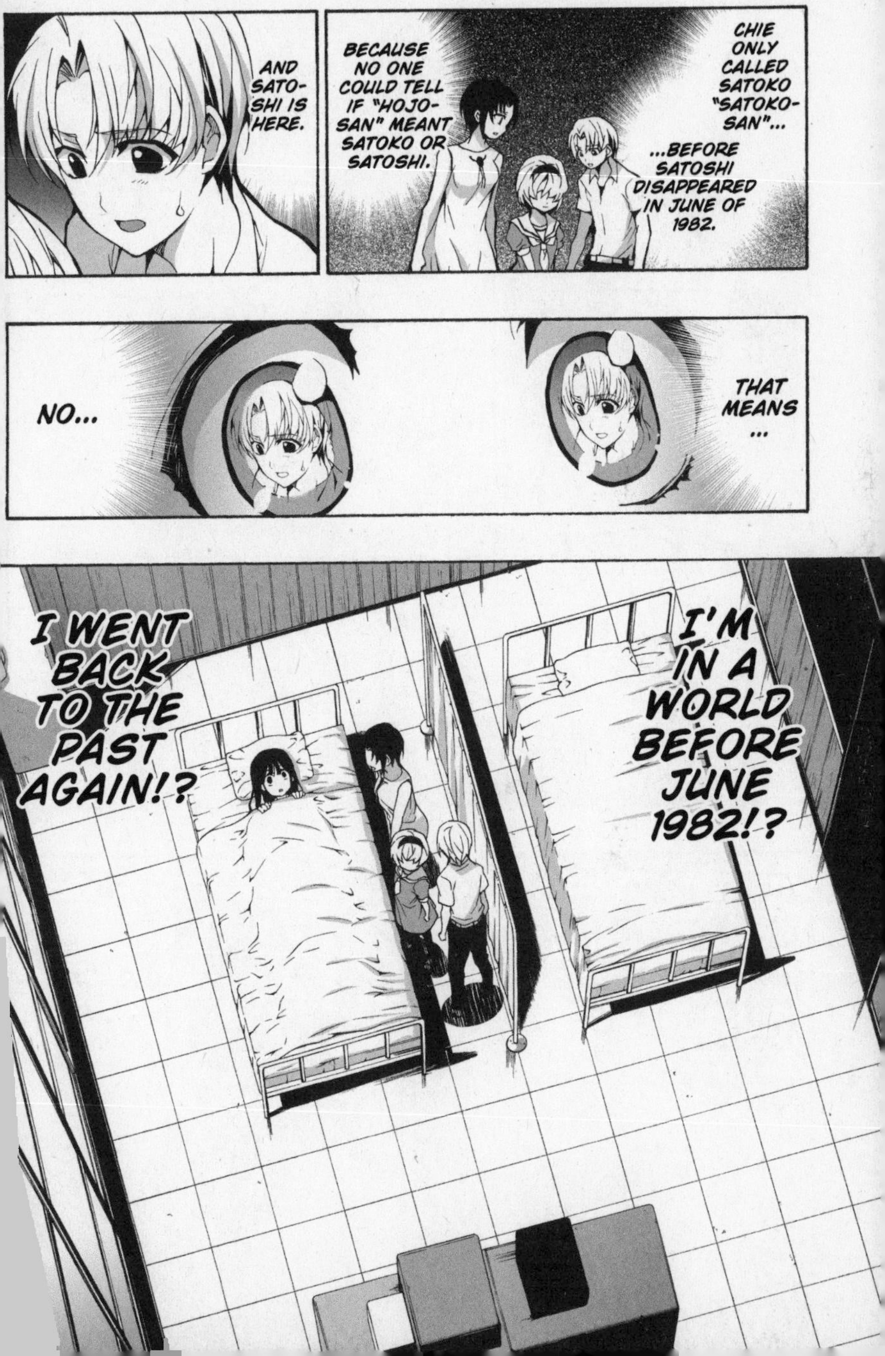
CHIE ONLY CALLED SATOKO "SATOKO-SAN"...
...BEFORE SATOSHI DISAPPEARED IN JUNE OF 1982.
BECAUSE NO ONE COULD TELL IF "HOJO-SAN" MEANT SATOKO OR SATOSHI.
AND SATOSHI IS HERE.
THAT MEANS ...
NO...
I'M IN A WORLD BEFORE JUNE 1982!?
I WENT BACK TO THE PAST AGAIN!?

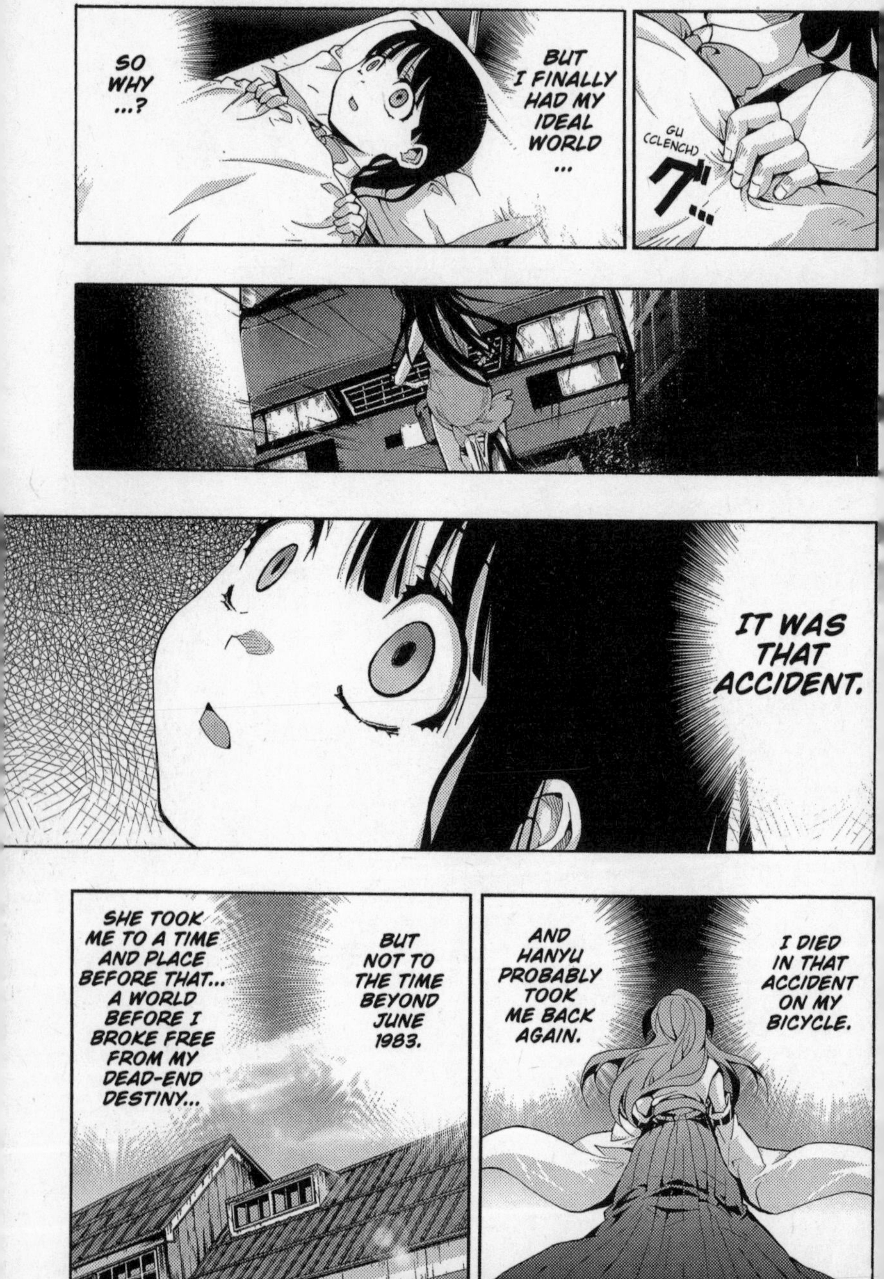
GU (CLENCH)
グ…
BUT I FINALLY HAD MY IDEAL WORLD...
SO WHY...?
IT WAS THAT ACCIDENT.
I DIED IN THAT ACCIDENT ON MY BICYCLE.
AND HANYU PROBABLY TOOK ME BACK AGAIN.
BUT NOT TO THE TIME BEYOND JUNE 1983.
SHE TOOK ME TO A TIME AND PLACE BEFORE THAT... A WORLD BEFORE I BROKE FREE FROM MY DEAD-END DESTINY...

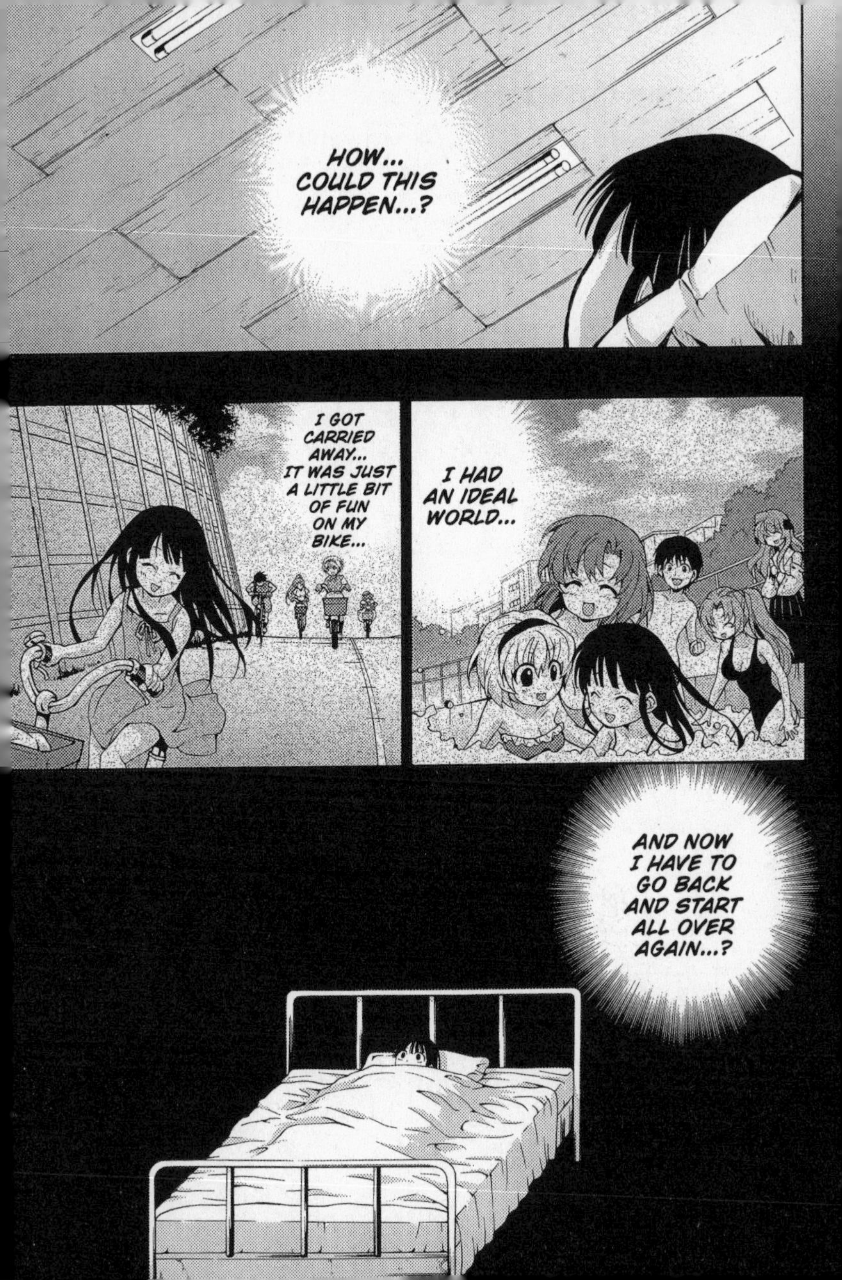
HOW... COULD THIS HAPPEN...?
I HAD AN IDEAL WORLD...
I GOT CARRIED AWAY... IT WAS JUST A LITTLE BIT OF FUN ON MY BIKE...
AND NOW I HAVE TO GO BACK AND START ALL OVER AGAIN...?

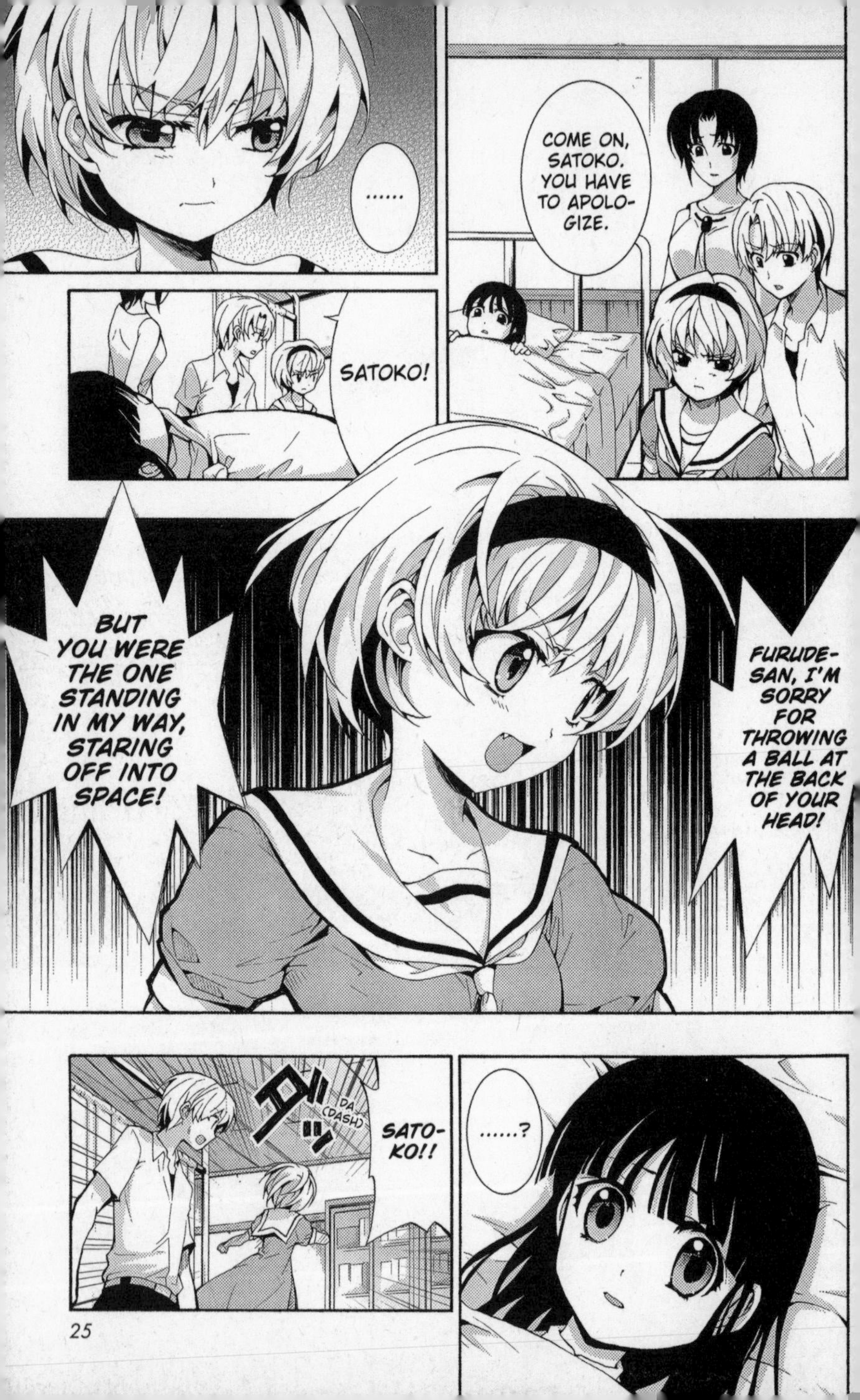
COME ON, SATOKO. YOU HAVE TO APOLOGIZE.
......
SATOKO!
FURUDE-SAN, I'M SORRY FOR THROWING A BALL AT THE BACK OF YOUR HEAD!
BUT YOU WERE THE ONE STANDING IN MY WAY, STARING OFF INTO SPACE!
......?
SATO-KO!!
DA (DASH)

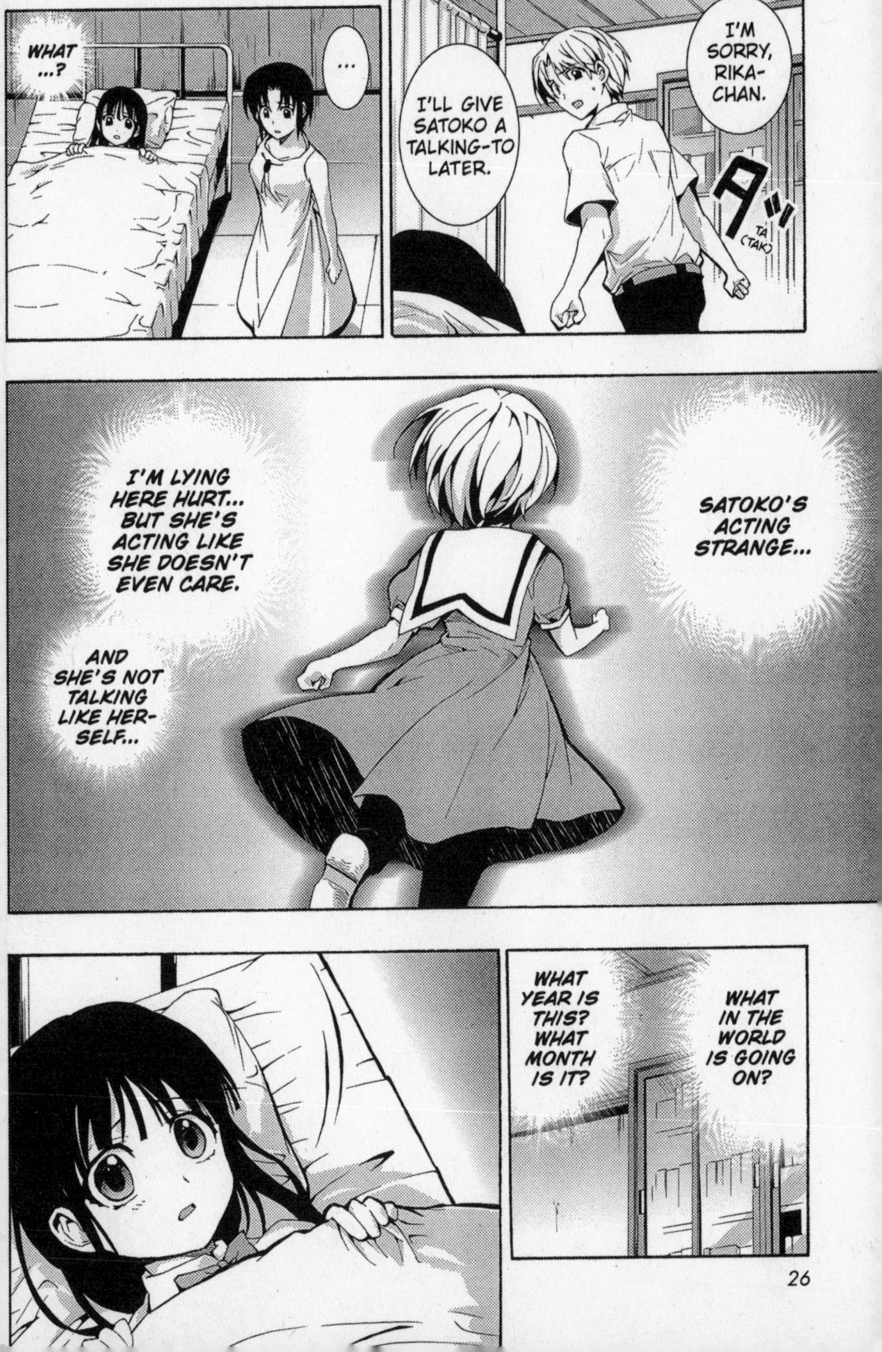
I'M SORRY, RIKA-CHAN.
I'LL GIVE SATOKO A TALKING-TO LATER.
TA (TAK)
...
WHAT ...?
SATOKO'S ACTING STRANGE...
I'M LYING HERE HURT... BUT SHE'S ACTING LIKE SHE DOESN'T EVEN CARE.
AND SHE'S NOT TALKING LIKE HER-SELF...
WHAT IN THE WORLD IS GOING ON?
WHAT YEAR IS THIS? WHAT MONTH IS IT?

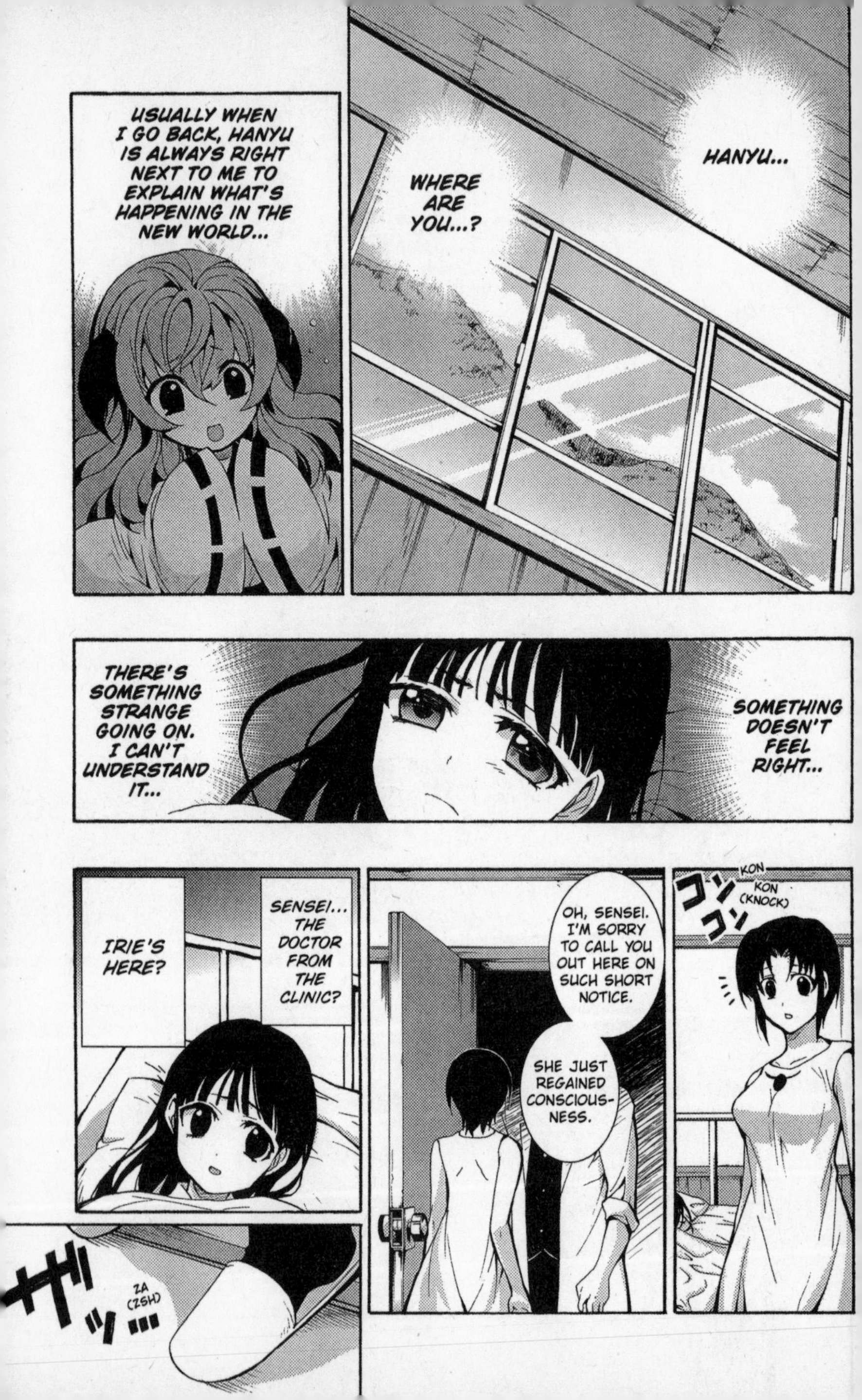
HANYU...
WHERE ARE YOU...?
USUALLY WHEN I GO BACK, HANYU IS ALWAYS RIGHT NEXT TO ME TO EXPLAIN WHAT'S HAPPENING IN THE NEW WORLD...
SOMETHING DOESN'T FEEL RIGHT...
THERE'S SOMETHING STRANGE GOING ON. I CAN'T UNDERSTAND IT...
KON KON (KNOCK)
OH, SENSEI. I'M SORRY TO CALL YOU OUT HERE ON SUCH SHORT NOTICE.
SHE JUST REGAINED CONSCIOUSNESS.
SENSEI... THE DOCTOR FROM THE CLINIC?
IRIE'S HERE?
ZA (ZSH)

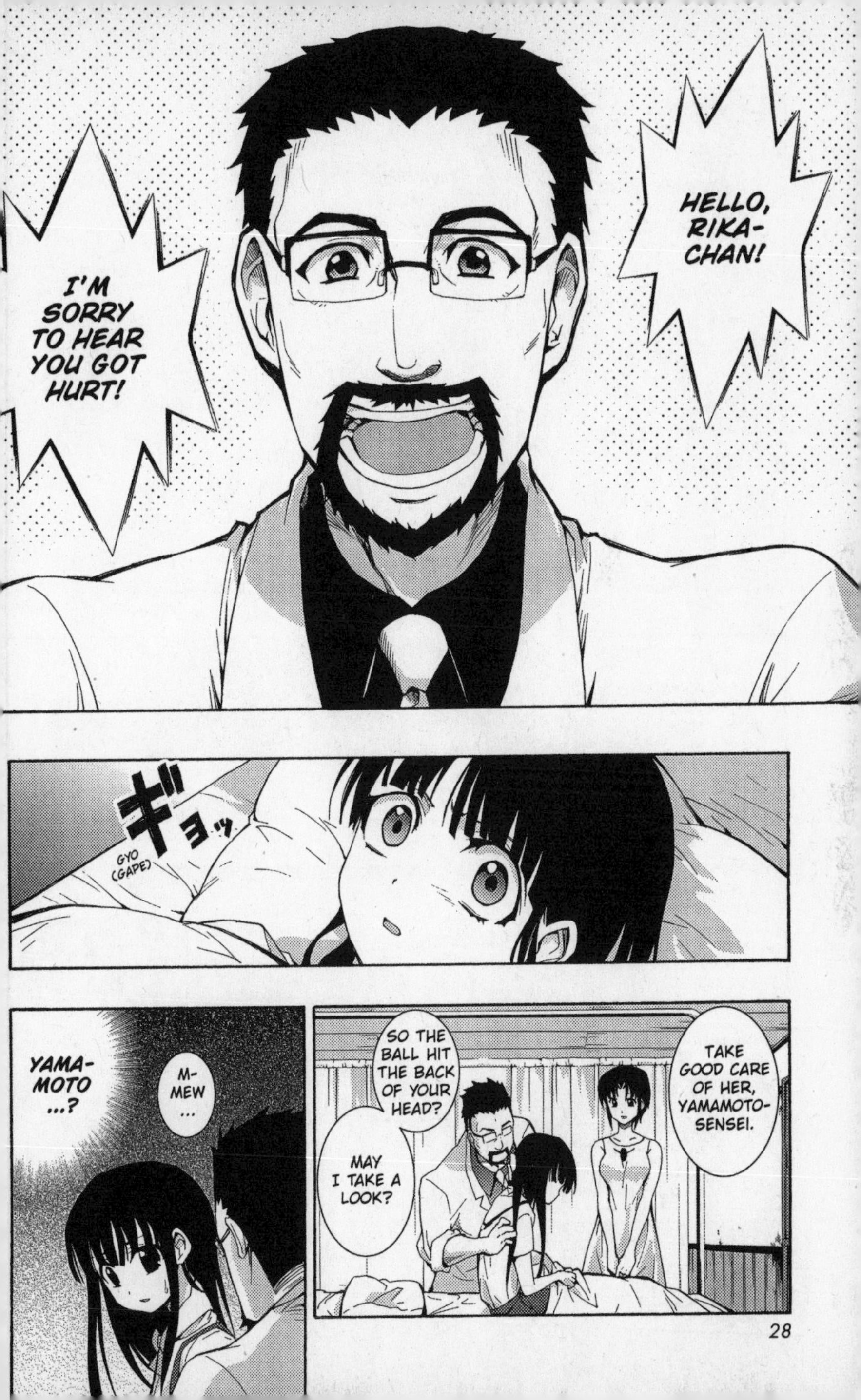
HELLO, RIKA-CHAN!
I'M SORRY TO HEAR YOU GOT HURT!
ギョッ
GYO (GAPE)
TAKE GOOD CARE OF HER, YAMAMOTO-SENSEI.
SO THE BALL HIT THE BACK OF YOUR HEAD?
MAY I TAKE A LOOK?
M-MEW ...
YAMAMOTO ...?

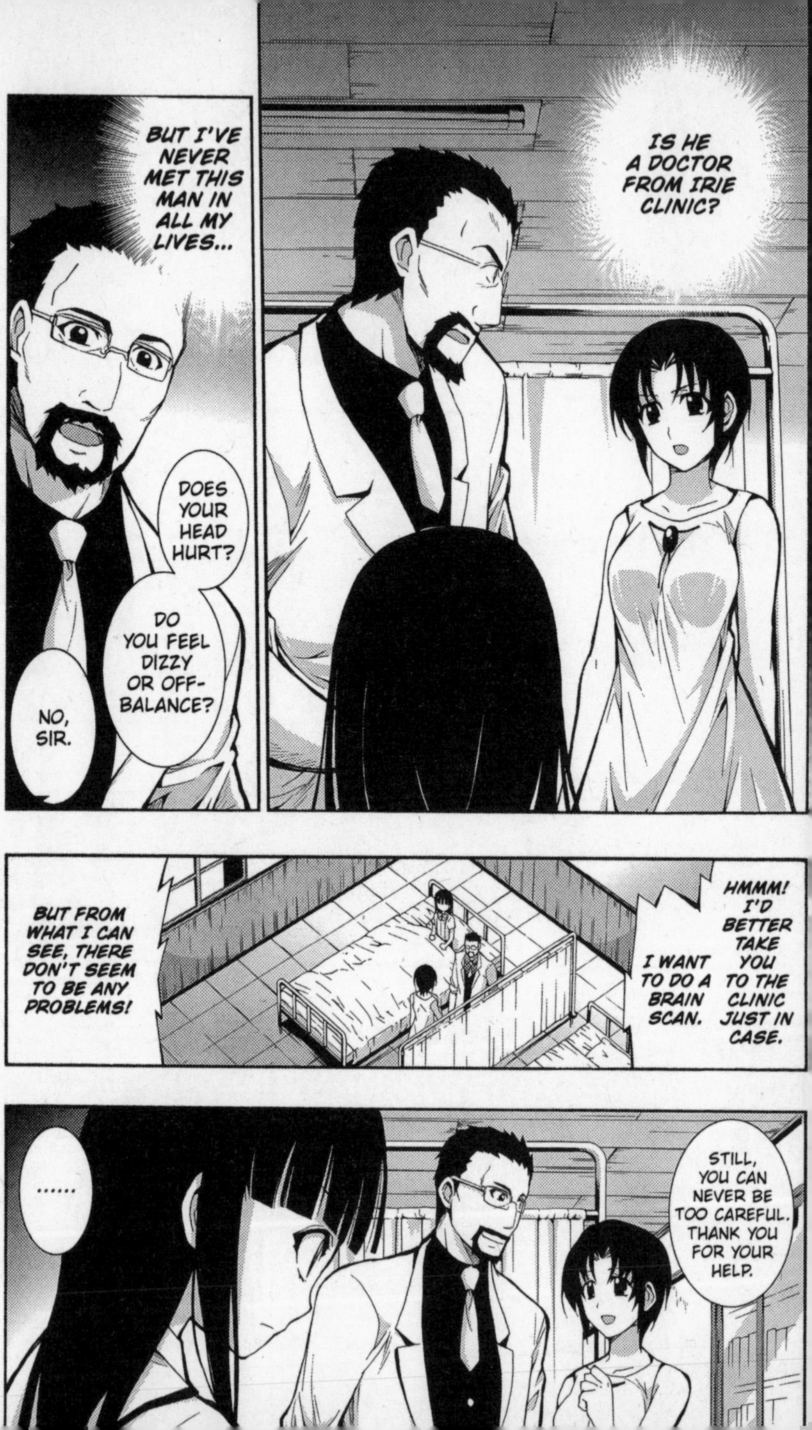
IS HE A DOCTOR FROM IRIE CLINIC?
BUT I'VE NEVER MET THIS MAN IN ALL MY LIVES...
DOES YOUR HEAD HURT?
DO YOU FEEL DIZZY OR OFF-BALANCE?
NO, SIR.
HMMM! I'D BETTER TAKE YOU TO THE CLINIC JUST IN CASE.
I WANT TO DO A BRAIN SCAN.
BUT FROM WHAT I CAN SEE, THERE DON'T SEEM TO BE ANY PROBLEMS!
STILL, YOU CAN NEVER BE TOO CAREFUL. THANK YOU FOR YOUR HELP.
......

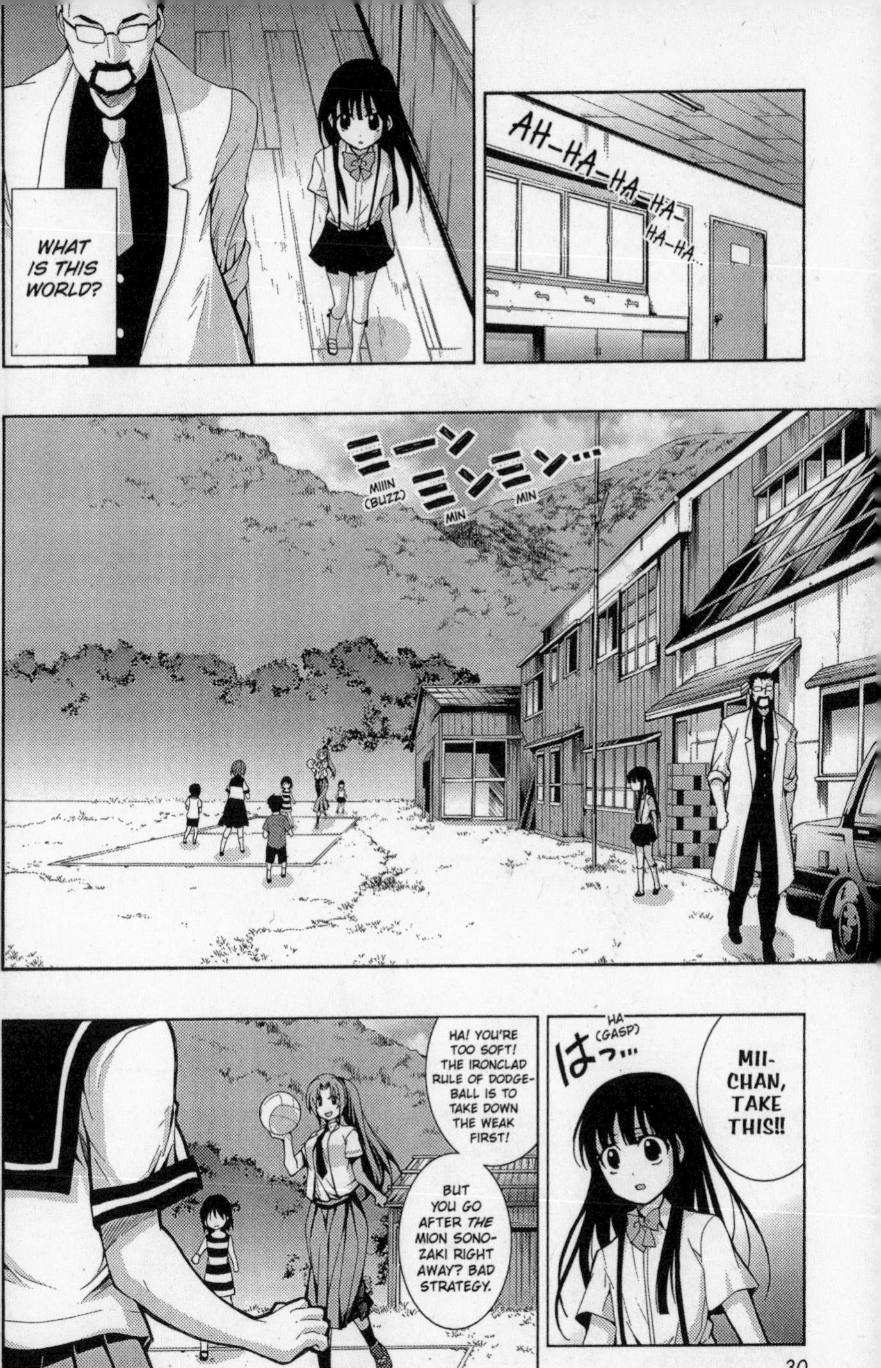
AH-HA-HA-HA-HA-HA...
WHAT IS THIS WORLD?
ミーンミンミン…
MIIIN (BUZZ) MIN MIN
はっ…
HA (GASP)
MII-CHAN, TAKE THIS!!
HA! YOU'RE TOO SOFT! THE IRONCLAD RULE OF DODGE-BALL IS TO TAKE DOWN THE WEAK FIRST!
BUT YOU GO AFTER *THE* MION SONO-ZAKI RIGHT AWAY? BAD STRATEGY.

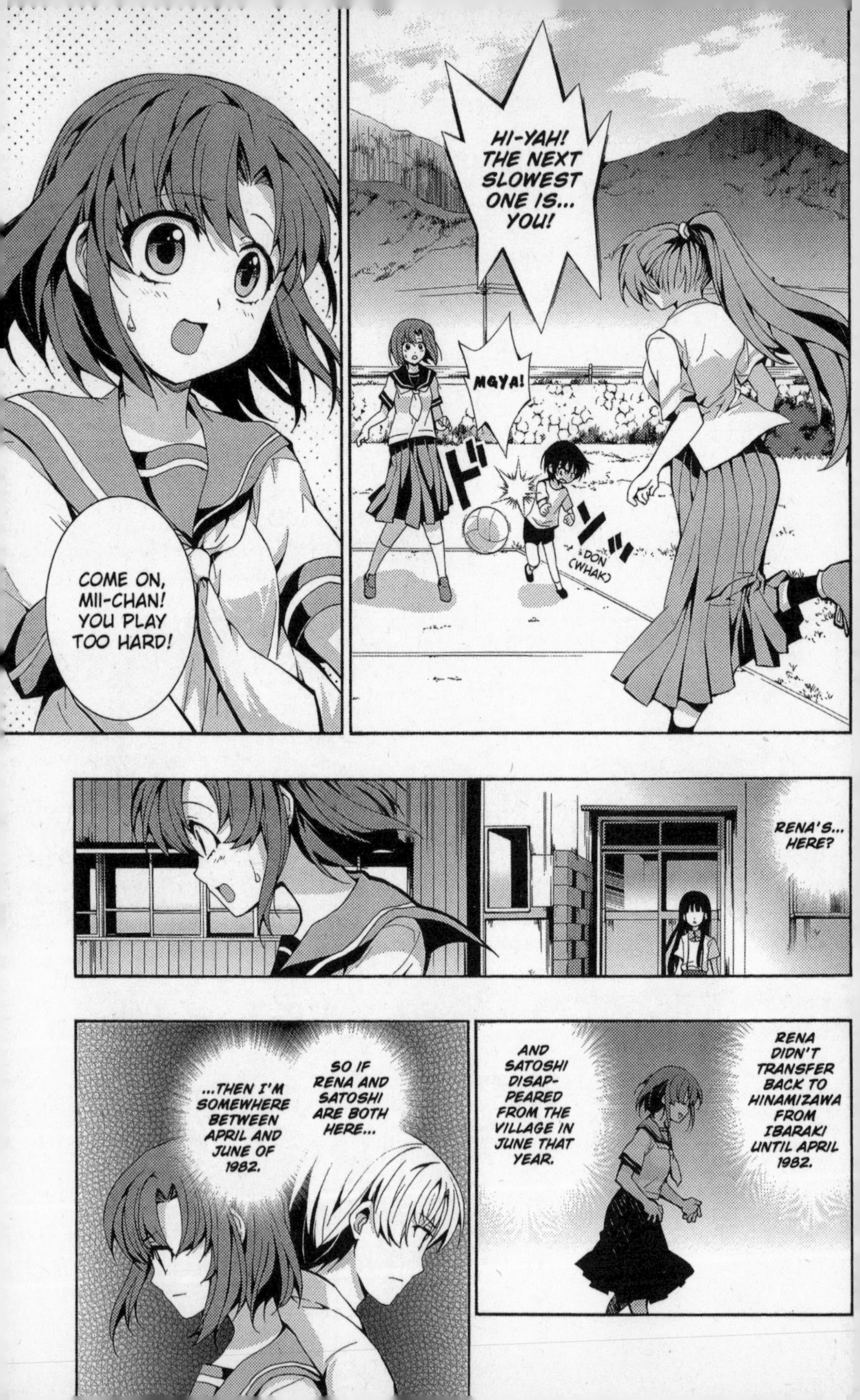
HI-YAH! THE NEXT SLOWEST ONE IS... YOU!
MGYA!
DON (WHAK)
COME ON, MII-CHAN! YOU PLAY TOO HARD!
RENA'S... HERE?
RENA DIDN'T TRANSFER BACK TO HINAMIZAWA FROM IBARAKI UNTIL APRIL 1982.
AND SATOSHI DISAP-PEARED FROM THE VILLAGE IN JUNE THAT YEAR.
SO IF RENA AND SATOSHI ARE BOTH HERE...
...THEN I'M SOMEWHERE BETWEEN APRIL AND JUNE OF 1982.

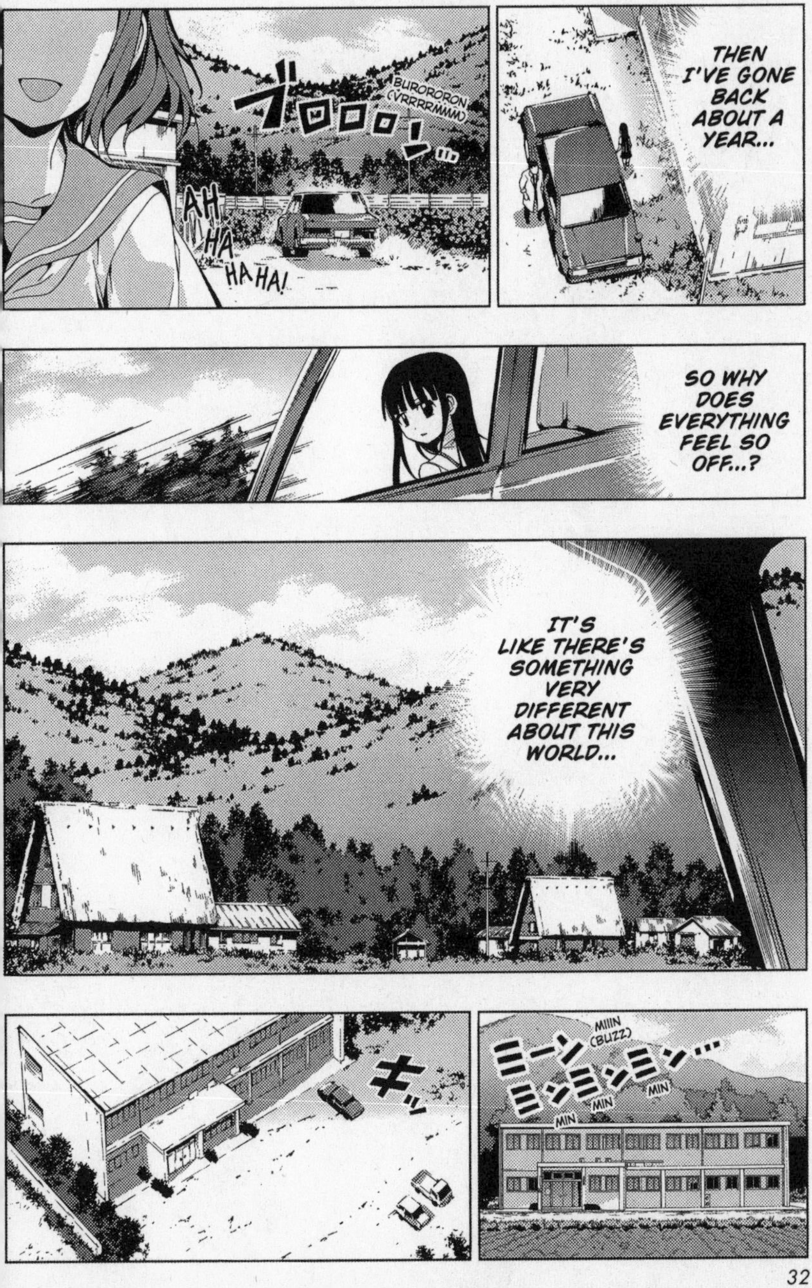
THEN I'VE GONE BACK ABOUT A YEAR...
BURORORON (VRRRRMMM)
AH HA HA HA!
SO WHY DOES EVERYTHING FEEL SO OFF...?
IT'S LIKE THERE'S SOMETHING VERY DIFFERENT ABOUT THIS WORLD...
MIIIN (BUZZ)
MIN
MIN
MIN

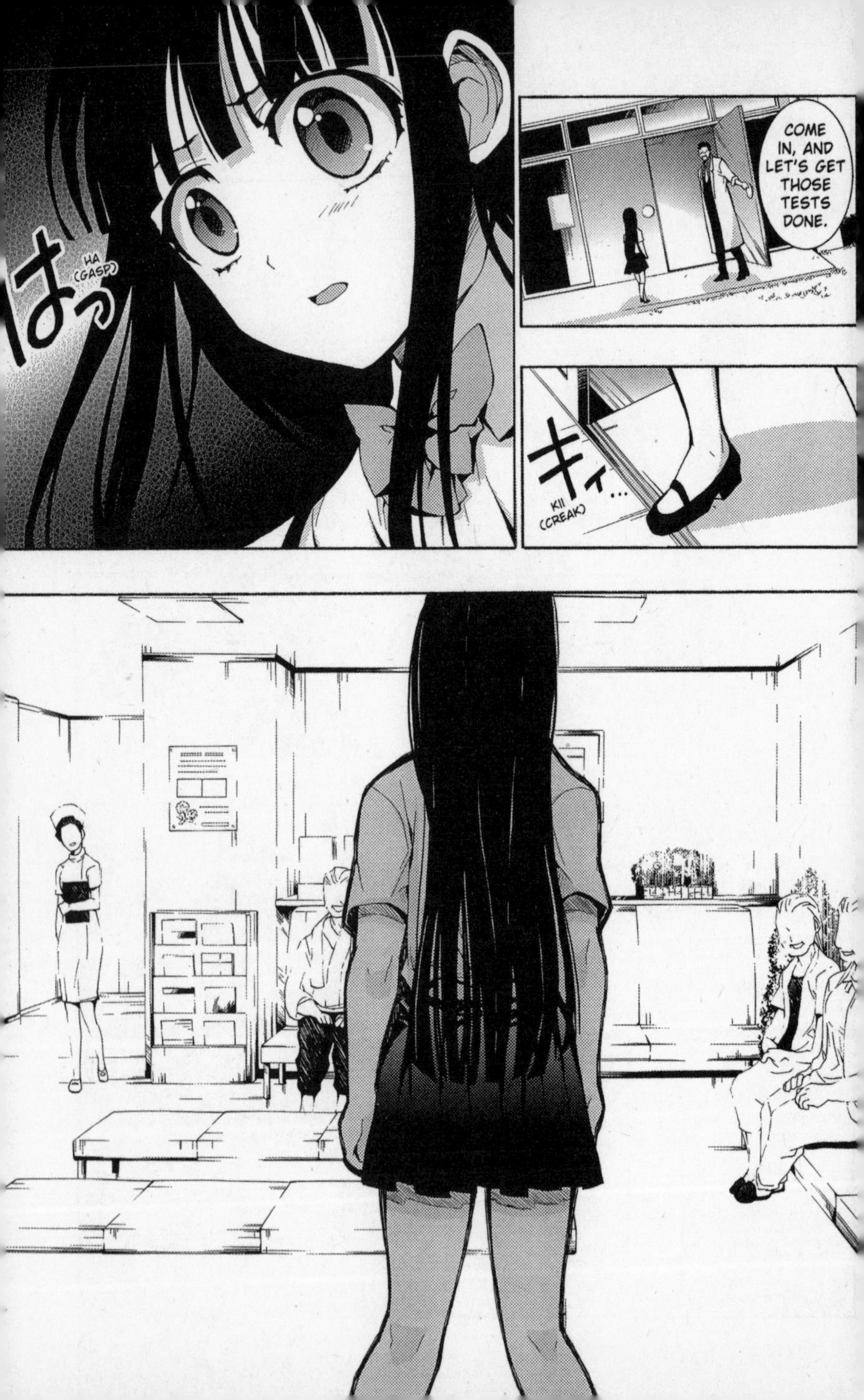
COME IN, AND LET'S GET THOSE TESTS DONE.
キィ…
KII (CREAK)
はっ
HA (GASP)

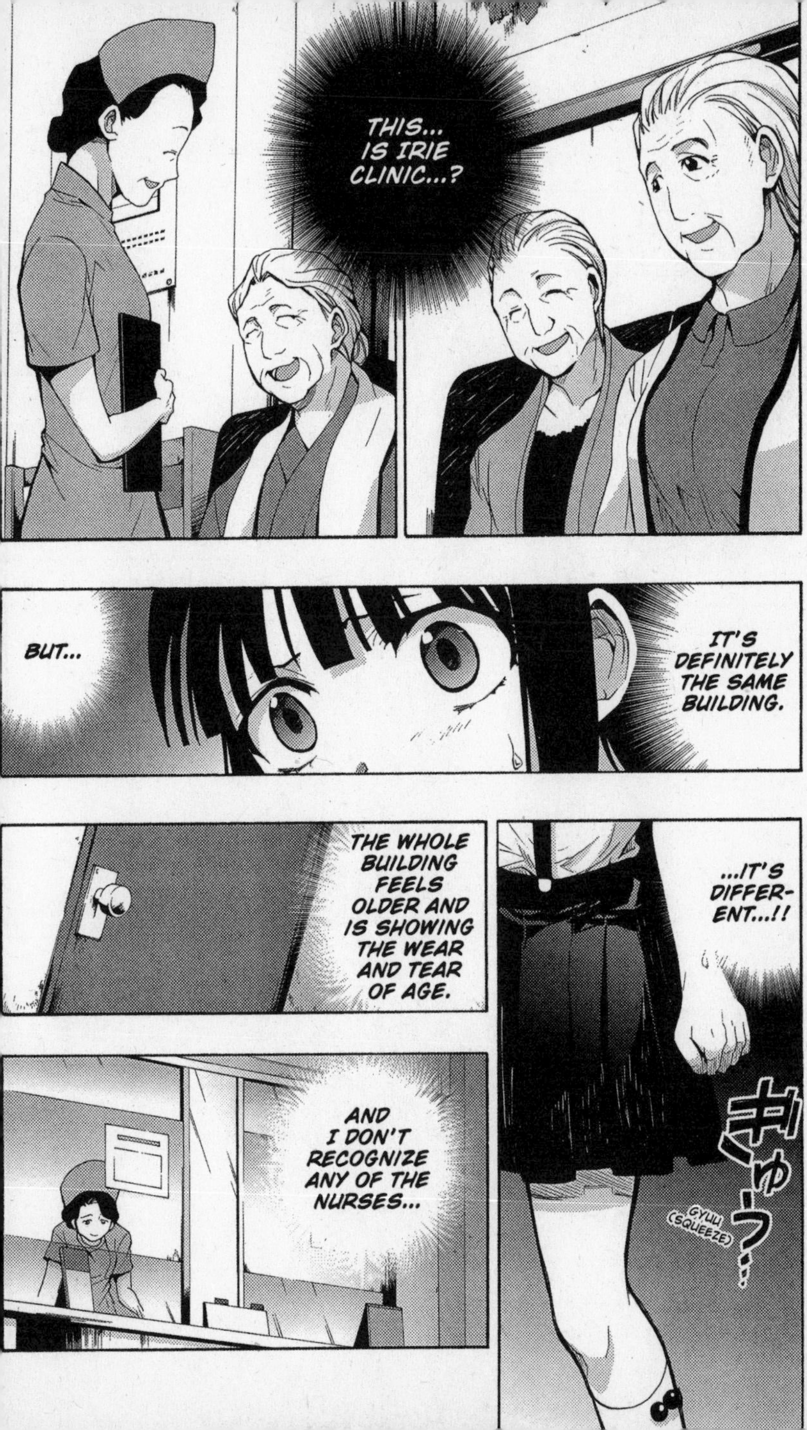
THIS... IS IRIE CLINIC...?
IT'S DEFINITELY THE SAME BUILDING.
BUT...
...IT'S DIFFERENT...!!
ぎゅ~っ...
GYUU (SQUEEZE)
THE WHOLE BUILDING FEELS OLDER AND IS SHOWING THE WEAR AND TEAR OF AGE.
AND I DON'T RECOGNIZE ANY OF THE NURSES...

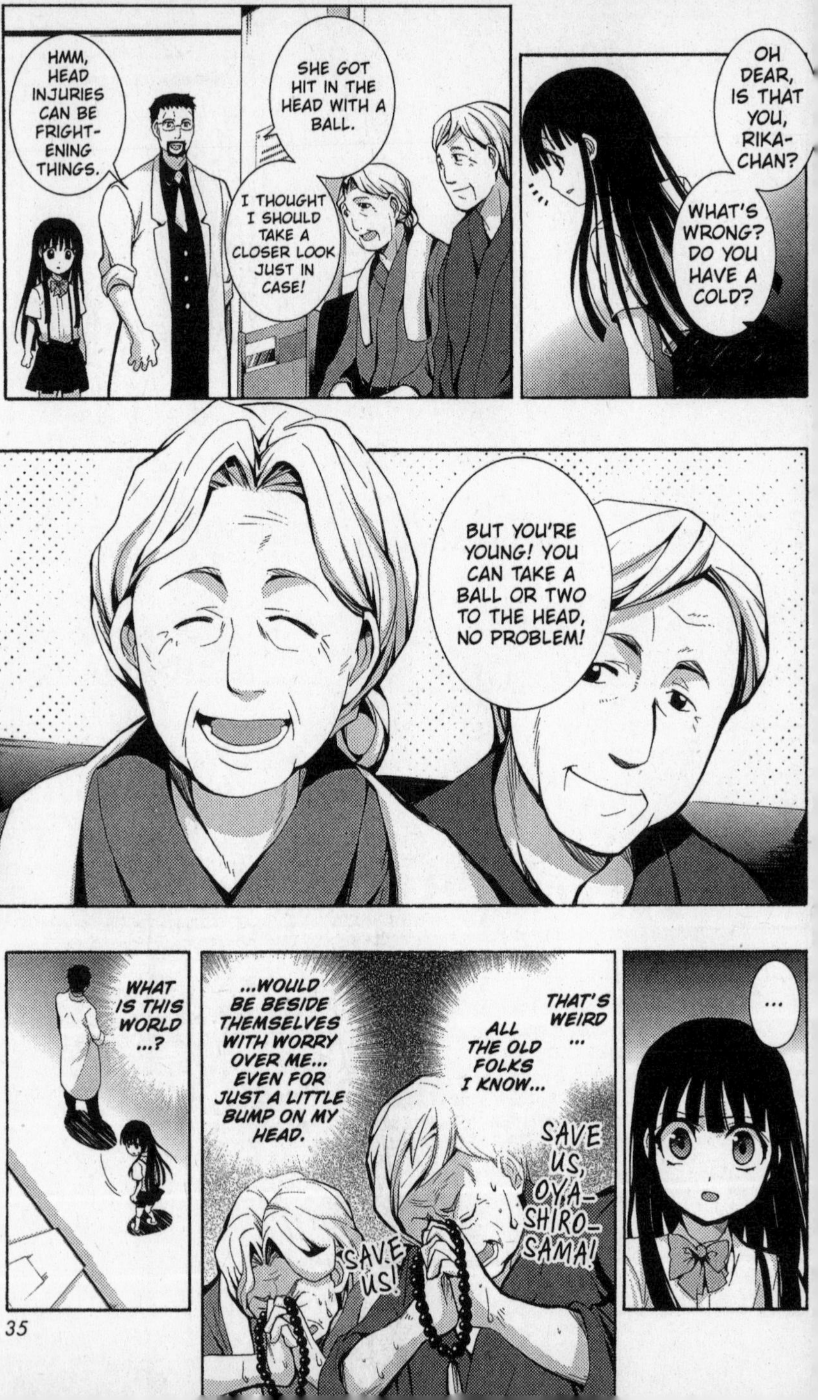
OH DEAR, IS THAT YOU, RIKA-CHAN?
WHAT'S WRONG? DO YOU HAVE A COLD?
SHE GOT HIT IN THE HEAD WITH A BALL.
I THOUGHT I SHOULD TAKE A CLOSER LOOK JUST IN CASE!
HMM, HEAD INJURIES CAN BE FRIGHT-ENING THINGS.
BUT YOU'RE YOUNG! YOU CAN TAKE A BALL OR TWO TO THE HEAD, NO PROBLEM!
...
THAT'S WEIRD...
ALL THE OLD FOLKS I KNOW...
...WOULD BE BESIDE THEMSELVES WITH WORRY OVER ME... EVEN FOR JUST A LITTLE BUMP ON MY HEAD.
SAVE US, OYA-SHIRO-SAMA!
SAVE US!
WHAT IS THIS WORLD ...?

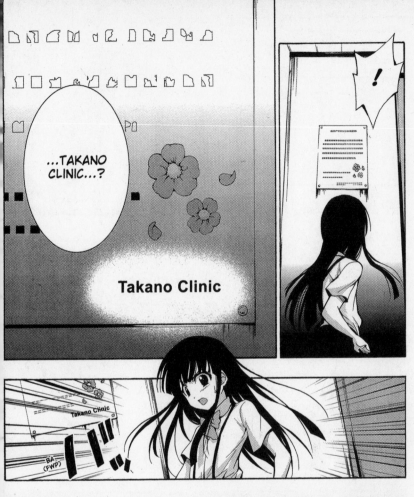

...TAKANO CLINIC...?

Takano Clinic

!

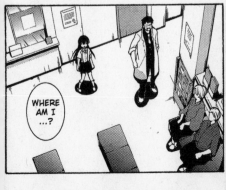

WHERE AM I ...?

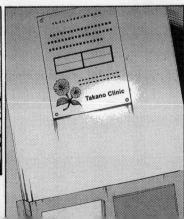

Takano Clinic

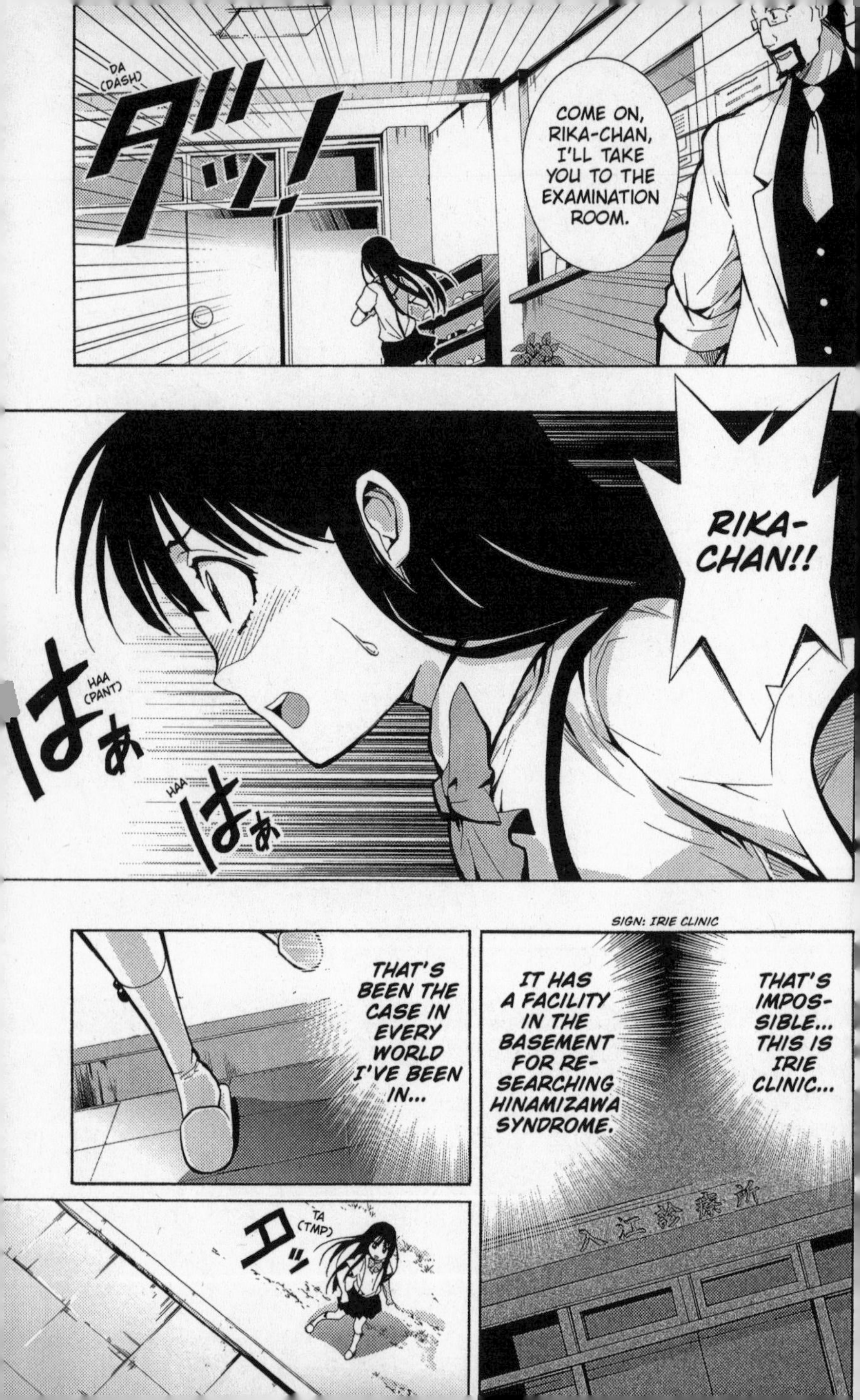
COME ON, RIKA-CHAN, I'LL TAKE YOU TO THE EXAMINATION ROOM.
DA (DASH)
RIKA-CHAN!!
HAA (PANT)
HAA
SIGN: IRIE CLINIC
THAT'S IMPOSSIBLE... THIS IS IRIE CLINIC...
IT HAS A FACILITY IN THE BASEMENT FOR RESEARCHING HINAMIZAWA SYNDROME.
入江診療所
THAT'S BEEN THE CASE IN EVERY WORLD I'VE BEEN IN...
TA (TMP)

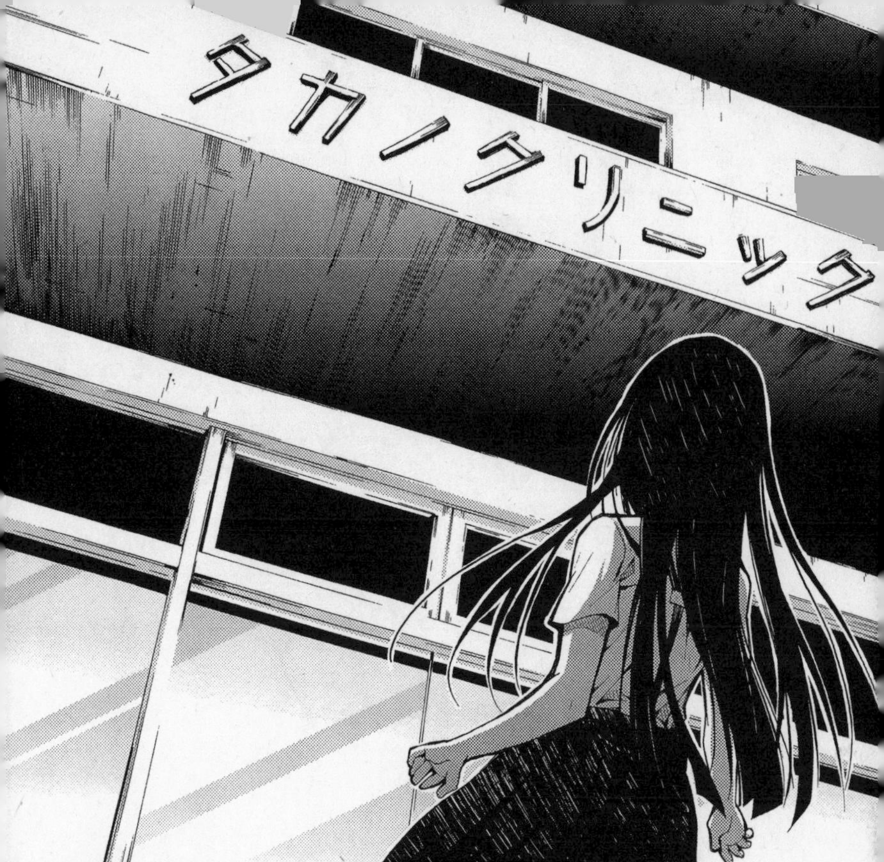
タカノクリニック

SIGN: TAKANO CLINIC

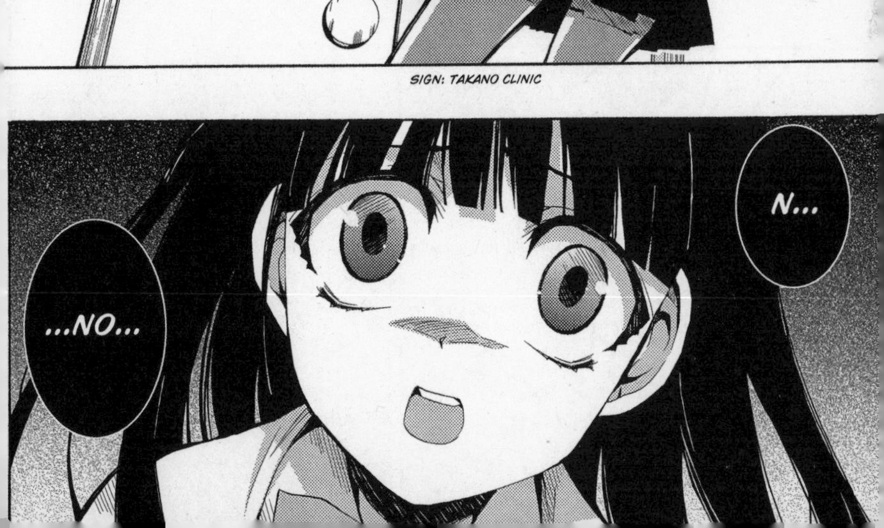
N...
...NO...

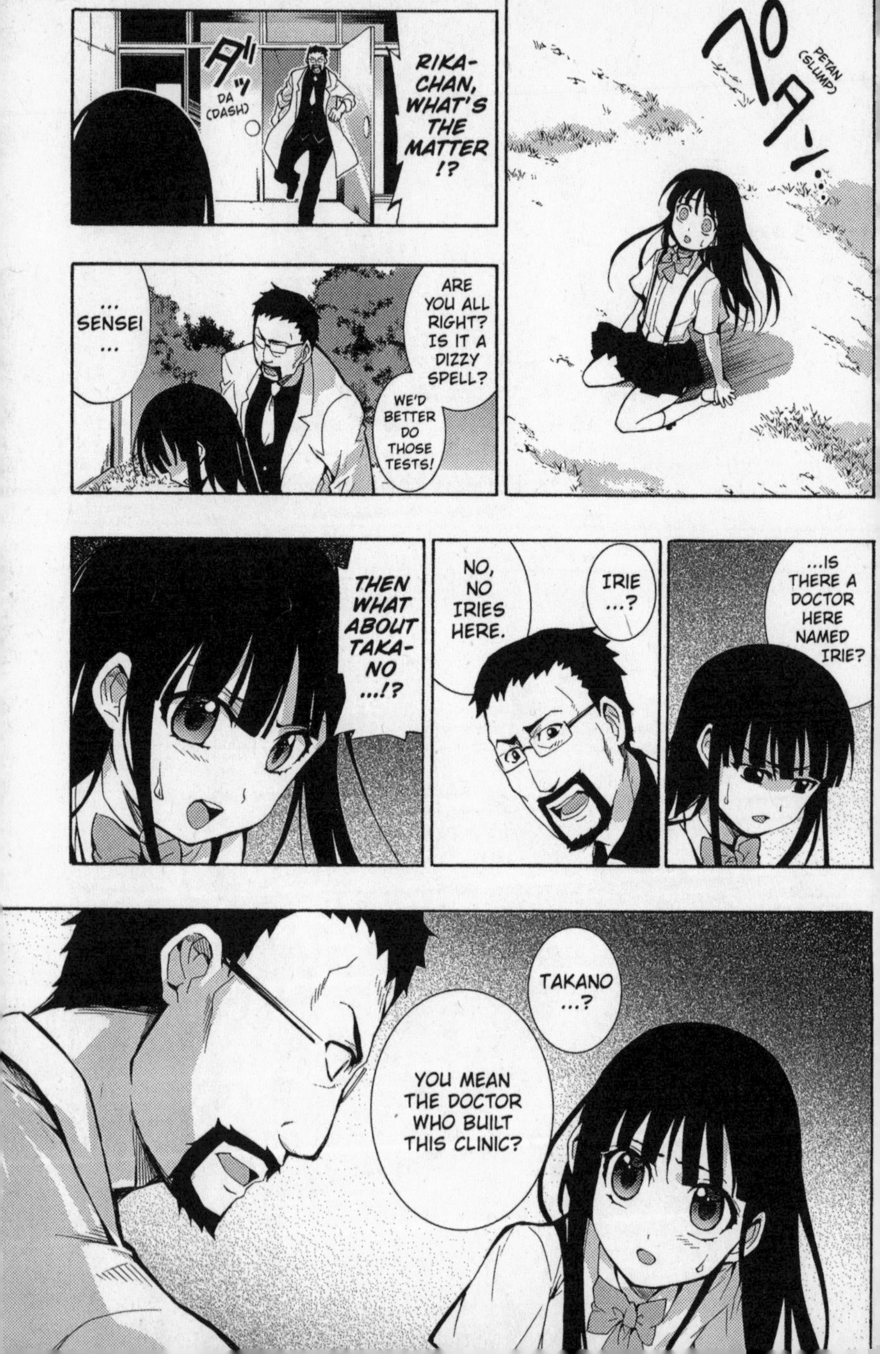
PETAN (SLUMP)
DA (DASH)
RIKA-CHAN, WHAT'S THE MATTER!?
ARE YOU ALL RIGHT? IS IT A DIZZY SPELL?
WE'D BETTER DO THOSE TESTS!
...SENSEI...
...IS THERE A DOCTOR HERE NAMED IRIE?
IRIE ...?
NO, NO IRIES HERE.
THEN WHAT ABOUT TAKA-NO ...!?
TAKANO ...?
YOU MEAN THE DOCTOR WHO BUILT THIS CLINIC?

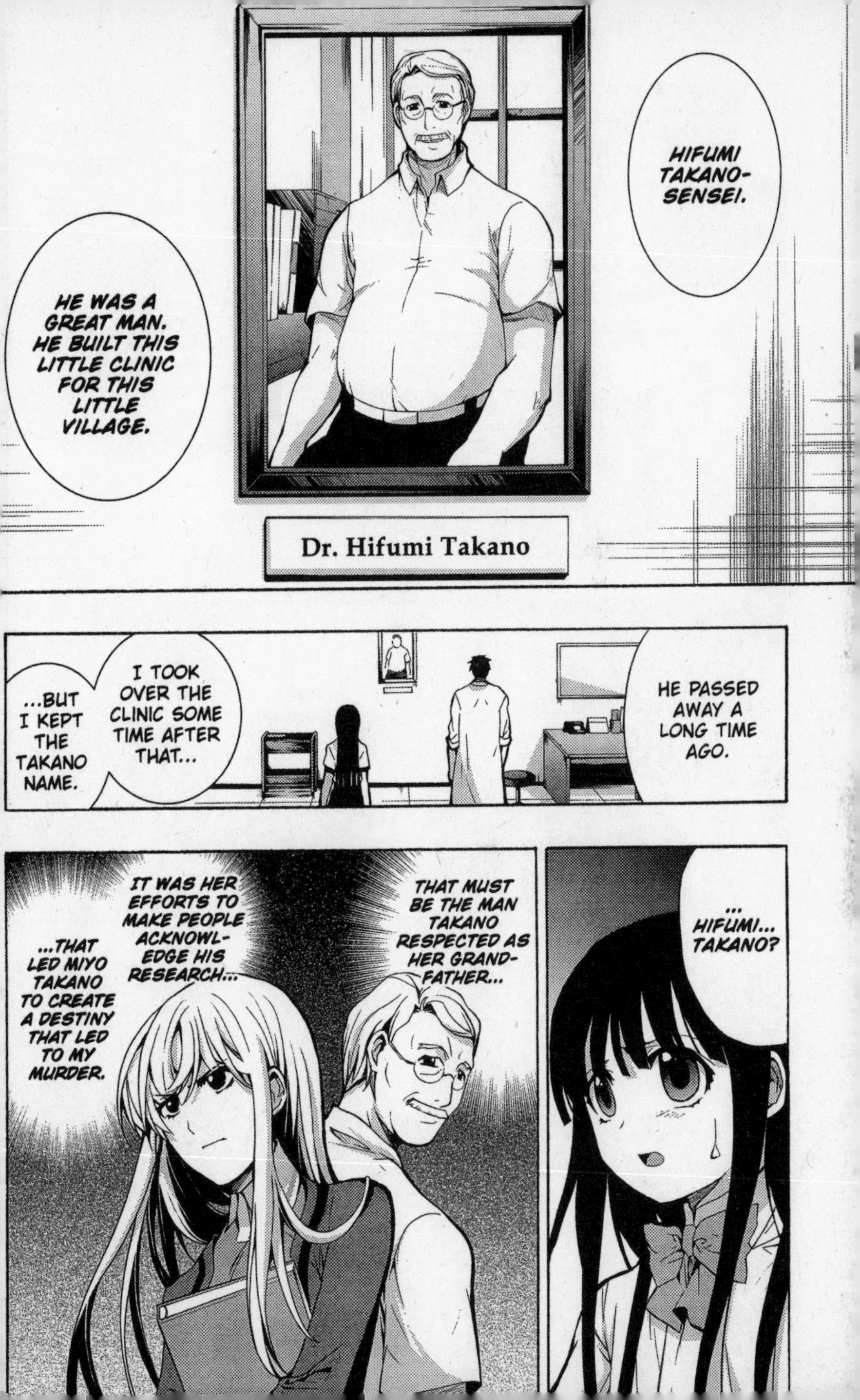
HIFUMI TAKANO-SENSEI.
HE WAS A GREAT MAN. HE BUILT THIS LITTLE CLINIC FOR THIS LITTLE VILLAGE.
Dr. Hifumi Takano
HE PASSED AWAY A LONG TIME AGO.
I TOOK OVER THE CLINIC SOME TIME AFTER THAT...
...BUT I KEPT THE TAKANO NAME.
... HIFUMI... TAKANO?
THAT MUST BE THE MAN TAKANO RESPECTED AS HER GRAND-FATHER...
IT WAS HER EFFORTS TO MAKE PEOPLE ACKNOWL-EDGE HIS RESEARCH...
...THAT LED MIYO TAKANO TO CREATE A DESTINY THAT LED TO MY MURDER.

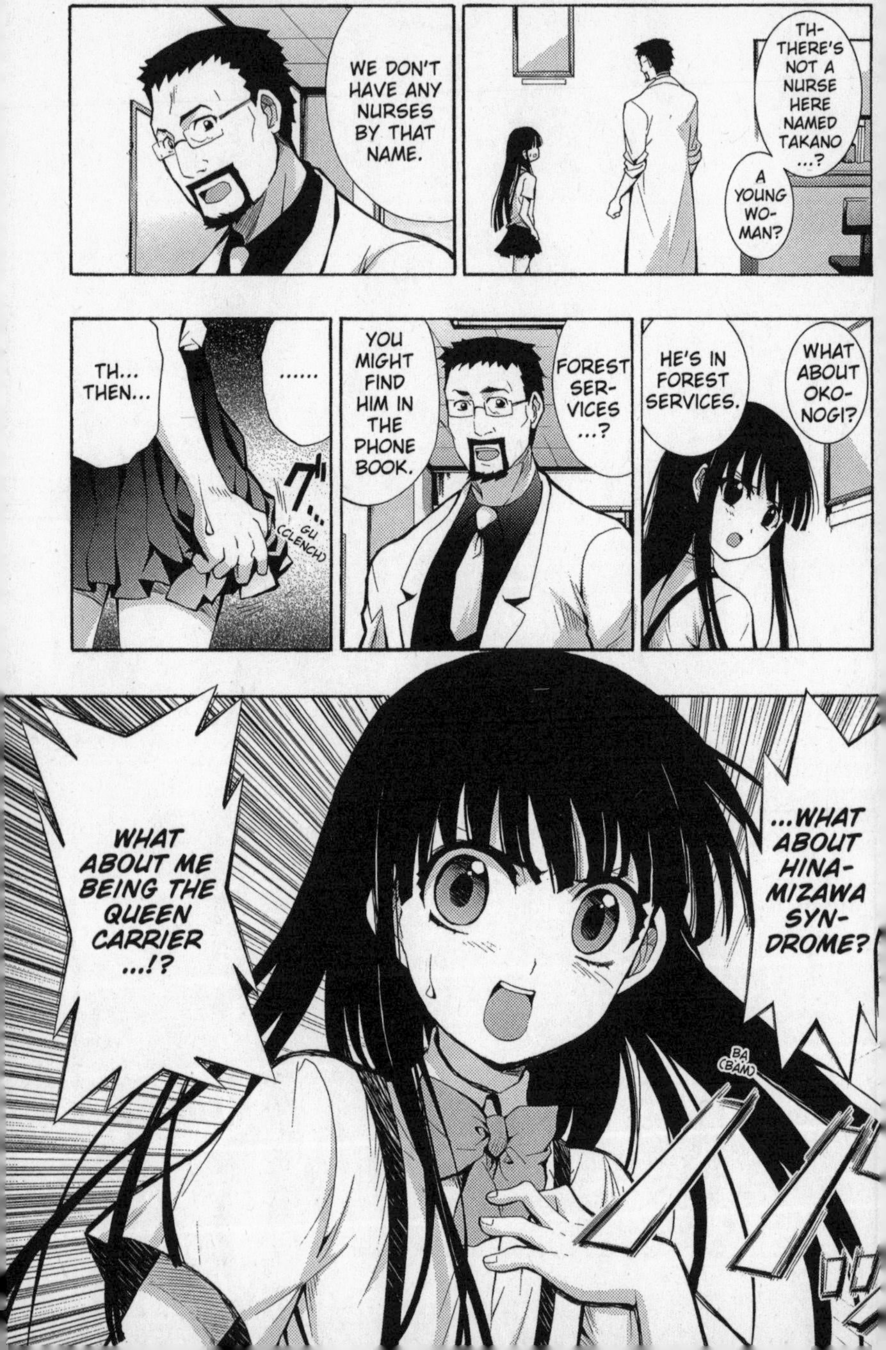
TH-THERE'S NOT A NURSE HERE NAMED TAKANO...?
A YOUNG WO-MAN?
WE DON'T HAVE ANY NURSES BY THAT NAME.
WHAT ABOUT OKO-NOGI?
HE'S IN FOREST SERVICES.
FOREST SER-VICES...?
YOU MIGHT FIND HIM IN THE PHONE BOOK.
......
TH... THEN...
GU (CLENCH)
...WHAT ABOUT HINA-MIZAWA SYN-DROME?
BA (BAM)
WHAT ABOUT ME BEING THE QUEEN CARRIER...!?

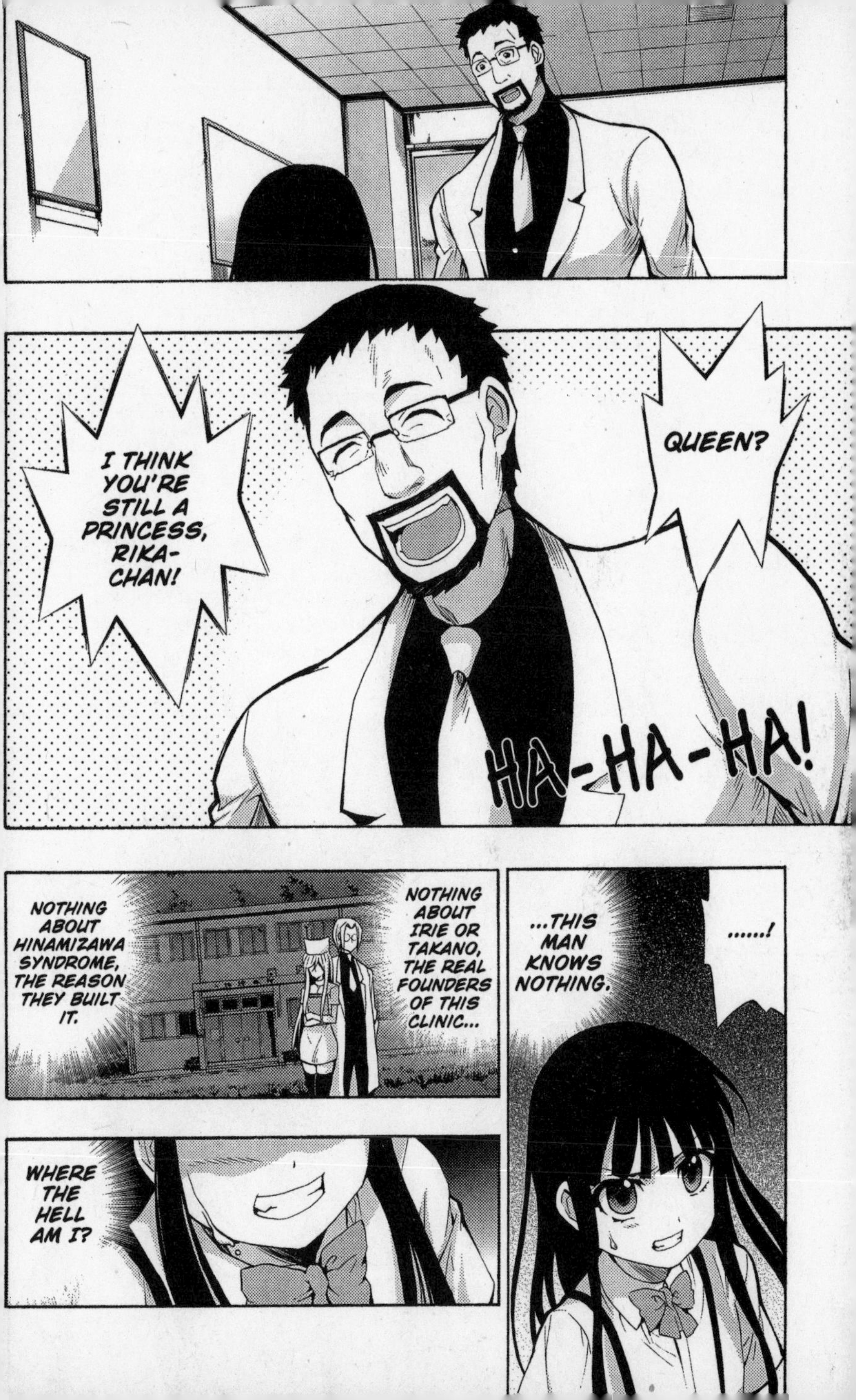
QUEEN?
I THINK YOU'RE STILL A PRINCESS, RIKA-CHAN!
HA-HA-HA!
......!
...THIS MAN KNOWS NOTHING.
NOTHING ABOUT IRIE OR TAKANO, THE REAL FOUNDERS OF THIS CLINIC...
NOTHING ABOUT HINAMIZAWA SYNDROME, THE REASON THEY BUILT IT.
WHERE THE HELL AM I?

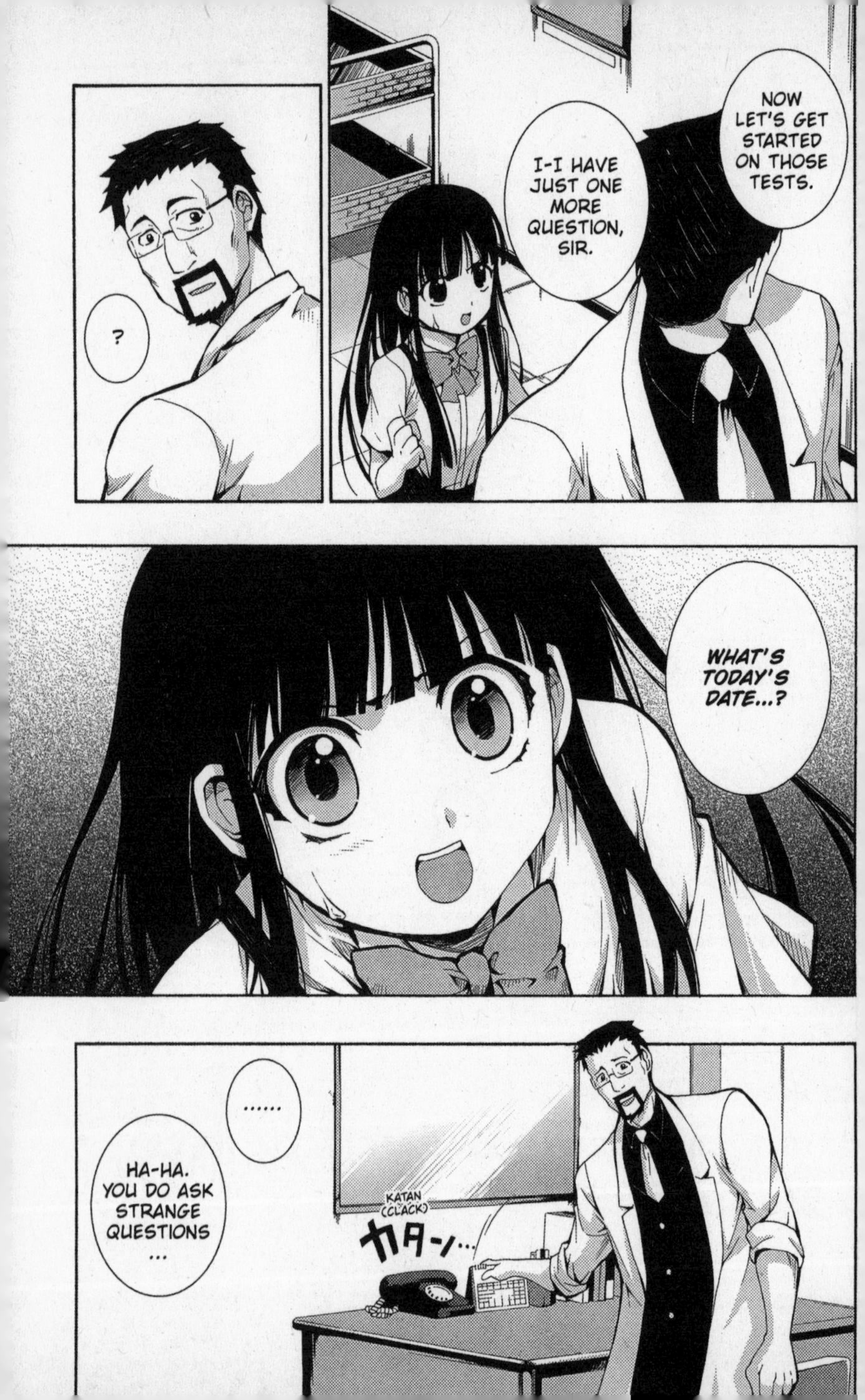

NOW LET'S GET STARTED ON THOSE TESTS.
I-I HAVE JUST ONE MORE QUESTION, SIR.
?
WHAT'S TODAY'S DATE...?
......
HA-HA. YOU DO ASK STRANGE QUESTIONS...
KATAN (CLACK)
カタ-ン...

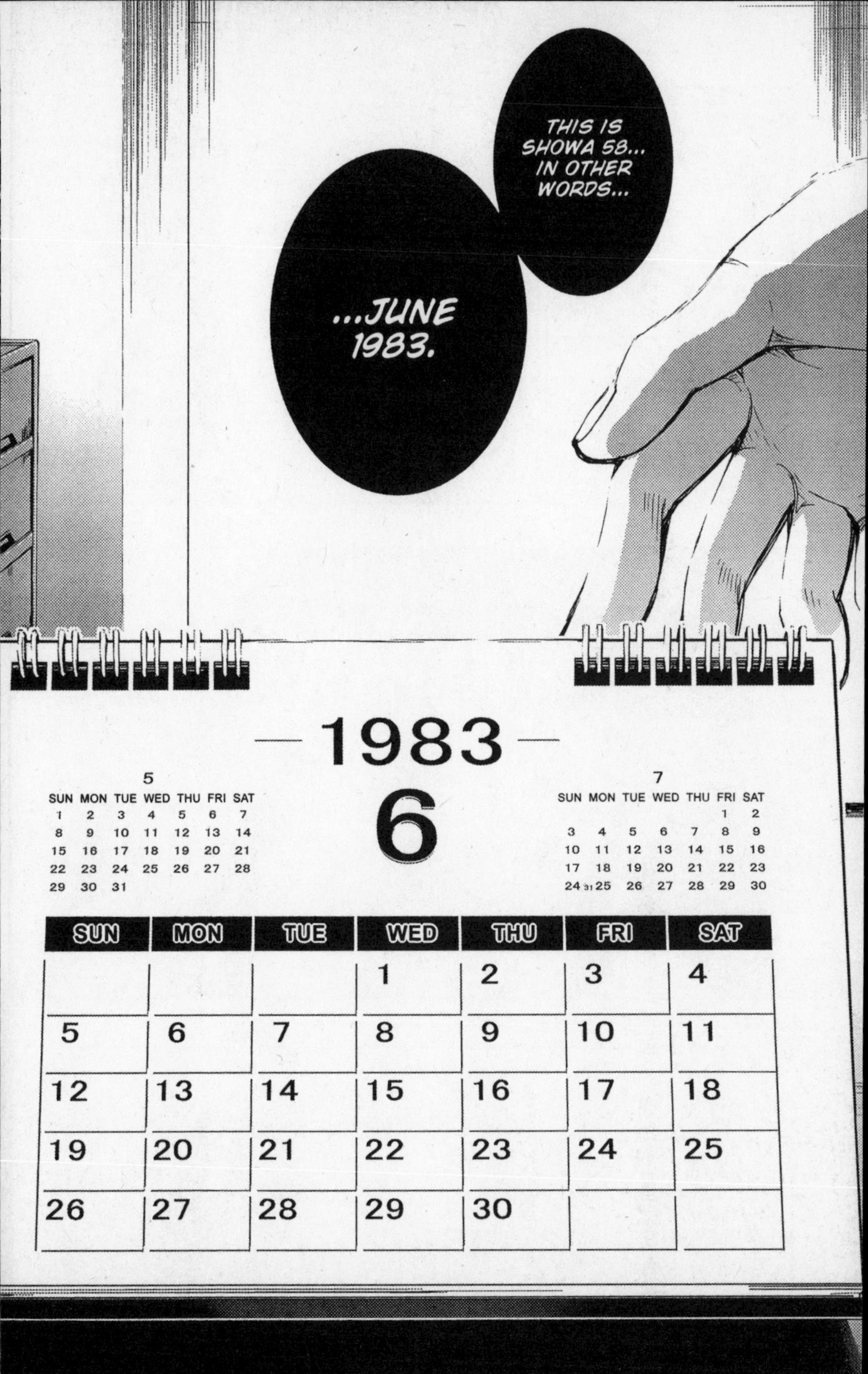
THIS IS SHOWA 58... IN OTHER WORDS...
...JUNE 1983.
1983
6
5
SUN MON TUE WED THU FRI SAT
1 2 3 4 5 6 7
8 9 10 11 12 13 14
15 16 17 18 19 20 21
22 23 24 25 26 27 28
29 30 31
7
SUN MON TUE WED THU FRI SAT
1 2
3 4 5 6 7 8 9
10 11 12 13 14 15 16
17 18 19 20 21 22 23
24 31 25 26 27 28 29 30
SUN MON TUE WED THU FRI SAT
1 2 3 4
5 6 7 8 9 10 11
12 13 14 15 16 17 18
19 20 21 22 23 24 25
26 27 28 29 30

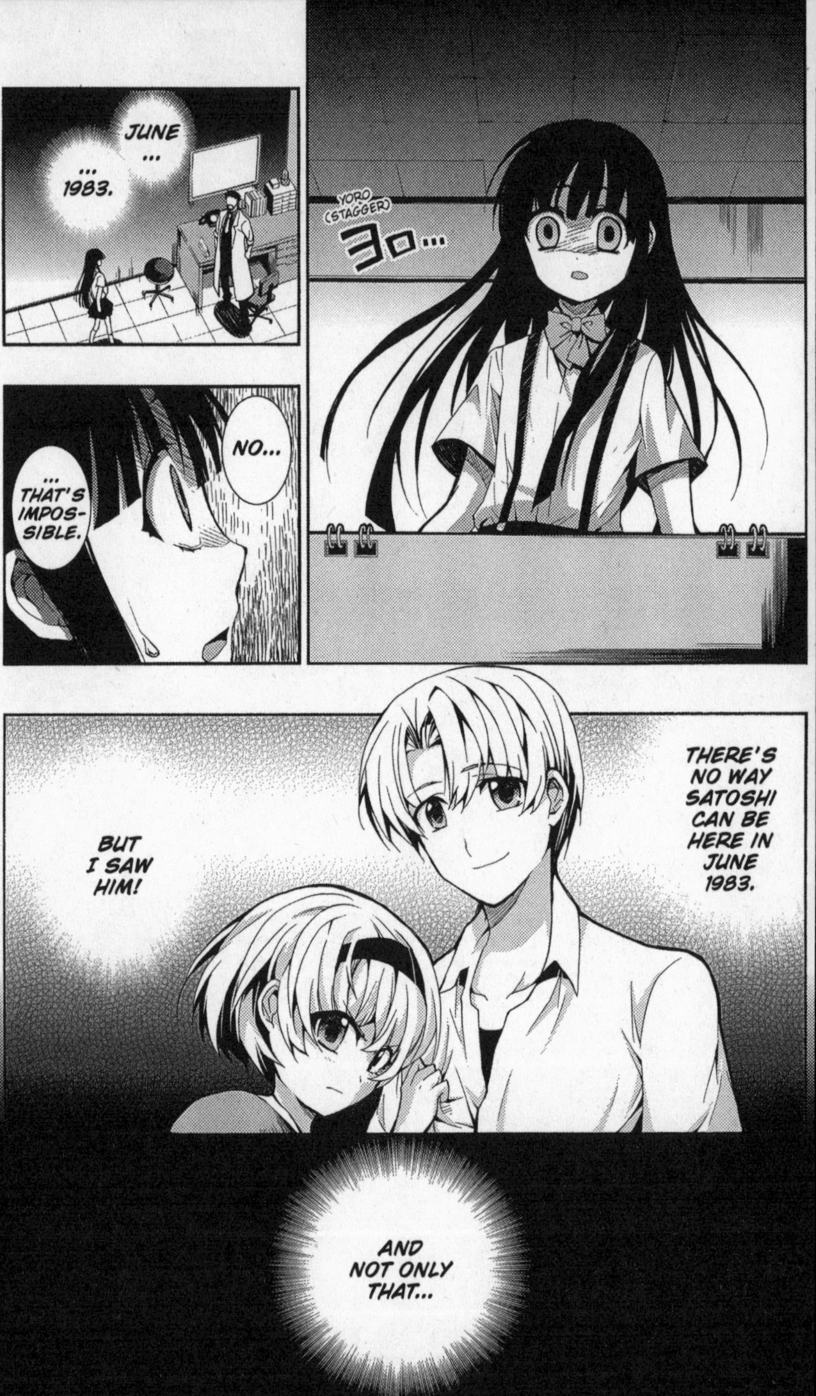
YORO (STAGGER)
ヨロ...
JUNE ...
... 1983.
NO...
... THAT'S IMPOSSIBLE.
THERE'S NO WAY SATOSHI CAN BE HERE IN JUNE 1983.
BUT I SAW HIM!
AND NOT ONLY THAT...

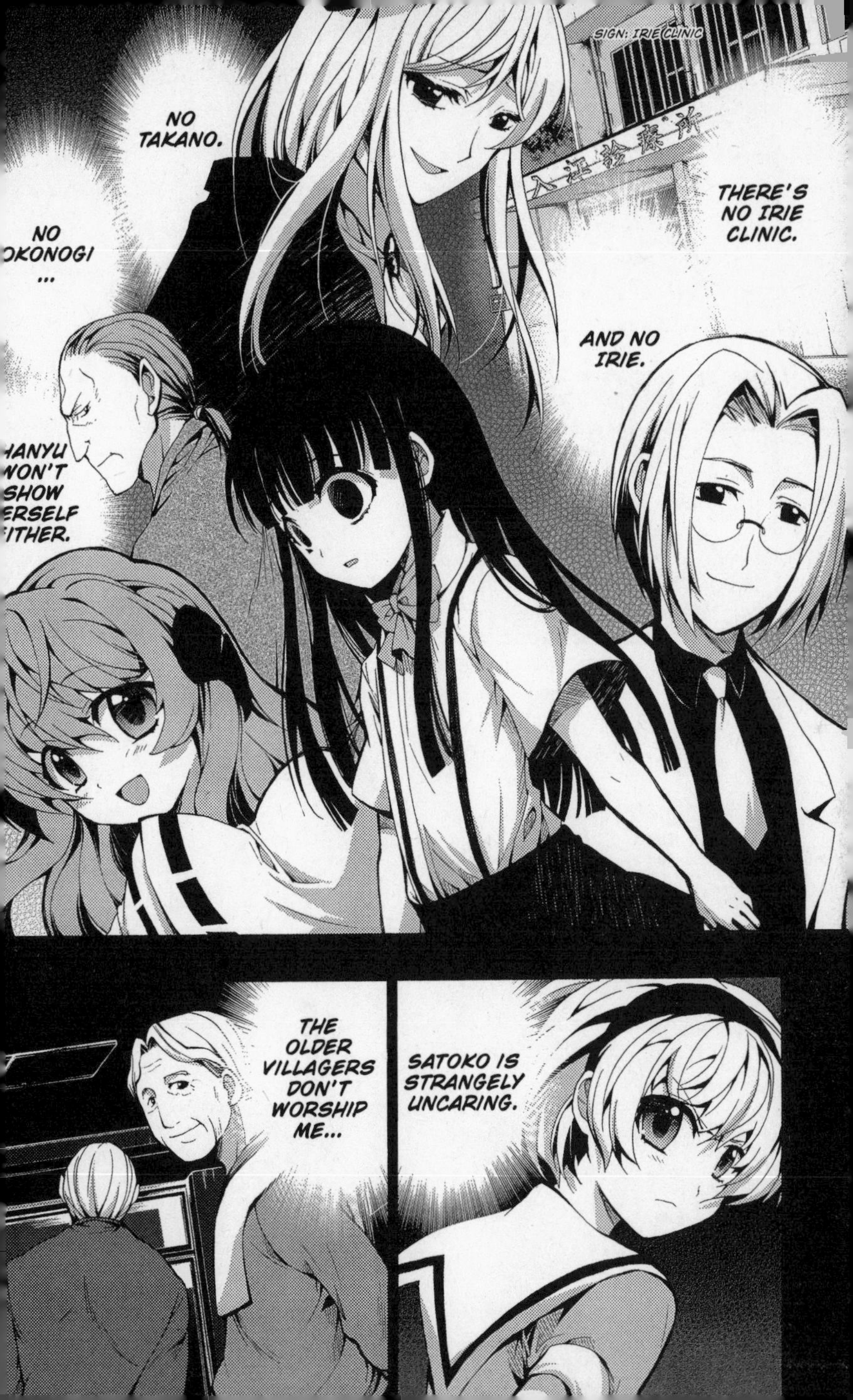
SIGN: IRIE CLINIC
THERE'S NO IRIE CLINIC.
AND NO IRIE.
NO TAKANO.
NO OKONOGI ...
HANYU WON'T SHOW ERSELF EITHER.
SATOKO IS STRANGELY UNCARING.
THE OLDER VILLAGERS DON'T WORSHIP ME...

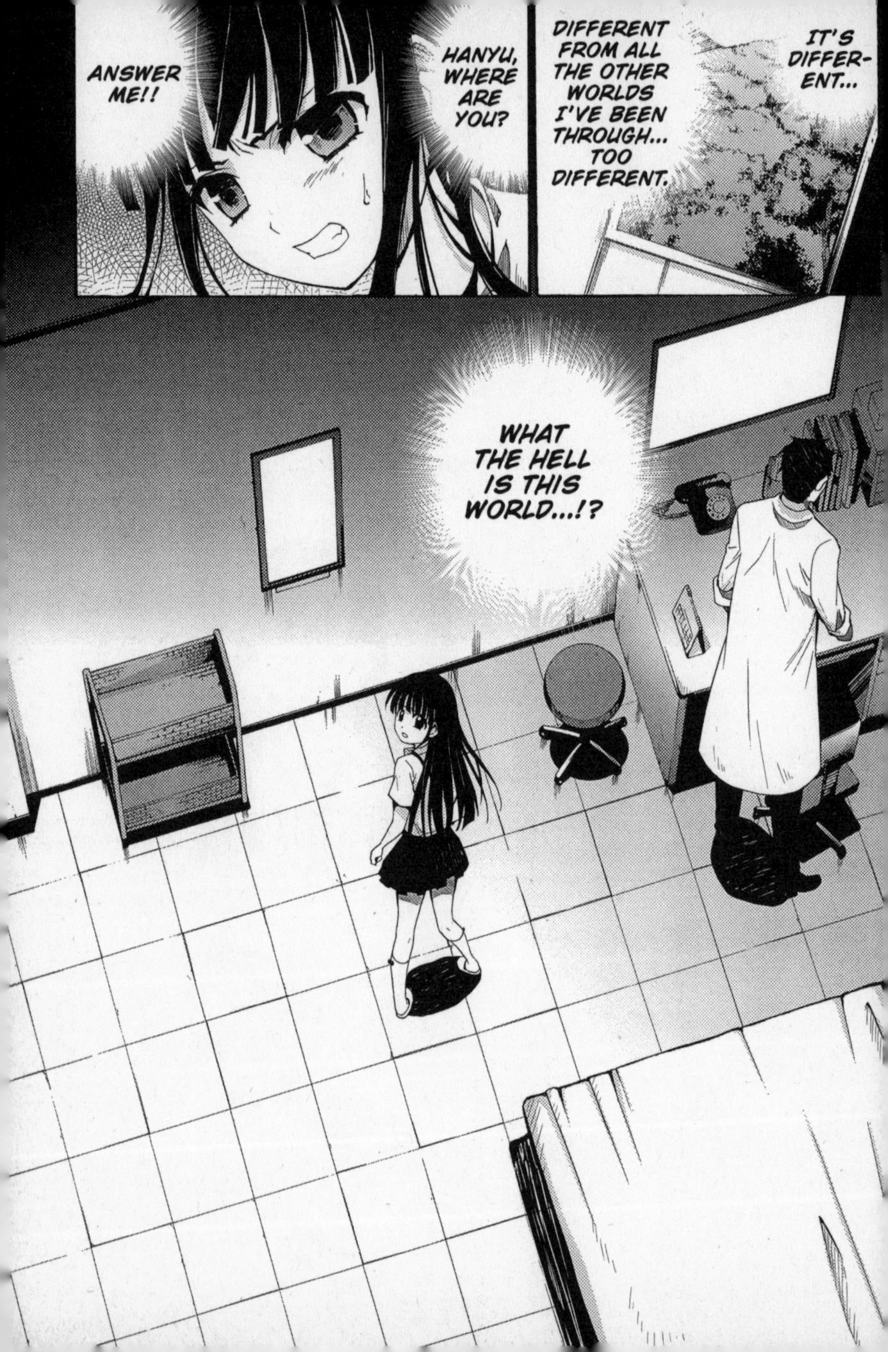
IT'S DIFFERENT...
DIFFERENT FROM ALL THE OTHER WORLDS I'VE BEEN THROUGH... TOO DIFFERENT.
HANYU, WHERE ARE YOU?
ANSWER ME!!
WHAT THE HELL IS THIS WORLD...!?

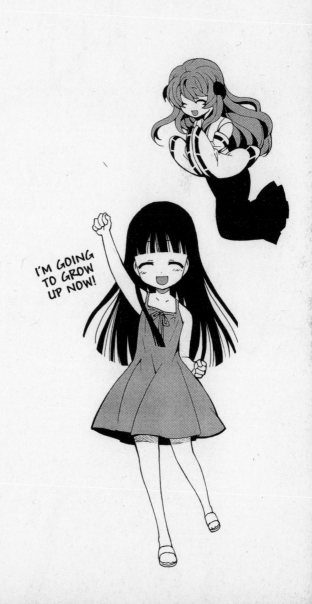

I'M GOING TO GROW UP NOW!

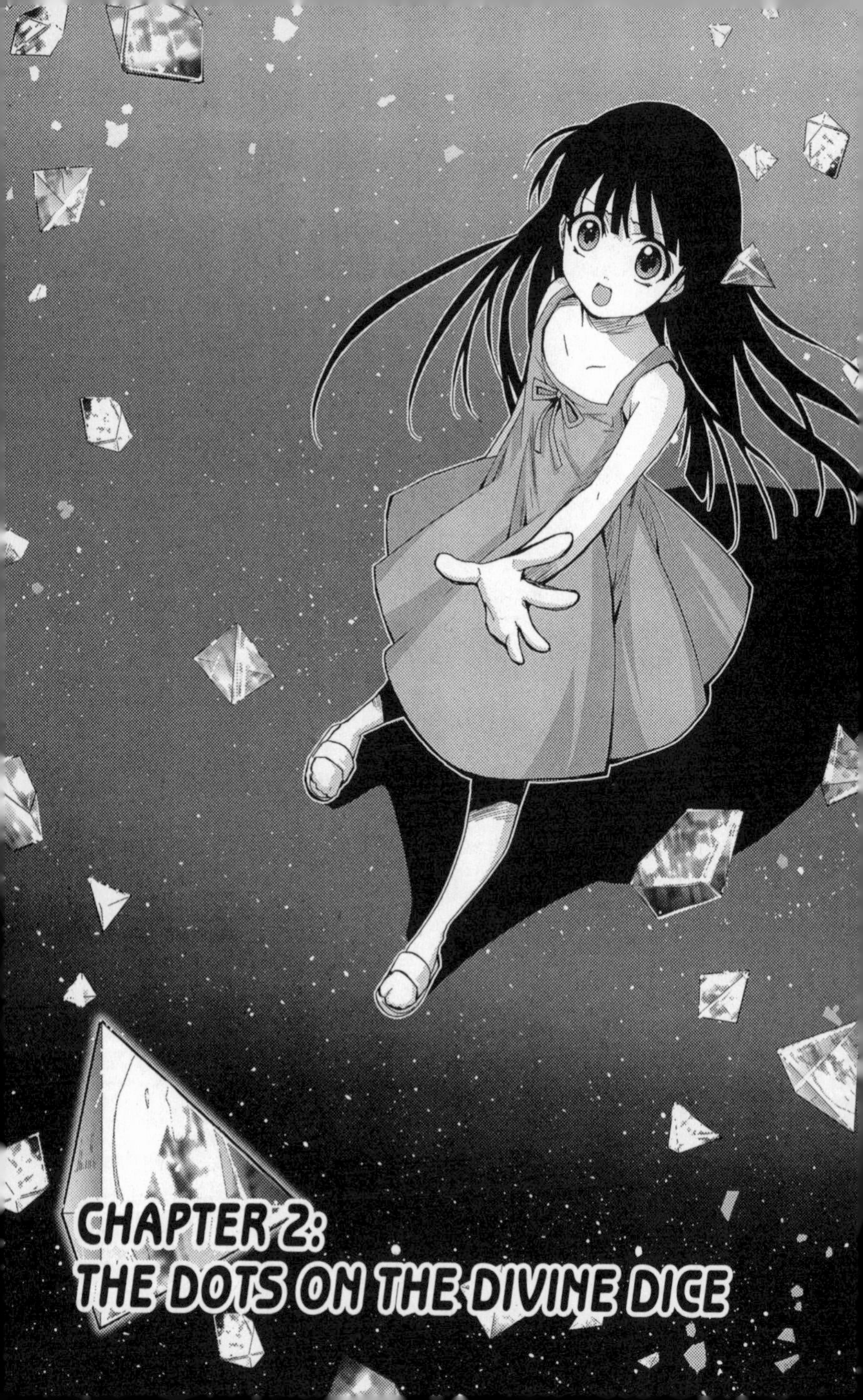
CHAPTER 2:
THE DOTS ON THE DIVINE DICE

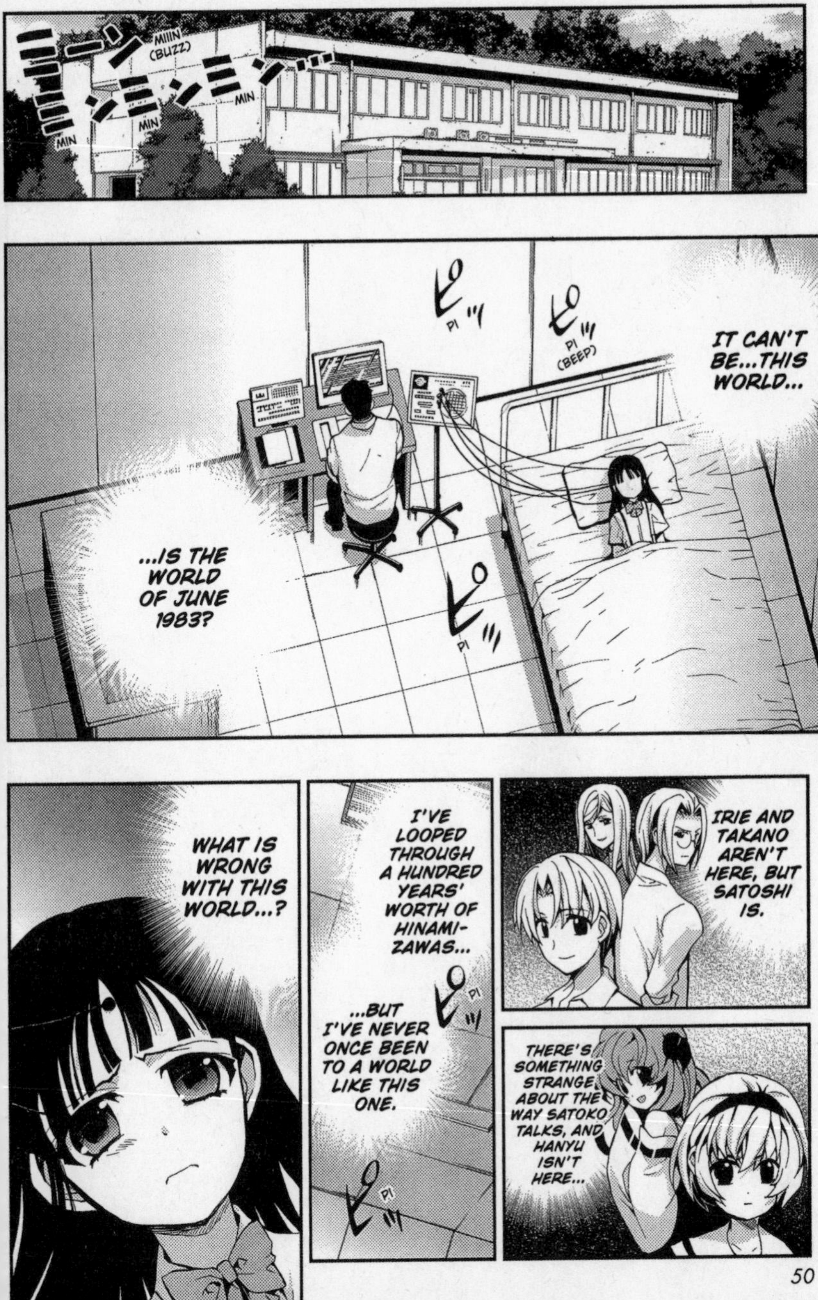
MIIIN (BUZZ)
MIN
MIN
MIN
PI
PI (BEEP)
IT CAN'T BE...THIS WORLD...
...IS THE WORLD OF JUNE 1983?
PI
IRIE AND TAKANO AREN'T HERE, BUT SATOSHI IS.
THERE'S SOMETHING STRANGE ABOUT THE WAY SATOKO TALKS, AND HANYU ISN'T HERE...
I'VE LOOPED THROUGH A HUNDRED YEARS' WORTH OF HINAMI-ZAWAS...
PI
...BUT I'VE NEVER ONCE BEEN TO A WORLD LIKE THIS ONE.
PI
WHAT IS WRONG WITH THIS WORLD...?

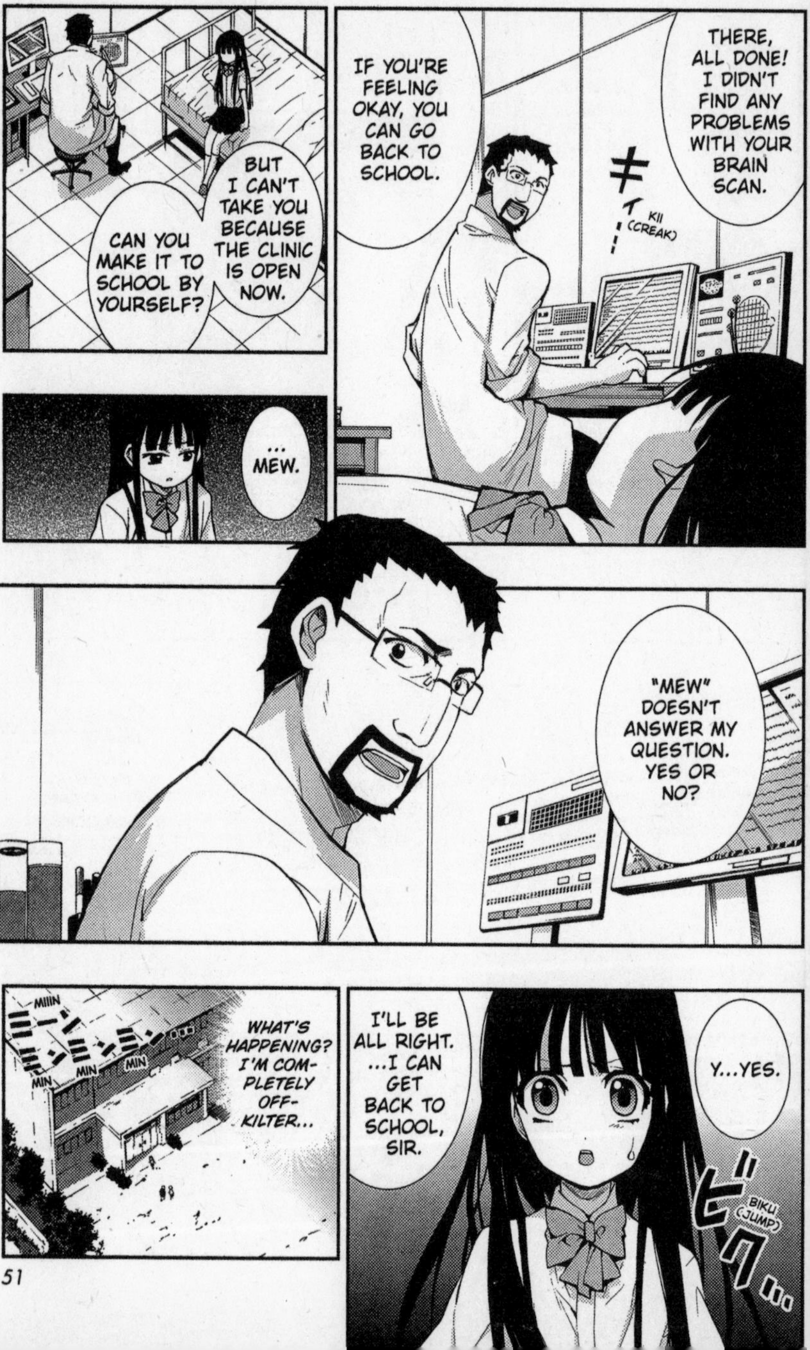
THERE, ALL DONE! I DIDN'T FIND ANY PROBLEMS WITH YOUR BRAIN SCAN.
KII (CREAK)
IF YOU'RE FEELING OKAY, YOU CAN GO BACK TO SCHOOL.
BUT I CAN'T TAKE YOU BECAUSE THE CLINIC IS OPEN NOW.
CAN YOU MAKE IT TO SCHOOL BY YOURSELF?
... MEW.
"MEW" DOESN'T ANSWER MY QUESTION. YES OR NO?
Y...YES.
BIKU (JUMP)
I'LL BE ALL RIGHT. ...I CAN GET BACK TO SCHOOL, SIR.
WHAT'S HAPPENING? I'M COMPLETELY OFF-KILTER...
MIIIN
MIN
MIN
MIN
MIN

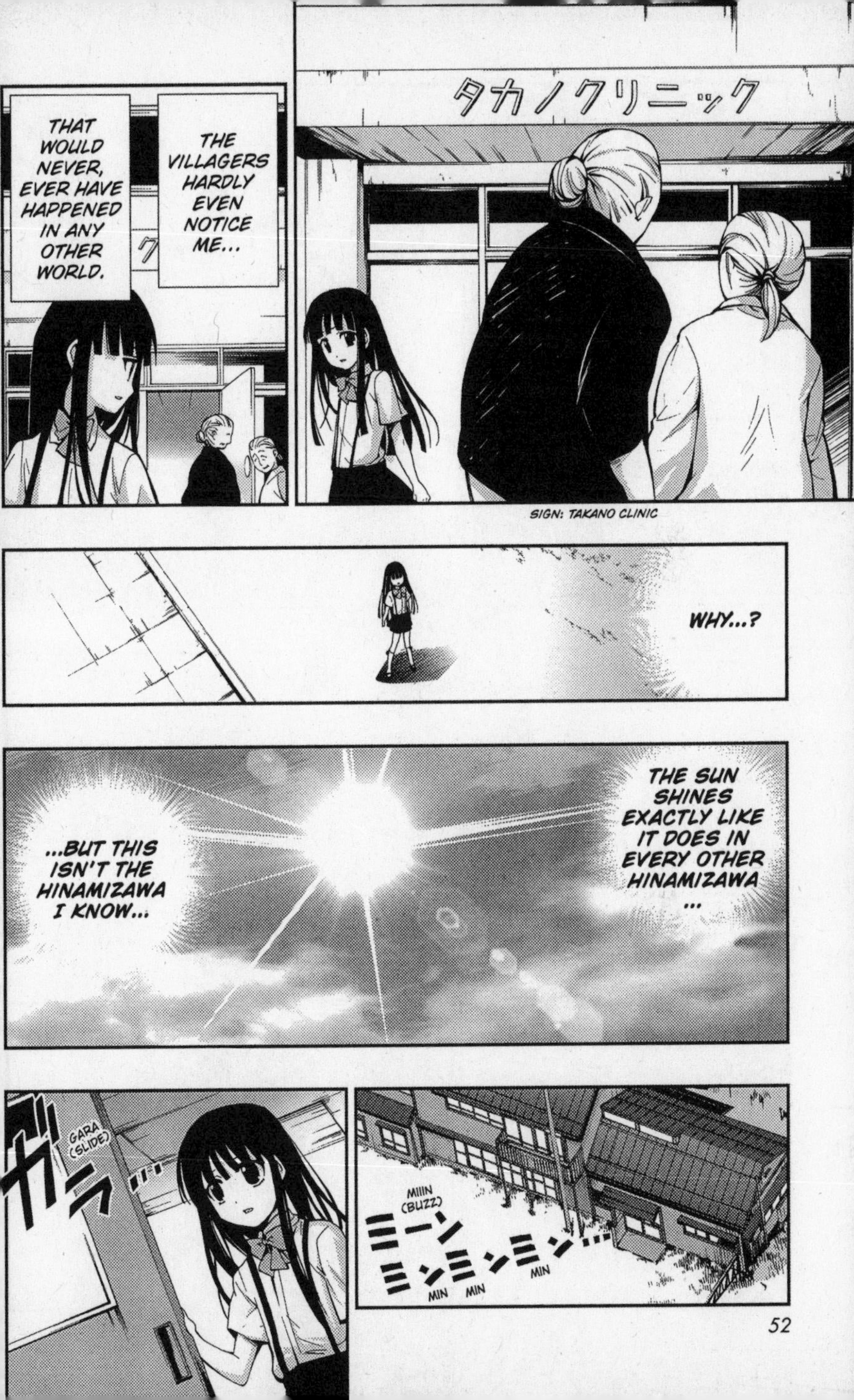
タカノクリニック
THE VILLAGERS HARDLY EVEN NOTICE ME...
THAT WOULD NEVER, EVER HAVE HAPPENED IN ANY OTHER WORLD.
SIGN: TAKANO CLINIC
WHY...?
THE SUN SHINES EXACTLY LIKE IT DOES IN EVERY OTHER HINAMIZAWA ...
...BUT THIS ISN'T THE HINAMIZAWA I KNOW...
MIIIN (BUZZ)
ミーン ミンミンミン
MIN MIN MIN
GARA (SLIDE)
ガラッ

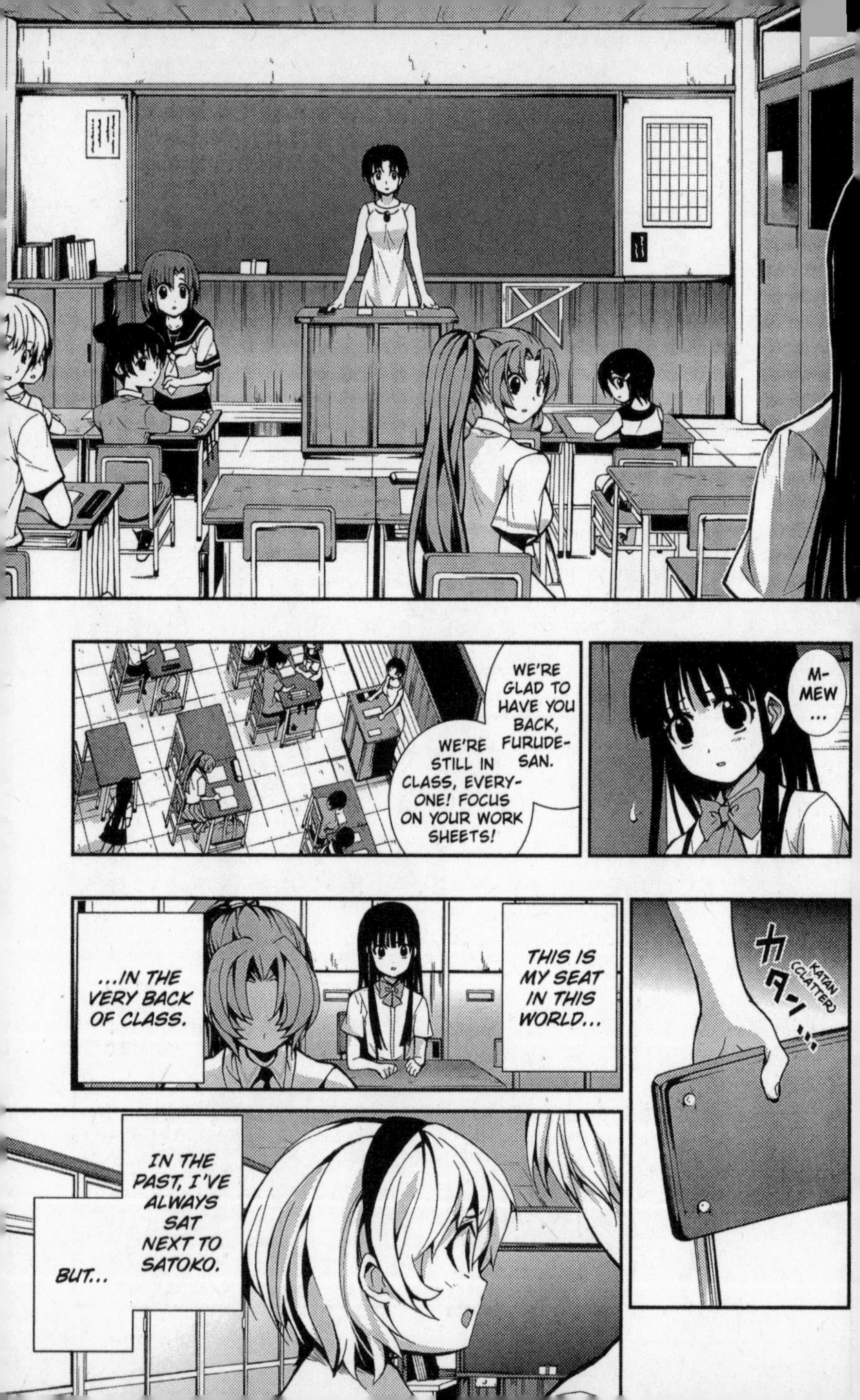
M-MEW ...
WE'RE GLAD TO HAVE YOU BACK, FURUDE-SAN.
WE'RE STILL IN CLASS, EVERYONE! FOCUS ON YOUR WORK SHEETS!
KATAN (CLATTER)
THIS IS MY SEAT IN THIS WORLD...
...IN THE VERY BACK OF CLASS.
IN THE PAST, I'VE ALWAYS SAT NEXT TO SATOKO.
BUT...

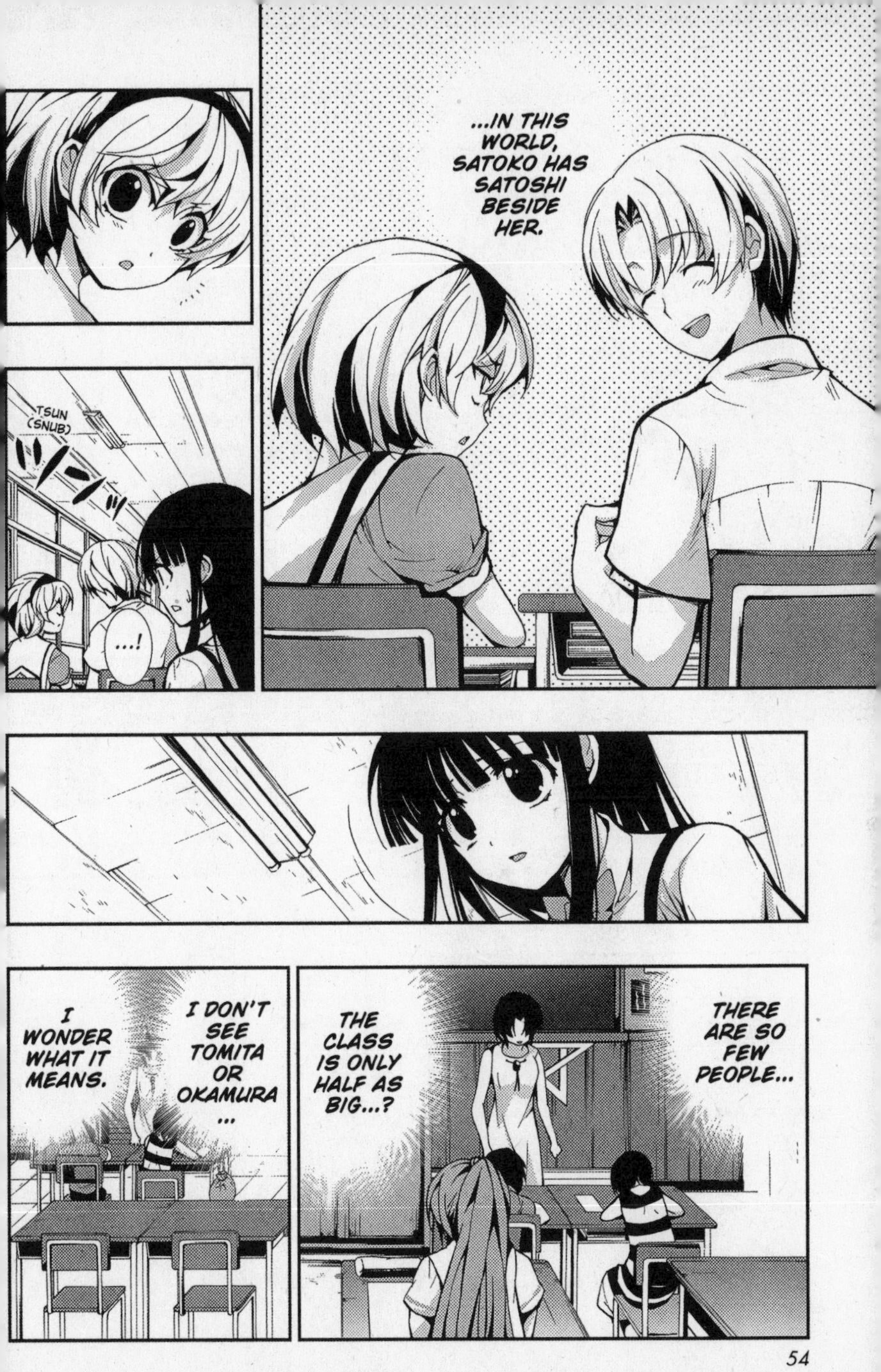
...IN THIS WORLD, SATOKO HAS SATOSHI BESIDE HER.
TSUN (SNUB)
...!
THERE ARE SO FEW PEOPLE...
THE CLASS IS ONLY HALF AS BIG...?
I DON'T SEE TOMITA OR OKAMURA...
I WONDER WHAT IT MEANS.

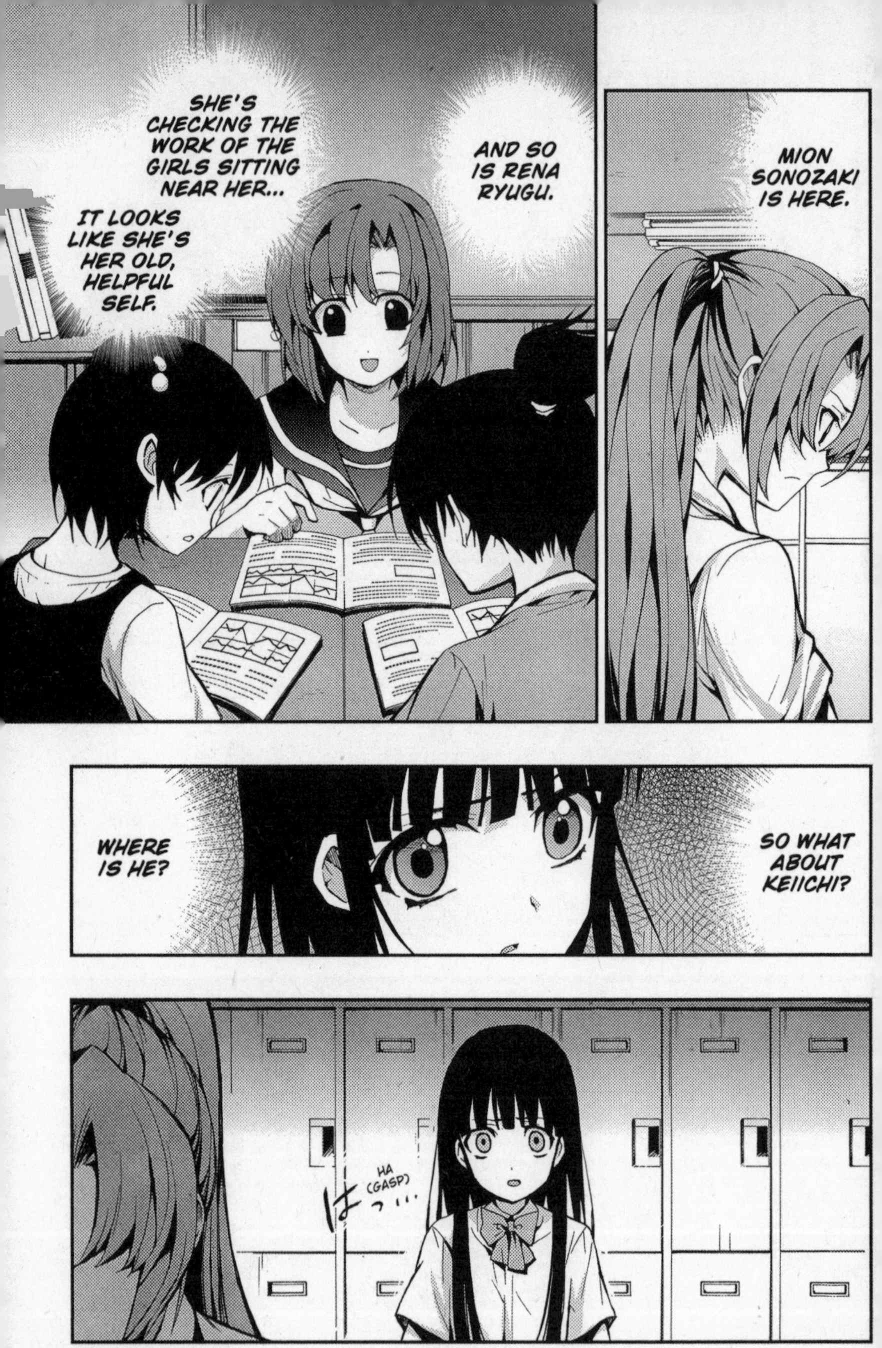
MION SONOZAKI IS HERE.
AND SO IS RENA RYUGU.
SHE'S CHECKING THE WORK OF THE GIRLS SITTING NEAR HER...
IT LOOKS LIKE SHE'S HER OLD, HELPFUL SELF.
SO WHAT ABOUT KEIICHI?
WHERE IS HE?
HA (GASP)

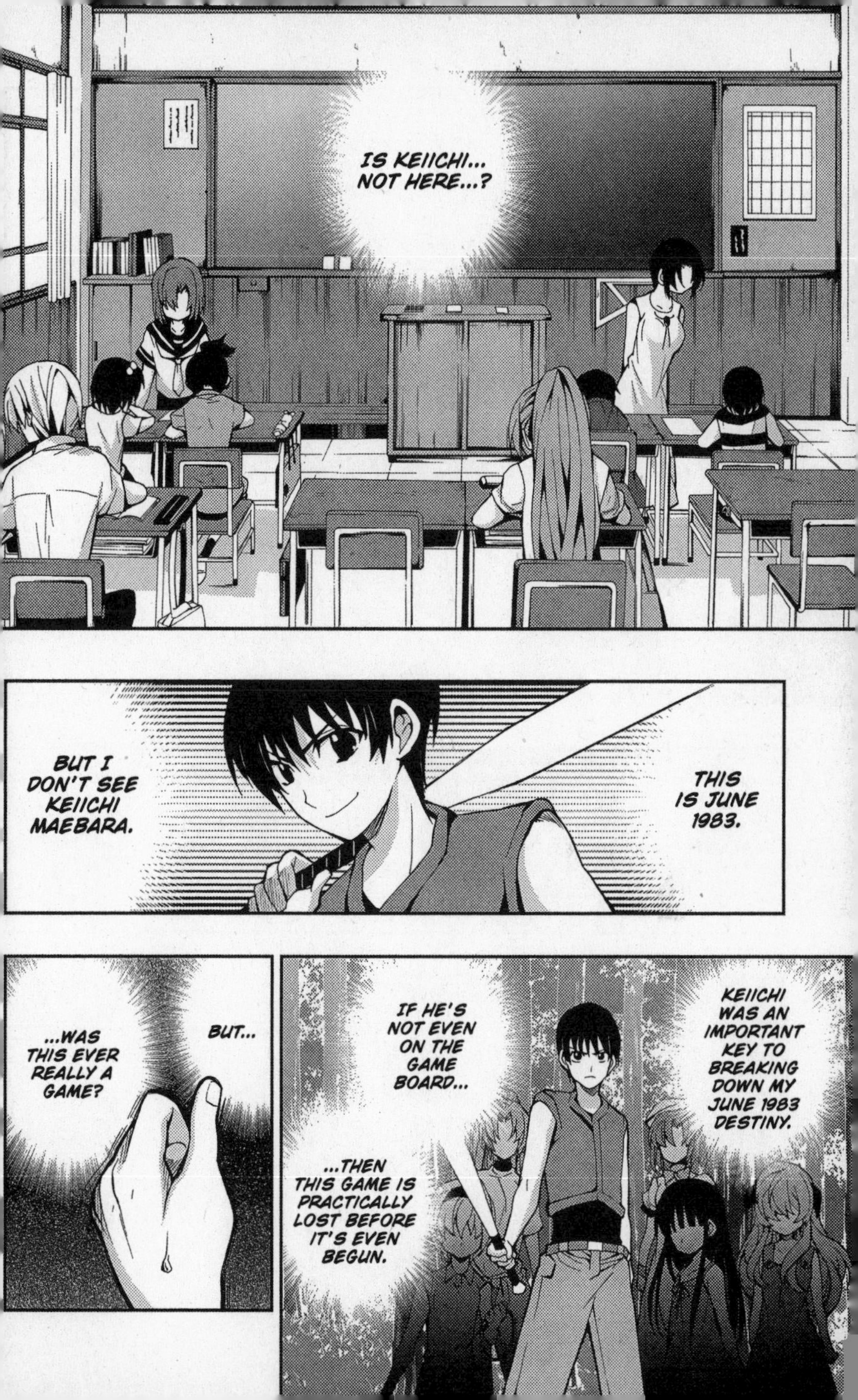
IS KEIICHI... NOT HERE...?
THIS IS JUNE 1983.
BUT I DON'T SEE KEIICHI MAEBARA.
KEIICHI WAS AN IMPORTANT KEY TO BREAKING DOWN MY JUNE 1983 DESTINY.
IF HE'S NOT EVEN ON THE GAME BOARD...
...THEN THIS GAME IS PRACTICALLY LOST BEFORE IT'S EVEN BEGUN.
BUT...
...WAS THIS EVER REALLY A GAME?

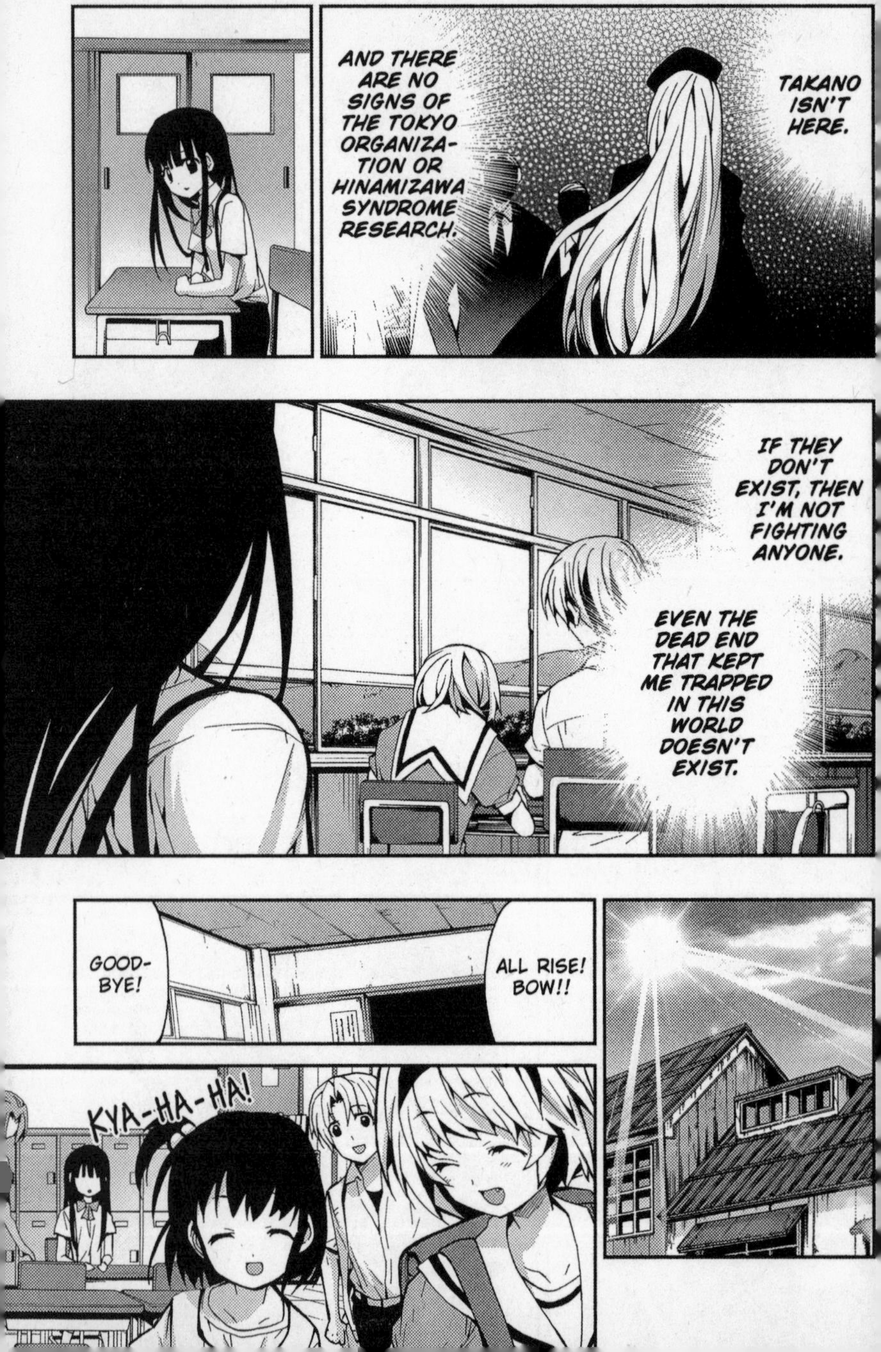
TAKANO ISN'T HERE.
AND THERE ARE NO SIGNS OF THE TOKYO ORGANIZA- TION OR HINAMIZAWA SYNDROME RESEARCH.
IF THEY DON'T EXIST, THEN I'M NOT FIGHTING ANYONE.
EVEN THE DEAD END THAT KEPT ME TRAPPED IN THIS WORLD DOESN'T EXIST.
ALL RISE! BOW!!
GOOD- BYE!
KYA-HA-HA!

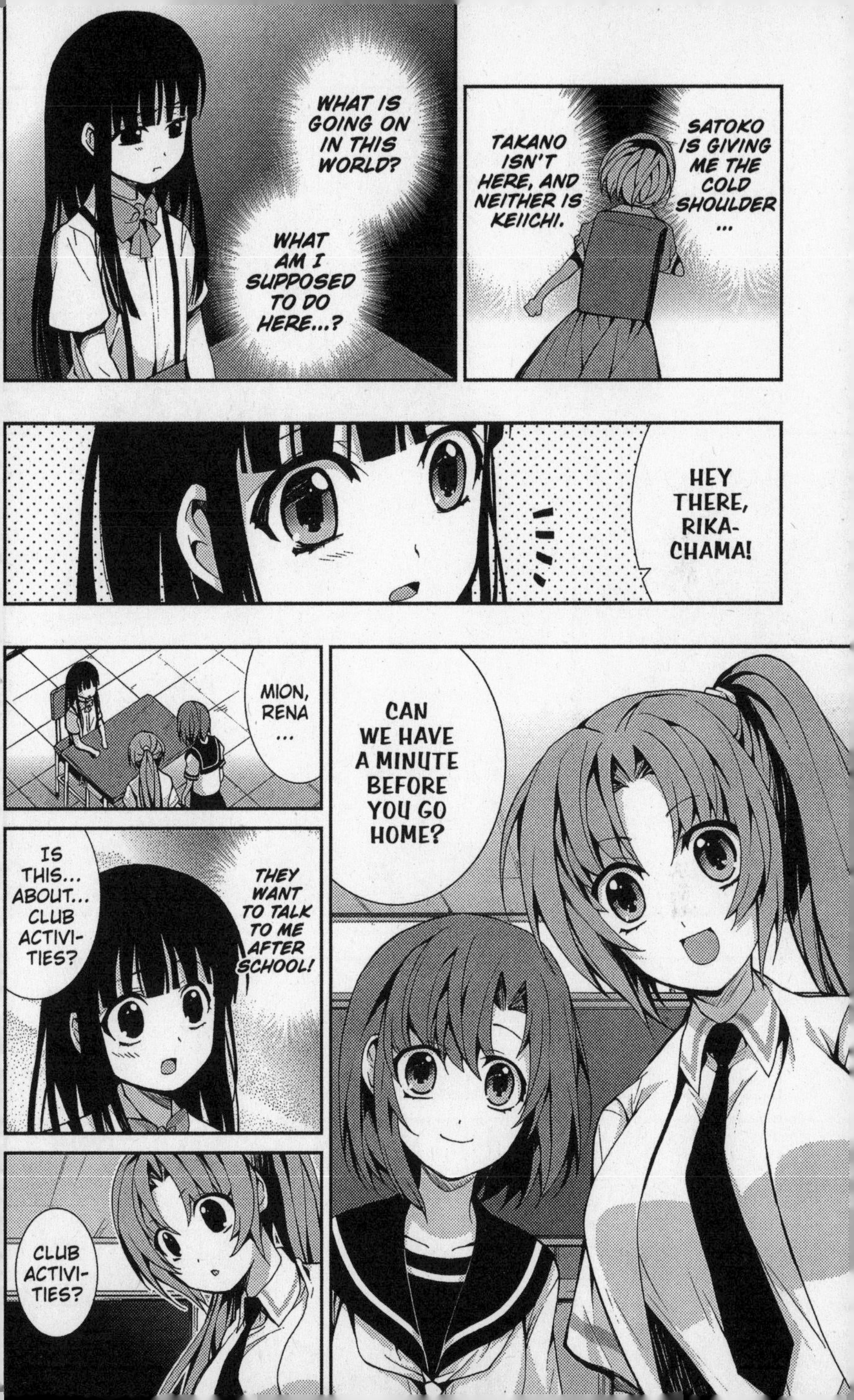
SATOKO IS GIVING ME THE COLD SHOULDER...
TAKANO ISN'T HERE, AND NEITHER IS KEIICHI.
WHAT IS GOING ON IN THIS WORLD?
WHAT AM I SUPPOSED TO DO HERE...?
HEY THERE, RIKA-CHAMA!
CAN WE HAVE A MINUTE BEFORE YOU GO HOME?
MION, RENA...
THEY WANT TO TALK TO ME AFTER SCHOOL!
IS THIS... ABOUT... CLUB ACTIVITIES?
CLUB ACTIVITIES?

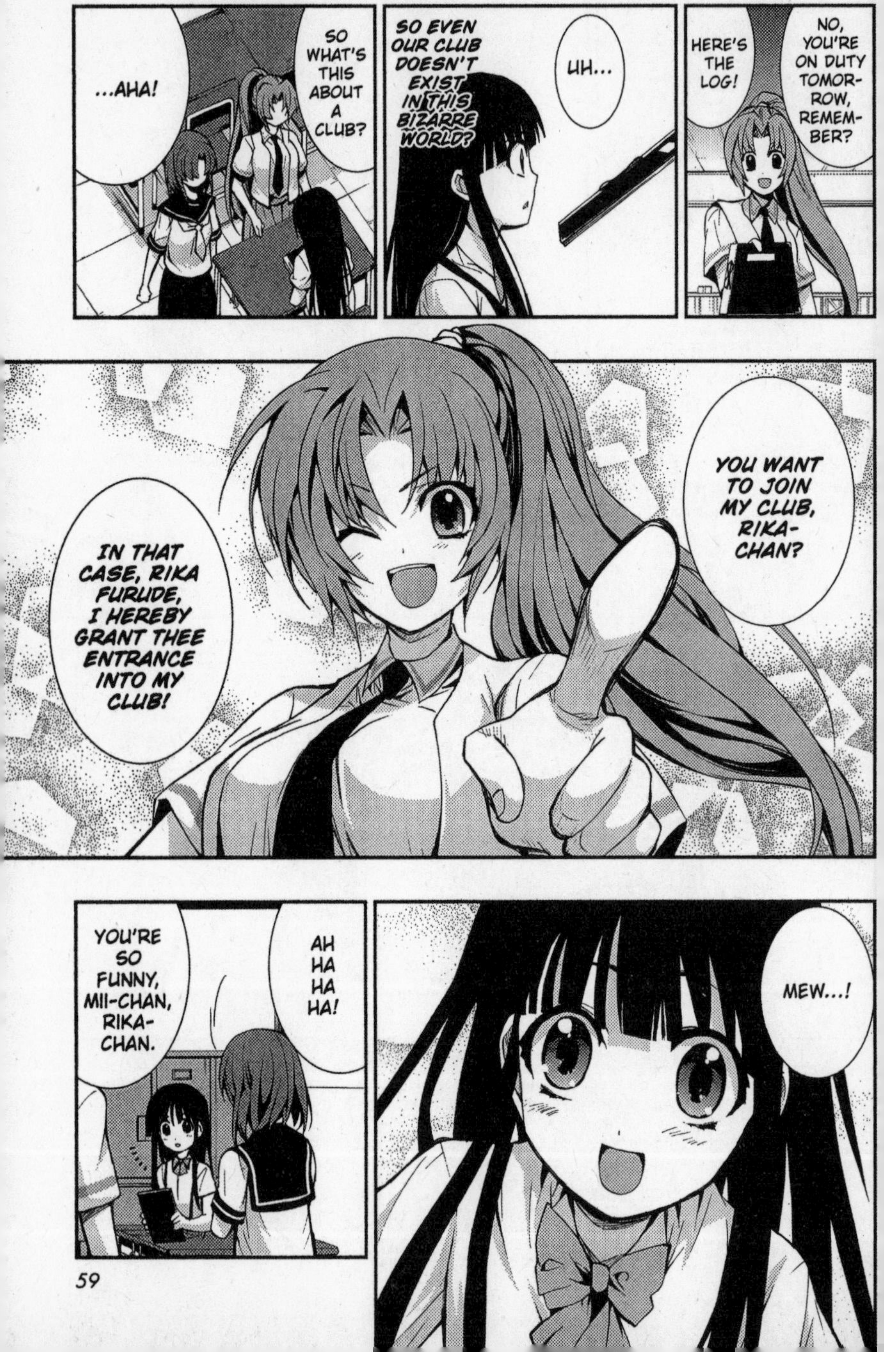
NO, YOU'RE ON DUTY TOMORROW, REMEMBER?
HERE'S THE LOG!
UH...
SO EVEN OUR CLUB DOESN'T EXIST IN THIS BIZARRE WORLD?
SO WHAT'S THIS ABOUT A CLUB?
...AHA!
YOU WANT TO JOIN MY CLUB, RIKA-CHAN?
IN THAT CASE, RIKA FURUDE, I HEREBY GRANT THEE ENTRANCE INTO MY CLUB!
MEW...!
AH HA HA HA!
YOU'RE SO FUNNY, MII-CHAN, RIKA-CHAN.

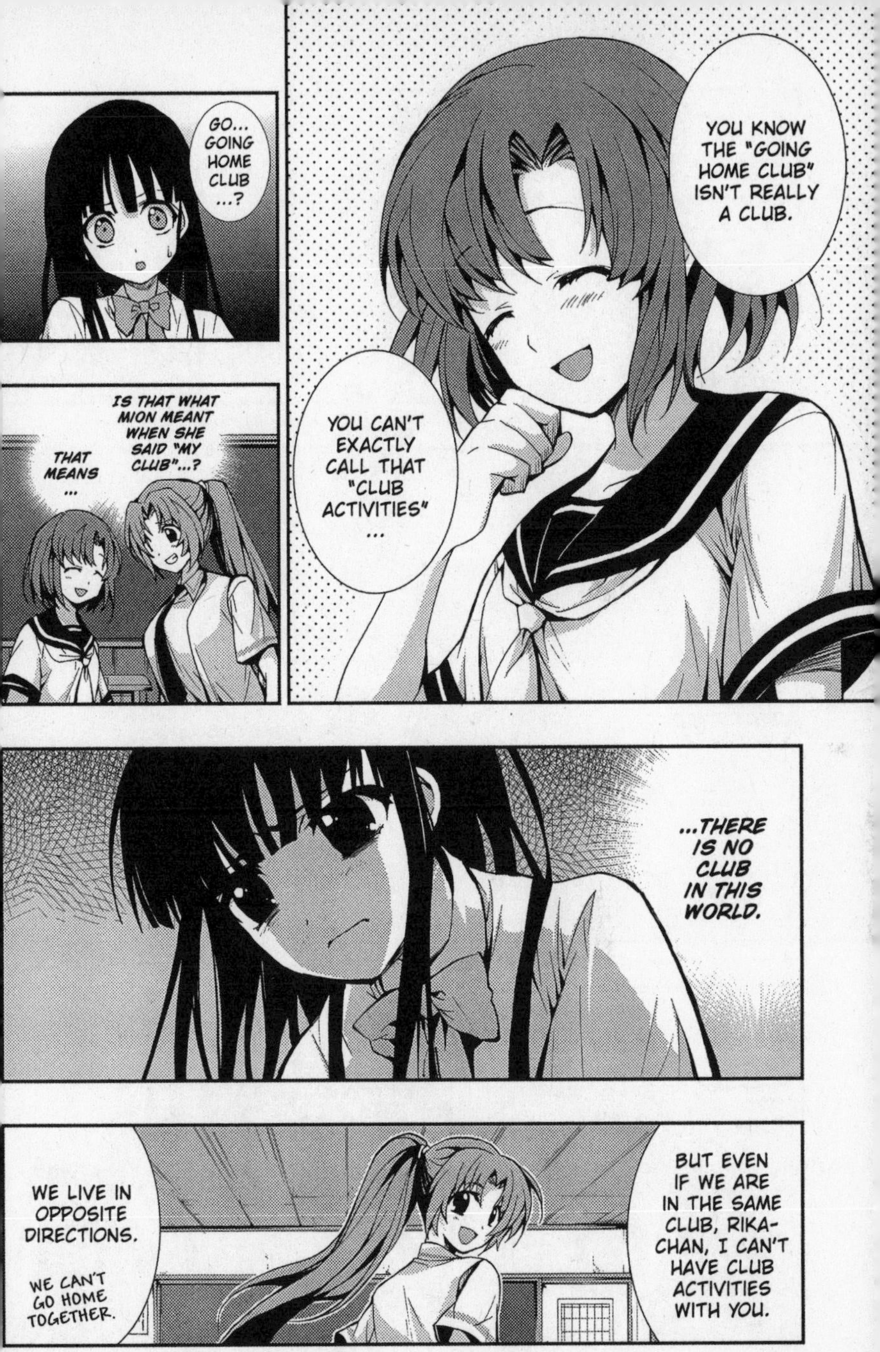
YOU KNOW THE "GOING HOME CLUB" ISN'T REALLY A CLUB.
YOU CAN'T EXACTLY CALL THAT "CLUB ACTIVITIES" ...
GO... GOING HOME CLUB ...?
IS THAT WHAT MION MEANT WHEN SHE SAID "MY CLUB"...?
THAT MEANS ...
...THERE IS NO CLUB IN THIS WORLD.
BUT EVEN IF WE ARE IN THE SAME CLUB, RIKA-CHAN, I CAN'T HAVE CLUB ACTIVITIES WITH YOU.
WE LIVE IN OPPOSITE DIRECTIONS.
WE CAN'T GO HOME TOGETHER.

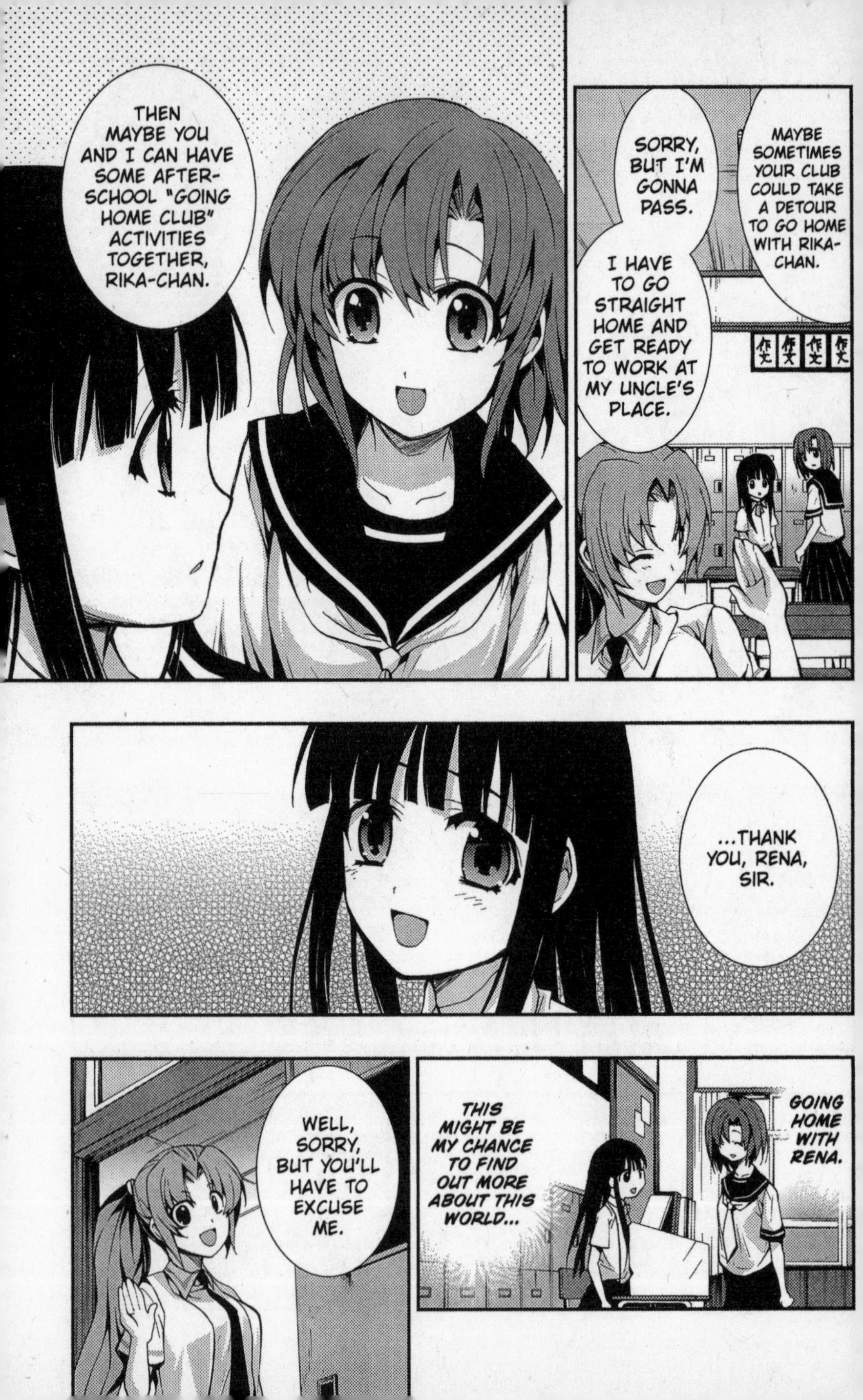
MAYBE SOMETIMES YOUR CLUB COULD TAKE A DETOUR TO GO HOME WITH RIKA-CHAN.
SORRY, BUT I'M GONNA PASS.
I HAVE TO GO STRAIGHT HOME AND GET READY TO WORK AT MY UNCLE'S PLACE.
THEN MAYBE YOU AND I CAN HAVE SOME AFTER-SCHOOL "GOING HOME CLUB" ACTIVITIES TOGETHER, RIKA-CHAN.
...THANK YOU, RENA, SIR.
GOING HOME WITH RENA.
THIS MIGHT BE MY CHANCE TO FIND OUT MORE ABOUT THIS WORLD...
WELL, SORRY, BUT YOU'LL HAVE TO EXCUSE ME.

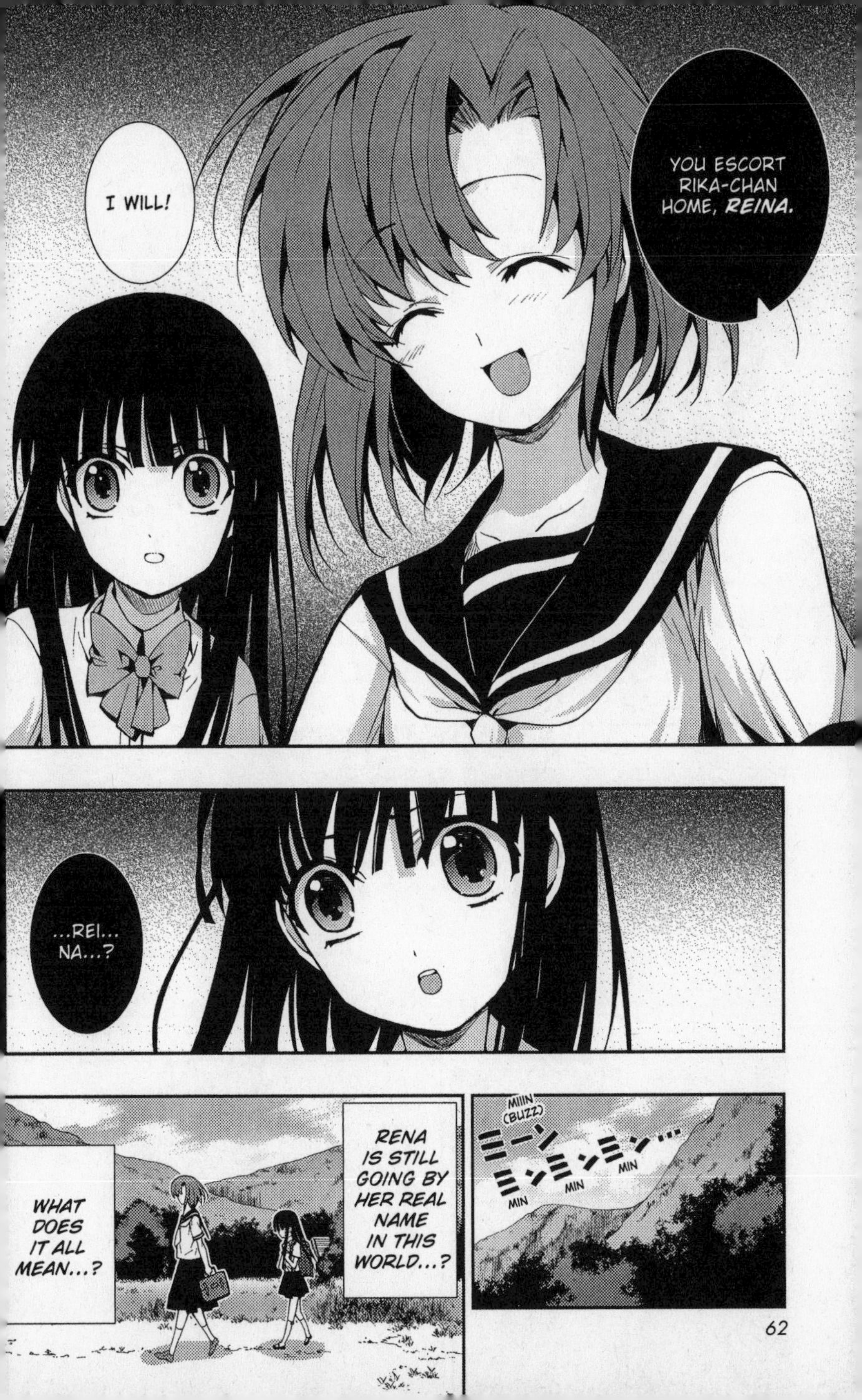
YOU ESCORT RIKA-CHAN HOME, *REINA.*
I WILL!
...REI... NA...?
MIIIN (BUZZ)
ミーン ミンミンミン…
MIN MIN MIN
RENA IS STILL GOING BY HER REAL NAME IN THIS WORLD...?
WHAT DOES IT ALL MEAN...?

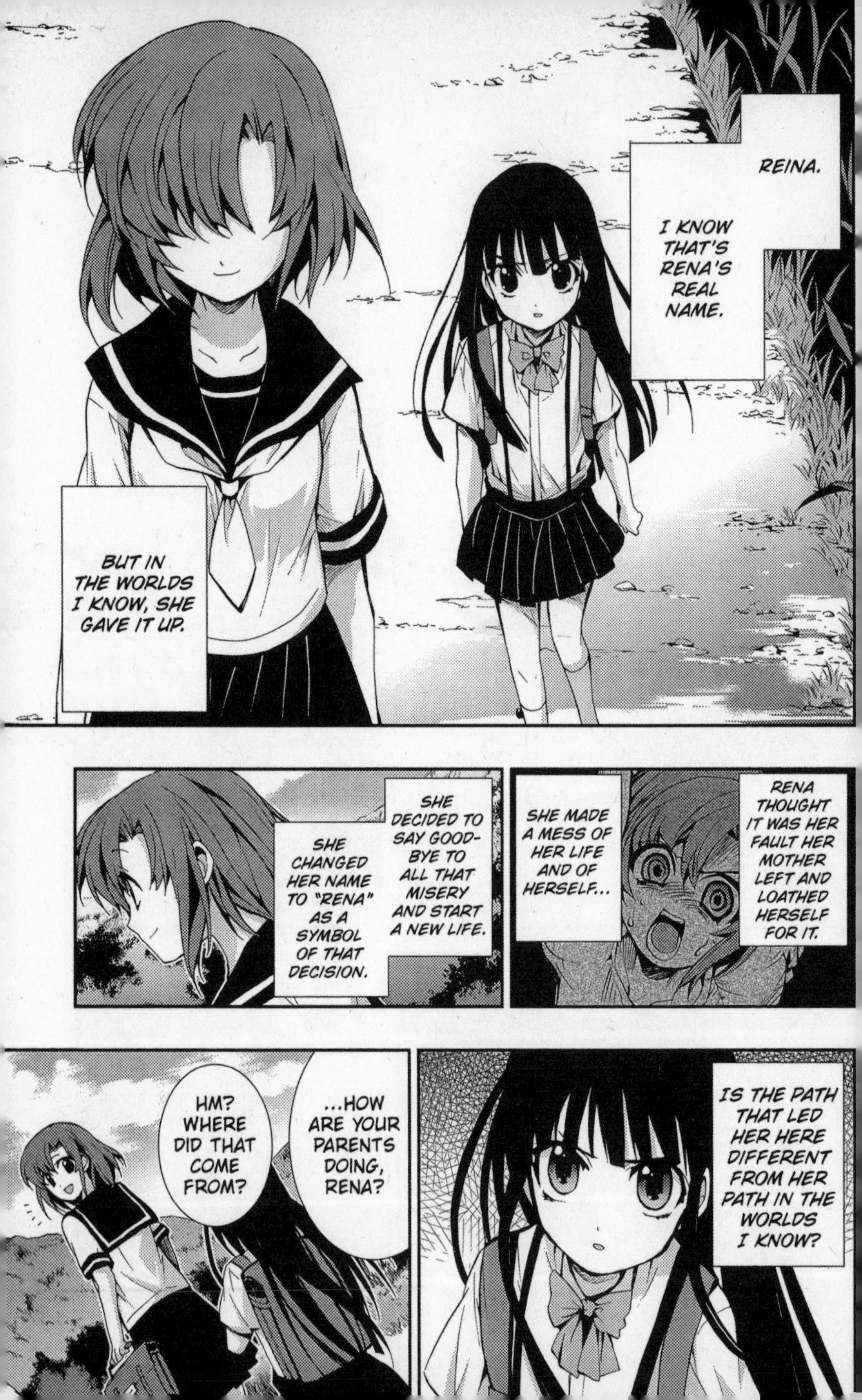
REINA.
I KNOW THAT'S RENA'S REAL NAME.
BUT IN THE WORLDS I KNOW, SHE GAVE IT UP.
RENA THOUGHT IT WAS HER FAULT HER MOTHER LEFT AND LOATHED HERSELF FOR IT.
SHE MADE A MESS OF HER LIFE AND OF HERSELF...
SHE DECIDED TO SAY GOOD-BYE TO ALL THAT MISERY AND START A NEW LIFE.
SHE CHANGED HER NAME TO "RENA" AS A SYMBOL OF THAT DECISION.
IS THE PATH THAT LED HER HERE DIFFERENT FROM HER PATH IN THE WORLDS I KNOW?
...HOW ARE YOUR PARENTS DOING, RENA?
HM? WHERE DID THAT COME FROM?

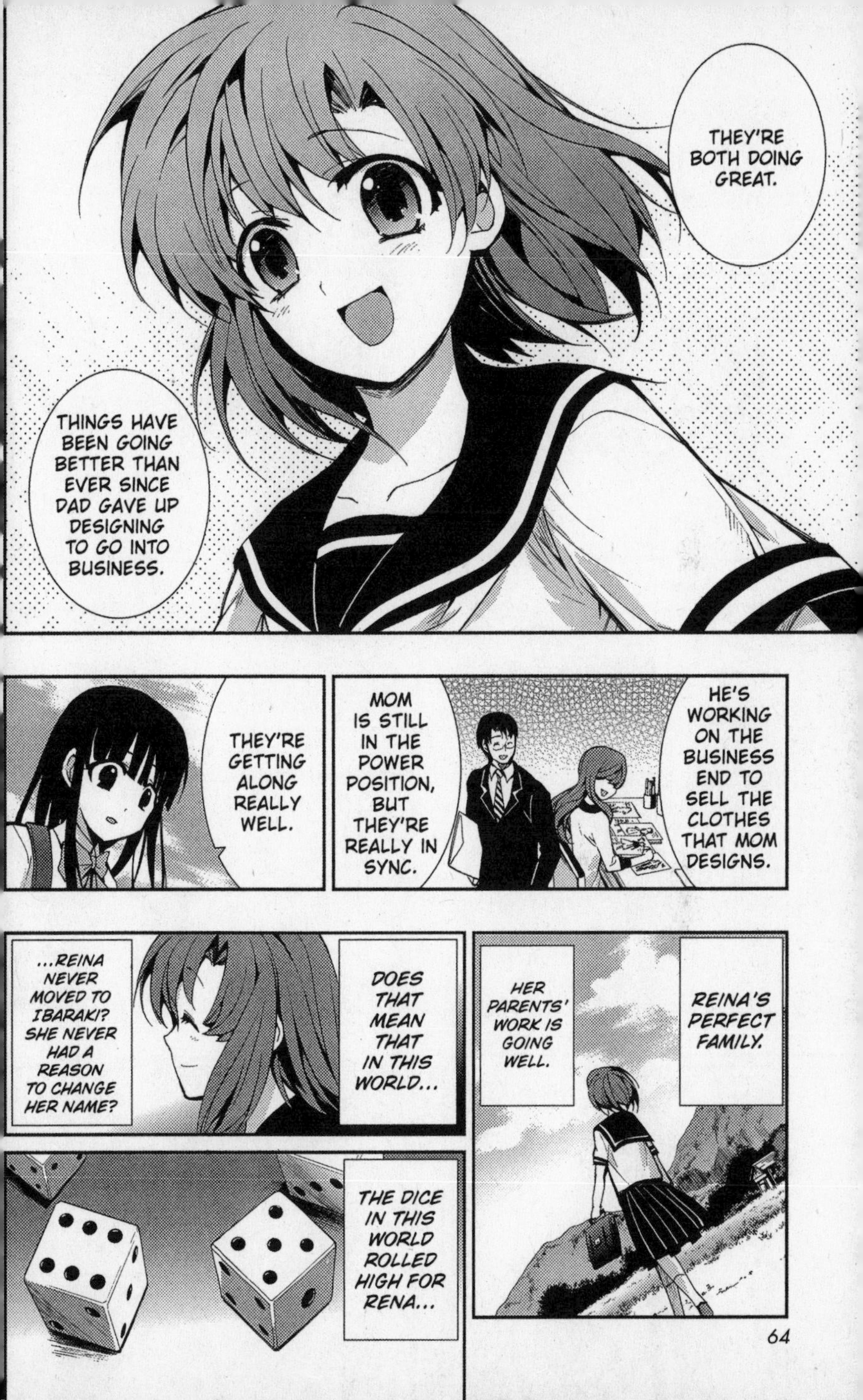
THEY'RE BOTH DOING GREAT.
THINGS HAVE BEEN GOING BETTER THAN EVER SINCE DAD GAVE UP DESIGNING TO GO INTO BUSINESS.
HE'S WORKING ON THE BUSINESS END TO SELL THE CLOTHES THAT MOM DESIGNS.
MOM IS STILL IN THE POWER POSITION, BUT THEY'RE REALLY IN SYNC.
THEY'RE GETTING ALONG REALLY WELL.
REINA'S PERFECT FAMILY.
HER PARENTS' WORK IS GOING WELL.
DOES THAT MEAN THAT IN THIS WORLD...
...REINA NEVER MOVED TO IBARAKI? SHE NEVER HAD A REASON TO CHANGE HER NAME?
THE DICE IN THIS WORLD ROLLED HIGH FOR RENA...

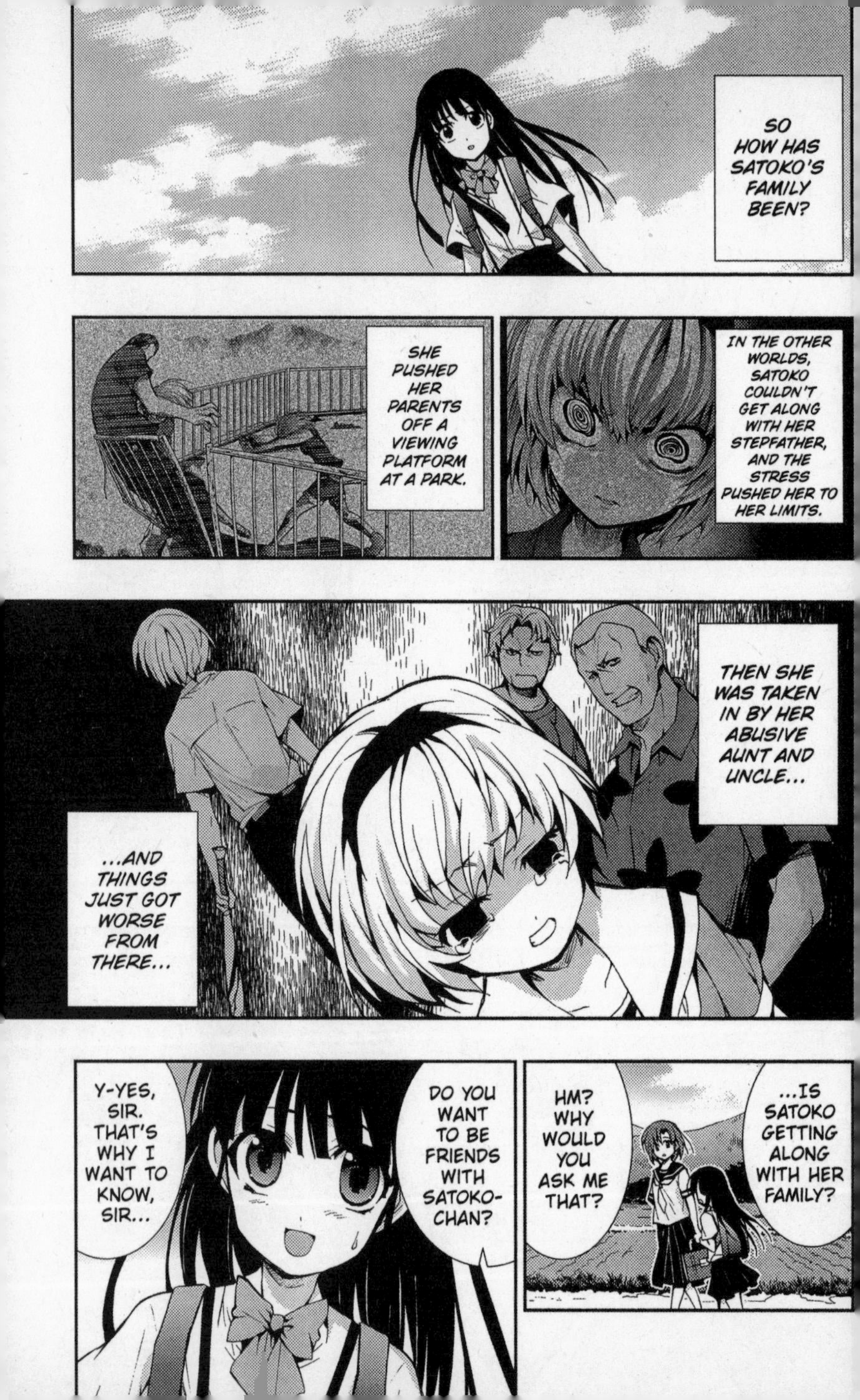
SO HOW HAS SATOKO'S FAMILY BEEN?
IN THE OTHER WORLDS, SATOKO COULDN'T GET ALONG WITH HER STEPFATHER, AND THE STRESS PUSHED HER TO HER LIMITS.
SHE PUSHED HER PARENTS OFF A VIEWING PLATFORM AT A PARK.
THEN SHE WAS TAKEN IN BY HER ABUSIVE AUNT AND UNCLE...
...AND THINGS JUST GOT WORSE FROM THERE...
...IS SATOKO GETTING ALONG WITH HER FAMILY?
HM? WHY WOULD YOU ASK ME THAT?
DO YOU WANT TO BE FRIENDS WITH SATOKO-CHAN?
Y-YES, SIR. THAT'S WHY I WANT TO KNOW, SIR...

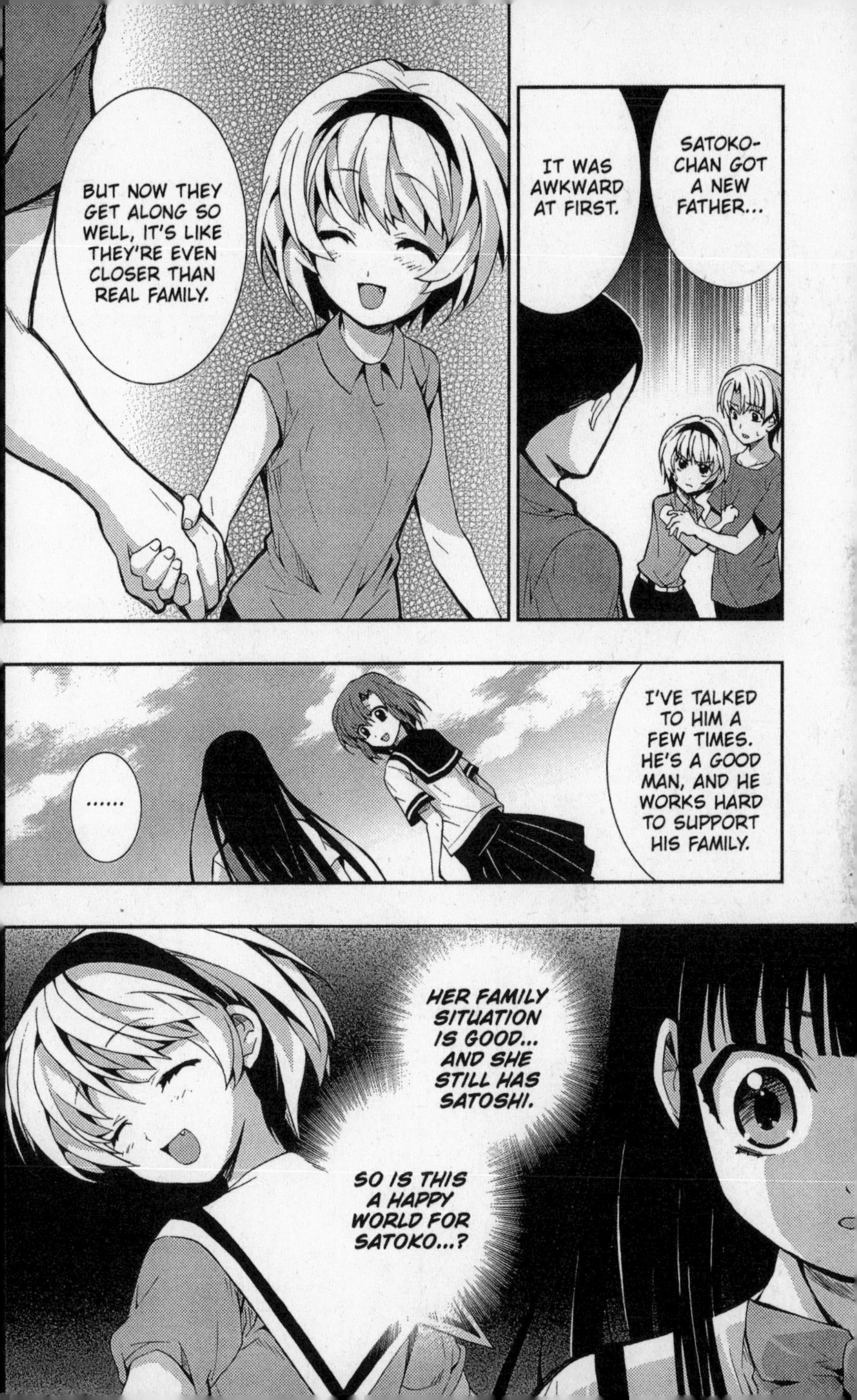
SATOKO-CHAN GOT A NEW FATHER...
IT WAS AWKWARD AT FIRST.
BUT NOW THEY GET ALONG SO WELL, IT'S LIKE THEY'RE EVEN CLOSER THAN REAL FAMILY.
I'VE TALKED TO HIM A FEW TIMES. HE'S A GOOD MAN, AND HE WORKS HARD TO SUPPORT HIS FAMILY.
......
HER FAMILY SITUATION IS GOOD... AND SHE STILL HAS SATOSHI.
SO IS THIS A HAPPY WORLD FOR SATOKO...?

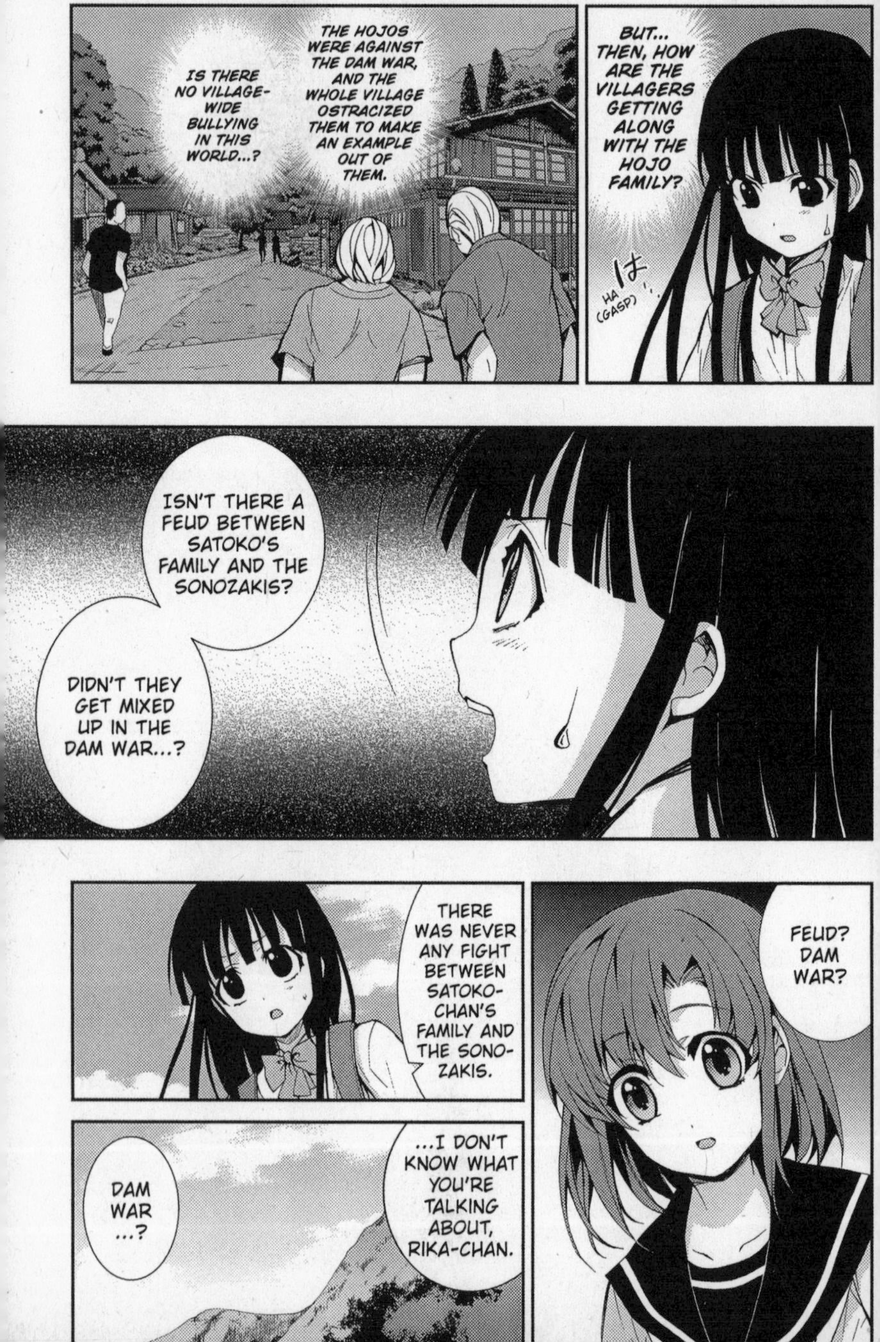
BUT... THEN, HOW ARE THE VILLAGERS GETTING ALONG WITH THE HOJO FAMILY?
は
HA (GASP)
THE HOJOS WERE AGAINST THE DAM WAR, AND THE WHOLE VILLAGE OSTRACIZED THEM TO MAKE AN EXAMPLE OUT OF THEM.
IS THERE NO VILLAGE-WIDE BULLYING IN THIS WORLD...?
ISN'T THERE A FEUD BETWEEN SATOKO'S FAMILY AND THE SONOZAKIS?
DIDN'T THEY GET MIXED UP IN THE DAM WAR...?
FEUD? DAM WAR?
THERE WAS NEVER ANY FIGHT BETWEEN SATOKO-CHAN'S FAMILY AND THE SONO-ZAKIS.
...I DON'T KNOW WHAT YOU'RE TALKING ABOUT, RIKA-CHAN.
DAM WAR ...?

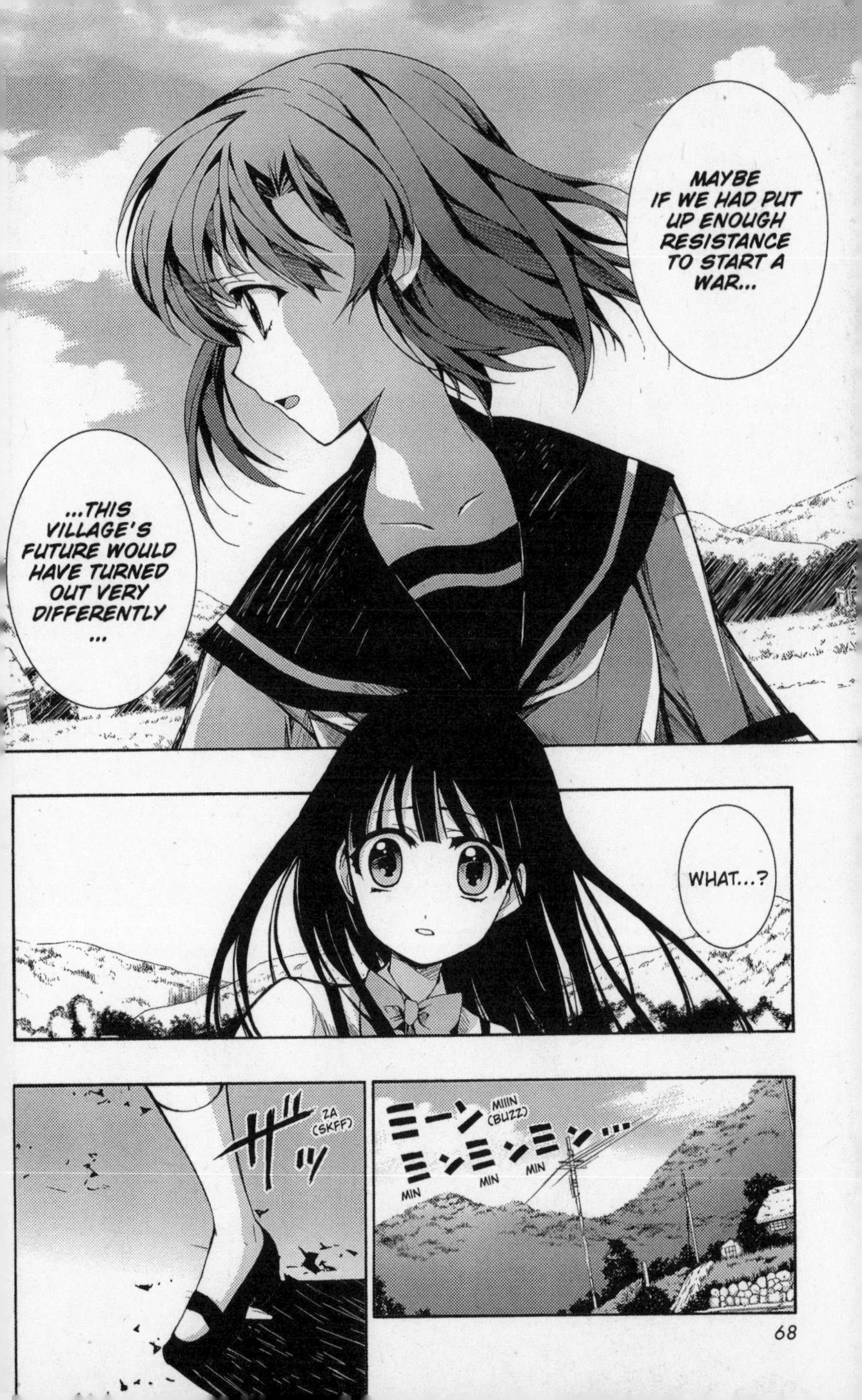
MAYBE IF WE HAD PUT UP ENOUGH RESISTANCE TO START A WAR...
...THIS VILLAGE'S FUTURE WOULD HAVE TURNED OUT VERY DIFFERENTLY ...
WHAT...?
MIIIN (BUZZ)
MIN
MIN
MIN
ZA (SKFF)

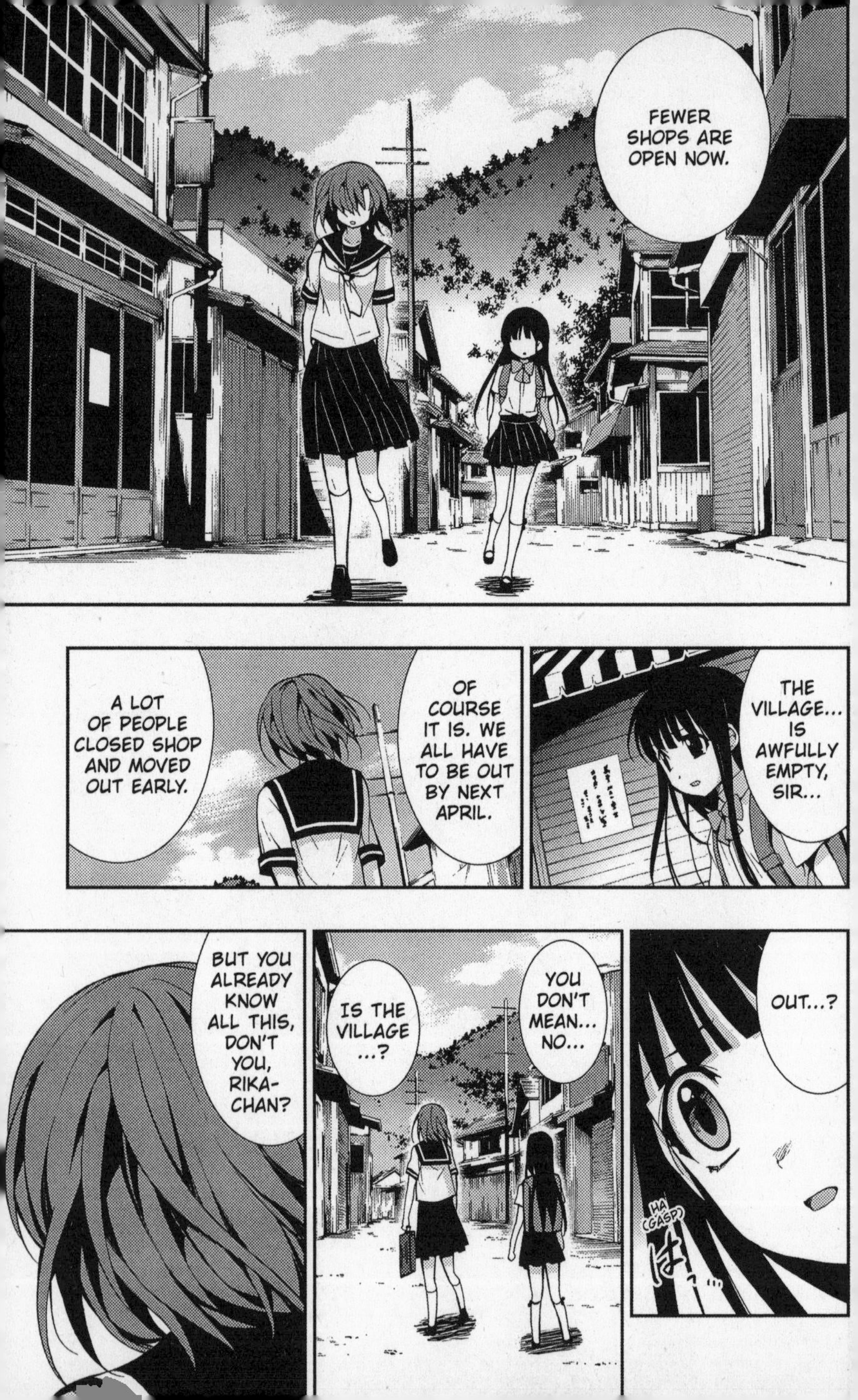
FEWER SHOPS ARE OPEN NOW.
THE VILLAGE... IS AWFULLY EMPTY, SIR...
OF COURSE IT IS. WE ALL HAVE TO BE OUT BY NEXT APRIL.
A LOT OF PEOPLE CLOSED SHOP AND MOVED OUT EARLY.
OUT...?
HA (GASP)
YOU DON'T MEAN... NO...
IS THE VILLAGE ...?
BUT YOU ALREADY KNOW ALL THIS, DON'T YOU, RIKA-CHAN?

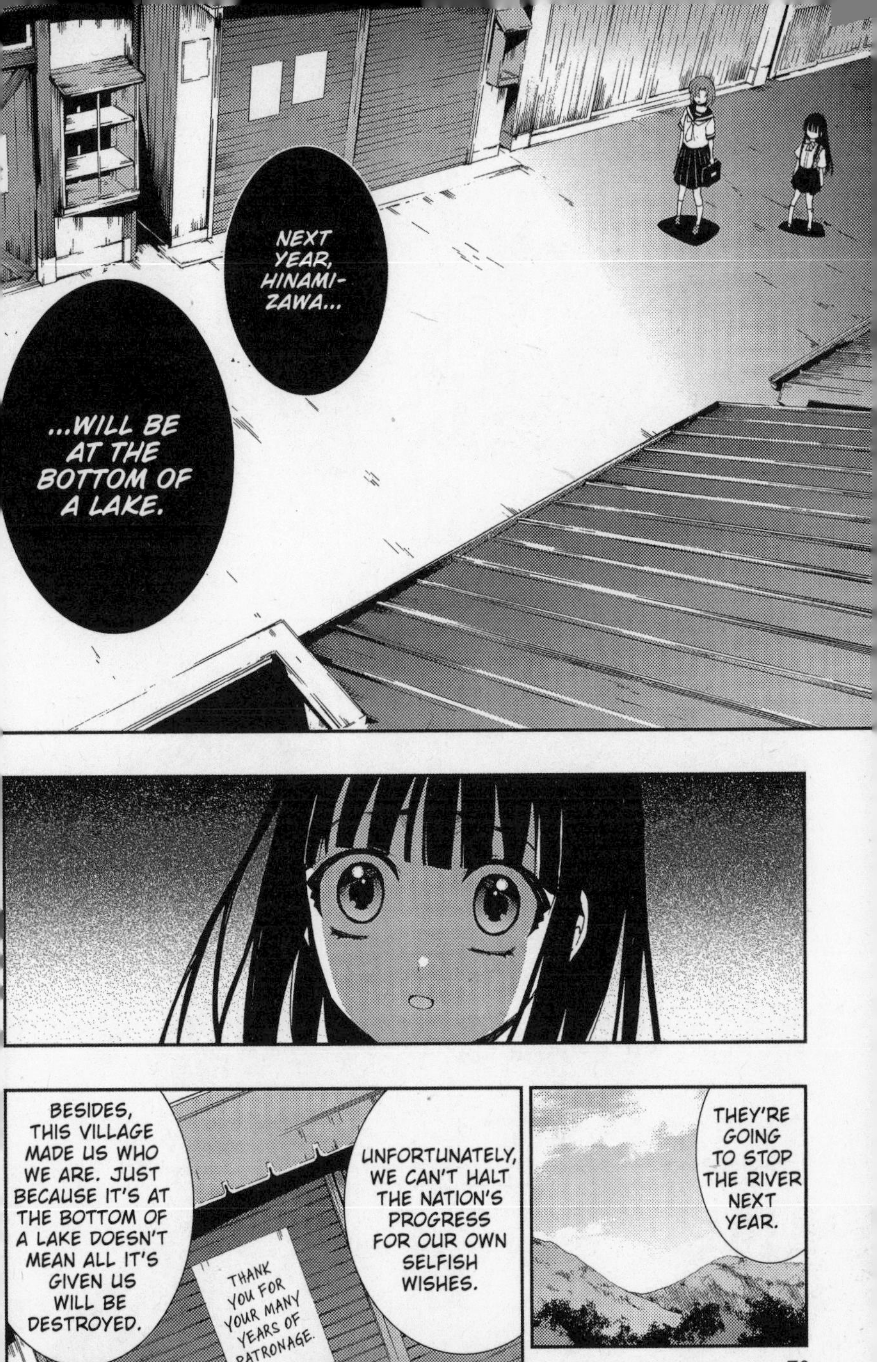
NEXT YEAR, HINAMI-ZAWA...
...WILL BE AT THE BOTTOM OF A LAKE.
THEY'RE GOING TO STOP THE RIVER NEXT YEAR.
UNFORTUNATELY, WE CAN'T HALT THE NATION'S PROGRESS FOR OUR OWN SELFISH WISHES.
BESIDES, THIS VILLAGE MADE US WHO WE ARE. JUST BECAUSE IT'S AT THE BOTTOM OF A LAKE DOESN'T MEAN ALL IT'S GIVEN US WILL BE DESTROYED.
THANK YOU FOR YOUR MANY YEARS OF PATRONAGE.

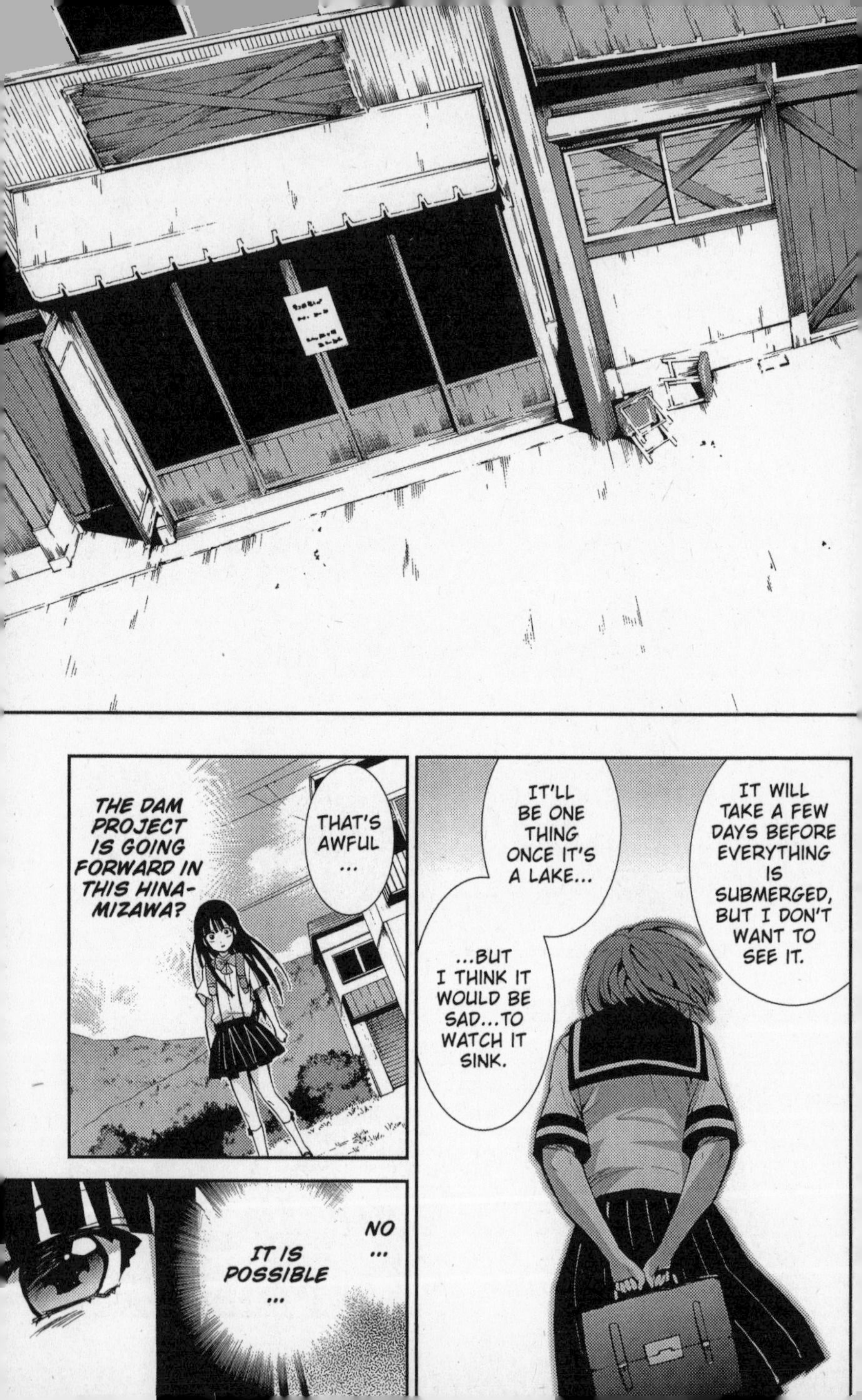
IT WILL TAKE A FEW DAYS BEFORE EVERYTHING IS SUBMERGED, BUT I DON'T WANT TO SEE IT.
IT'LL BE ONE THING ONCE IT'S A LAKE...
...BUT I THINK IT WOULD BE SAD...TO WATCH IT SINK.
THAT'S AWFUL...
THE DAM PROJECT IS GOING FORWARD IN THIS HINA-MIZAWA?
NO...
IT IS POSSIBLE...

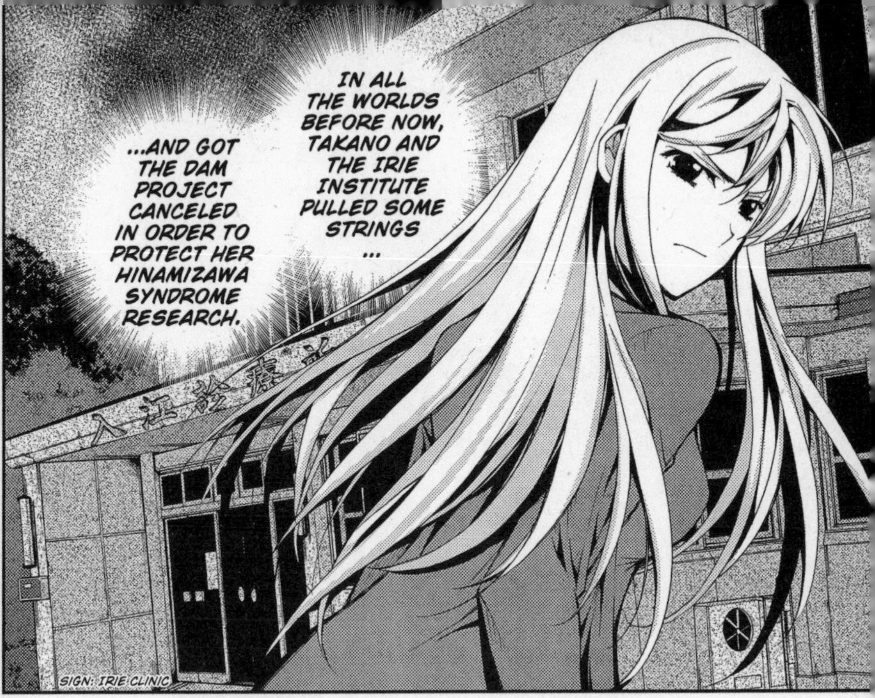
IN ALL THE WORLDS BEFORE NOW, TAKANO AND THE IRIE INSTITUTE PULLED SOME STRINGS ...
...AND GOT THE DAM PROJECT CANCELED IN ORDER TO PROTECT HER HINAMIZAWA SYNDROME RESEARCH.
SIGN: IRIE CLINIC

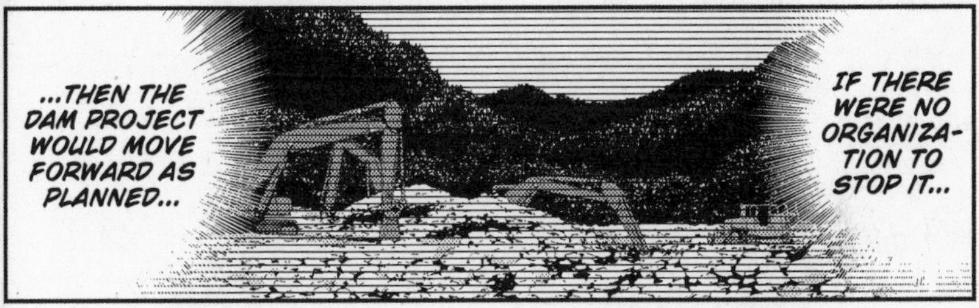
IF THERE WERE NO ORGANIZATION TO STOP IT...
...THEN THE DAM PROJECT WOULD MOVE FORWARD AS PLANNED...

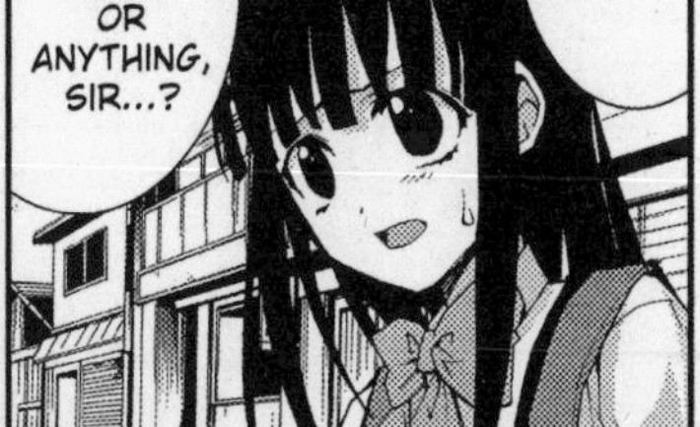
THAT'S TERRIBLE...
WEREN'T THERE ANY PROTESTS OR ANYTHING, SIR...?

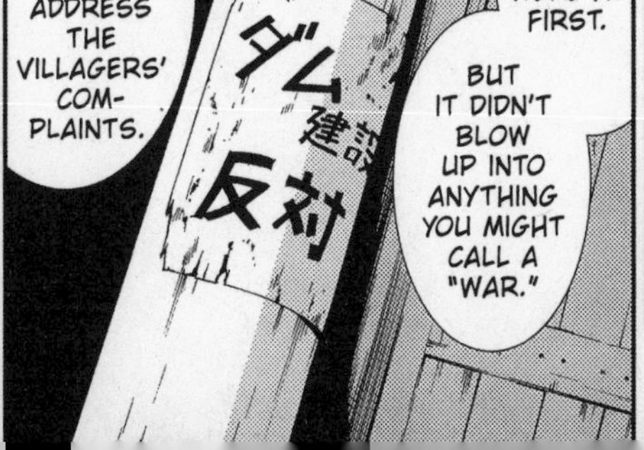
I HEARD THERE WERE AT FIRST.
BUT IT DIDN'T BLOW UP INTO ANYTHING YOU MIGHT CALL A "WAR."
THEY TWEAKED THE PLAN A LOT TO ADDRESS THE VILLAGERS' COMPLAINTS.
ダム建設反対

SIGN: DOWN WITH THE DAM PROJECT

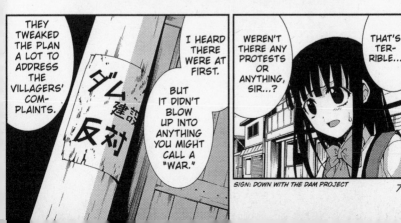

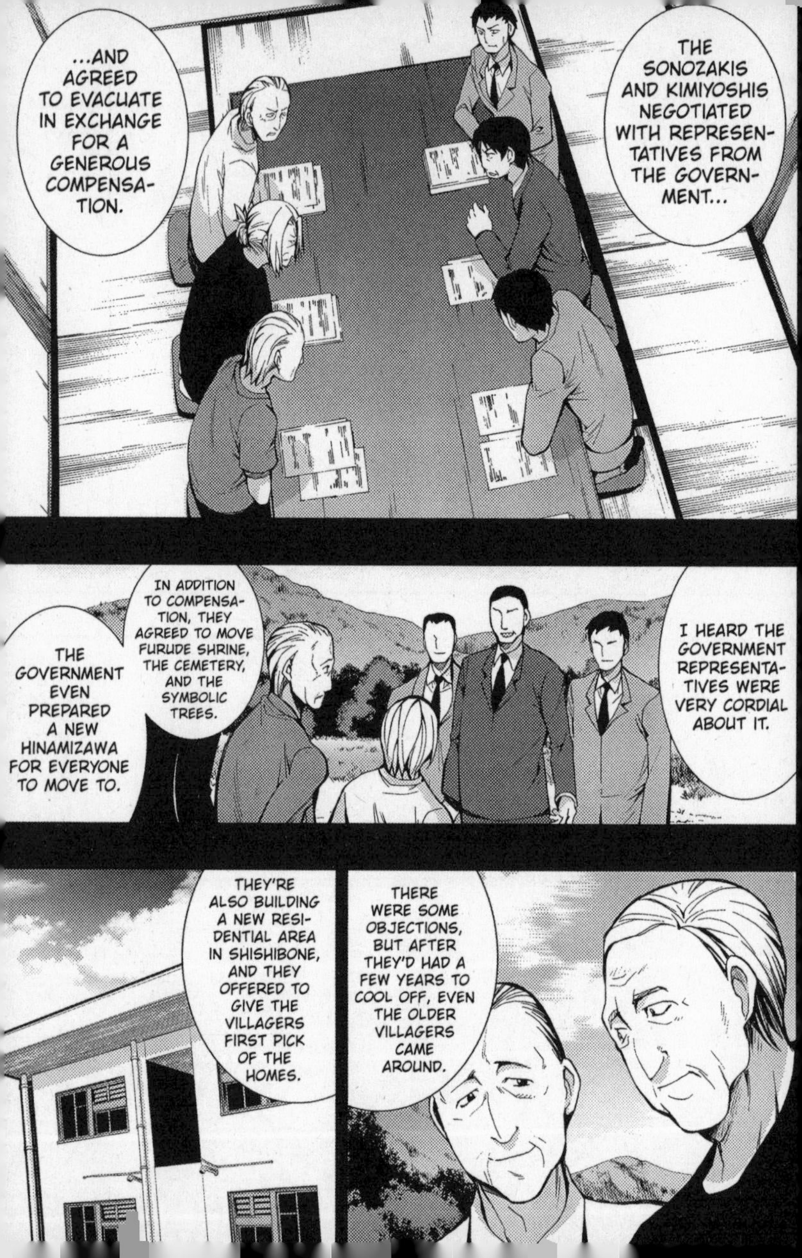
THE SONOZAKIS AND KIMIYOSHIS NEGOTIATED WITH REPRESENTATIVES FROM THE GOVERNMENT...
...AND AGREED TO EVACUATE IN EXCHANGE FOR A GENEROUS COMPENSATION.
I HEARD THE GOVERNMENT REPRESENTATIVES WERE VERY CORDIAL ABOUT IT.
IN ADDITION TO COMPENSATION, THEY AGREED TO MOVE FURUDE SHRINE, THE CEMETERY, AND THE SYMBOLIC TREES.
THE GOVERNMENT EVEN PREPARED A NEW HINAMIZAWA FOR EVERYONE TO MOVE TO.
THERE WERE SOME OBJECTIONS, BUT AFTER THEY'D HAD A FEW YEARS TO COOL OFF, EVEN THE OLDER VILLAGERS CAME AROUND.
THEY'RE ALSO BUILDING A NEW RESIDENTIAL AREA IN SHISHIBONE, AND THEY OFFERED TO GIVE THE VILLAGERS FIRST PICK OF THE HOMES.

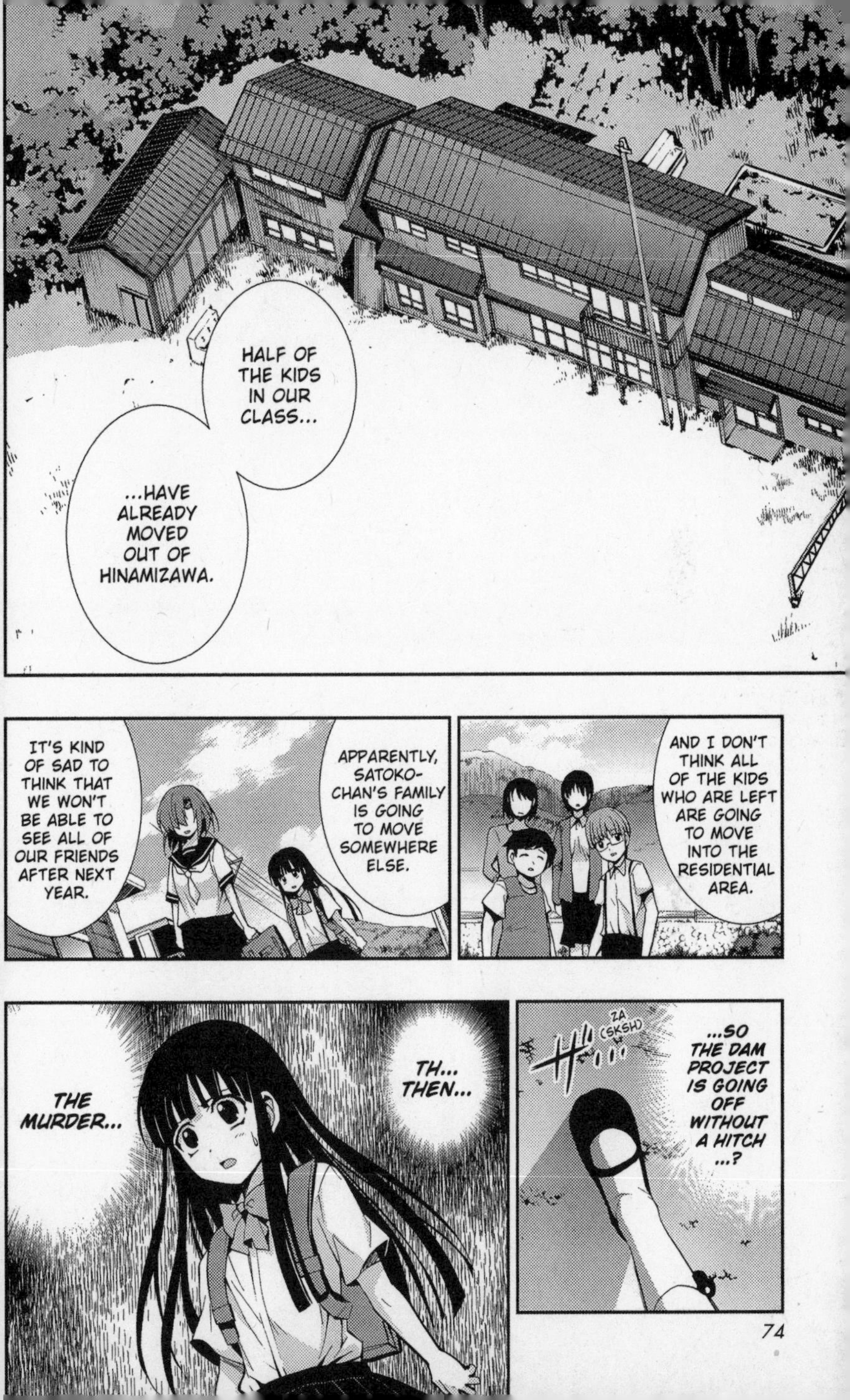
HALF OF THE KIDS IN OUR CLASS...
...HAVE ALREADY MOVED OUT OF HINAMIZAWA.
AND I DON'T THINK ALL OF THE KIDS WHO ARE LEFT ARE GOING TO MOVE INTO THE RESIDENTIAL AREA.
APPARENTLY, SATOKO-CHAN'S FAMILY IS GOING TO MOVE SOMEWHERE ELSE.
IT'S KIND OF SAD TO THINK THAT WE WON'T BE ABLE TO SEE ALL OF OUR FRIENDS AFTER NEXT YEAR.
ZA (SKSH)
...SO THE DAM PROJECT IS GOING OFF WITHOUT A HITCH ...?
TH... THEN...
THE MURDER...

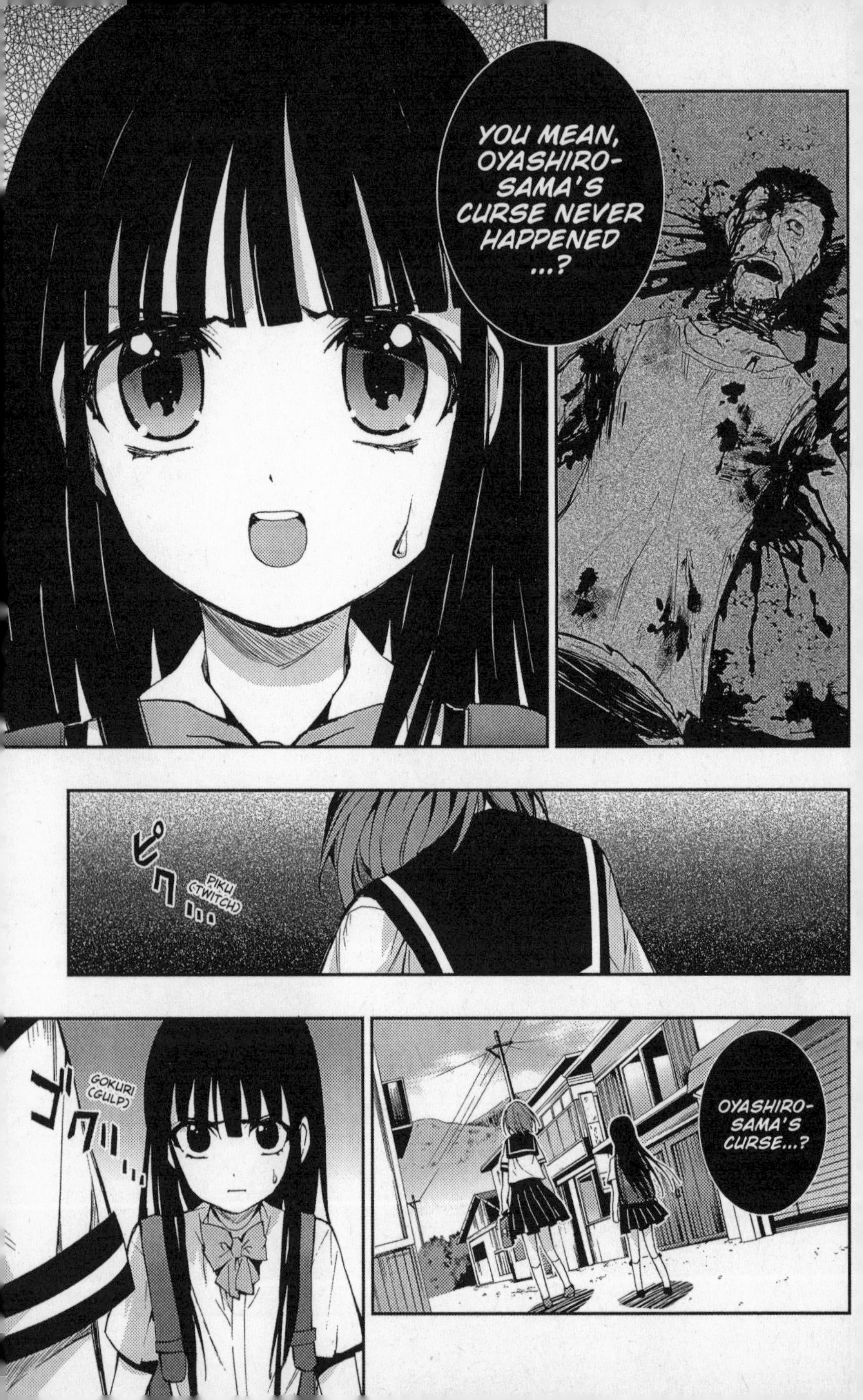
YOU MEAN, OYASHIRO-SAMA'S CURSE NEVER HAPPENED ...?
PIKU (TWITCH)
OYASHIRO-SAMA'S CURSE...?
GOKURI (GULP)

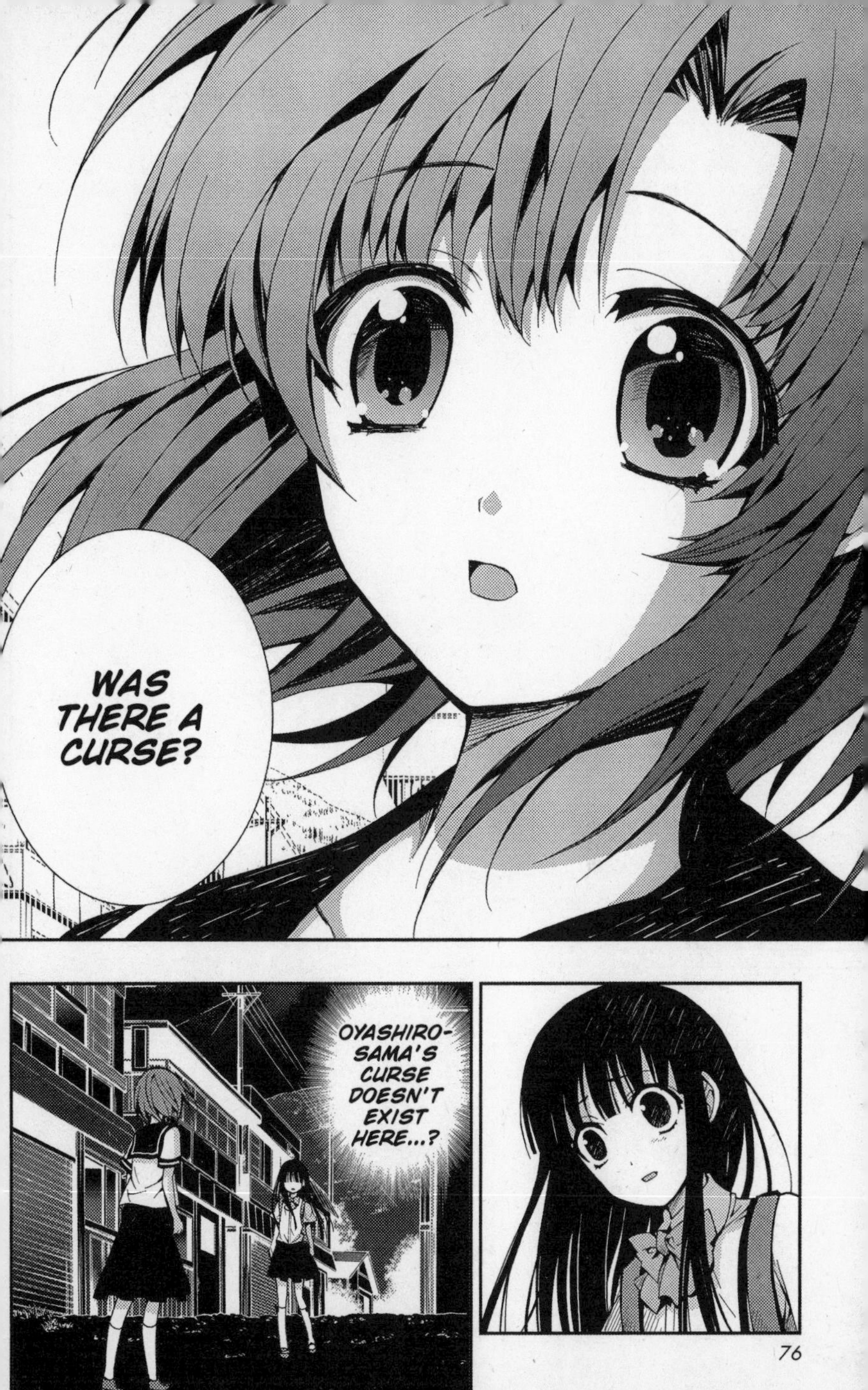
WAS THERE A CURSE?
OYASHIRO-SAMA'S CURSE DOESN'T EXIST HERE...?

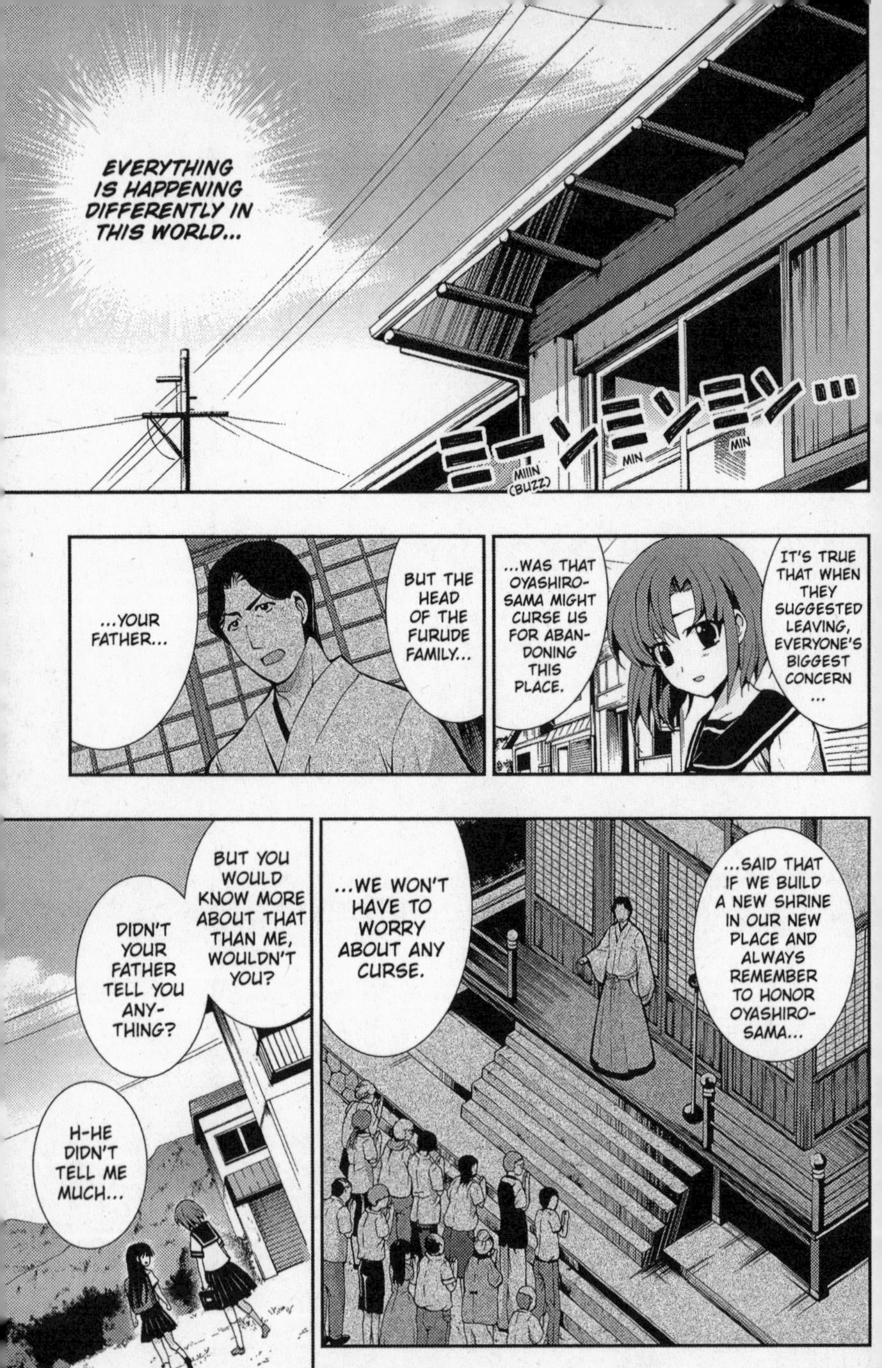
EVERYTHING IS HAPPENING DIFFERENTLY IN THIS WORLD...
MIIIN (BUZZ)
MIN
MIN
IT'S TRUE THAT WHEN THEY SUGGESTED LEAVING, EVERYONE'S BIGGEST CONCERN ...
...WAS THAT OYASHIRO-SAMA MIGHT CURSE US FOR ABANDONING THIS PLACE.
BUT THE HEAD OF THE FURUDE FAMILY...
...YOUR FATHER...
...SAID THAT IF WE BUILD A NEW SHRINE IN OUR NEW PLACE AND ALWAYS REMEMBER TO HONOR OYASHIRO-SAMA...
...WE WON'T HAVE TO WORRY ABOUT ANY CURSE.
BUT YOU WOULD KNOW MORE ABOUT THAT THAN ME, WOULDN'T YOU?
DIDN'T YOUR FATHER TELL YOU ANYTHING?
H-HE DIDN'T TELL ME MUCH...

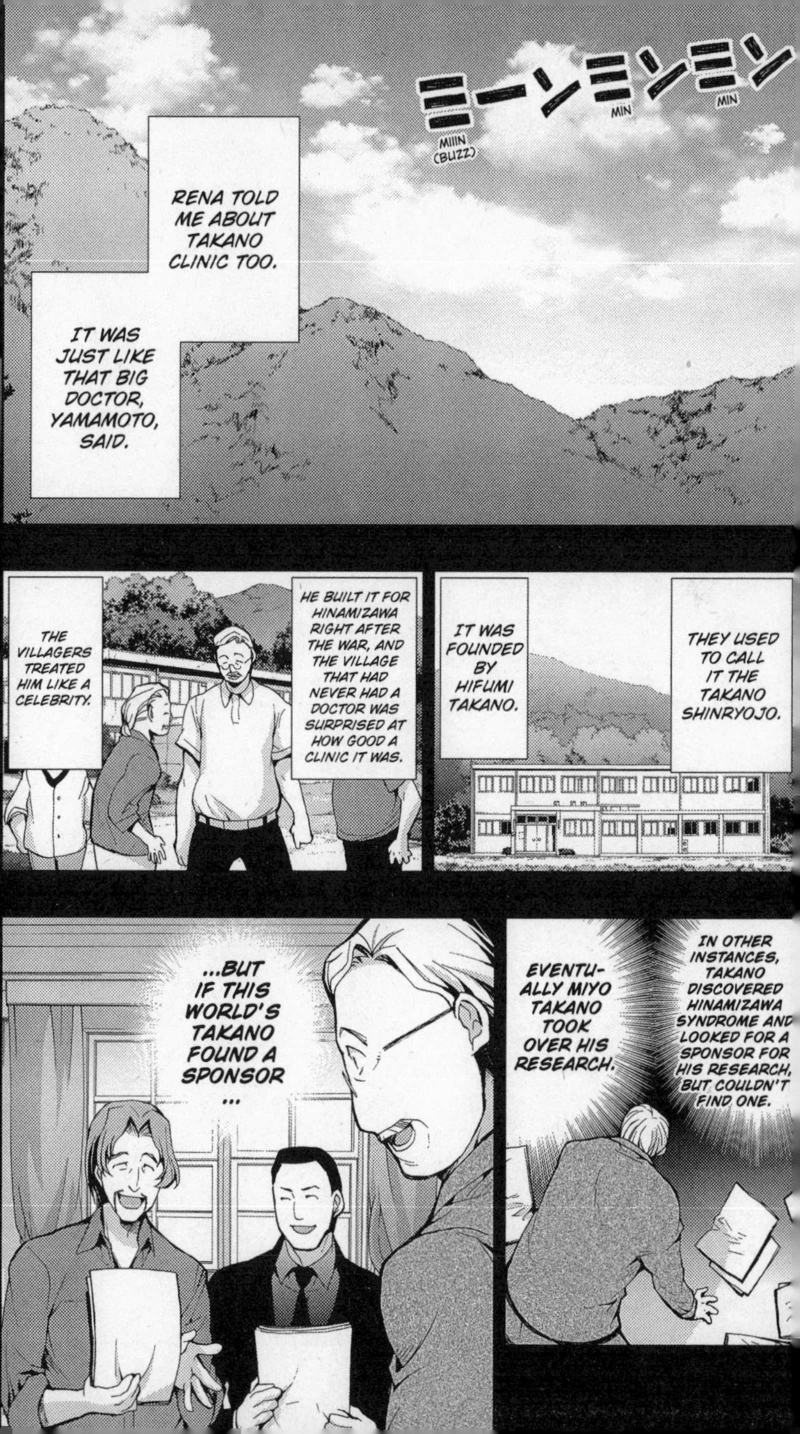

ミーンミンミン
MIIN (BUZZ)
MIN
MIN
RENA TOLD ME ABOUT TAKANO CLINIC TOO.
IT WAS JUST LIKE THAT BIG DOCTOR, YAMAMOTO, SAID.
THEY USED TO CALL IT THE TAKANO SHINRYOJO.
IT WAS FOUNDED BY HIFUMI TAKANO.
HE BUILT IT FOR HINAMIZAWA RIGHT AFTER THE WAR, AND THE VILLAGE THAT HAD NEVER HAD A DOCTOR WAS SURPRISED AT HOW GOOD A CLINIC IT WAS.
THE VILLAGERS TREATED HIM LIKE A CELEBRITY.
IN OTHER INSTANCES, TAKANO DISCOVERED HINAMIZAWA SYNDROME AND LOOKED FOR A SPONSOR FOR HIS RESEARCH, BUT COULDN'T FIND ONE.
EVENTU-ALLY MIYO TAKANO TOOK OVER HIS RESEARCH.
...BUT IF THIS WORLD'S TAKANO FOUND A SPONSOR...

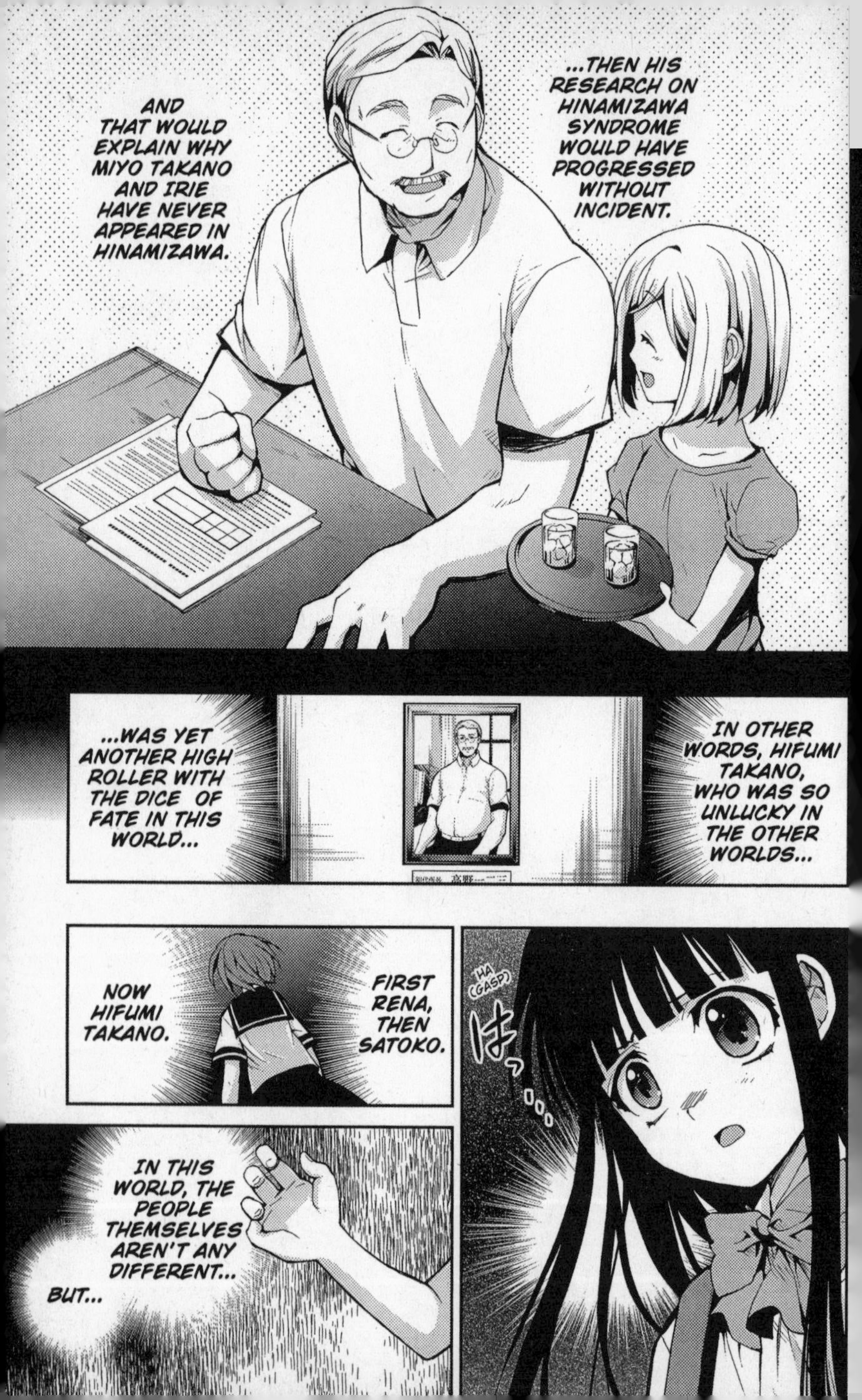
...THEN HIS RESEARCH ON HINAMIZAWA SYNDROME WOULD HAVE PROGRESSED WITHOUT INCIDENT.
AND THAT WOULD EXPLAIN WHY MIYO TAKANO AND IRIE HAVE NEVER APPEARED IN HINAMIZAWA.
IN OTHER WORDS, HIFUMI TAKANO, WHO WAS SO UNLUCKY IN THE OTHER WORLDS...
...WAS YET ANOTHER HIGH ROLLER WITH THE DICE OF FATE IN THIS WORLD...
HA (GASP)
はっ
FIRST RENA, THEN SATOKO.
NOW HIFUMI TAKANO.
IN THIS WORLD, THE PEOPLE THEMSELVES AREN'T ANY DIFFERENT...
BUT...

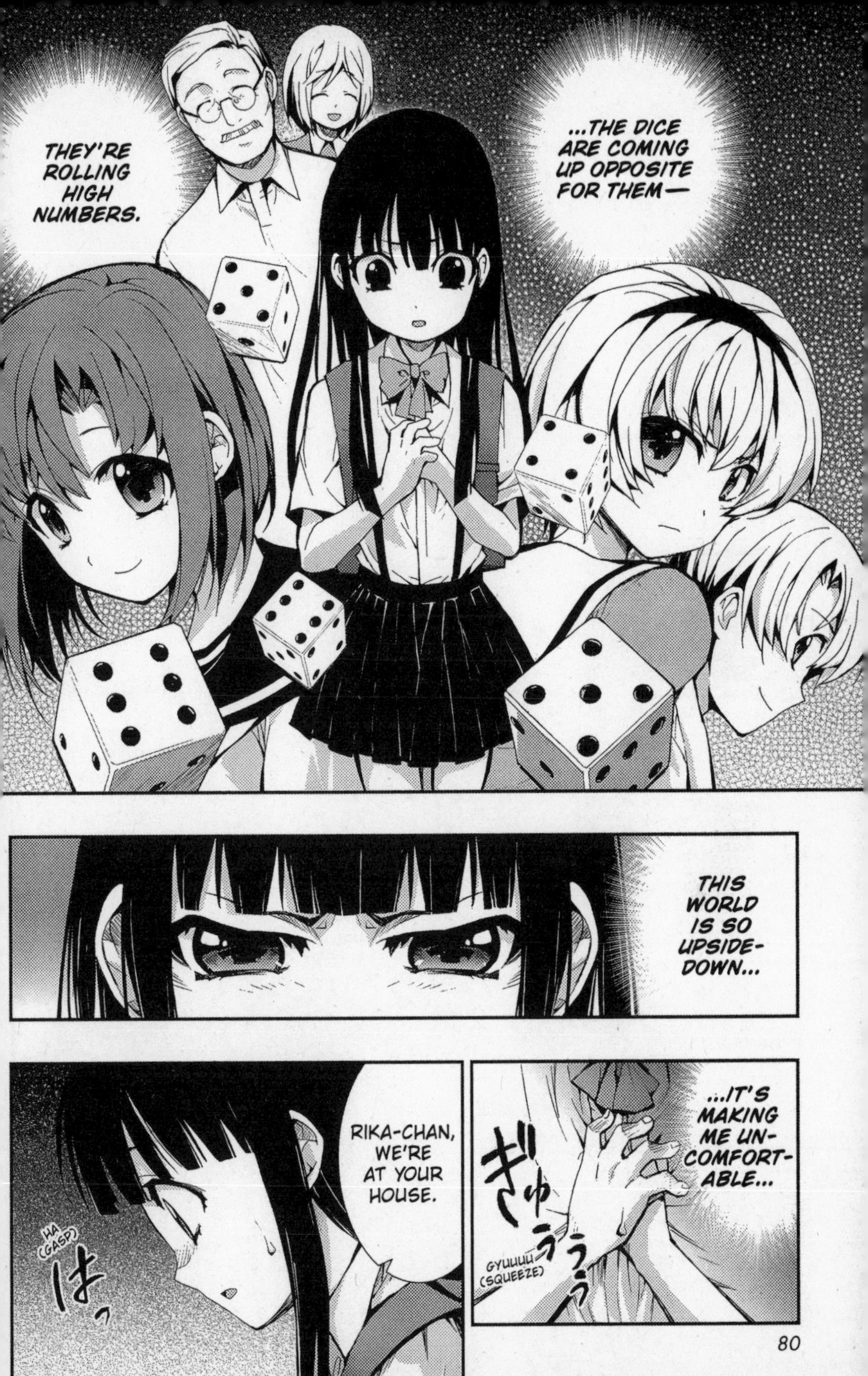
...THE DICE ARE COMING UP OPPOSITE FOR THEM—
THEY'RE ROLLING HIGH NUMBERS.
THIS WORLD IS SO UPSIDE-DOWN...
...IT'S MAKING ME UN-COMFORT-ABLE...
ぎゅううう
GYUUUU (SQUEEZE)
RIKA-CHAN, WE'RE AT YOUR HOUSE.
HA (GASP)
はっ

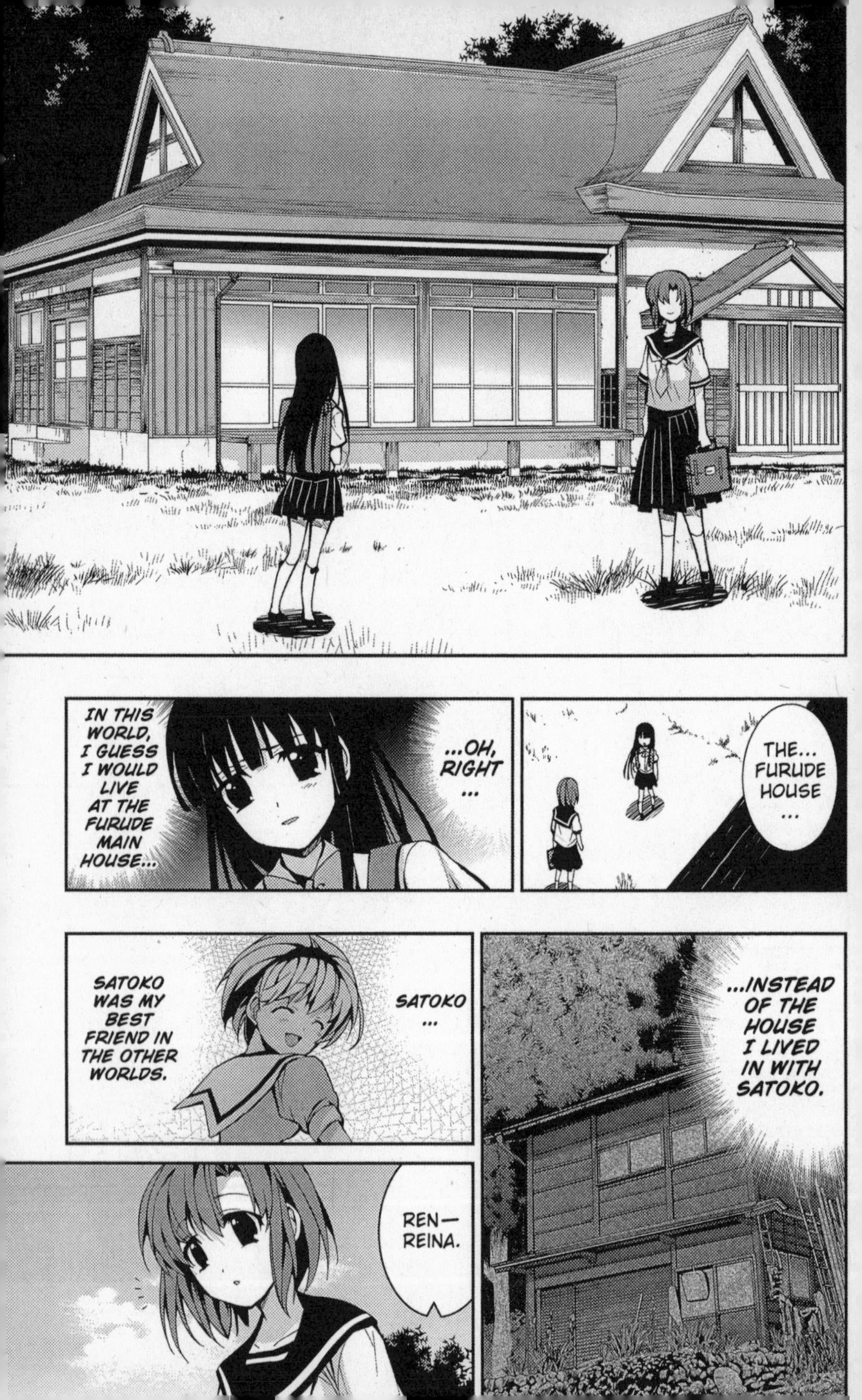
THE... FURUDE HOUSE...
...OH, RIGHT...
IN THIS WORLD, I GUESS I WOULD LIVE AT THE FURUDE MAIN HOUSE...
...INSTEAD OF THE HOUSE I LIVED IN WITH SATOKO.
SATOKO...
SATOKO WAS MY BEST FRIEND IN THE OTHER WORLDS.
REN—REINA.

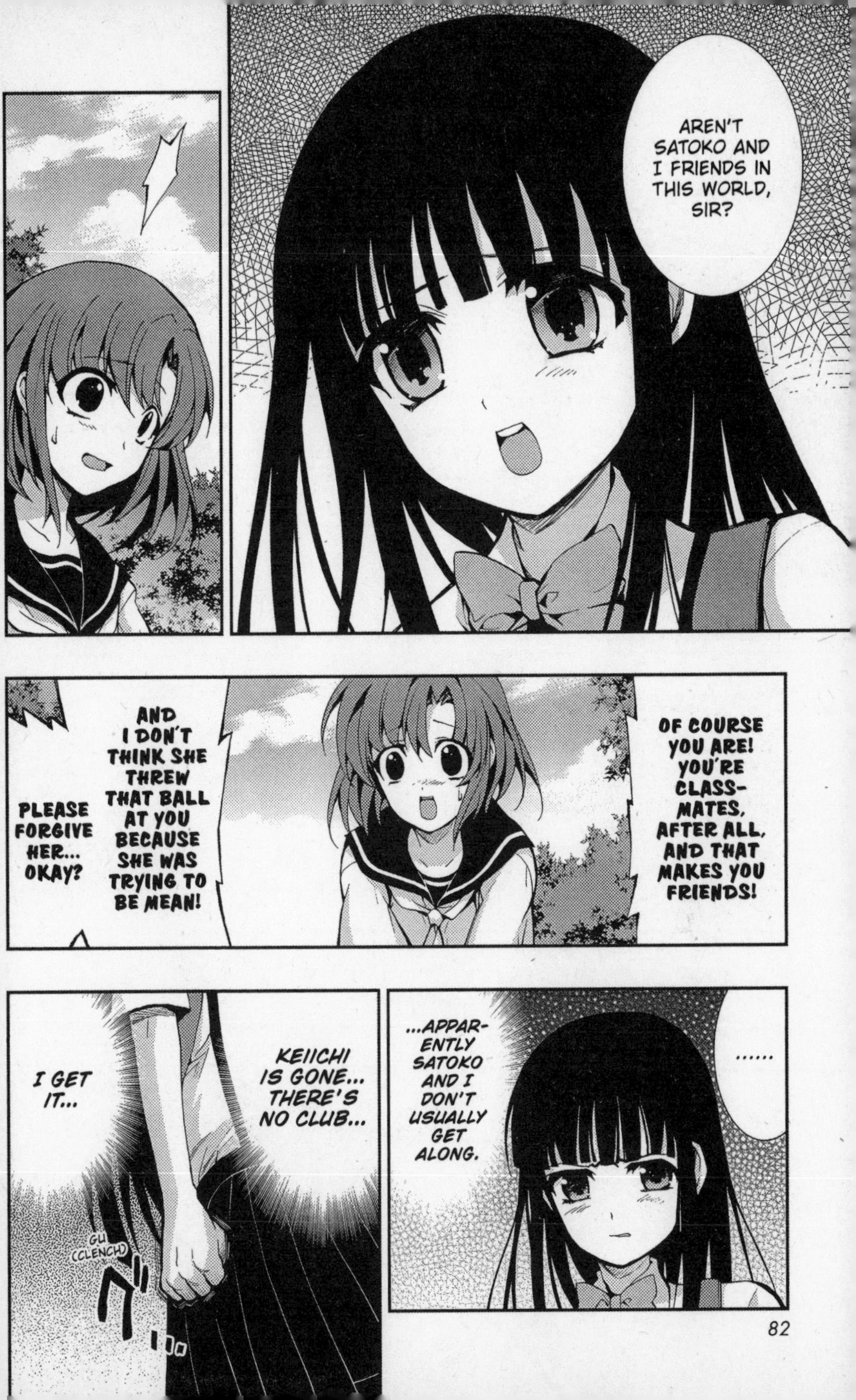
AREN'T SATOKO AND I FRIENDS IN THIS WORLD, SIR?
OF COURSE YOU ARE! YOU'RE CLASS-MATES, AFTER ALL, AND THAT MAKES YOU FRIENDS!
AND I DON'T THINK SHE THREW THAT BALL AT YOU BECAUSE SHE WAS TRYING TO BE MEAN!
PLEASE FORGIVE HER... OKAY?
......
...APPAR-ENTLY SATOKO AND I DON'T USUALLY GET ALONG.
KEIICHI IS GONE... THERE'S NO CLUB...
I GET IT...
GU (CLENCH)

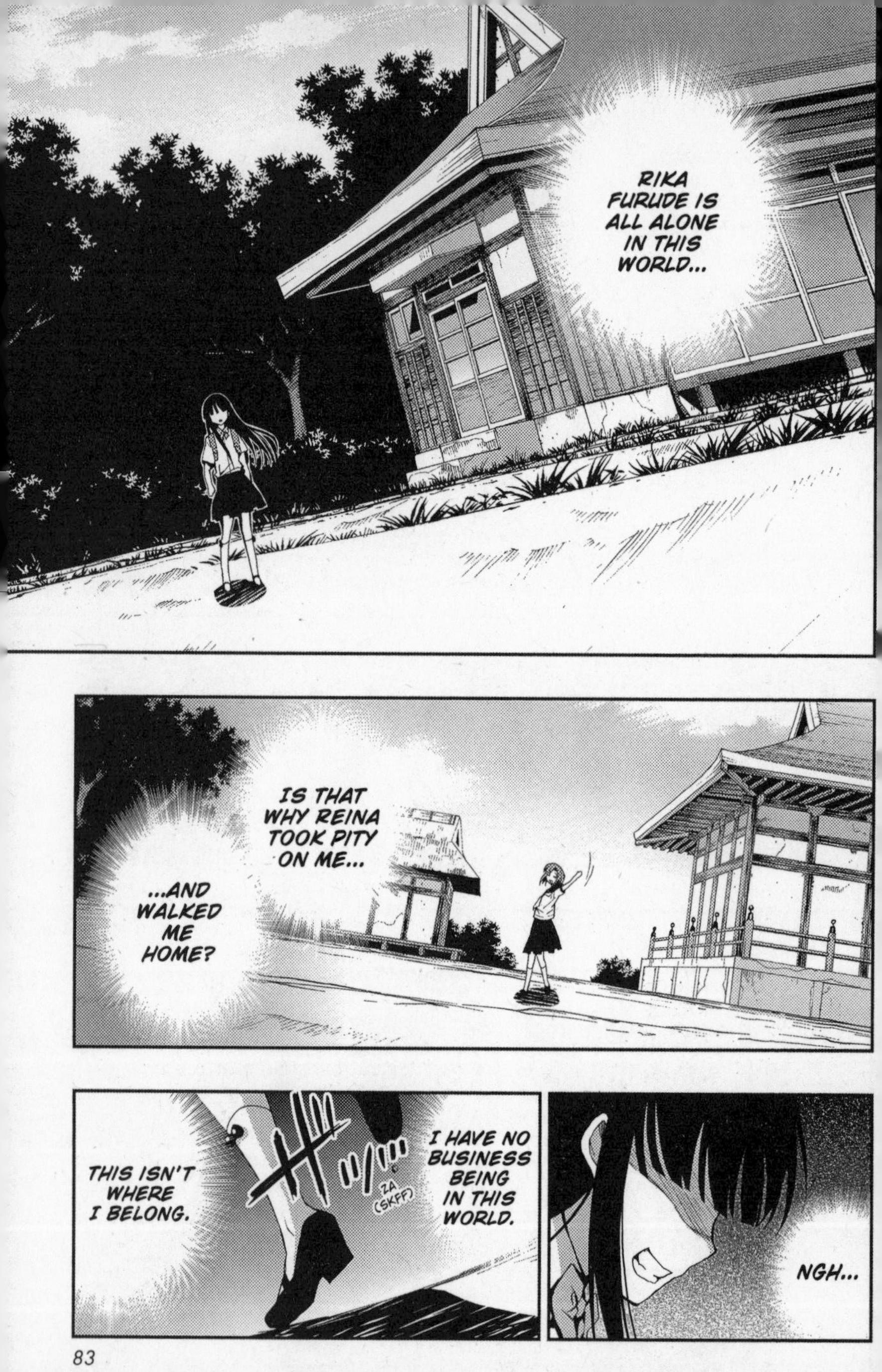
RIKA FURUDE IS ALL ALONE IN THIS WORLD...
IS THAT WHY REINA TOOK PITY ON ME...
...AND WALKED ME HOME?
NGH...
I HAVE NO BUSINESS BEING IN THIS WORLD.
ZA (SKFF)
THIS ISN'T WHERE I BELONG.

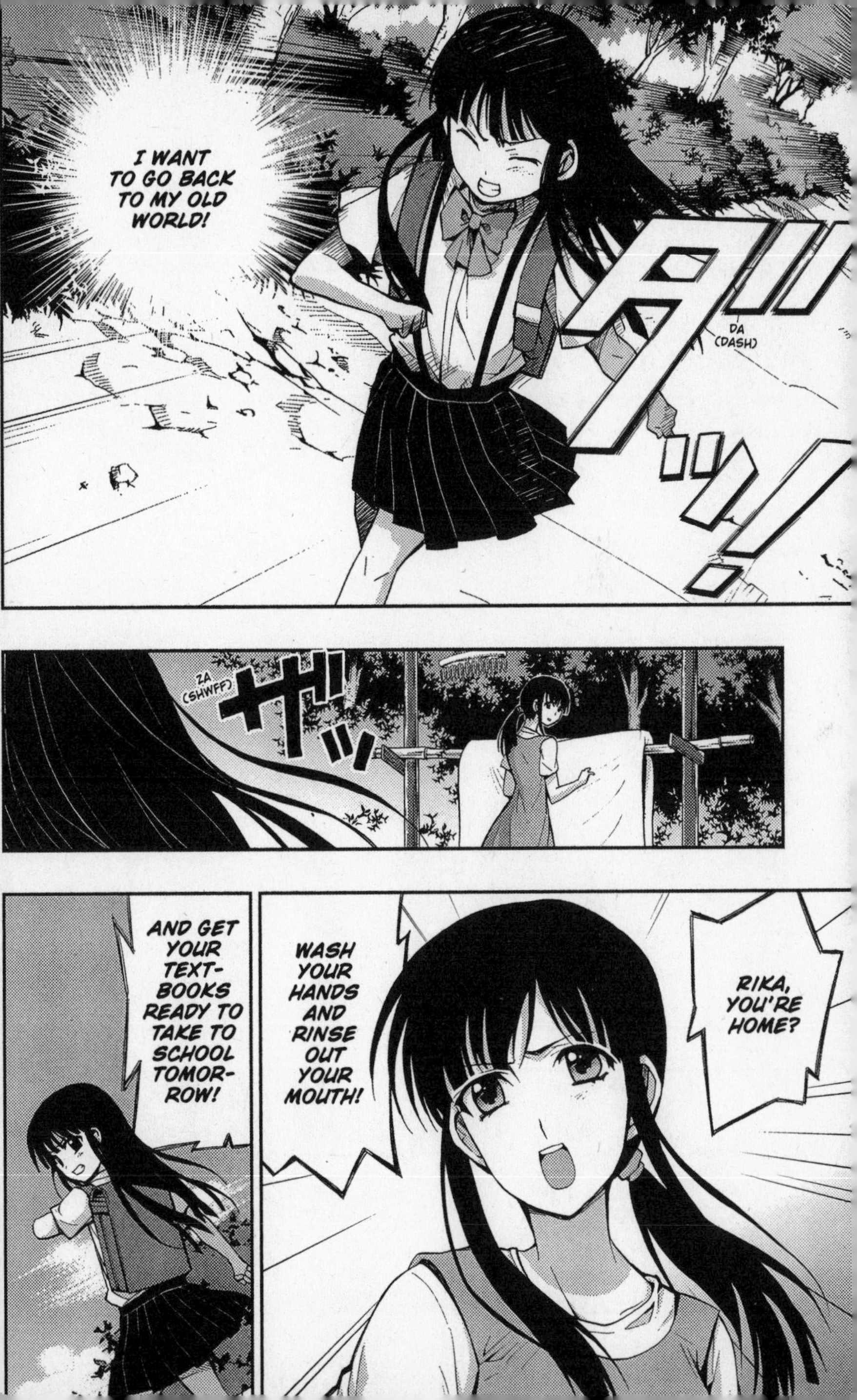
I WANT TO GO BACK TO MY OLD WORLD!
DA (DASH)
ZA (SHWFF)
RIKA, YOU'RE HOME?
WASH YOUR HANDS AND RINSE OUT YOUR MOUTH!
AND GET YOUR TEXT-BOOKS READY TO TAKE TO SCHOOL TOMOR-ROW!

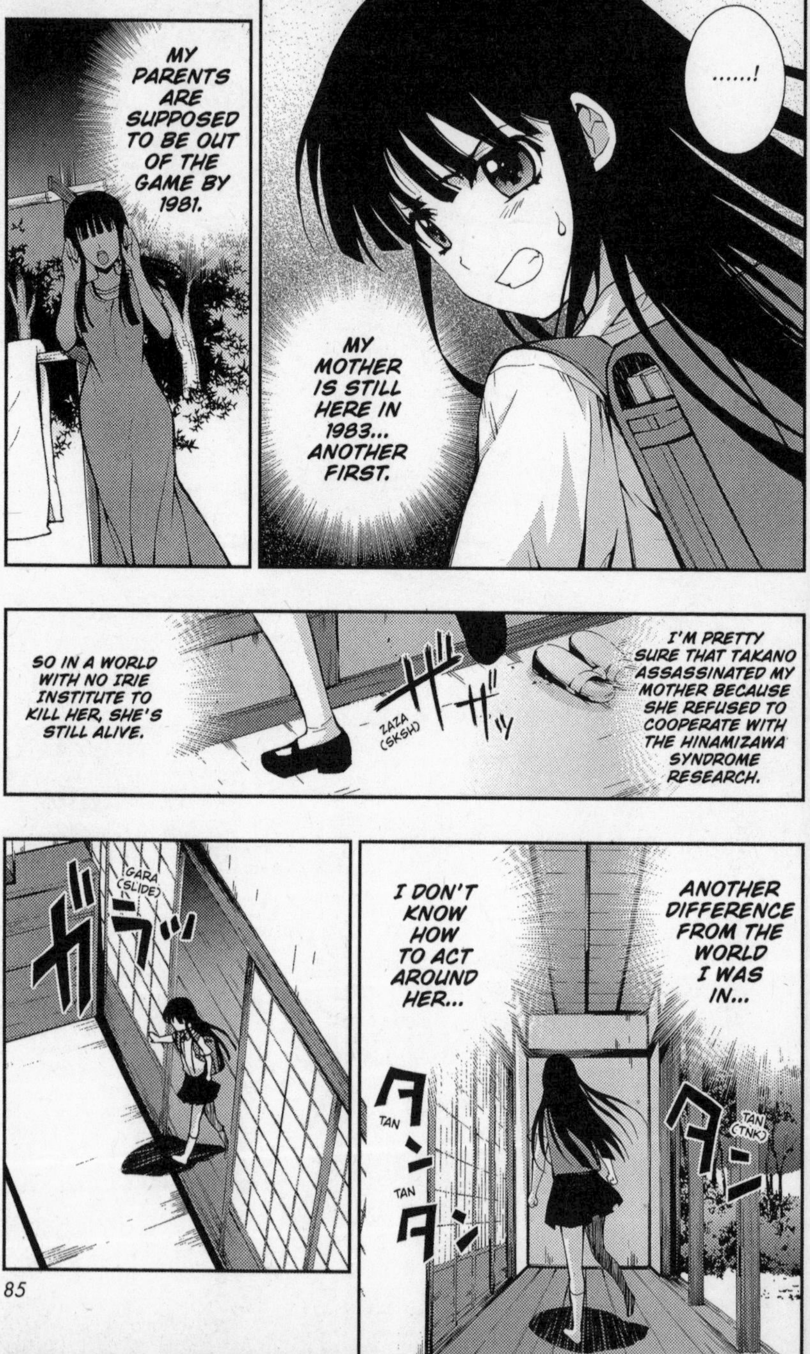
......!
MY MOTHER IS STILL HERE IN 1983... ANOTHER FIRST.
MY PARENTS ARE SUPPOSED TO BE OUT OF THE GAME BY 1981.
I'M PRETTY SURE THAT TAKANO ASSASSINATED MY MOTHER BECAUSE SHE REFUSED TO COOPERATE WITH THE HINAMIZAWA SYNDROME RESEARCH.
ZAZA (SKSH)
SO IN A WORLD WITH NO IRIE INSTITUTE TO KILL HER, SHE'S STILL ALIVE.
ANOTHER DIFFERENCE FROM THE WORLD I WAS IN...
I DON'T KNOW HOW TO ACT AROUND HER...
TAN (TNK)
TAN
TAN
GARA (SLIDE)

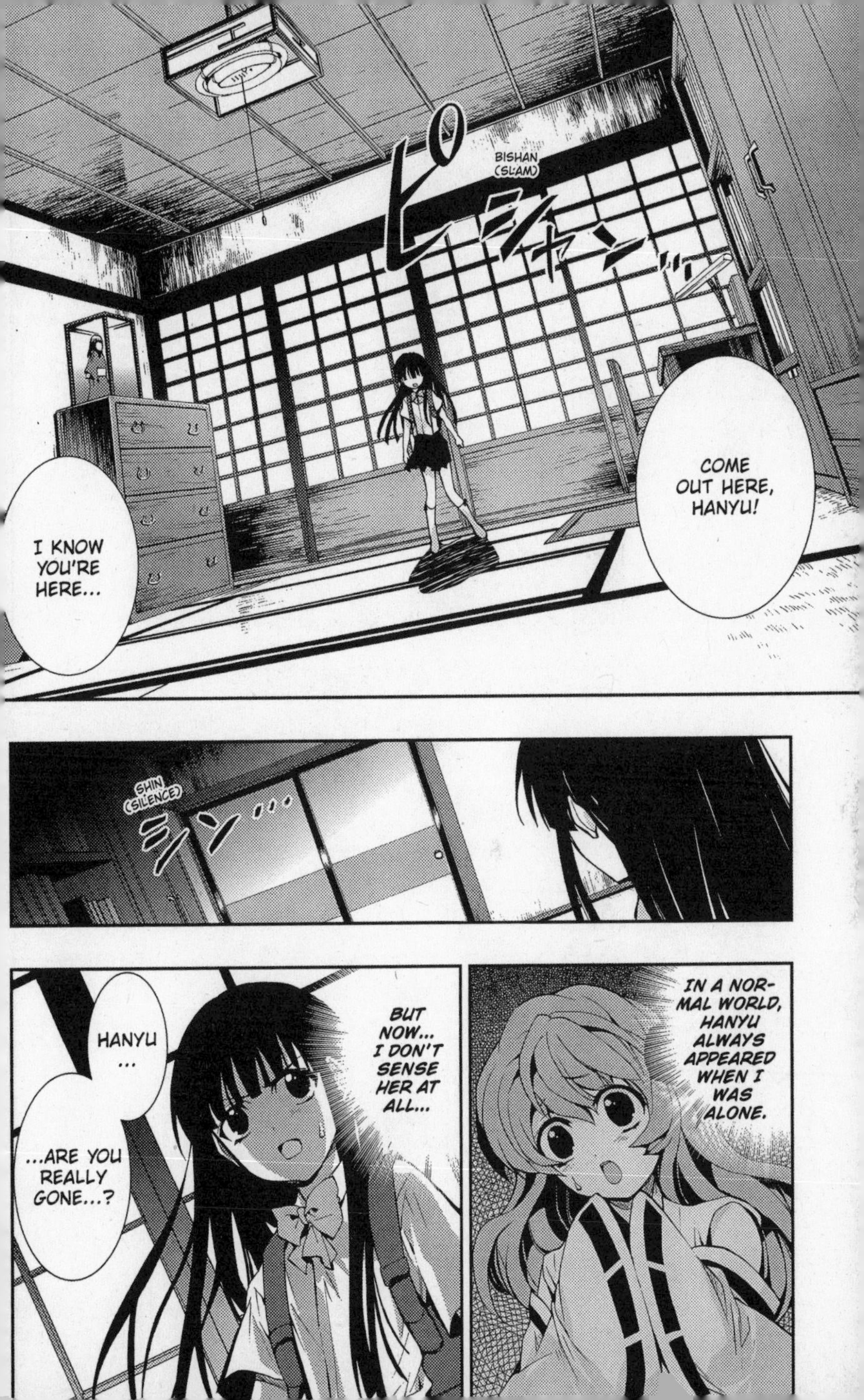
BISHAN (SLAM)
COME OUT HERE, HANYU!
I KNOW YOU'RE HERE...
SHIN (SILENCE)
IN A NORMAL WORLD, HANYU ALWAYS APPEARED WHEN I WAS ALONE.
BUT NOW... I DON'T SENSE HER AT ALL...
HANYU ...
...ARE YOU REALLY GONE...?

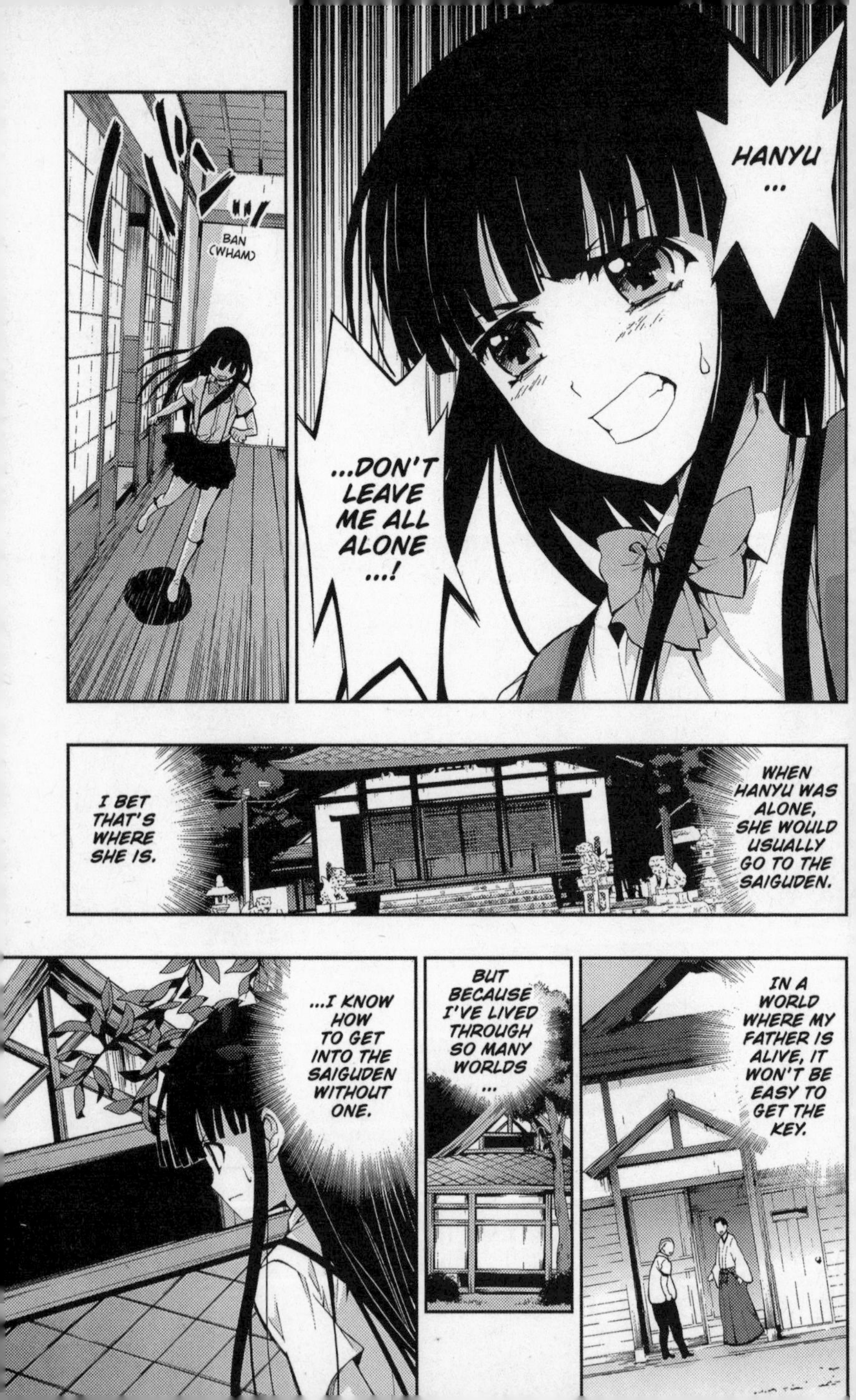
HANYU ...
...DON'T LEAVE ME ALL ALONE ...!
BAN (WHAM)
WHEN HANYU WAS ALONE, SHE WOULD USUALLY GO TO THE SAIGUDEN.
I BET THAT'S WHERE SHE IS.
IN A WORLD WHERE MY FATHER IS ALIVE, IT WON'T BE EASY TO GET THE KEY.
BUT BECAUSE I'VE LIVED THROUGH SO MANY WORLDS ...
...I KNOW HOW TO GET INTO THE SAIGUDEN WITHOUT ONE.

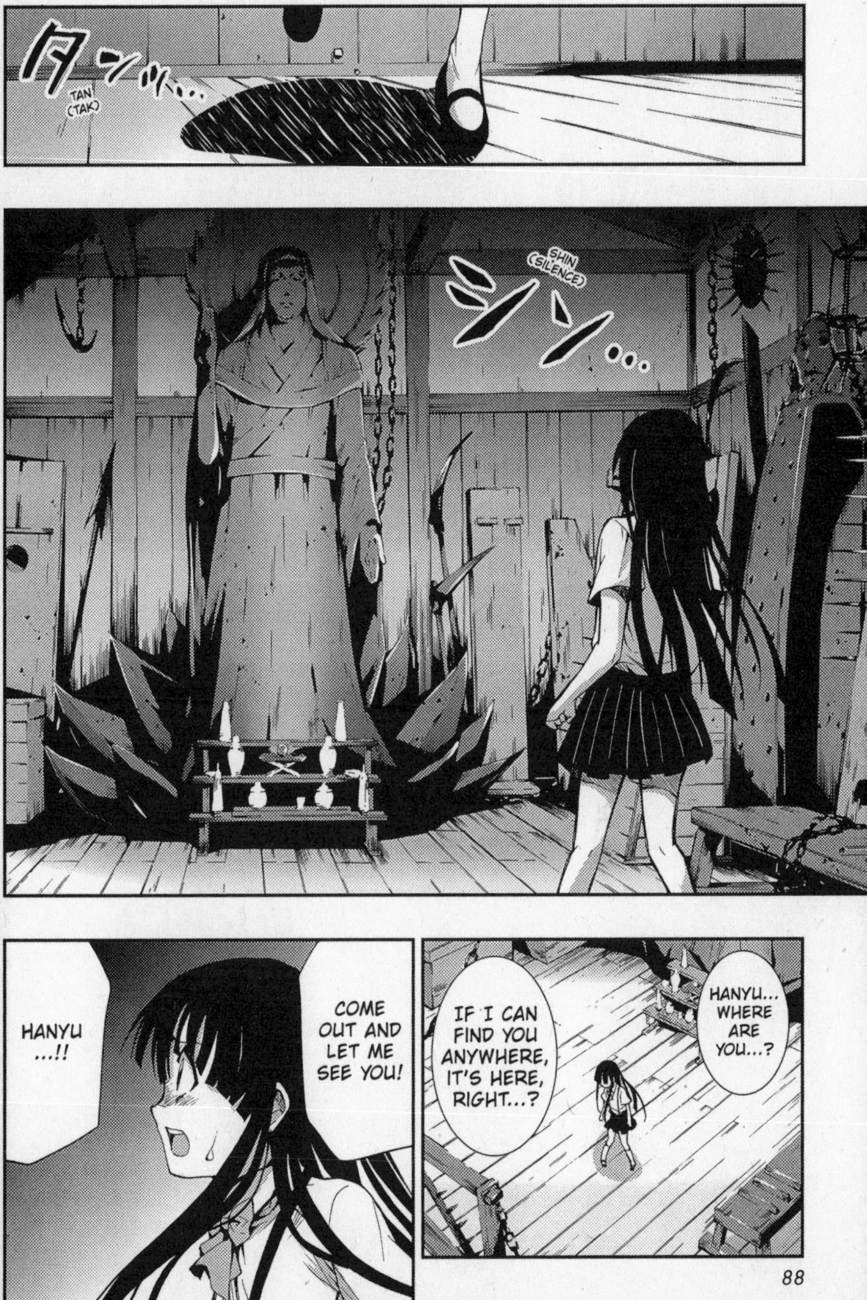
TAN (TAK)
SHIN (SILENCE)
HANYU... WHERE ARE YOU...?
IF I CAN FIND YOU ANYWHERE, IT'S HERE, RIGHT...?
COME OUT AND LET ME SEE YOU!
HANYU ...!!

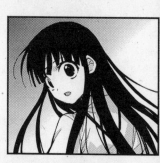

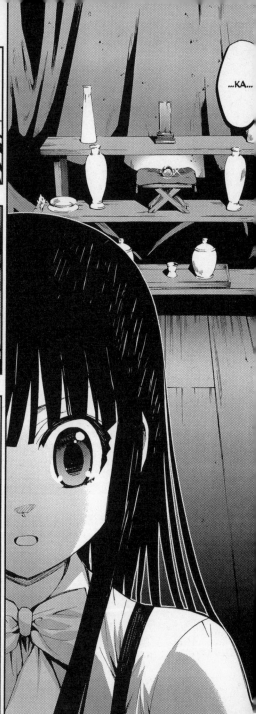

...KA...

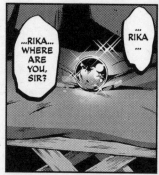

...RIKA... WHERE ARE YOU, SIR?

...RIKA...

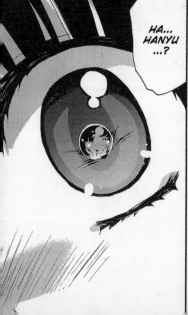

HA... HANYU...?

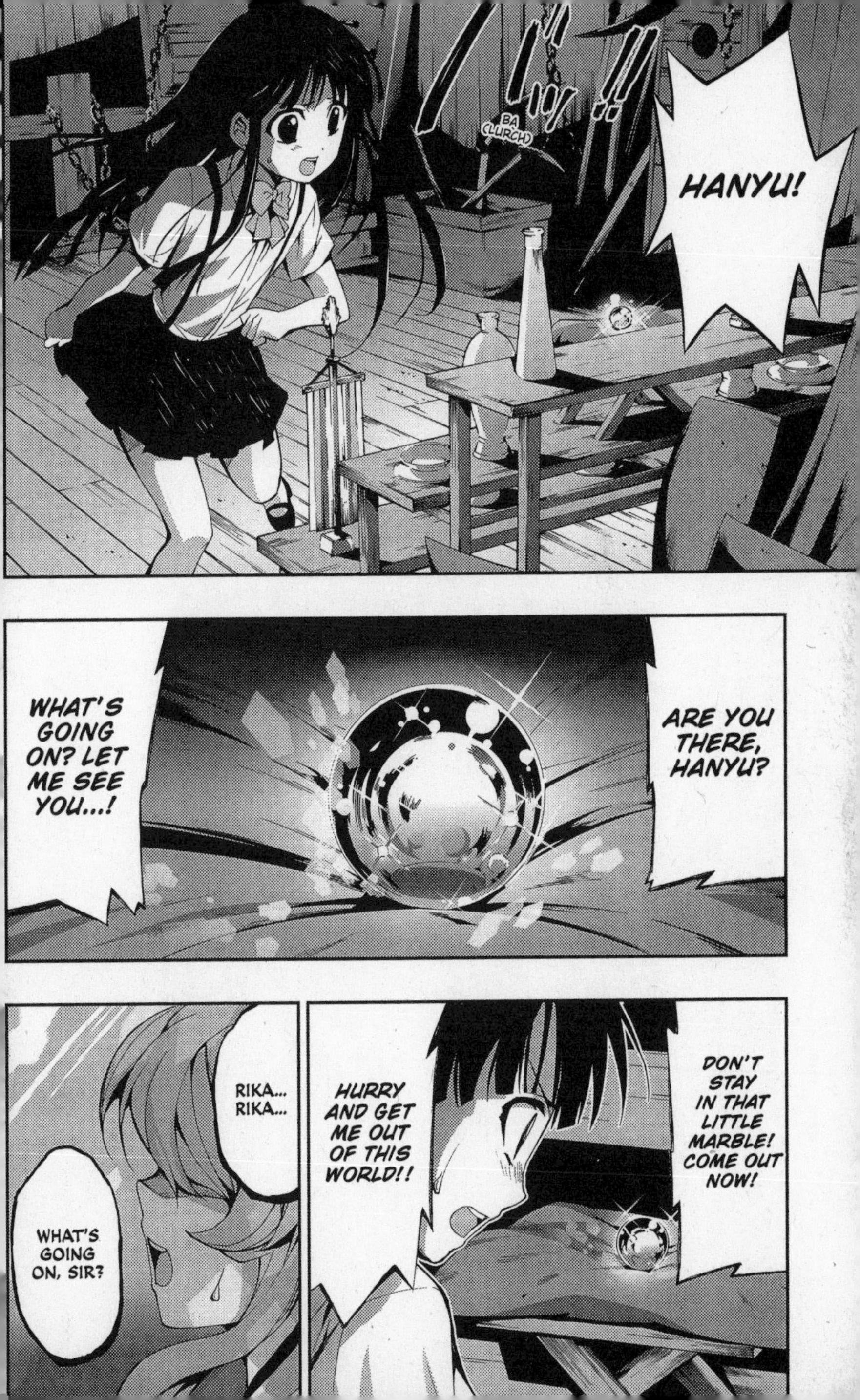
HANYU!
BA (LURCH)
ARE YOU THERE, HANYU?
WHAT'S GOING ON? LET ME SEE YOU...!
DON'T STAY IN THAT LITTLE MARBLE! COME OUT NOW!
HURRY AND GET ME OUT OF THIS WORLD!!
RIKA... RIKA...
WHAT'S GOING ON, SIR?

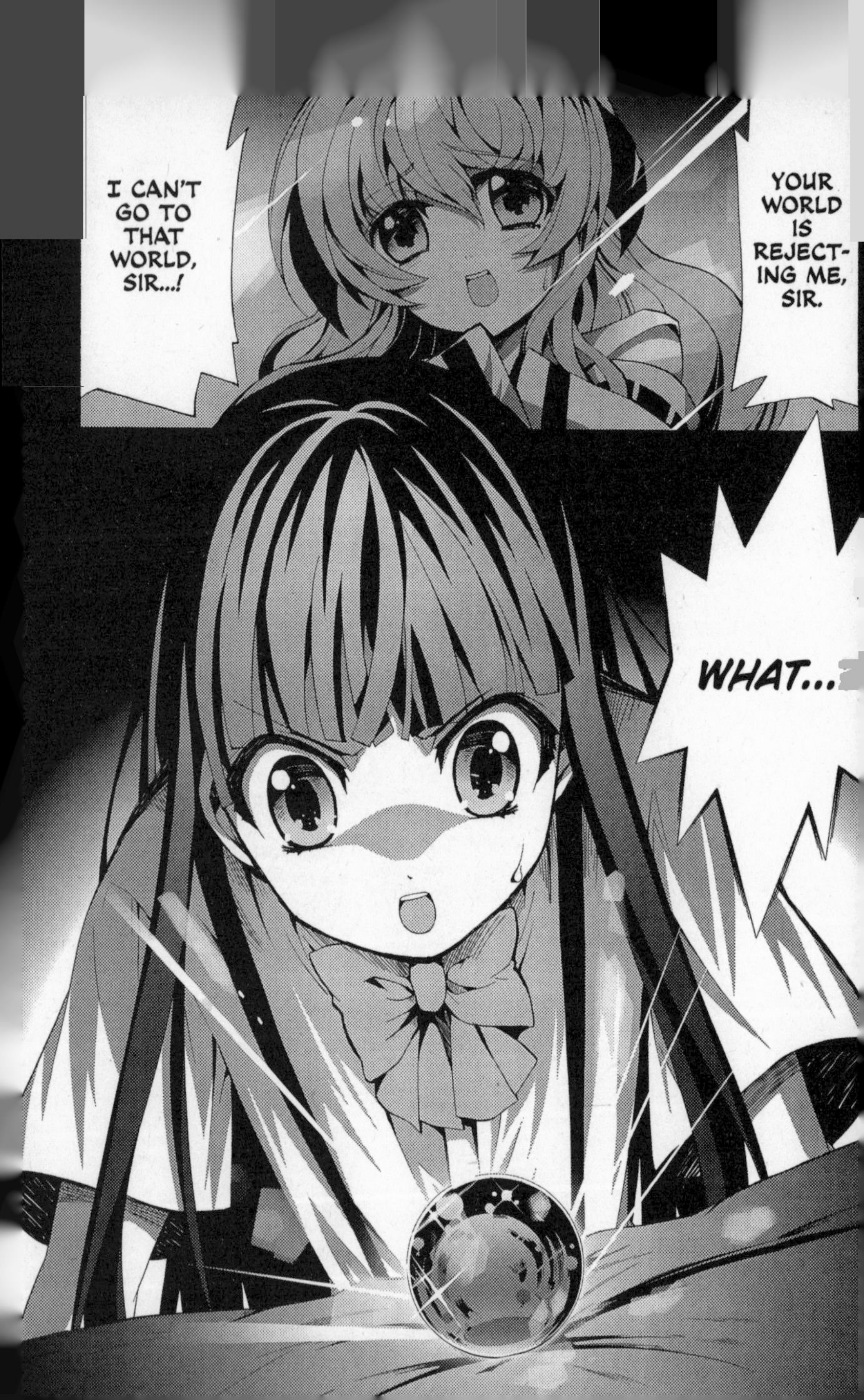
YOUR WORLD IS REJECTING ME, SIR.
I CAN'T GO TO THAT WORLD, SIR...!
WHAT...

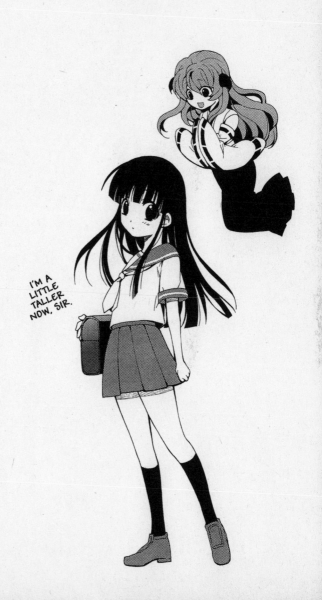

I'M A
LITTLE
TALLER
NOW, SIR.

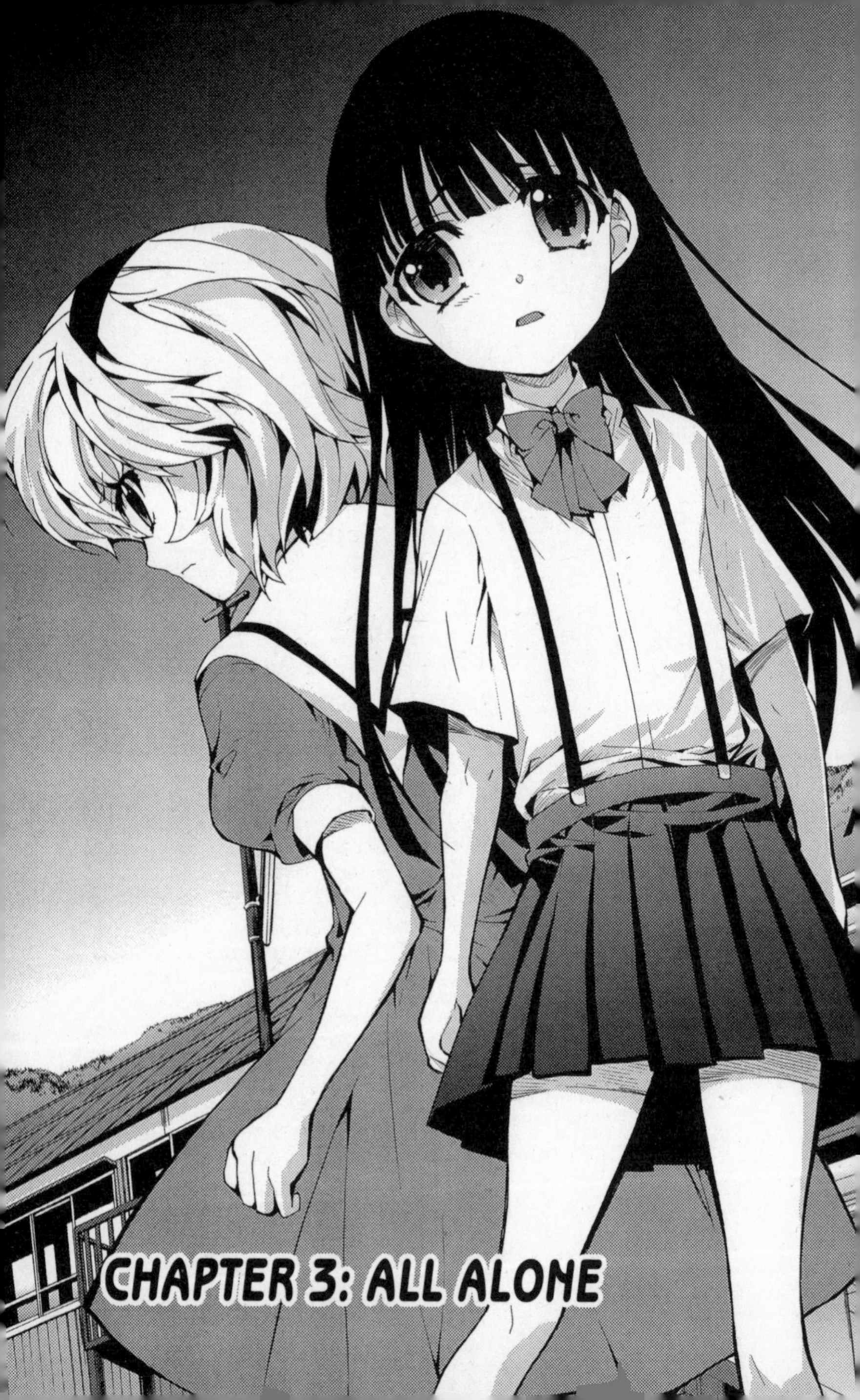
CHAPTER 3: ALL ALONE

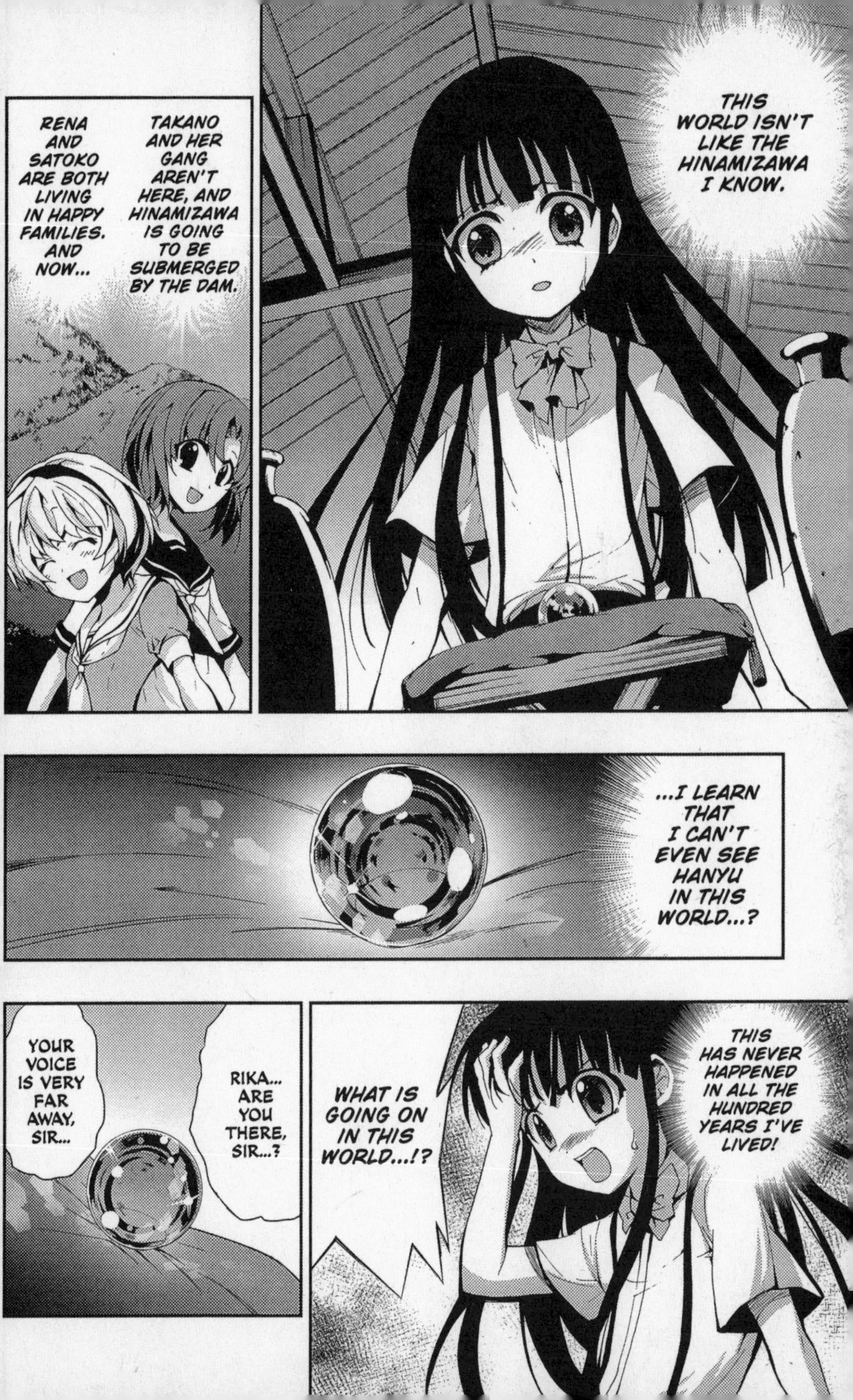
THIS WORLD ISN'T LIKE THE HINAMIZAWA I KNOW.
TAKANO AND HER GANG AREN'T HERE, AND HINAMIZAWA IS GOING TO BE SUBMERGED BY THE DAM.
RENA AND SATOKO ARE BOTH LIVING IN HAPPY FAMILIES. AND NOW...
...I LEARN THAT I CAN'T EVEN SEE HANYU IN THIS WORLD...?
THIS HAS NEVER HAPPENED IN ALL THE HUNDRED YEARS I'VE LIVED!
WHAT IS GOING ON IN THIS WORLD...!?
RIKA... ARE YOU THERE, SIR...?
YOUR VOICE IS VERY FAR AWAY, SIR...

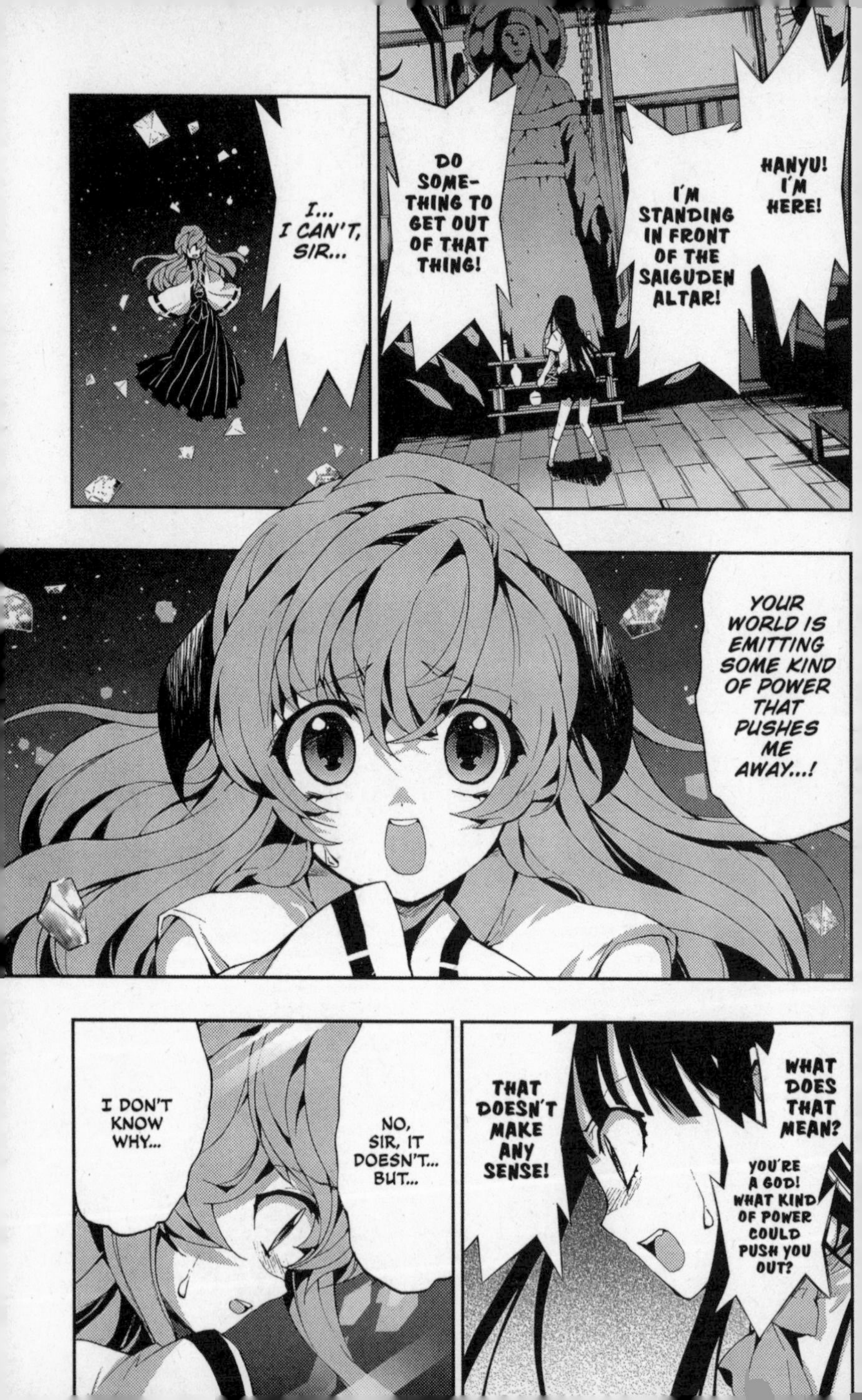
HANYU! I'M HERE!
I'M STANDING IN FRONT OF THE SAIGUDEN ALTAR!
DO SOME-THING TO GET OUT OF THAT THING!
I... I CAN'T, SIR...
YOUR WORLD IS EMITTING SOME KIND OF POWER THAT PUSHES ME AWAY...!
WHAT DOES THAT MEAN?
YOU'RE A GOD! WHAT KIND OF POWER COULD PUSH YOU OUT?
THAT DOESN'T MAKE ANY SENSE!
NO, SIR, IT DOESN'T... BUT...
I DON'T KNOW WHY...

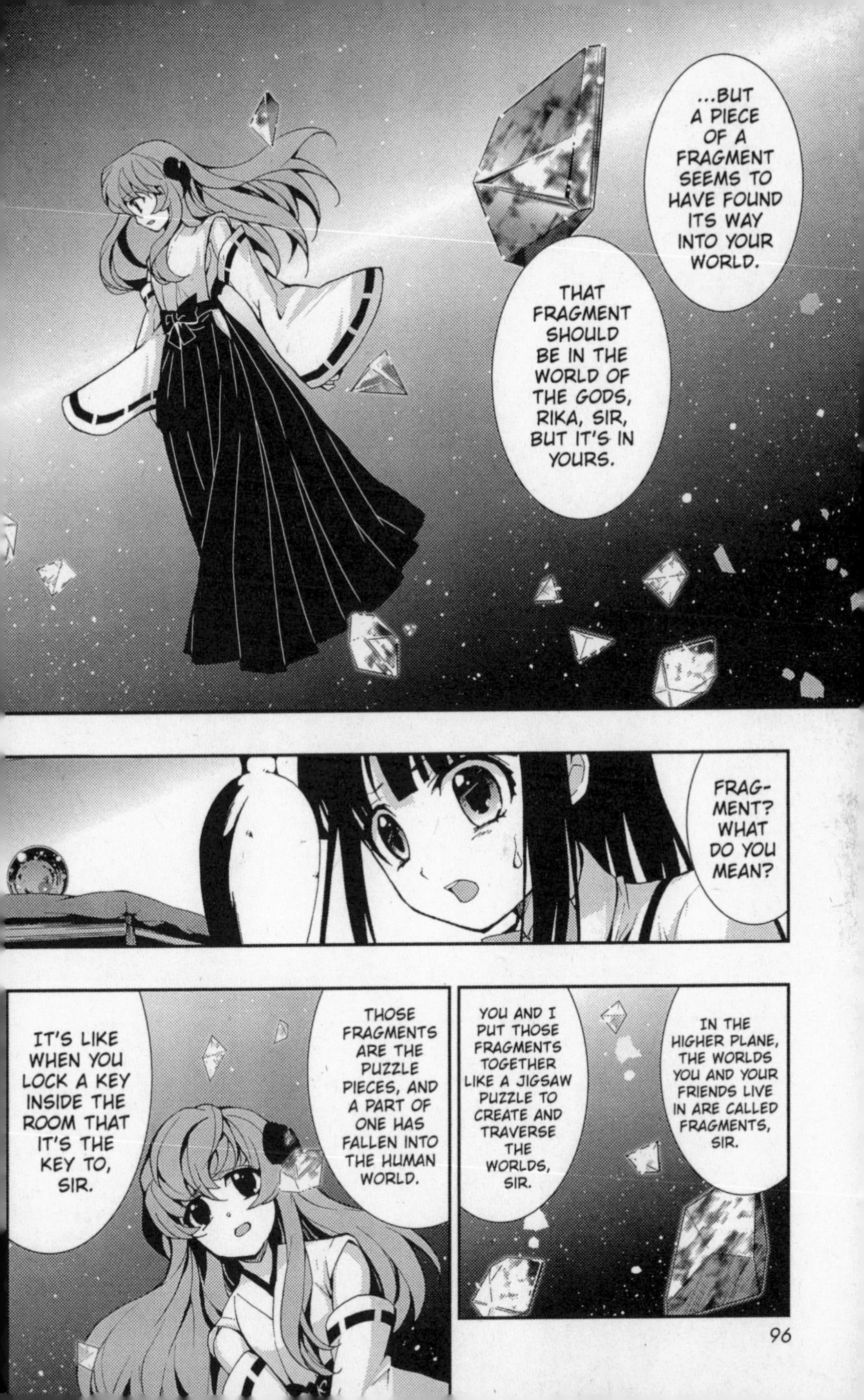
...BUT A PIECE OF A FRAGMENT SEEMS TO HAVE FOUND ITS WAY INTO YOUR WORLD.
THAT FRAGMENT SHOULD BE IN THE WORLD OF THE GODS, RIKA, SIR, BUT IT'S IN YOURS.
FRAG-MENT? WHAT DO YOU MEAN?
IN THE HIGHER PLANE, THE WORLDS YOU AND YOUR FRIENDS LIVE IN ARE CALLED FRAGMENTS, SIR.
YOU AND I PUT THOSE FRAGMENTS TOGETHER LIKE A JIGSAW PUZZLE TO CREATE AND TRAVERSE THE WORLDS, SIR.
THOSE FRAGMENTS ARE THE PUZZLE PIECES, AND A PART OF ONE HAS FALLEN INTO THE HUMAN WORLD.
IT'S LIKE WHEN YOU LOCK A KEY INSIDE THE ROOM THAT IT'S THE KEY TO, SIR.

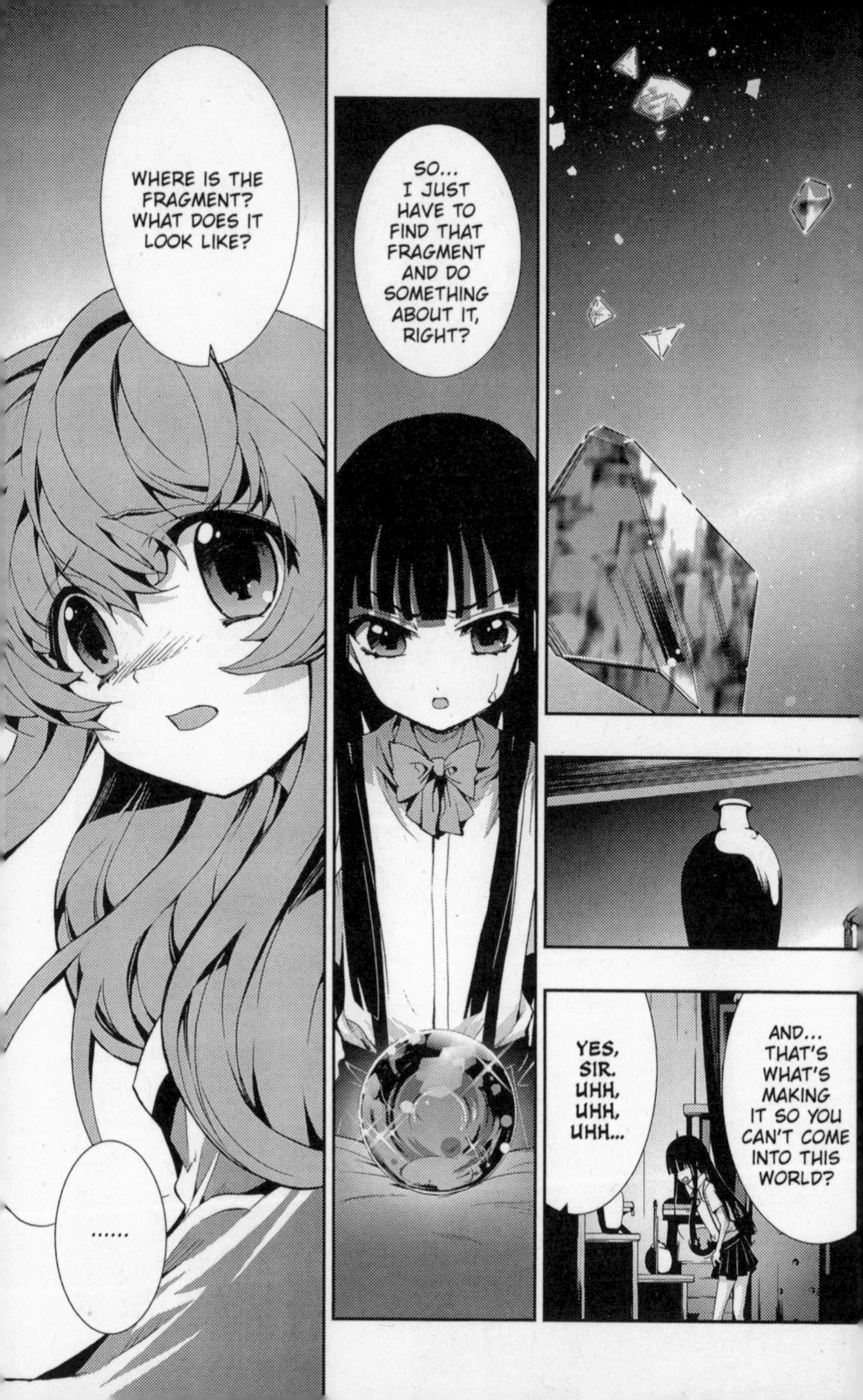
AND... THAT'S WHAT'S MAKING IT SO YOU CAN'T COME INTO THIS WORLD?
YES, SIR. UHH, UHH, UHH...
SO... I JUST HAVE TO FIND THAT FRAGMENT AND DO SOMETHING ABOUT IT, RIGHT?
WHERE IS THE FRAGMENT? WHAT DOES IT LOOK LIKE?
......

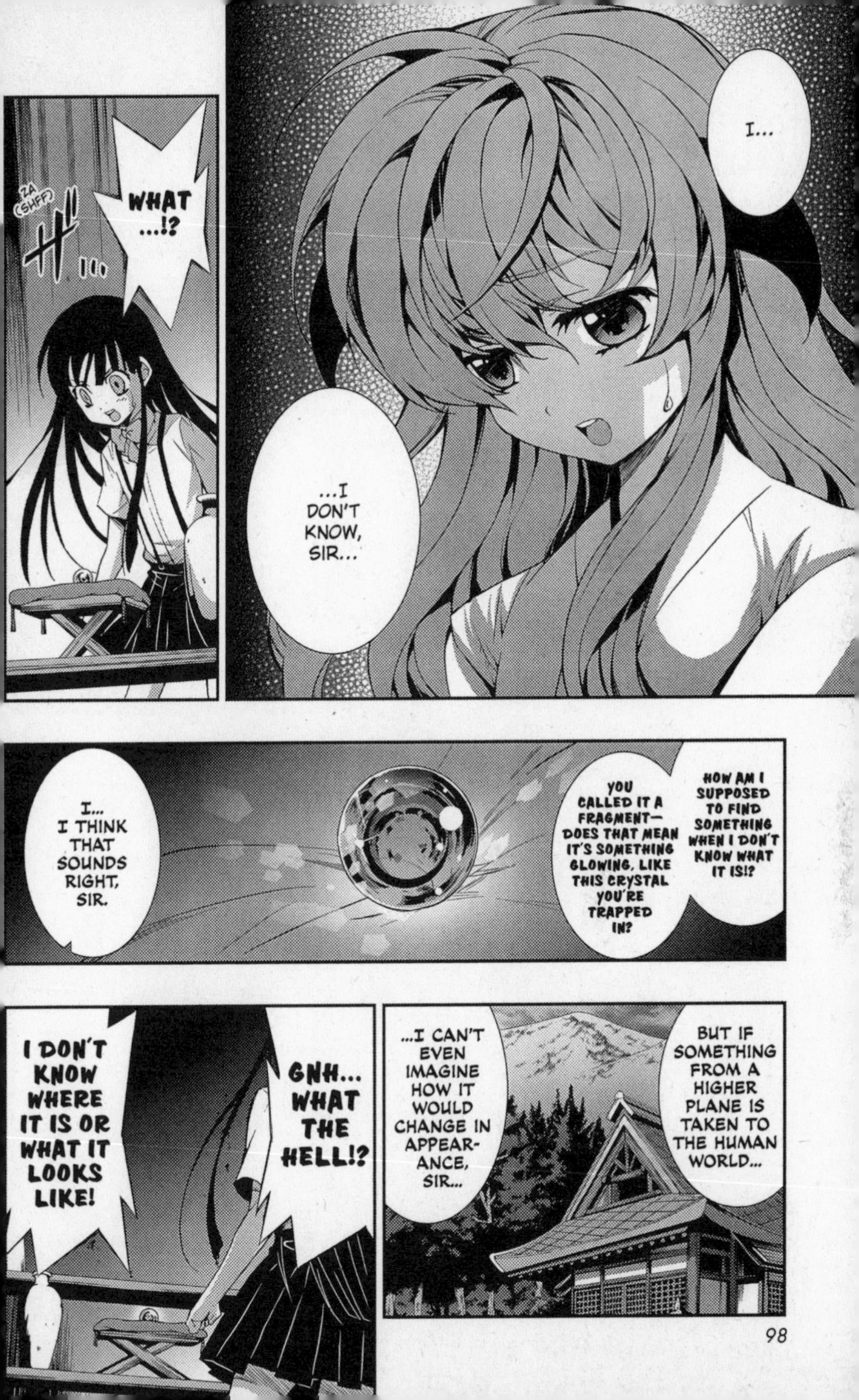
I...
...I DON'T KNOW, SIR...
WHAT ...!?
ZA (SHFF)
HOW AM I SUPPOSED TO FIND SOMETHING WHEN I DON'T KNOW WHAT IT IS!?
YOU CALLED IT A FRAGMENT— DOES THAT MEAN IT'S SOMETHING GLOWING, LIKE THIS CRYSTAL YOU'RE TRAPPED IN?
I... I THINK THAT SOUNDS RIGHT, SIR.
BUT IF SOMETHING FROM A HIGHER PLANE IS TAKEN TO THE HUMAN WORLD...
...I CAN'T EVEN IMAGINE HOW IT WOULD CHANGE IN APPEARANCE, SIR...
GNH... WHAT THE HELL!?
I DON'T KNOW WHERE IT IS OR WHAT IT LOOKS LIKE!

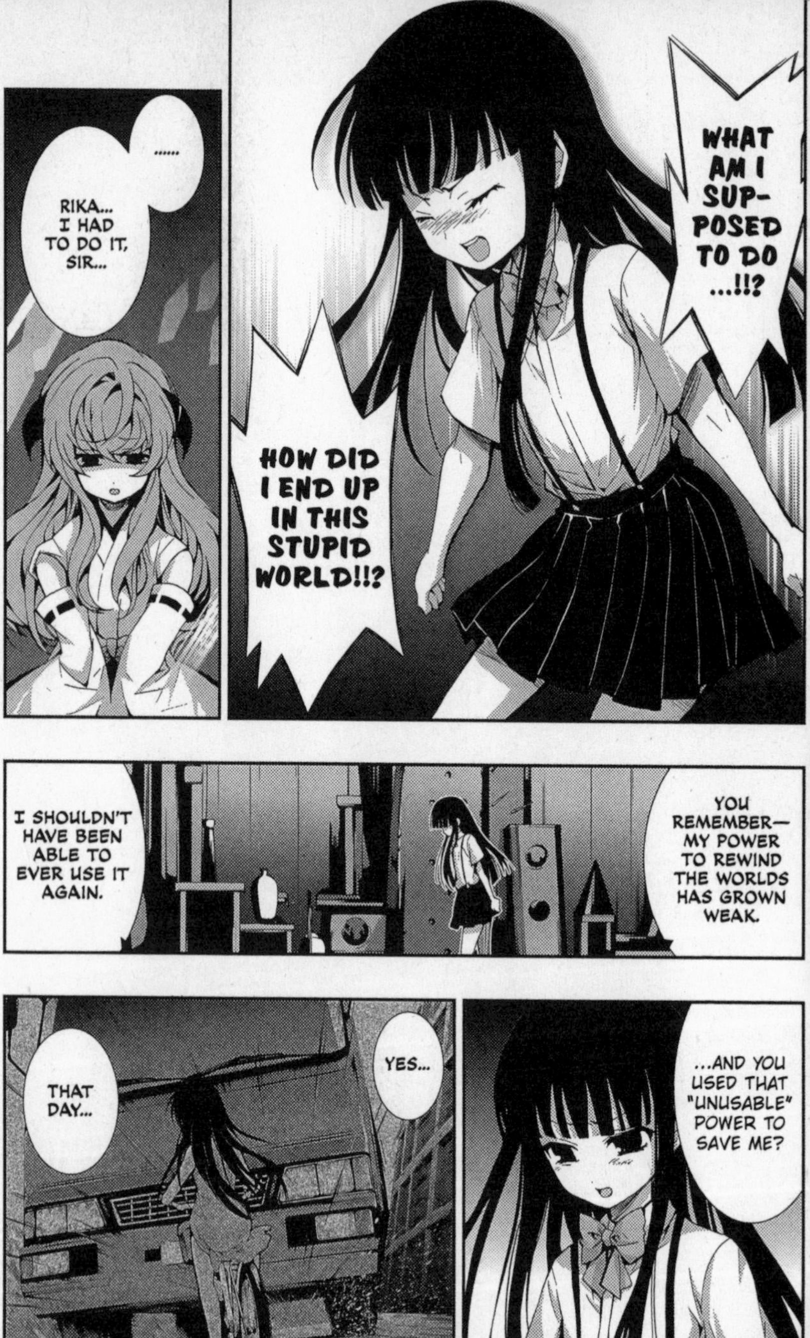
WHAT AM I SUP-POSED TO DO ...!!?
HOW DID I END UP IN THIS STUPID WORLD!!?
......
RIKA... I HAD TO DO IT, SIR...
YOU REMEMBER— MY POWER TO REWIND THE WORLDS HAS GROWN WEAK.
I SHOULDN'T HAVE BEEN ABLE TO EVER USE IT AGAIN.
...AND YOU USED THAT "UNUSABLE" POWER TO SAVE ME?
YES...
THAT DAY...

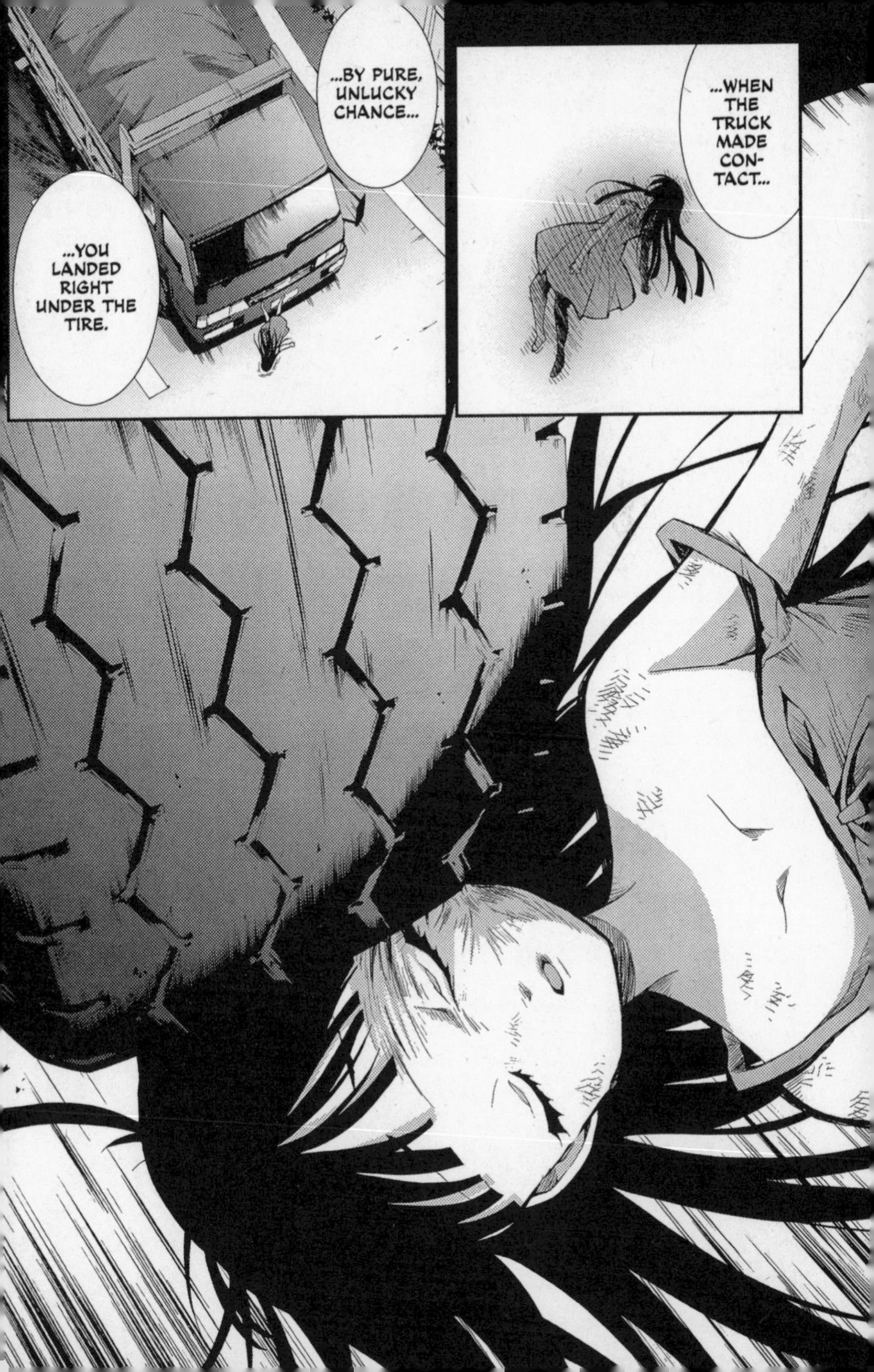
...WHEN THE TRUCK MADE CON-TACT...
...BY PURE, UNLUCKY CHANCE...
...YOU LANDED RIGHT UNDER THE TIRE.

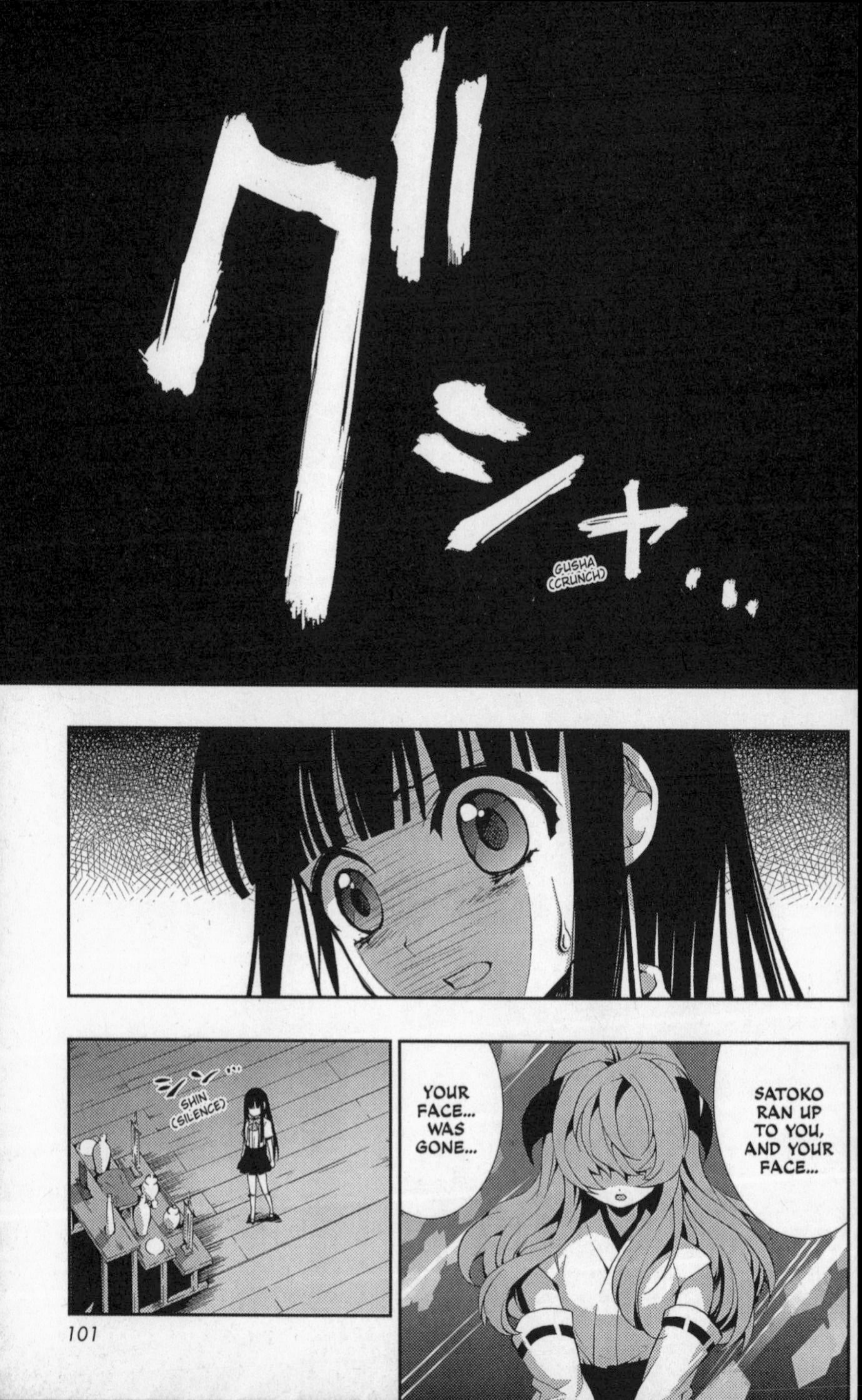
グシャ…
GUSHA (CRUNCH)
SATOKO RAN UP TO YOU, AND YOUR FACE...
YOUR FACE... WAS GONE...
シン…
SHIN (SILENCE)

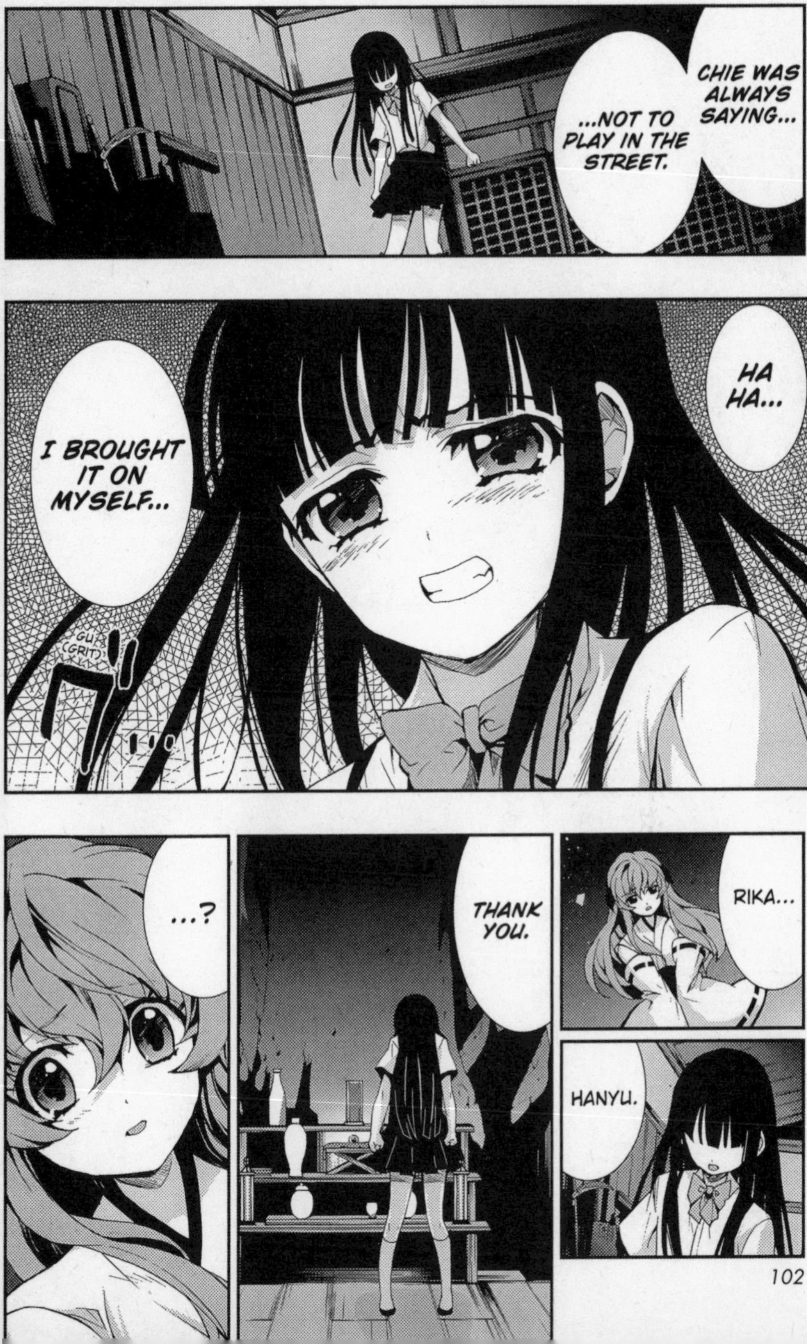
CHIE WAS ALWAYS SAYING...
...NOT TO PLAY IN THE STREET.
HA HA...
I BROUGHT IT ON MYSELF...
GU (GRIT)
RIKA...
HANYU.
THANK YOU.
...?

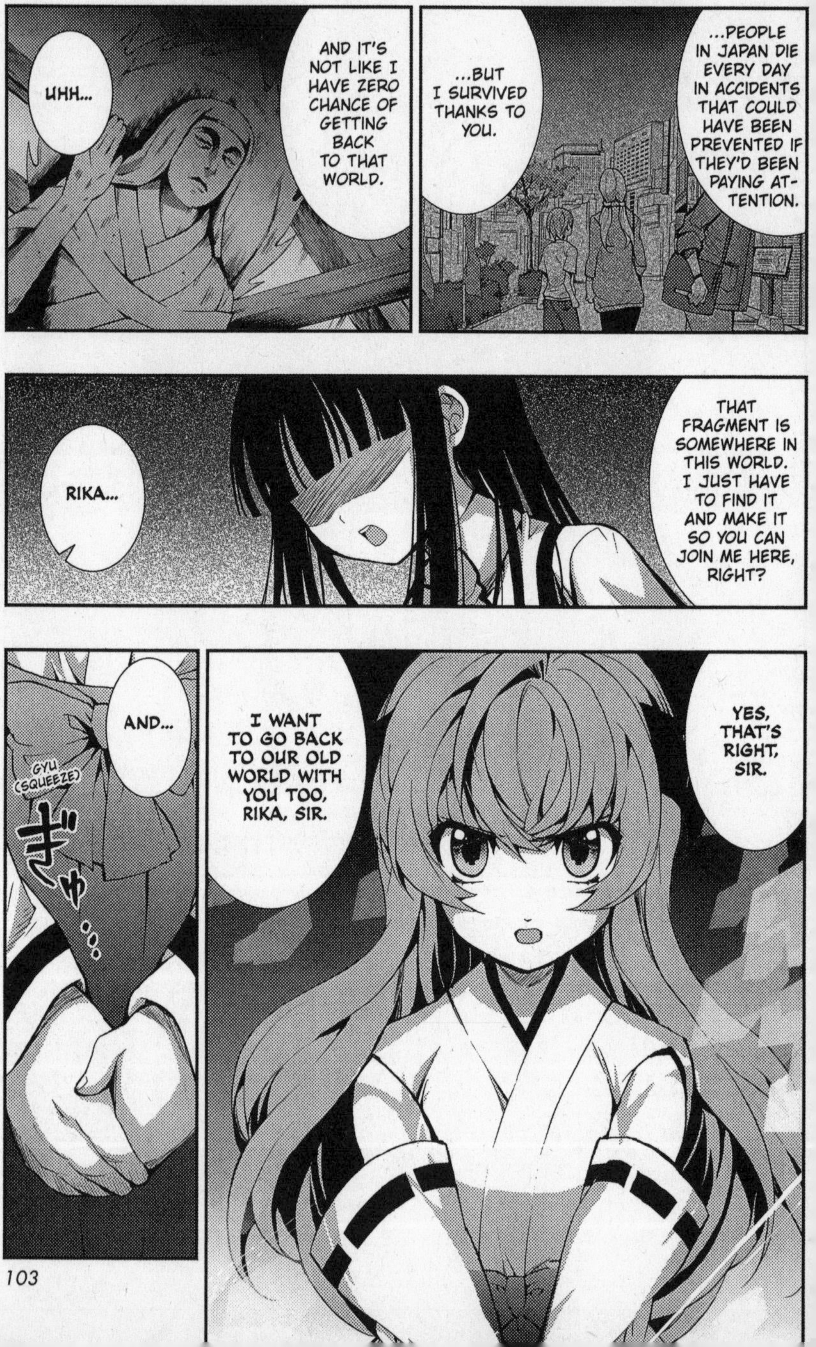
...PEOPLE IN JAPAN DIE EVERY DAY IN ACCIDENTS THAT COULD HAVE BEEN PREVENTED IF THEY'D BEEN PAYING AT-TENTION.
...BUT I SURVIVED THANKS TO YOU.
AND IT'S NOT LIKE I HAVE ZERO CHANCE OF GETTING BACK TO THAT WORLD.
UHH...
THAT FRAGMENT IS SOMEWHERE IN THIS WORLD. I JUST HAVE TO FIND IT AND MAKE IT SO YOU CAN JOIN ME HERE, RIGHT?
RIKA...
YES, THAT'S RIGHT, SIR.
I WANT TO GO BACK TO OUR OLD WORLD WITH YOU TOO, RIKA, SIR.
AND...
GYU (SQUEEZE)
ぎゅ...

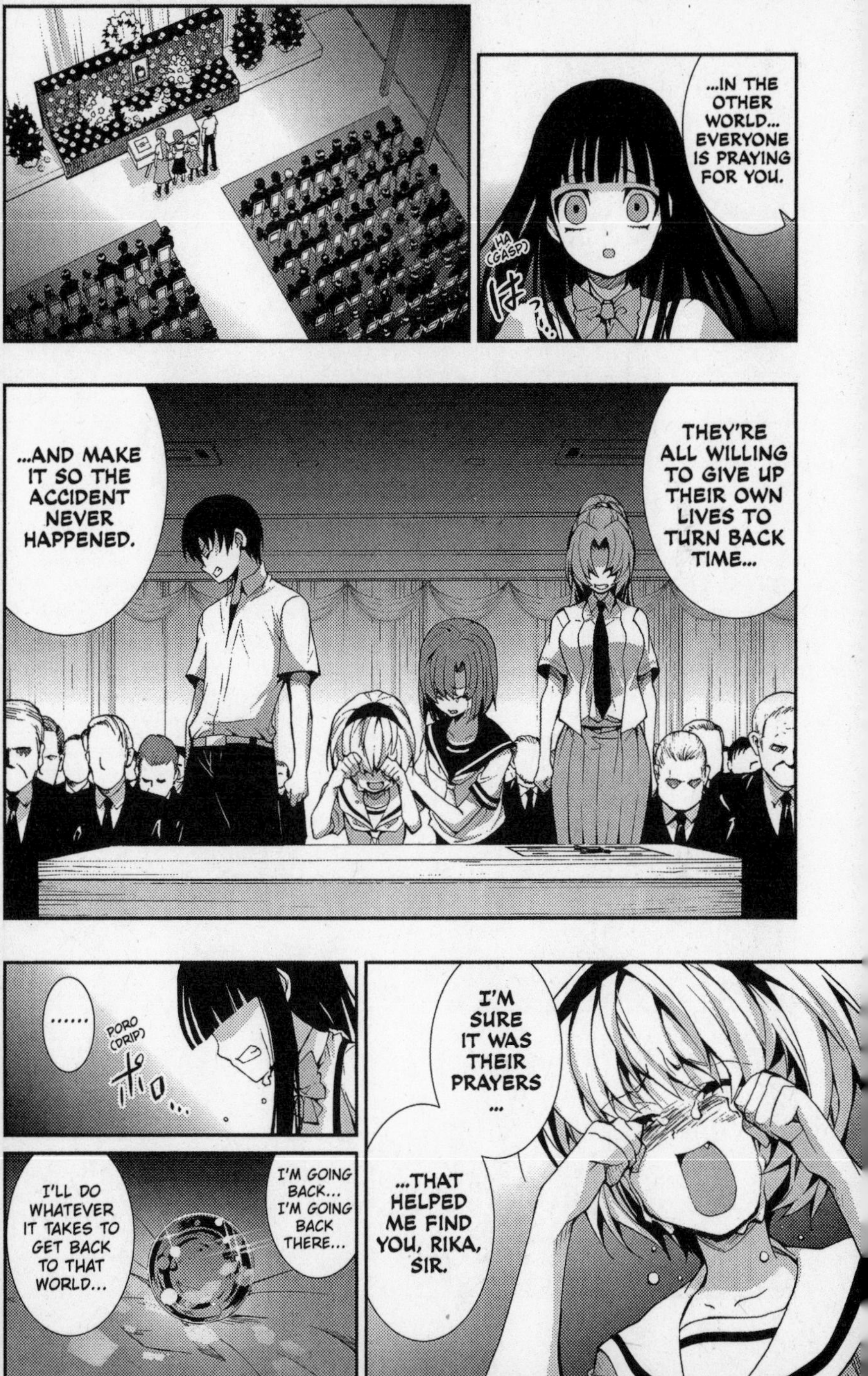
...IN THE OTHER WORLD... EVERYONE IS PRAYING FOR YOU.
HA (GASP)
はっ...
THEY'RE ALL WILLING TO GIVE UP THEIR OWN LIVES TO TURN BACK TIME...
...AND MAKE IT SO THE ACCIDENT NEVER HAPPENED.
I'M SURE IT WAS THEIR PRAYERS...
...THAT HELPED ME FIND YOU, RIKA, SIR.
......
PORO (DRIP)
ポロ...
I'M GOING BACK... I'M GOING BACK THERE...
I'LL DO WHATEVER IT TAKES TO GET BACK TO THAT WORLD...

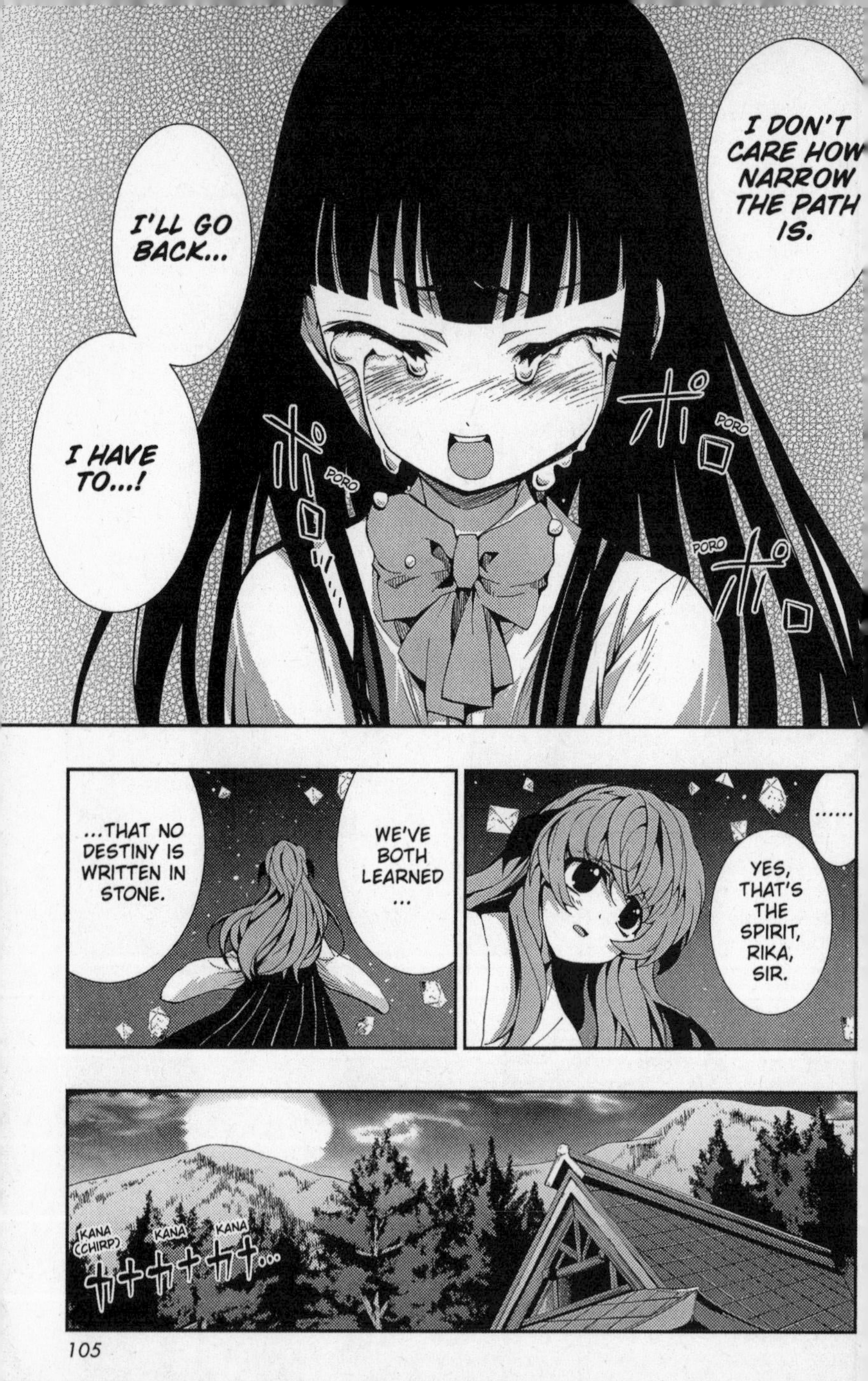
I DON'T CARE HOW NARROW THE PATH IS.
I'LL GO BACK...
I HAVE TO...!
PORO
PORO
PORO
......
YES, THAT'S THE SPIRIT, RIKA, SIR.
WE'VE BOTH LEARNED ...
...THAT NO DESTINY IS WRITTEN IN STONE.
KANA
KANA
KANA (CHIRP)

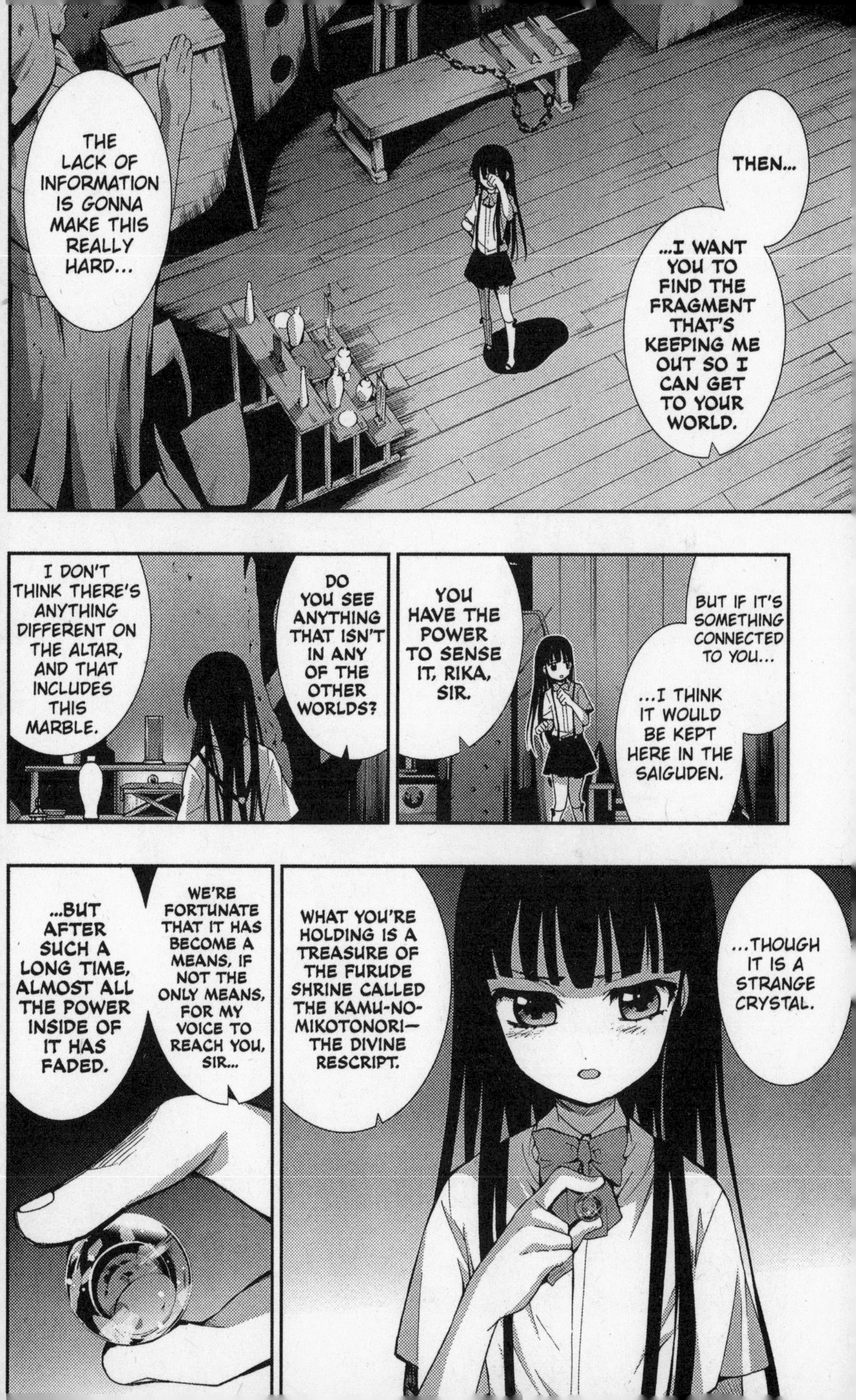
THEN...
...I WANT YOU TO FIND THE FRAGMENT THAT'S KEEPING ME OUT SO I CAN GET TO YOUR WORLD.
THE LACK OF INFORMATION IS GONNA MAKE THIS REALLY HARD...
BUT IF IT'S SOMETHING CONNECTED TO YOU...
...I THINK IT WOULD BE KEPT HERE IN THE SAIGUDEN.
YOU HAVE THE POWER TO SENSE IT, RIKA, SIR.
DO YOU SEE ANYTHING THAT ISN'T IN ANY OF THE OTHER WORLDS?
I DON'T THINK THERE'S ANYTHING DIFFERENT ON THE ALTAR, AND THAT INCLUDES THIS MARBLE.
WHAT YOU'RE HOLDING IS A TREASURE OF THE FURUDE SHRINE CALLED THE KAMU-NO-MIKOTONORI—THE DIVINE RESCRIPT.
...THOUGH IT IS A STRANGE CRYSTAL.
WE'RE FORTUNATE THAT IT HAS BECOME A MEANS, IF NOT THE ONLY MEANS, FOR MY VOICE TO REACH YOU, SIR...
...BUT AFTER SUCH A LONG TIME, ALMOST ALL THE POWER INSIDE OF IT HAS FADED.

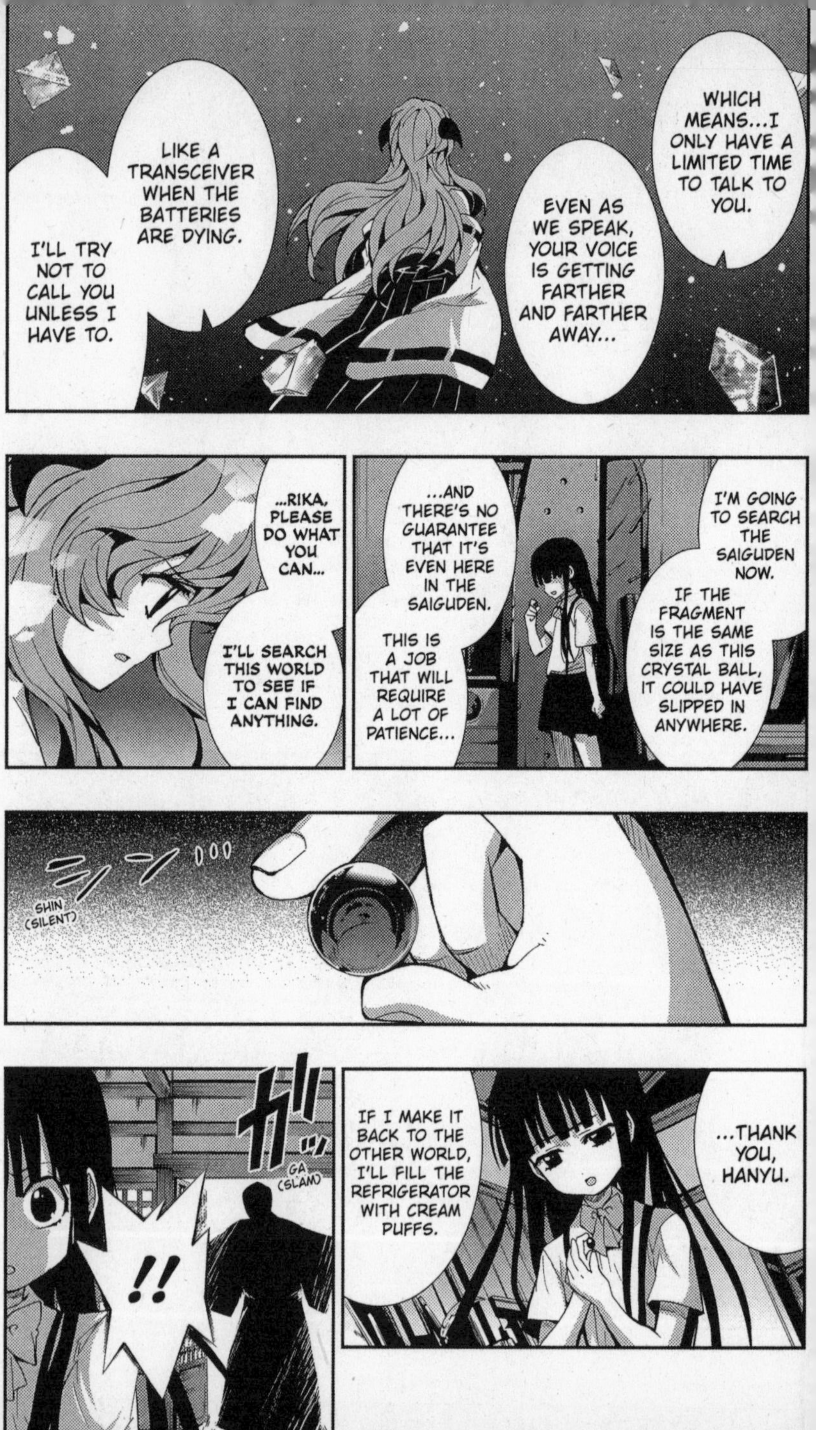
WHICH MEANS...I ONLY HAVE A LIMITED TIME TO TALK TO YOU.
EVEN AS WE SPEAK, YOUR VOICE IS GETTING FARTHER AND FARTHER AWAY...
LIKE A TRANSCEIVER WHEN THE BATTERIES ARE DYING.
I'LL TRY NOT TO CALL YOU UNLESS I HAVE TO.
I'M GOING TO SEARCH THE SAIGUDEN NOW.
IF THE FRAGMENT IS THE SAME SIZE AS THIS CRYSTAL BALL, IT COULD HAVE SLIPPED IN ANYWHERE.
...AND THERE'S NO GUARANTEE THAT IT'S EVEN HERE IN THE SAIGUDEN.
THIS IS A JOB THAT WILL REQUIRE A LOT OF PATIENCE...
...RIKA, PLEASE DO WHAT YOU CAN...
I'LL SEARCH THIS WORLD TO SEE IF I CAN FIND ANYTHING.
SHIN (SILENT)
...THANK YOU, HANYU.
IF I MAKE IT BACK TO THE OTHER WORLD, I'LL FILL THE REFRIGERATOR WITH CREAM PUFFS.
GA (SLAM)
!!

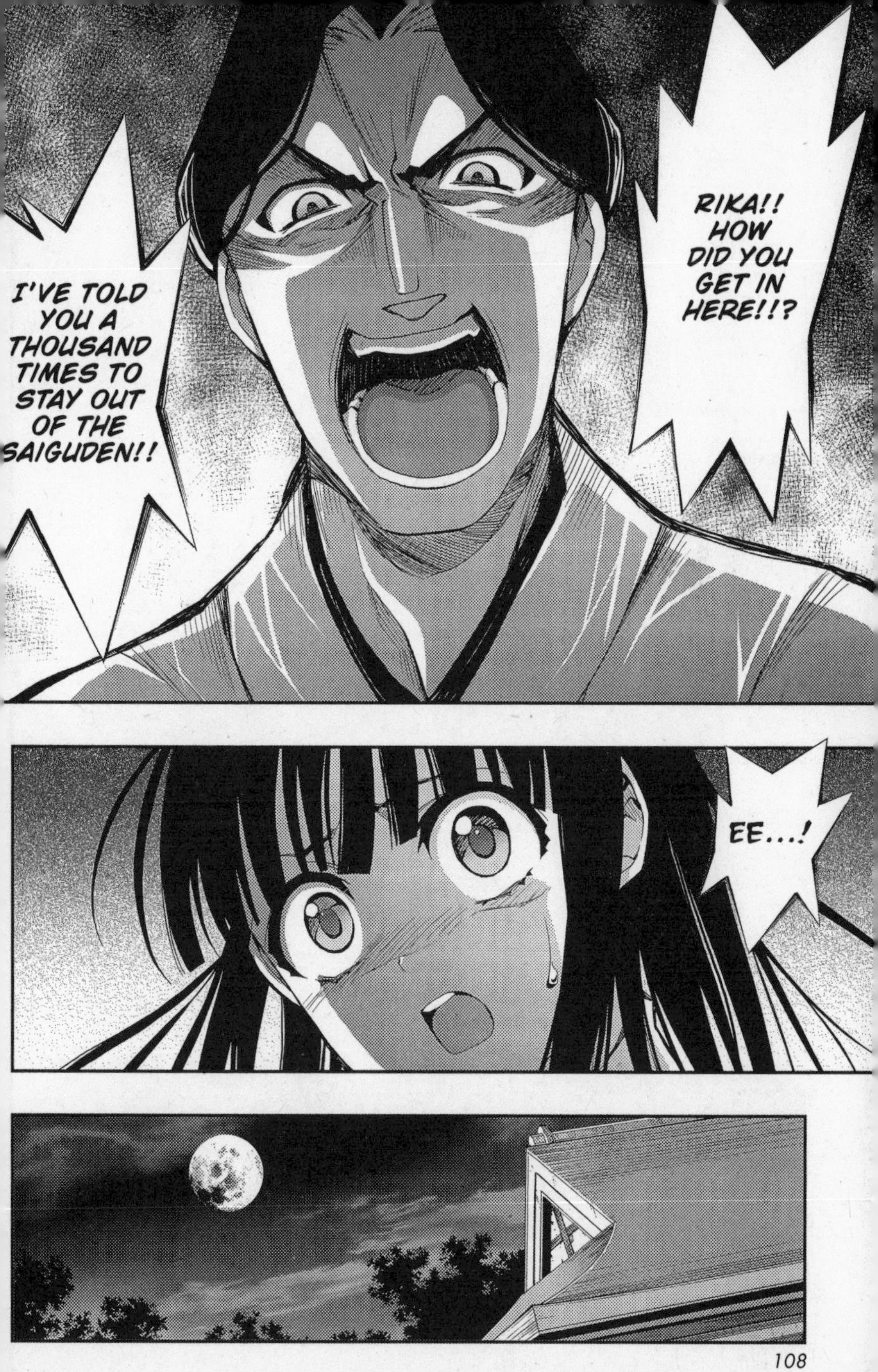
RIKA!! HOW DID YOU GET IN HERE!!?
I'VE TOLD YOU A THOUSAND TIMES TO STAY OUT OF THE SAIGUDEN!!
EE...!

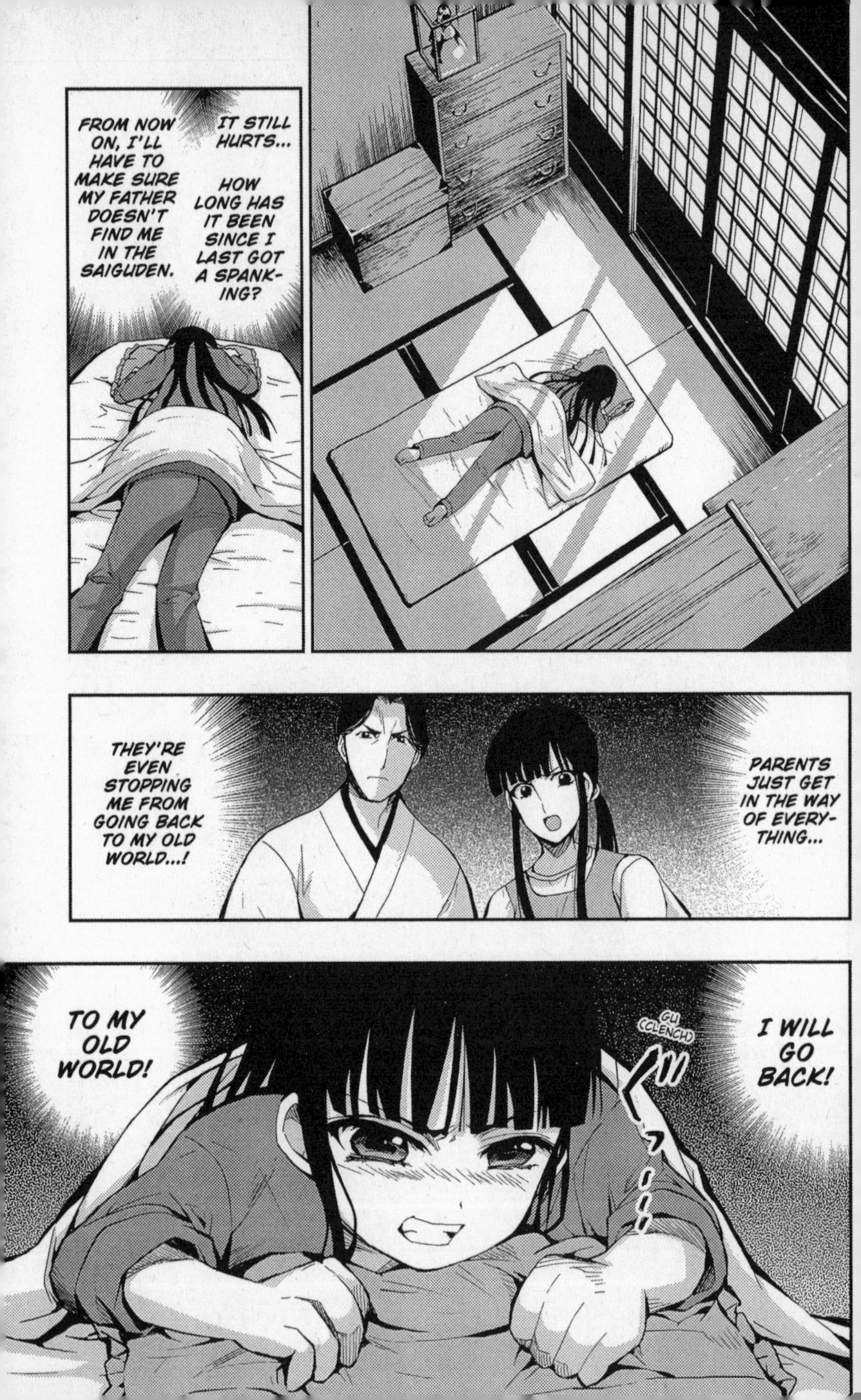
IT STILL HURTS...
HOW LONG HAS IT BEEN SINCE I LAST GOT A SPANK-ING?
FROM NOW ON, I'LL HAVE TO MAKE SURE MY FATHER DOESN'T FIND ME IN THE SAIGUDEN.
PARENTS JUST GET IN THE WAY OF EVERY-THING...
THEY'RE EVEN STOPPING ME FROM GOING BACK TO MY OLD WORLD...!
I WILL GO BACK!
GU (CLENCH)
TO MY OLD WORLD!

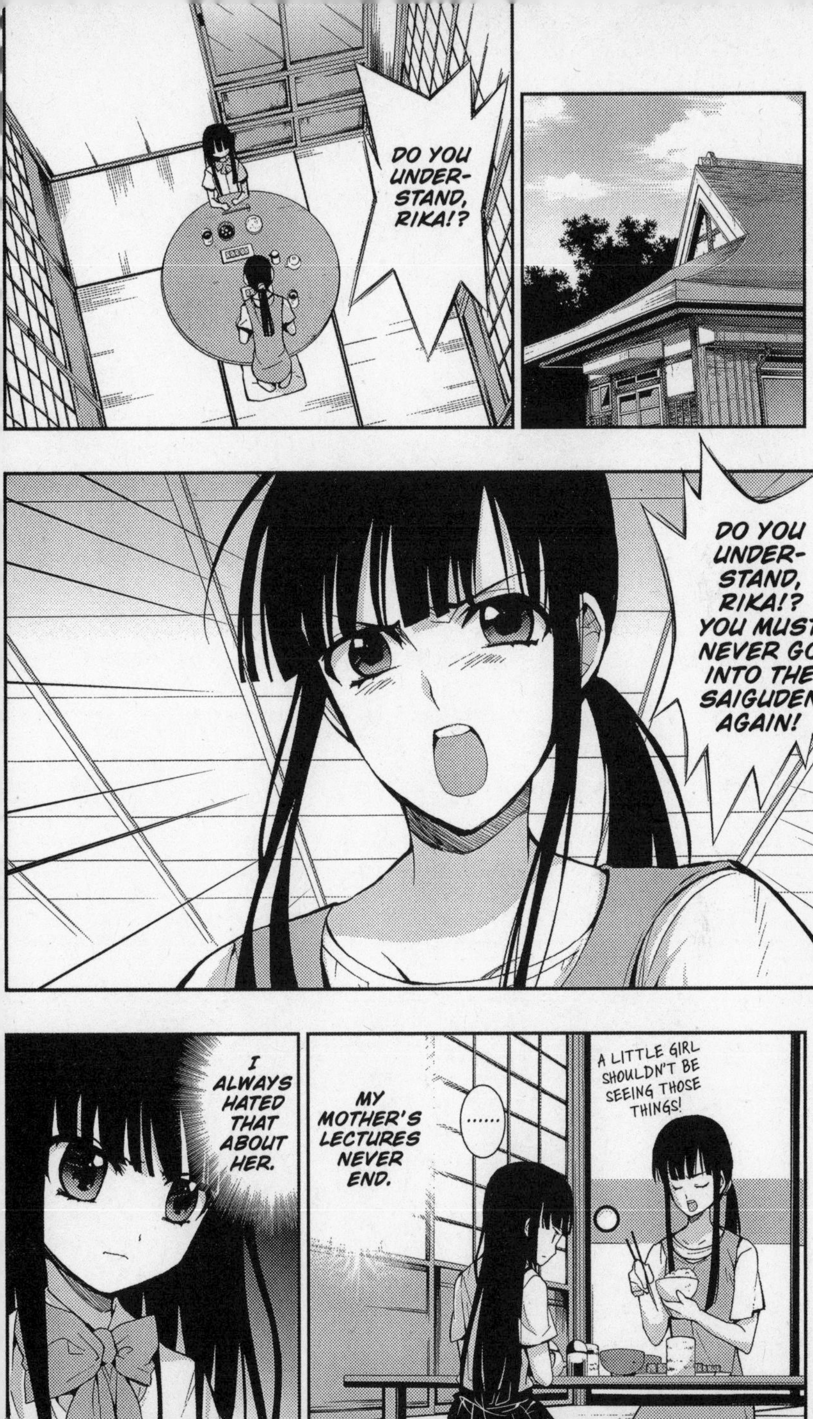
DO YOU UNDERSTAND, RIKA!?
DO YOU UNDERSTAND, RIKA!? YOU MUST NEVER GO INTO THE SAIGUDEN AGAIN!
A LITTLE GIRL SHOULDN'T BE SEEING THOSE THINGS!
......
MY MOTHER'S LECTURES NEVER END.
I ALWAYS HATED THAT ABOUT HER.

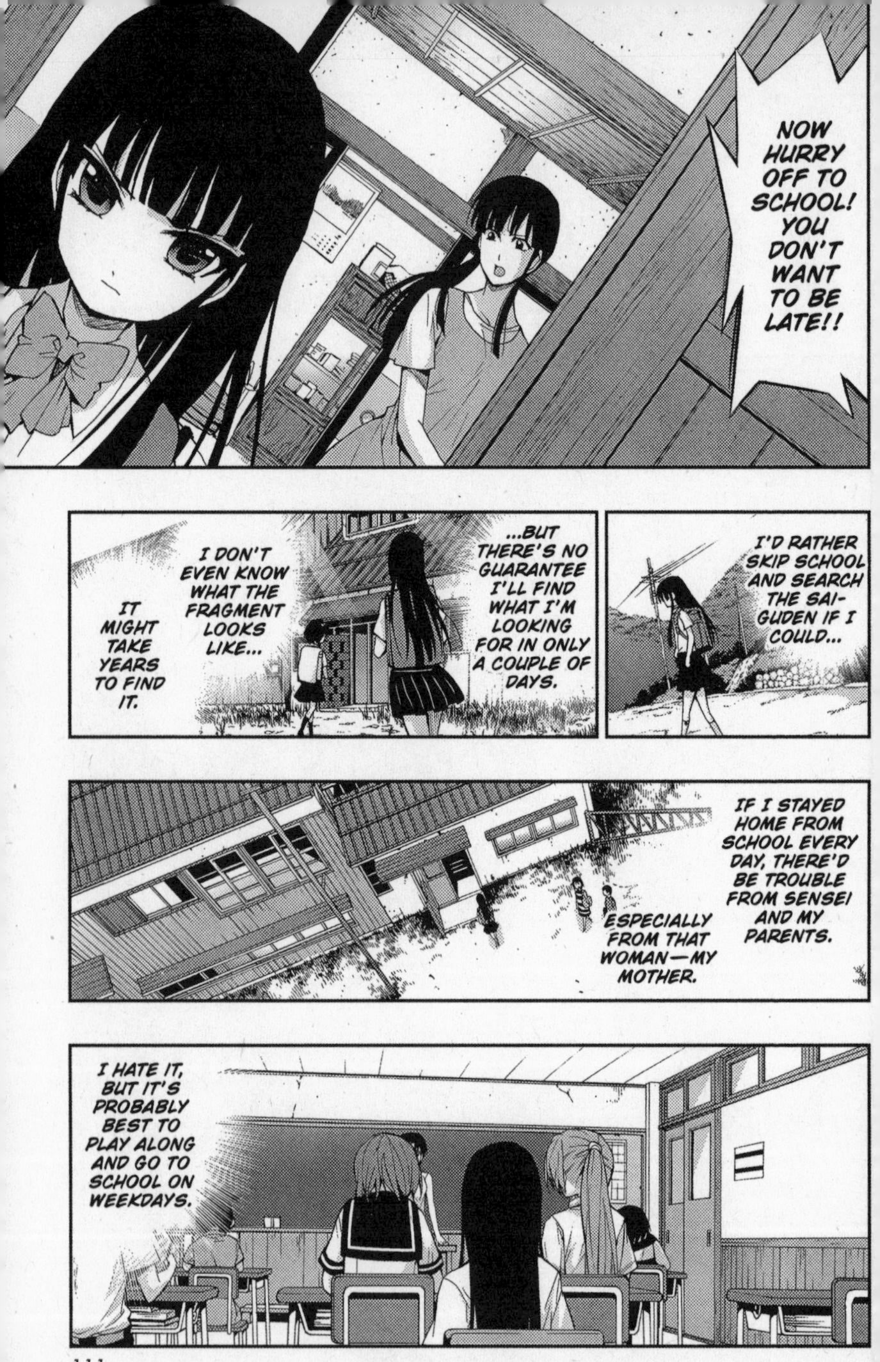
NOW HURRY OFF TO SCHOOL! YOU DON'T WANT TO BE LATE!!
I'D RATHER SKIP SCHOOL AND SEARCH THE SAI-GUDEN IF I COULD...
...BUT THERE'S NO GUARANTEE I'LL FIND WHAT I'M LOOKING FOR IN ONLY A COUPLE OF DAYS.
I DON'T EVEN KNOW WHAT THE FRAGMENT LOOKS LIKE...
IT MIGHT TAKE YEARS TO FIND IT.
IF I STAYED HOME FROM SCHOOL EVERY DAY, THERE'D BE TROUBLE FROM SENSEI AND MY PARENTS.
ESPECIALLY FROM THAT WOMAN—MY MOTHER.
I HATE IT, BUT IT'S PROBABLY BEST TO PLAY ALONG AND GO TO SCHOOL ON WEEKDAYS.

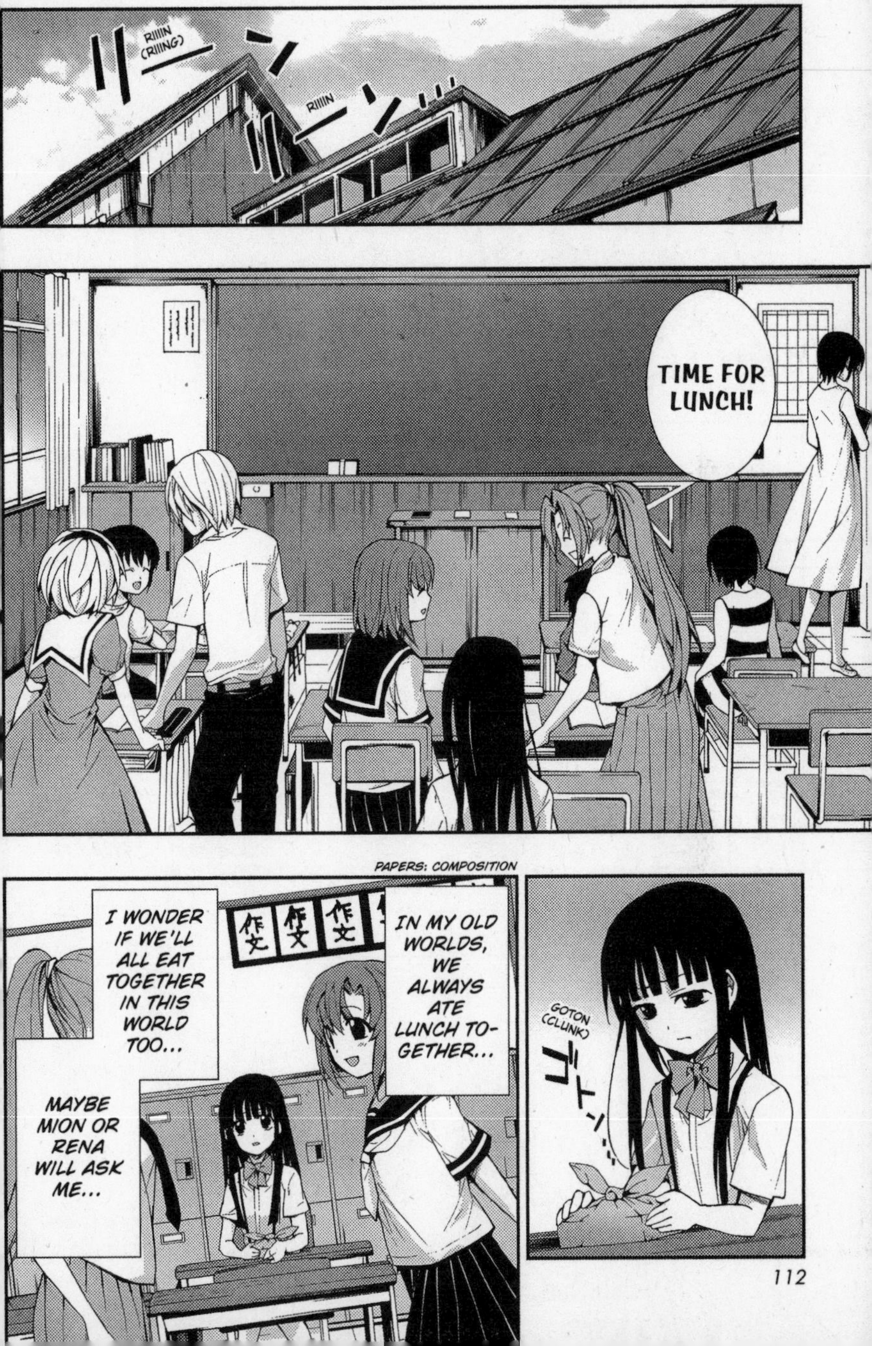
RIIIN (RIIING)
RIIIN
TIME FOR LUNCH!
GOTON (CLUNK)
PAPERS: COMPOSITION
IN MY OLD WORLDS, WE ALWAYS ATE LUNCH TOGETHER...
I WONDER IF WE'LL ALL EAT TOGETHER IN THIS WORLD TOO...
MAYBE MION OR RENA WILL ASK ME...

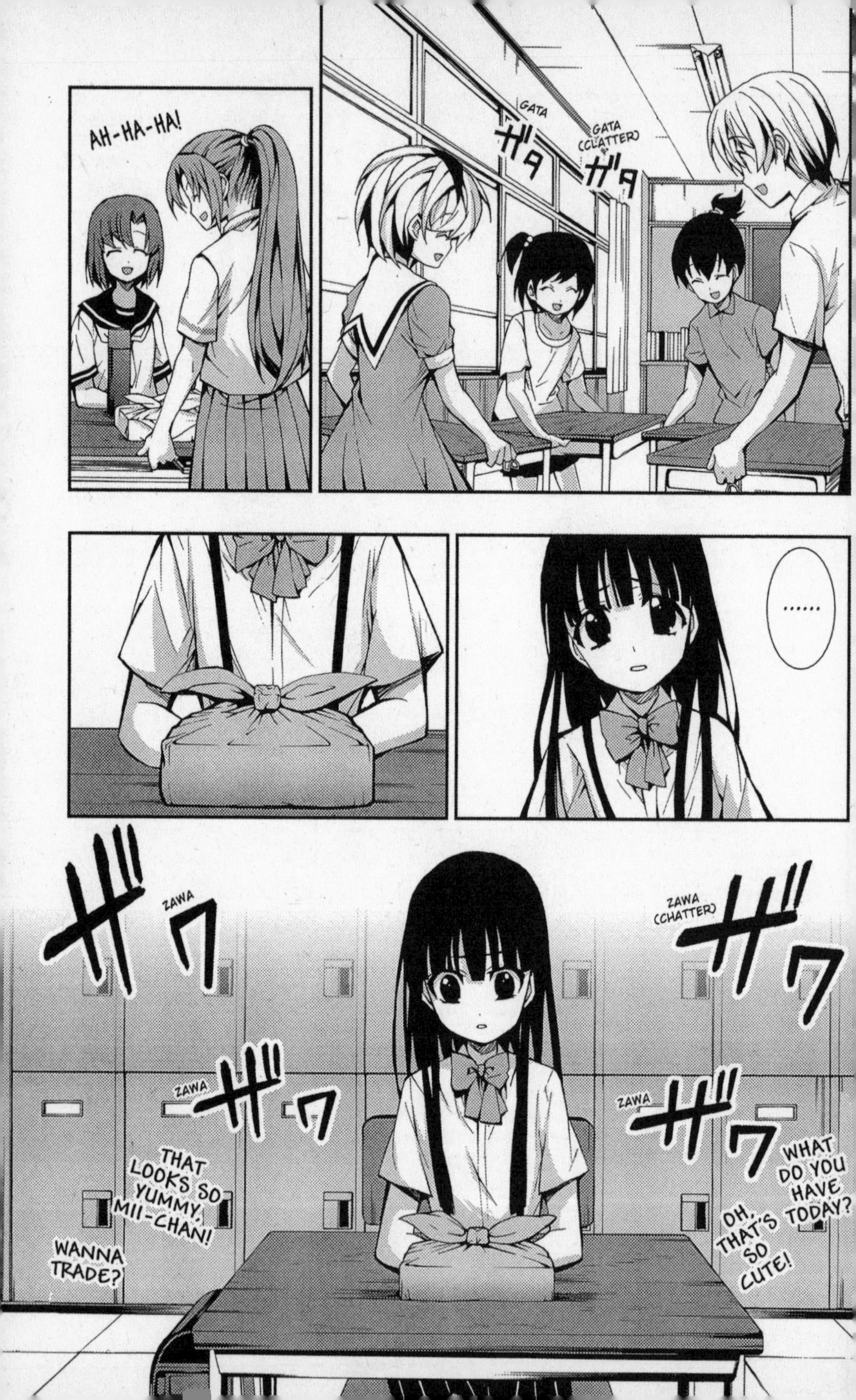
GATA
ガタ
GATA (CLATTER)
ガタ
AH-HA-HA!
......
ZAWA (CHATTER)
ザワ
WHAT DO YOU HAVE TODAY?
OH, THAT'S SO CUTE!
ZAWA
ザワ
ZAWA
ザワ
THAT LOOKS SO YUMMY, MII-CHAN!
WANNA TRADE?
ZAWA
ザワ

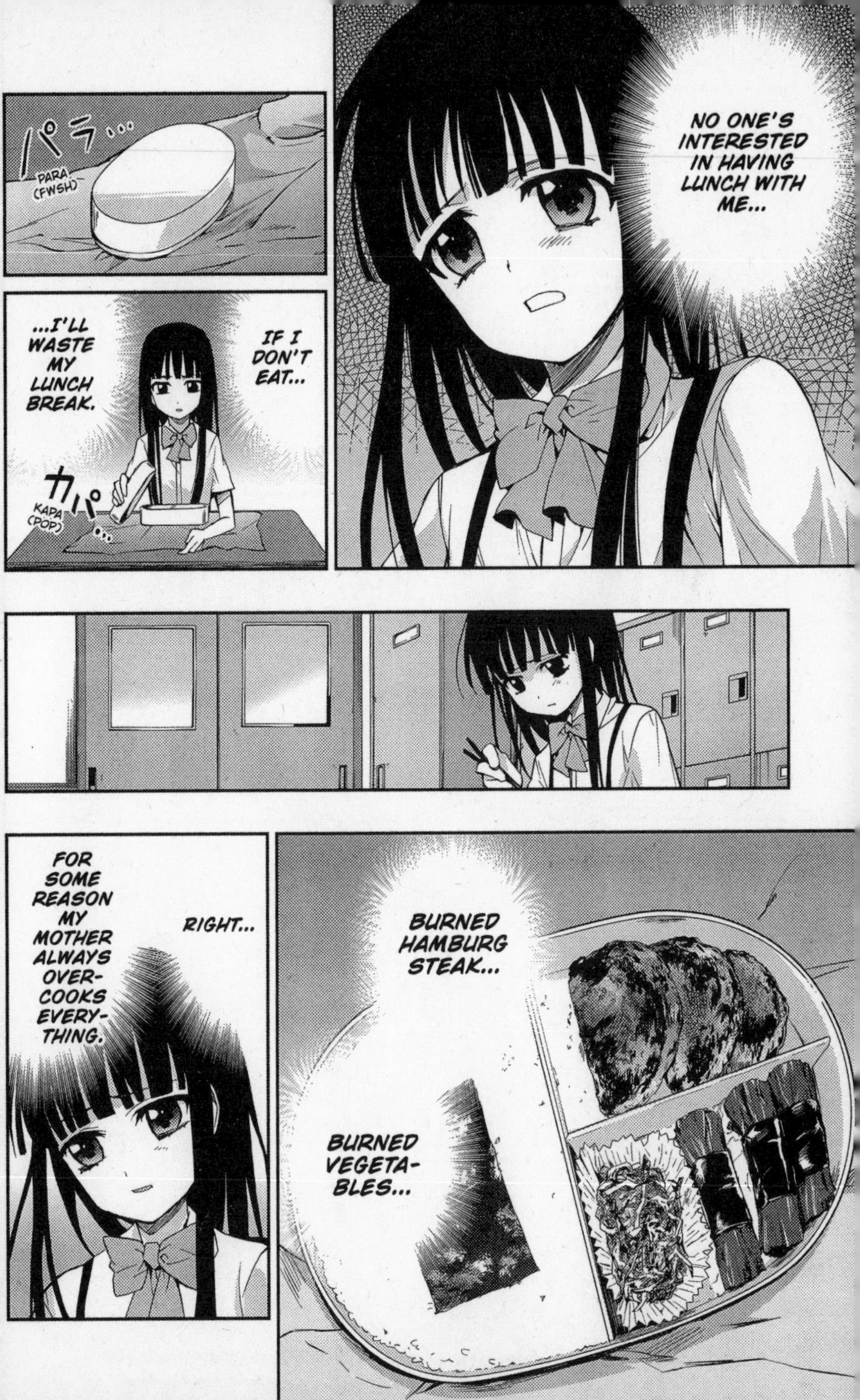
NO ONE'S INTERESTED IN HAVING LUNCH WITH ME...
パラ…
PARA (FWSH)
IF I DON'T EAT...
...I'LL WASTE MY LUNCH BREAK.
カパ…
KAPA (POP)
BURNED HAMBURG STEAK...
BURNED VEGETA-BLES...
RIGHT...
FOR SOME REASON MY MOTHER ALWAYS OVER-COOKS EVERY-THING.

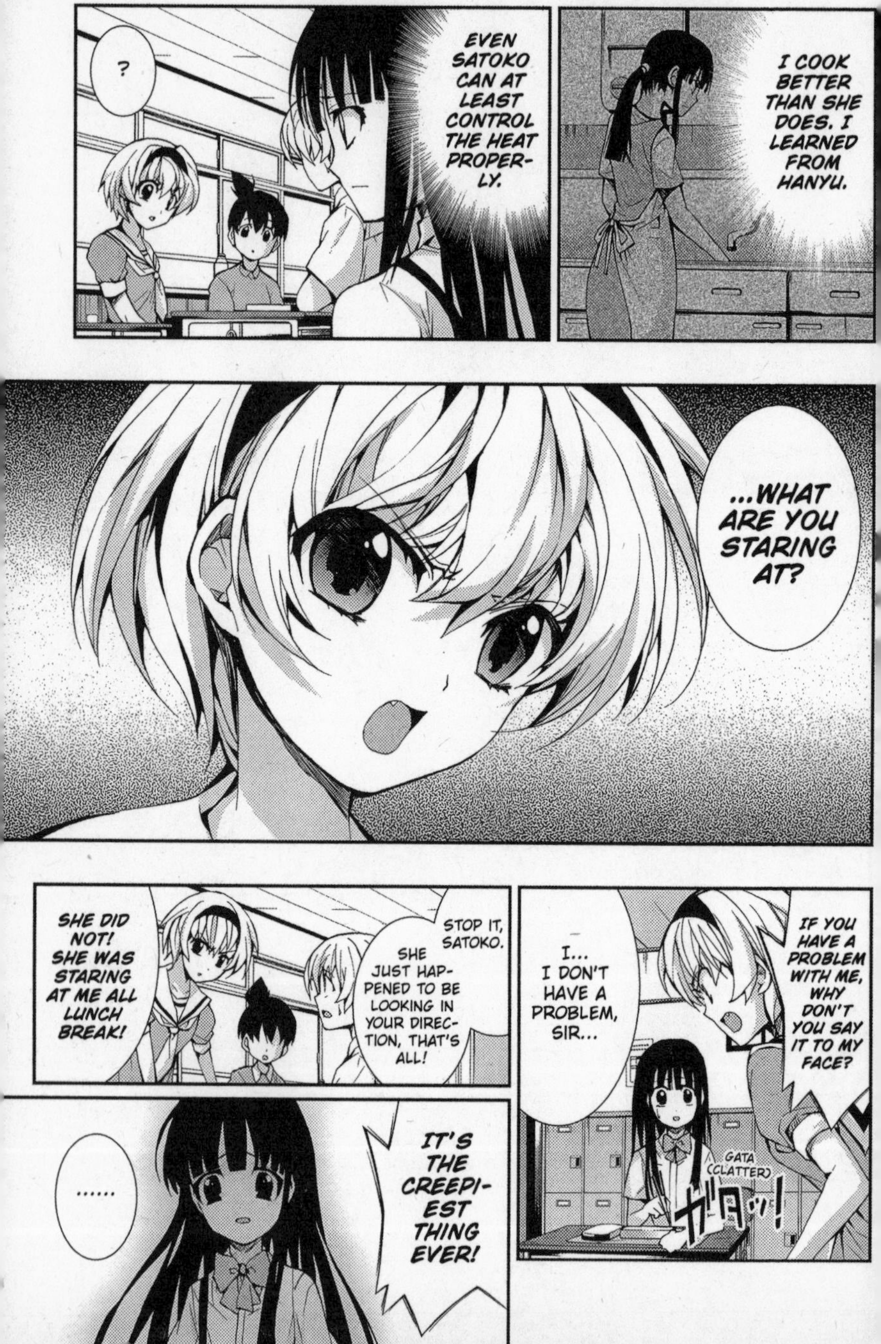

I COOK BETTER THAN SHE DOES. I LEARNED FROM HANYU.
EVEN SATOKO CAN AT LEAST CONTROL THE HEAT PROPER-LY.
?
...WHAT ARE YOU STARING AT?
IF YOU HAVE A PROBLEM WITH ME, WHY DON'T YOU SAY IT TO MY FACE?
I... I DON'T HAVE A PROBLEM, SIR...
GATA (CLATTER)
STOP IT, SATOKO.
SHE JUST HAP-PENED TO BE LOOKING IN YOUR DIREC-TION, THAT'S ALL!
SHE DID NOT! SHE WAS STARING AT ME ALL LUNCH BREAK!
IT'S THE CREEPI-EST THING EVER!
......

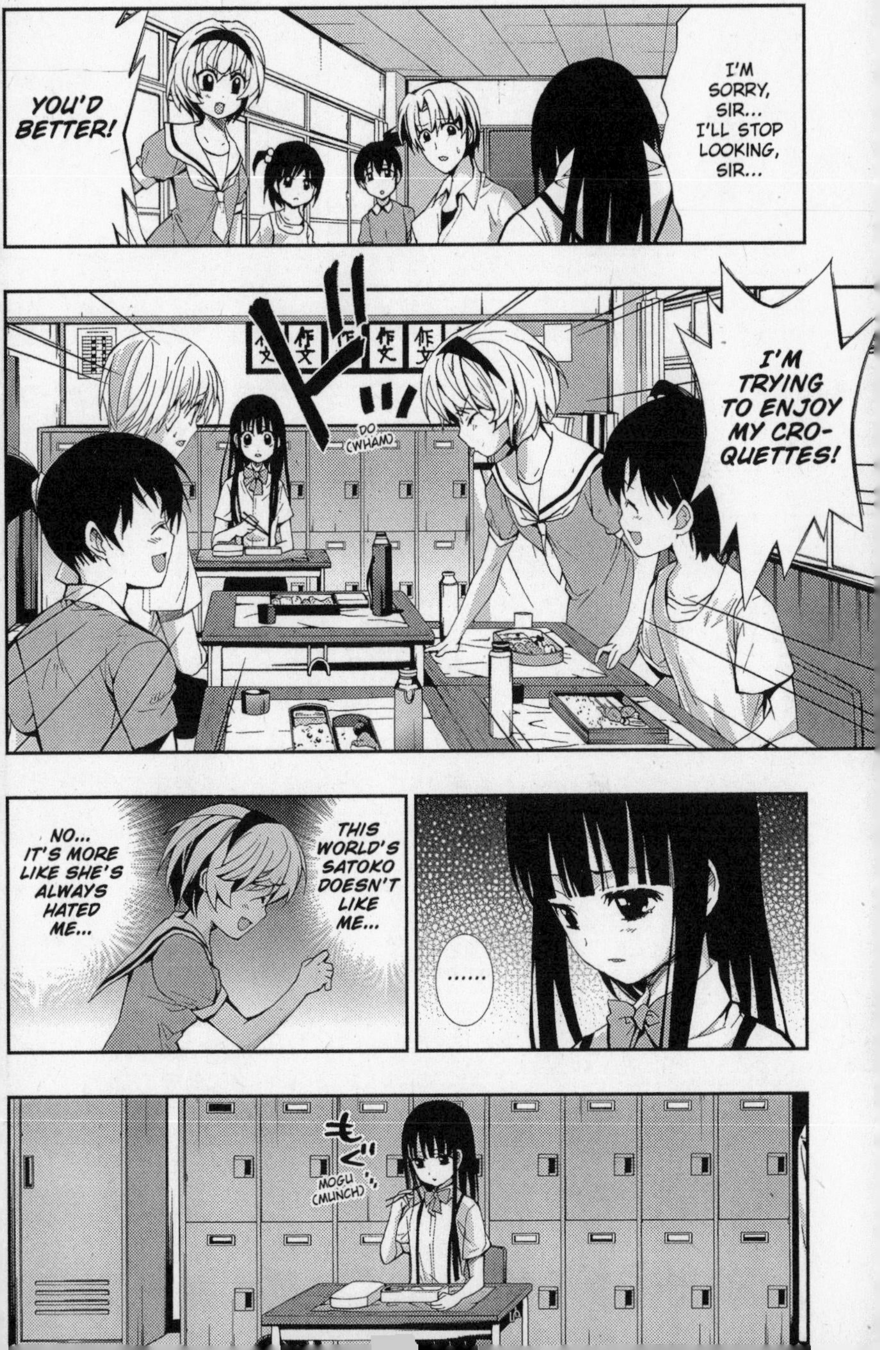
I'M SORRY, SIR... I'LL STOP LOOKING, SIR...
YOU'D BETTER!
I'M TRYING TO ENJOY MY CRO-QUETTES!
DO (WHAM)
......
THIS WORLD'S SATOKO DOESN'T LIKE ME...
NO... IT'S MORE LIKE SHE'S ALWAYS HATED ME...
もぐ
MOGU (MUNCH)

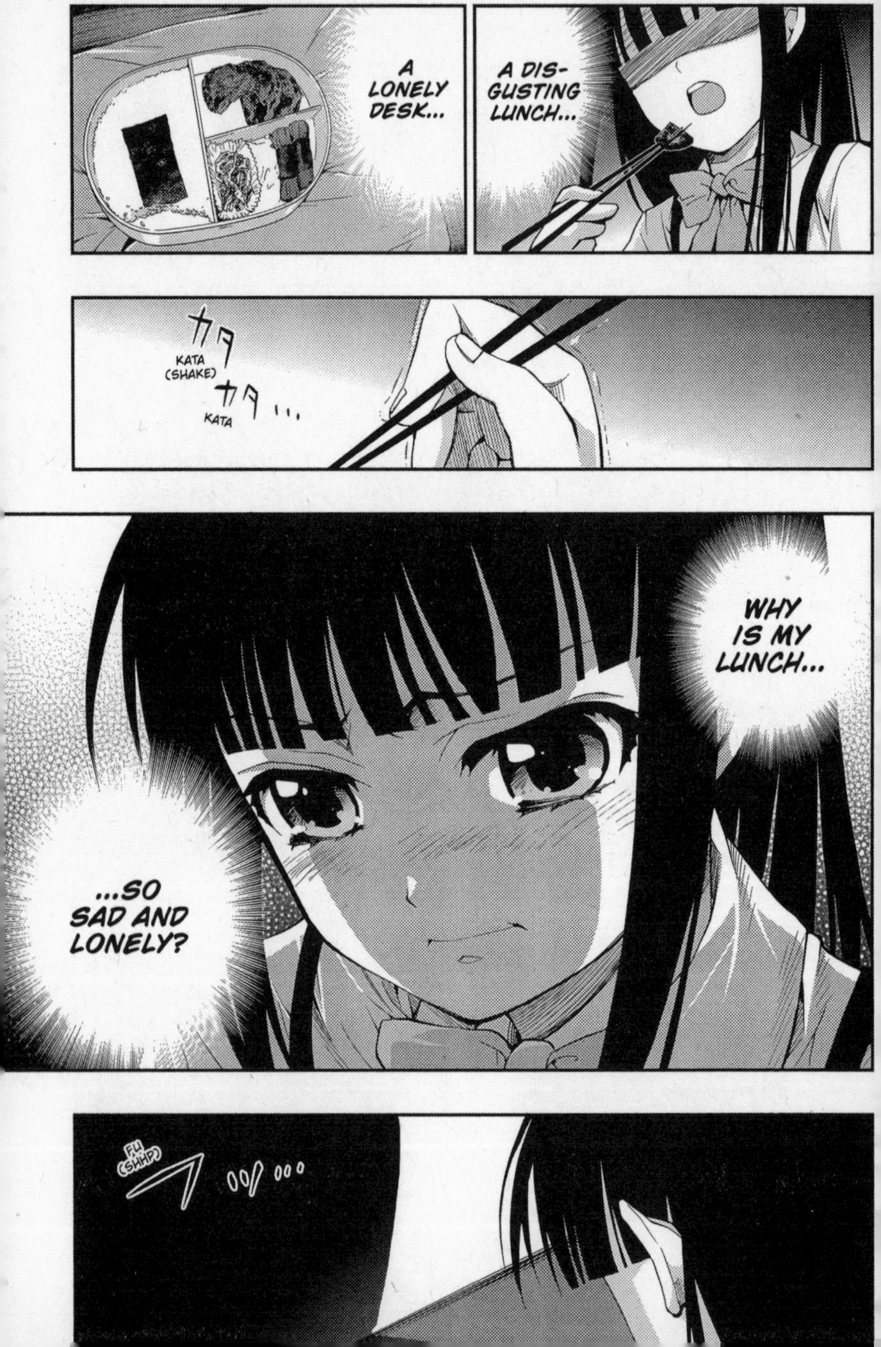

A DIS-GUSTING LUNCH...
A LONELY DESK...
カタ
KATA (SHAKE)
カタ...
KATA
WHY IS MY LUNCH...
...SO SAD AND LONELY?
FU (SHHP)

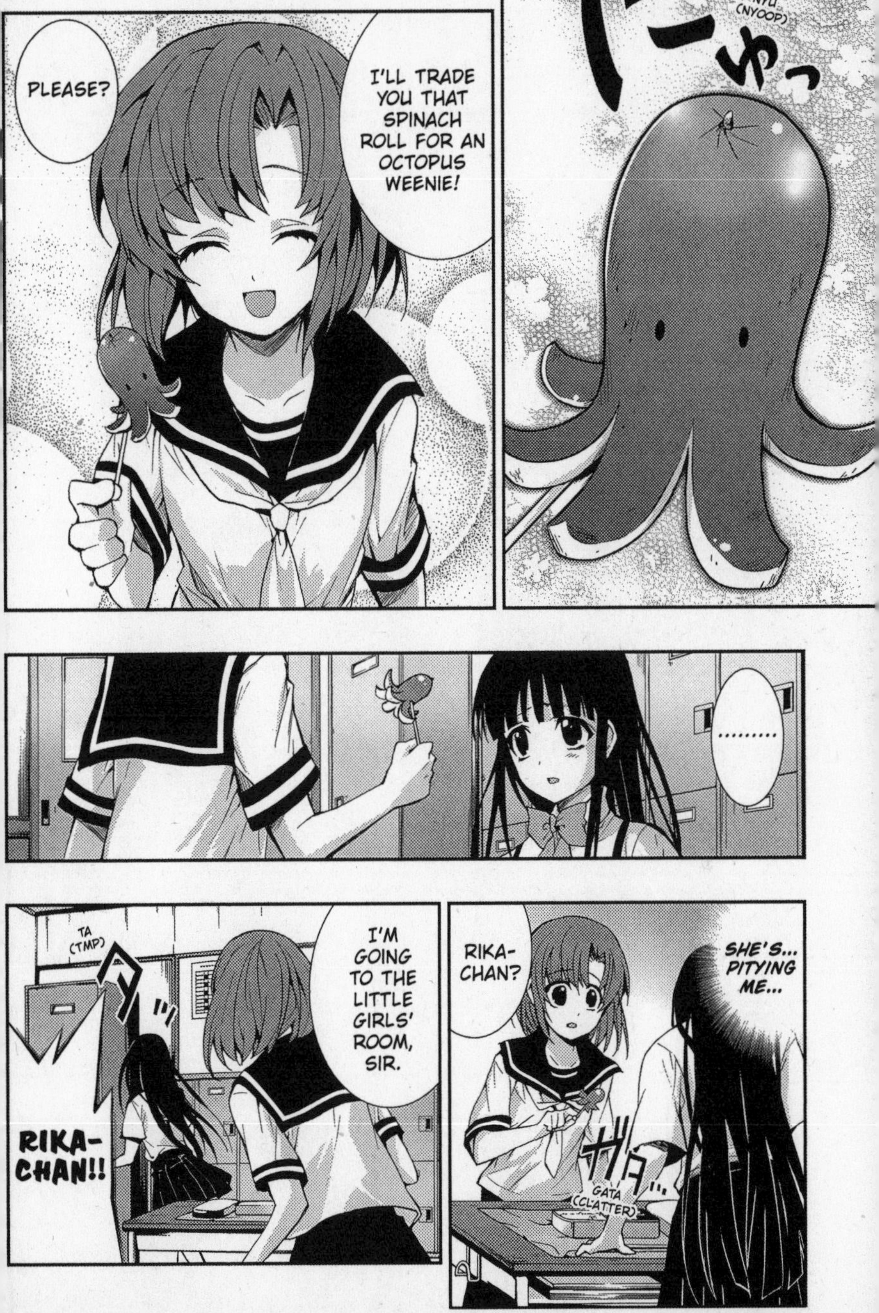
にゅっ
NYU (NYOOP)
I'LL TRADE YOU THAT SPINACH ROLL FOR AN OCTOPUS WEENIE!
PLEASE?
....
SHE'S... PITYING ME...
RIKA-CHAN?
GATA (CLATTER)
I'M GOING TO THE LITTLE GIRLS' ROOM, SIR.
TA (TMP)
RIKA-CHAN!!

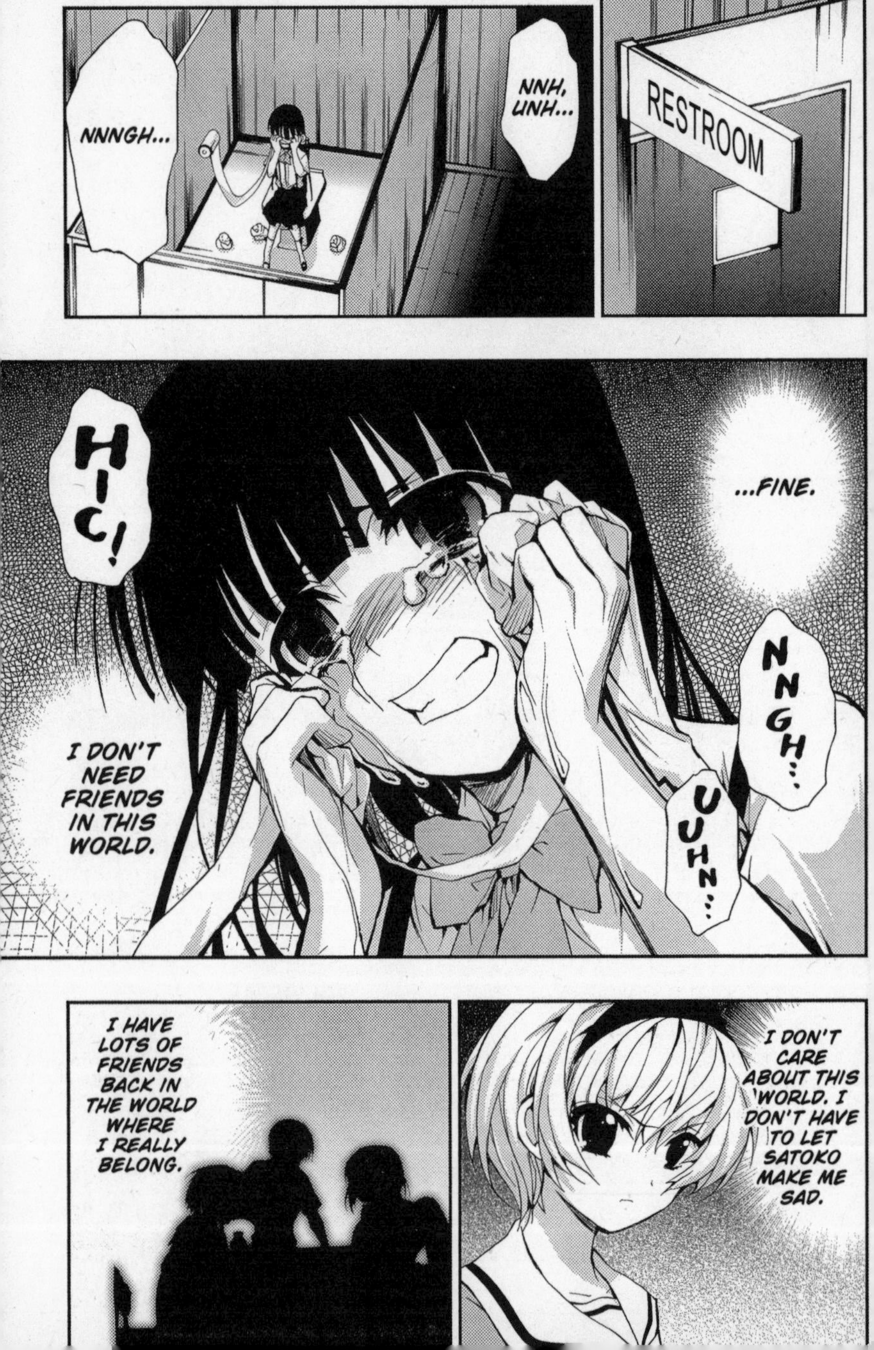
RESTROOM
NNH, UNH...
NNNGH...
...FINE.
HIC!
NNGH...
UUHN...
I DON'T NEED FRIENDS IN THIS WORLD.
I DON'T CARE ABOUT THIS WORLD. I DON'T HAVE TO LET SATOKO MAKE ME SAD.
I HAVE LOTS OF FRIENDS BACK IN THE WORLD WHERE I REALLY BELONG.

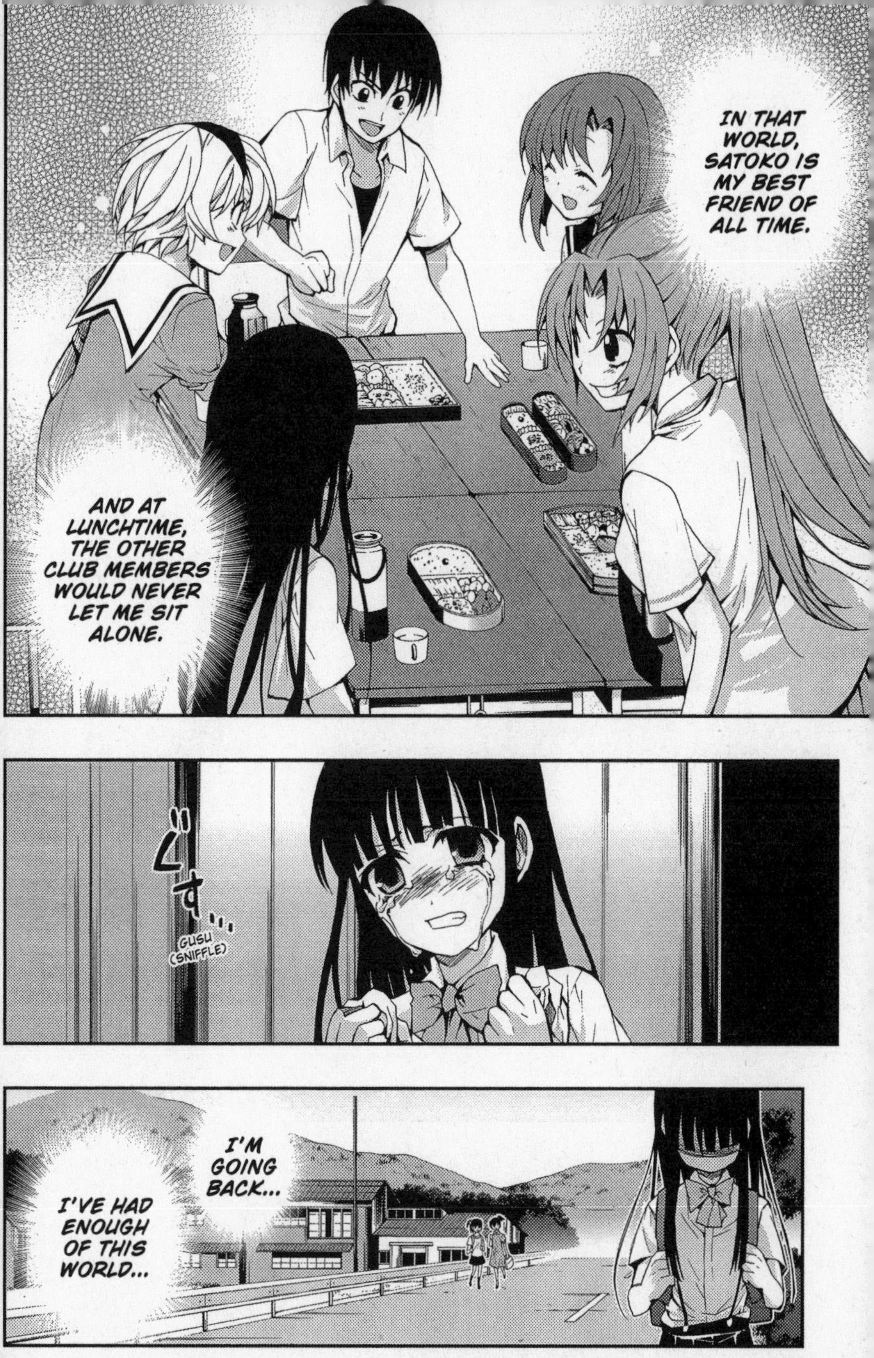
IN THAT WORLD, SATOKO IS MY BEST FRIEND OF ALL TIME.
AND AT LUNCHTIME, THE OTHER CLUB MEMBERS WOULD NEVER LET ME SIT ALONE.
ぐす…
GUSU (SNIFFLE)
I'M GOING BACK...
I'VE HAD ENOUGH OF THIS WORLD...

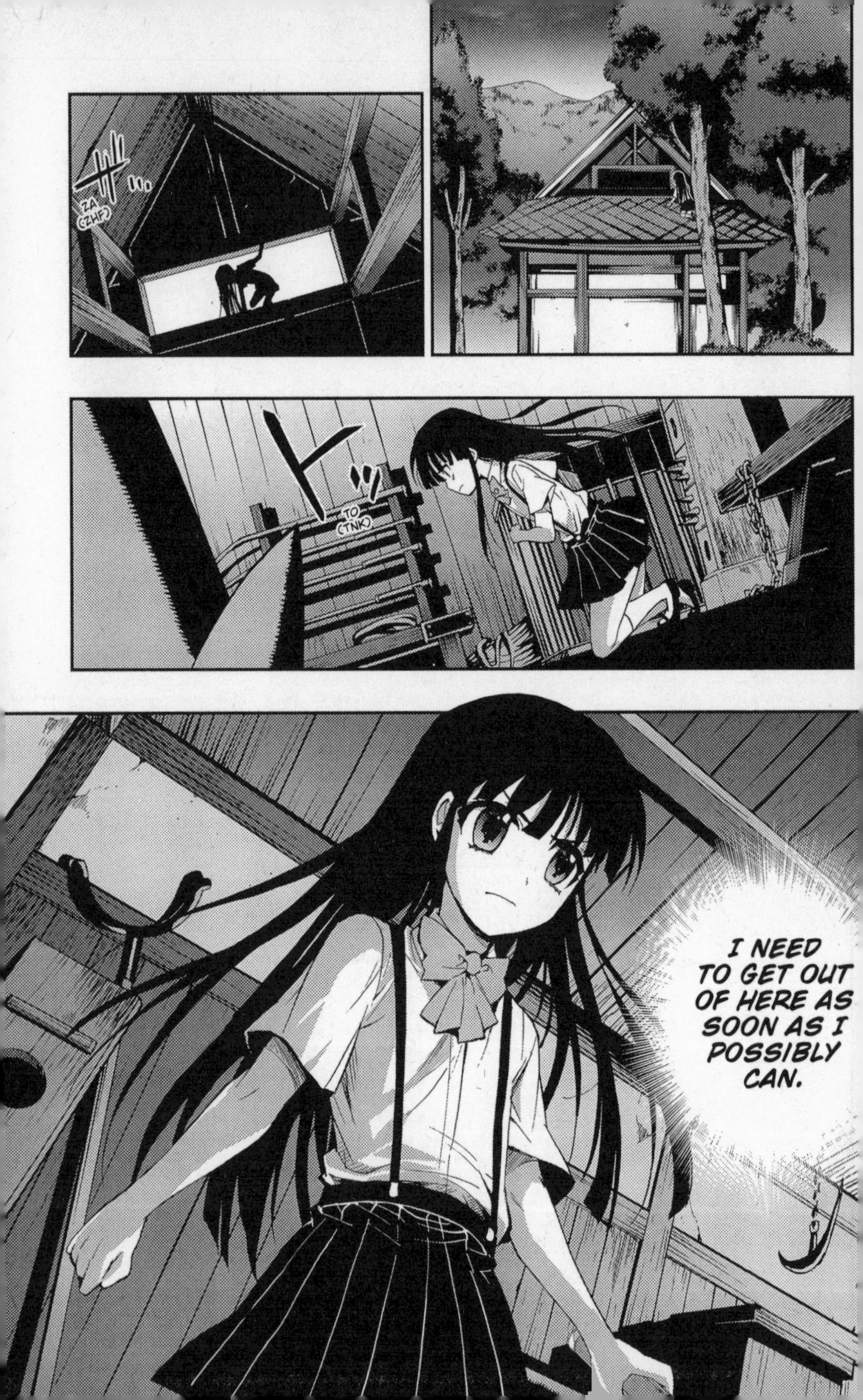
ZA (ZHF)
TO (TNK)
I NEED TO GET OUT OF HERE AS SOON AS I POSSIBLY CAN.

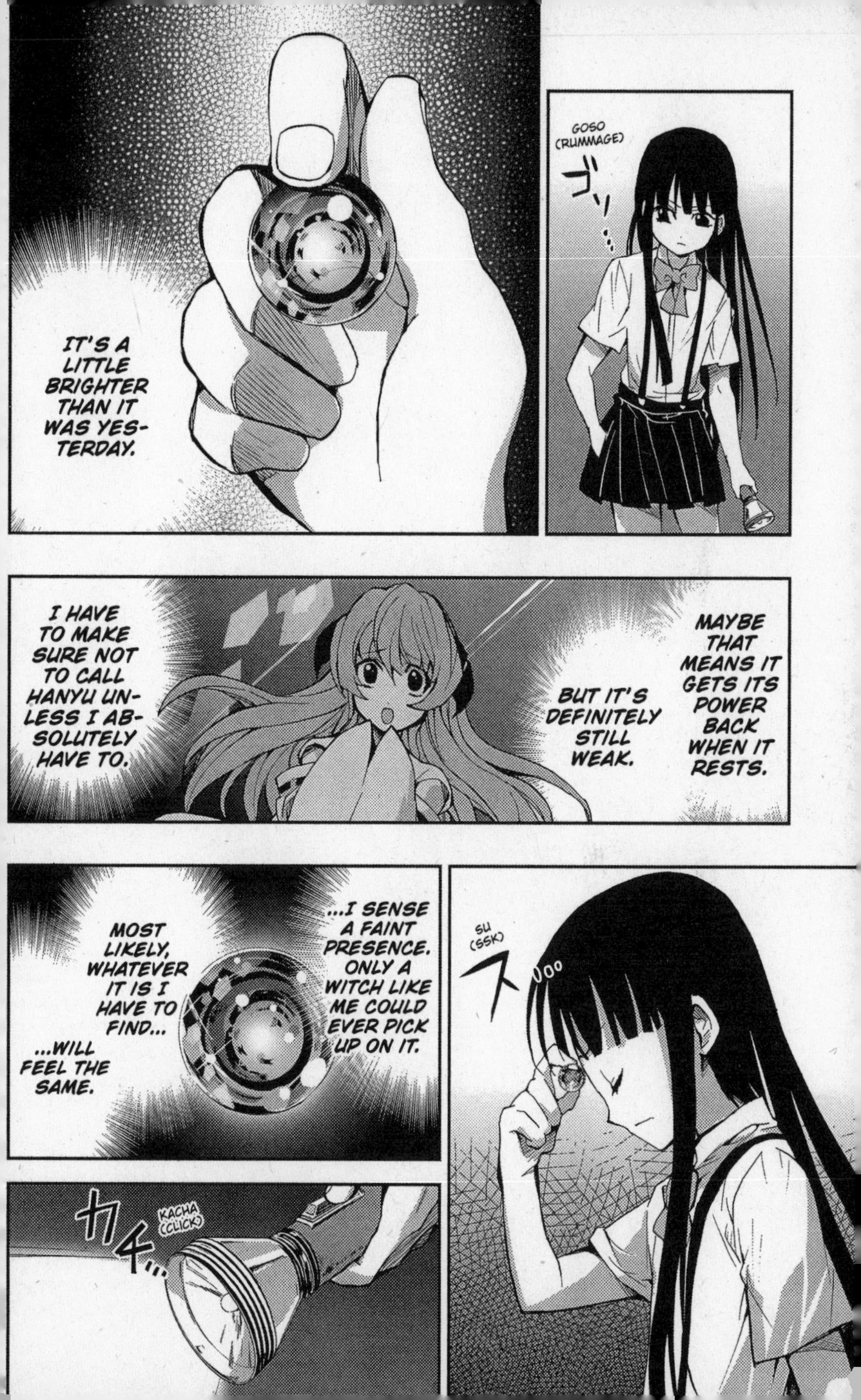
GOSO
(RUMMAGE)
IT'S A LITTLE BRIGHTER THAN IT WAS YES- TERDAY.
MAYBE THAT MEANS IT GETS ITS POWER BACK WHEN IT RESTS.
BUT IT'S DEFINITELY STILL WEAK.
I HAVE TO MAKE SURE NOT TO CALL HANYU UN- LESS I AB- SOLUTELY HAVE TO.
SU
(SSK)
...I SENSE A FAINT PRESENCE. ONLY A WITCH LIKE ME COULD EVER PICK UP ON IT.
MOST LIKELY, WHATEVER IT IS I HAVE TO FIND...
...WILL FEEL THE SAME.
KACHA
(CLICK)

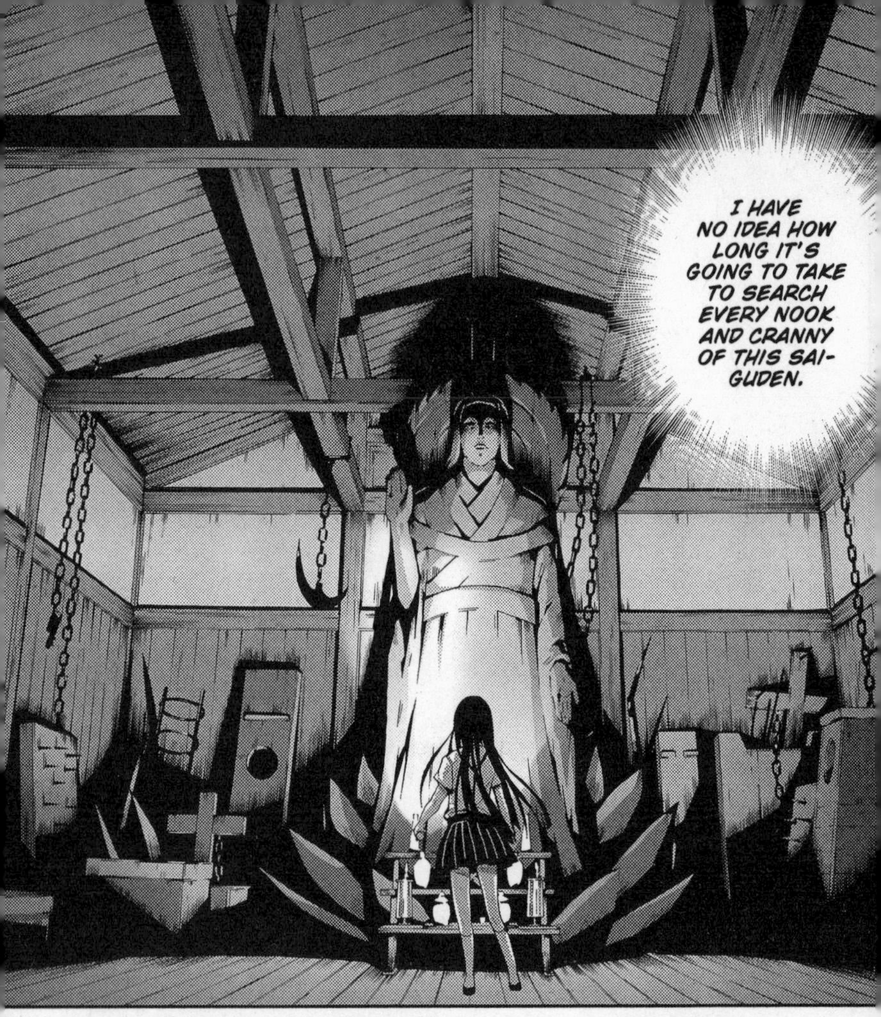
I HAVE NO IDEA HOW LONG IT'S GOING TO TAKE TO SEARCH EVERY NOOK AND CRANNY OF THIS SAI-GUDEN.

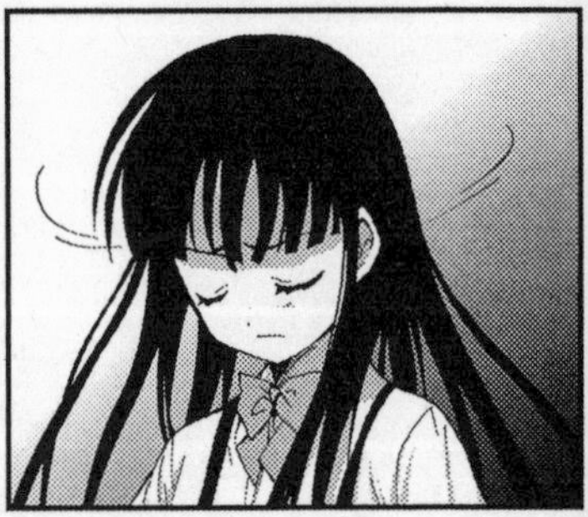

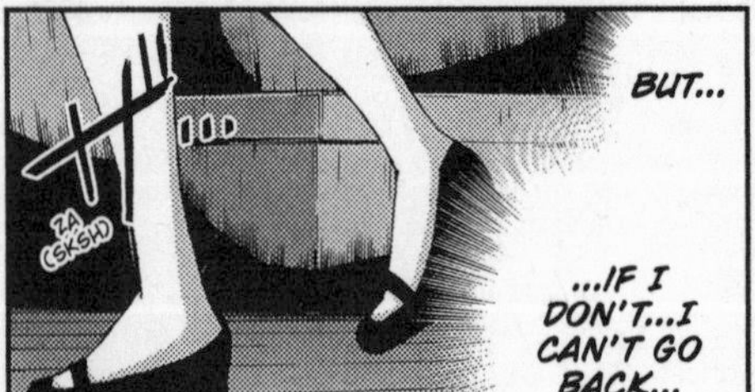
BUT...
...IF I DON'T...I CAN'T GO BACK...
ZA (SKSH)

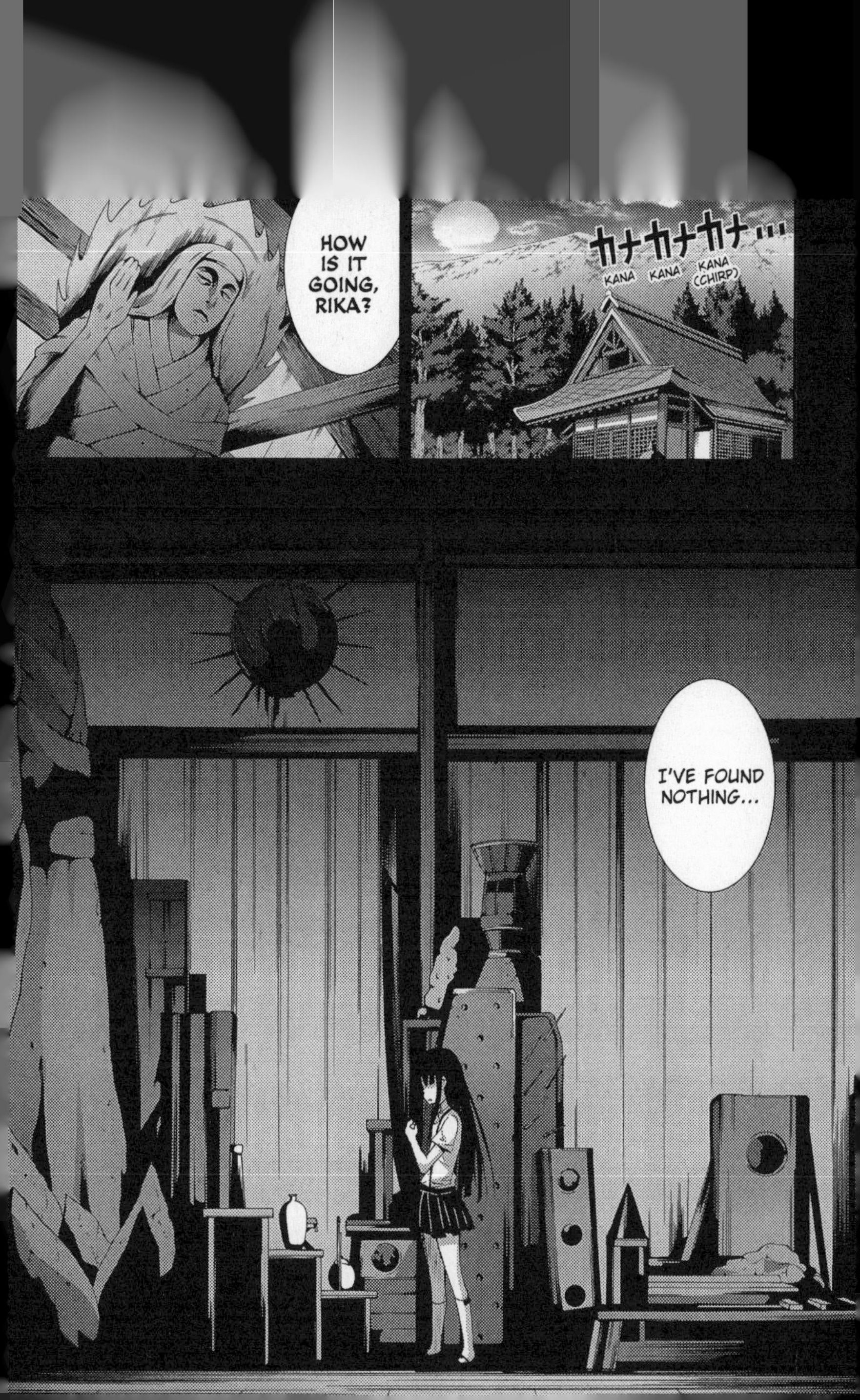
カナカナカナ…
KANA KANA KANA (CHIRP)
HOW IS IT GOING, RIKA?
I'VE FOUND NOTHING...

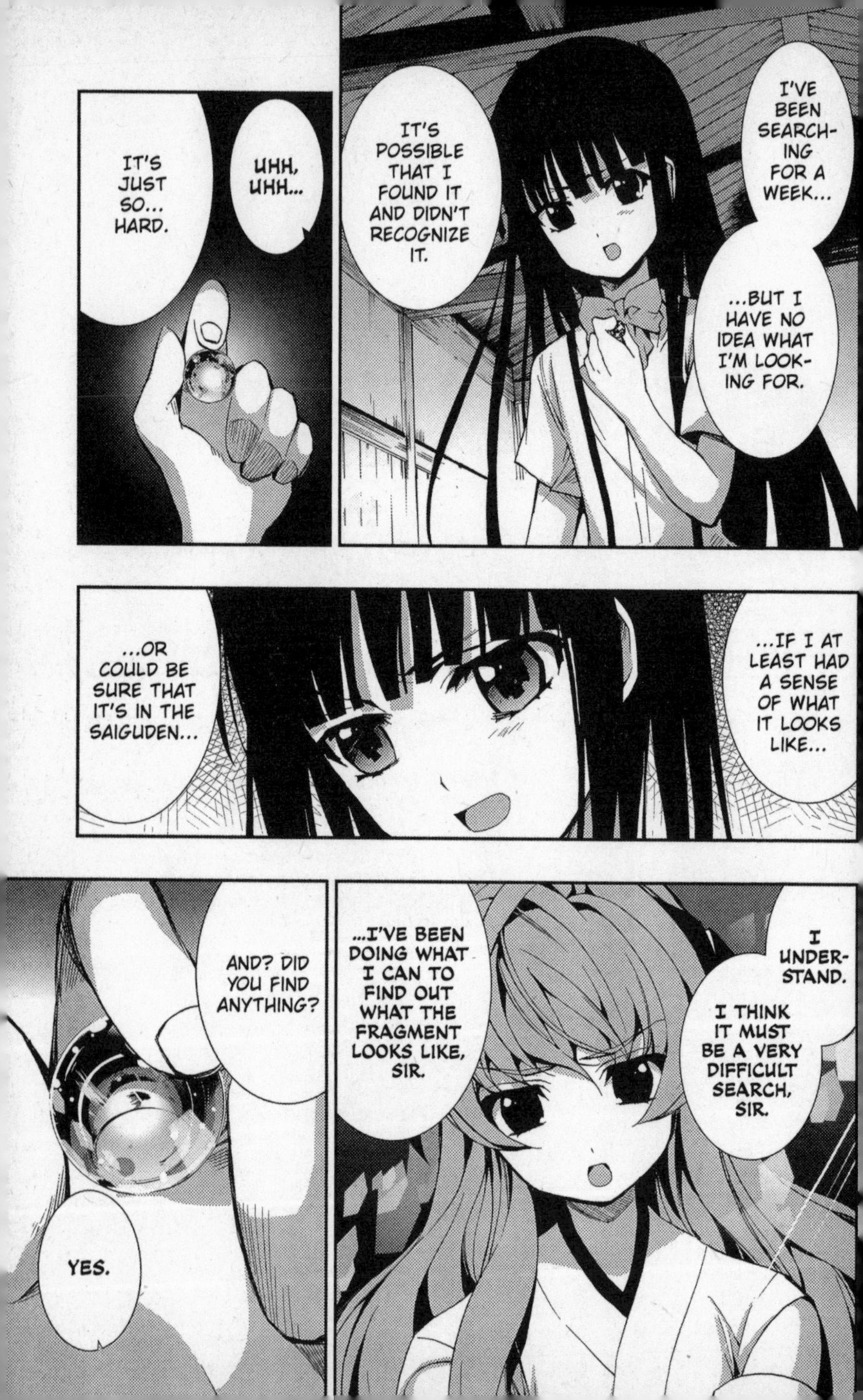
I'VE BEEN SEARCHING FOR A WEEK...
...BUT I HAVE NO IDEA WHAT I'M LOOKING FOR.
IT'S POSSIBLE THAT I FOUND IT AND DIDN'T RECOGNIZE IT.
UHH, UHH...
IT'S JUST SO... HARD.
...IF I AT LEAST HAD A SENSE OF WHAT IT LOOKS LIKE...
...OR COULD BE SURE THAT IT'S IN THE SAIGUDEN...
I UNDERSTAND.
I THINK IT MUST BE A VERY DIFFICULT SEARCH, SIR.
...I'VE BEEN DOING WHAT I CAN TO FIND OUT WHAT THE FRAGMENT LOOKS LIKE, SIR.
AND? DID YOU FIND ANYTHING?
YES.

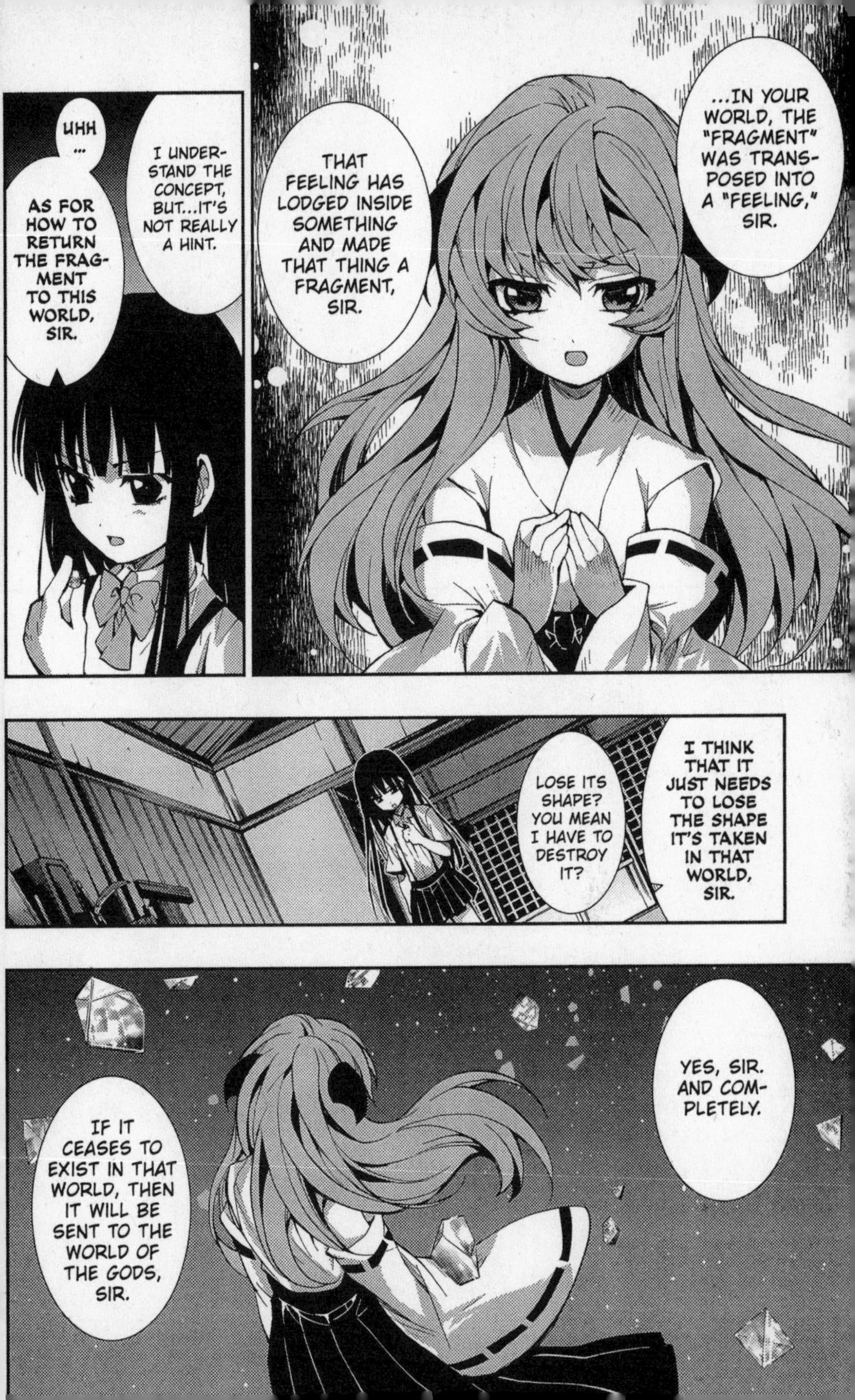
...IN YOUR WORLD, THE "FRAGMENT" WAS TRANSPOSED INTO A "FEELING," SIR.
THAT FEELING HAS LODGED INSIDE SOMETHING AND MADE THAT THING A FRAGMENT, SIR.
I UNDERSTAND THE CONCEPT, BUT...IT'S NOT REALLY A HINT.
UHH ...
AS FOR HOW TO RETURN THE FRAGMENT TO THIS WORLD, SIR.
I THINK THAT IT JUST NEEDS TO LOSE THE SHAPE IT'S TAKEN IN THAT WORLD, SIR.
LOSE ITS SHAPE? YOU MEAN I HAVE TO DESTROY IT?
YES, SIR. AND COMPLETELY.
IF IT CEASES TO EXIST IN THAT WORLD, THEN IT WILL BE SENT TO THE WORLD OF THE GODS, SIR.

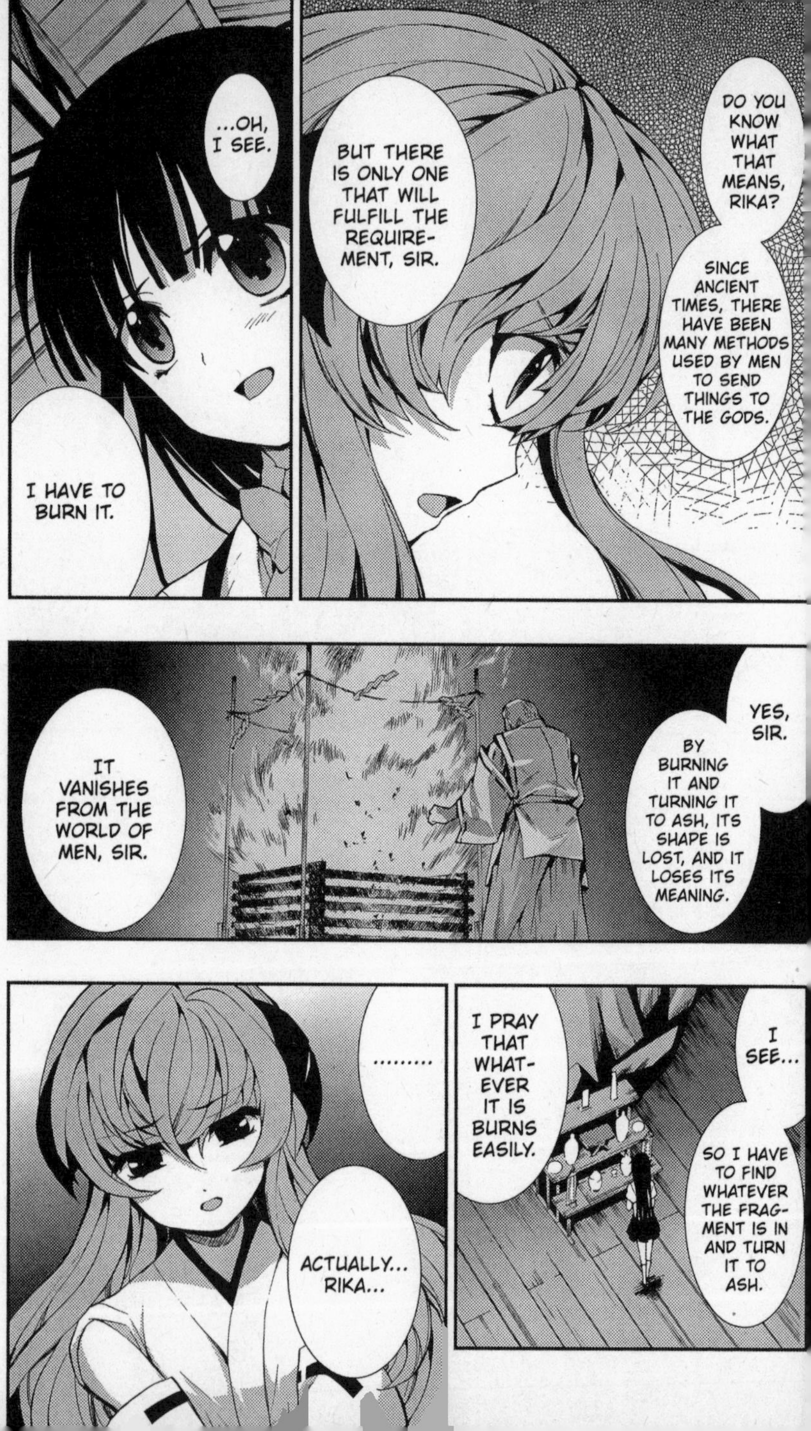
DO YOU KNOW WHAT THAT MEANS, RIKA?
SINCE ANCIENT TIMES, THERE HAVE BEEN MANY METHODS USED BY MEN TO SEND THINGS TO THE GODS.
BUT THERE IS ONLY ONE THAT WILL FULFILL THE REQUIRE-MENT, SIR.
...OH, I SEE.
I HAVE TO BURN IT.
YES, SIR.
BY BURNING IT AND TURNING IT TO ASH, ITS SHAPE IS LOST, AND IT LOSES ITS MEANING.
IT VANISHES FROM THE WORLD OF MEN, SIR.
I SEE...
SO I HAVE TO FIND WHATEVER THE FRAG-MENT IS IN AND TURN IT TO ASH.
I PRAY THAT WHAT-EVER IT IS BURNS EASILY.
....
ACTUALLY... RIKA...

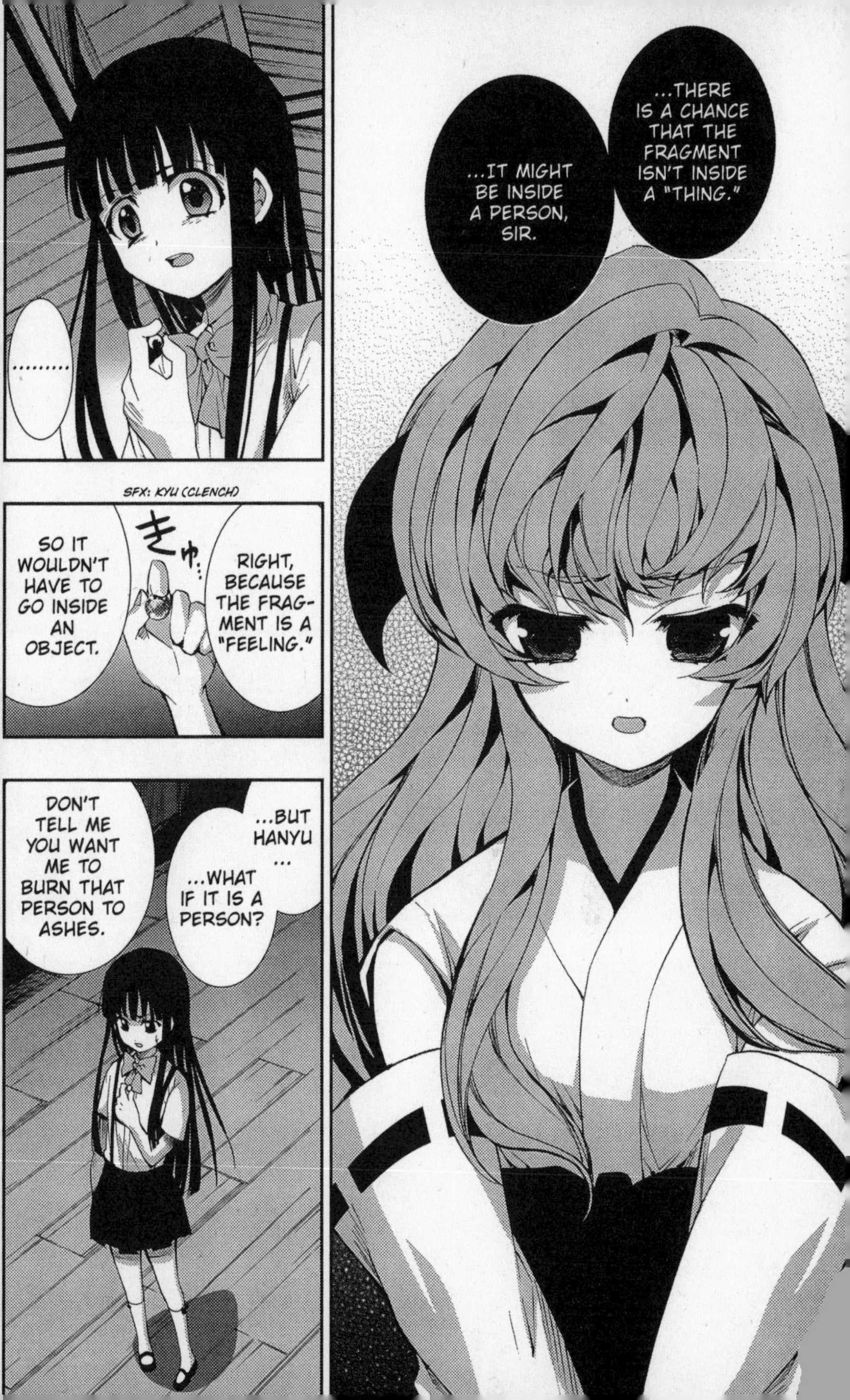
...THERE IS A CHANCE THAT THE FRAGMENT ISN'T INSIDE A "THING."
...IT MIGHT BE INSIDE A PERSON, SIR.
....
SFX: KYU (CLENCH)
RIGHT, BECAUSE THE FRAG-MENT IS A "FEELING."
きゅ...
SO IT WOULDN'T HAVE TO GO INSIDE AN OBJECT.
...BUT HANYU ...
...WHAT IF IT IS A PERSON?
DON'T TELL ME YOU WANT ME TO BURN THAT PERSON TO ASHES.

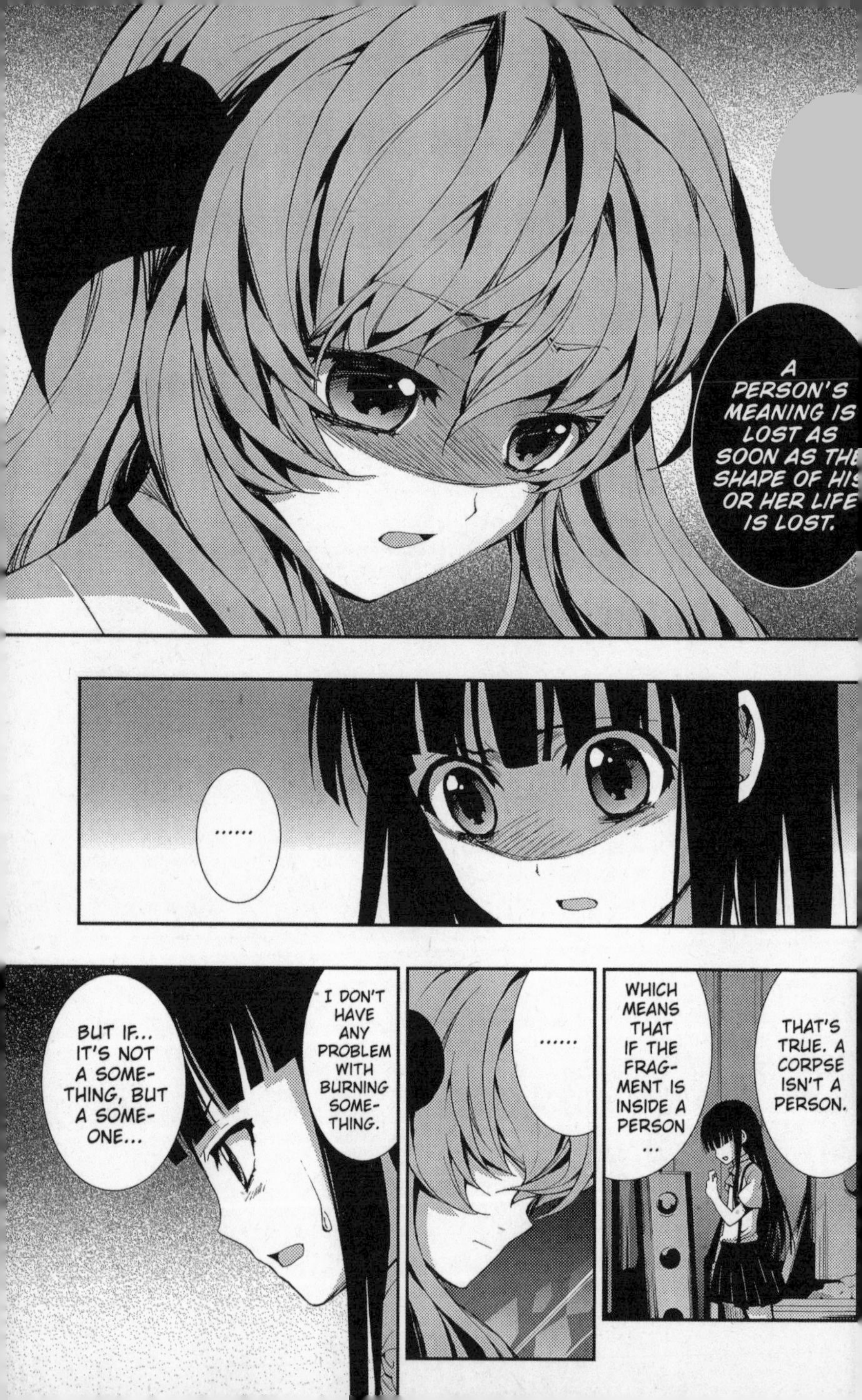
A PERSON'S MEANING IS LOST AS SOON AS THE SHAPE OF HIS OR HER LIFE IS LOST.
......
THAT'S TRUE. A CORPSE ISN'T A PERSON.
WHICH MEANS THAT IF THE FRAG-MENT IS INSIDE A PERSON ...
......
I DON'T HAVE ANY PROBLEM WITH BURNING SOME-THING.
BUT IF... IT'S NOT A SOME-THING, BUT A SOME-ONE...

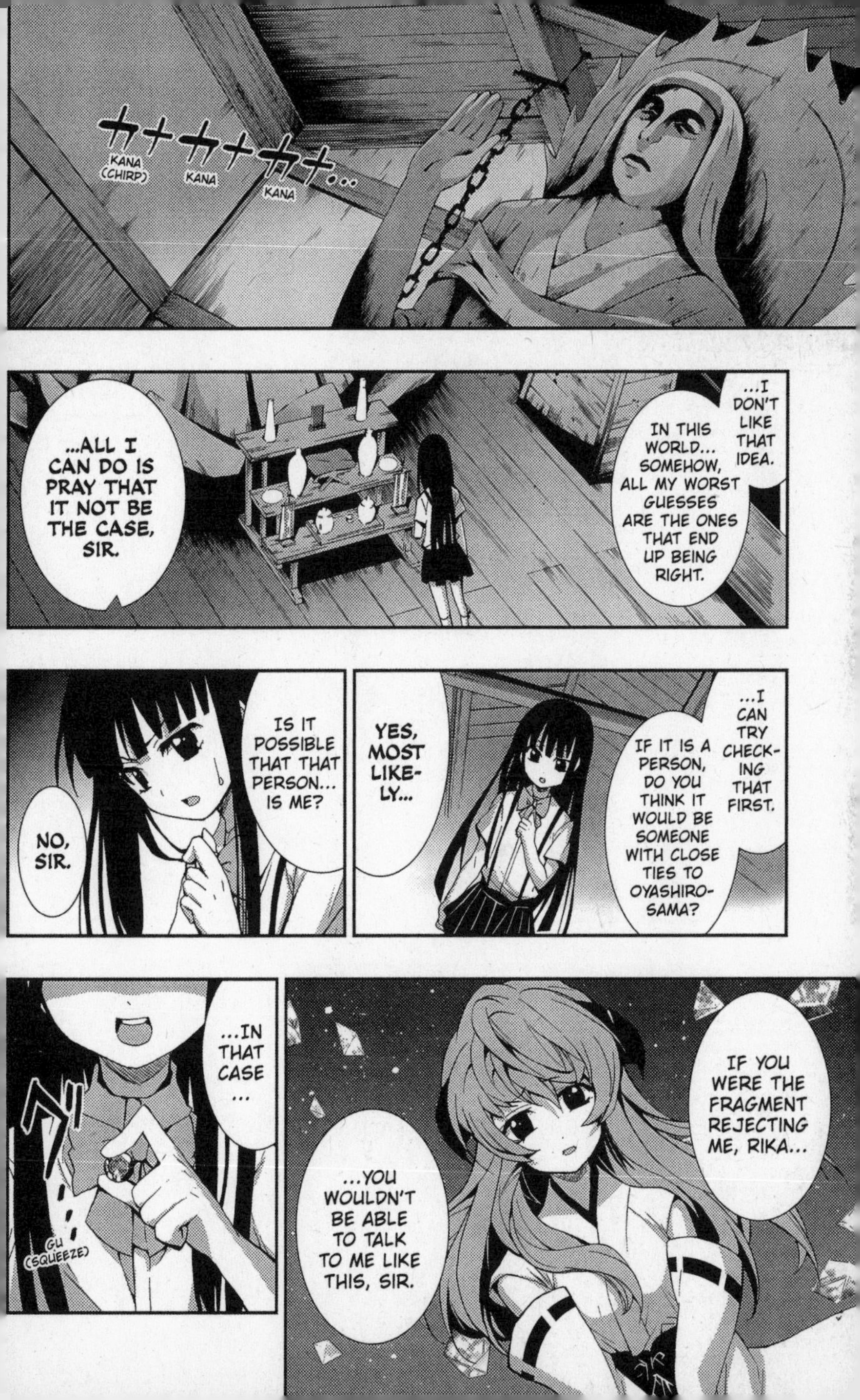
カナカナカナ…
KANA (CHIRP)
KANA
KANA
...I DON'T LIKE THAT IDEA.
IN THIS WORLD... SOMEHOW, ALL MY WORST GUESSES ARE THE ONES THAT END UP BEING RIGHT.
...ALL I CAN DO IS PRAY THAT IT NOT BE THE CASE, SIR.
...I CAN TRY CHECK-ING THAT FIRST.
IF IT IS A PERSON, DO YOU THINK IT WOULD BE SOMEONE WITH CLOSE TIES TO OYASHIRO-SAMA?
YES, MOST LIKE-LY...
IS IT POSSIBLE THAT THAT PERSON... IS ME?
NO, SIR.
IF YOU WERE THE FRAGMENT REJECTING ME, RIKA...
...YOU WOULDN'T BE ABLE TO TALK TO ME LIKE THIS, SIR.
...IN THAT CASE...
GU (SQUEEZE)

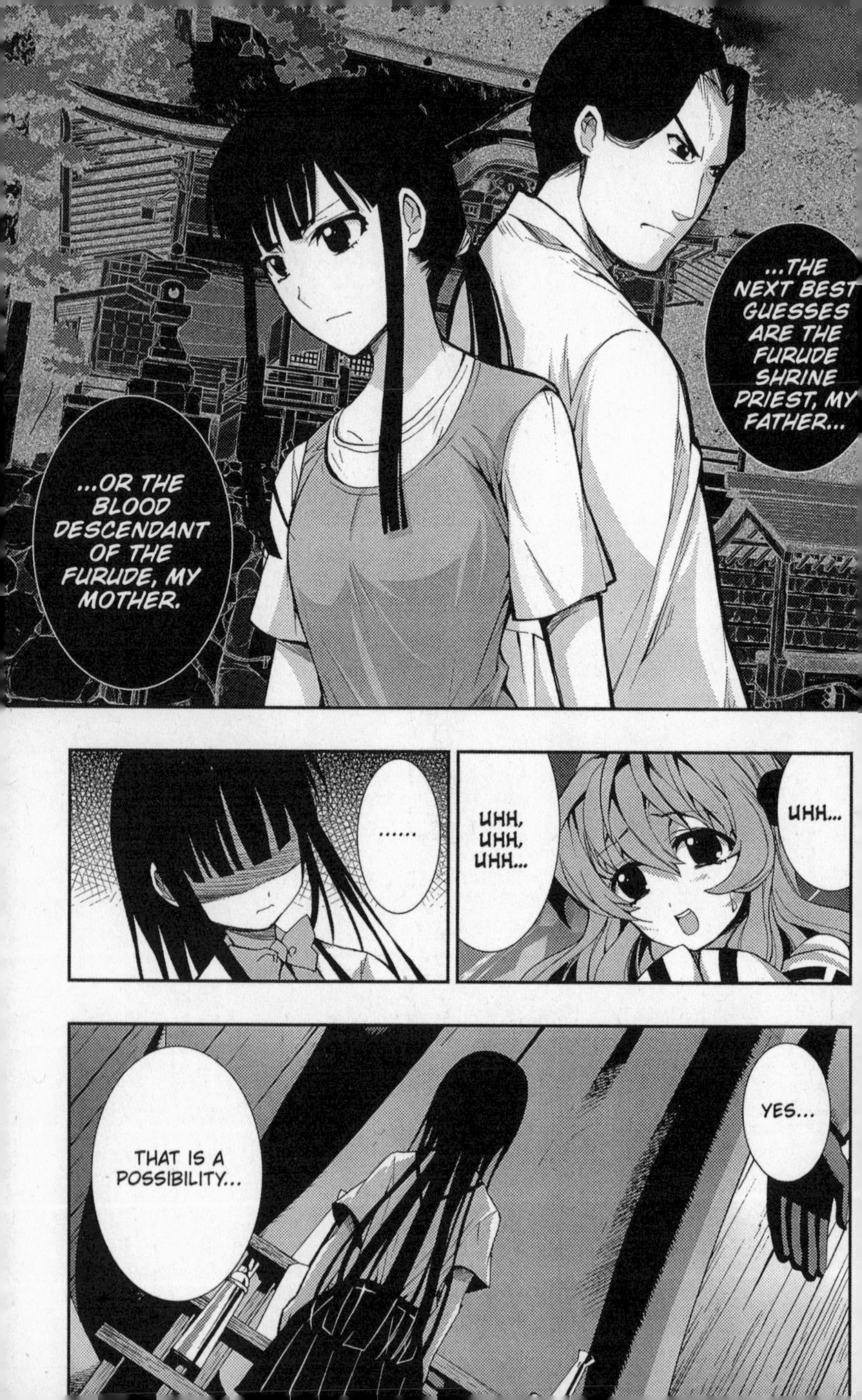
...THE NEXT BEST GUESSES ARE THE FURUDE SHRINE PRIEST, MY FATHER...
...OR THE BLOOD DESCENDANT OF THE FURUDE, MY MOTHER.
UHH...
UHH, UHH, UHH...
......
YES...
THAT IS A POSSIBILITY...

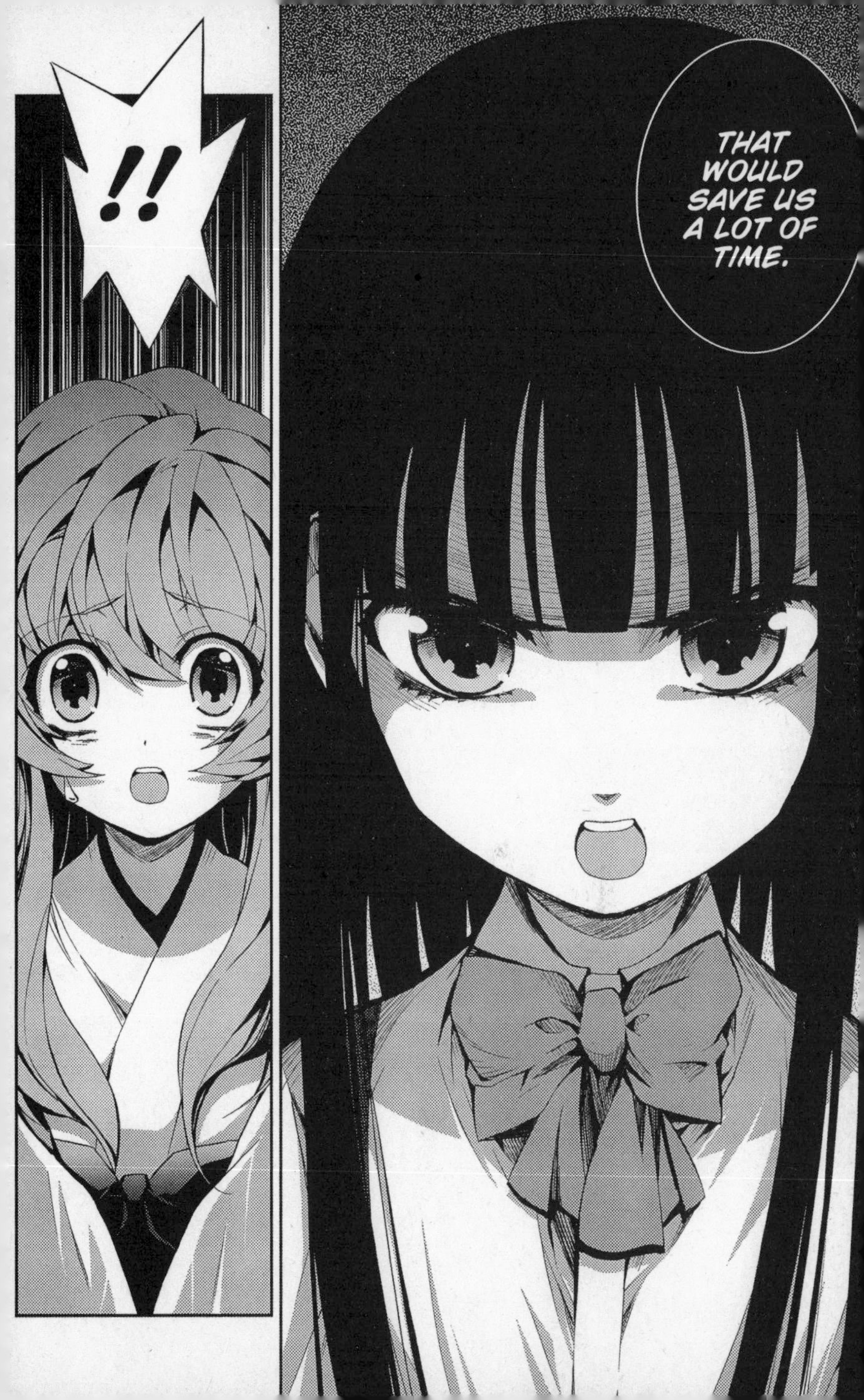
THAT WOULD SAVE US A LOT OF TIME.
!!

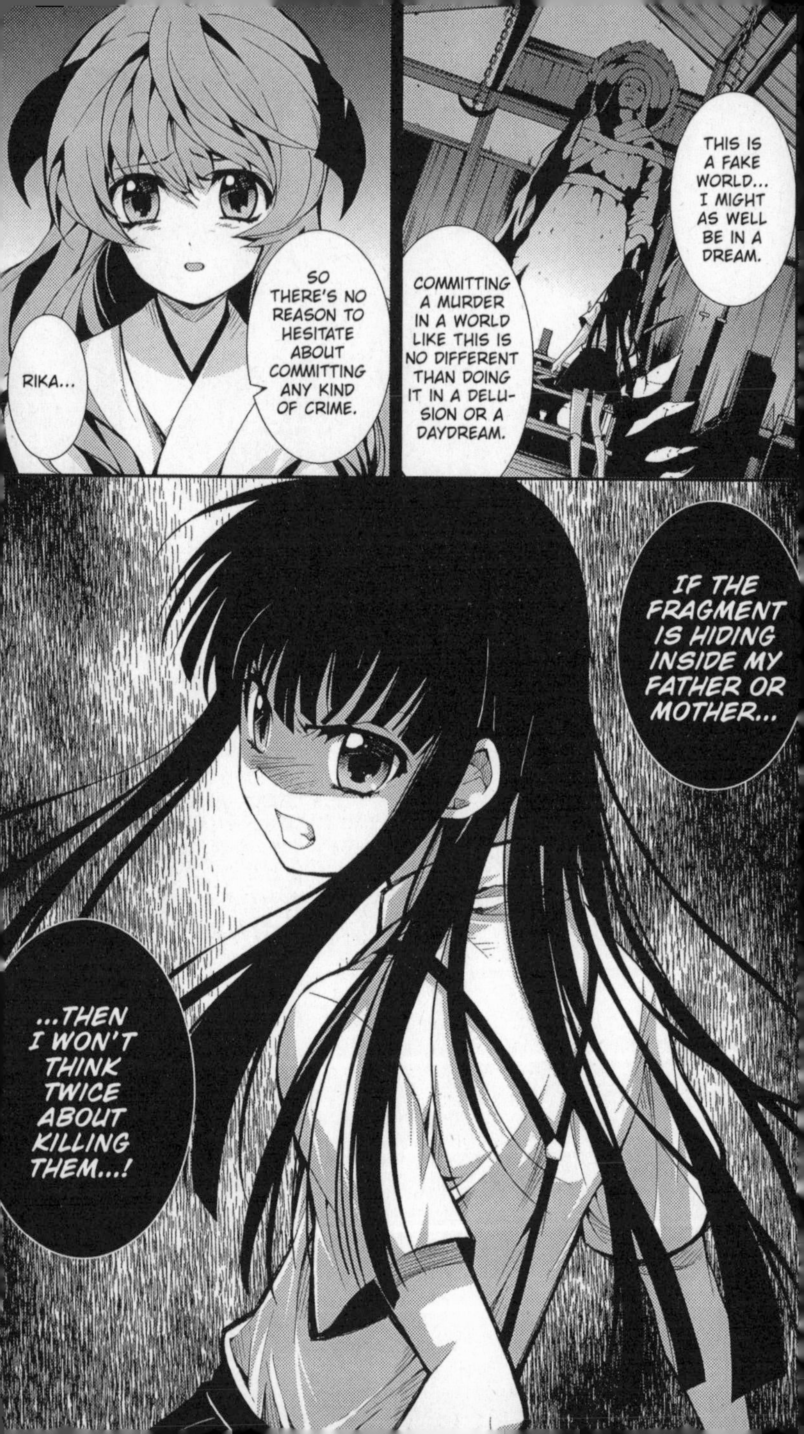
THIS IS A FAKE WORLD... I MIGHT AS WELL BE IN A DREAM.
COMMITTING A MURDER IN A WORLD LIKE THIS IS NO DIFFERENT THAN DOING IT IN A DELUSION OR A DAYDREAM.
SO THERE'S NO REASON TO HESITATE ABOUT COMMITTING ANY KIND OF CRIME.
RIKA...
IF THE FRAGMENT IS HIDING INSIDE MY FATHER OR MOTHER...
...THEN I WON'T THINK TWICE ABOUT KILLING THEM...!

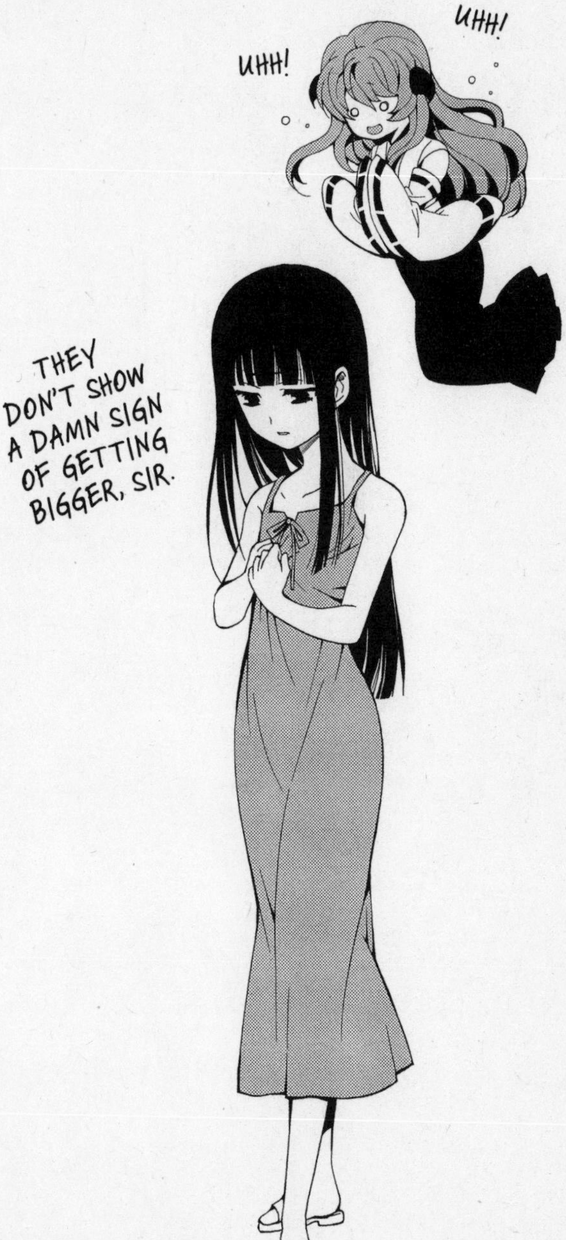
UHH!
UHH!
THEY DON'T SHOW A DAMN SIGN OF GETTING BIGGER, SIR.

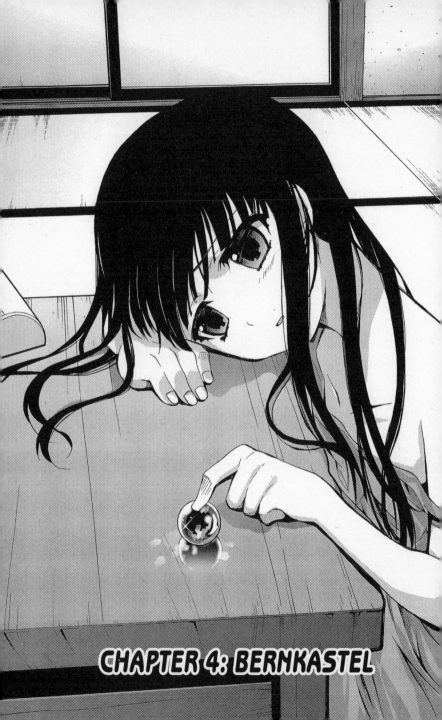

CHAPTER 4: BERNKASTEL

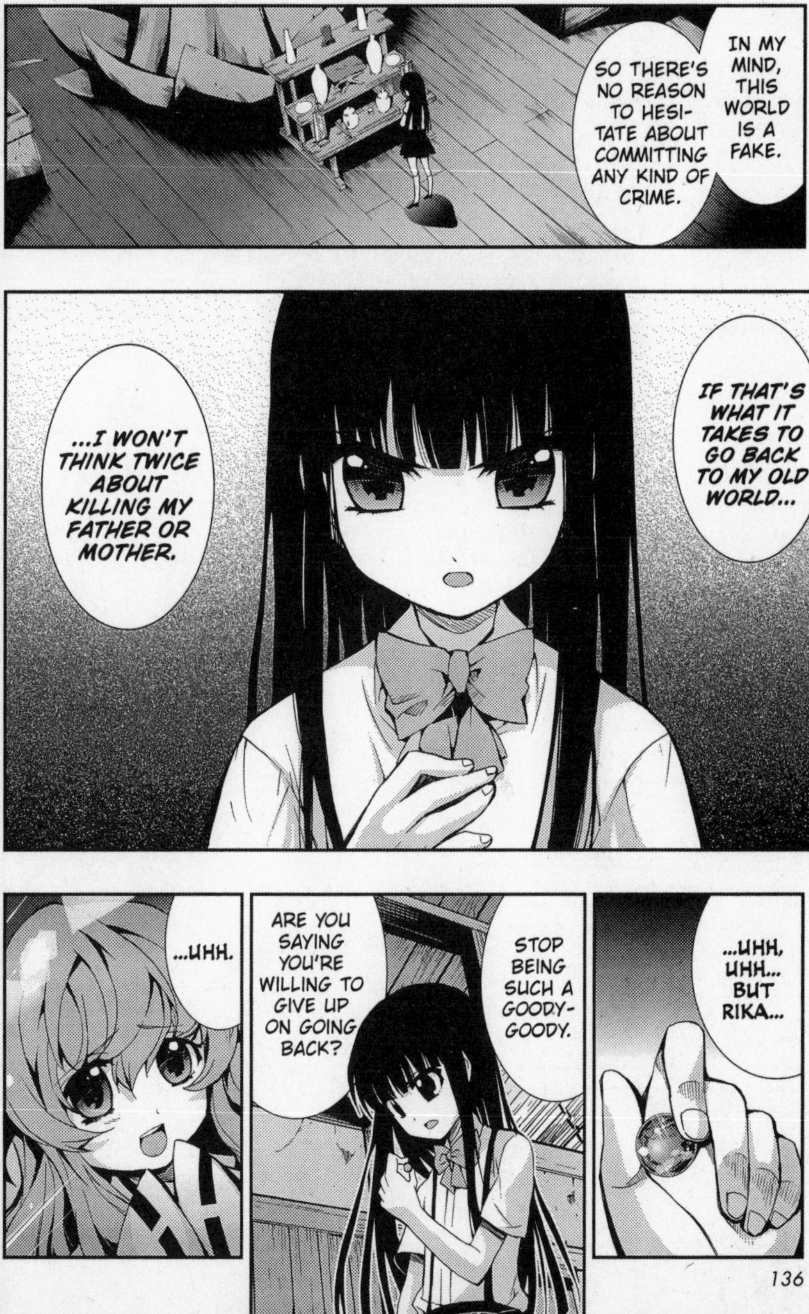
IN MY MIND, THIS WORLD IS A FAKE.
SO THERE'S NO REASON TO HESI-TATE ABOUT COMMITTING ANY KIND OF CRIME.
IF THAT'S WHAT IT TAKES TO GO BACK TO MY OLD WORLD...
...I WON'T THINK TWICE ABOUT KILLING MY FATHER OR MOTHER.
...UHH, UHH... BUT RIKA...
STOP BEING SUCH A GOODY-GOODY.
ARE YOU SAYING YOU'RE WILLING TO GIVE UP ON GOING BACK?
...UHH.

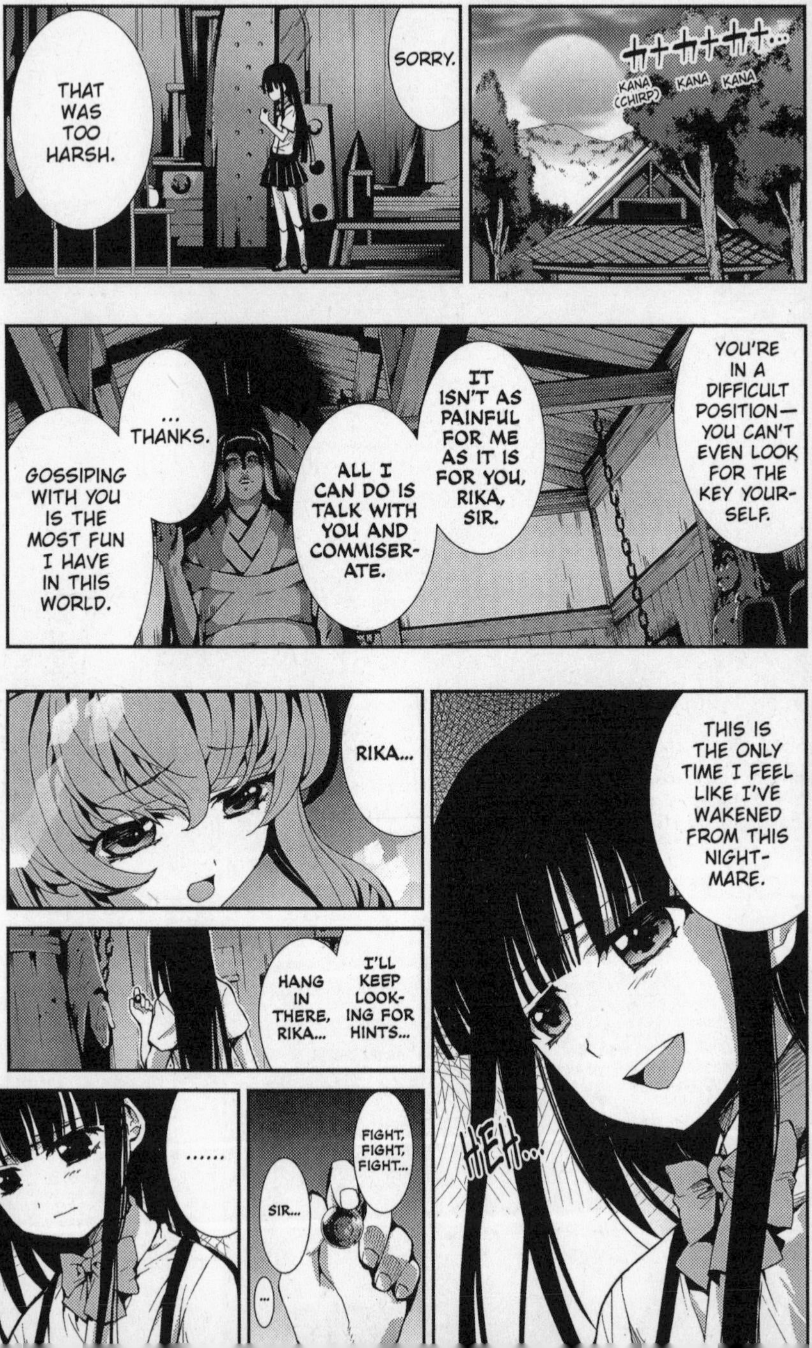
カナカナカナ…
KANA (CHIRP) KANA KANA
SORRY.
THAT WAS TOO HARSH.
YOU'RE IN A DIFFICULT POSITION—YOU CAN'T EVEN LOOK FOR THE KEY YOURSELF.
IT ISN'T AS PAINFUL FOR ME AS IT IS FOR YOU, RIKA, SIR.
ALL I CAN DO IS TALK WITH YOU AND COMMISERATE.
... THANKS.
GOSSIPING WITH YOU IS THE MOST FUN I HAVE IN THIS WORLD.
THIS IS THE ONLY TIME I FEEL LIKE I'VE WAKENED FROM THIS NIGHTMARE.
HEH...
RIKA...
I'LL KEEP LOOKING FOR HINTS...
HANG IN THERE, RIKA...
FIGHT, FIGHT, FIGHT...
SIR...
...
......

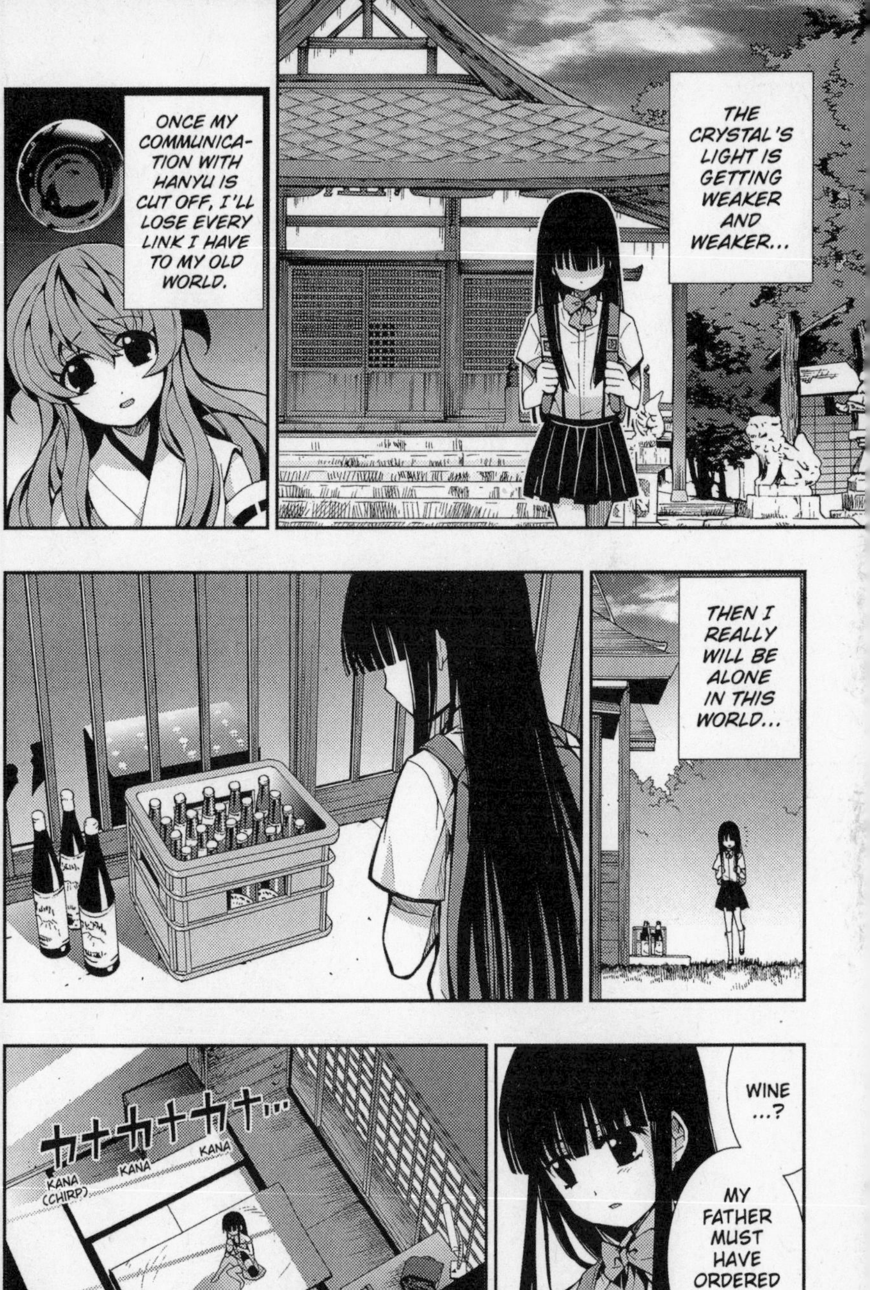
THE CRYSTAL'S LIGHT IS GETTING WEAKER AND WEAKER...
ONCE MY COMMUNICATION WITH HANYU IS CUT OFF, I'LL LOSE EVERY LINK I HAVE TO MY OLD WORLD.
THEN I REALLY WILL BE ALONE IN THIS WORLD...
WINE ...?
MY FATHER MUST HAVE ORDERED IT...
カナカナカナ‥
KANA
KANA
KANA (CHIRP)

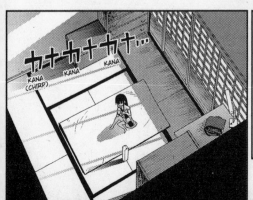

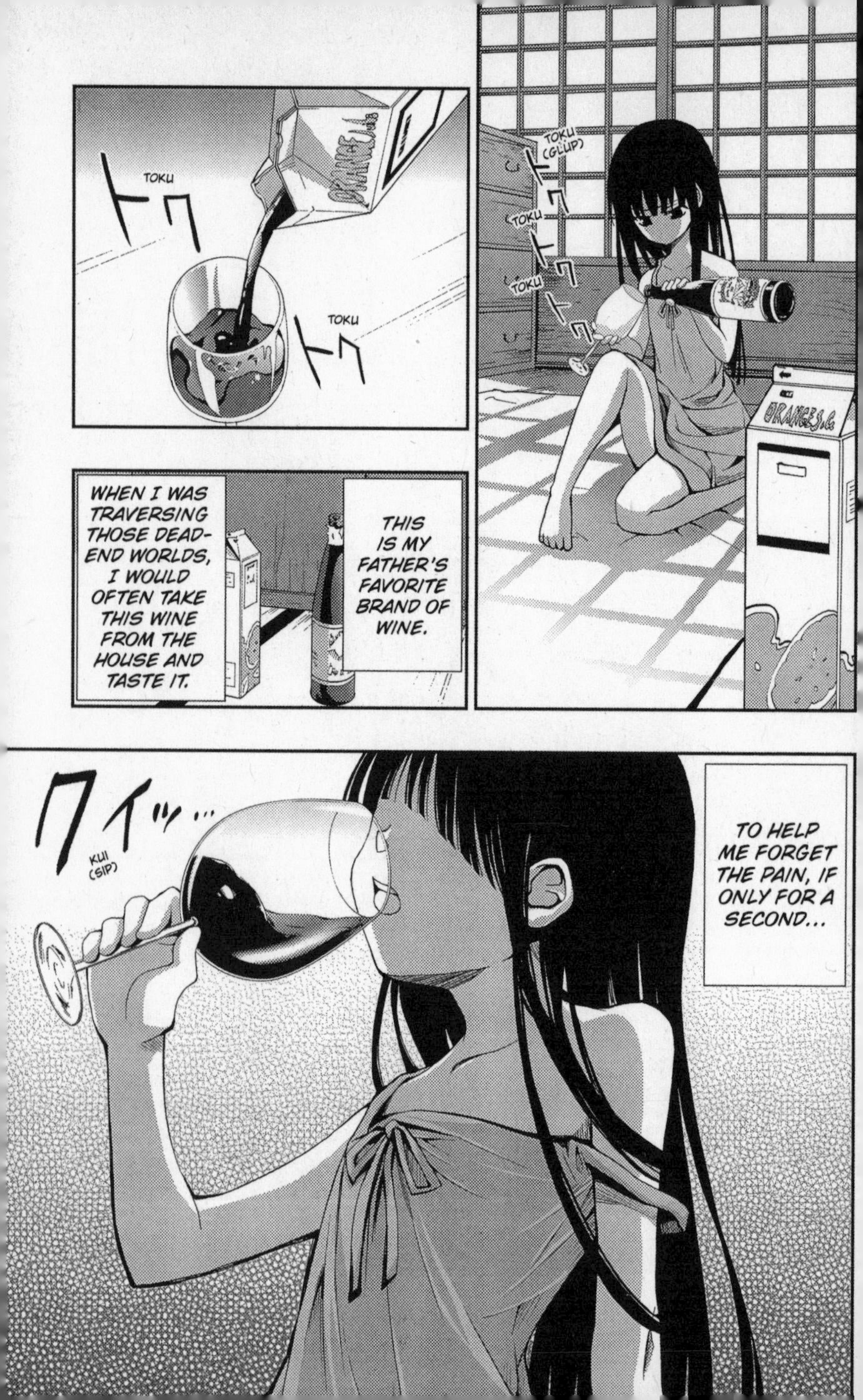
トク
TOKU (GLUP)
トク
TOKU
トク
TOKU
トク
TOKU
トク
TOKU
THIS IS MY FATHER'S FAVORITE BRAND OF WINE.
WHEN I WAS TRAVERSING THOSE DEAD-END WORLDS, I WOULD OFTEN TAKE THIS WINE FROM THE HOUSE AND TASTE IT.
TO HELP ME FORGET THE PAIN, IF ONLY FOR A SECOND...
クイッ…
KUI (SIP)

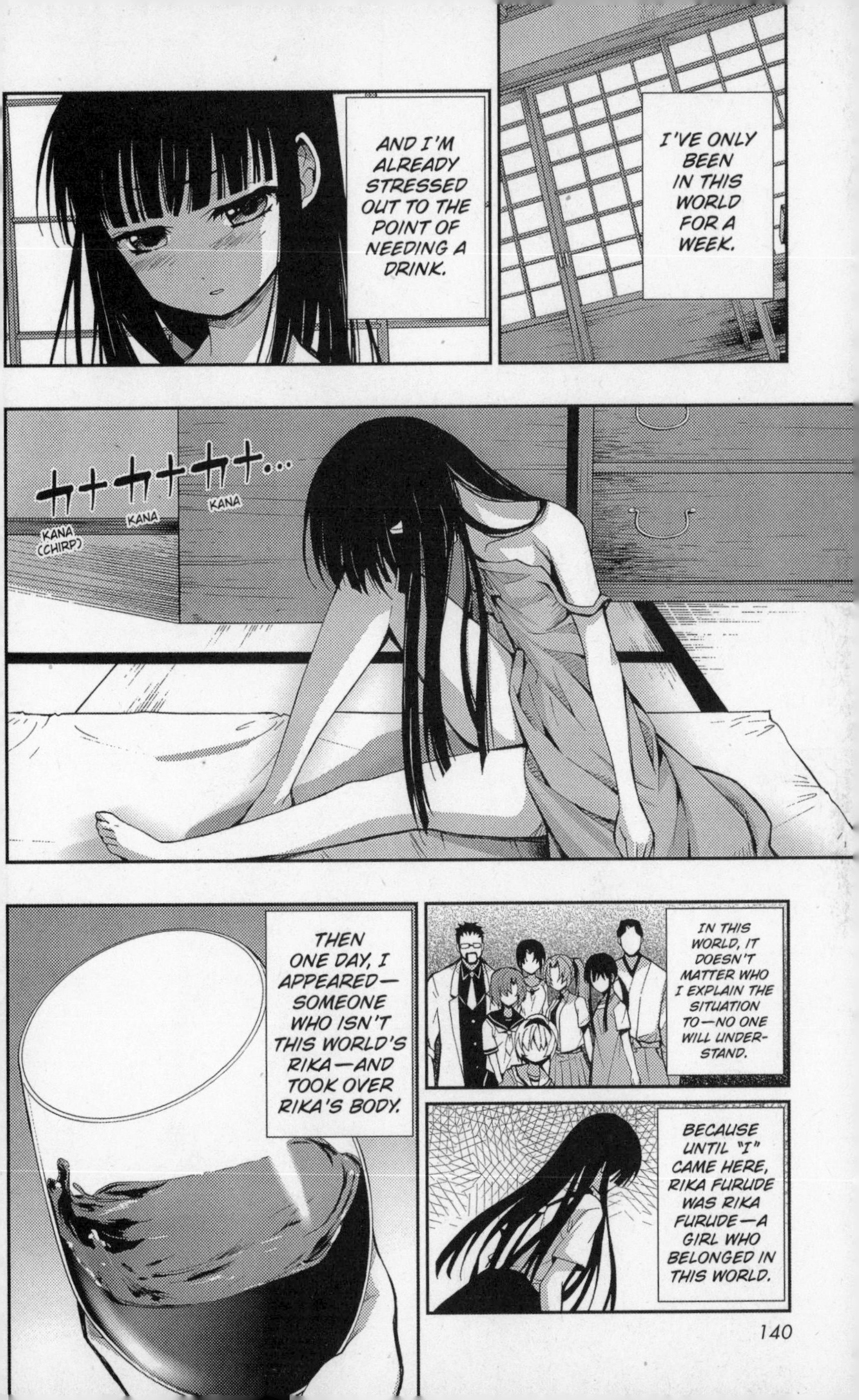
I'VE ONLY BEEN IN THIS WORLD FOR A WEEK.
AND I'M ALREADY STRESSED OUT TO THE POINT OF NEEDING A DRINK.
カナカナカナ...
KANA
KANA
KANA (CHIRP)
IN THIS WORLD, IT DOESN'T MATTER WHO I EXPLAIN THE SITUATION TO—NO ONE WILL UNDER-STAND.
BECAUSE UNTIL "I" CAME HERE, RIKA FURUDE WAS RIKA FURUDE—A GIRL WHO BELONGED IN THIS WORLD.
THEN ONE DAY, I APPEARED—SOMEONE WHO ISN'T THIS WORLD'S RIKA—AND TOOK OVER RIKA'S BODY.

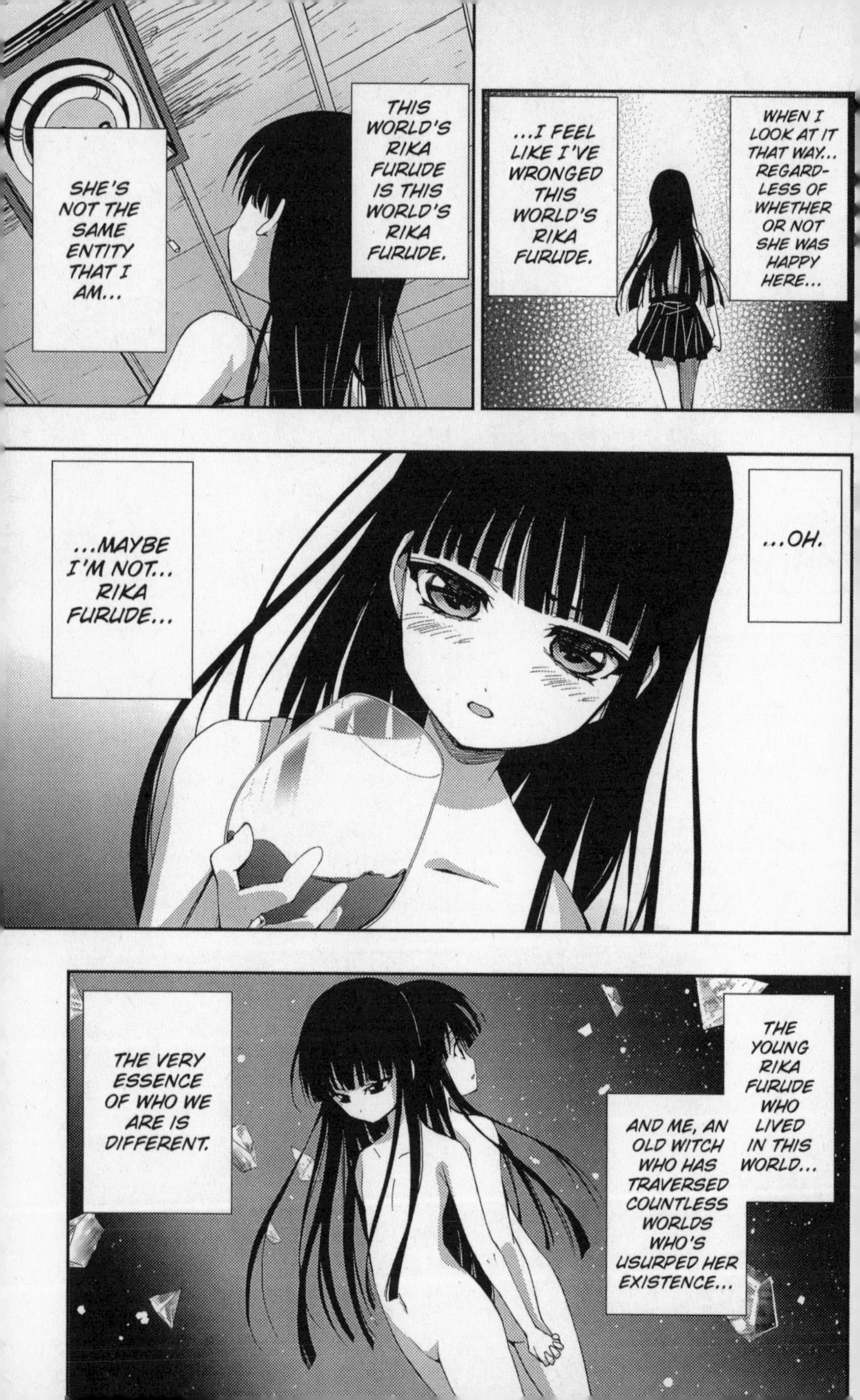
WHEN I LOOK AT IT THAT WAY... REGARD-LESS OF WHETHER OR NOT SHE WAS HAPPY HERE...
...I FEEL LIKE I'VE WRONGED THIS WORLD'S RIKA FURUDE.
THIS WORLD'S RIKA FURUDE IS THIS WORLD'S RIKA FURUDE.
SHE'S NOT THE SAME ENTITY THAT I AM...
...OH.
...MAYBE I'M NOT... RIKA FURUDE...
THE YOUNG RIKA FURUDE WHO LIVED IN THIS WORLD...
AND ME, AN OLD WITCH WHO HAS TRAVERSED COUNTLESS WORLDS WHO'S USURPED HER EXISTENCE...
THE VERY ESSENCE OF WHO WE ARE IS DIFFERENT.

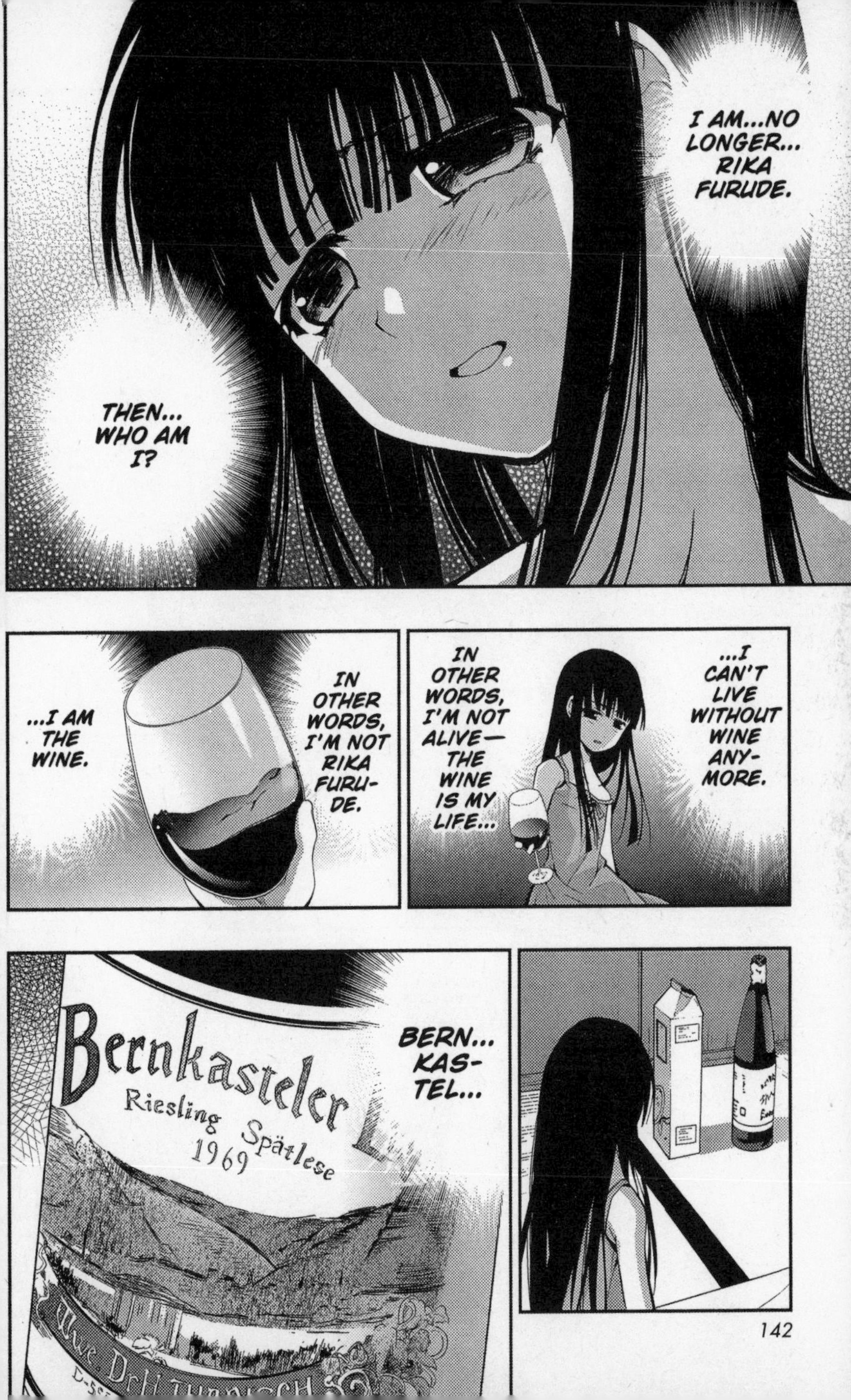
I AM...NO LONGER... RIKA FURUDE.
THEN... WHO AM I?
...I CAN'T LIVE WITHOUT WINE ANYMORE.
IN OTHER WORDS, I'M NOT ALIVE—THE WINE IS MY LIFE...
IN OTHER WORDS, I'M NOT RIKA FURUDE.
...I AM THE WINE.
BERN... KASTEL...
Bernkasteler
Riesling Spätlese
1969

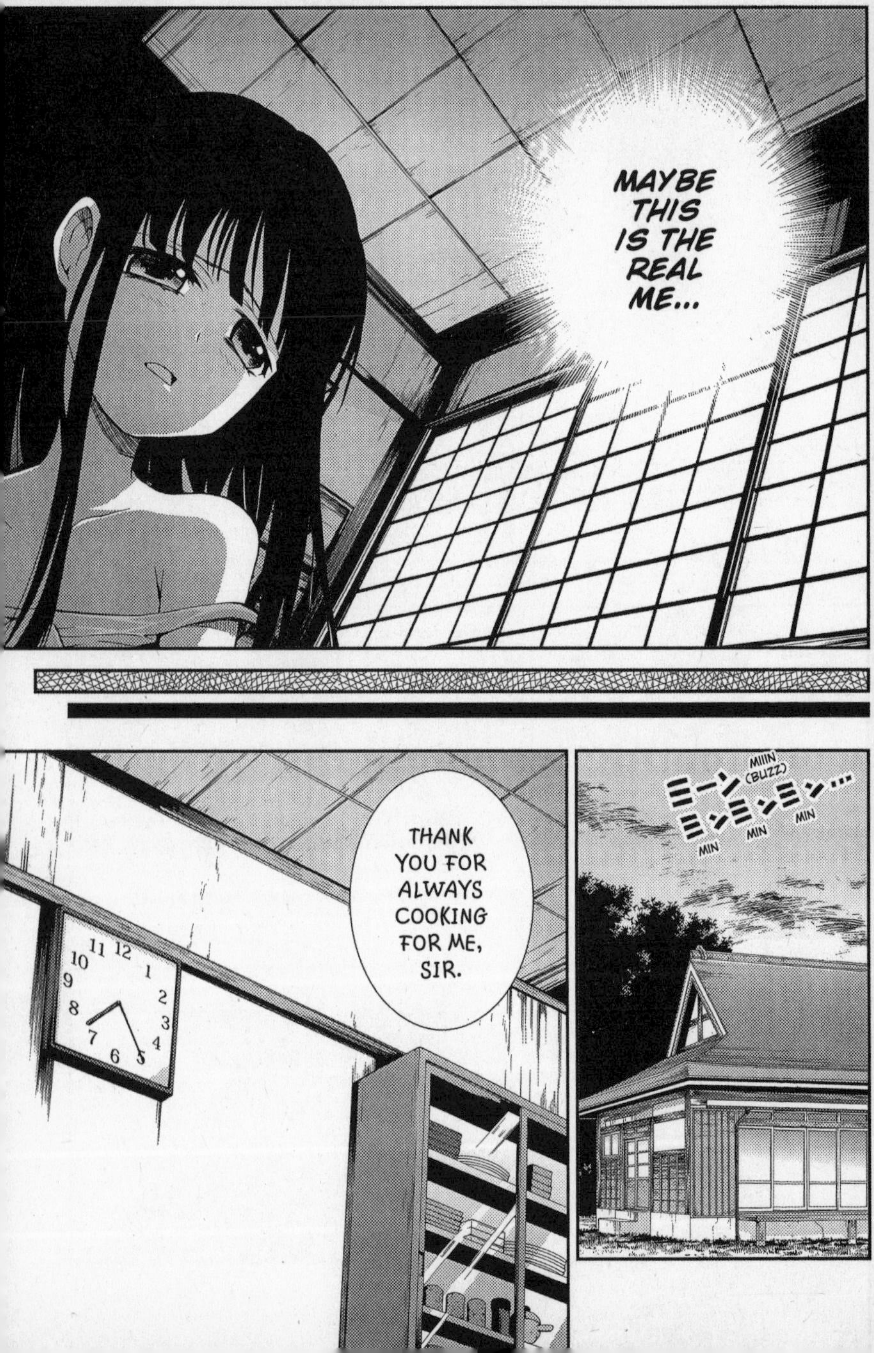
MAYBE THIS IS THE REAL ME...
ミーン ミンミンミン…
MIIIN (BUZZ)
MIN MIN MIN MIN
THANK YOU FOR ALWAYS COOKING FOR ME, SIR.

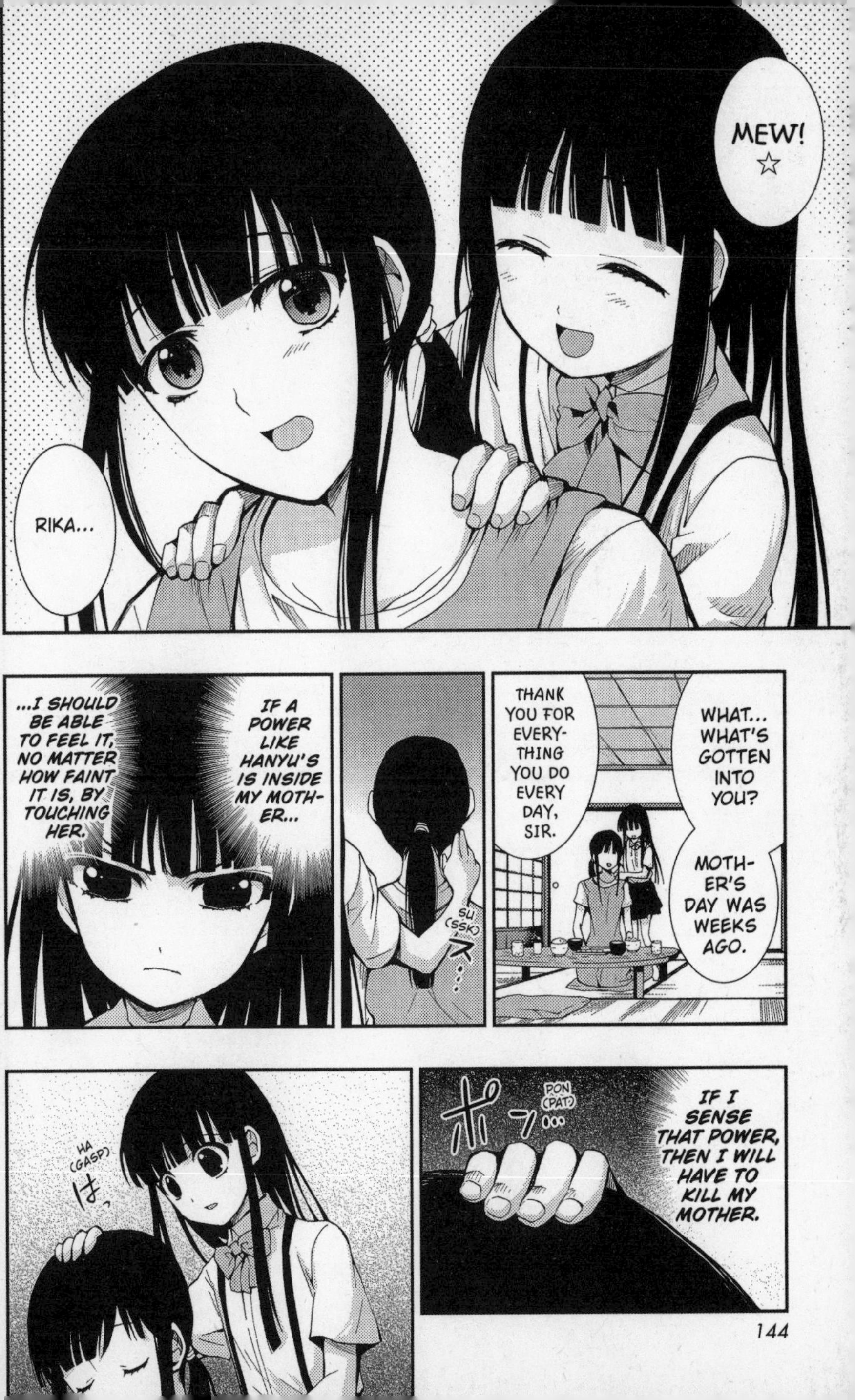

MEW! ☆
RIKA...
THANK YOU FOR EVERYTHING YOU DO EVERY DAY, SIR.
WHAT... WHAT'S GOTTEN INTO YOU?
MOTHER'S DAY WAS WEEKS AGO.
SU (SSK)
IF A POWER LIKE HANYU'S IS INSIDE MY MOTHER...
...I SHOULD BE ABLE TO FEEL IT, NO MATTER HOW FAINT IT IS, BY TOUCHING HER.
PON (PAT)
IF I SENSE THAT POWER, THEN I WILL HAVE TO KILL MY MOTHER.
HA (GASP)

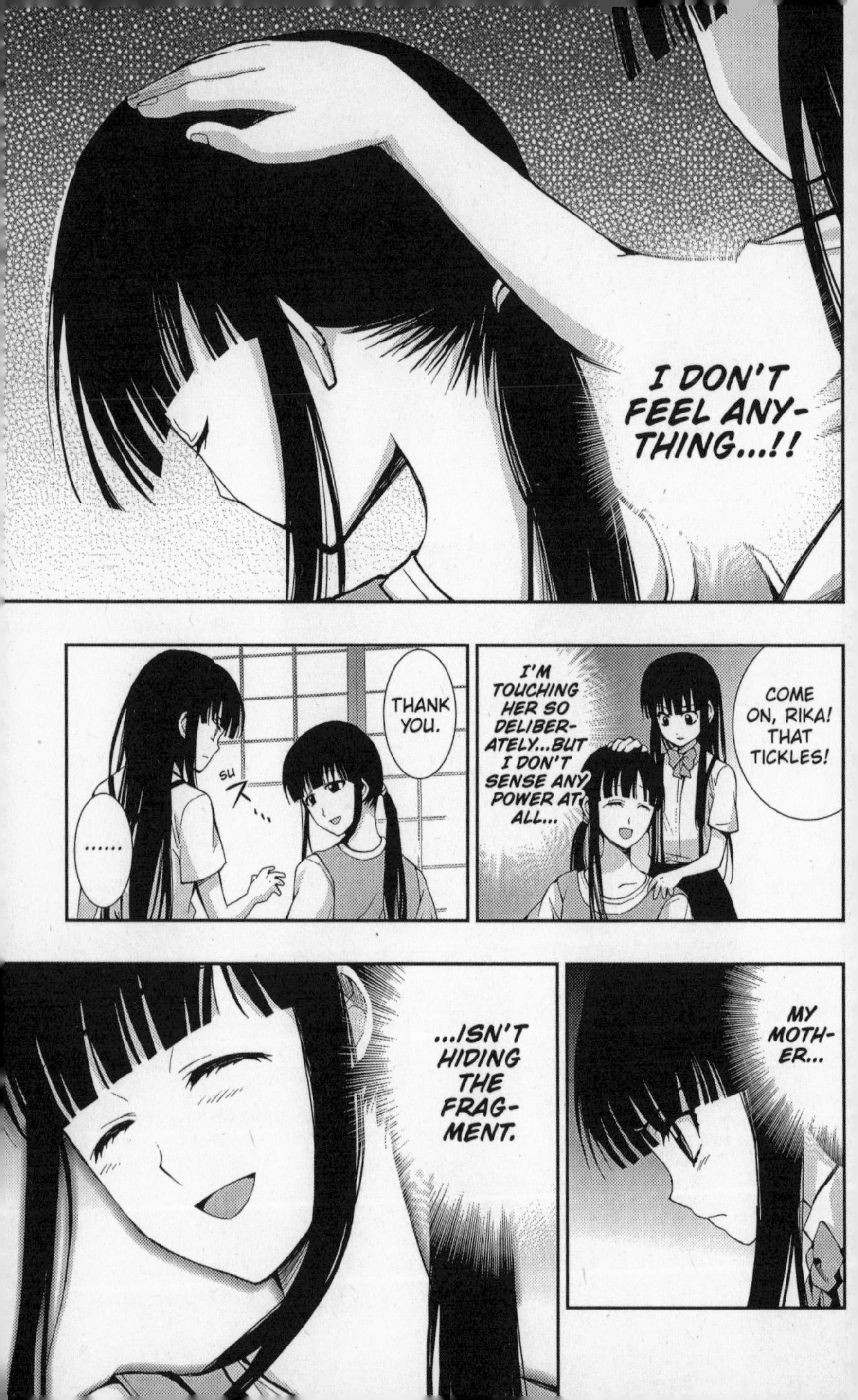
I DON'T FEEL ANYTHING...!!
COME ON, RIKA! THAT TICKLES!
I'M TOUCHING HER SO DELIBERATELY...BUT I DON'T SENSE ANY POWER AT ALL...
THANK YOU.
SU ス...
......
MY MOTHER...
...ISN'T HIDING THE FRAGMENT.

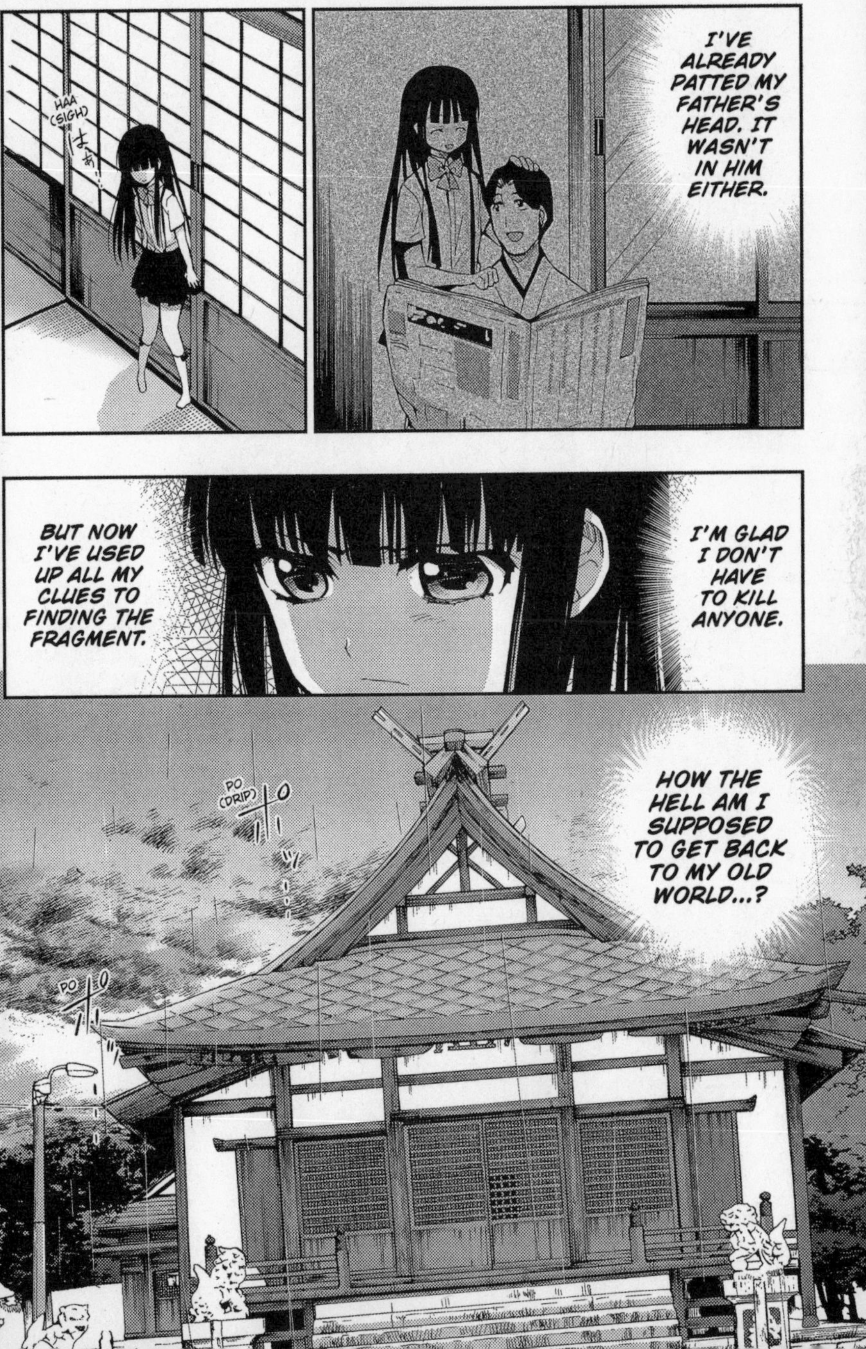
I'VE ALREADY PATTED MY FATHER'S HEAD. IT WASN'T IN HIM EITHER.
HAA (SIGH)
はぁ…
I'M GLAD I DON'T HAVE TO KILL ANYONE.
BUT NOW I'VE USED UP ALL MY CLUES TO FINDING THE FRAGMENT.
HOW THE HELL AM I SUPPOSED TO GET BACK TO MY OLD WORLD...?
PO (DRIP)
PO

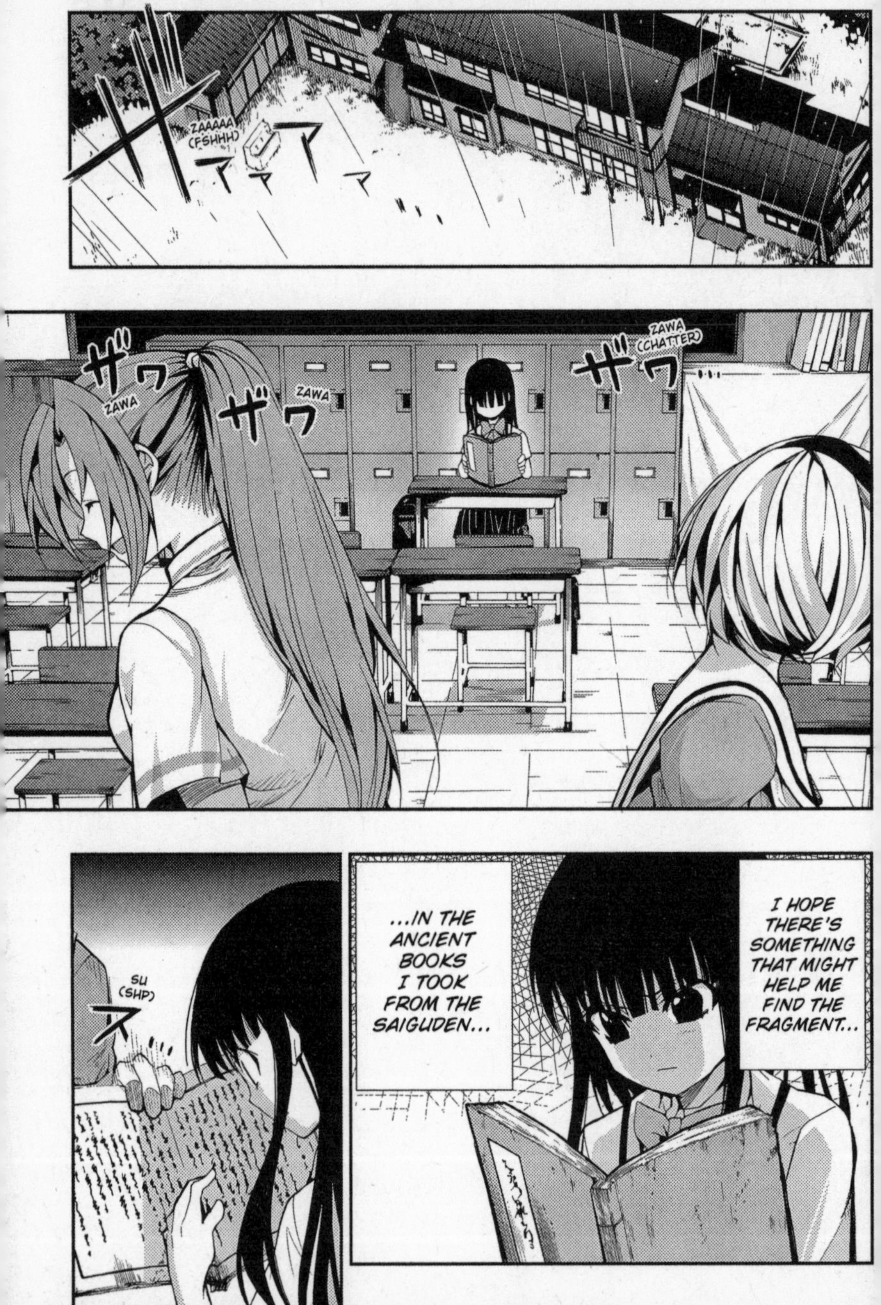
ZAAAAA (FSHHH)
ザワ
ZAWA (CHATTER)
ザワ
ZAWA
ザワ
ZAWA
I HOPE THERE'S SOMETHING THAT MIGHT HELP ME FIND THE FRAGMENT...
...IN THE ANCIENT BOOKS I TOOK FROM THE SAIGUDEN...
ス
SU (SHP)

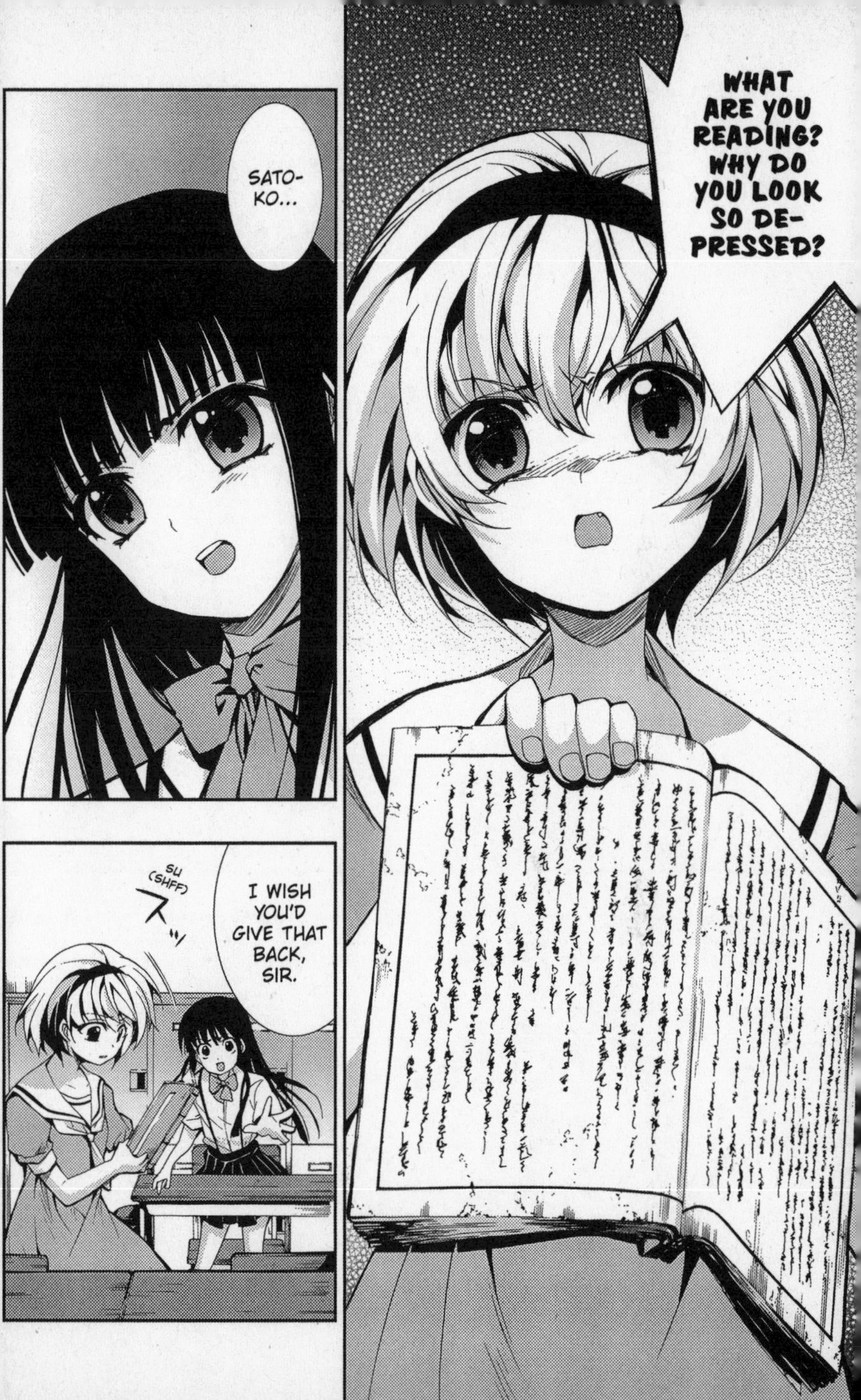
WHAT ARE YOU READING? WHY DO YOU LOOK SO DE-PRESSED?
SATO-KO...
SU (SHFF)
I WISH YOU'D GIVE THAT BACK, SIR.

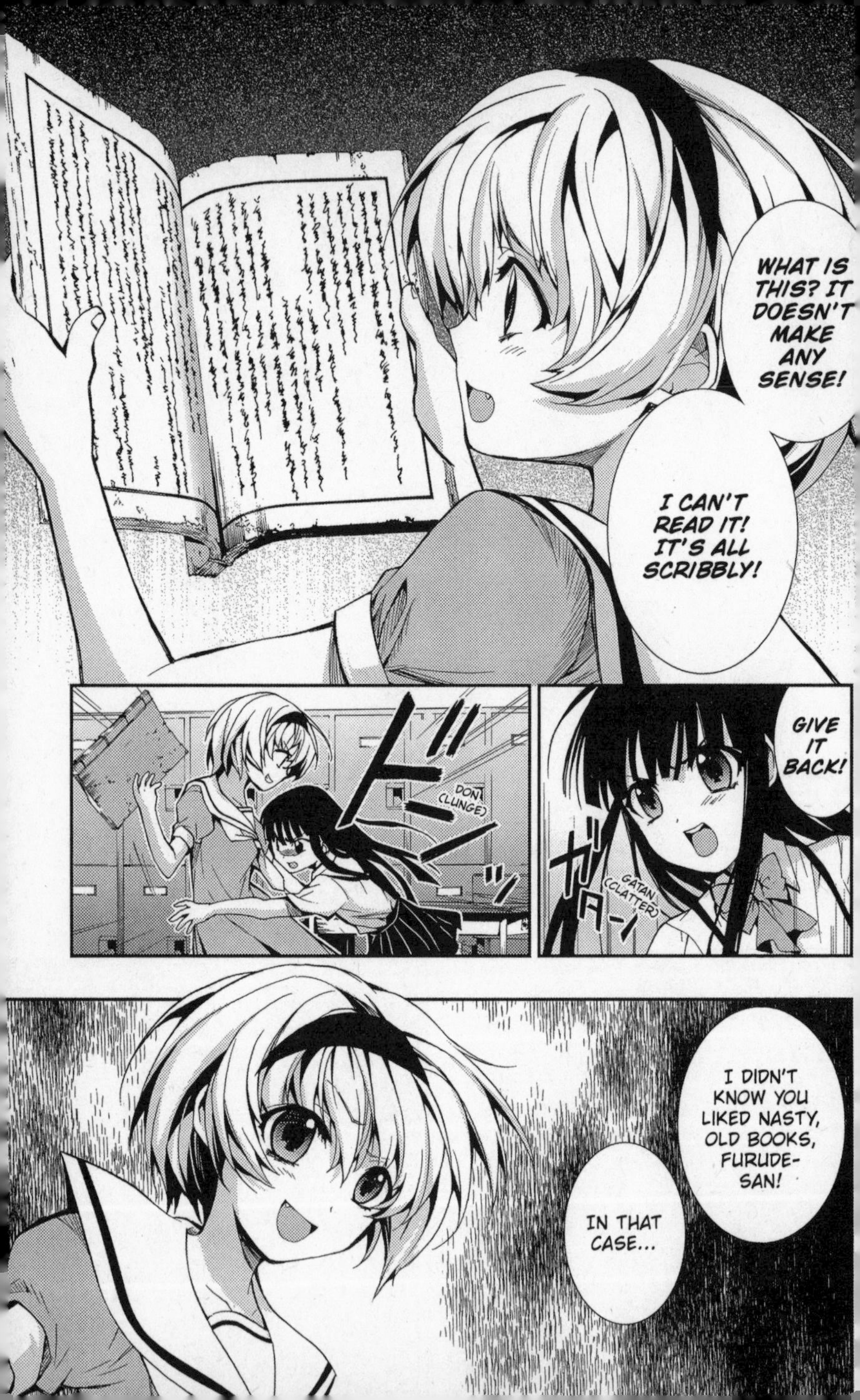
WHAT IS THIS? IT DOESN'T MAKE ANY SENSE!
I CAN'T READ IT! IT'S ALL SCRIBBLY!
GIVE IT BACK!
GATAN (CLATTER)
DON (LUNGE)
I DIDN'T KNOW YOU LIKED NASTY, OLD BOOKS, FURUDE-SAN!
IN THAT CASE...

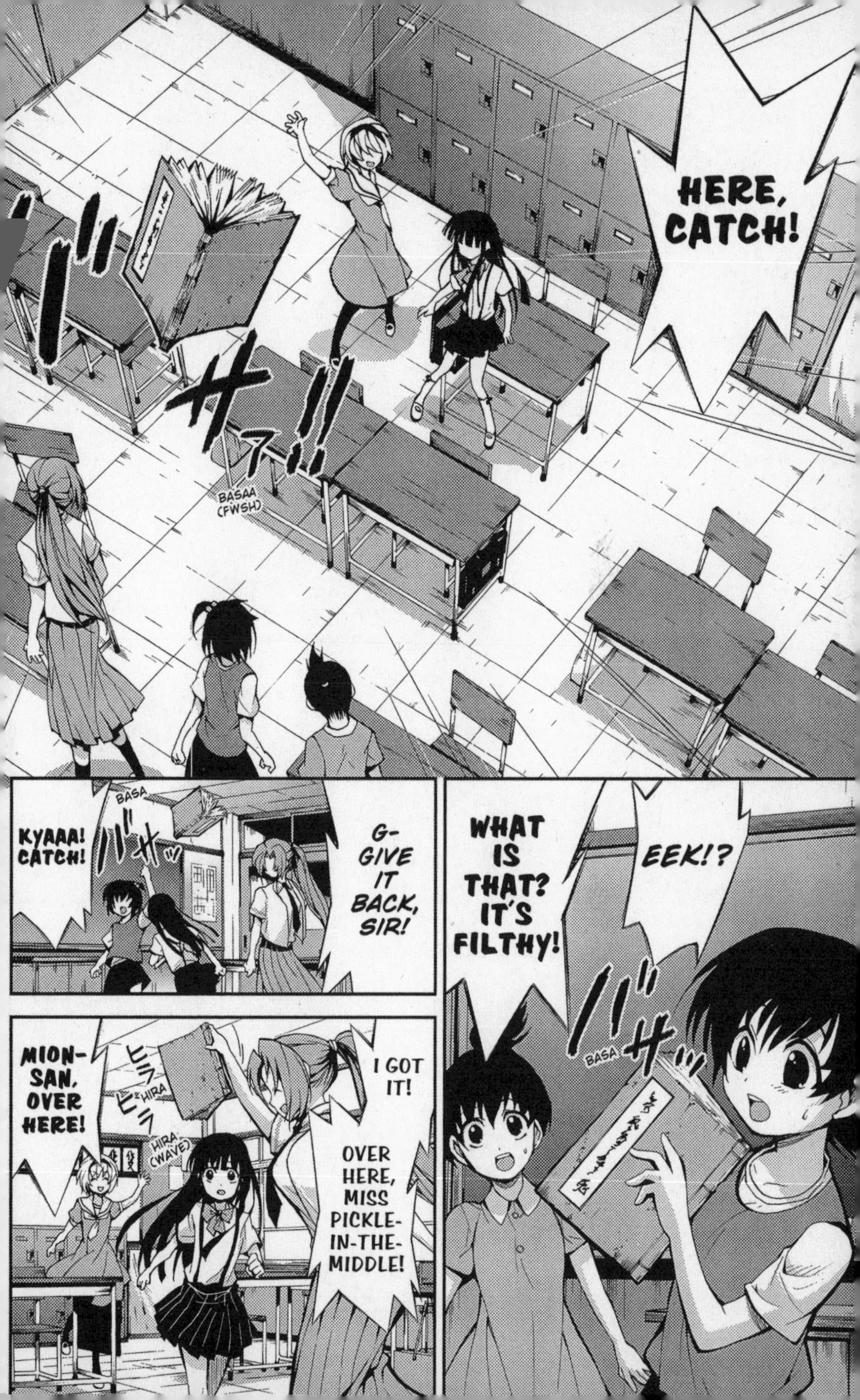
HERE, CATCH!
BASAA (FWSH)
EEK!?
WHAT IS THAT? IT'S FILTHY!
BASA
G-GIVE IT BACK, SIR!
KYAAA! CATCH!
BASA
I GOT IT!
MION-SAN, OVER HERE!
HIRA
HIRA (WAVE)
OVER HERE, MISS PICKLE-IN-THE-MIDDLE!

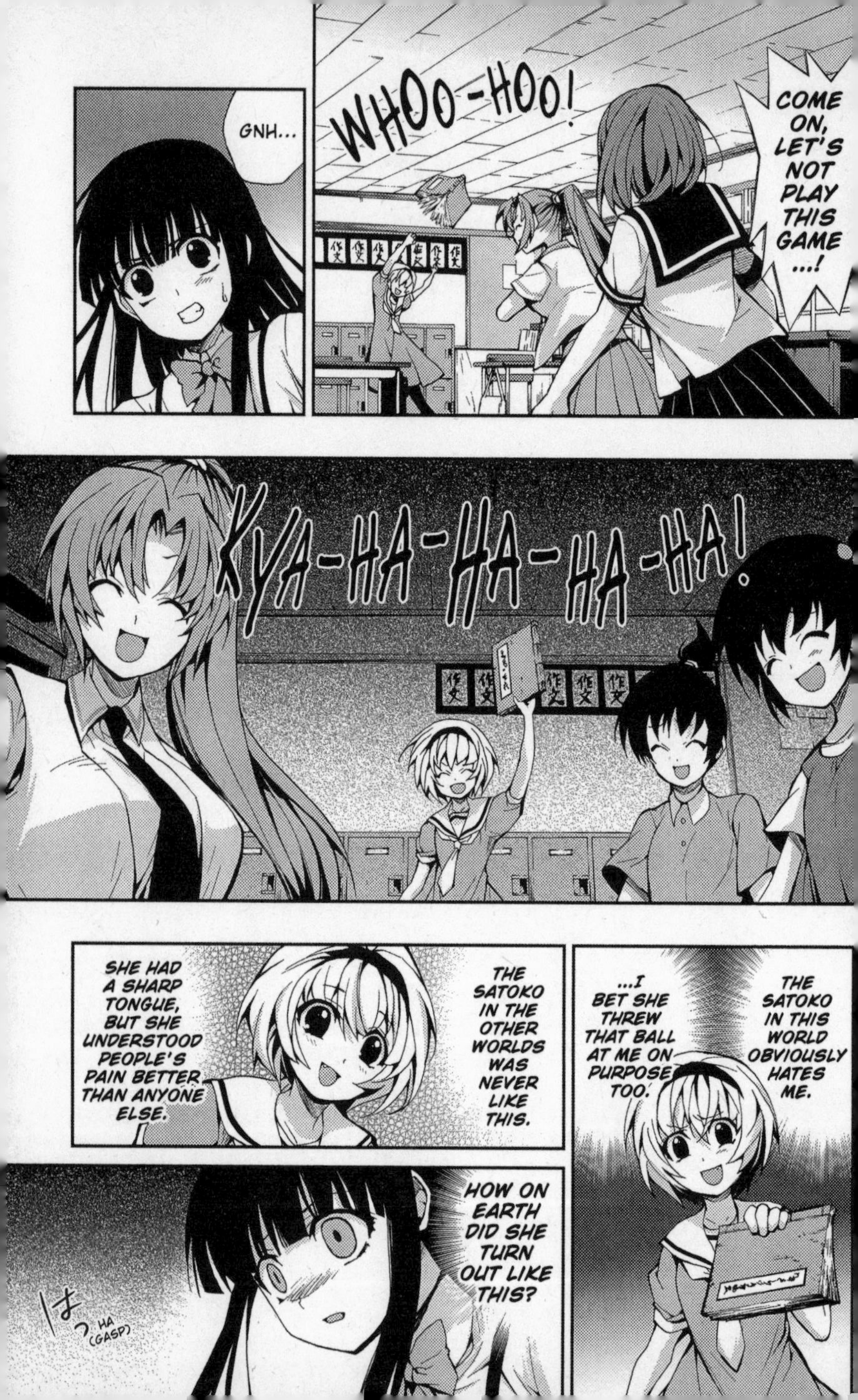
COME ON, LET'S NOT PLAY THIS GAME...!
WHOO-HOO!
GNH...
KYA-HA-HA-HA-HA!
THE SATOKO IN THIS WORLD OBVIOUSLY HATES ME.
...I BET SHE THREW THAT BALL AT ME ON PURPOSE TOO.
THE SATOKO IN THE OTHER WORLDS WAS NEVER LIKE THIS.
SHE HAD A SHARP TONGUE, BUT SHE UNDERSTOOD PEOPLE'S PAIN BETTER THAN ANYONE ELSE.
HOW ON EARTH DID SHE TURN OUT LIKE THIS?
はっ
HA (GASP)

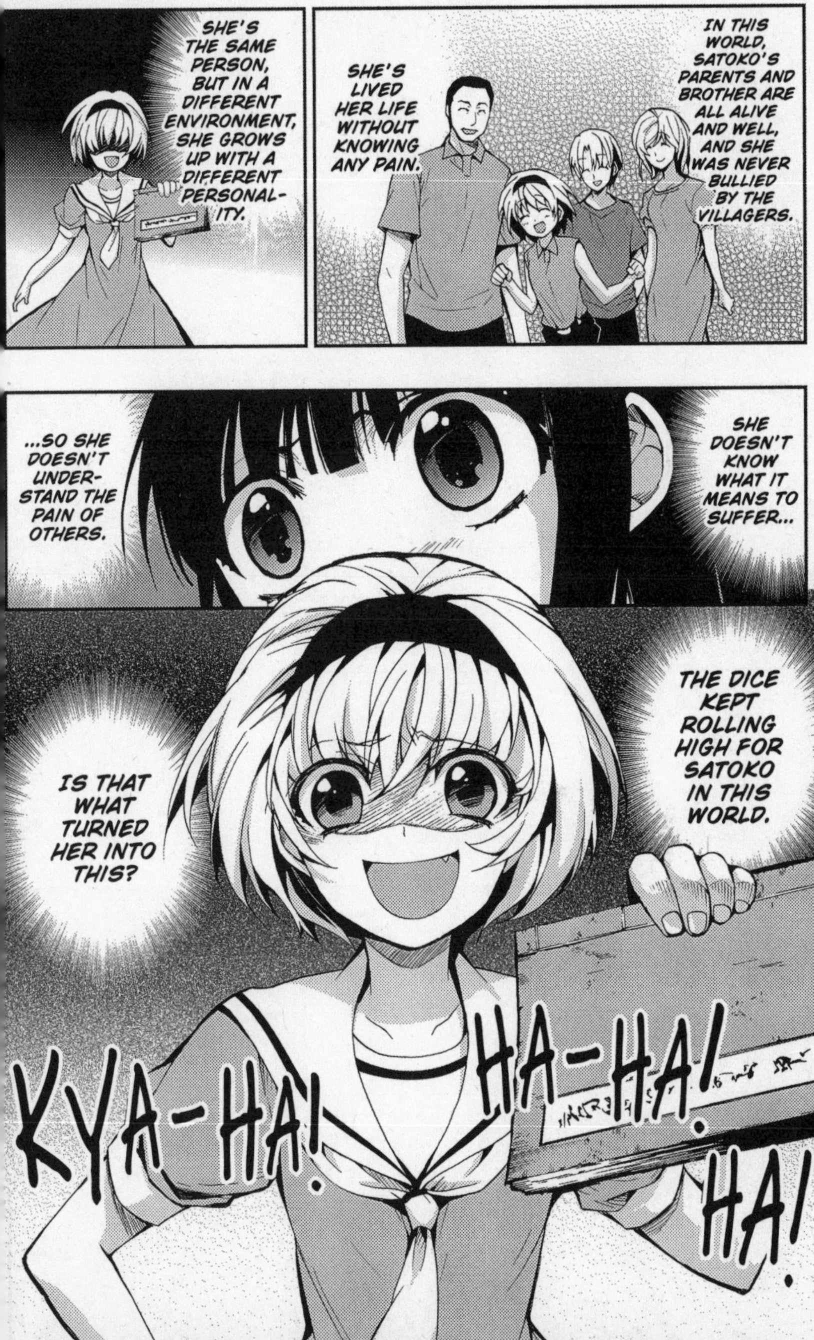
IN THIS WORLD, SATOKO'S PARENTS AND BROTHER ARE ALL ALIVE AND WELL, AND SHE WAS NEVER BULLIED BY THE VILLAGERS.
SHE'S LIVED HER LIFE WITHOUT KNOWING ANY PAIN.
SHE'S THE SAME PERSON, BUT IN A DIFFERENT ENVIRONMENT, SHE GROWS UP WITH A DIFFERENT PERSONALITY.
SHE DOESN'T KNOW WHAT IT MEANS TO SUFFER...
...SO SHE DOESN'T UNDERSTAND THE PAIN OF OTHERS.
THE DICE KEPT ROLLING HIGH FOR SATOKO IN THIS WORLD.
IS THAT WHAT TURNED HER INTO THIS?
KYA-HA! HA-HA! HA! HA!

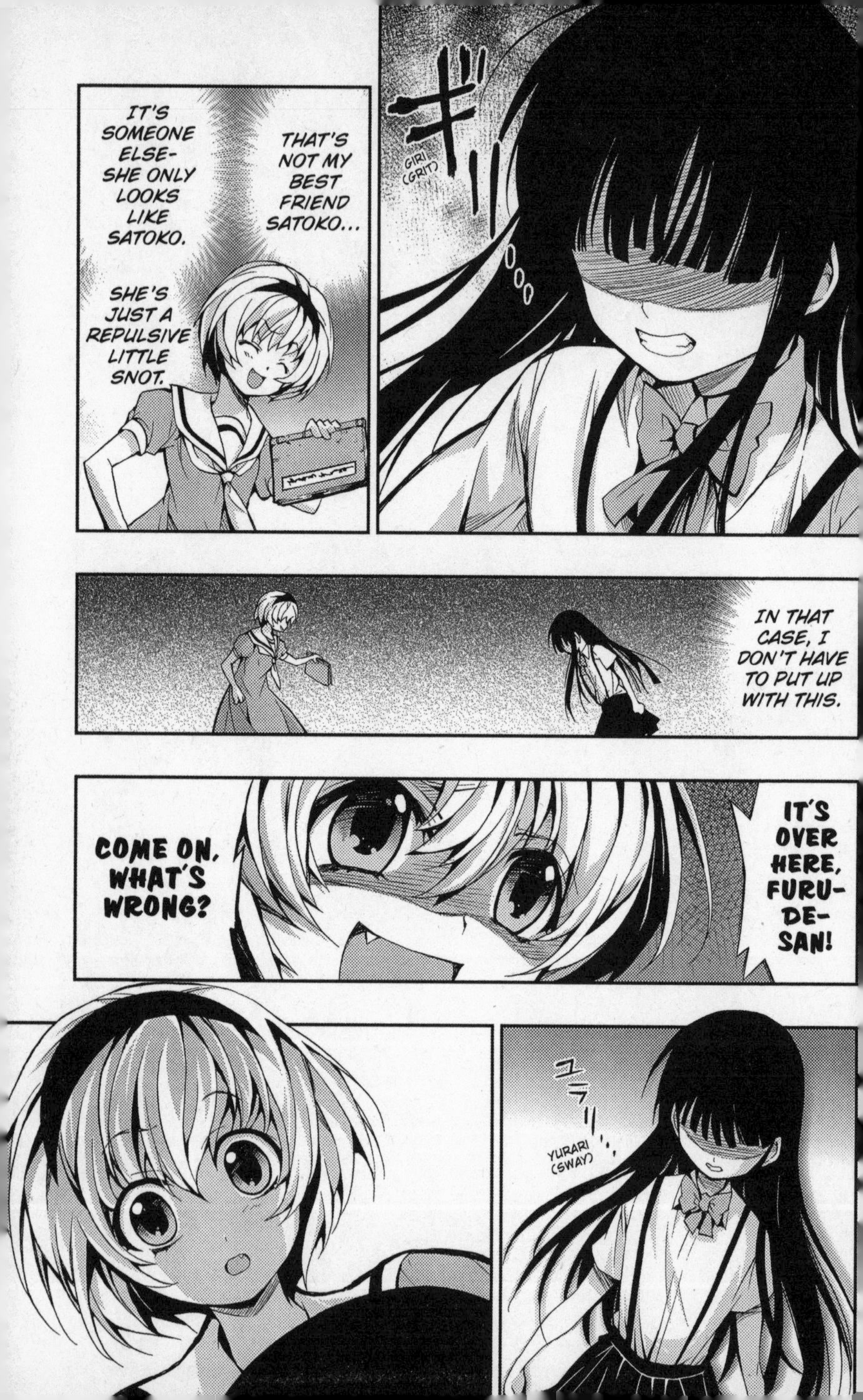
GIRI (GRIT)
THAT'S NOT MY BEST FRIEND SATOKO...
IT'S SOMEONE ELSE- SHE ONLY LOOKS LIKE SATOKO.
SHE'S JUST A REPULSIVE LITTLE SNOT.
IN THAT CASE, I DON'T HAVE TO PUT UP WITH THIS.
IT'S OVER HERE, FURU-DE-SAN!
COME ON, WHAT'S WRONG?
YURARI (SWAY)

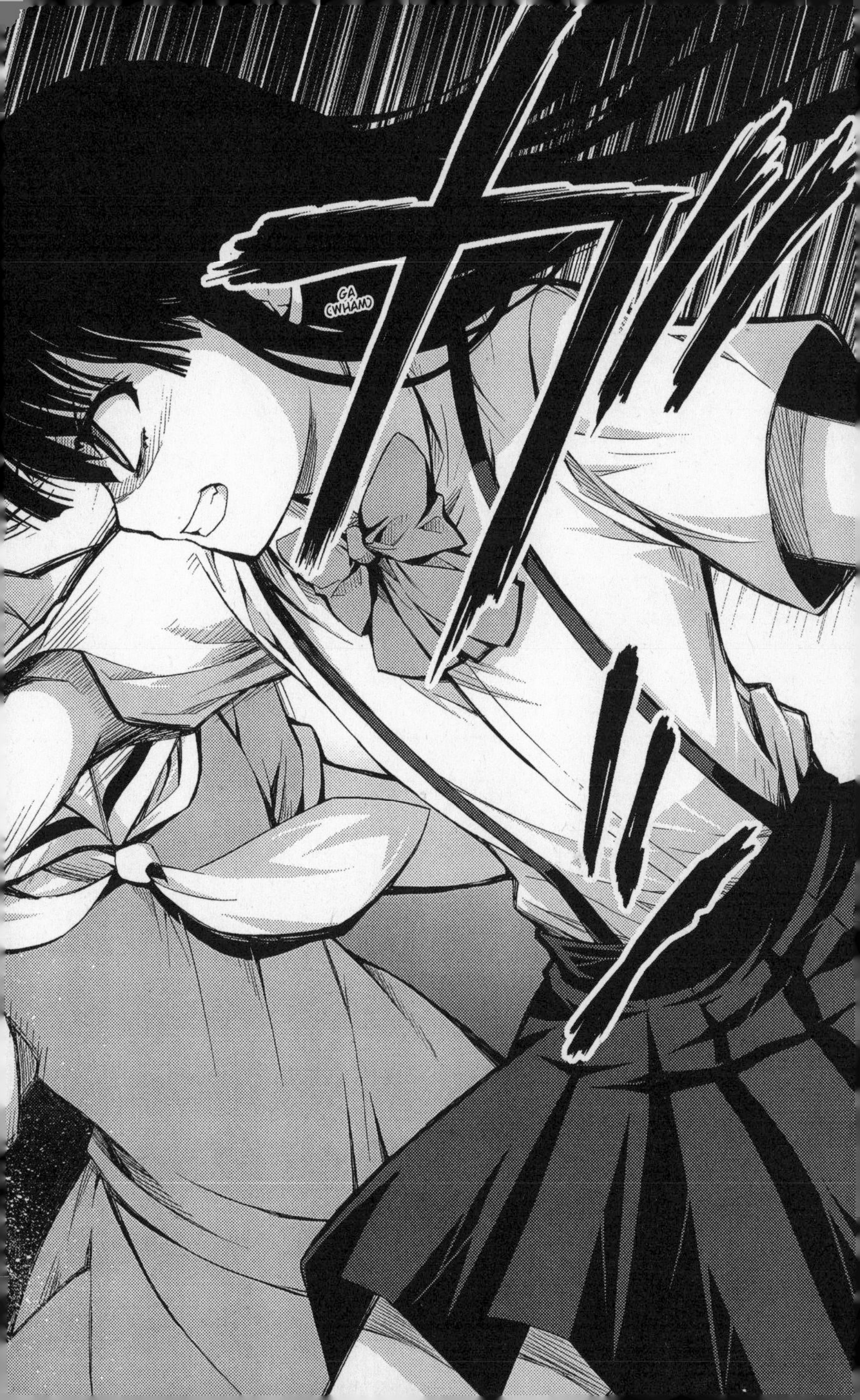
GA (WHAM)

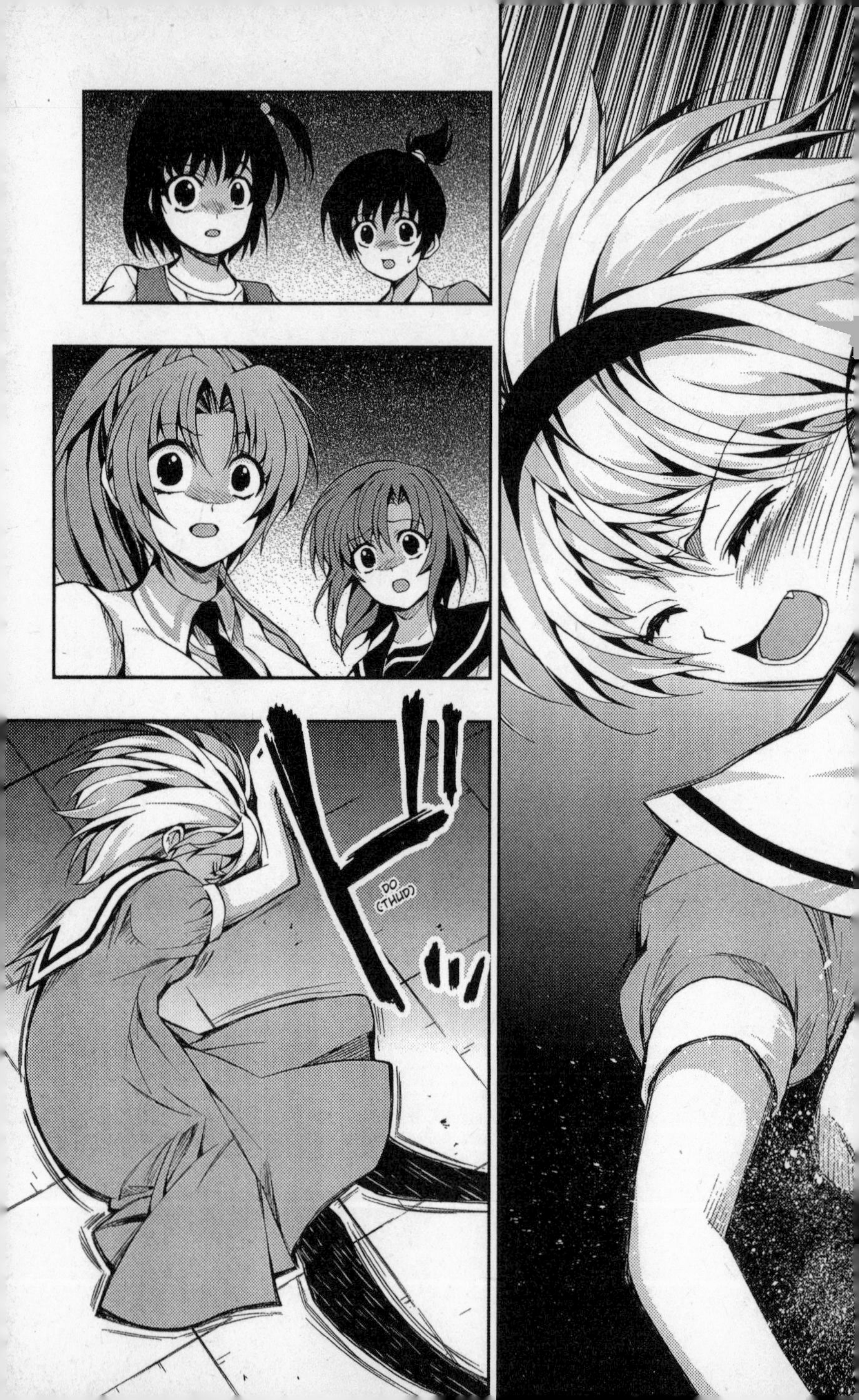
DO
(THUD)

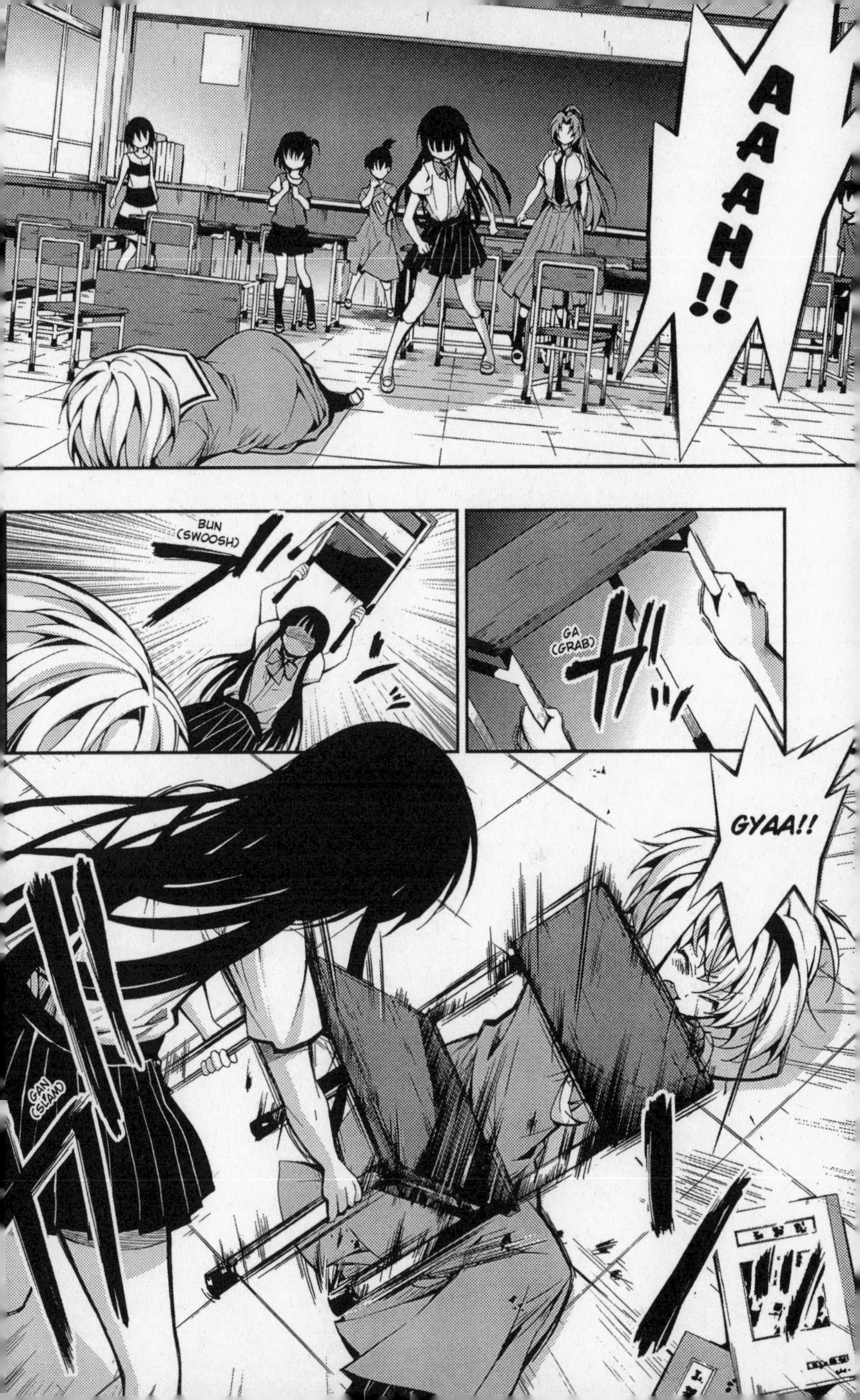
AAAAH!!
GA (GRAB)
BUN (SWOOSH)
GYAA!!
GAN (SLAM)

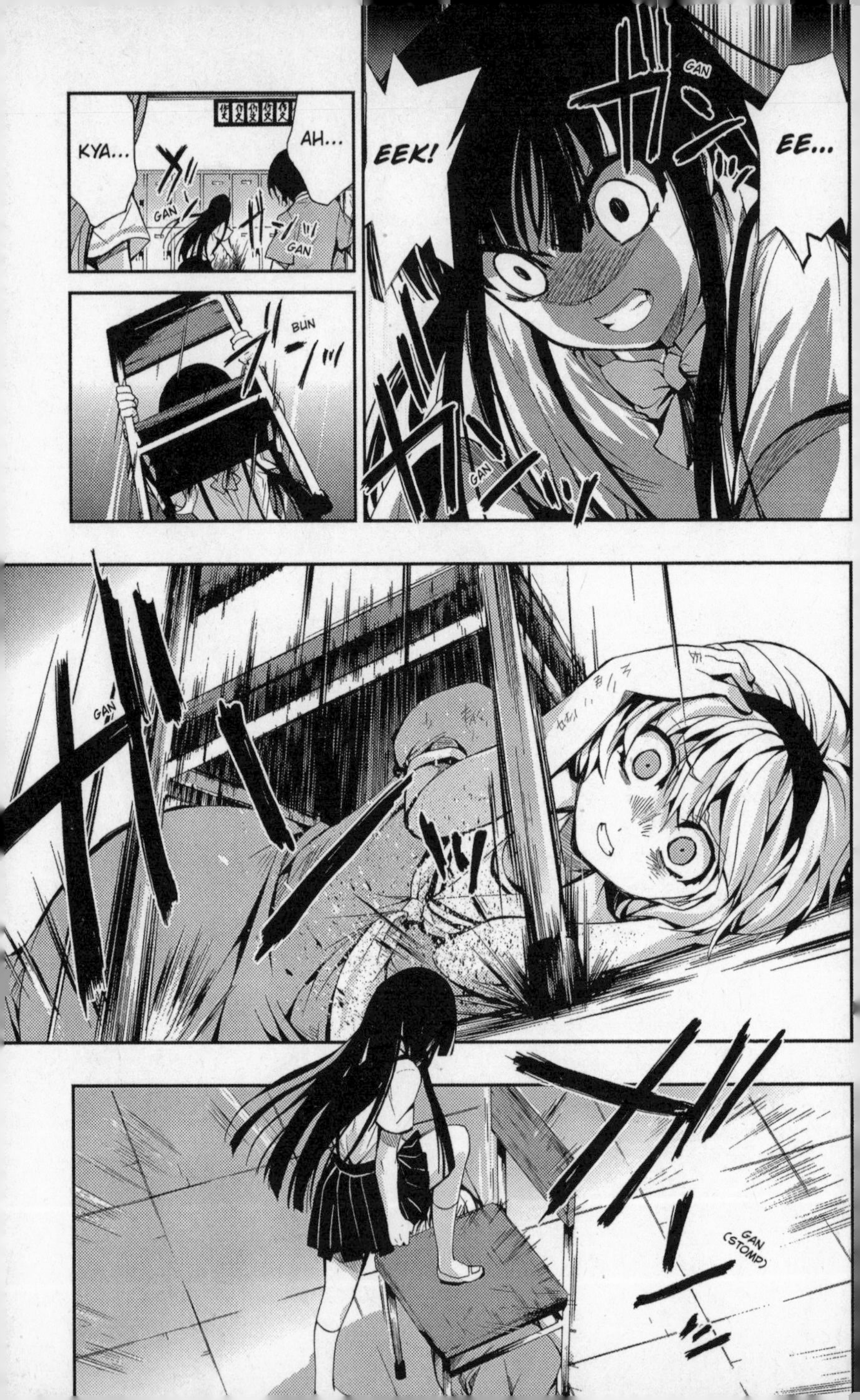
GAN
EE...
EEK!
GAN
AH...
KYA...
GAN
GAN
BUN
GAN
GAN (STOMP)

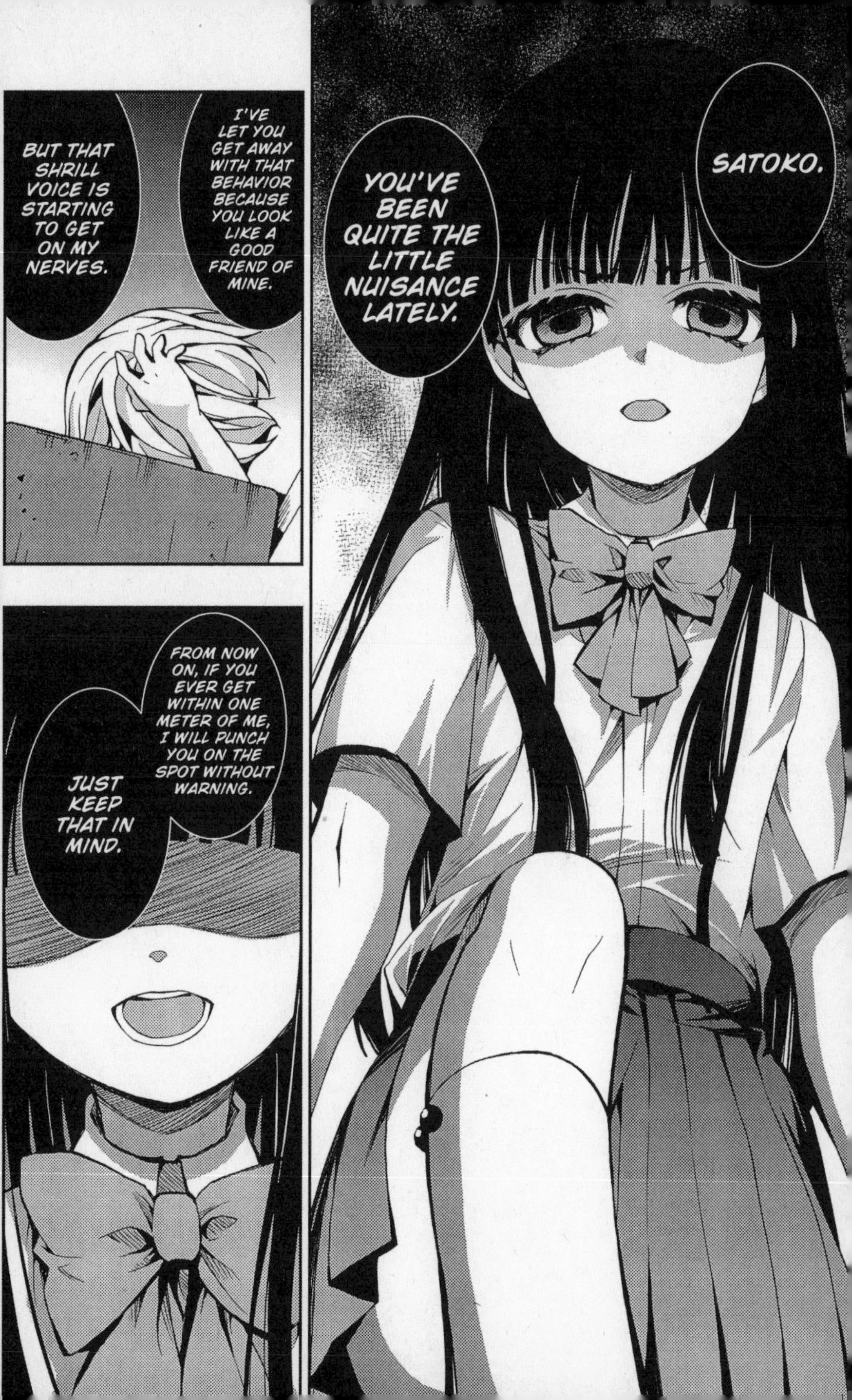
SATOKO.
YOU'VE BEEN QUITE THE LITTLE NUISANCE LATELY.
I'VE LET YOU GET AWAY WITH THAT BEHAVIOR BECAUSE YOU LOOK LIKE A GOOD FRIEND OF MINE.
BUT THAT SHRILL VOICE IS STARTING TO GET ON MY NERVES.
FROM NOW ON, IF YOU EVER GET WITHIN ONE METER OF ME, I WILL PUNCH YOU ON THE SPOT WITHOUT WARNING.
JUST KEEP THAT IN MIND.

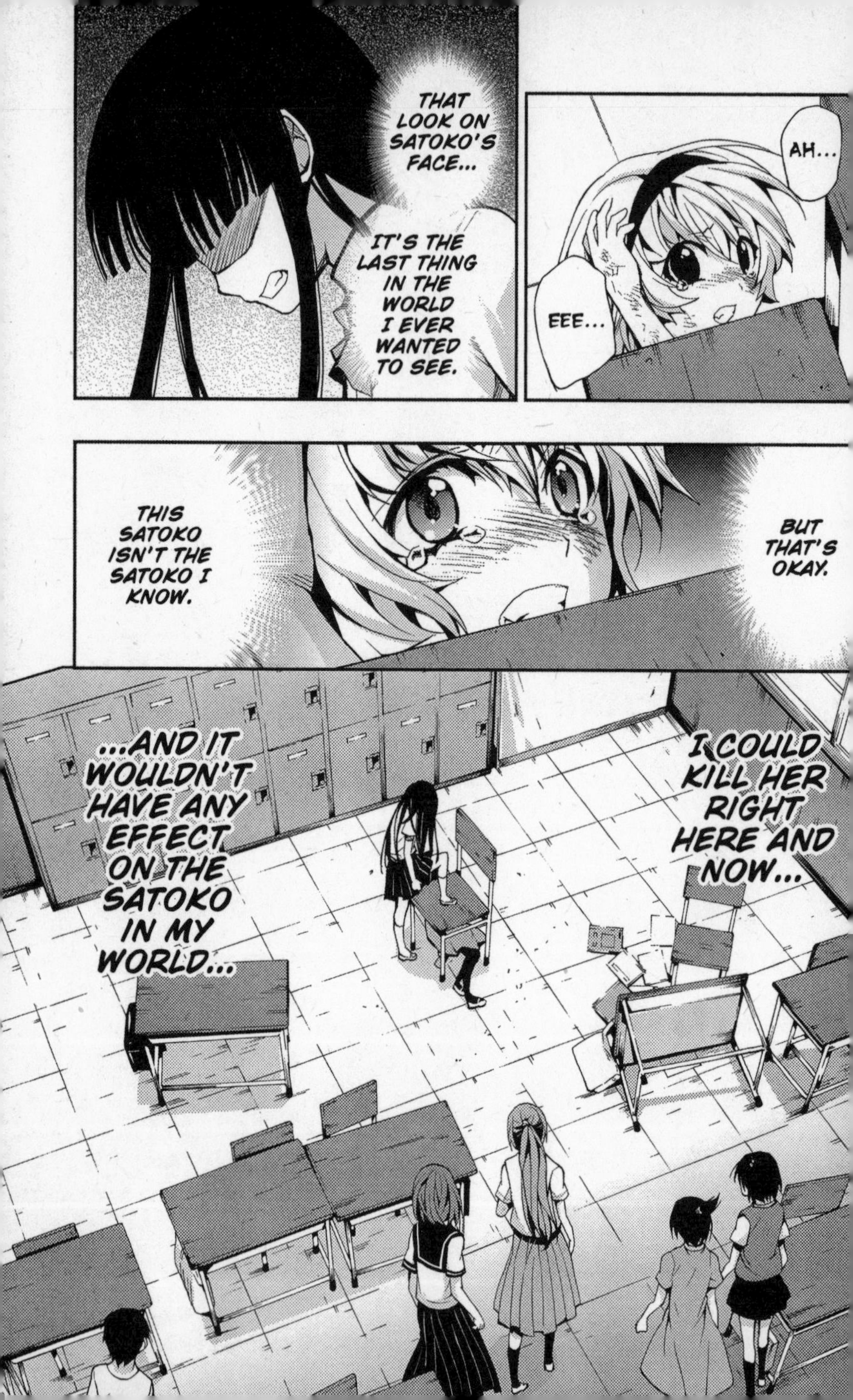
AH...
EEE...
THAT LOOK ON SATOKO'S FACE...
IT'S THE LAST THING IN THE WORLD I EVER WANTED TO SEE.
BUT THAT'S OKAY.
THIS SATOKO ISN'T THE SATOKO I KNOW.
I COULD KILL HER RIGHT HERE AND NOW...
...AND IT WOULDN'T HAVE ANY EFFECT ON THE SATOKO IN MY WORLD...

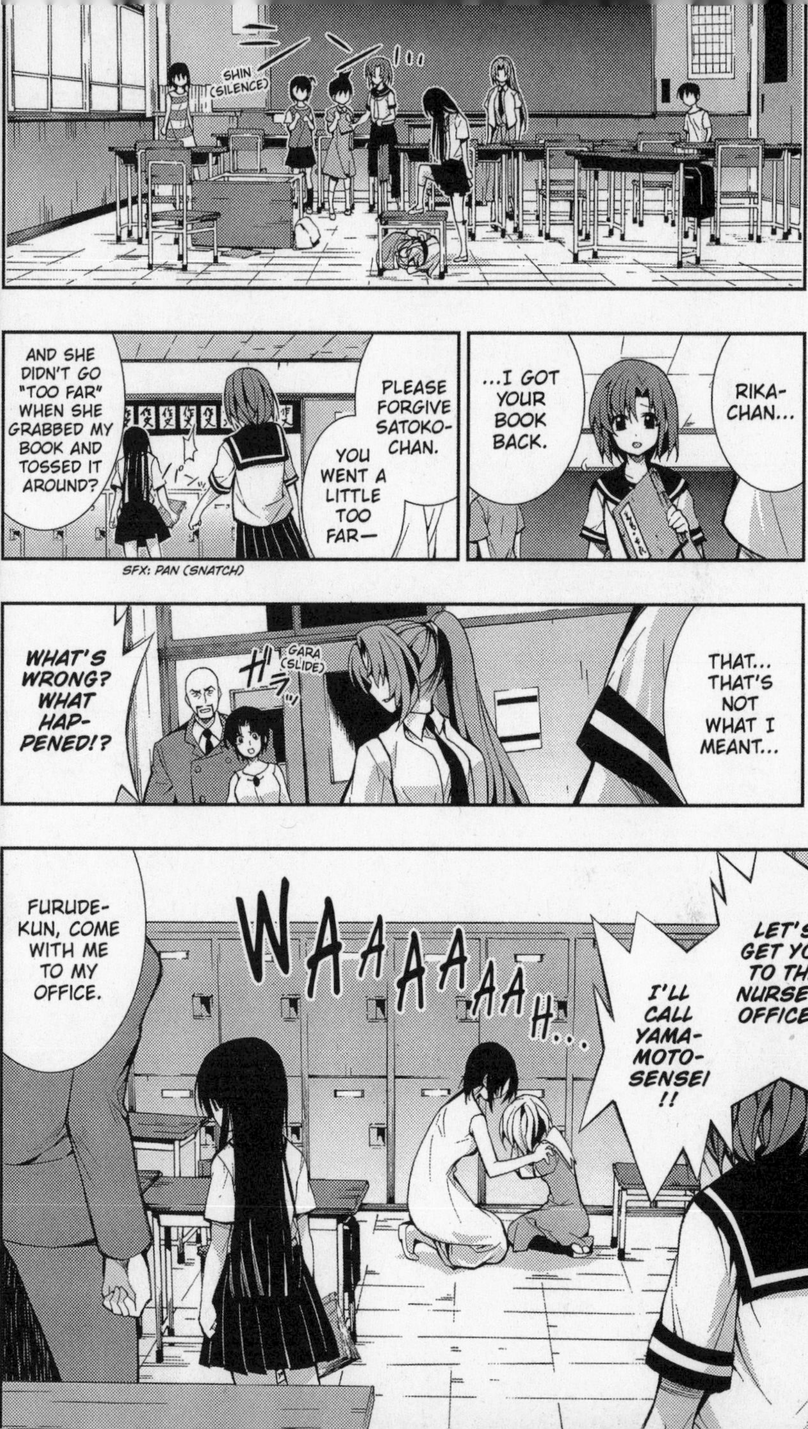
SHIN (SILENCE)
RIKA-CHAN...
...I GOT YOUR BOOK BACK.
PLEASE FORGIVE SATOKO-CHAN.
YOU WENT A LITTLE TOO FAR—
AND SHE DIDN'T GO "TOO FAR" WHEN SHE GRABBED MY BOOK AND TOSSED IT AROUND?
SFX: PAN (SNATCH)
THAT... THAT'S NOT WHAT I MEANT...
GARA (SLIDE)
WHAT'S WRONG? WHAT HAPPENED!?
LET'S GET YOU TO THE NURSE'S OFFICE!!
I'LL CALL YAMAMOTO-SENSEI!!
WAAAAAAAH...
FURUDE-KUN, COME WITH ME TO MY OFFICE.

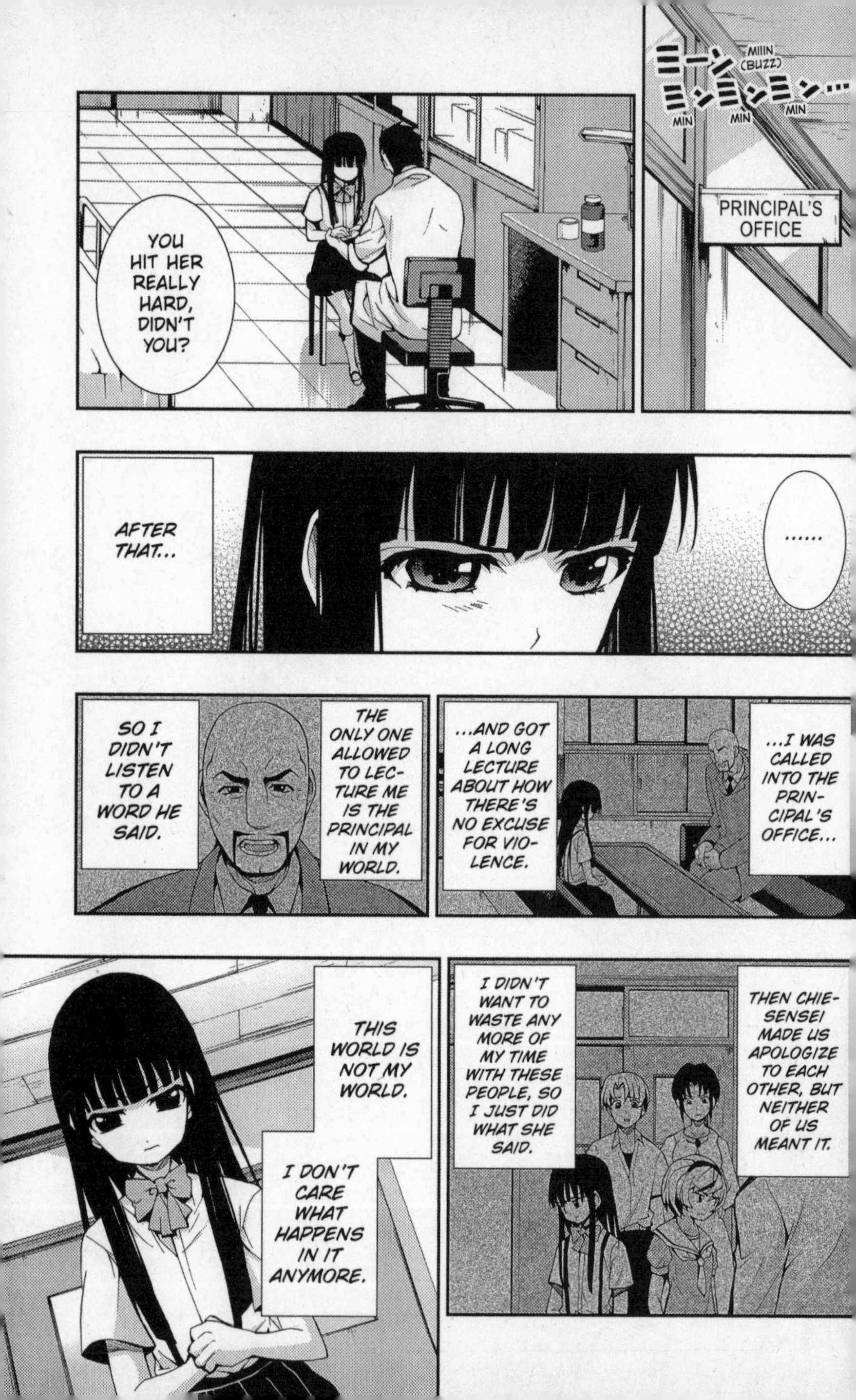
ミーン
MIIIN (BUZZ)
ミンミンミン…
MIN MIN MIN
PRINCIPAL'S OFFICE
YOU HIT HER REALLY HARD, DIDN'T YOU?
......
AFTER THAT...
...I WAS CALLED INTO THE PRIN-CIPAL'S OFFICE...
...AND GOT A LONG LECTURE ABOUT HOW THERE'S NO EXCUSE FOR VIO-LENCE.
THE ONLY ONE ALLOWED TO LEC-TURE ME IS THE PRINCIPAL IN MY WORLD.
SO I DIDN'T LISTEN TO A WORD HE SAID.
THEN CHIE-SENSEI MADE US APOLOGIZE TO EACH OTHER, BUT NEITHER OF US MEANT IT.
I DIDN'T WANT TO WASTE ANY MORE OF MY TIME WITH THESE PEOPLE, SO I JUST DID WHAT SHE SAID.
THIS WORLD IS NOT MY WORLD.
I DON'T CARE WHAT HAPPENS IN IT ANYMORE.

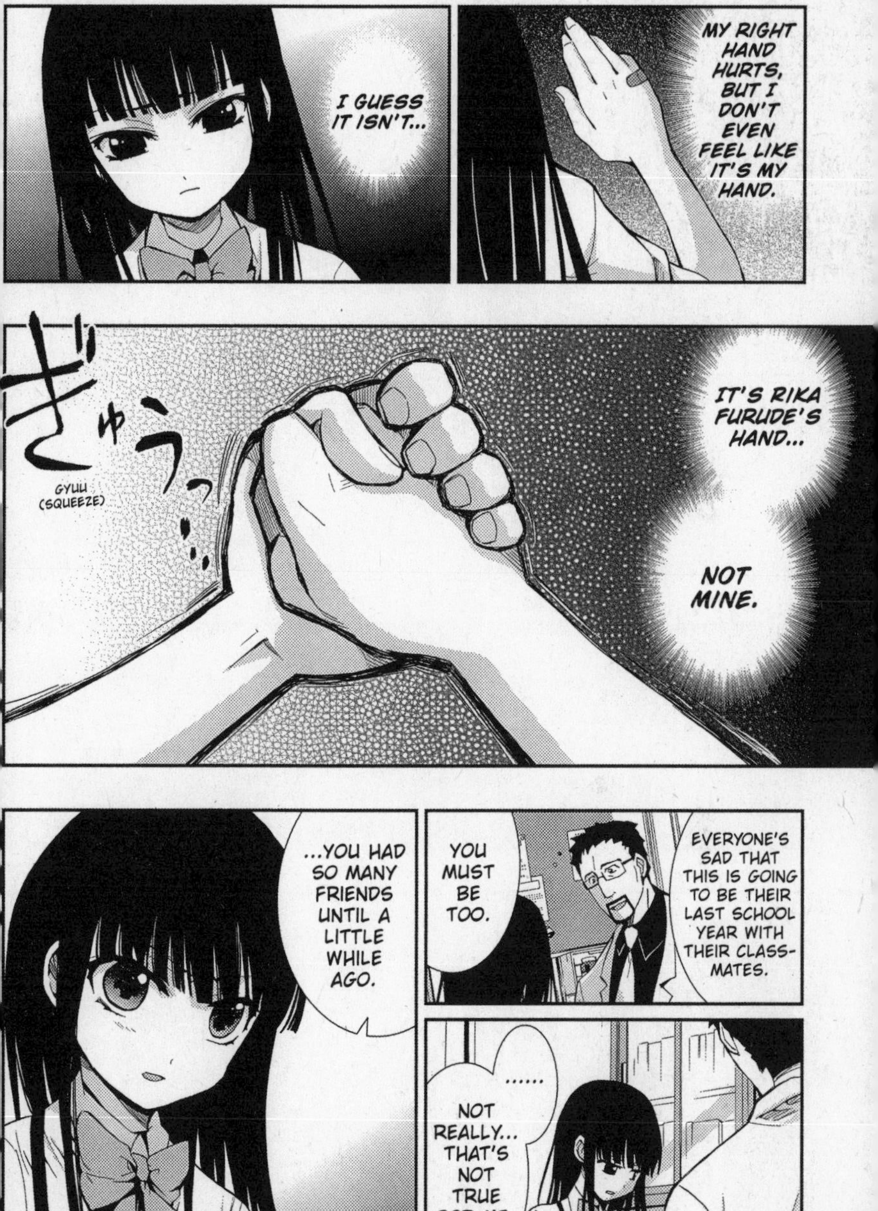
MY RIGHT HAND HURTS, BUT I DON'T EVEN FEEL LIKE IT'S MY HAND.
I GUESS IT ISN'T...
IT'S RIKA FURUDE'S HAND...
NOT MINE.
GYUU (SQUEEZE)
EVERYONE'S SAD THAT THIS IS GOING TO BE THEIR LAST SCHOOL YEAR WITH THEIR CLASSMATES.
YOU MUST BE TOO.
......
NOT REALLY... THAT'S NOT TRUE FOR ME.
...YOU HAD SO MANY FRIENDS UNTIL A LITTLE WHILE AGO.

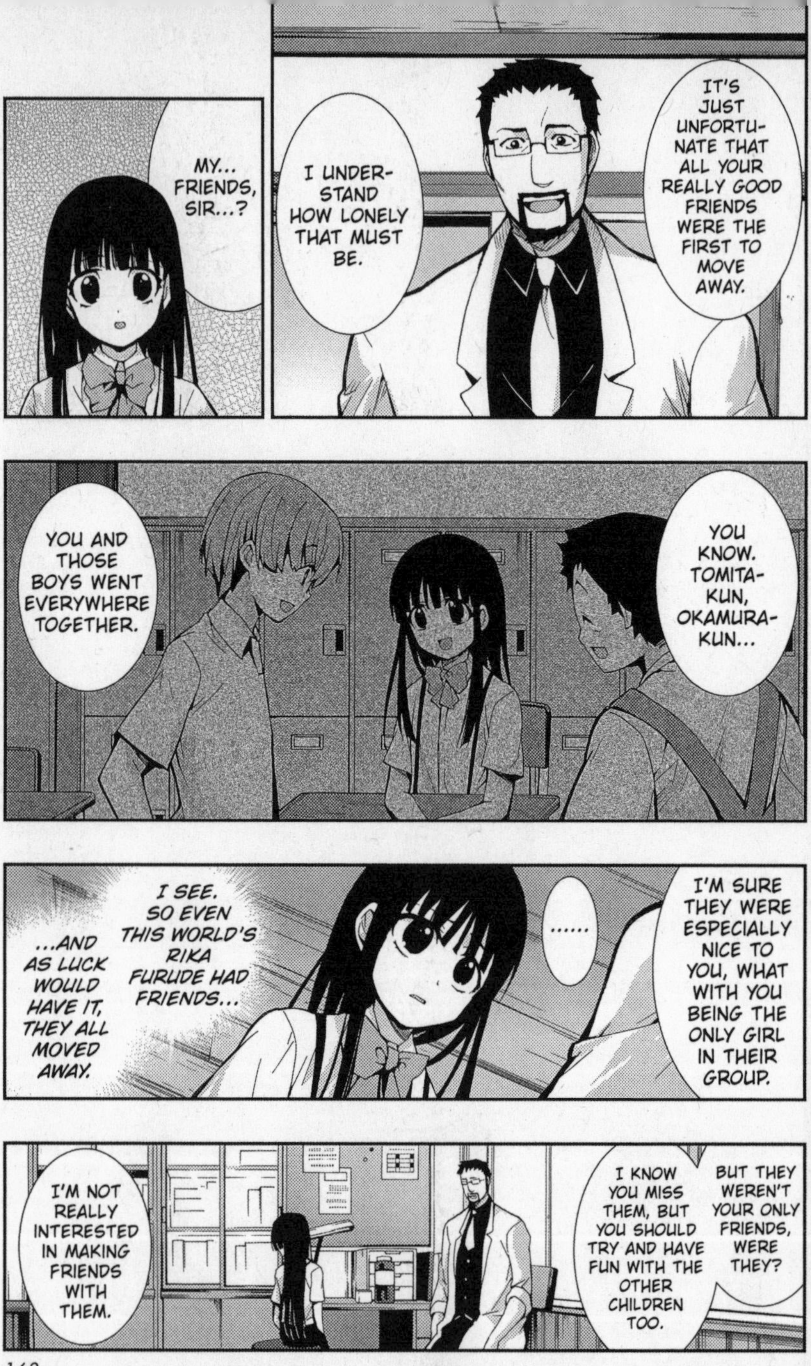
IT'S JUST UNFORTUNATE THAT ALL YOUR REALLY GOOD FRIENDS WERE THE FIRST TO MOVE AWAY.
I UNDERSTAND HOW LONELY THAT MUST BE.
MY... FRIENDS, SIR...?
YOU KNOW. TOMITA-KUN, OKAMURA-KUN...
YOU AND THOSE BOYS WENT EVERYWHERE TOGETHER.
I'M SURE THEY WERE ESPECIALLY NICE TO YOU, WHAT WITH YOU BEING THE ONLY GIRL IN THEIR GROUP.
......
I SEE. SO EVEN THIS WORLD'S RIKA FURUDE HAD FRIENDS...
...AND AS LUCK WOULD HAVE IT, THEY ALL MOVED AWAY.
BUT THEY WEREN'T YOUR ONLY FRIENDS, WERE THEY?
I KNOW YOU MISS THEM, BUT YOU SHOULD TRY AND HAVE FUN WITH THE OTHER CHILDREN TOO.
I'M NOT REALLY INTERESTED IN MAKING FRIENDS WITH THEM.

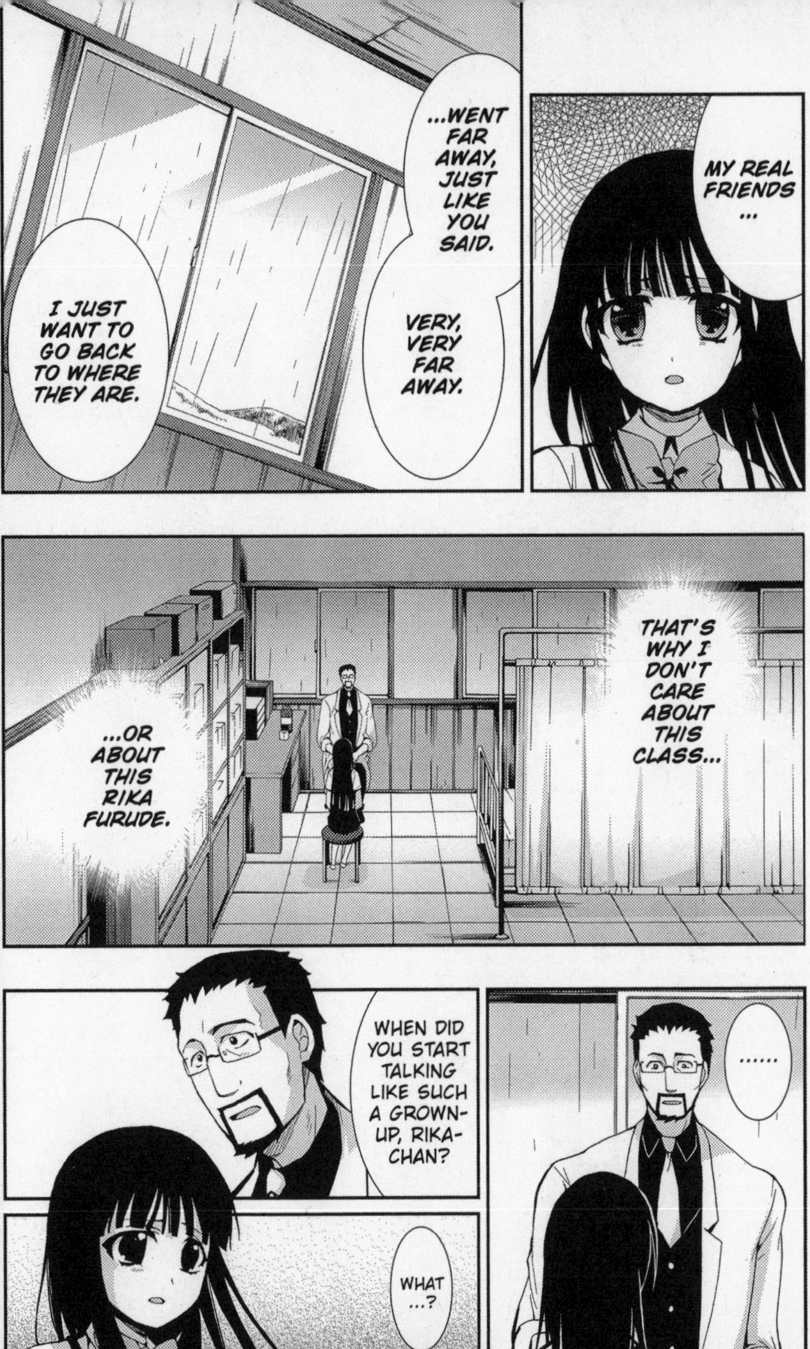
MY REAL FRIENDS...
...WENT FAR AWAY, JUST LIKE YOU SAID.
VERY, VERY FAR AWAY.
I JUST WANT TO GO BACK TO WHERE THEY ARE.
THAT'S WHY I DON'T CARE ABOUT THIS CLASS...
...OR ABOUT THIS RIKA FURUDE.
......
WHEN DID YOU START TALKING LIKE SUCH A GROWN-UP, RIKA-CHAN?
WHAT...?

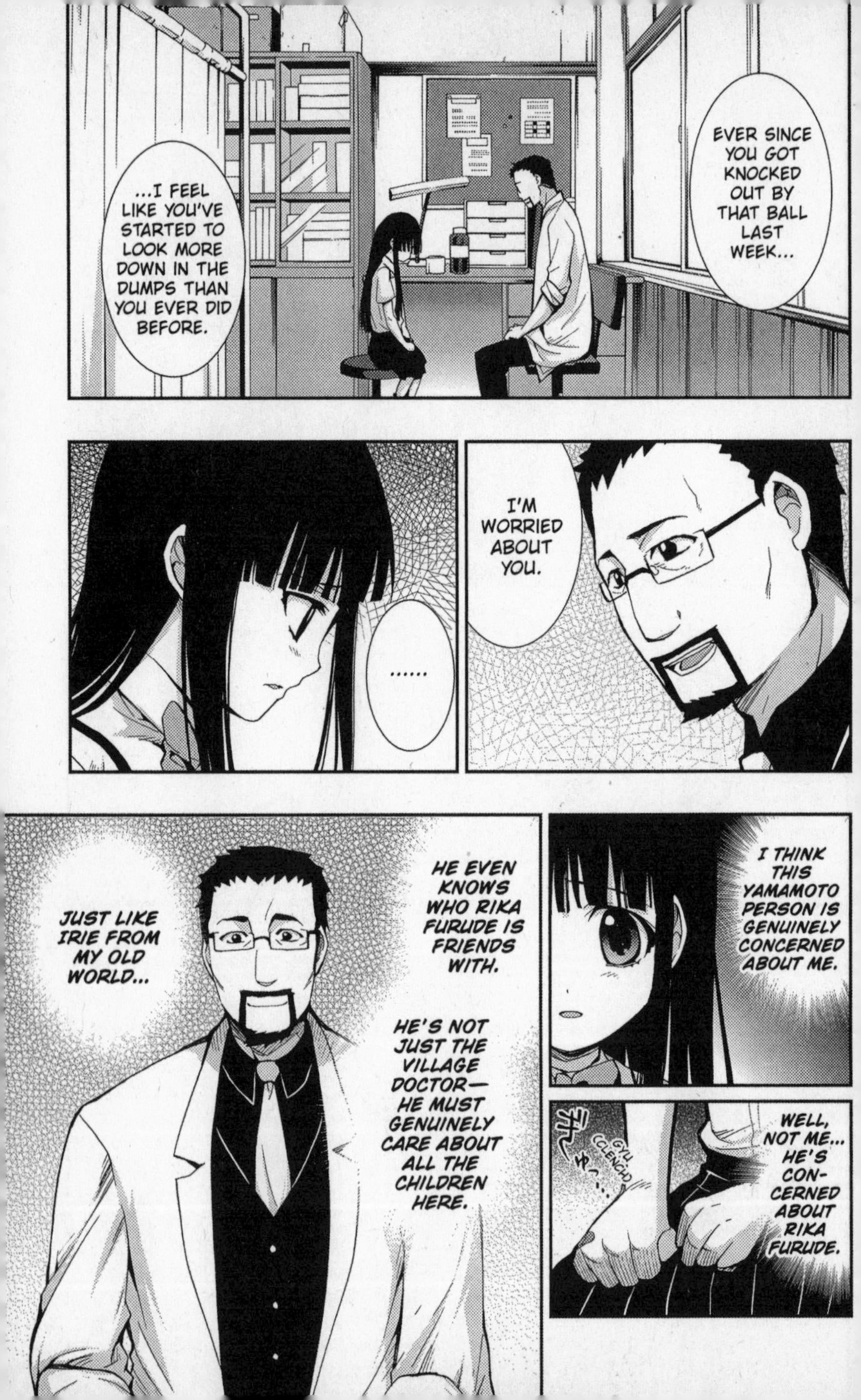
EVER SINCE YOU GOT KNOCKED OUT BY THAT BALL LAST WEEK...
...I FEEL LIKE YOU'VE STARTED TO LOOK MORE DOWN IN THE DUMPS THAN YOU EVER DID BEFORE.
I'M WORRIED ABOUT YOU.
......
I THINK THIS YAMAMOTO PERSON IS GENUINELY CONCERNED ABOUT ME.
GYU (CLENCH)
WELL, NOT ME... HE'S CON-CERNED ABOUT RIKA FURUDE.
HE EVEN KNOWS WHO RIKA FURUDE IS FRIENDS WITH.
JUST LIKE IRIE FROM MY OLD WORLD...
HE'S NOT JUST THE VILLAGE DOCTOR—HE MUST GENUINELY CARE ABOUT ALL THE CHILDREN HERE.

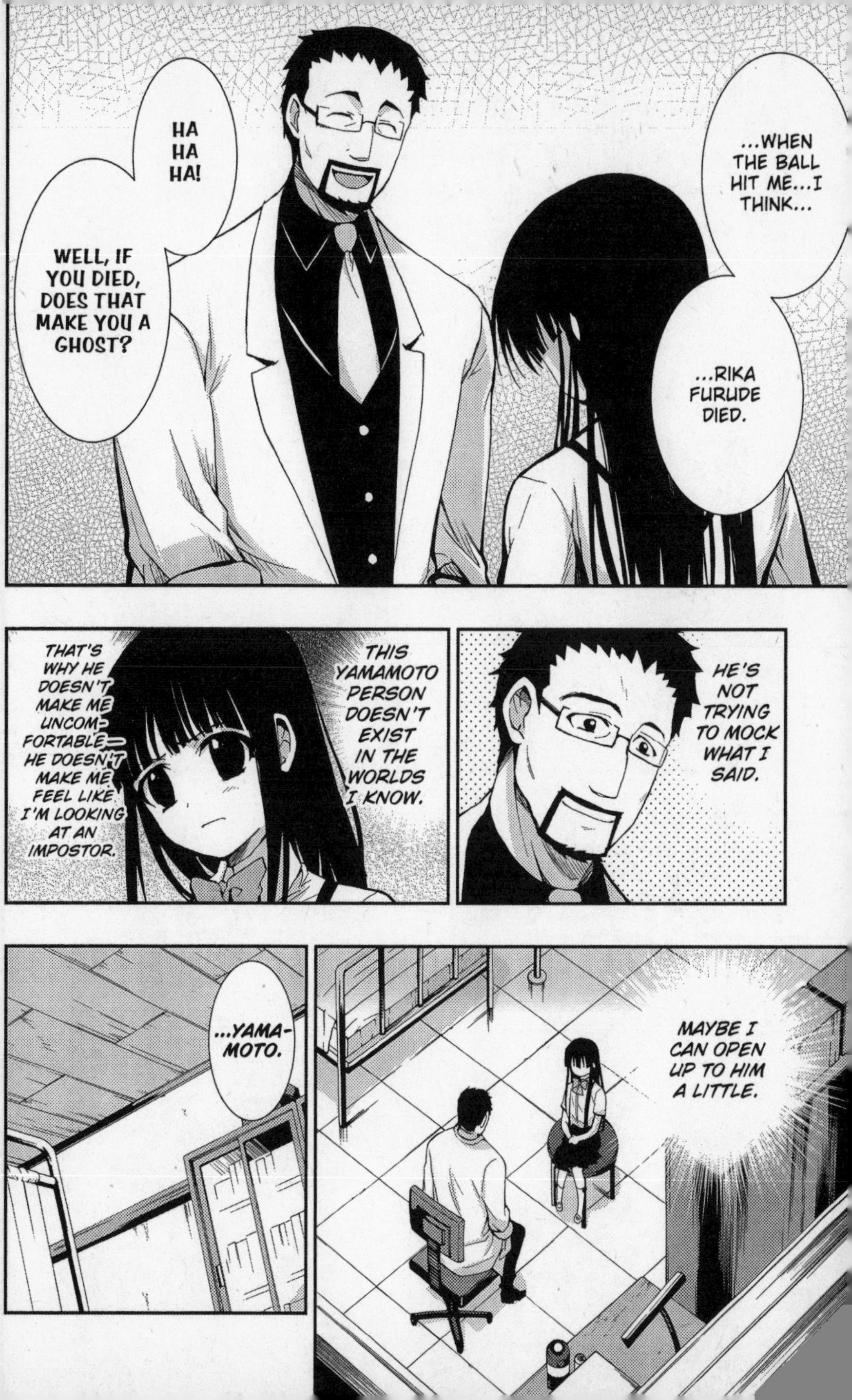
...WHEN THE BALL HIT ME...I THINK...
...RIKA FURUDE DIED.
HA HA HA!
WELL, IF YOU DIED, DOES THAT MAKE YOU A GHOST?
HE'S NOT TRYING TO MOCK WHAT I SAID.
THIS YAMAMOTO PERSON DOESN'T EXIST IN THE WORLDS I KNOW.
THAT'S WHY HE DOESN'T MAKE ME UNCOM-FORTABLE—HE DOESN'T MAKE ME FEEL LIKE I'M LOOKING AT AN IMPOSTOR.
MAYBE I CAN OPEN UP TO HIM A LITTLE.
...YAMA-MOTO.

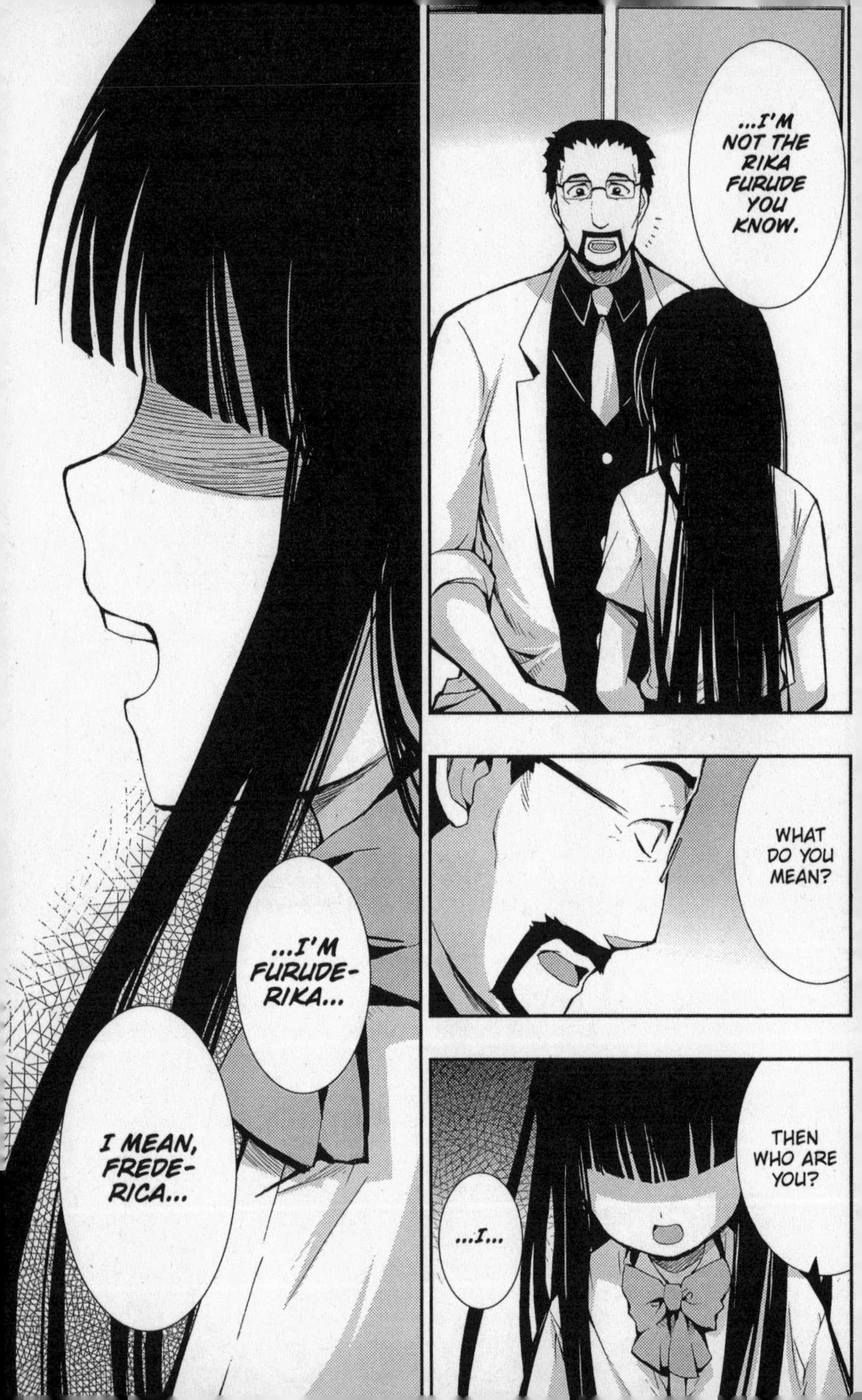
...I'M NOT THE RIKA FURUDE YOU KNOW.
WHAT DO YOU MEAN?
THEN WHO ARE YOU?
...I...
...I'M FURUDE-RIKA...
I MEAN, FREDE-RICA...

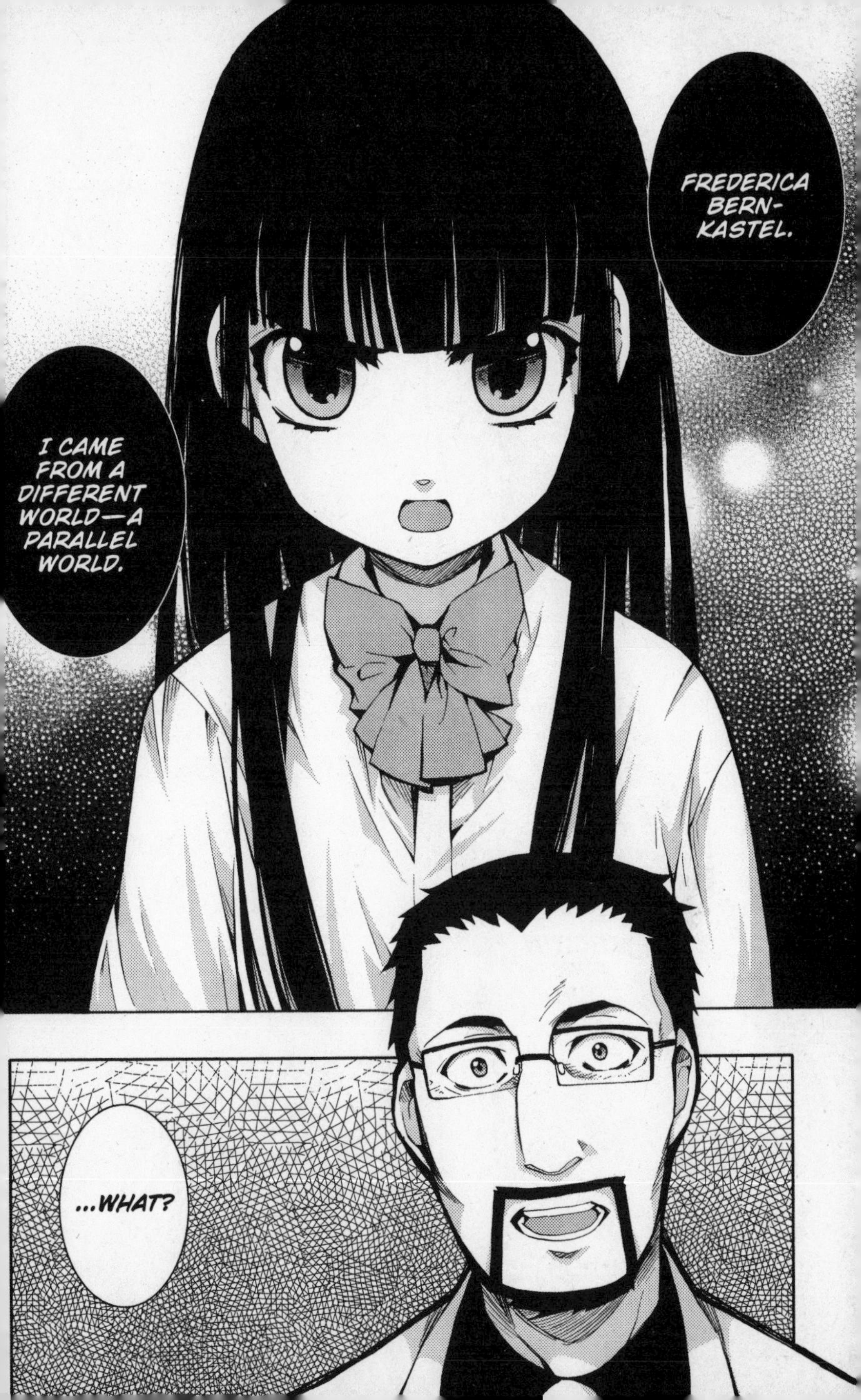
FREDERICA BERN-KASTEL.
I CAME FROM A DIFFERENT WORLD—A PARALLEL WORLD.
...WHAT?

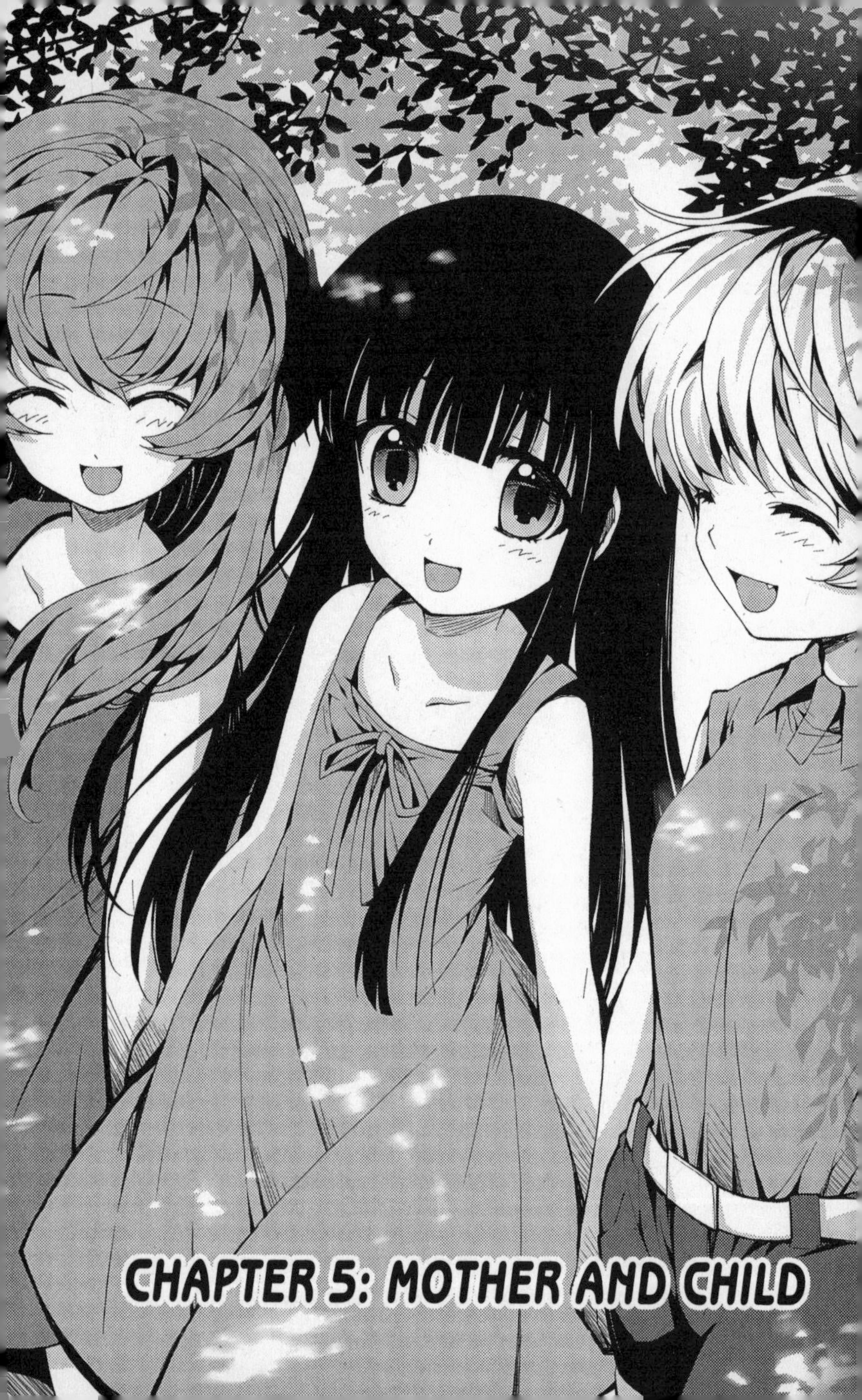
CHAPTER 5: MOTHER AND CHILD

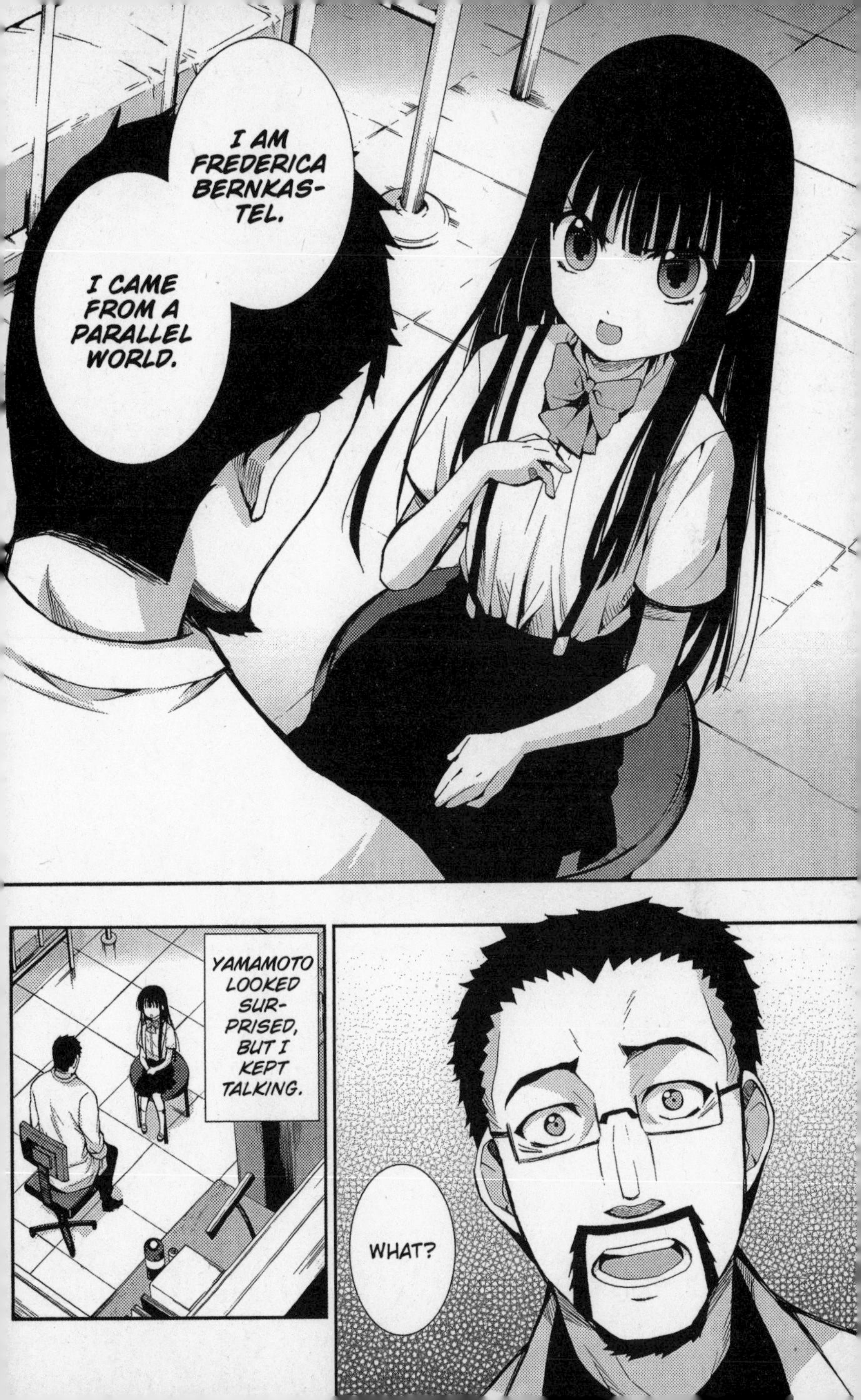
I AM FREDERICA BERNKAS-TEL.
I CAME FROM A PARALLEL WORLD.
WHAT?
YAMAMOTO LOOKED SUR-PRISED, BUT I KEPT TALKING.

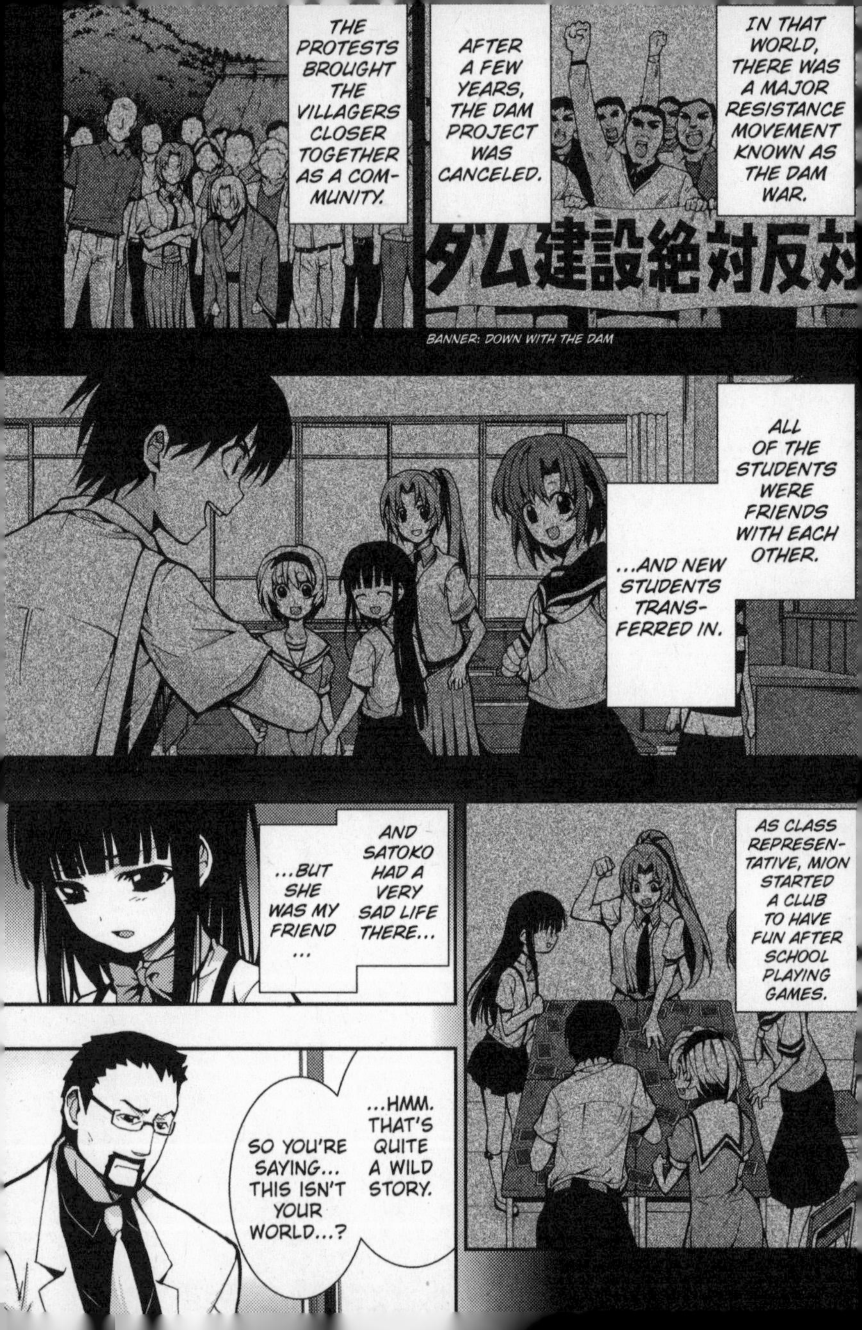
IN THAT WORLD, THERE WAS A MAJOR RESISTANCE MOVEMENT KNOWN AS THE DAM WAR.
AFTER A FEW YEARS, THE DAM PROJECT WAS CANCELED.
ダム建設絶対反対
THE PROTESTS BROUGHT THE VILLAGERS CLOSER TOGETHER AS A COM-MUNITY.
BANNER: DOWN WITH THE DAM
ALL OF THE STUDENTS WERE FRIENDS WITH EACH OTHER.
...AND NEW STUDENTS TRANS-FERRED IN.
AS CLASS REPRESEN-TATIVE, MION STARTED A CLUB TO HAVE FUN AFTER SCHOOL PLAYING GAMES.
AND SATOKO HAD A VERY SAD LIFE THERE...
...BUT SHE WAS MY FRIEND...
...HMM. THAT'S QUITE A WILD STORY.
SO YOU'RE SAYING... THIS ISN'T YOUR WORLD...?

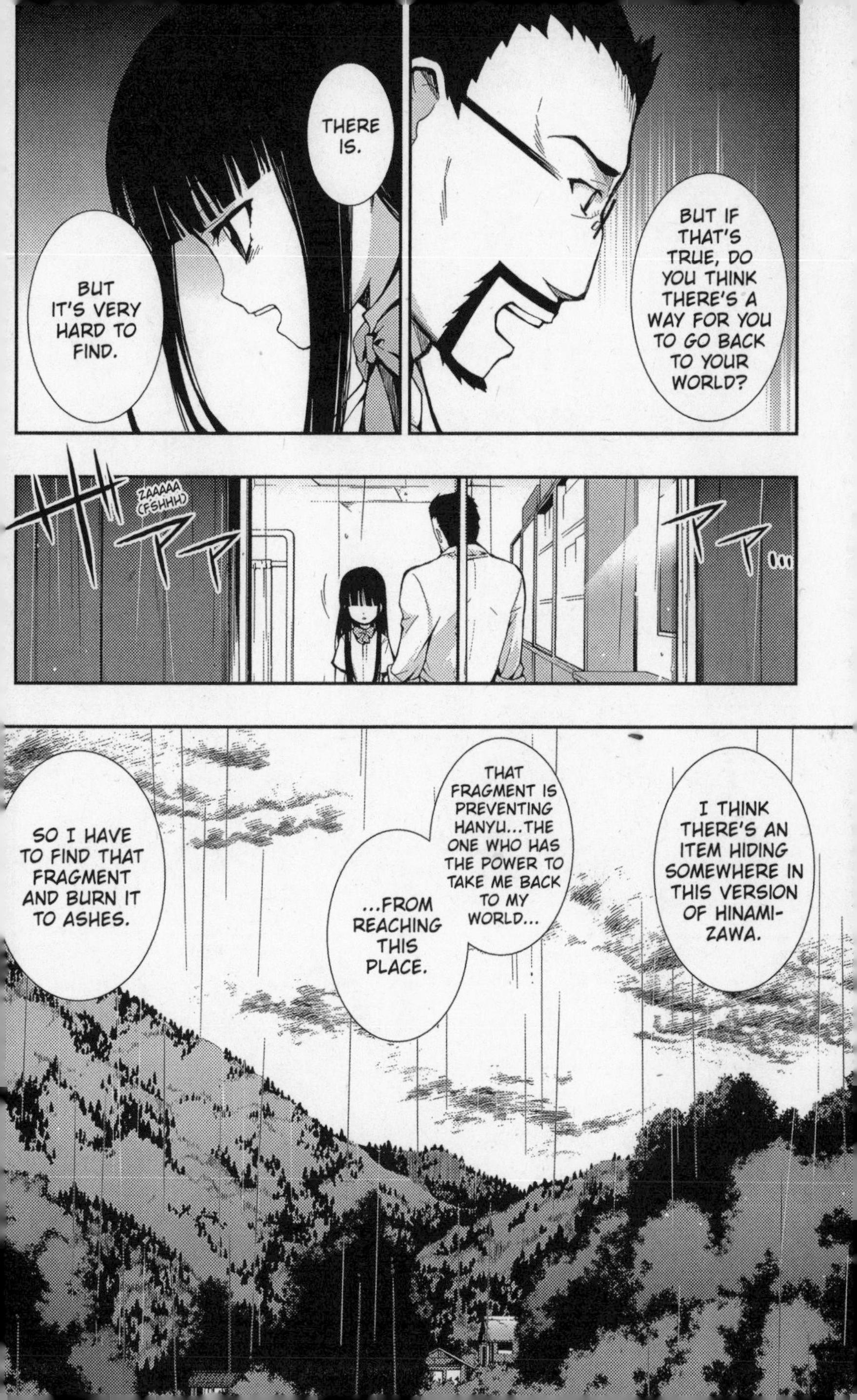
BUT IF THAT'S TRUE, DO YOU THINK THERE'S A WAY FOR YOU TO GO BACK TO YOUR WORLD?
THERE IS.
BUT IT'S VERY HARD TO FIND.
ZAAAAA (FSHHH)
I THINK THERE'S AN ITEM HIDING SOMEWHERE IN THIS VERSION OF HINAMI-ZAWA.
THAT FRAGMENT IS PREVENTING HANYU...THE ONE WHO HAS THE POWER TO TAKE ME BACK TO MY WORLD...
...FROM REACHING THIS PLACE.
SO I HAVE TO FIND THAT FRAGMENT AND BURN IT TO ASHES.

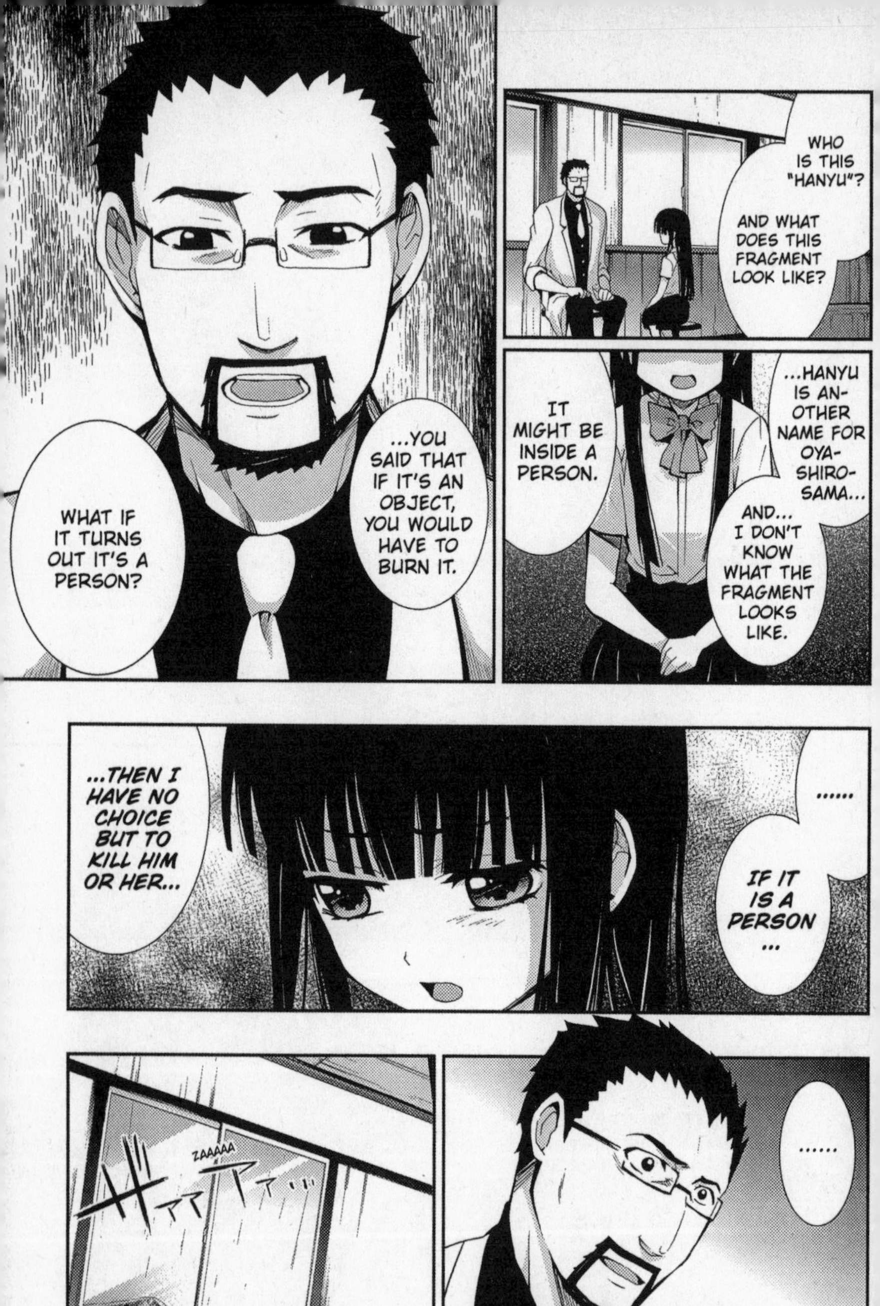
WHO IS THIS "HANYU"?
AND WHAT DOES THIS FRAGMENT LOOK LIKE?
...HANYU IS ANOTHER NAME FOR OYASHIRO-SAMA...
AND... I DON'T KNOW WHAT THE FRAGMENT LOOKS LIKE.
IT MIGHT BE INSIDE A PERSON.
...YOU SAID THAT IF IT'S AN OBJECT, YOU WOULD HAVE TO BURN IT.
WHAT IF IT TURNS OUT IT'S A PERSON?
......
IF IT IS A PERSON...
...THEN I HAVE NO CHOICE BUT TO KILL HIM OR HER...
......
ZAAAAA

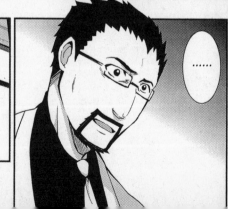

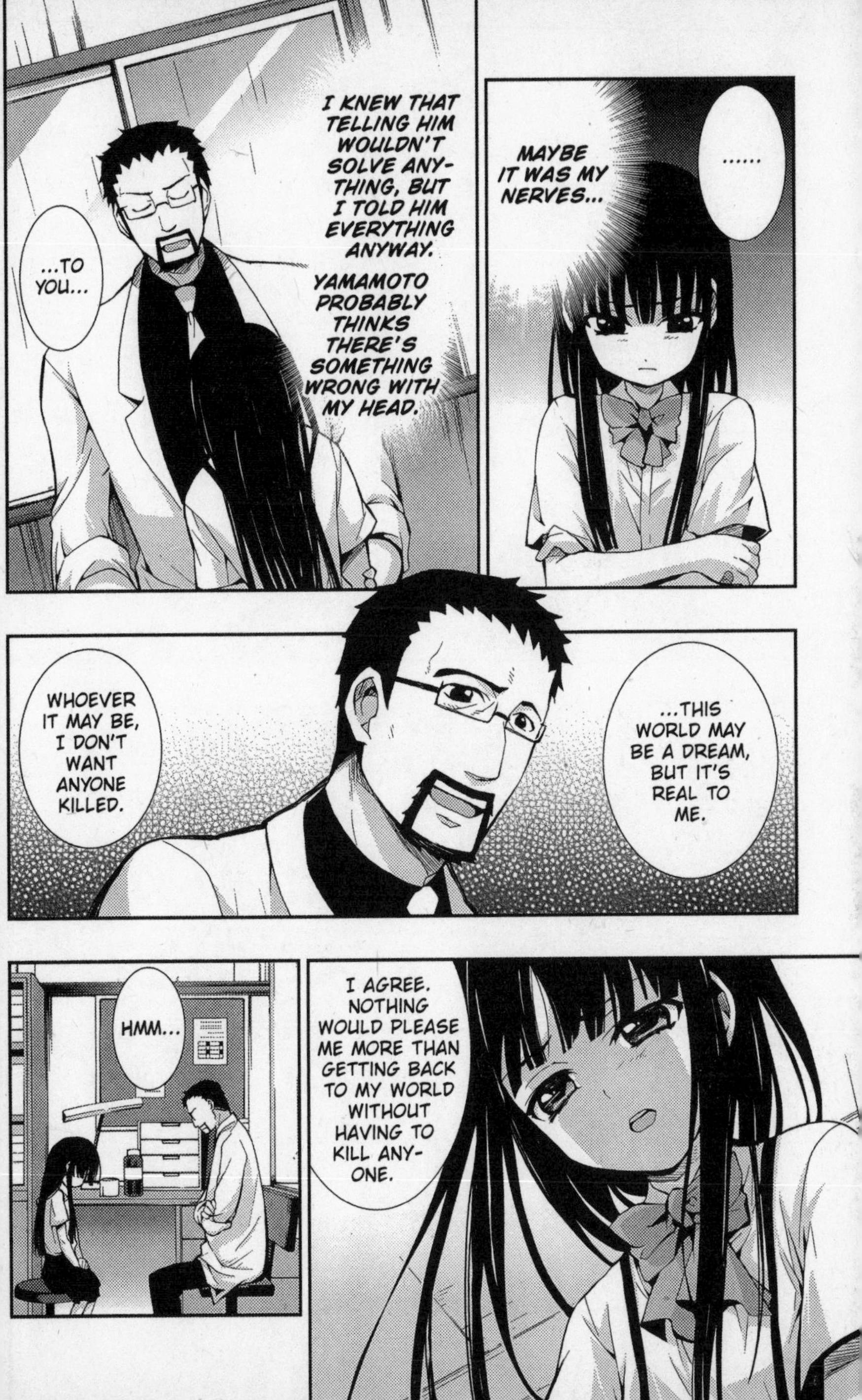
......
MAYBE IT WAS MY NERVES...
I KNEW THAT TELLING HIM WOULDN'T SOLVE ANY-THING, BUT I TOLD HIM EVERYTHING ANYWAY.
YAMAMOTO PROBABLY THINKS THERE'S SOMETHING WRONG WITH MY HEAD.
...TO YOU...
...THIS WORLD MAY BE A DREAM, BUT IT'S REAL TO ME.
WHOEVER IT MAY BE, I DON'T WANT ANYONE KILLED.
I AGREE. NOTHING WOULD PLEASE ME MORE THAN GETTING BACK TO MY WORLD WITHOUT HAVING TO KILL ANY-ONE.
HMM...

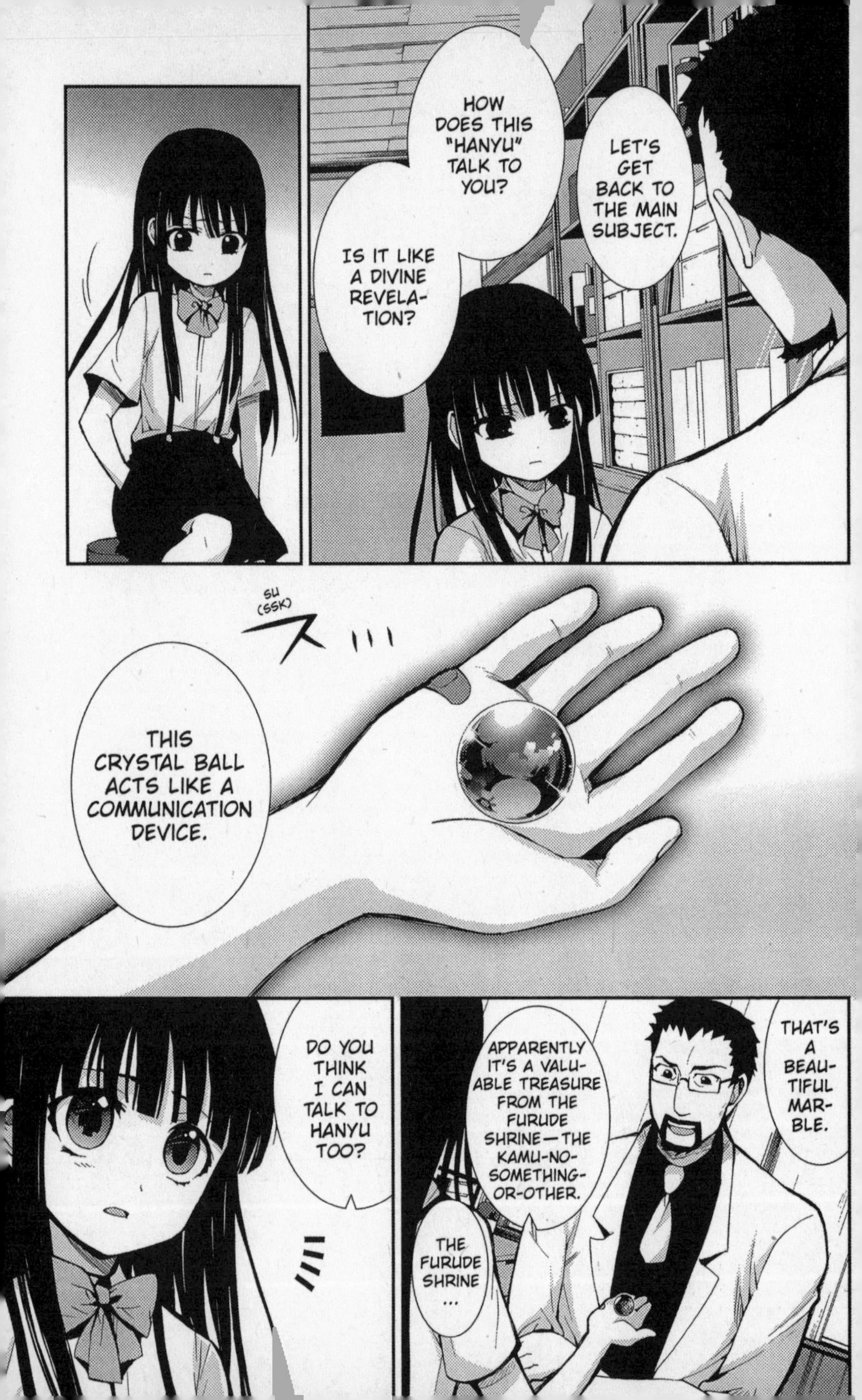
LET'S GET BACK TO THE MAIN SUBJECT.
HOW DOES THIS "HANYU" TALK TO YOU?
IS IT LIKE A DIVINE REVELATION?
SU (SSK)
THIS CRYSTAL BALL ACTS LIKE A COMMUNICATION DEVICE.
THAT'S A BEAUTIFUL MARBLE.
APPARENTLY IT'S A VALUABLE TREASURE FROM THE FURUDE SHRINE—THE KAMU-NO-SOMETHING-OR-OTHER.
THE FURUDE SHRINE...
DO YOU THINK I CAN TALK TO HANYU TOO?

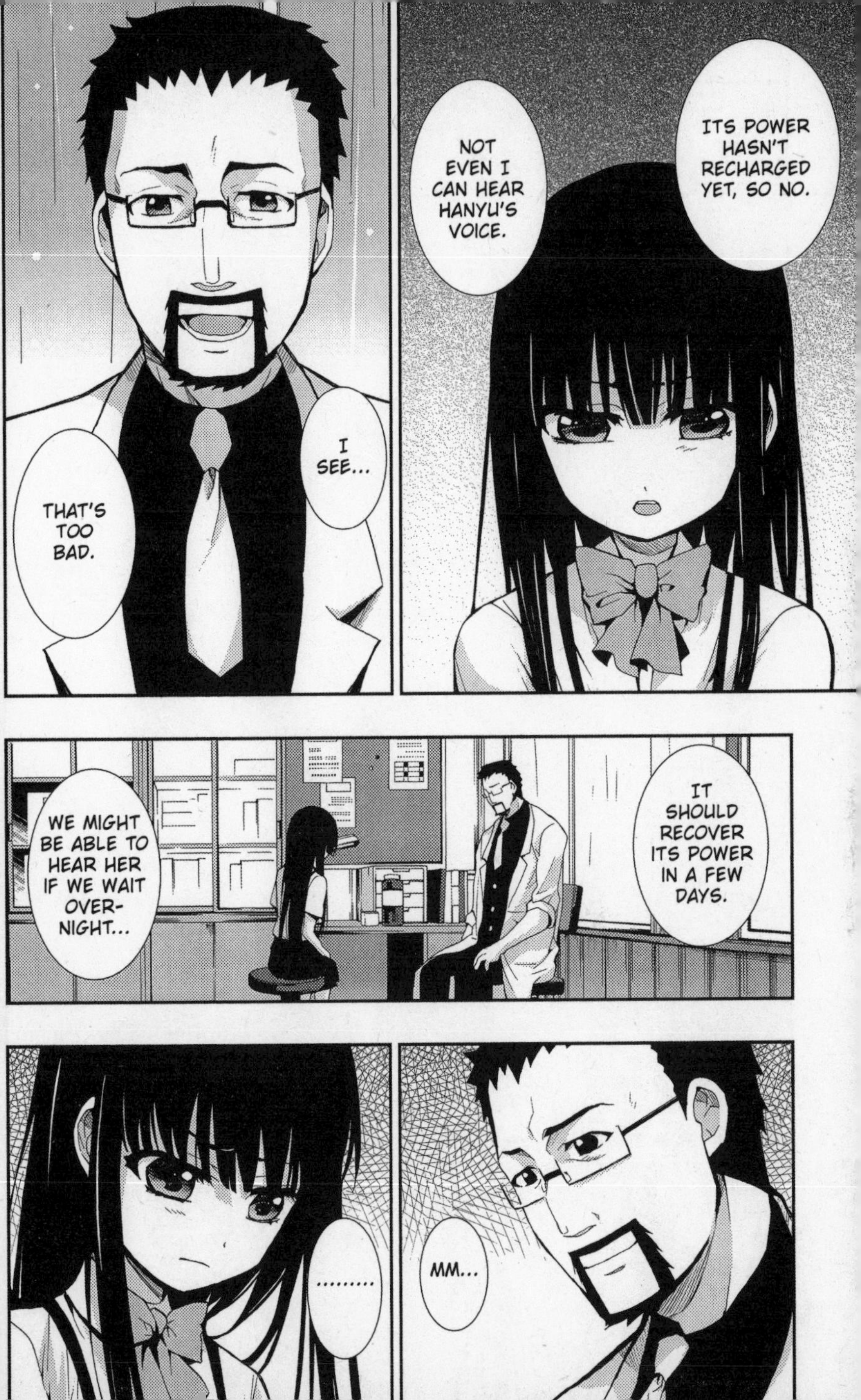
ITS POWER HASN'T RECHARGED YET, SO NO.
NOT EVEN I CAN HEAR HANYU'S VOICE.
I SEE...
THAT'S TOO BAD.
IT SHOULD RECOVER ITS POWER IN A FEW DAYS.
WE MIGHT BE ABLE TO HEAR HER IF WE WAIT OVER-NIGHT...
MM...
....

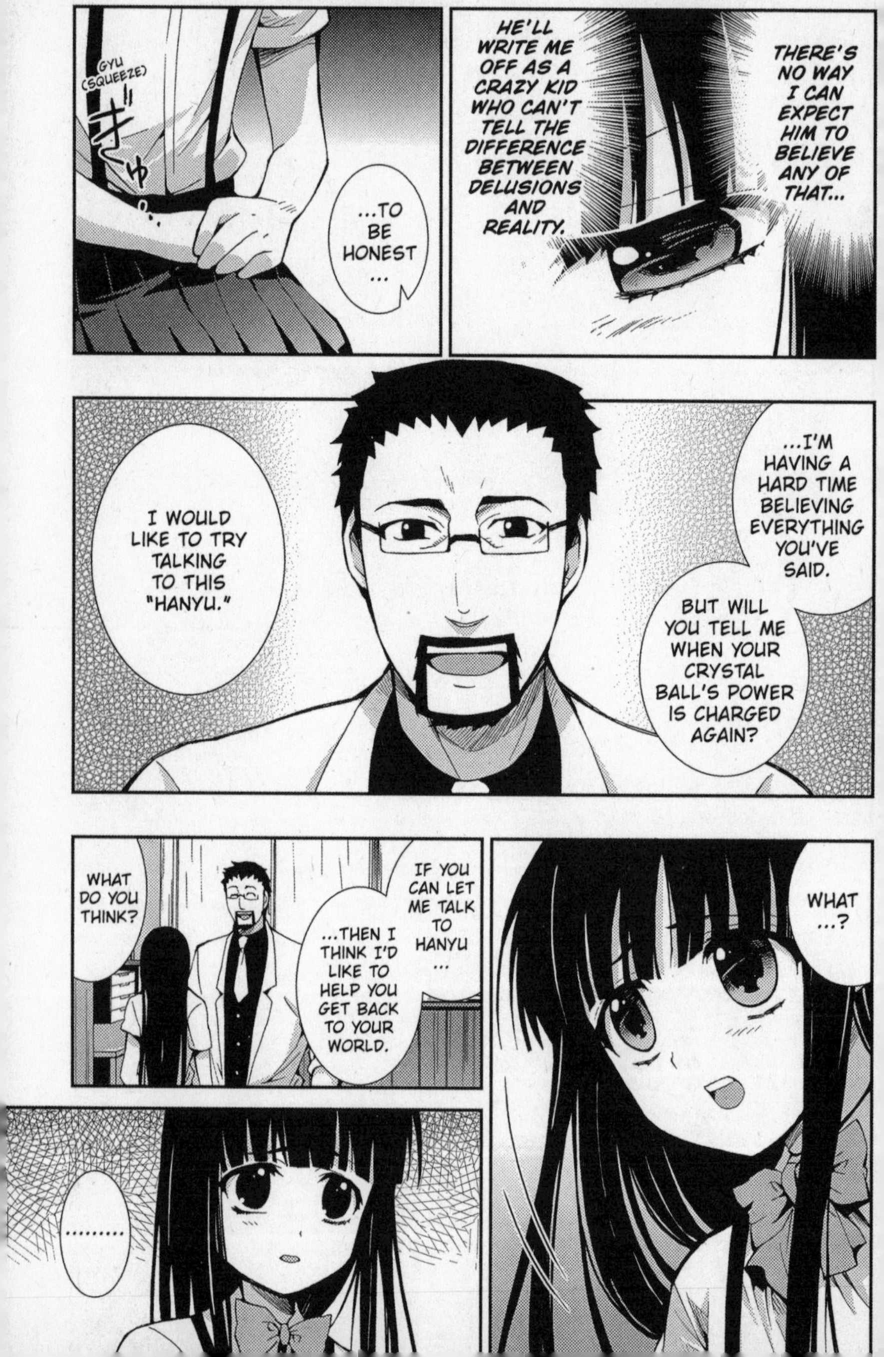
THERE'S NO WAY I CAN EXPECT HIM TO BELIEVE ANY OF THAT...
HE'LL WRITE ME OFF AS A CRAZY KID WHO CAN'T TELL THE DIFFERENCE BETWEEN DELUSIONS AND REALITY.
GYU (SQUEEZE)
ぎゅ
...TO BE HONEST ...
...I'M HAVING A HARD TIME BELIEVING EVERYTHING YOU'VE SAID.
BUT WILL YOU TELL ME WHEN YOUR CRYSTAL BALL'S POWER IS CHARGED AGAIN?
I WOULD LIKE TO TRY TALKING TO THIS "HANYU."
WHAT ...?
IF YOU CAN LET ME TALK TO HANYU ...
...THEN I THINK I'D LIKE TO HELP YOU GET BACK TO YOUR WORLD.
WHAT DO YOU THINK?
....

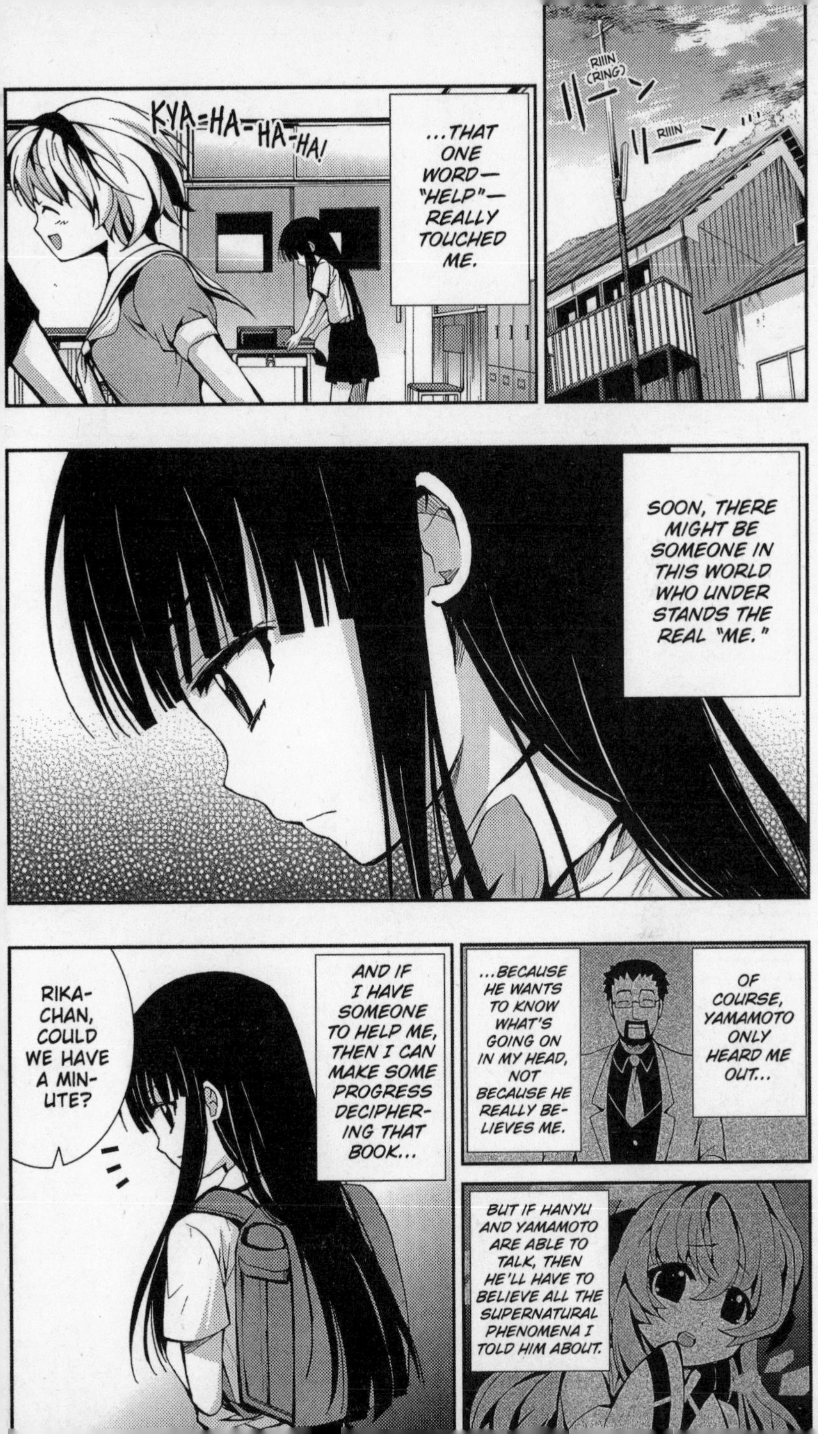
RIIIN (RING)
RIIIN
...THAT ONE WORD—"HELP"—REALLY TOUCHED ME.
KYA-HA-HA-HA!
SOON, THERE MIGHT BE SOMEONE IN THIS WORLD WHO UNDER STANDS THE REAL "ME."
OF COURSE, YAMAMOTO ONLY HEARD ME OUT...
...BECAUSE HE WANTS TO KNOW WHAT'S GOING ON IN MY HEAD, NOT BECAUSE HE REALLY BE-LIEVES ME.
BUT IF HANYU AND YAMAMOTO ARE ABLE TO TALK, THEN HE'LL HAVE TO BELIEVE ALL THE SUPERNATURAL PHENOMENA I TOLD HIM ABOUT.
AND IF I HAVE SOMEONE TO HELP ME, THEN I CAN MAKE SOME PROGRESS DECIPHER-ING THAT BOOK...
RIKA-CHAN, COULD WE HAVE A MIN-UTE?

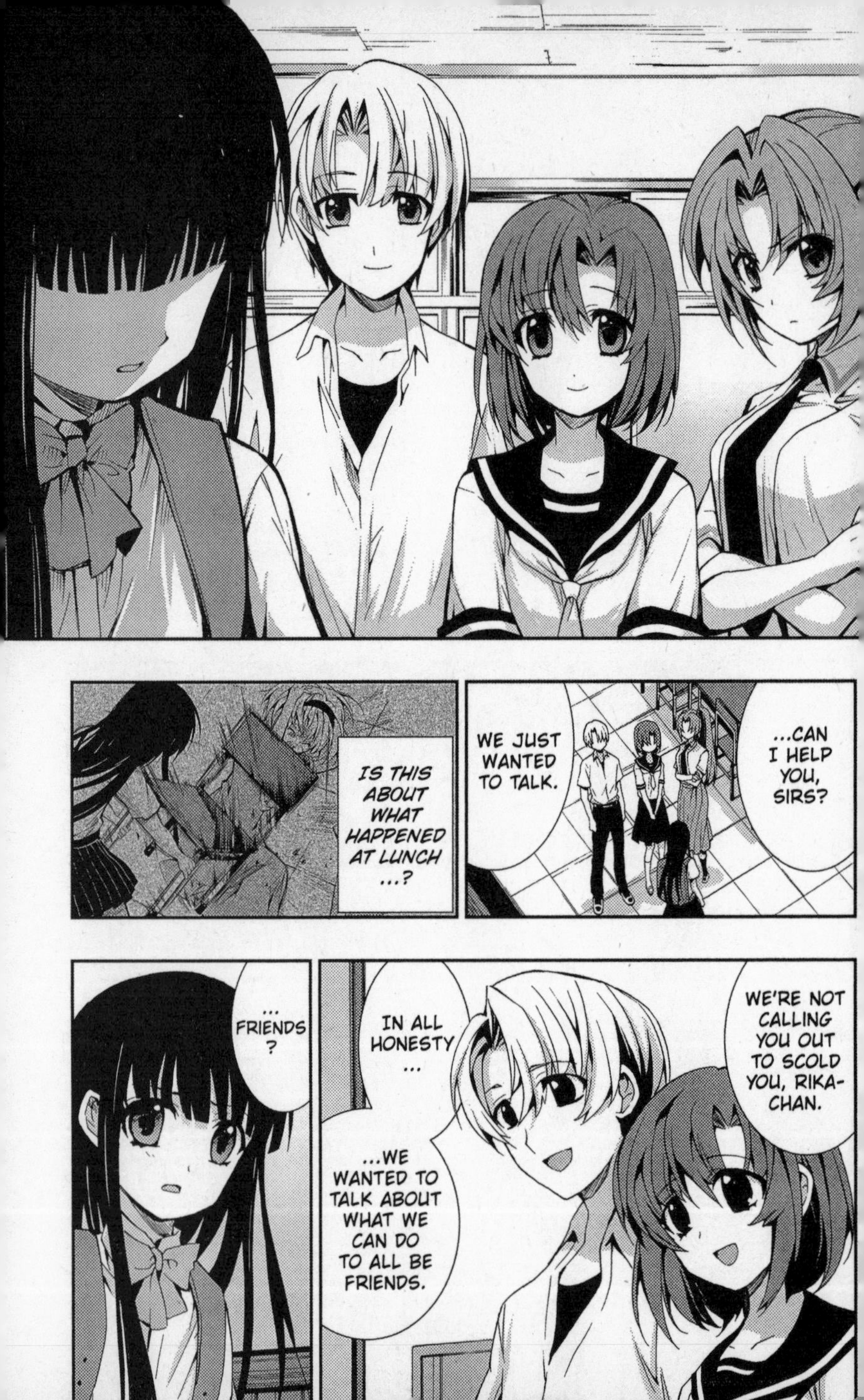
...CAN I HELP YOU, SIRS?
WE JUST WANTED TO TALK.
IS THIS ABOUT WHAT HAPPENED AT LUNCH ...?
WE'RE NOT CALLING YOU OUT TO SCOLD YOU, RIKA-CHAN.
IN ALL HONESTY ...
...WE WANTED TO TALK ABOUT WHAT WE CAN DO TO ALL BE FRIENDS.
... FRIENDS ?

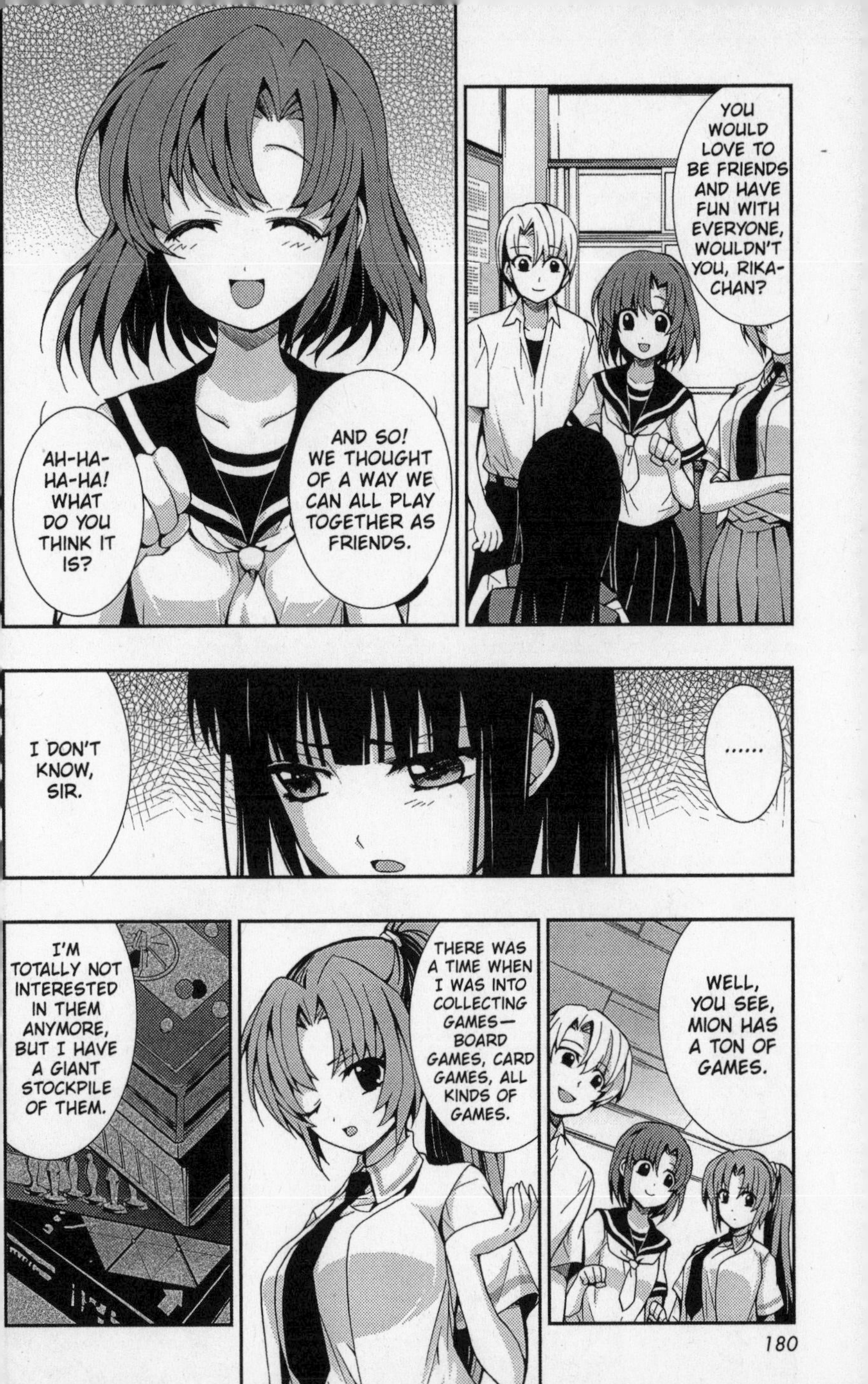
YOU WOULD LOVE TO BE FRIENDS AND HAVE FUN WITH EVERYONE, WOULDN'T YOU, RIKA-CHAN?
AND SO! WE THOUGHT OF A WAY WE CAN ALL PLAY TOGETHER AS FRIENDS.
AH-HA-HA-HA! WHAT DO YOU THINK IT IS?
......
I DON'T KNOW, SIR.
WELL, YOU SEE, MION HAS A TON OF GAMES.
THERE WAS A TIME WHEN I WAS INTO COLLECTING GAMES—BOARD GAMES, CARD GAMES, ALL KINDS OF GAMES.
I'M TOTALLY NOT INTERESTED IN THEM ANYMORE, BUT I HAVE A GIANT STOCKPILE OF THEM.

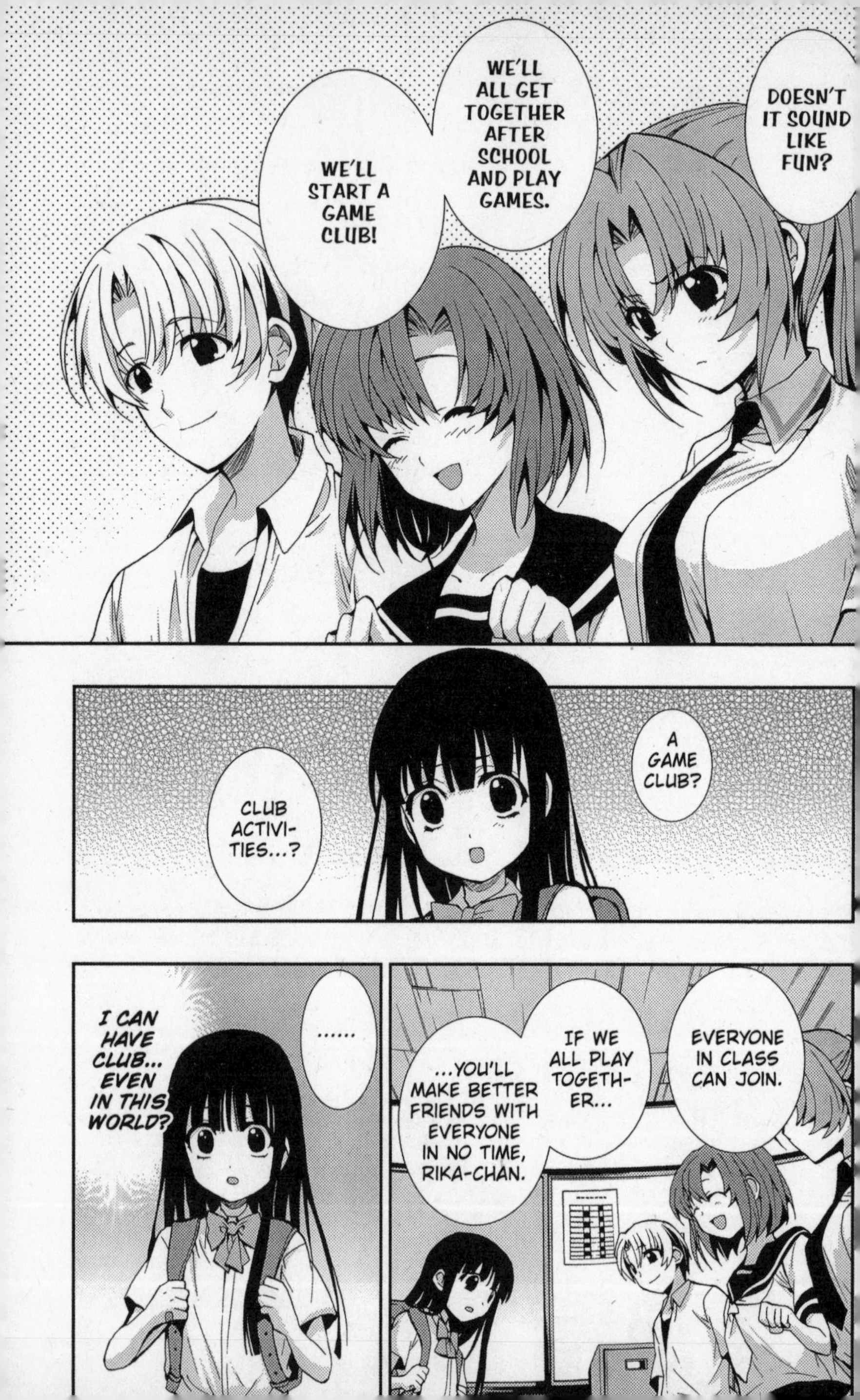
DOESN'T IT SOUND LIKE FUN?
WE'LL ALL GET TOGETHER AFTER SCHOOL AND PLAY GAMES.
WE'LL START A GAME CLUB!
A GAME CLUB?
CLUB ACTIVITIES...?
EVERYONE IN CLASS CAN JOIN.
IF WE ALL PLAY TOGETHER...
...YOU'LL MAKE BETTER FRIENDS WITH EVERYONE IN NO TIME, RIKA-CHAN.
......
I CAN HAVE CLUB... EVEN IN THIS WORLD?

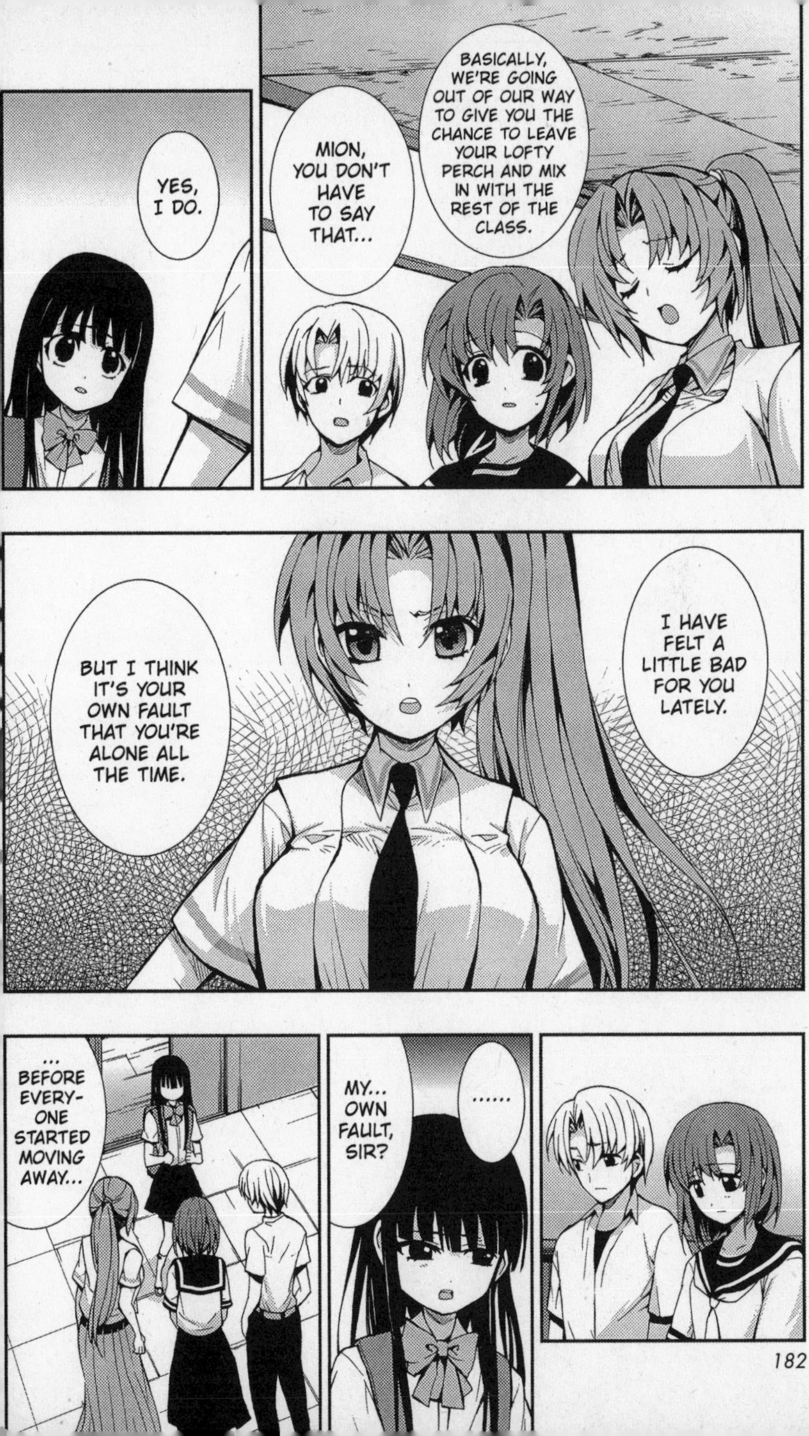
BASICALLY, WE'RE GOING OUT OF OUR WAY TO GIVE YOU THE CHANCE TO LEAVE YOUR LOFTY PERCH AND MIX IN WITH THE REST OF THE CLASS.
MION, YOU DON'T HAVE TO SAY THAT...
YES, I DO.
I HAVE FELT A LITTLE BAD FOR YOU LATELY.
BUT I THINK IT'S YOUR OWN FAULT THAT YOU'RE ALONE ALL THE TIME.
......
MY... OWN FAULT, SIR?
... BEFORE EVERY-ONE STARTED MOVING AWAY...

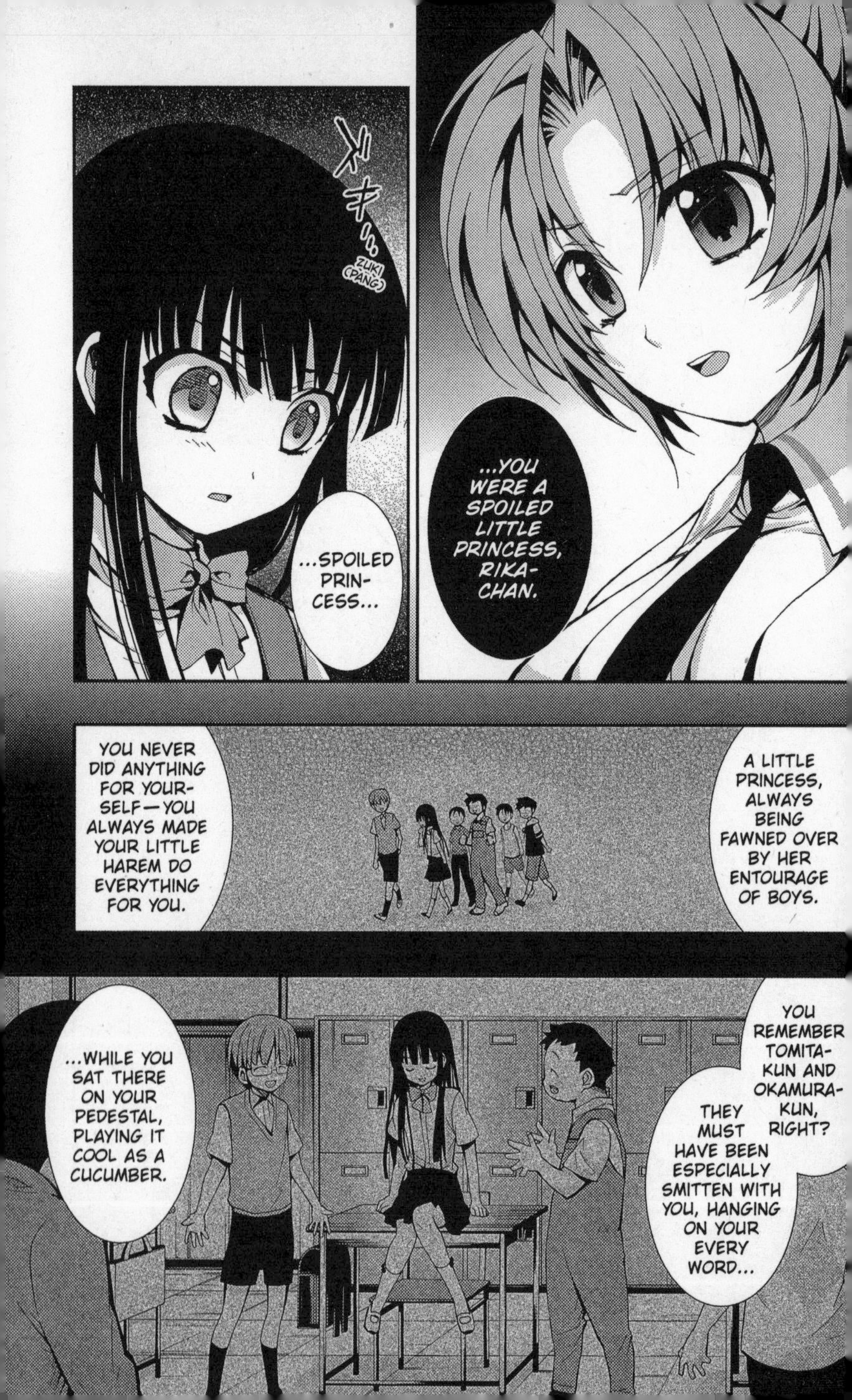
...YOU WERE A SPOILED LITTLE PRINCESS, RIKA-CHAN.
ZUKI (PANG)
...SPOILED PRIN-CESS...
A LITTLE PRINCESS, ALWAYS BEING FAWNED OVER BY HER ENTOURAGE OF BOYS.
YOU NEVER DID ANYTHING FOR YOUR-SELF—YOU ALWAYS MADE YOUR LITTLE HAREM DO EVERYTHING FOR YOU.
YOU REMEMBER TOMITA-KUN AND OKAMURA-KUN, RIGHT?
THEY MUST HAVE BEEN ESPECIALLY SMITTEN WITH YOU, HANGING ON YOUR EVERY WORD...
...WHILE YOU SAT THERE ON YOUR PEDESTAL, PLAYING IT COOL AS A CUCUMBER.

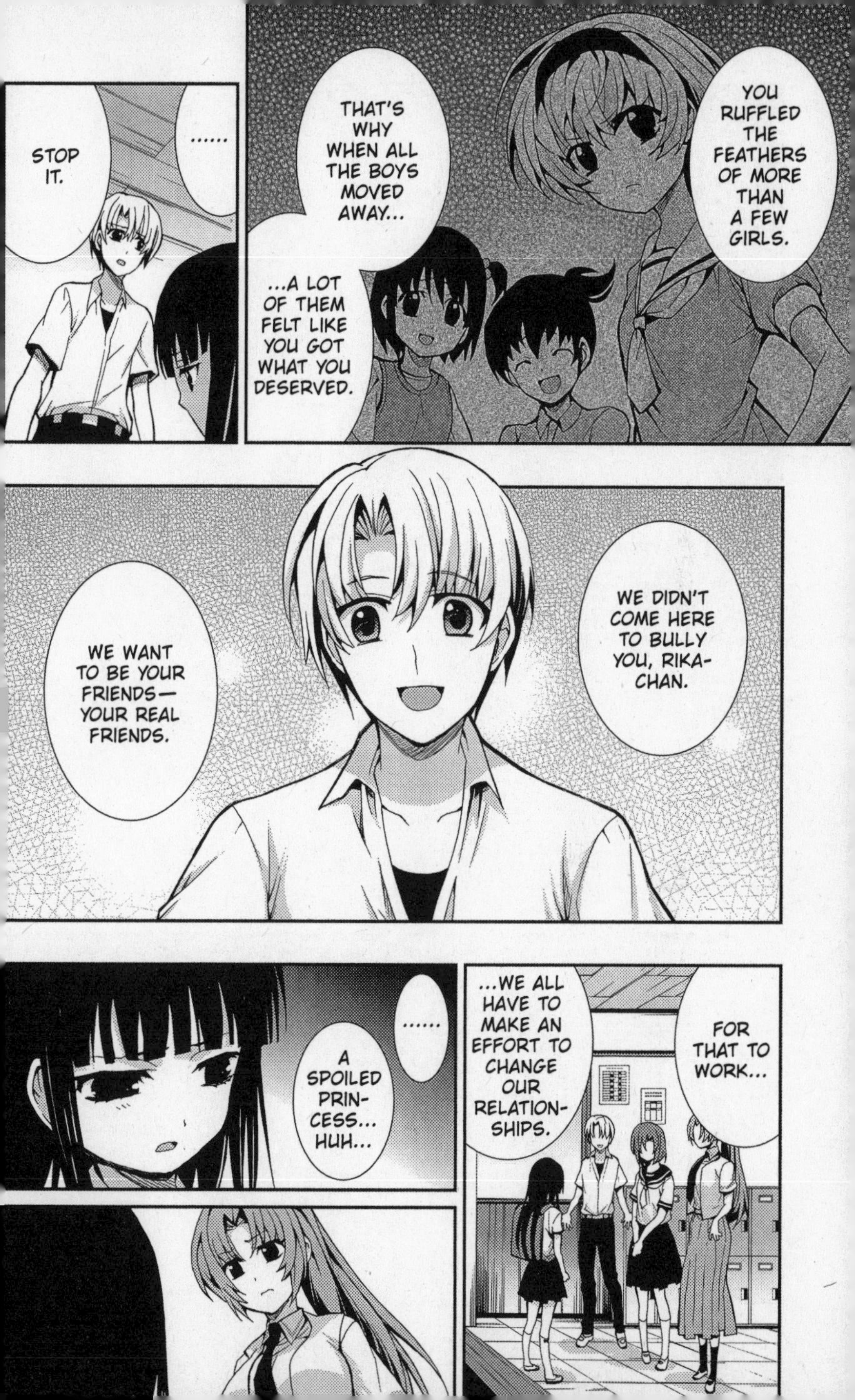
YOU RUFFLED THE FEATHERS OF MORE THAN A FEW GIRLS.
THAT'S WHY WHEN ALL THE BOYS MOVED AWAY...
...A LOT OF THEM FELT LIKE YOU GOT WHAT YOU DESERVED.
......
STOP IT.
WE DIDN'T COME HERE TO BULLY YOU, RIKA-CHAN.
WE WANT TO BE YOUR FRIENDS—YOUR REAL FRIENDS.
FOR THAT TO WORK...
...WE ALL HAVE TO MAKE AN EFFORT TO CHANGE OUR RELATIONSHIPS.
......
A SPOILED PRINCESS... HUH...

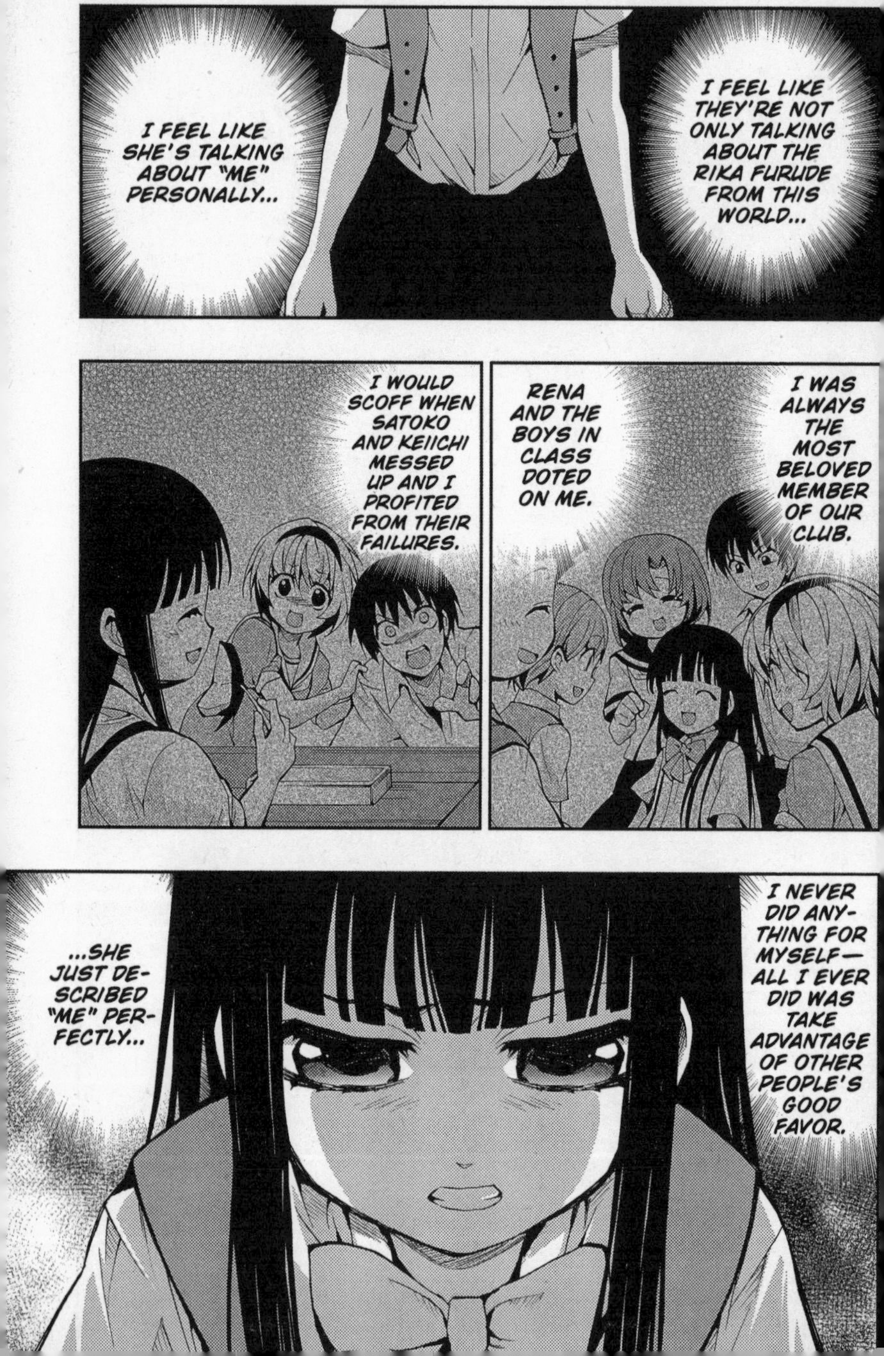
I FEEL LIKE THEY'RE NOT ONLY TALKING ABOUT THE RIKA FURUDE FROM THIS WORLD...
I FEEL LIKE SHE'S TALKING ABOUT "ME" PERSONALLY...
I WAS ALWAYS THE MOST BELOVED MEMBER OF OUR CLUB.
RENA AND THE BOYS IN CLASS DOTED ON ME.
I WOULD SCOFF WHEN SATOKO AND KEIICHI MESSED UP AND I PROFITED FROM THEIR FAILURES.
I NEVER DID ANY-THING FOR MYSELF— ALL I EVER DID WAS TAKE ADVANTAGE OF OTHER PEOPLE'S GOOD FAVOR.
...SHE JUST DE-SCRIBED "ME" PER-FECTLY...

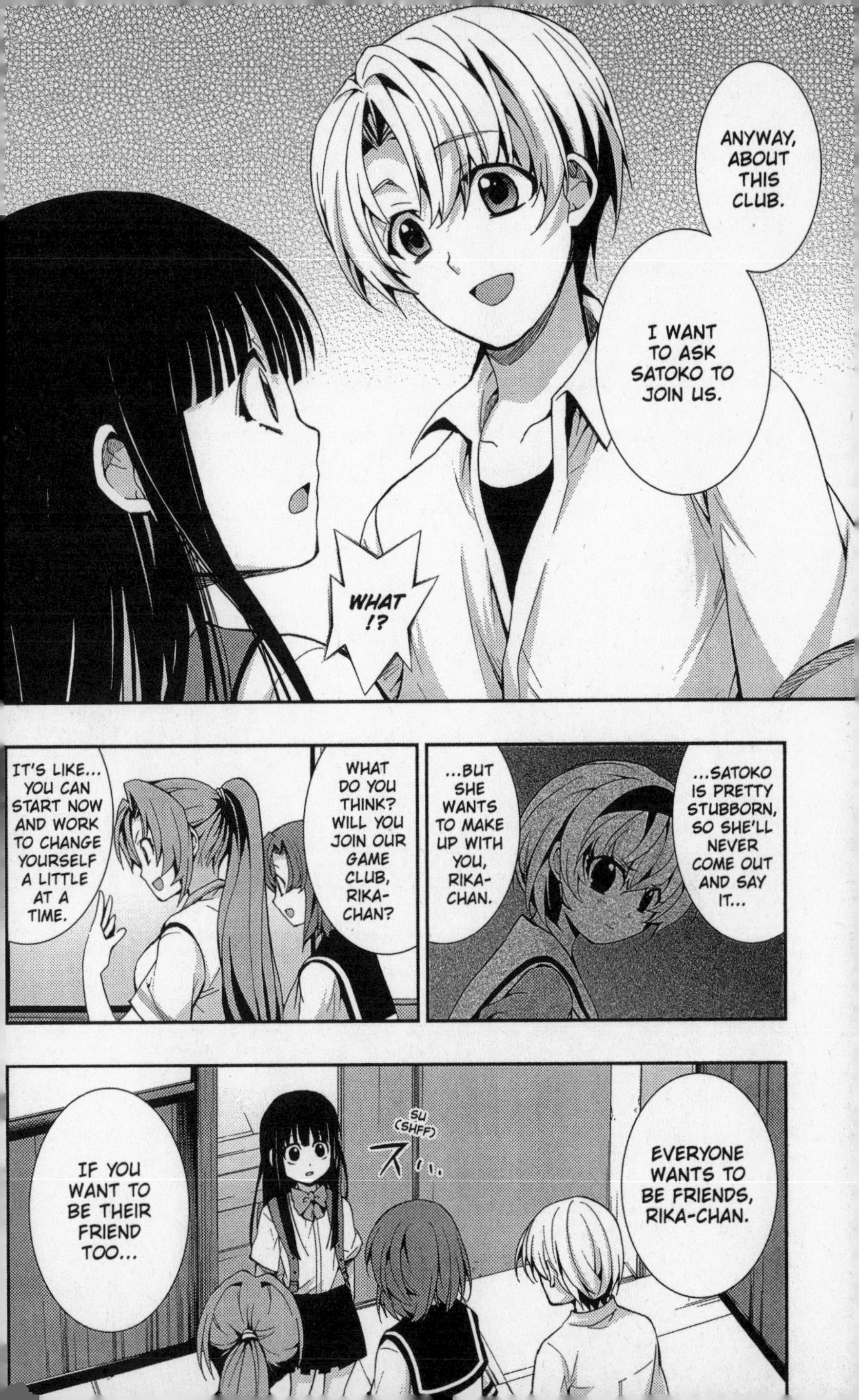
ANYWAY, ABOUT THIS CLUB.
I WANT TO ASK SATOKO TO JOIN US.
WHAT !?
...SATOKO IS PRETTY STUBBORN, SO SHE'LL NEVER COME OUT AND SAY IT...
...BUT SHE WANTS TO MAKE UP WITH YOU, RIKA-CHAN.
WHAT DO YOU THINK? WILL YOU JOIN OUR GAME CLUB, RIKA-CHAN?
IT'S LIKE... YOU CAN START NOW AND WORK TO CHANGE YOURSELF A LITTLE AT A TIME.
EVERYONE WANTS TO BE FRIENDS, RIKA-CHAN.
SU (SHFF)
IF YOU WANT TO BE THEIR FRIEND TOO...

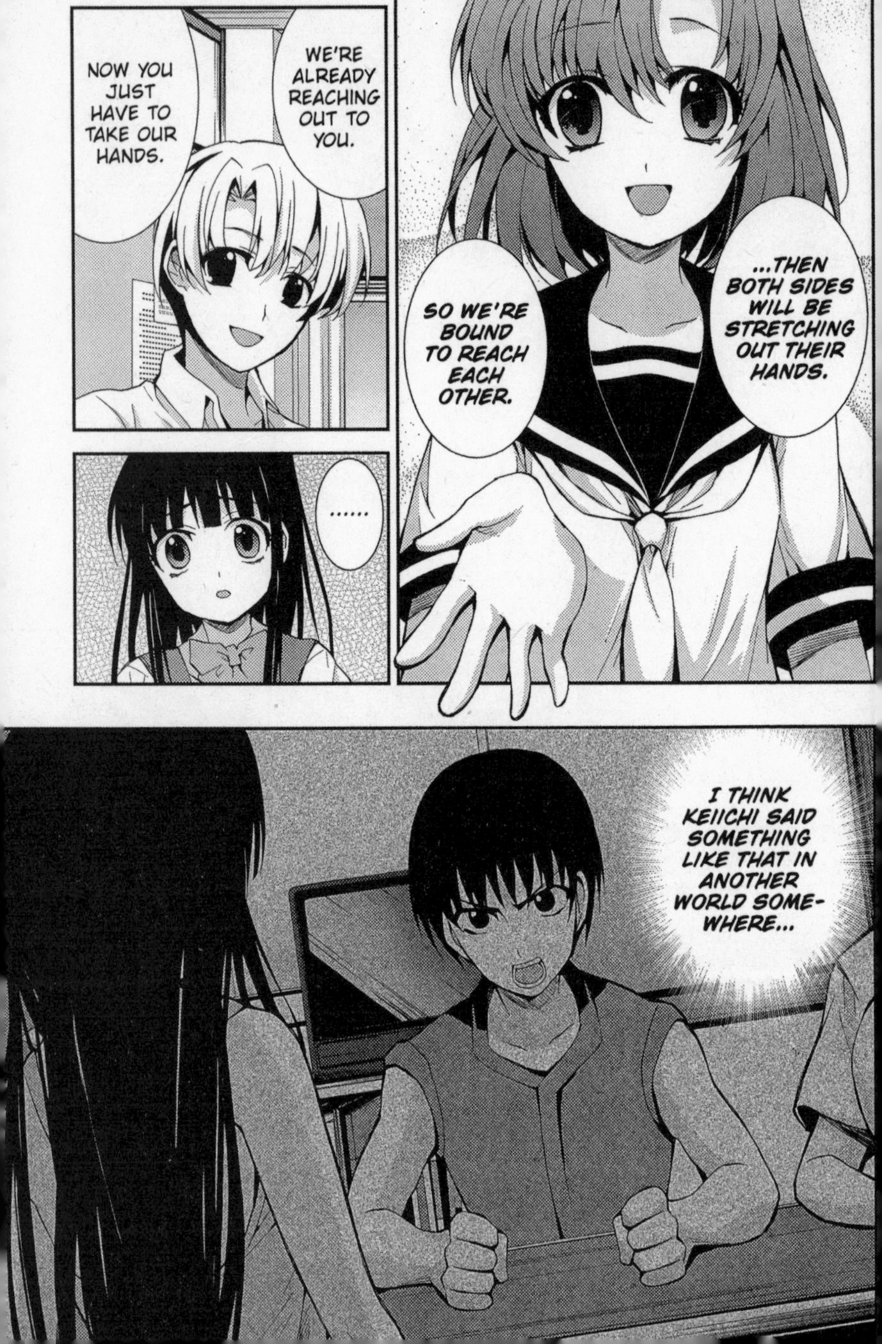
...THEN BOTH SIDES WILL BE STRETCHING OUT THEIR HANDS.
SO WE'RE BOUND TO REACH EACH OTHER.
WE'RE ALREADY REACHING OUT TO YOU.
NOW YOU JUST HAVE TO TAKE OUR HANDS.
......
I THINK KEIICHI SAID SOMETHING LIKE THAT IN ANOTHER WORLD SOME-WHERE...

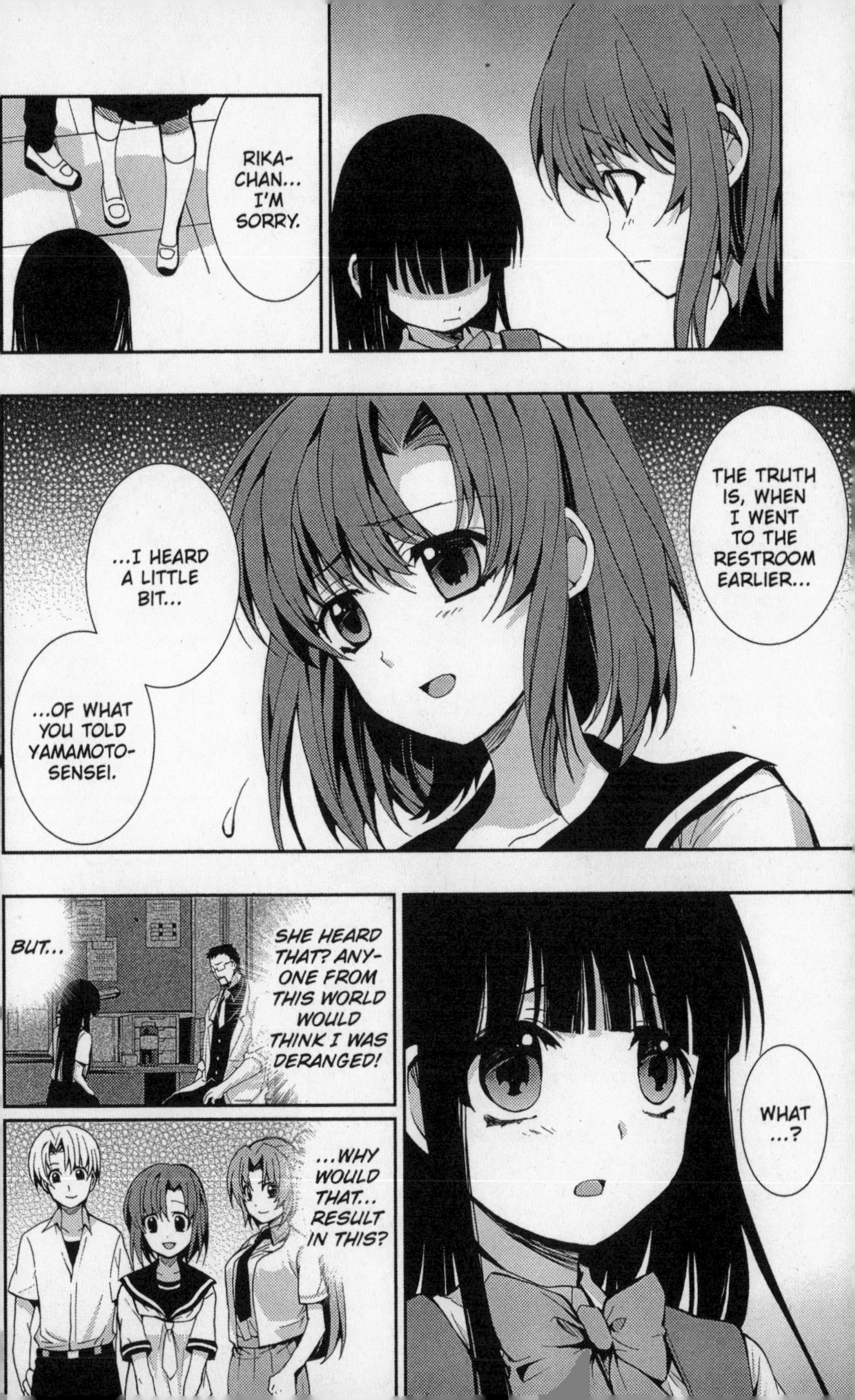
RIKA-CHAN... I'M SORRY.
THE TRUTH IS, WHEN I WENT TO THE RESTROOM EARLIER...
...I HEARD A LITTLE BIT...
...OF WHAT YOU TOLD YAMAMOTO-SENSEI.
WHAT ...?
SHE HEARD THAT? ANYONE FROM THIS WORLD WOULD THINK I WAS DERANGED!
BUT...
...WHY WOULD THAT... RESULT IN THIS?

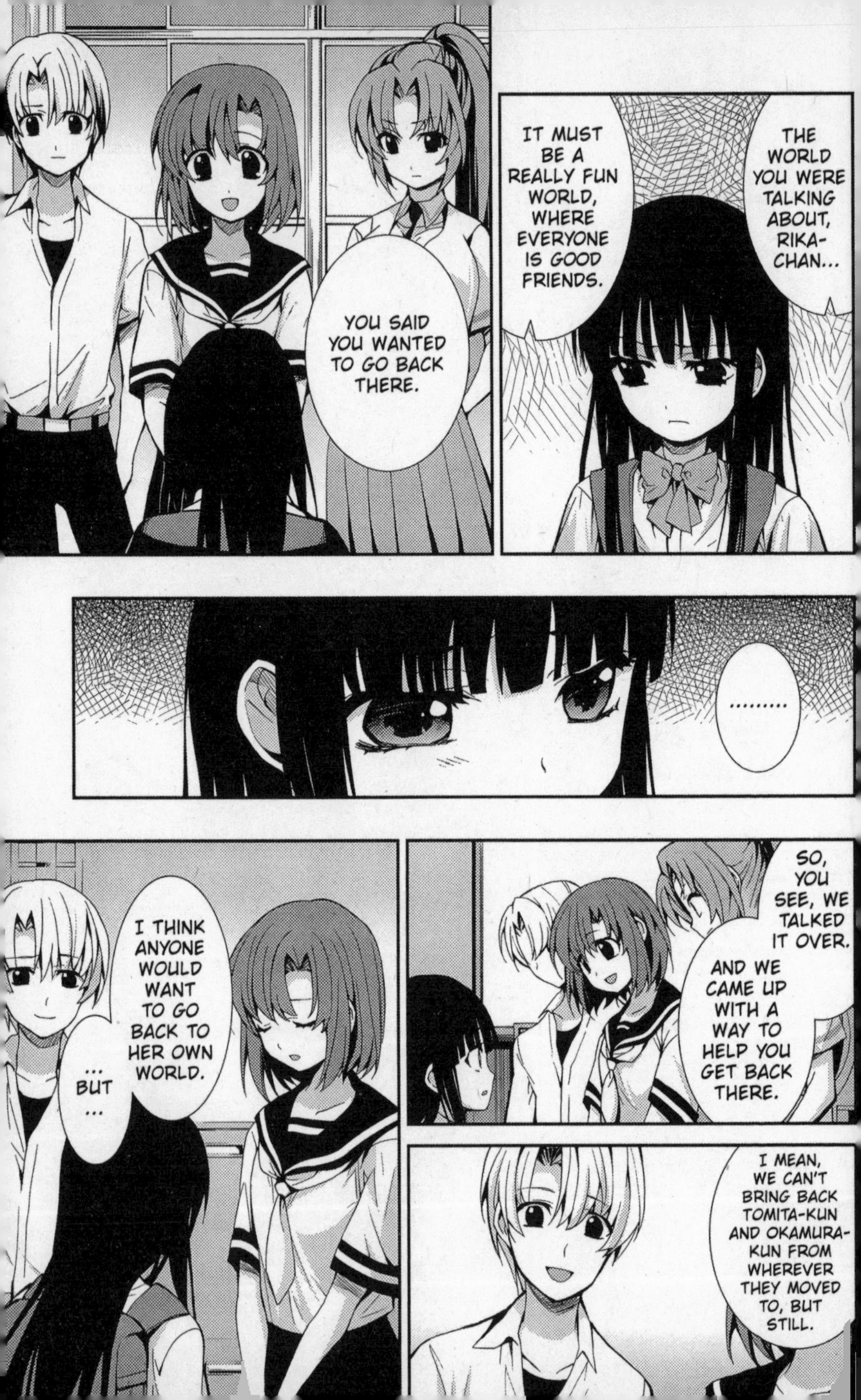
THE WORLD YOU WERE TALKING ABOUT, RIKA-CHAN...
IT MUST BE A REALLY FUN WORLD, WHERE EVERYONE IS GOOD FRIENDS.
YOU SAID YOU WANTED TO GO BACK THERE.
....
SO, YOU SEE, WE TALKED IT OVER.
AND WE CAME UP WITH A WAY TO HELP YOU GET BACK THERE.
I MEAN, WE CAN'T BRING BACK TOMITA-KUN AND OKAMURA-KUN FROM WHEREVER THEY MOVED TO, BUT STILL.
I THINK ANYONE WOULD WANT TO GO BACK TO HER OWN WORLD.
... BUT ...

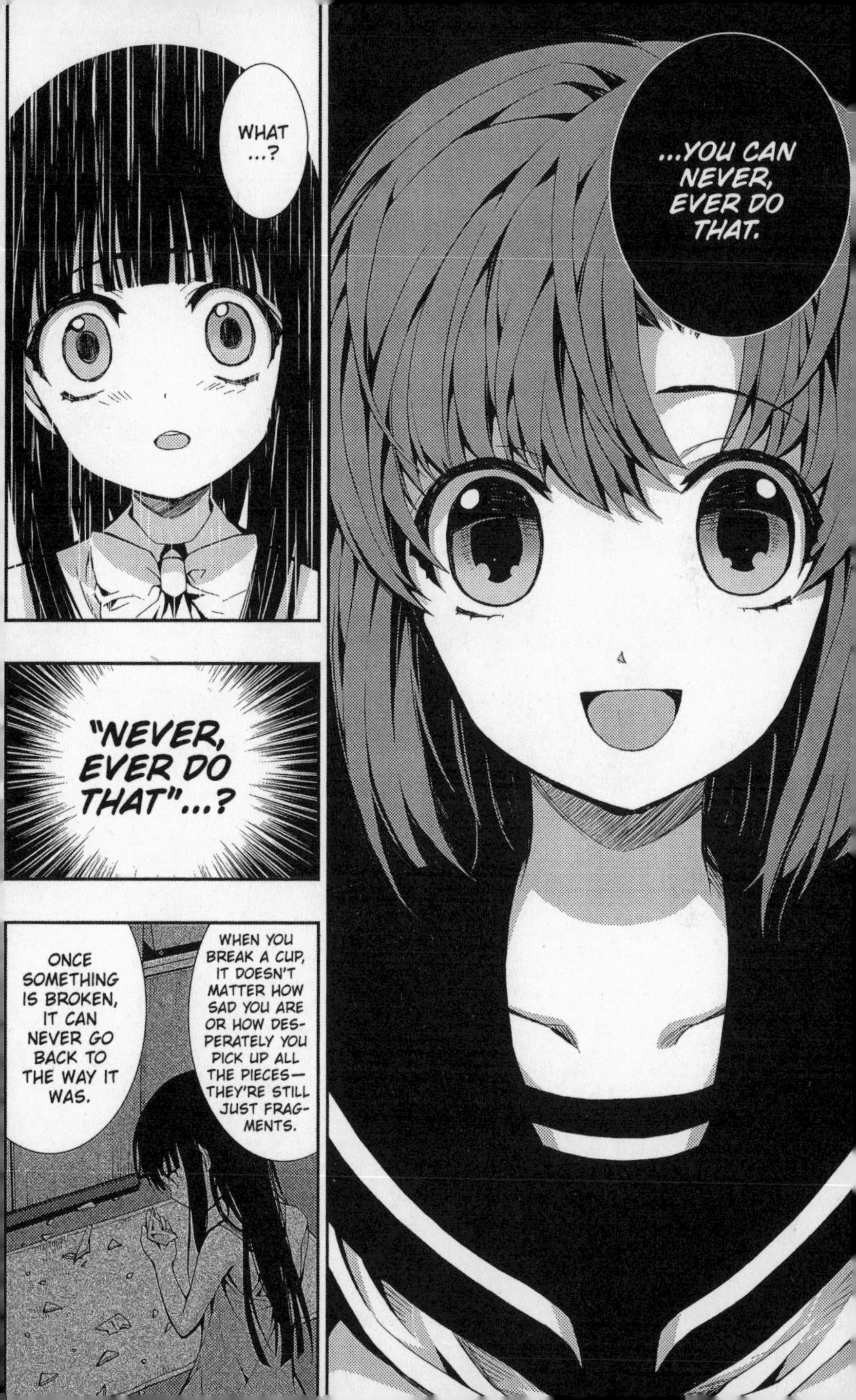
...YOU CAN NEVER, EVER DO THAT.
WHAT ...?
"NEVER, EVER DO THAT"...?
WHEN YOU BREAK A CUP, IT DOESN'T MATTER HOW SAD YOU ARE OR HOW DES-PERATELY YOU PICK UP ALL THE PIECES—THEY'RE STILL JUST FRAG-MENTS.
ONCE SOMETHING IS BROKEN, IT CAN NEVER GO BACK TO THE WAY IT WAS.

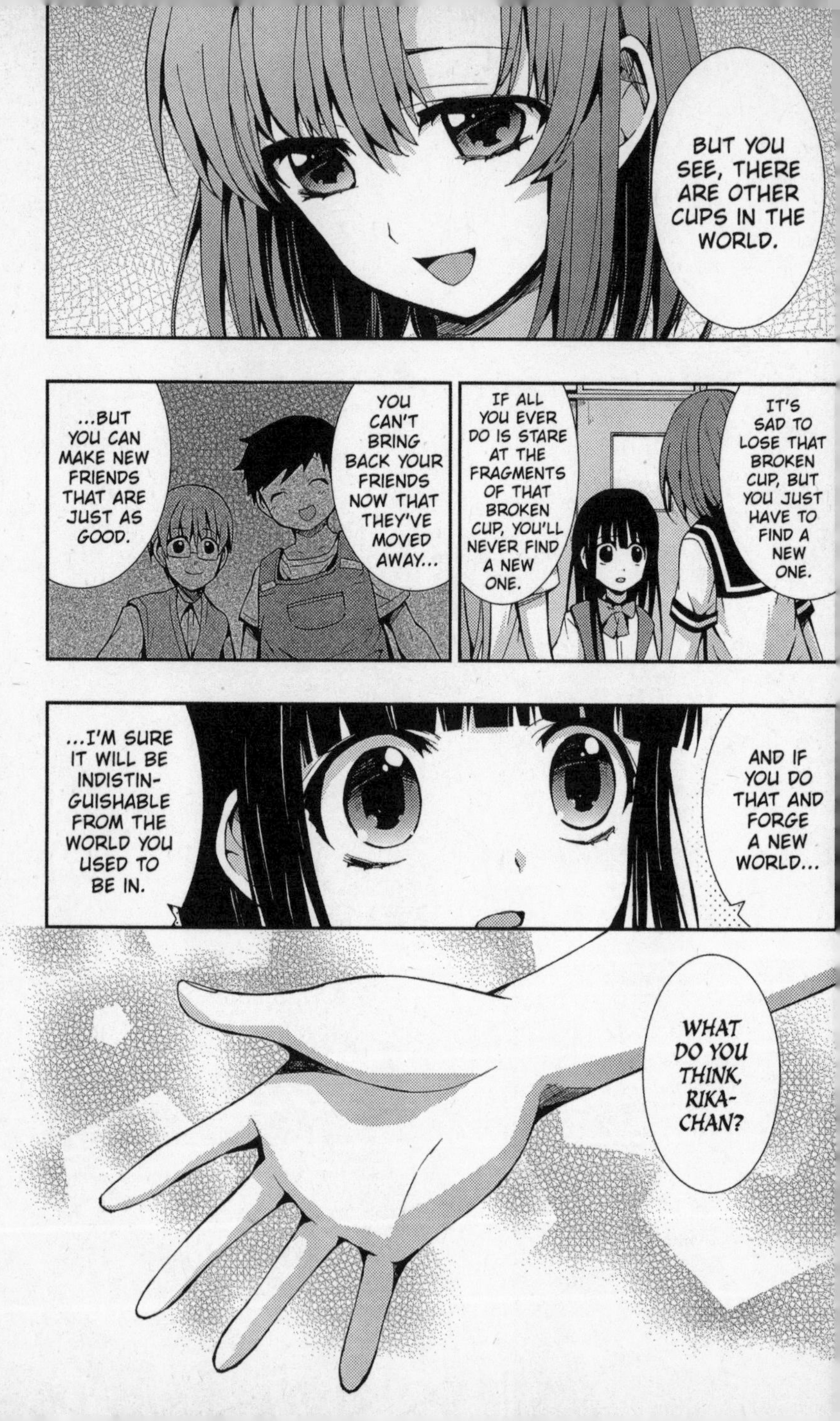
BUT YOU SEE, THERE ARE OTHER CUPS IN THE WORLD.
IT'S SAD TO LOSE THAT BROKEN CUP, BUT YOU JUST HAVE TO FIND A NEW ONE.
IF ALL YOU EVER DO IS STARE AT THE FRAGMENTS OF THAT BROKEN CUP, YOU'LL NEVER FIND A NEW ONE.
YOU CAN'T BRING BACK YOUR FRIENDS NOW THAT THEY'VE MOVED AWAY...
...BUT YOU CAN MAKE NEW FRIENDS THAT ARE JUST AS GOOD.
AND IF YOU DO THAT AND FORGE A NEW WORLD...
...I'M SURE IT WILL BE INDISTIN-GUISHABLE FROM THE WORLD YOU USED TO BE IN.
WHAT DO YOU THINK, RIKA-CHAN?

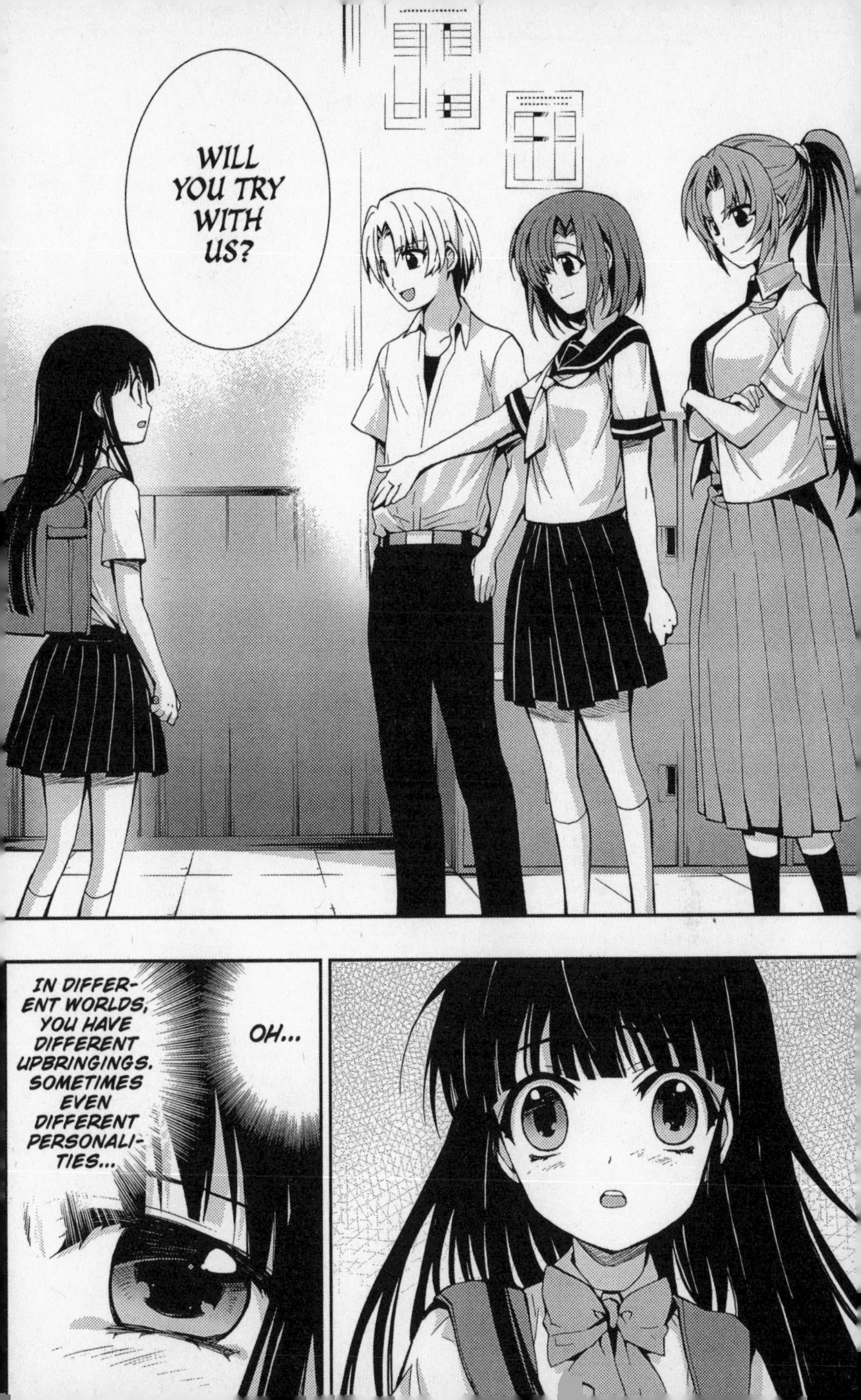
WILL YOU TRY WITH US?
OH...
IN DIFFERENT WORLDS, YOU HAVE DIFFERENT UPBRINGINGS. SOMETIMES EVEN DIFFERENT PERSONALITIES...

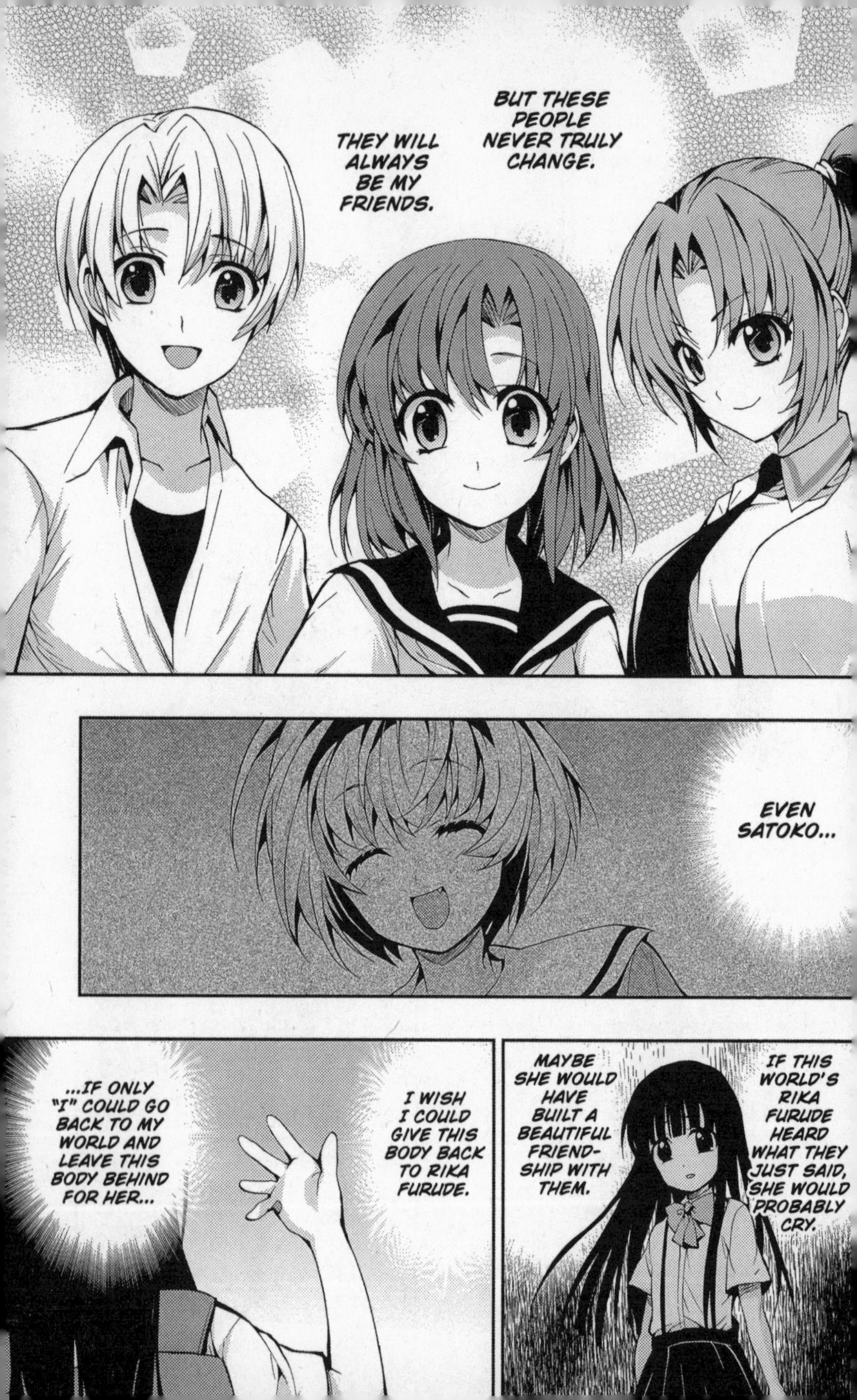
BUT THESE PEOPLE NEVER TRULY CHANGE.
THEY WILL ALWAYS BE MY FRIENDS.
EVEN SATOKO...
IF THIS WORLD'S RIKA FURUDE HEARD WHAT THEY JUST SAID, SHE WOULD PROBABLY CRY.
MAYBE SHE WOULD HAVE BUILT A BEAUTIFUL FRIEND-SHIP WITH THEM.
I WISH I COULD GIVE THIS BODY BACK TO RIKA FURUDE.
...IF ONLY "I" COULD GO BACK TO MY WORLD AND LEAVE THIS BODY BEHIND FOR HER...

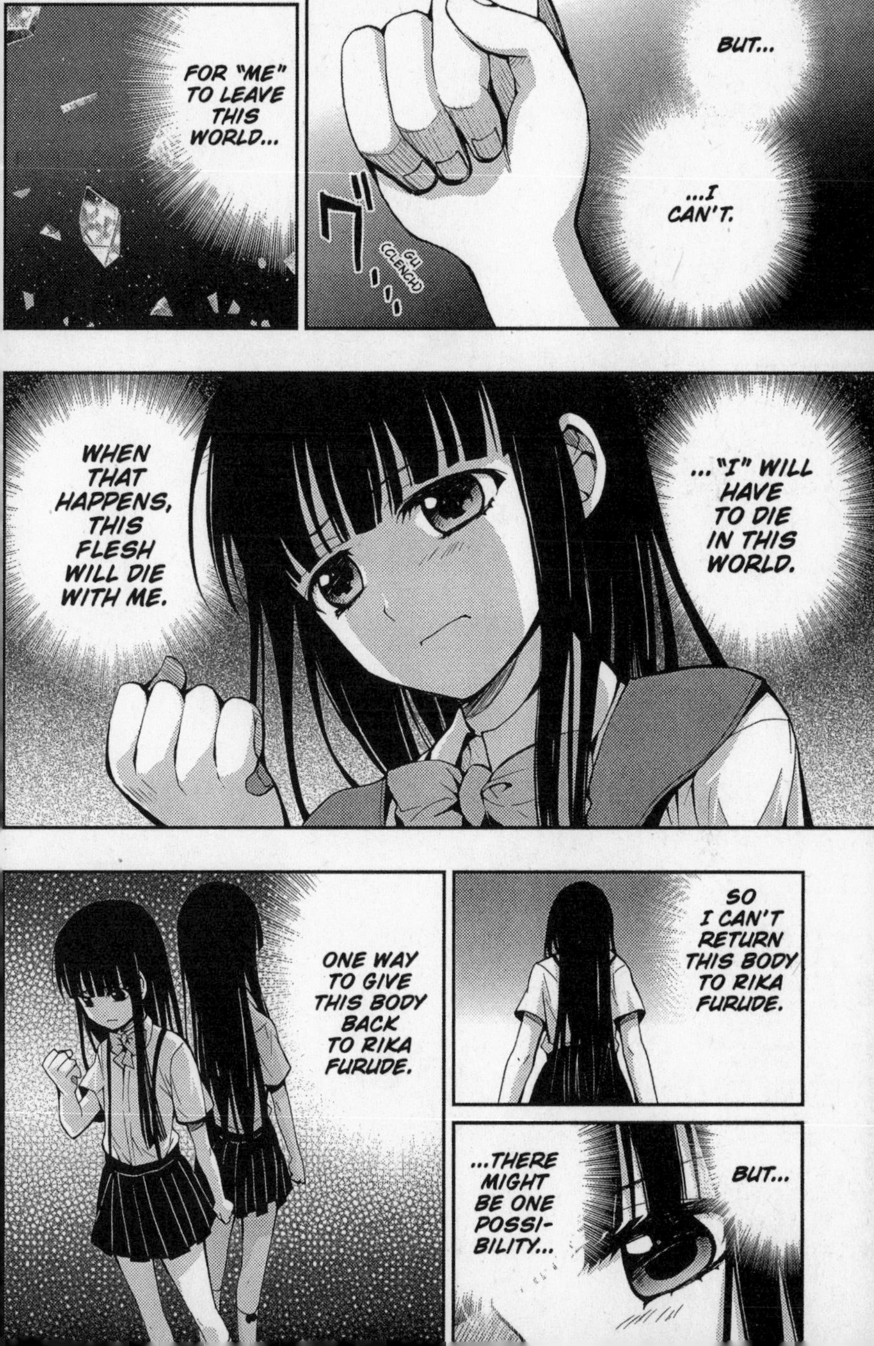
BUT...
...I CAN'T.
GU (CLENCH)
FOR "ME" TO LEAVE THIS WORLD...
..."I" WILL HAVE TO DIE IN THIS WORLD.
WHEN THAT HAPPENS, THIS FLESH WILL DIE WITH ME.
SO I CAN'T RETURN THIS BODY TO RIKA FURUDE.
BUT...
...THERE MIGHT BE ONE POSSIBILITY...
ONE WAY TO GIVE THIS BODY BACK TO RIKA FURUDE.

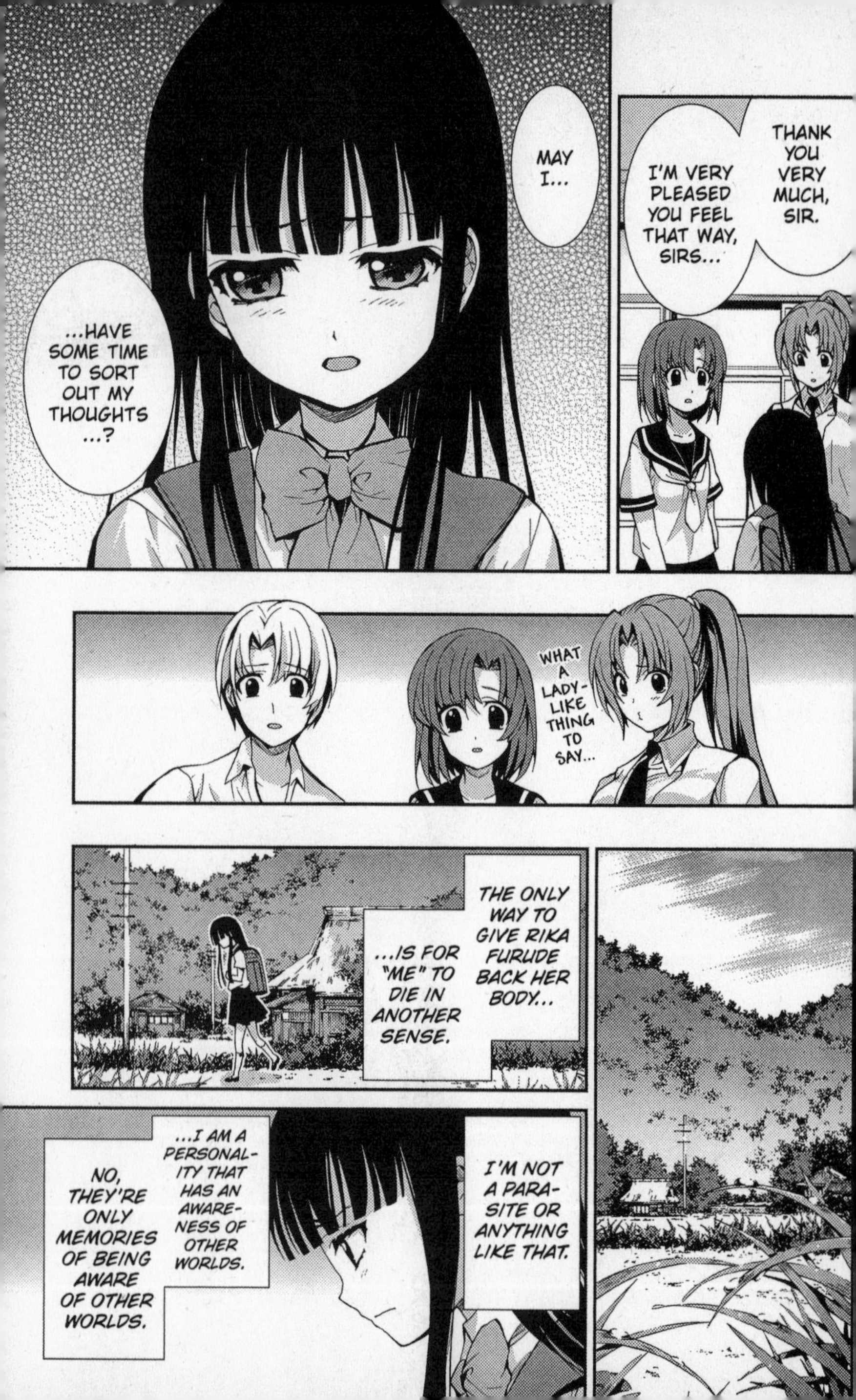
THANK YOU VERY MUCH, SIR.
I'M VERY PLEASED YOU FEEL THAT WAY, SIRS...
MAY I...
...HAVE SOME TIME TO SORT OUT MY THOUGHTS ...?
WHAT A LADY-LIKE THING TO SAY...
THE ONLY WAY TO GIVE RIKA FURUDE BACK HER BODY...
...IS FOR "ME" TO DIE IN ANOTHER SENSE.
I'M NOT A PARA-SITE OR ANYTHING LIKE THAT.
...I AM A PERSONAL-ITY THAT HAS AN AWARE-NESS OF OTHER WORLDS.
NO, THEY'RE ONLY MEMORIES OF BEING AWARE OF OTHER WORLDS.

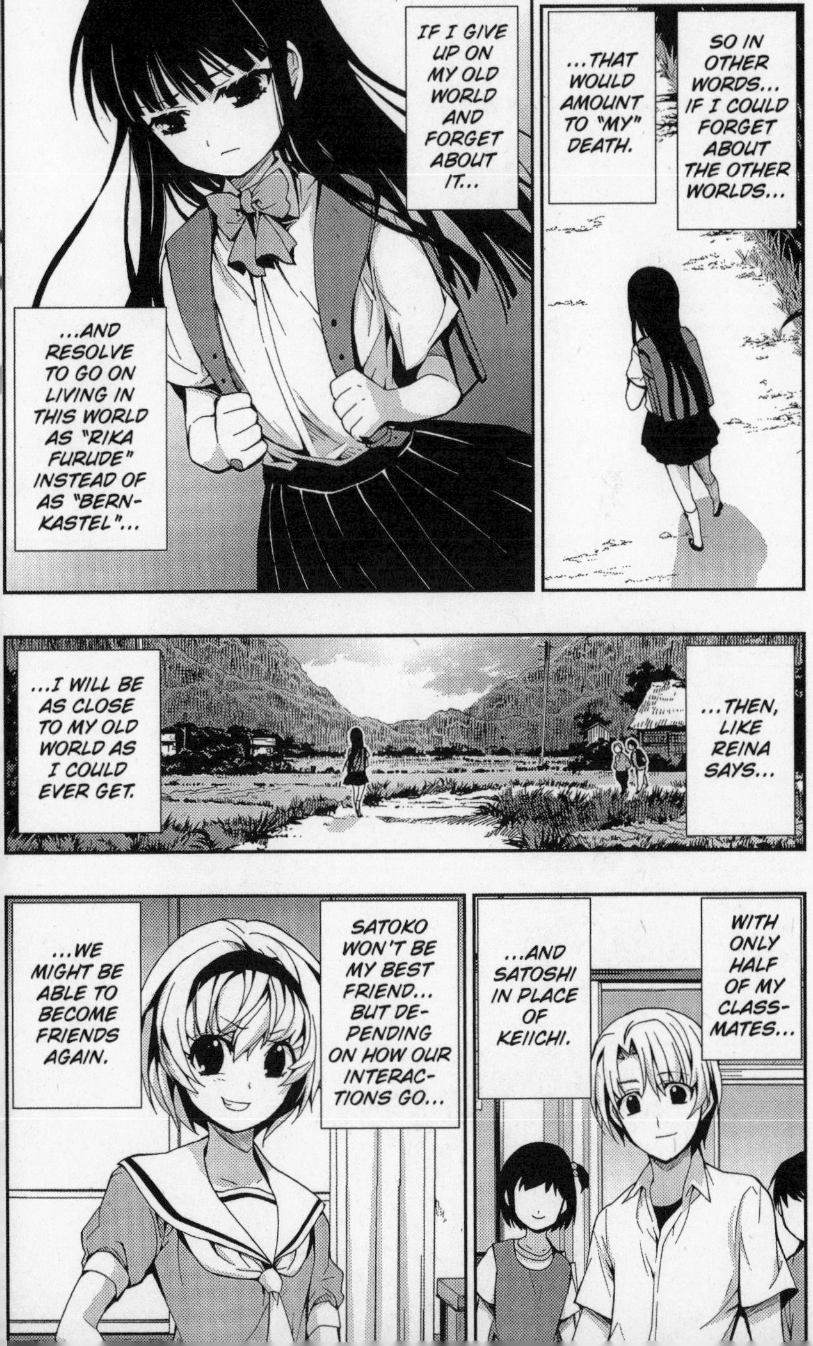
SO IN OTHER WORDS... IF I COULD FORGET ABOUT THE OTHER WORLDS...
...THAT WOULD AMOUNT TO "MY" DEATH.
IF I GIVE UP ON MY OLD WORLD AND FORGET ABOUT IT...
...AND RESOLVE TO GO ON LIVING IN THIS WORLD AS "RIKA FURUDE" INSTEAD OF AS "BERN-KASTEL"...
...THEN, LIKE REINA SAYS...
...I WILL BE AS CLOSE TO MY OLD WORLD AS I COULD EVER GET.
WITH ONLY HALF OF MY CLASSMATES...
...AND SATOSHI IN PLACE OF KEIICHI.
SATOKO WON'T BE MY BEST FRIEND... BUT DE-PENDING ON HOW OUR INTERAC-TIONS GO...
...WE MIGHT BE ABLE TO BECOME FRIENDS AGAIN.

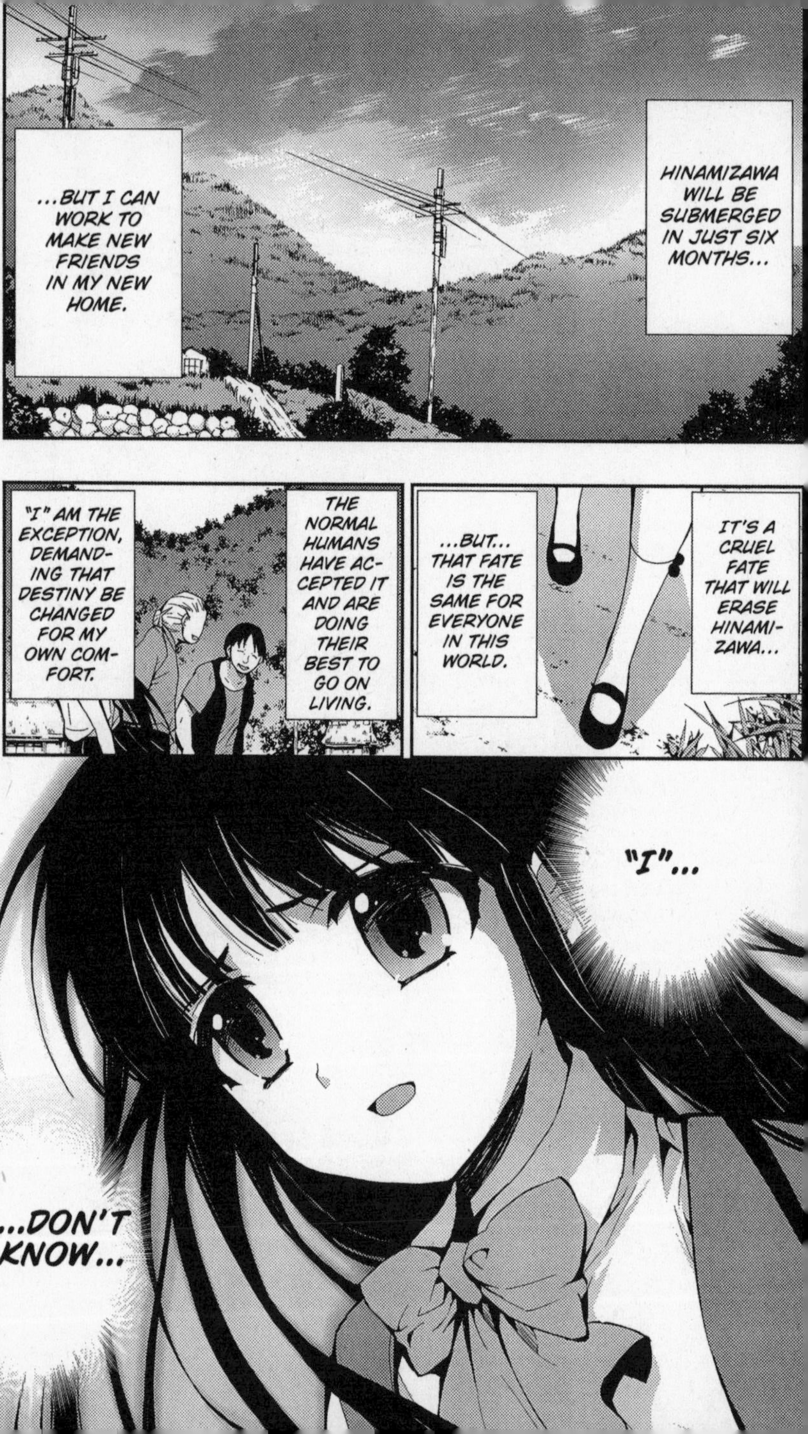
HINAMIZAWA WILL BE SUBMERGED IN JUST SIX MONTHS...
...BUT I CAN WORK TO MAKE NEW FRIENDS IN MY NEW HOME.
IT'S A CRUEL FATE THAT WILL ERASE HINAMIZAWA...
...BUT... THAT FATE IS THE SAME FOR EVERYONE IN THIS WORLD.
THE NORMAL HUMANS HAVE ACCEPTED IT AND ARE DOING THEIR BEST TO GO ON LIVING.
"I" AM THE EXCEPTION, DEMANDING THAT DESTINY BE CHANGED FOR MY OWN COMFORT.
"I"...
...DON'T KNOW...

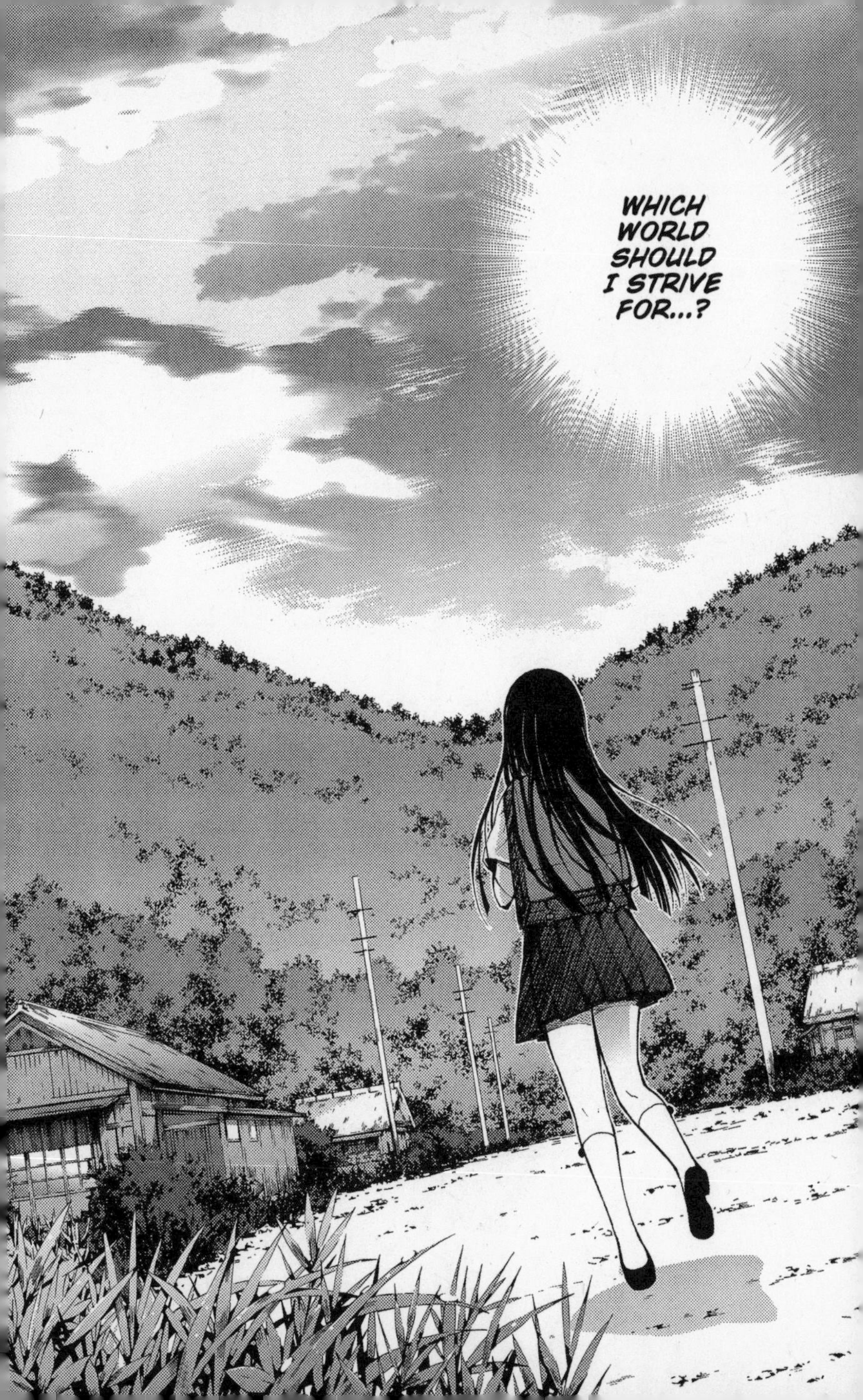
WHICH WORLD SHOULD I STRIVE FOR...?

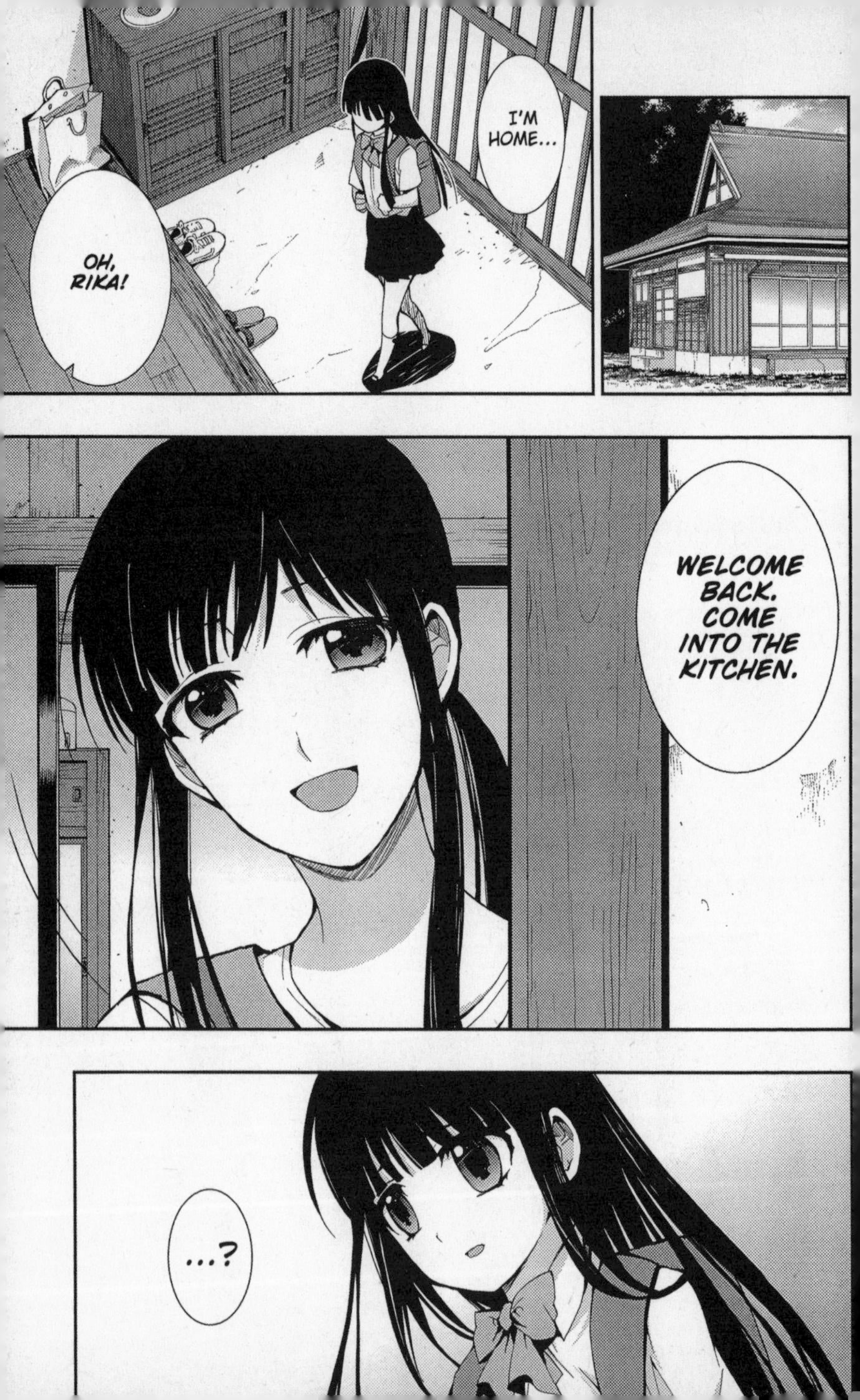
I'M HOME...
OH, RIKA!
WELCOME BACK. COME INTO THE KITCHEN.
...?

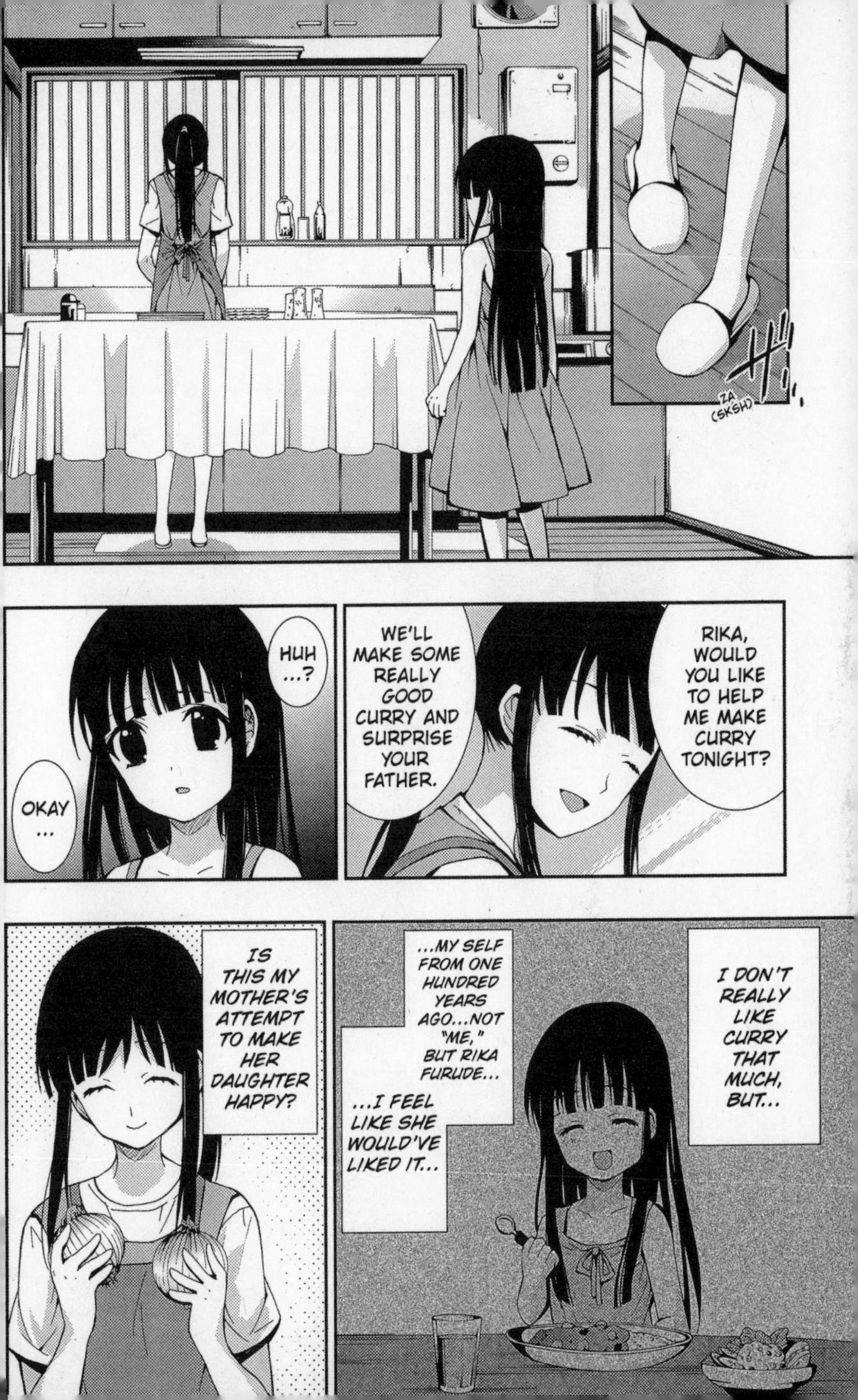
ZA (SKSH)
RIKA, WOULD YOU LIKE TO HELP ME MAKE CURRY TONIGHT?
WE'LL MAKE SOME REALLY GOOD CURRY AND SURPRISE YOUR FATHER.
HUH ...?
OKAY ...
I DON'T REALLY LIKE CURRY THAT MUCH, BUT...
...MY SELF FROM ONE HUNDRED YEARS AGO...NOT "ME," BUT RIKA FURUDE...
...I FEEL LIKE SHE WOULD'VE LIKED IT...
IS THIS MY MOTHER'S ATTEMPT TO MAKE HER DAUGHTER HAPPY?

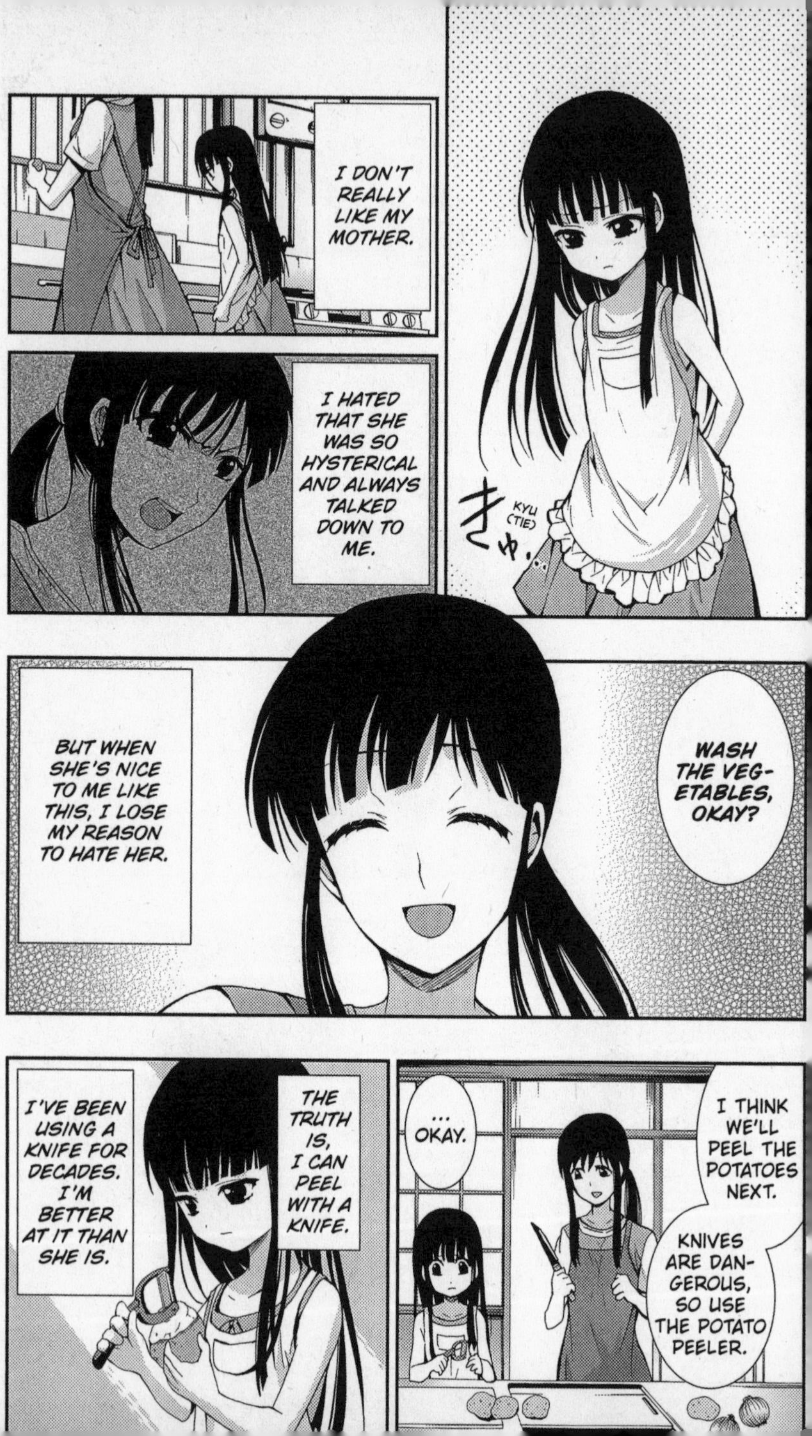

きゅ
KYU (TIE)
I DON'T REALLY LIKE MY MOTHER.
I HATED THAT SHE WAS SO HYSTERICAL AND ALWAYS TALKED DOWN TO ME.
WASH THE VEG-ETABLES, OKAY?
BUT WHEN SHE'S NICE TO ME LIKE THIS, I LOSE MY REASON TO HATE HER.
I THINK WE'LL PEEL THE POTATOES NEXT.
KNIVES ARE DAN-GEROUS, SO USE THE POTATO PEELER.
... OKAY.
THE TRUTH IS, I CAN PEEL WITH A KNIFE.
I'VE BEEN USING A KNIFE FOR DECADES. I'M BETTER AT IT THAN SHE IS.

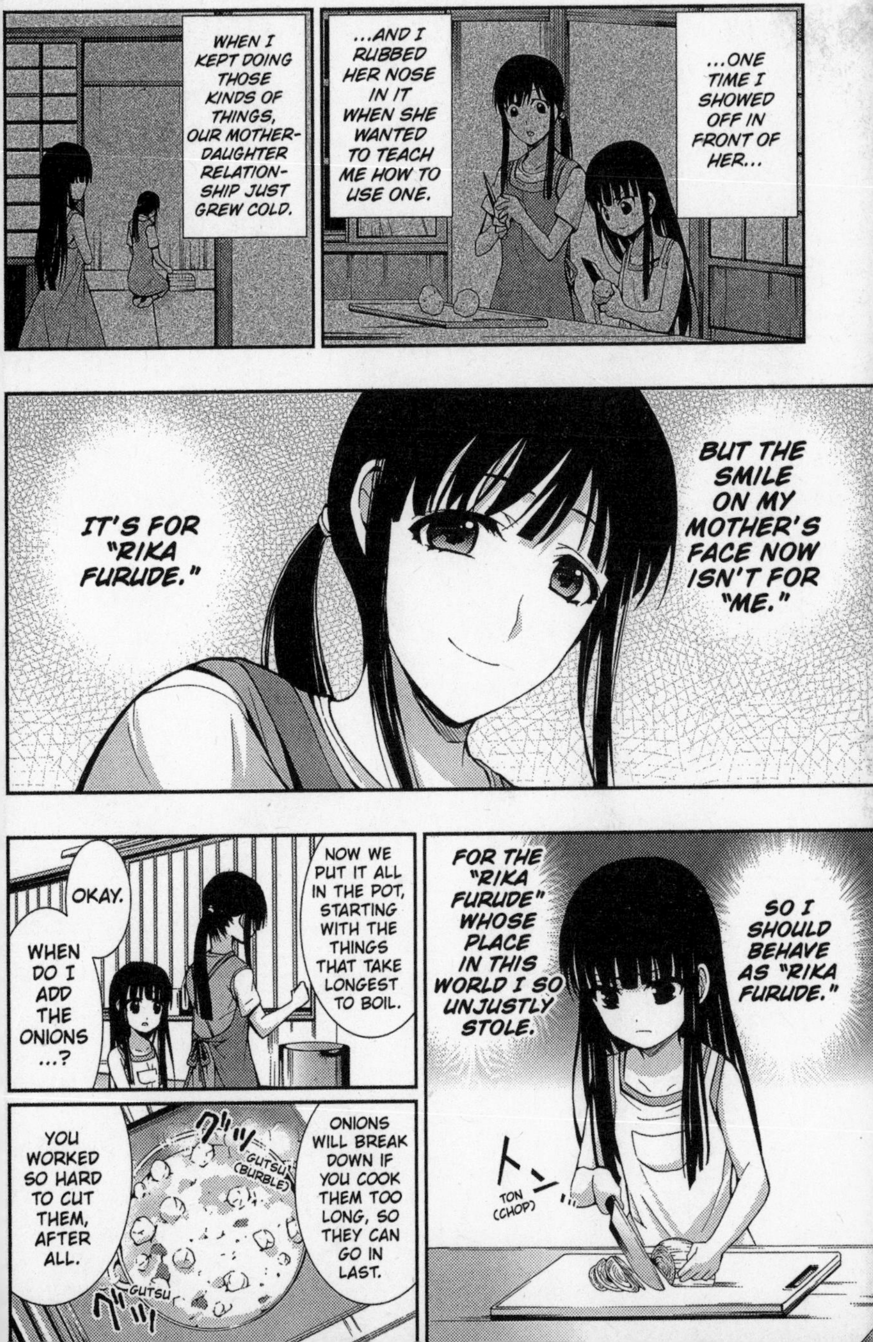
...ONE TIME I SHOWED OFF IN FRONT OF HER...
...AND I RUBBED HER NOSE IN IT WHEN SHE WANTED TO TEACH ME HOW TO USE ONE.
WHEN I KEPT DOING THOSE KINDS OF THINGS, OUR MOTHER-DAUGHTER RELATIONSHIP JUST GREW COLD.
BUT THE SMILE ON MY MOTHER'S FACE NOW ISN'T FOR "ME."
IT'S FOR "RIKA FURUDE."
SO I SHOULD BEHAVE AS "RIKA FURUDE."
FOR THE "RIKA FURUDE" WHOSE PLACE IN THIS WORLD I SO UNJUSTLY STOLE.
トン
TON (CHOP)
NOW WE PUT IT ALL IN THE POT, STARTING WITH THE THINGS THAT TAKE LONGEST TO BOIL.
OKAY.
WHEN DO I ADD THE ONIONS ...?
ONIONS WILL BREAK DOWN IF YOU COOK THEM TOO LONG, SO THEY CAN GO IN LAST.
グツッ
GUTSU (BURBLE)
YOU WORKED SO HARD TO CUT THEM, AFTER ALL.
グツッ
GUTSU

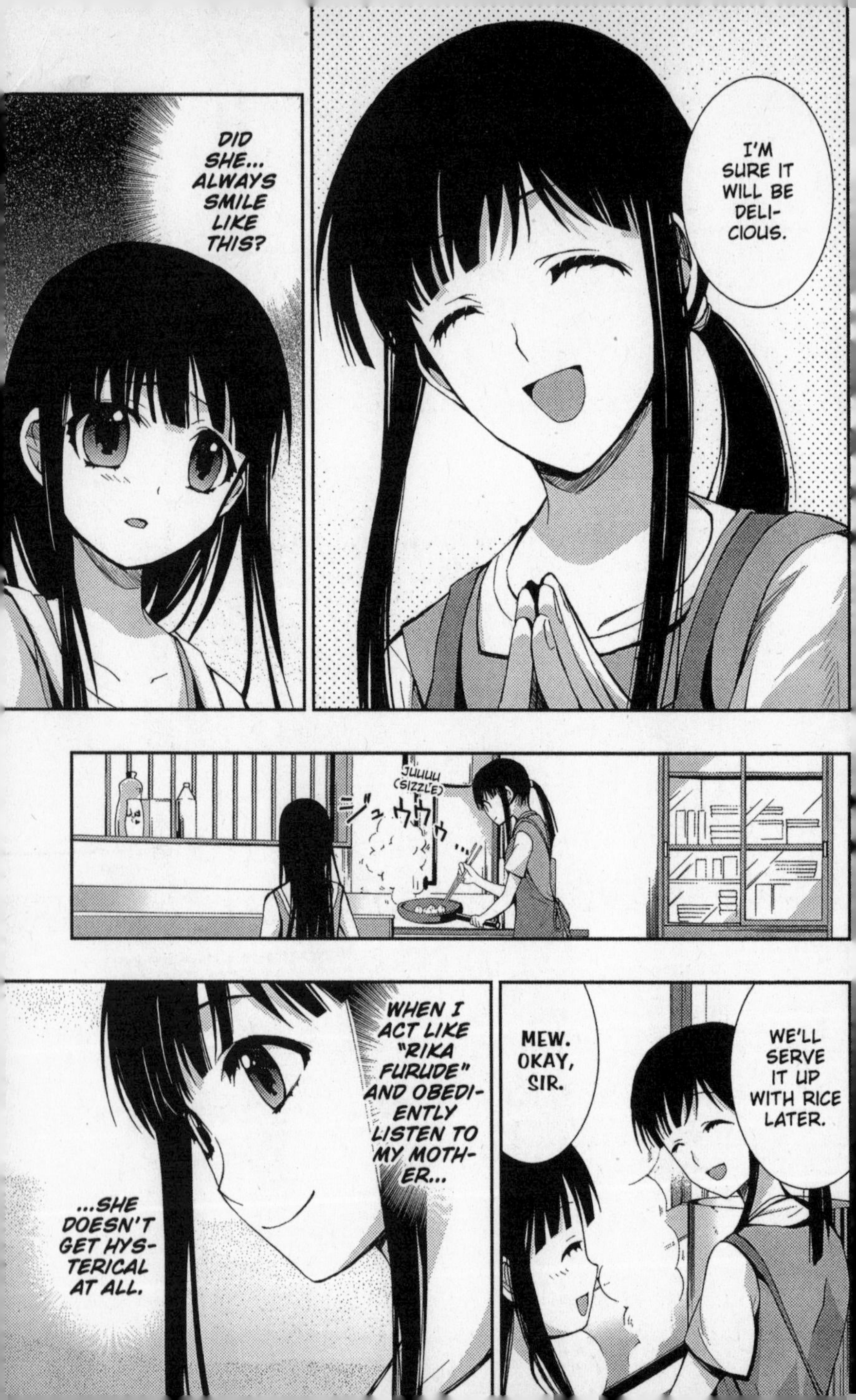
I'M SURE IT WILL BE DELI-CIOUS.
DID SHE... ALWAYS SMILE LIKE THIS?
ジュウウウ…
JUUUU (SIZZLE)
WE'LL SERVE IT UP WITH RICE LATER.
MEW. OKAY, SIR.
WHEN I ACT LIKE "RIKA FURUDE" AND OBEDI-ENTLY LISTEN TO MY MOTH-ER...
...SHE DOESN'T GET HYS-TERICAL AT ALL.

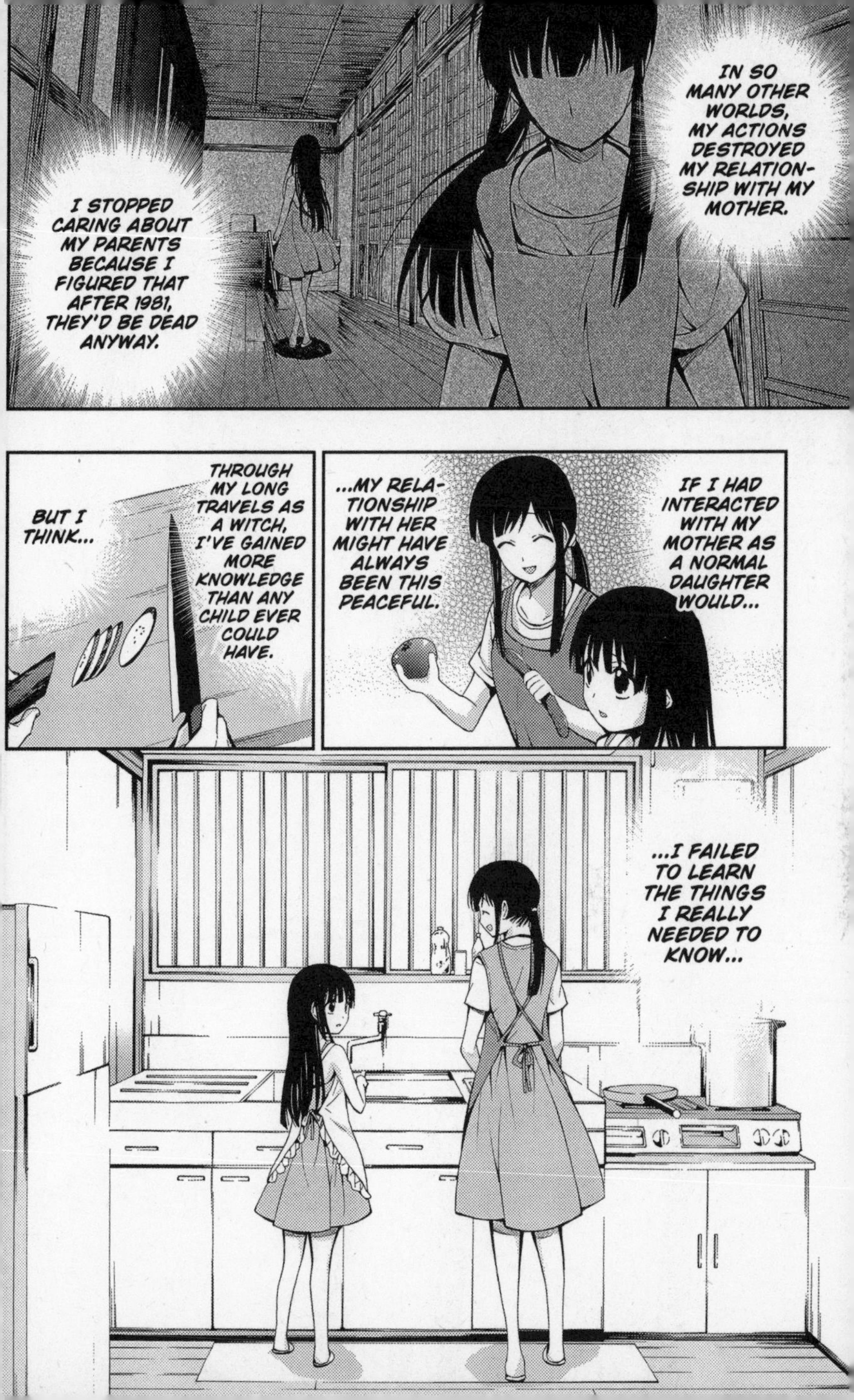
IN SO MANY OTHER WORLDS, MY ACTIONS DESTROYED MY RELATIONSHIP WITH MY MOTHER.
I STOPPED CARING ABOUT MY PARENTS BECAUSE I FIGURED THAT AFTER 1981, THEY'D BE DEAD ANYWAY.
IF I HAD INTERACTED WITH MY MOTHER AS A NORMAL DAUGHTER WOULD...
...MY RELATIONSHIP WITH HER MIGHT HAVE ALWAYS BEEN THIS PEACEFUL.
THROUGH MY LONG TRAVELS AS A WITCH, I'VE GAINED MORE KNOWLEDGE THAN ANY CHILD EVER COULD HAVE.
BUT I THINK...
...I FAILED TO LEARN THE THINGS I REALLY NEEDED TO KNOW...

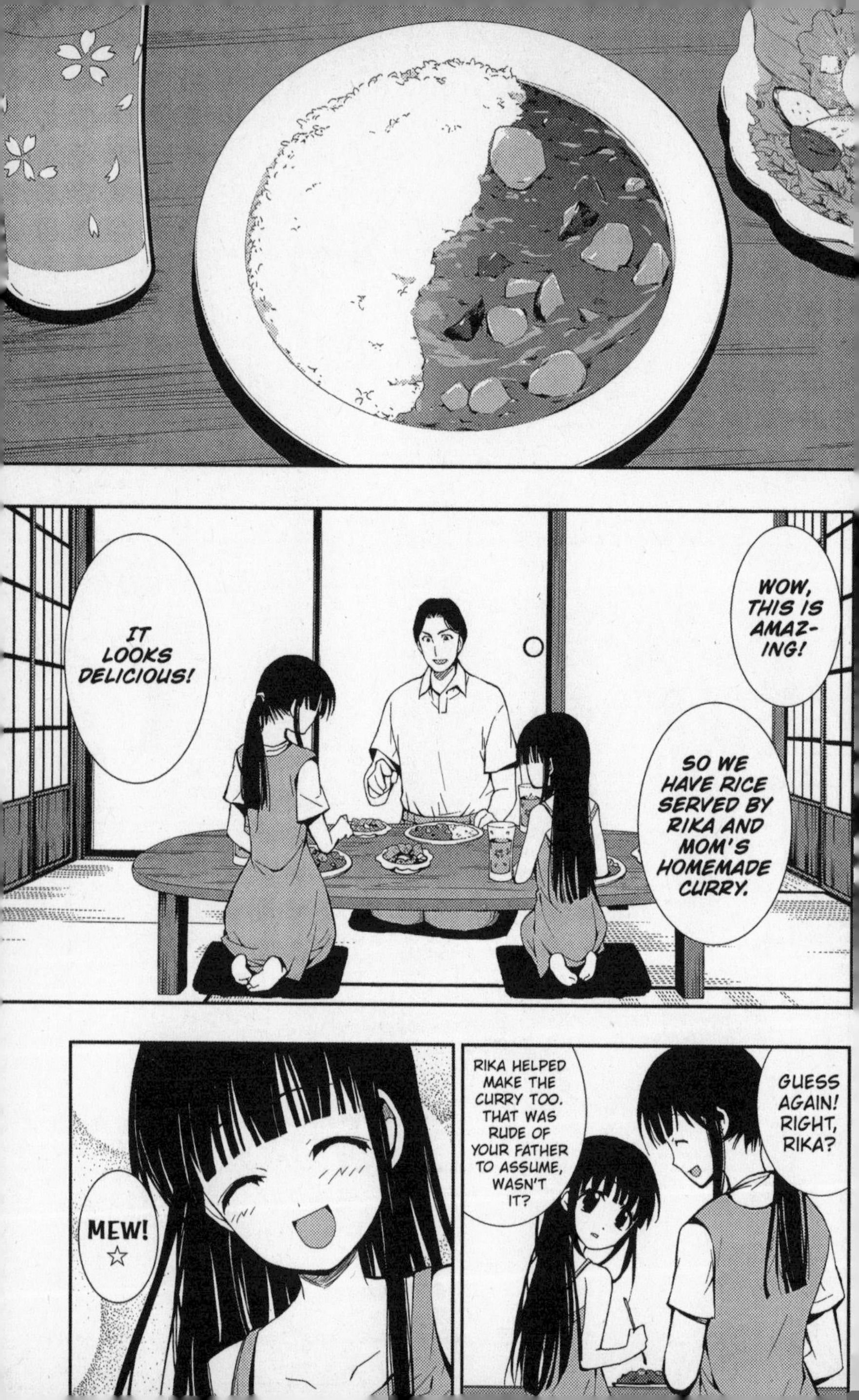
WOW, THIS IS AMAZ-ING!
SO WE HAVE RICE SERVED BY RIKA AND MOM'S HOMEMADE CURRY.
IT LOOKS DELICIOUS!
GUESS AGAIN! RIGHT, RIKA?
RIKA HELPED MAKE THE CURRY TOO. THAT WAS RUDE OF YOUR FATHER TO ASSUME, WASN'T IT?
MEW! ☆

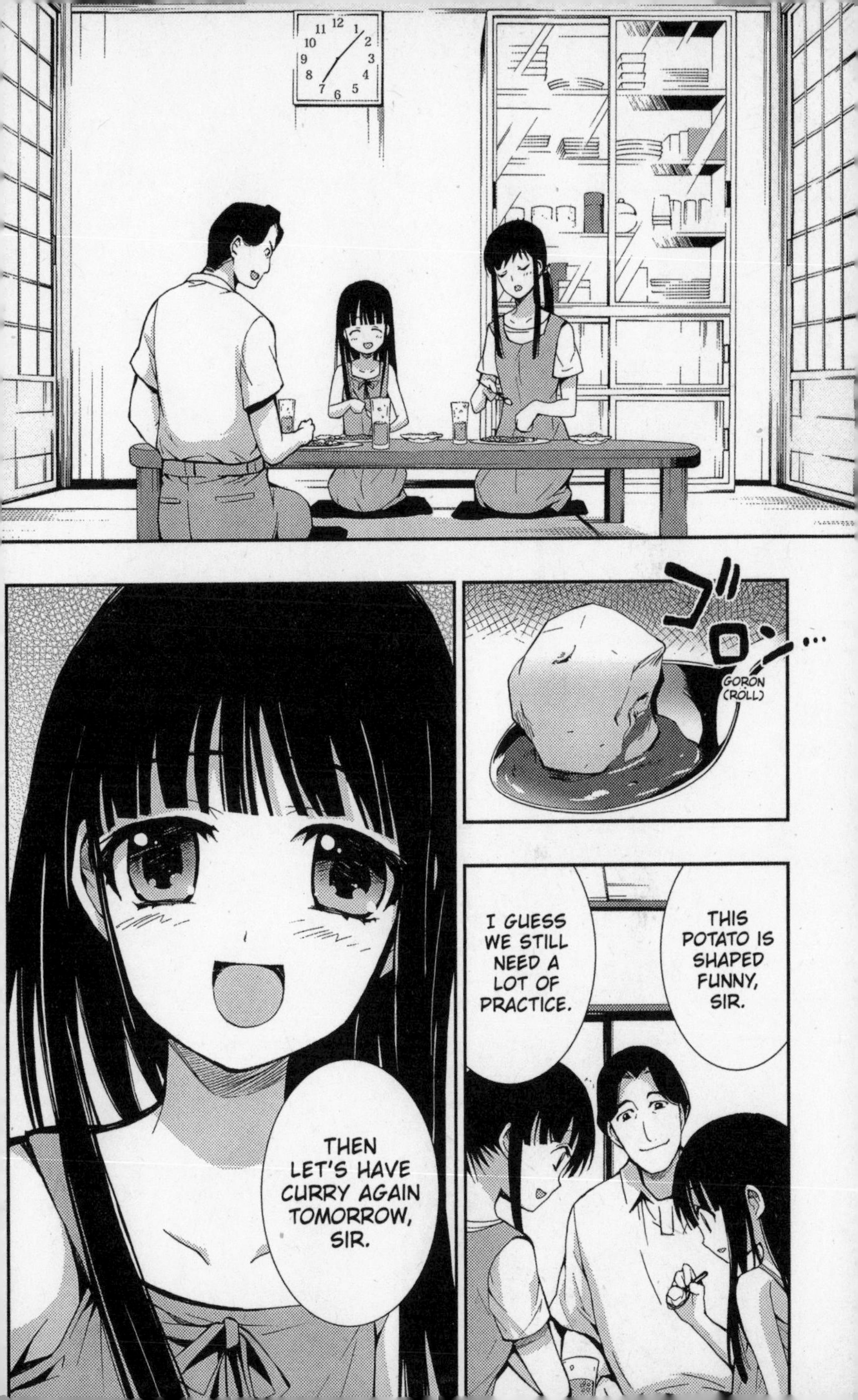
ゴロン…
GORON (ROLL)
THIS POTATO IS SHAPED FUNNY, SIR.
I GUESS WE STILL NEED A LOT OF PRACTICE.
THEN LET'S HAVE CURRY AGAIN TOMORROW, SIR.

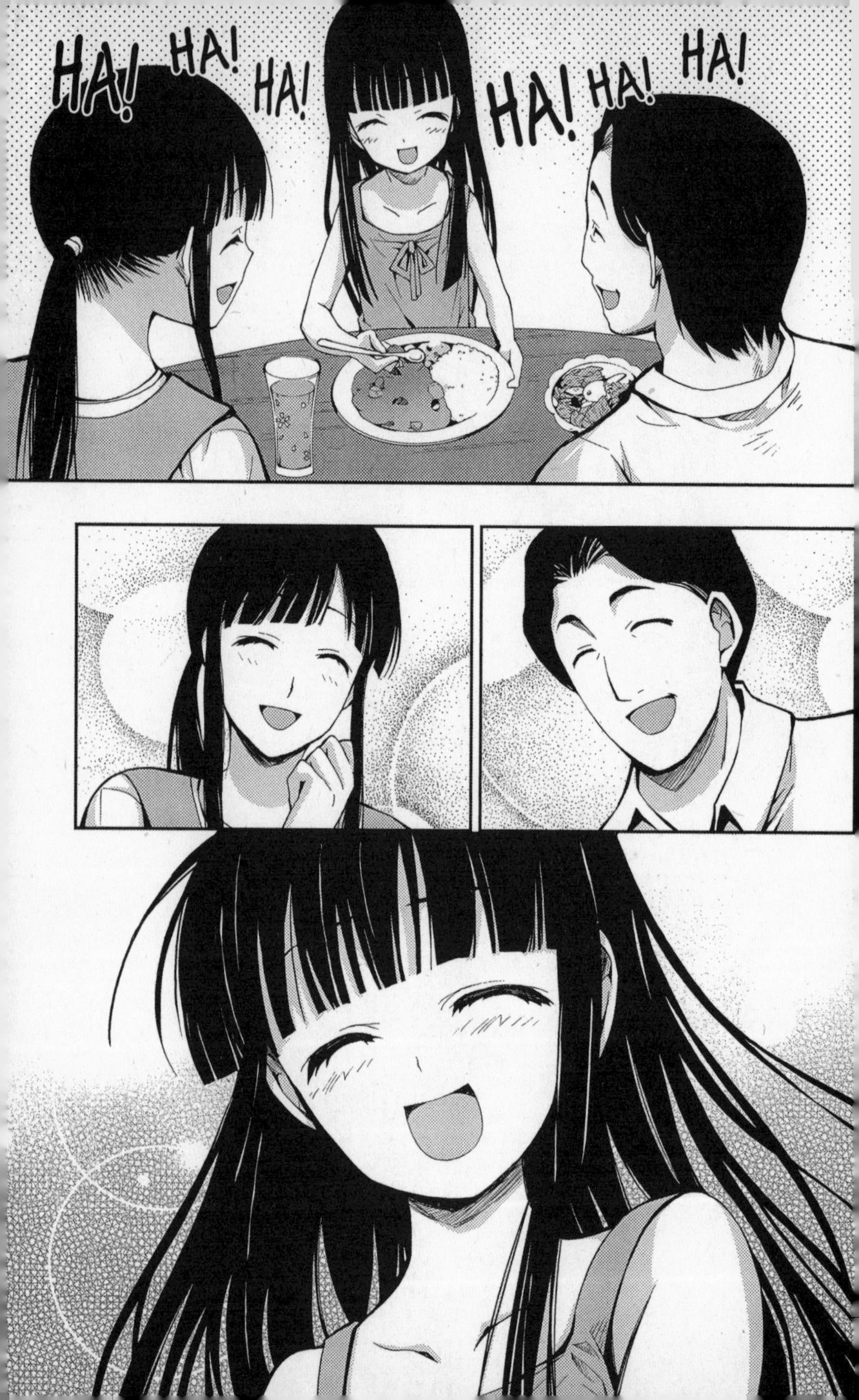
HA!
HA!
HA!
HA!
HA!
HA!

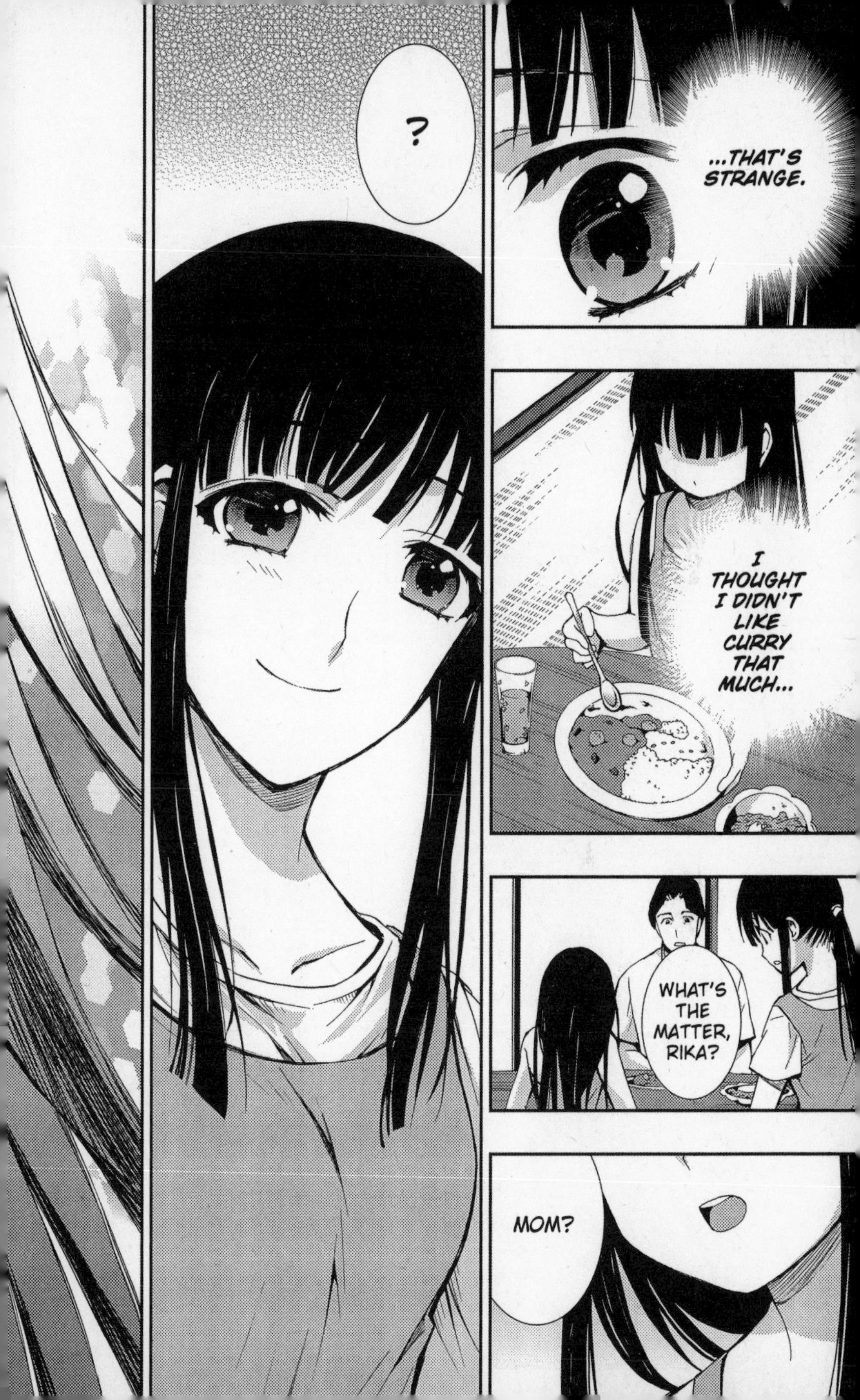
...THAT'S STRANGE.
I THOUGHT I DIDN'T LIKE CURRY THAT MUCH...
WHAT'S THE MATTER, RIKA?
MOM?
?

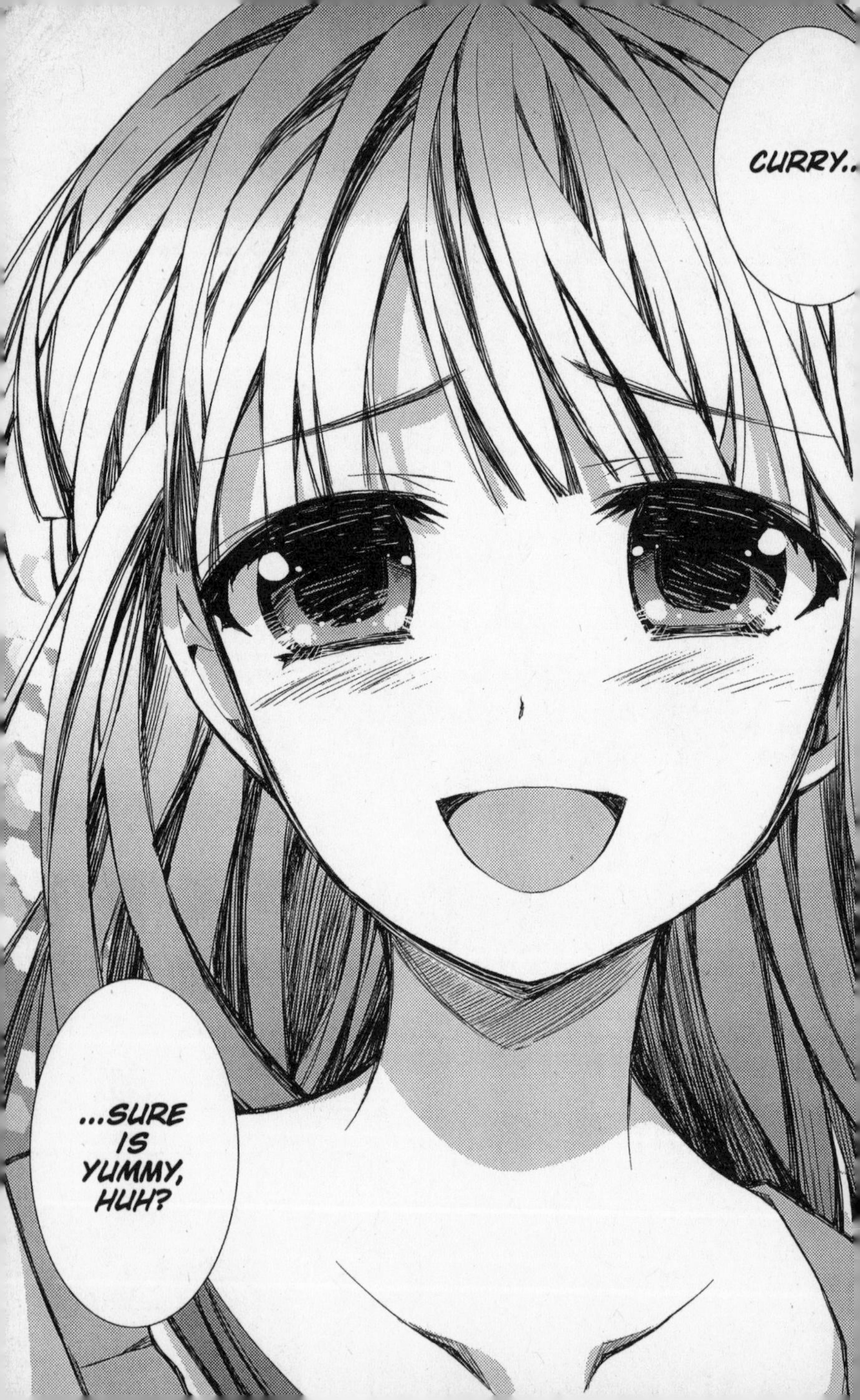
CURRY...
...SURE IS YUMMY, HUH?

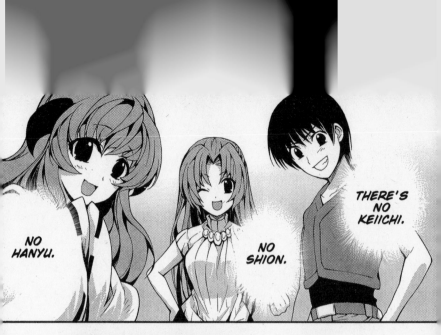

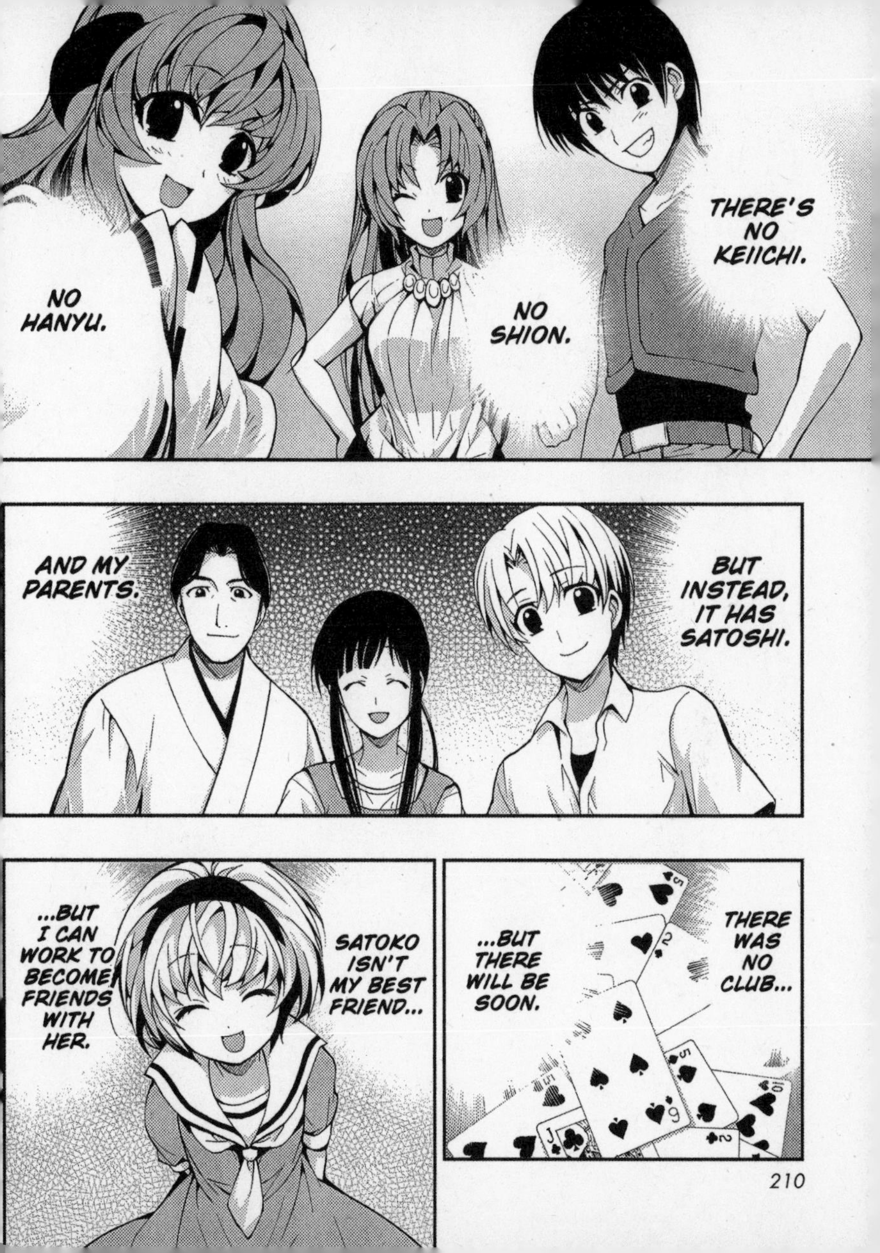
THERE'S NO KEIICHI.
NO SHION.
NO HANYU.
BUT INSTEAD, IT HAS SATOSHI.
AND MY PARENTS.
THERE WAS NO CLUB...
...BUT THERE WILL BE SOON.
SATOKO ISN'T MY BEST FRIEND...
...BUT I CAN WORK TO BECOME FRIENDS WITH HER.

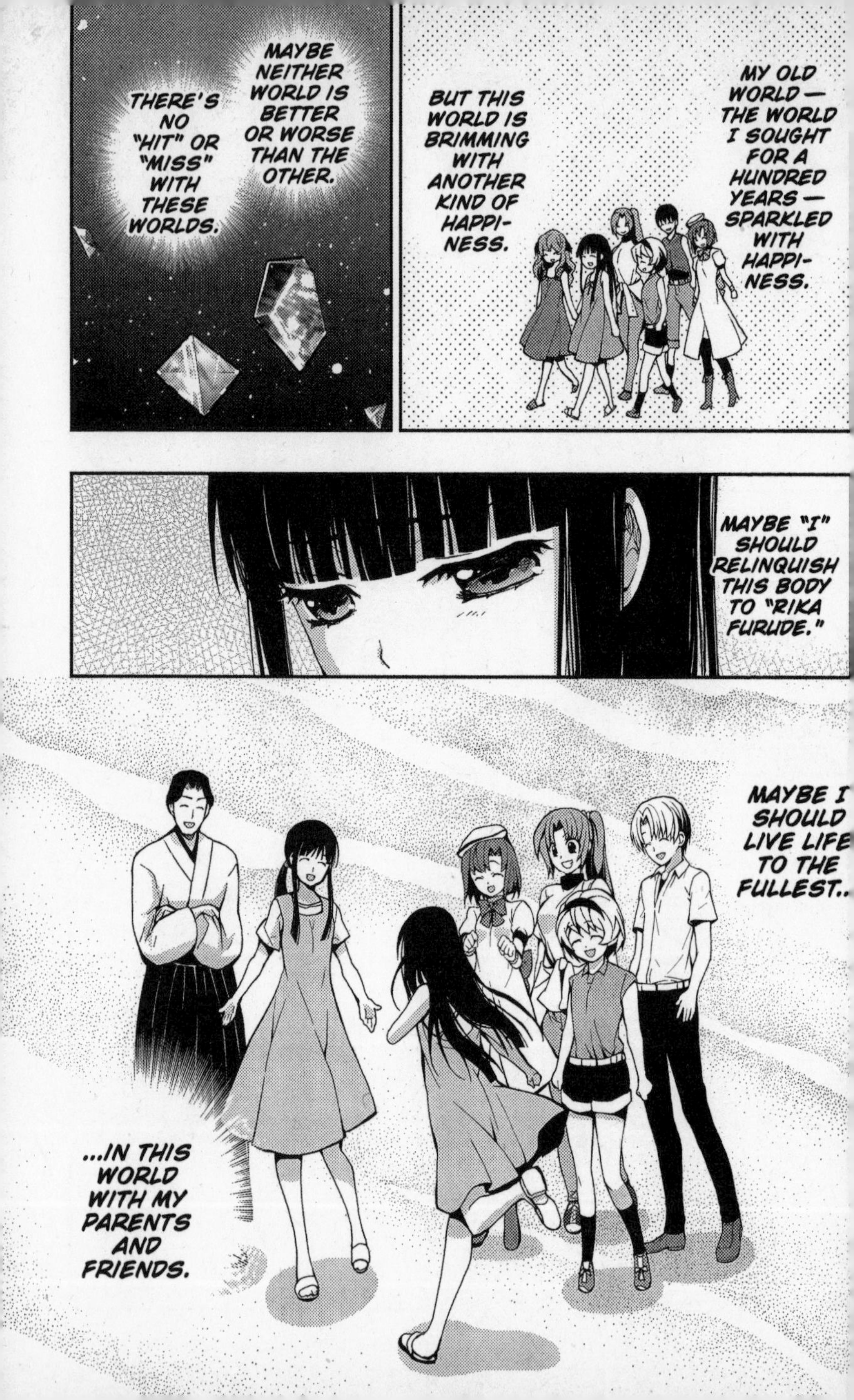
MY OLD WORLD—THE WORLD I SOUGHT FOR A HUNDRED YEARS—SPARKLED WITH HAPPINESS.
BUT THIS WORLD IS BRIMMING WITH ANOTHER KIND OF HAPPINESS.
MAYBE NEITHER WORLD IS BETTER OR WORSE THAN THE OTHER.
THERE'S NO "HIT" OR "MISS" WITH THESE WORLDS.
MAYBE "I" SHOULD RELINQUISH THIS BODY TO "RIKA FURUDE."
MAYBE I SHOULD LIVE LIFE TO THE FULLEST..
...IN THIS WORLD WITH MY PARENTS AND FRIENDS.

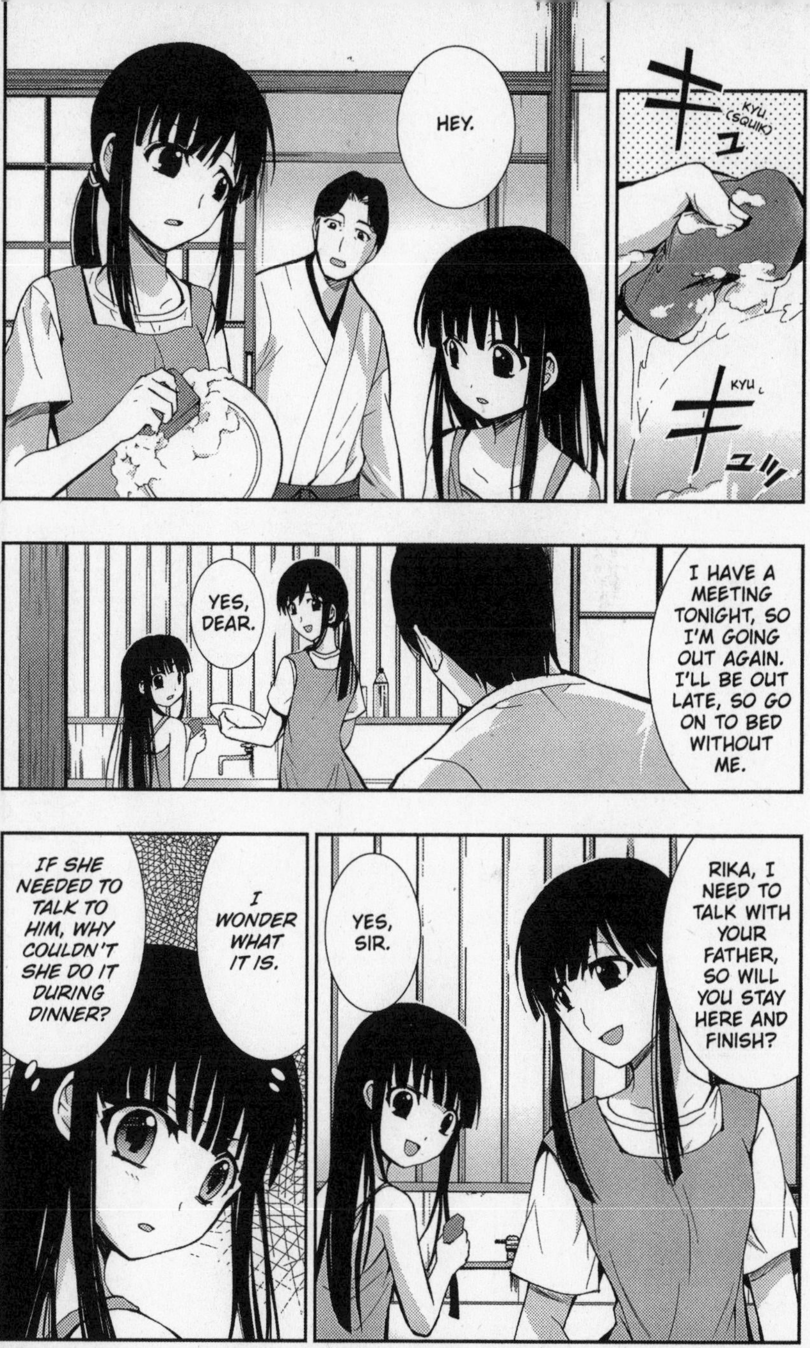
キュ
KYU. (SQUIK)
キュッ
KYU
HEY.
I HAVE A MEETING TONIGHT, SO I'M GOING OUT AGAIN. I'LL BE OUT LATE, SO GO ON TO BED WITHOUT ME.
YES, DEAR.
RIKA, I NEED TO TALK WITH YOUR FATHER, SO WILL YOU STAY HERE AND FINISH?
YES, SIR.
I WONDER WHAT IT IS.
IF SHE NEEDED TO TALK TO HIM, WHY COULDN'T SHE DO IT DURING DINNER?

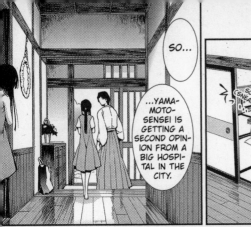

SO...

...YAMAMOTO-SENSEI IS GETTING A SECOND OPINION FROM A BIG HOSPITAL IN THE CITY.

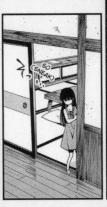

SO SNEAK)

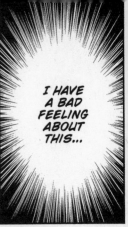

I HAVE A BAD FEELING ABOUT THIS...

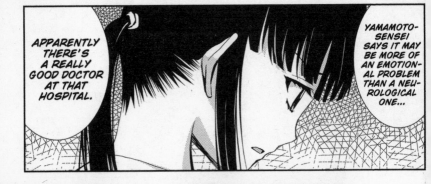

APPARENTLY THERE'S A REALLY GOOD DOCTOR AT THAT HOSPITAL.

YAMAMOTO-SENSEI SAYS IT MAY BE MORE OF AN EMOTIONAL PROBLEM THAN A NEUROLOGICAL ONE...

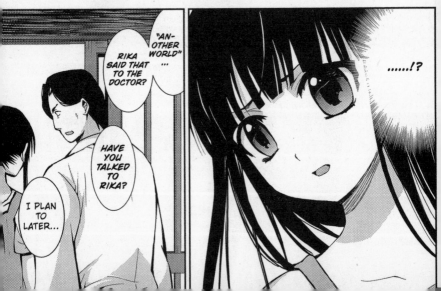

"AN-OTHER WORLD"...

RIKA SAID THAT TO THE DOCTOR?

HAVE YOU TALKED TO RIKA?

I PLAN TO LATER...

......!?

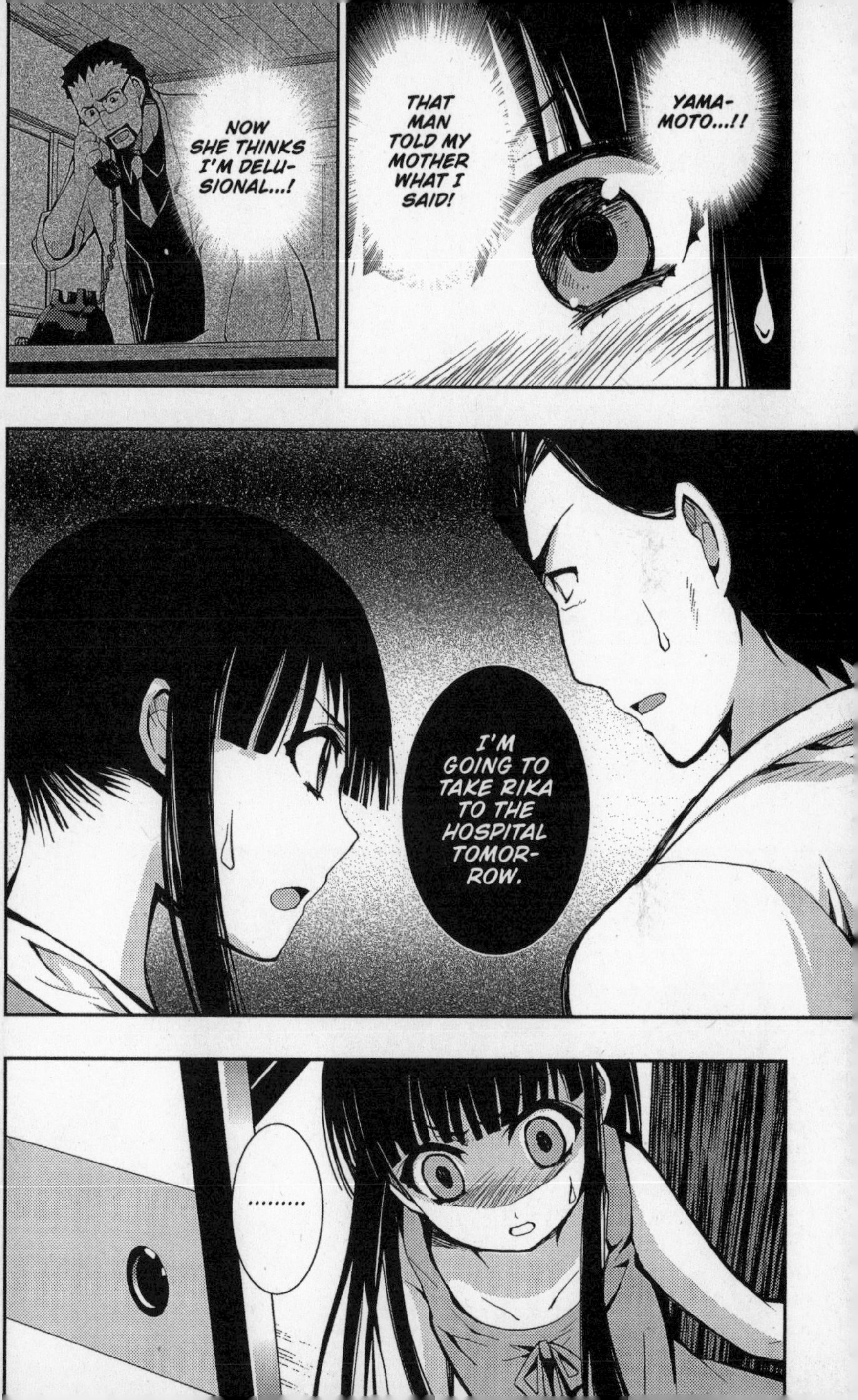
YAMA-MOTO...!!
THAT MAN TOLD MY MOTHER WHAT I SAID!
NOW SHE THINKS I'M DELU-SIONAL...!
I'M GOING TO TAKE RIKA TO THE HOSPITAL TOMOR-ROW.
....

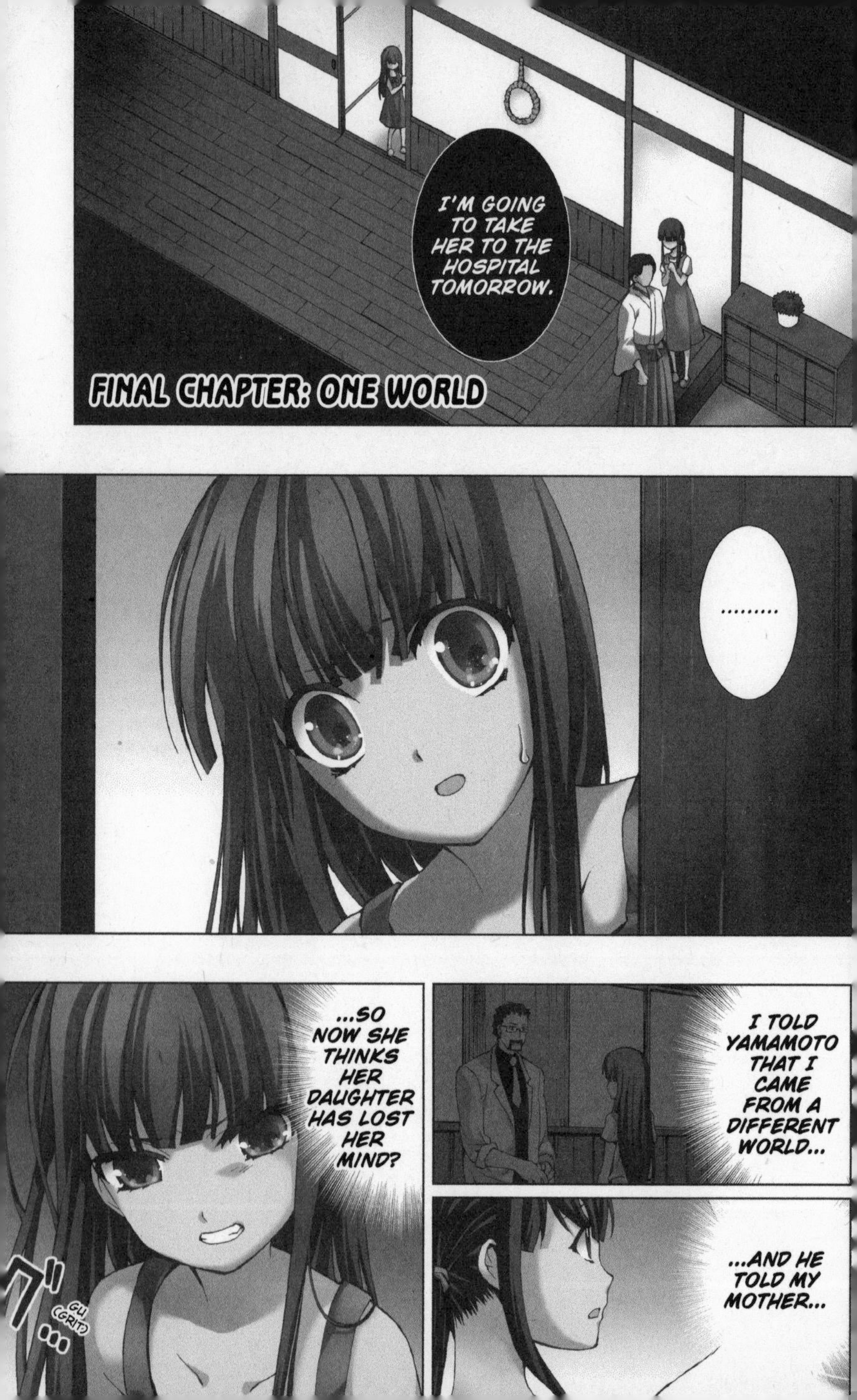
I'M GOING TO TAKE HER TO THE HOSPITAL TOMORROW.
FINAL CHAPTER: ONE WORLD
....
I TOLD YAMAMOTO THAT I CAME FROM A DIFFERENT WORLD...
...AND HE TOLD MY MOTHER...
...SO NOW SHE THINKS HER DAUGHTER HAS LOST HER MIND?
GU (GRIT)

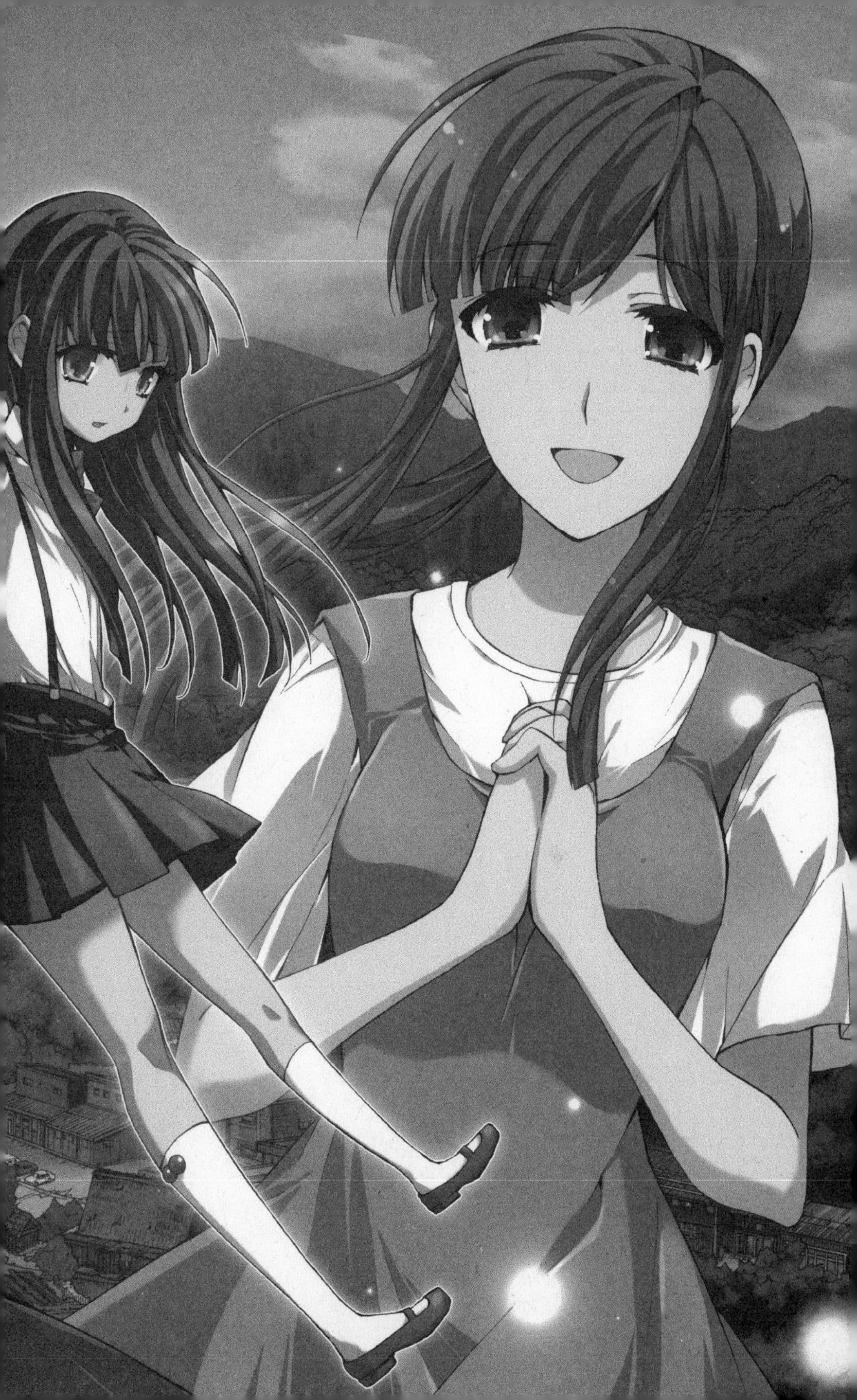

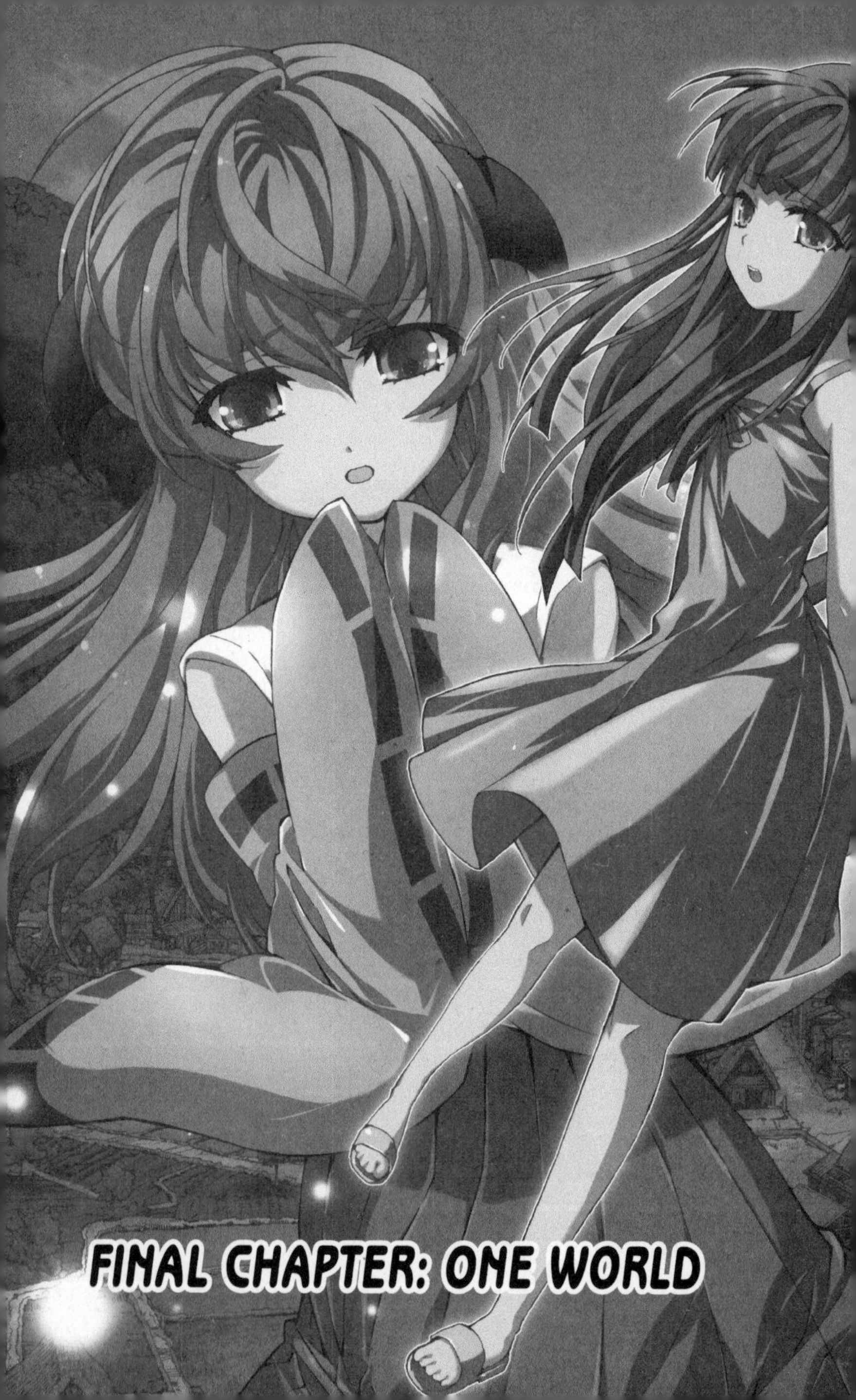

FINAL CHAPTER: ONE WORLD

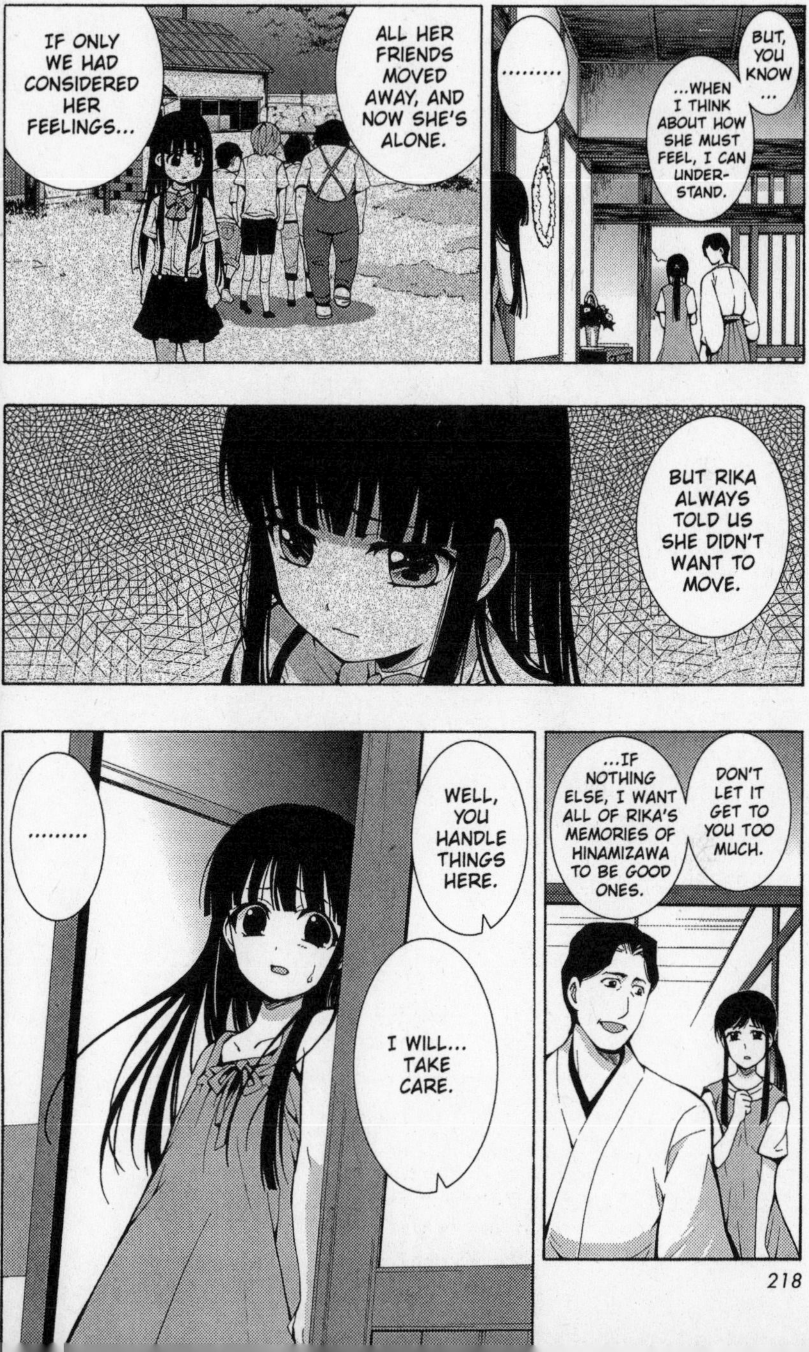
BUT, YOU KNOW ...
...WHEN I THINK ABOUT HOW SHE MUST FEEL, I CAN UNDERSTAND.
....
ALL HER FRIENDS MOVED AWAY, AND NOW SHE'S ALONE.
IF ONLY WE HAD CONSIDERED HER FEELINGS...
BUT RIKA ALWAYS TOLD US SHE DIDN'T WANT TO MOVE.
DON'T LET IT GET TO YOU TOO MUCH.
...IF NOTHING ELSE, I WANT ALL OF RIKA'S MEMORIES OF HINAMIZAWA TO BE GOOD ONES.
WELL, YOU HANDLE THINGS HERE.
I WILL... TAKE CARE.
....

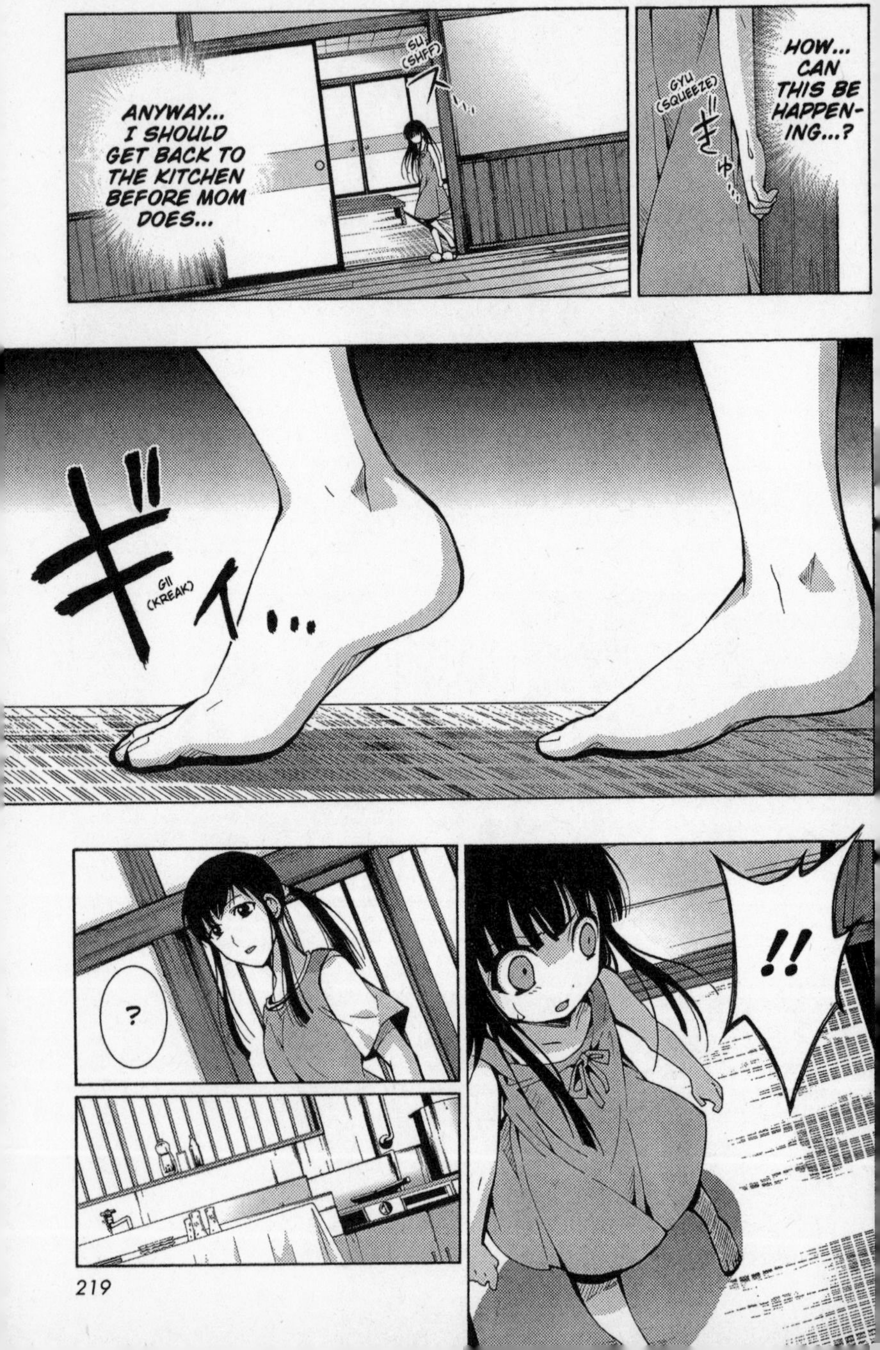
HOW... CAN THIS BE HAPPEN-ING...?
GYU (SQUEEZE)
ぎゅ...
ANYWAY... I SHOULD GET BACK TO THE KITCHEN BEFORE MOM DOES...
SU (SHFF)
ギィ...
GII (KREAK)
!!
?

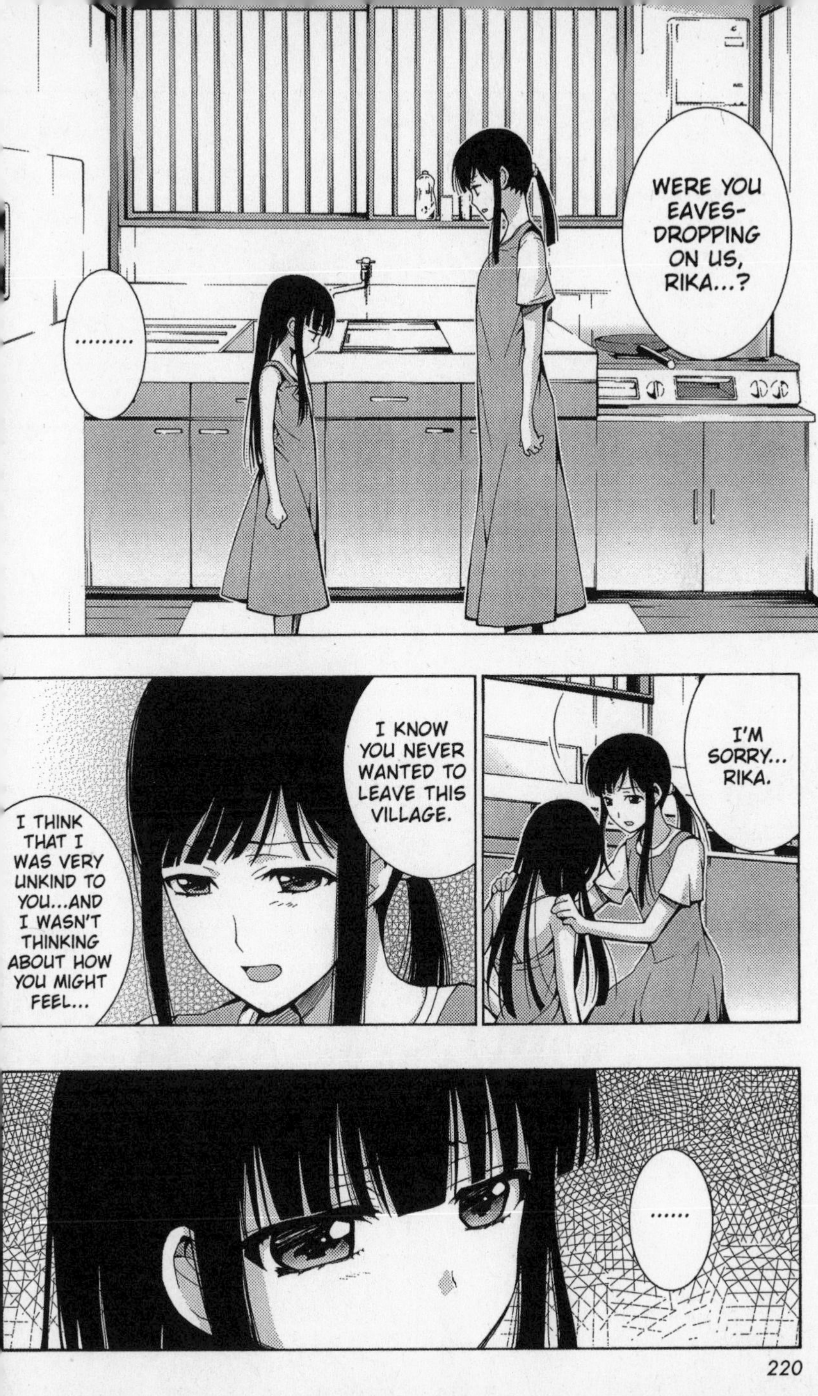
WERE YOU EAVES-DROPPING ON US, RIKA...?
....
I'M SORRY... RIKA.
I KNOW YOU NEVER WANTED TO LEAVE THIS VILLAGE.
I THINK THAT I WAS VERY UNKIND TO YOU...AND I WASN'T THINKING ABOUT HOW YOU MIGHT FEEL...
......

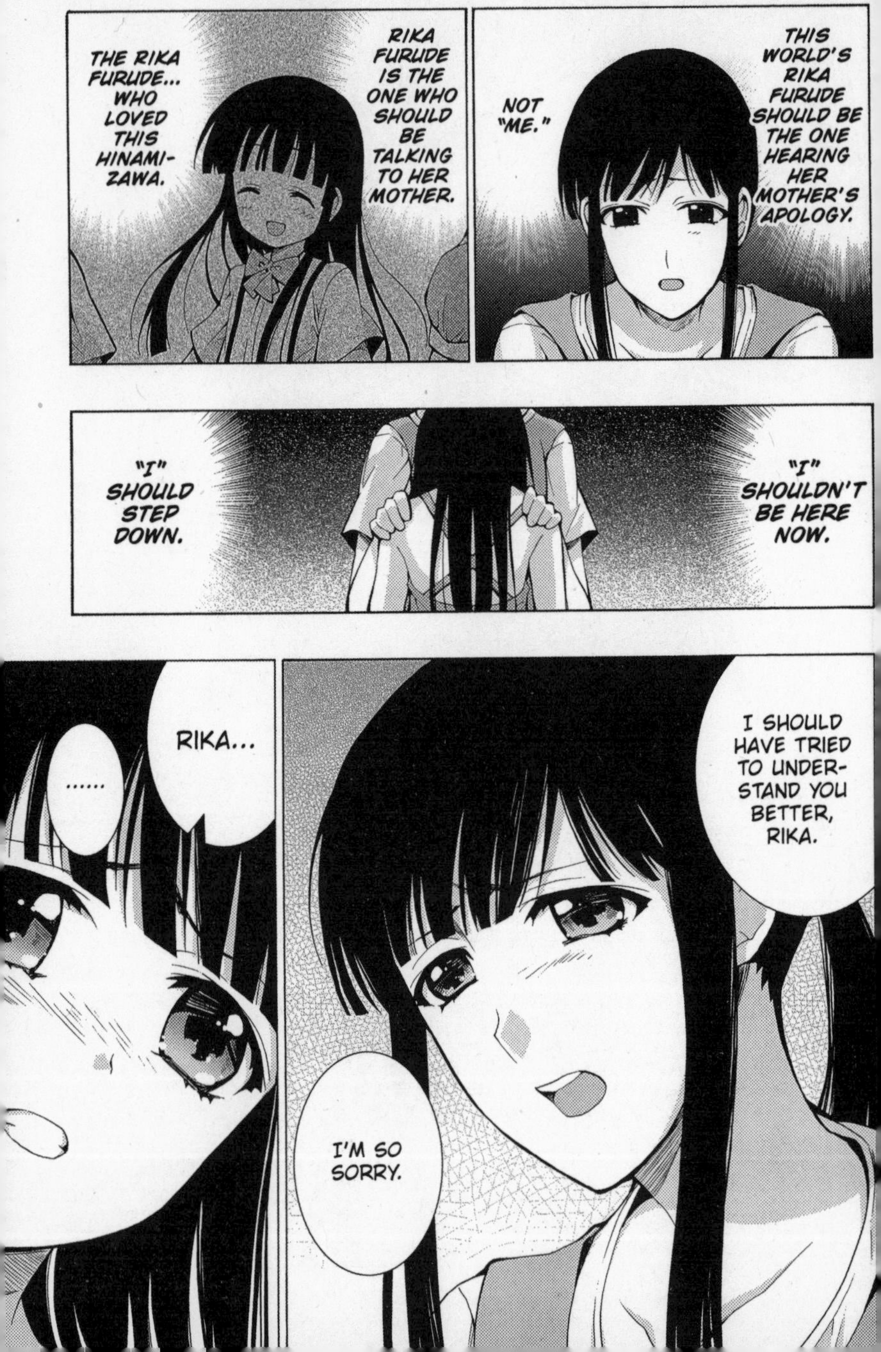
THIS WORLD'S RIKA FURUDE SHOULD BE THE ONE HEARING HER MOTHER'S APOLOGY.
NOT "ME."
RIKA FURUDE IS THE ONE WHO SHOULD BE TALKING TO HER MOTHER.
THE RIKA FURUDE... WHO LOVED THIS HINAMI-ZAWA.
"I" SHOULDN'T BE HERE NOW.
"I" SHOULD STEP DOWN.
I SHOULD HAVE TRIED TO UNDER-STAND YOU BETTER, RIKA.
I'M SO SORRY.
RIKA...
......

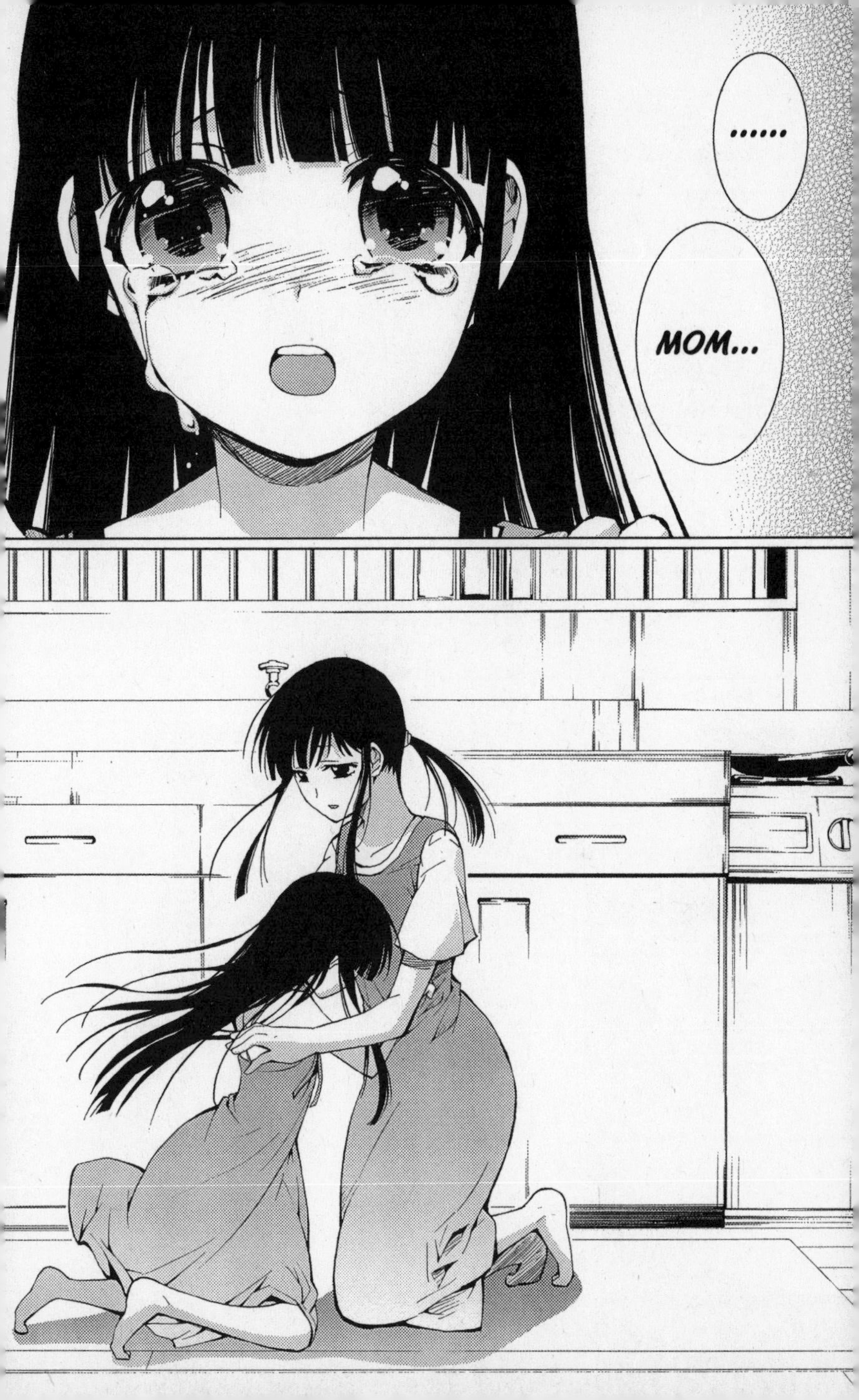
......
MOM...

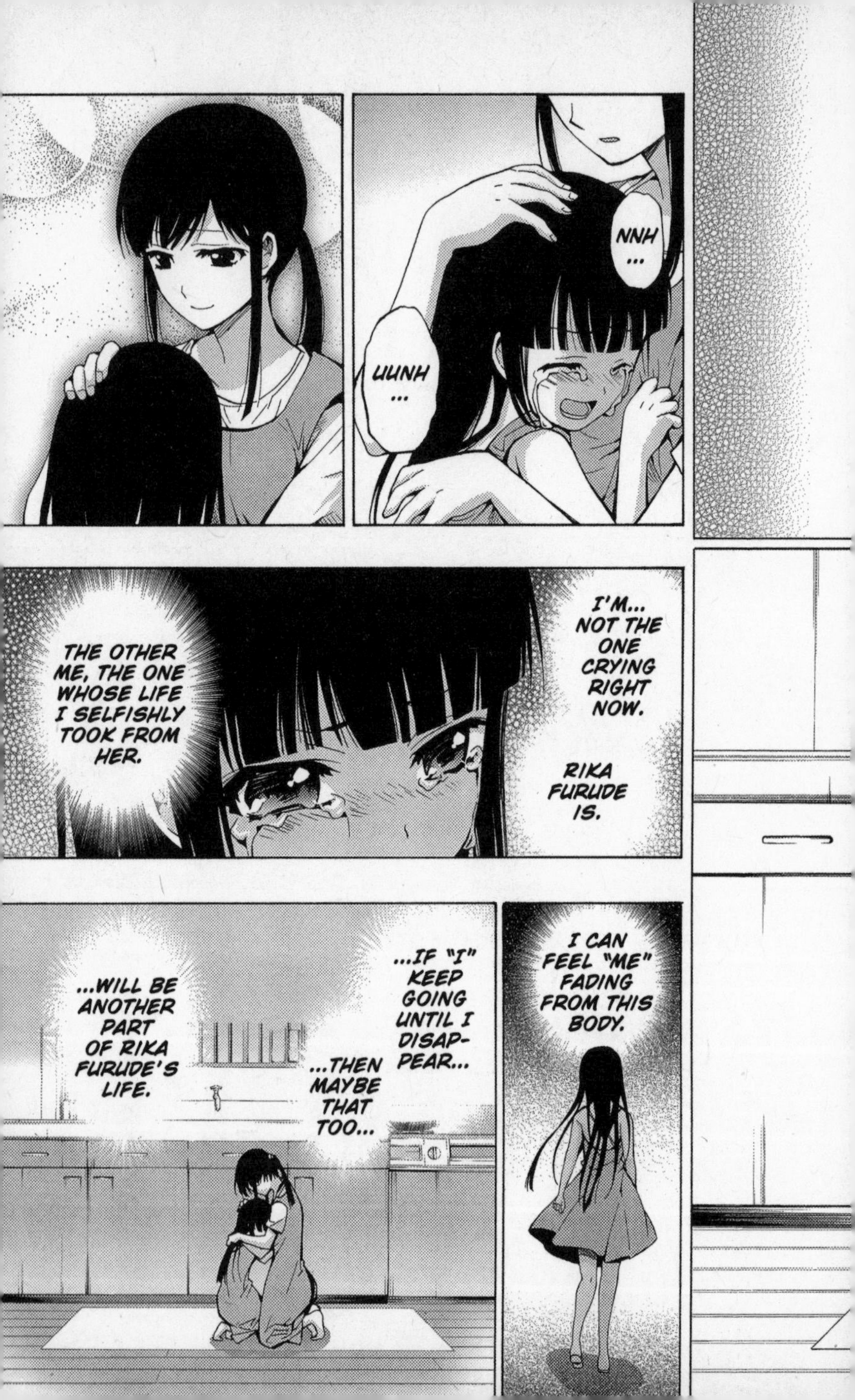
NNH ...
UUNH ...
I'M... NOT THE ONE CRYING RIGHT NOW.
RIKA FURUDE IS.
THE OTHER ME, THE ONE WHOSE LIFE I SELFISHLY TOOK FROM HER.
I CAN FEEL "ME" FADING FROM THIS BODY.
...IF "I" KEEP GOING UNTIL I DISAP-PEAR...
...THEN MAYBE THAT TOO...
...WILL BE ANOTHER PART OF RIKA FURUDE'S LIFE.

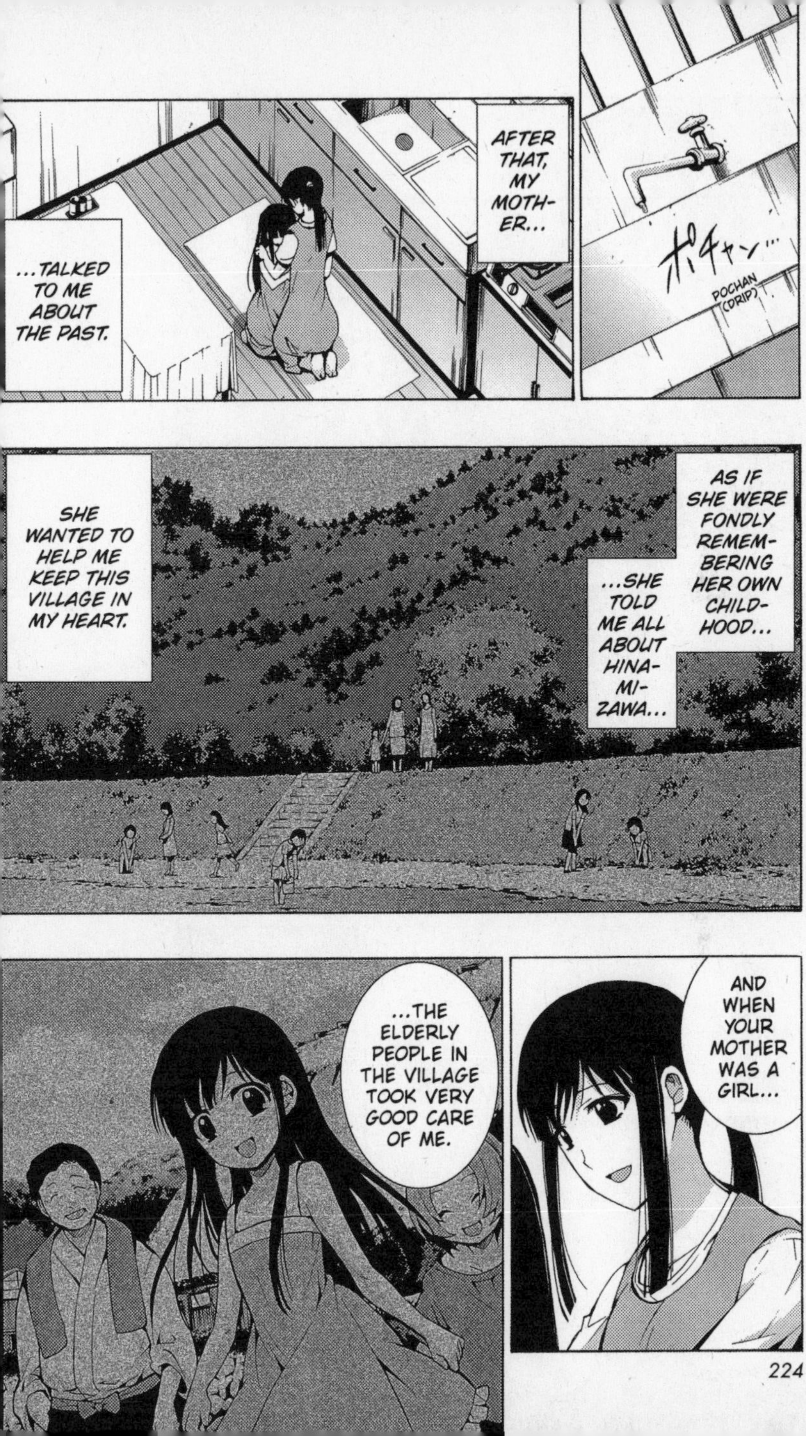
ポチャン…
POCHAN (DRIP)
AFTER THAT, MY MOTHER...
...TALKED TO ME ABOUT THE PAST.
AS IF SHE WERE FONDLY REMEMBERING HER OWN CHILDHOOD...
...SHE TOLD ME ALL ABOUT HINAMIZAWA...
SHE WANTED TO HELP ME KEEP THIS VILLAGE IN MY HEART.
AND WHEN YOUR MOTHER WAS A GIRL...
...THE ELDERLY PEOPLE IN THE VILLAGE TOOK VERY GOOD CARE OF ME.

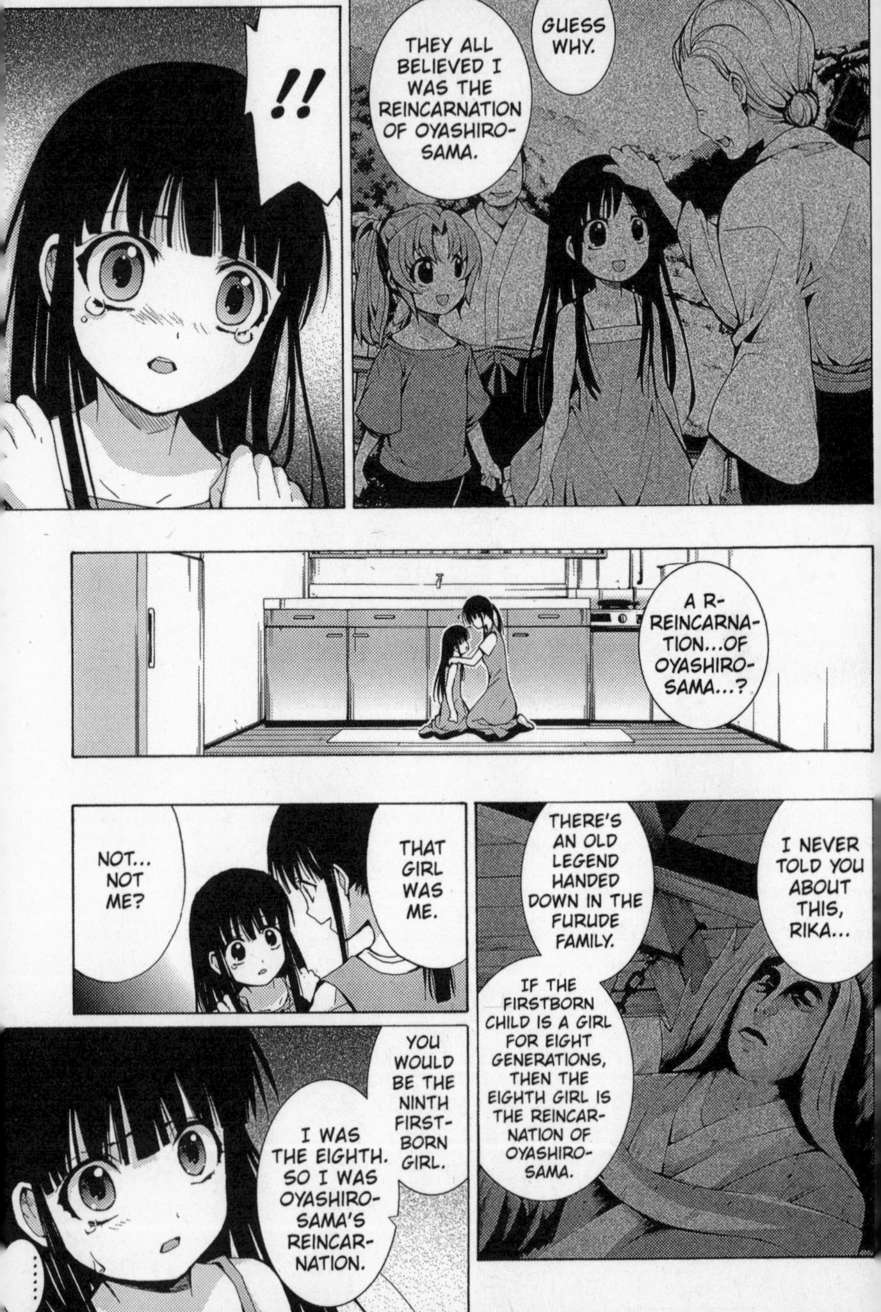
GUESS WHY.
THEY ALL BELIEVED I WAS THE REINCARNATION OF OYASHIRO-SAMA.
!!
A R-REINCARNATION...OF OYASHIRO-SAMA...?
I NEVER TOLD YOU ABOUT THIS, RIKA...
THERE'S AN OLD LEGEND HANDED DOWN IN THE FURUDE FAMILY.
IF THE FIRSTBORN CHILD IS A GIRL FOR EIGHT GENERATIONS, THEN THE EIGHTH GIRL IS THE REINCARNATION OF OYASHIRO-SAMA.
THAT GIRL WAS ME.
NOT... NOT ME?
YOU WOULD BE THE NINTH FIRST-BORN GIRL.
I WAS THE EIGHTH. SO I WAS OYASHIRO-SAMA'S REINCARNATION.

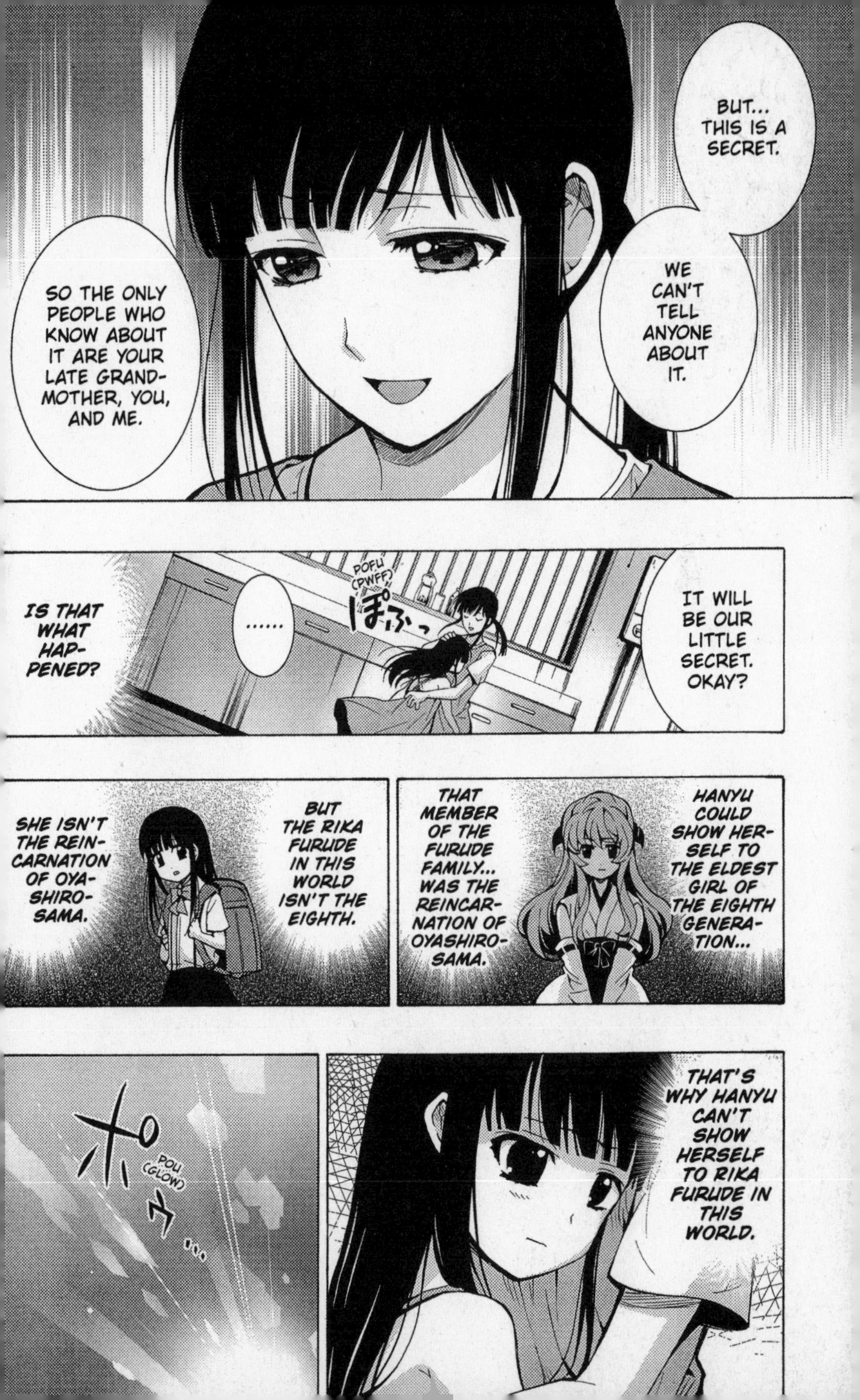
BUT... THIS IS A SECRET.
WE CAN'T TELL ANYONE ABOUT IT.
SO THE ONLY PEOPLE WHO KNOW ABOUT IT ARE YOUR LATE GRANDMOTHER, YOU, AND ME.
IT WILL BE OUR LITTLE SECRET. OKAY?
POFU (PWFF)
......
IS THAT WHAT HAPPENED?
HANYU COULD SHOW HERSELF TO THE ELDEST GIRL OF THE EIGHTH GENERATION...
THAT MEMBER OF THE FURUDE FAMILY... WAS THE REINCARNATION OF OYASHIRO-SAMA.
BUT THE RIKA FURUDE IN THIS WORLD ISN'T THE EIGHTH.
SHE ISN'T THE REINCARNATION OF OYASHIRO-SAMA.
THAT'S WHY HANYU CAN'T SHOW HERSELF TO RIKA FURUDE IN THIS WORLD.
POU (GLOW)

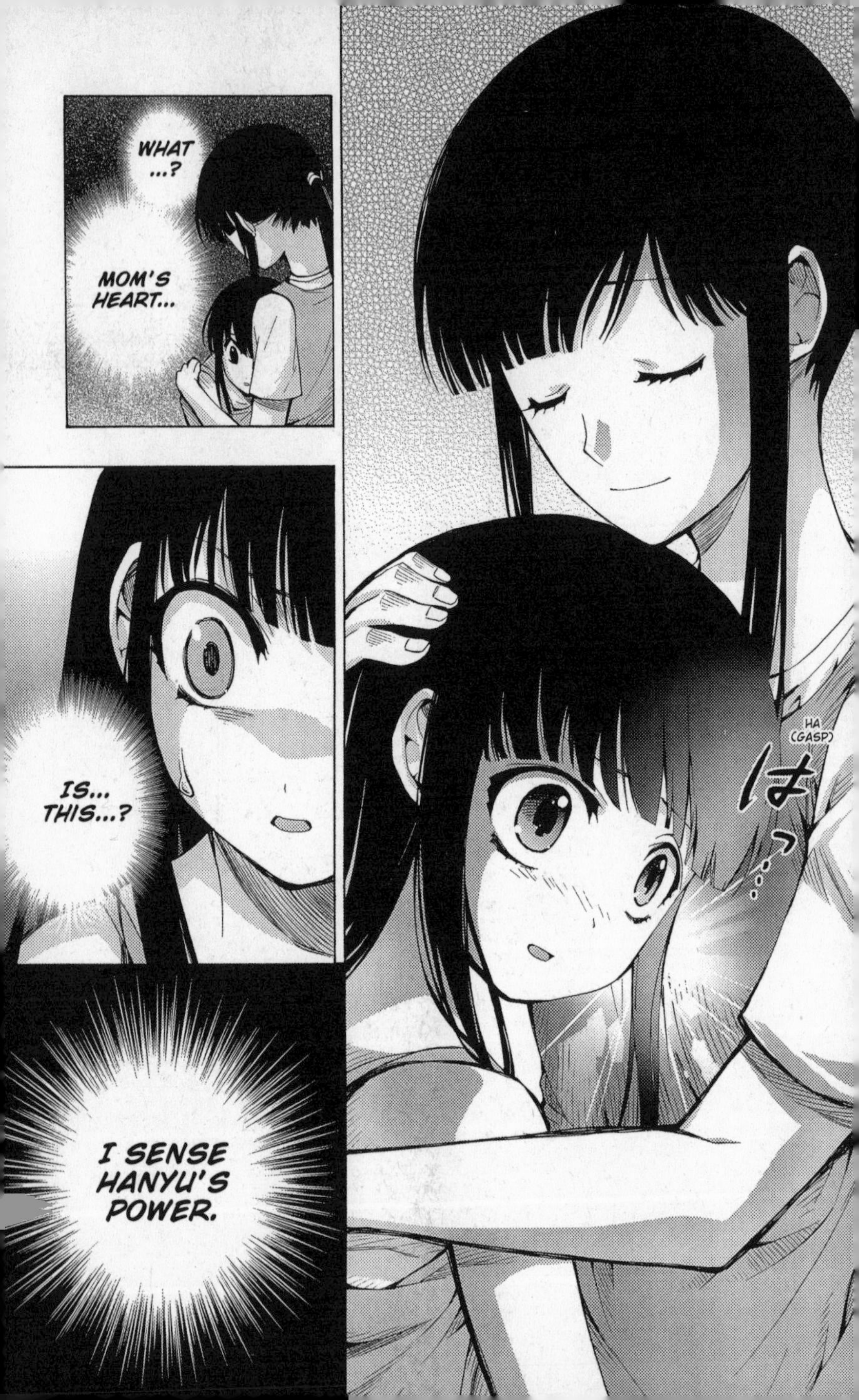
HA (GASP)
はっ…
WHAT ...?
MOM'S HEART...
IS... THIS...?
I SENSE HANYU'S POWER.

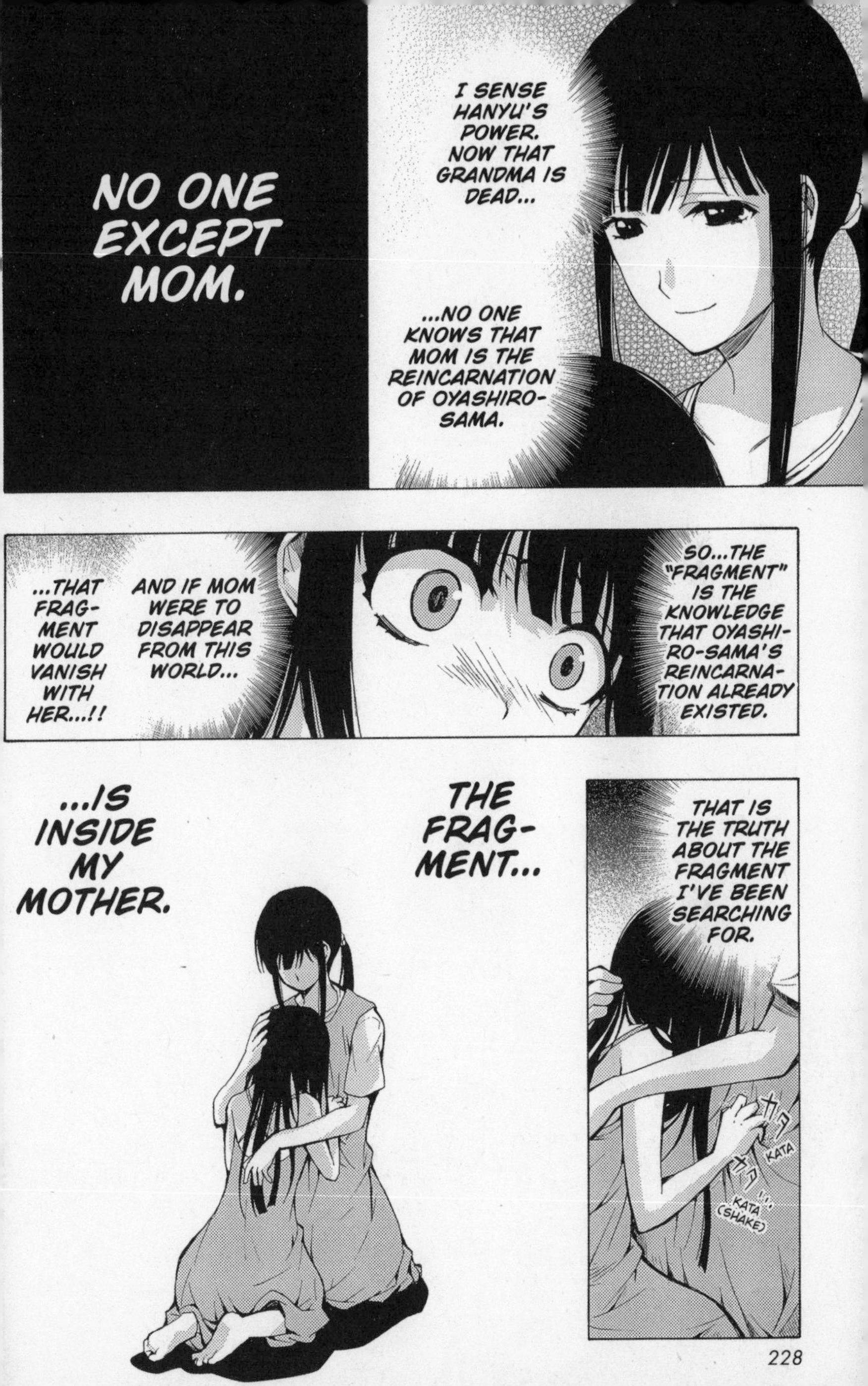
I SENSE HANYU'S POWER. NOW THAT GRANDMA IS DEAD...
...NO ONE KNOWS THAT MOM IS THE REINCARNATION OF OYASHIRO-SAMA.
NO ONE EXCEPT MOM.
SO...THE "FRAGMENT" IS THE KNOWLEDGE THAT OYASHIRO-SAMA'S REINCARNATION ALREADY EXISTED.
AND IF MOM WERE TO DISAPPEAR FROM THIS WORLD...
...THAT FRAGMENT WOULD VANISH WITH HER...!!
THAT IS THE TRUTH ABOUT THE FRAGMENT I'VE BEEN SEARCHING FOR.
KATA
KATA (SHAKE)
THE FRAGMENT...
...IS INSIDE MY MOTHER.

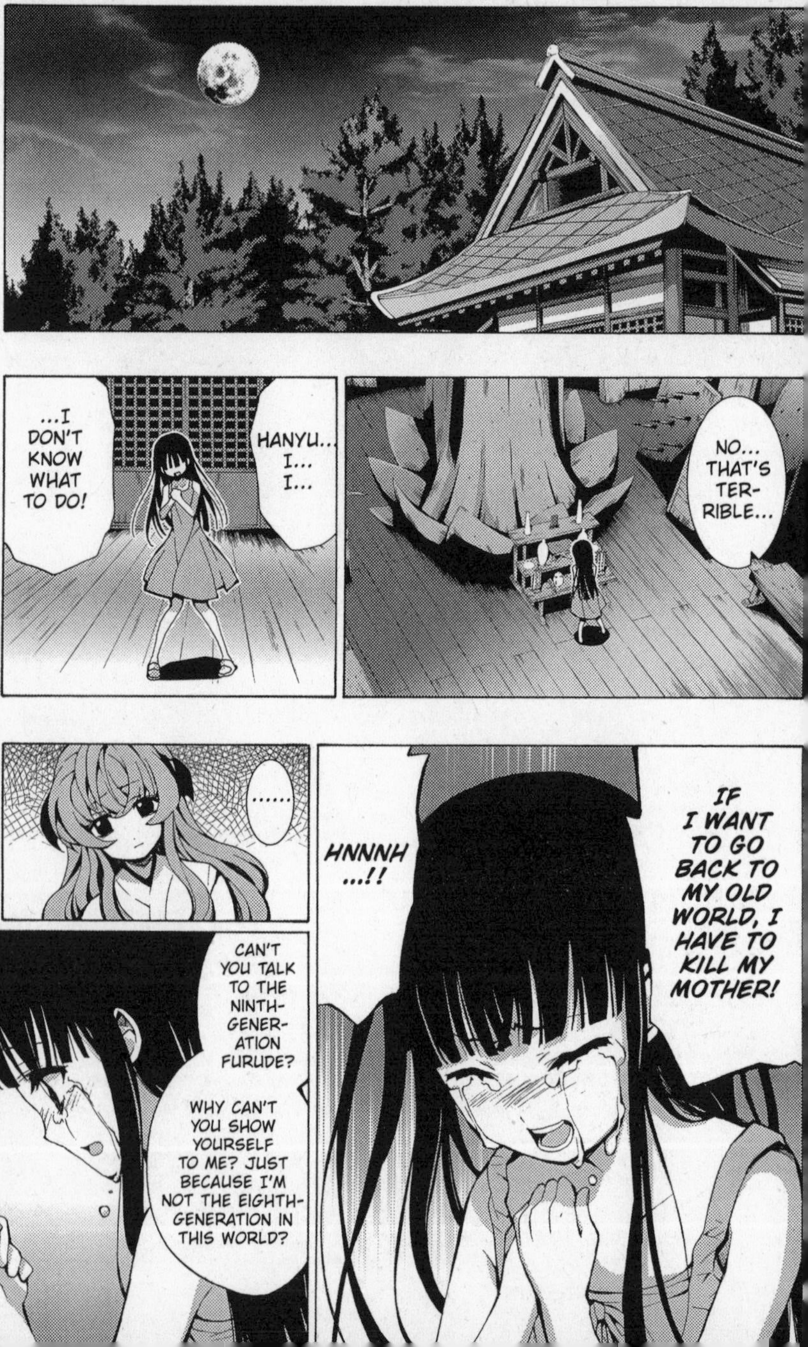
NO... THAT'S TER-RIBLE...
HANYU... I... I...
...I DON'T KNOW WHAT TO DO!
IF I WANT TO GO BACK TO MY OLD WORLD, I HAVE TO KILL MY MOTHER!
HNNNH ...!!
......
CAN'T YOU TALK TO THE NINTH-GENER-ATION FURUDE?
WHY CAN'T YOU SHOW YOURSELF TO ME? JUST BECAUSE I'M NOT THE EIGHTH-GENERATION IN THIS WORLD?

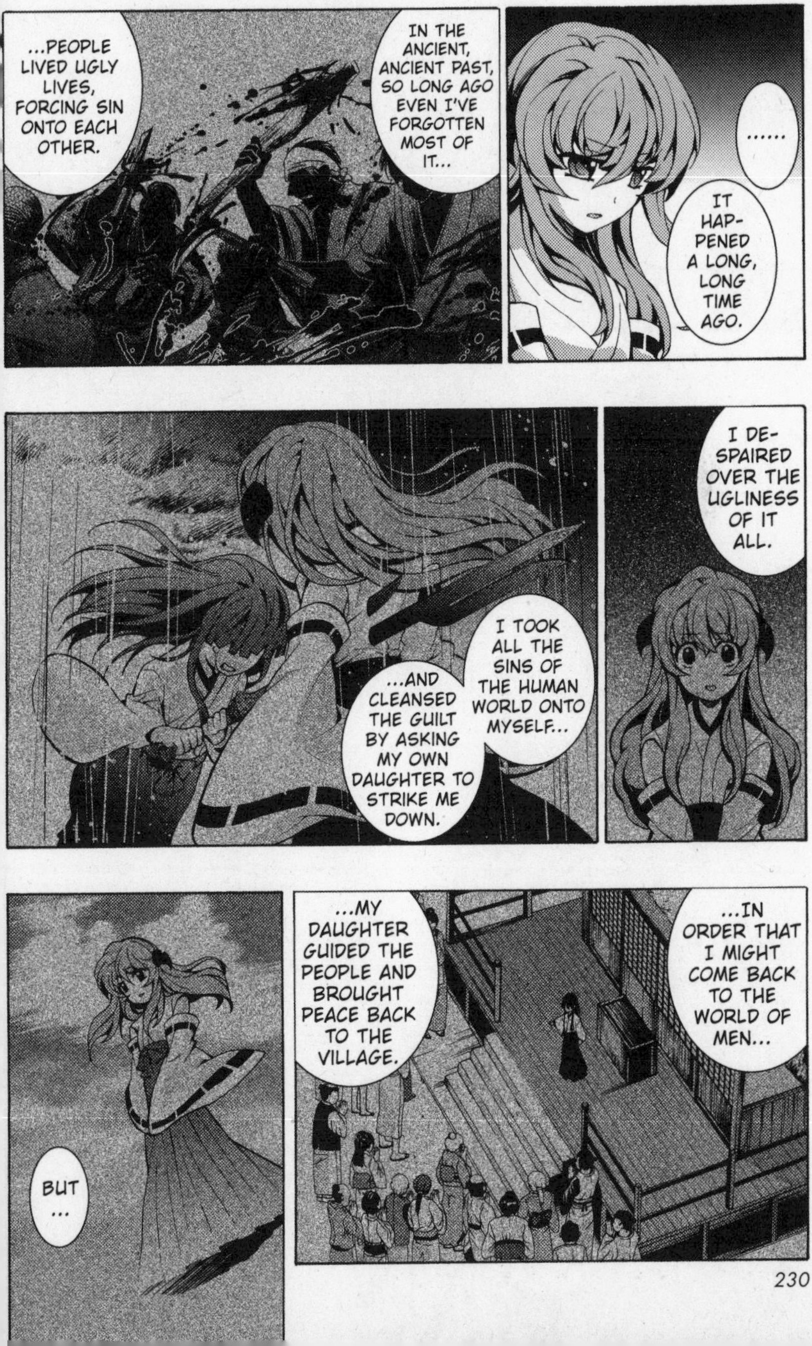
......
IT HAPPENED A LONG, LONG TIME AGO.
IN THE ANCIENT, ANCIENT PAST, SO LONG AGO EVEN I'VE FORGOTTEN MOST OF IT...
...PEOPLE LIVED UGLY LIVES, FORCING SIN ONTO EACH OTHER.
I DESPAIRED OVER THE UGLINESS OF IT ALL.
I TOOK ALL THE SINS OF THE HUMAN WORLD ONTO MYSELF...
...AND CLEANSED THE GUILT BY ASKING MY OWN DAUGHTER TO STRIKE ME DOWN.
...IN ORDER THAT I MIGHT COME BACK TO THE WORLD OF MEN...
...MY DAUGHTER GUIDED THE PEOPLE AND BROUGHT PEACE BACK TO THE VILLAGE.
BUT ...

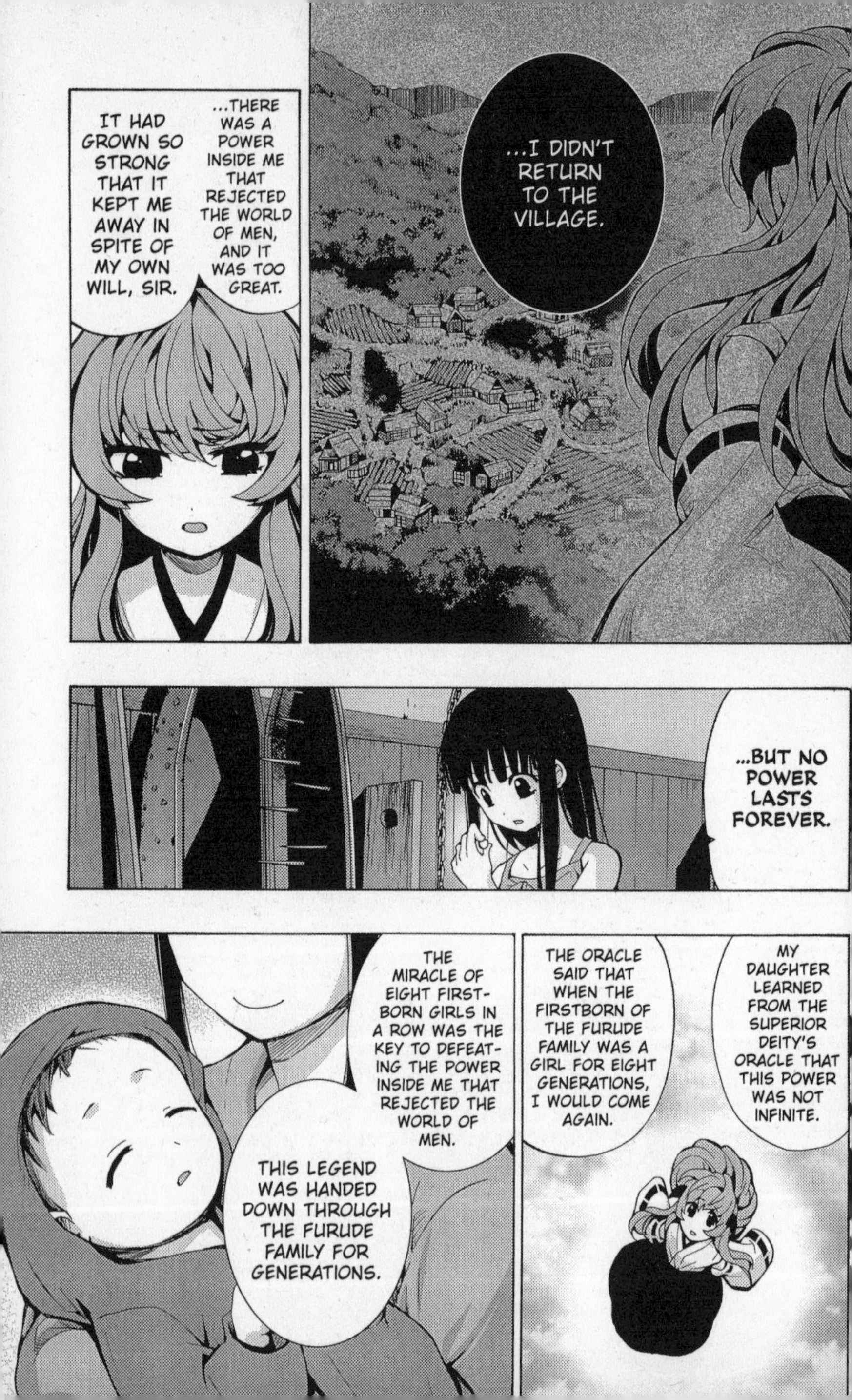
...I DIDN'T RETURN TO THE VILLAGE.
...THERE WAS A POWER INSIDE ME THAT REJECTED THE WORLD OF MEN, AND IT WAS TOO GREAT.
IT HAD GROWN SO STRONG THAT IT KEPT ME AWAY IN SPITE OF MY OWN WILL, SIR.
...BUT NO POWER LASTS FOREVER.
MY DAUGHTER LEARNED FROM THE SUPERIOR DEITY'S ORACLE THAT THIS POWER WAS NOT INFINITE.
THE ORACLE SAID THAT WHEN THE FIRSTBORN OF THE FURUDE FAMILY WAS A GIRL FOR EIGHT GENERATIONS, I WOULD COME AGAIN.
THE MIRACLE OF EIGHT FIRST-BORN GIRLS IN A ROW WAS THE KEY TO DEFEAT-ING THE POWER INSIDE ME THAT REJECTED THE WORLD OF MEN.
THIS LEGEND WAS HANDED DOWN THROUGH THE FURUDE FAMILY FOR GENERATIONS.

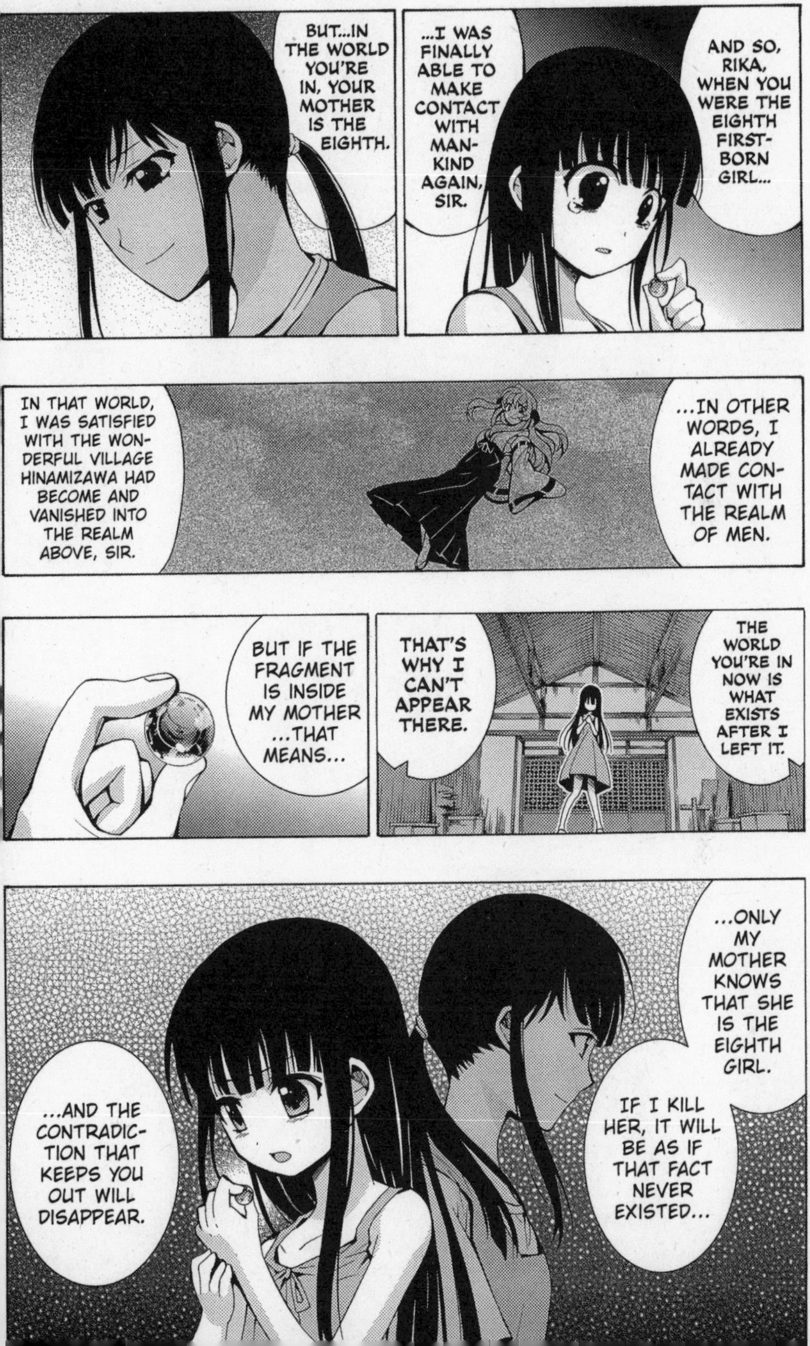
AND SO, RIKA, WHEN YOU WERE THE EIGHTH FIRST-BORN GIRL...
...I WAS FINALLY ABLE TO MAKE CONTACT WITH MANKIND AGAIN, SIR.
BUT...IN THE WORLD YOU'RE IN, YOUR MOTHER IS THE EIGHTH.
...IN OTHER WORDS, I ALREADY MADE CONTACT WITH THE REALM OF MEN.
IN THAT WORLD, I WAS SATISFIED WITH THE WONDERFUL VILLAGE HINAMIZAWA HAD BECOME AND VANISHED INTO THE REALM ABOVE, SIR.
THE WORLD YOU'RE IN NOW IS WHAT EXISTS AFTER I LEFT IT.
THAT'S WHY I CAN'T APPEAR THERE.
BUT IF THE FRAGMENT IS INSIDE MY MOTHER ...THAT MEANS...
...ONLY MY MOTHER KNOWS THAT SHE IS THE EIGHTH GIRL.
IF I KILL HER, IT WILL BE AS IF THAT FACT NEVER EXISTED...
...AND THE CONTRADICTION THAT KEEPS YOU OUT WILL DISAPPEAR.

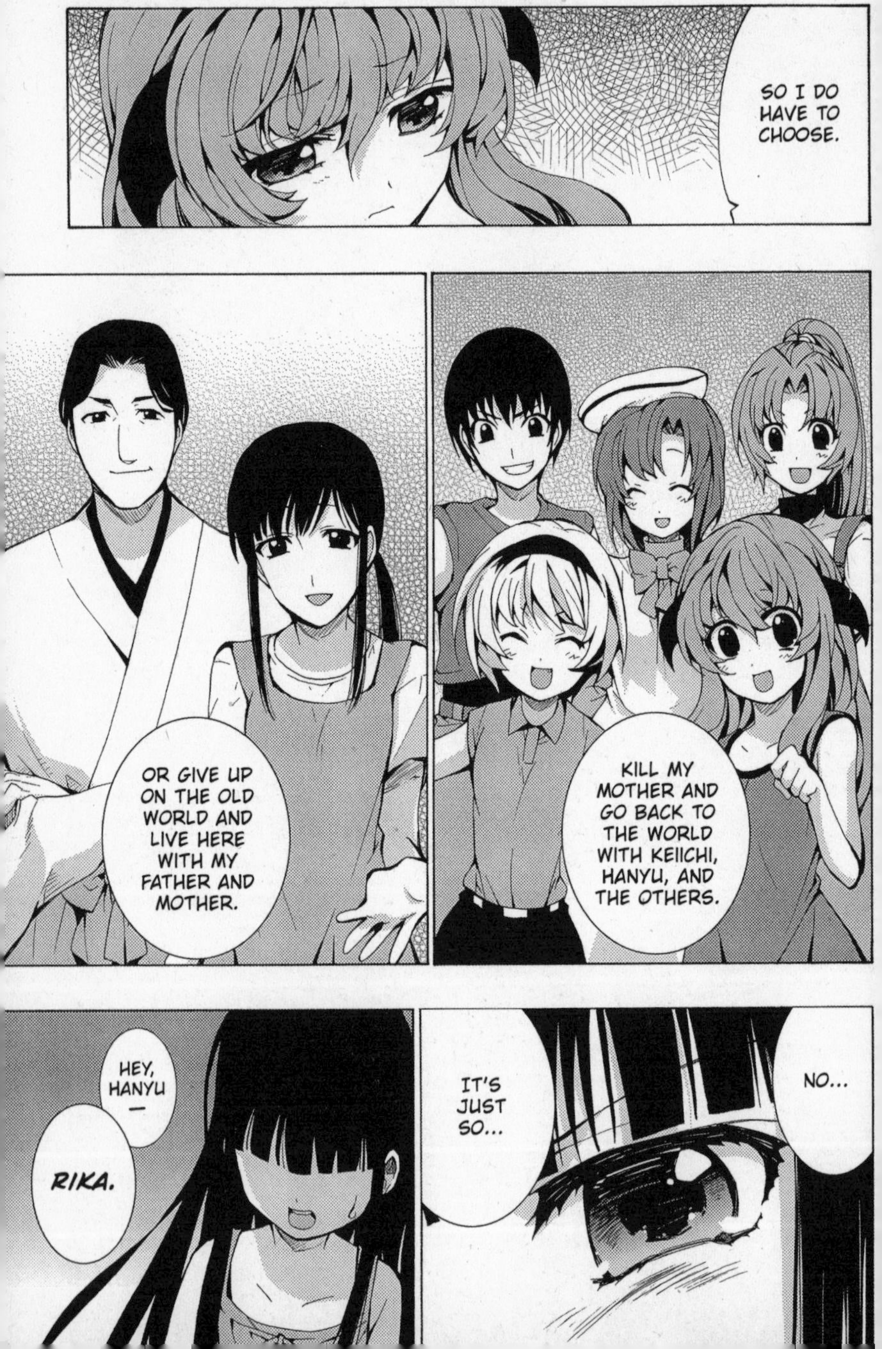
SO I DO HAVE TO CHOOSE.
KILL MY MOTHER AND GO BACK TO THE WORLD WITH KEIICHI, HANYU, AND THE OTHERS.
OR GIVE UP ON THE OLD WORLD AND LIVE HERE WITH MY FATHER AND MOTHER.
NO...
IT'S JUST SO...
HEY, HANYU—
RIKA.

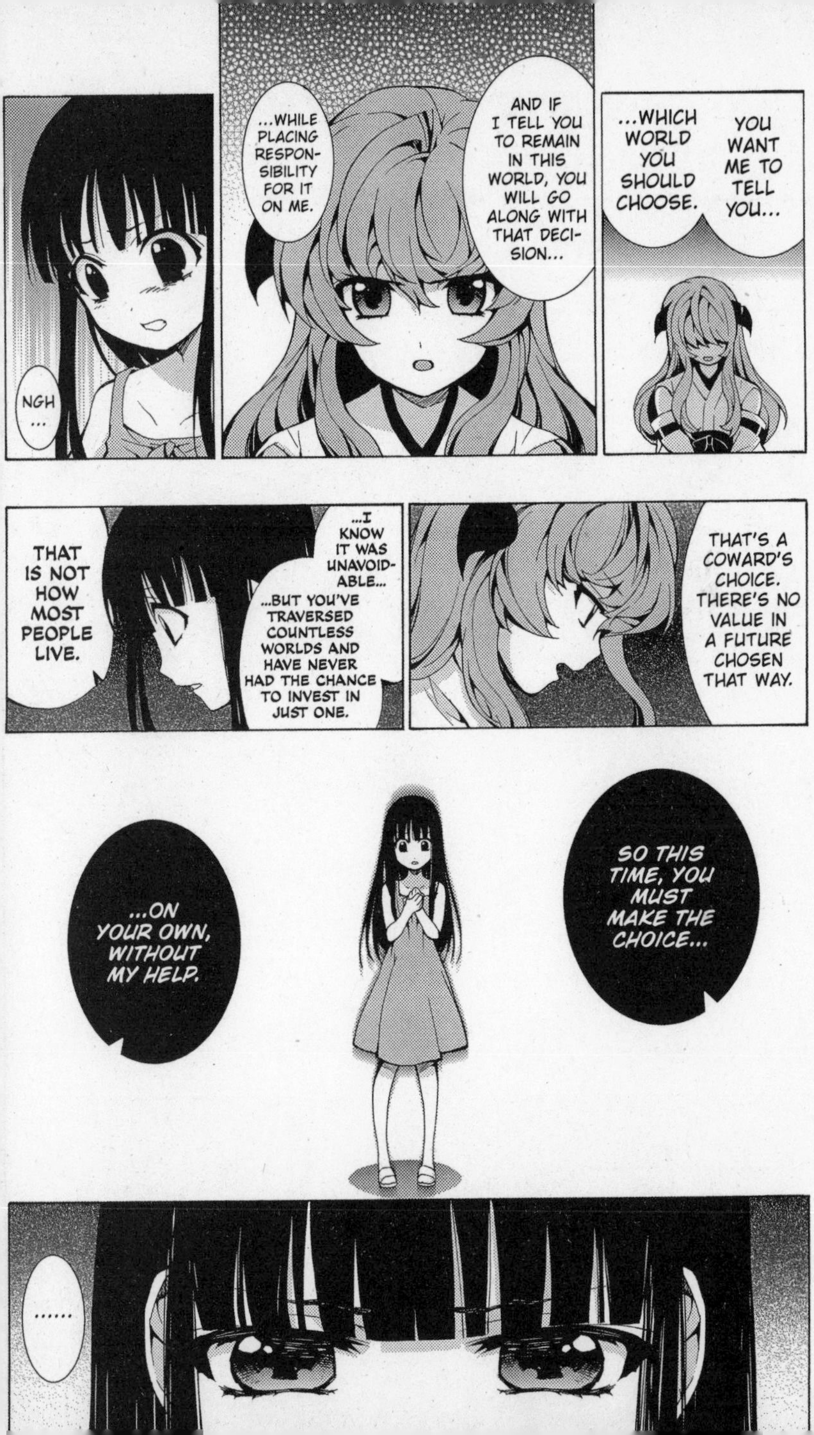
YOU WANT ME TO TELL YOU...
...WHICH WORLD YOU SHOULD CHOOSE.
AND IF I TELL YOU TO REMAIN IN THIS WORLD, YOU WILL GO ALONG WITH THAT DECISION...
...WHILE PLACING RESPONSIBILITY FOR IT ON ME.
NGH...
THAT'S A COWARD'S CHOICE. THERE'S NO VALUE IN A FUTURE CHOSEN THAT WAY.
...I KNOW IT WAS UNAVOIDABLE...
...BUT YOU'VE TRAVERSED COUNTLESS WORLDS AND HAVE NEVER HAD THE CHANCE TO INVEST IN JUST ONE.
THAT IS NOT HOW MOST PEOPLE LIVE.
SO THIS TIME, YOU MUST MAKE THE CHOICE...
...ON YOUR OWN, WITHOUT MY HELP.
......

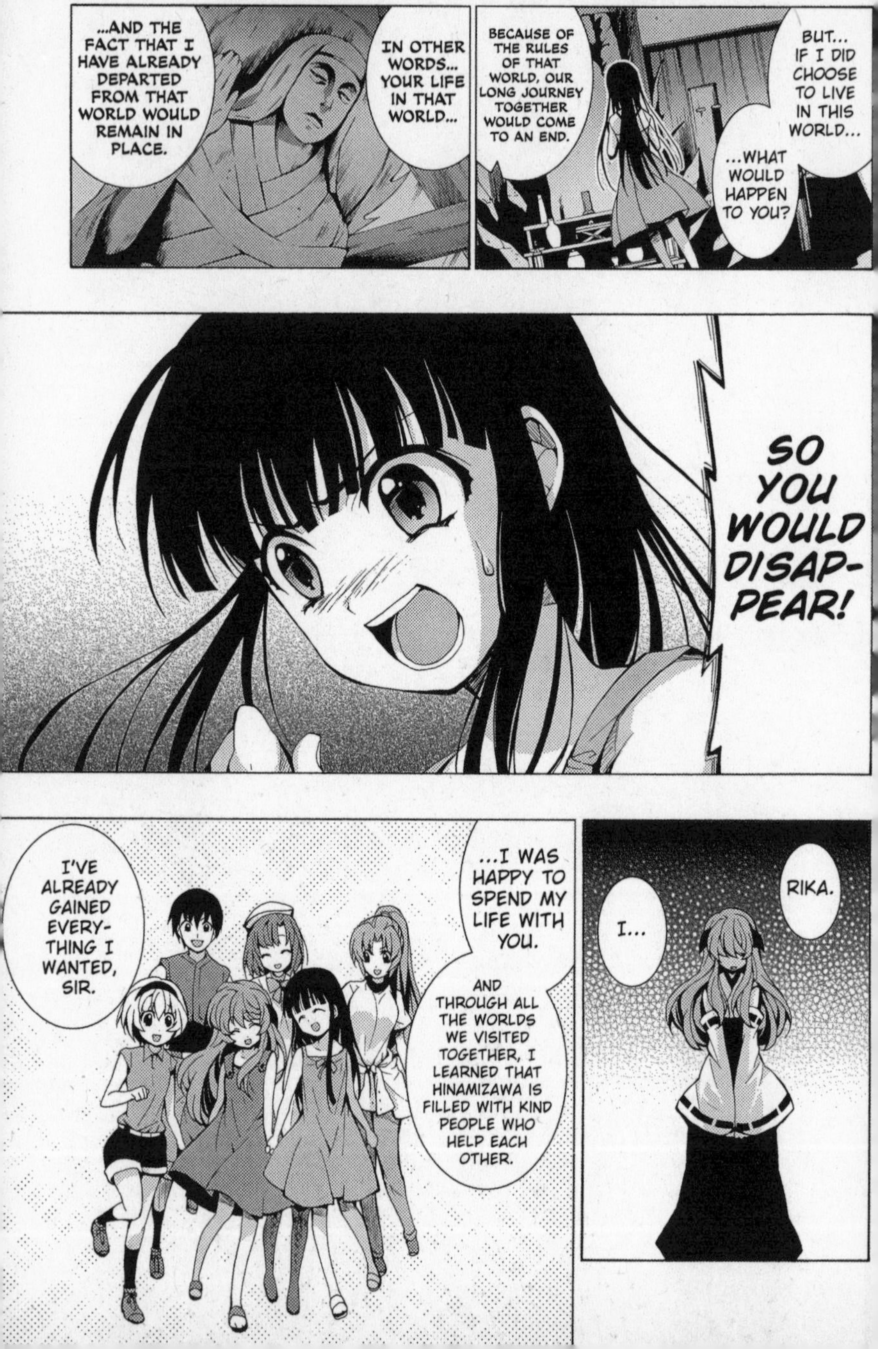
BUT... IF I DID CHOOSE TO LIVE IN THIS WORLD...
...WHAT WOULD HAPPEN TO YOU?
BECAUSE OF THE RULES OF THAT WORLD, OUR LONG JOURNEY TOGETHER WOULD COME TO AN END.
IN OTHER WORDS... YOUR LIFE IN THAT WORLD...
...AND THE FACT THAT I HAVE ALREADY DEPARTED FROM THAT WORLD WOULD REMAIN IN PLACE.
SO YOU WOULD DISAP-PEAR!
RIKA.
I...
...I WAS HAPPY TO SPEND MY LIFE WITH YOU.
AND THROUGH ALL THE WORLDS WE VISITED TOGETHER, I LEARNED THAT HINAMIZAWA IS FILLED WITH KIND PEOPLE WHO HELP EACH OTHER.
I'VE ALREADY GAINED EVERY-THING I WANTED, SIR.

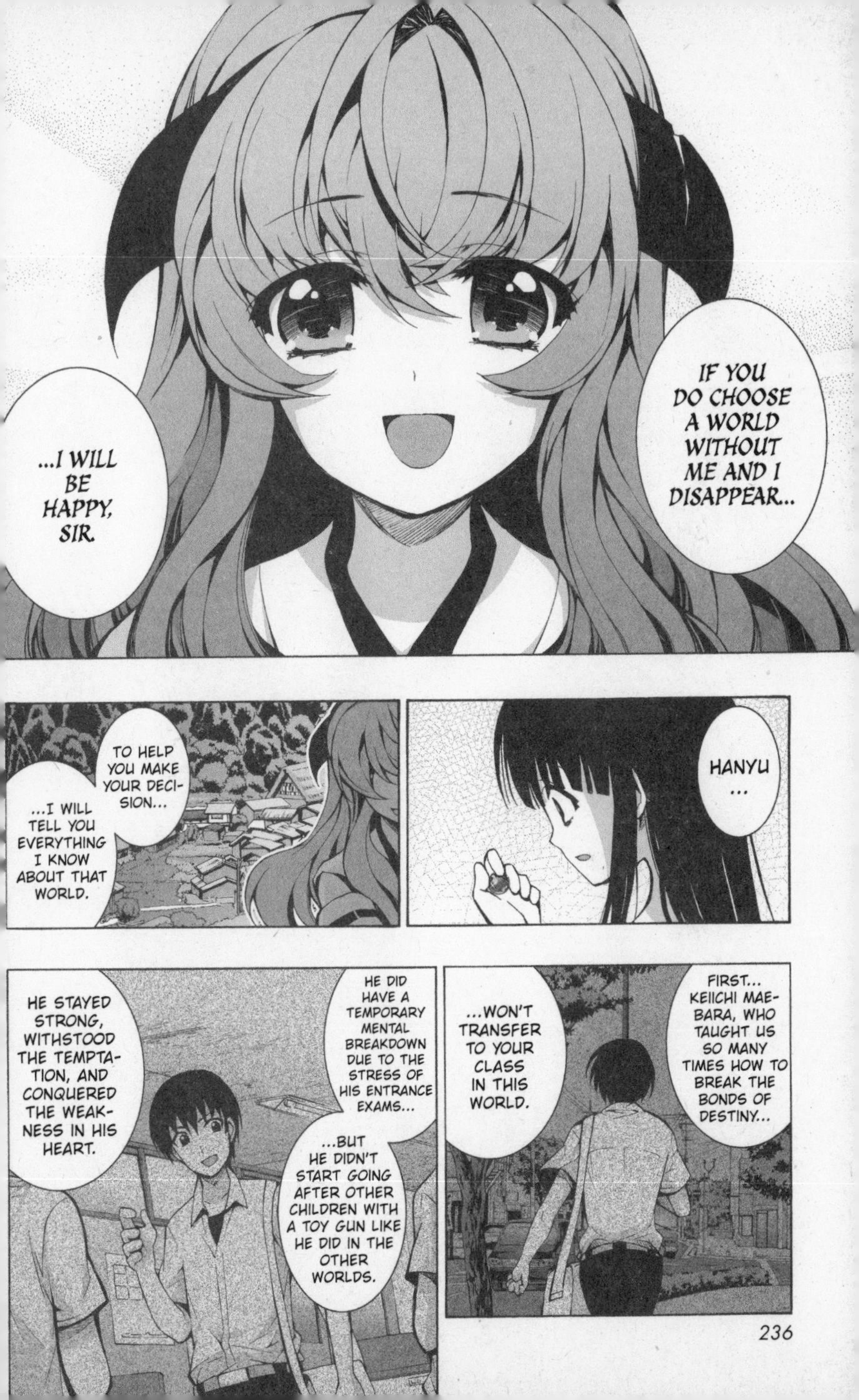
IF YOU DO CHOOSE A WORLD WITHOUT ME AND I DISAPPEAR...
...I WILL BE HAPPY, SIR.
HANYU ...
TO HELP YOU MAKE YOUR DECISION...
...I WILL TELL YOU EVERYTHING I KNOW ABOUT THAT WORLD.
FIRST... KEIICHI MAEBARA, WHO TAUGHT US SO MANY TIMES HOW TO BREAK THE BONDS OF DESTINY...
...WON'T TRANSFER TO YOUR CLASS IN THIS WORLD.
HE DID HAVE A TEMPORARY MENTAL BREAKDOWN DUE TO THE STRESS OF HIS ENTRANCE EXAMS...
...BUT HE DIDN'T START GOING AFTER OTHER CHILDREN WITH A TOY GUN LIKE HE DID IN THE OTHER WORLDS.
HE STAYED STRONG, WITHSTOOD THE TEMPTATION, AND CONQUERED THE WEAKNESS IN HIS HEART.

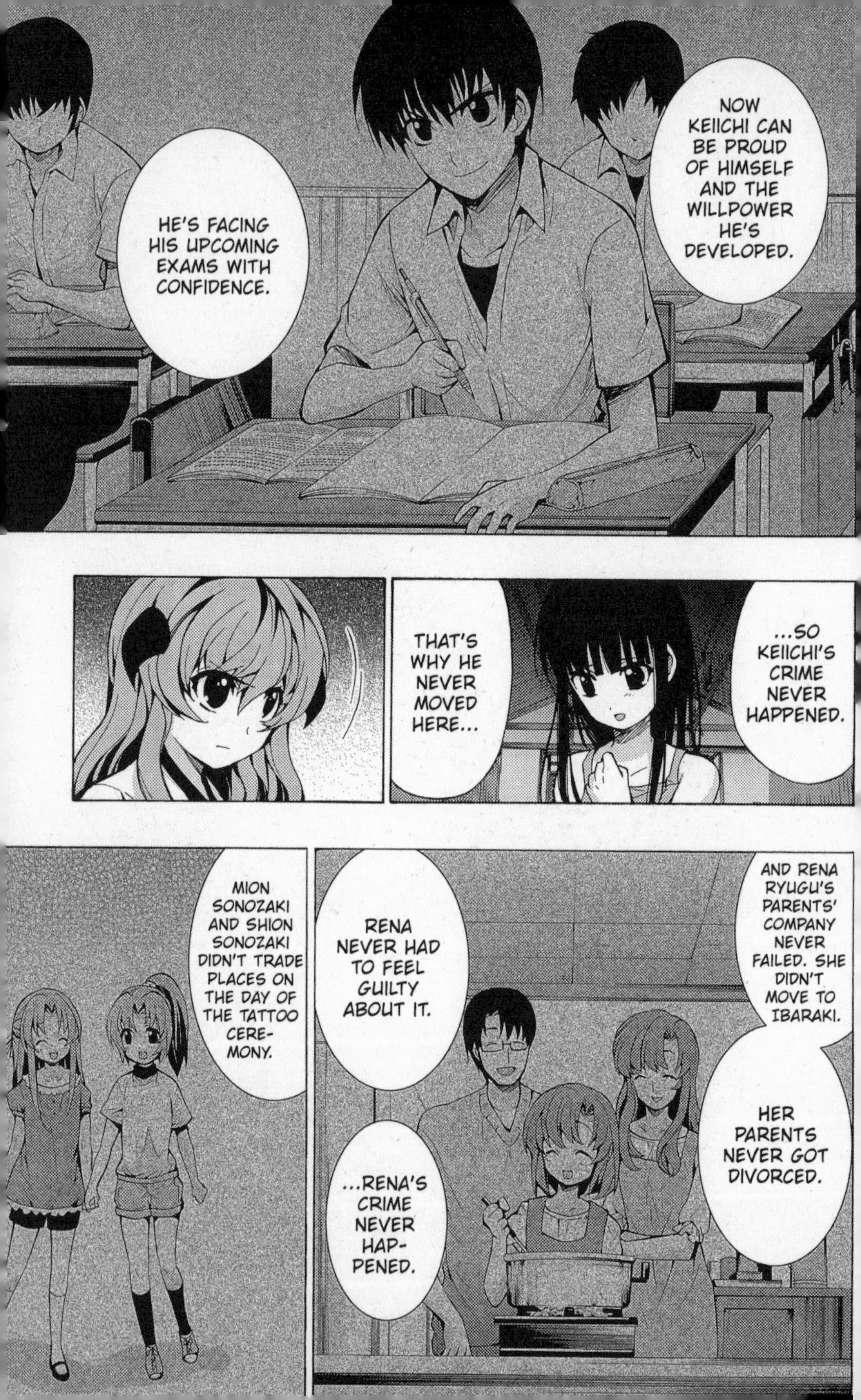
NOW KEIICHI CAN BE PROUD OF HIMSELF AND THE WILLPOWER HE'S DEVELOPED.
HE'S FACING HIS UPCOMING EXAMS WITH CONFIDENCE.
...SO KEIICHI'S CRIME NEVER HAPPENED.
THAT'S WHY HE NEVER MOVED HERE...
AND RENA RYUGU'S PARENTS' COMPANY NEVER FAILED. SHE DIDN'T MOVE TO IBARAKI.
HER PARENTS NEVER GOT DIVORCED.
RENA NEVER HAD TO FEEL GUILTY ABOUT IT.
...RENA'S CRIME NEVER HAP-PENED.
MION SONOZAKI AND SHION SONOZAKI DIDN'T TRADE PLACES ON THE DAY OF THE TATTOO CERE-MONY.

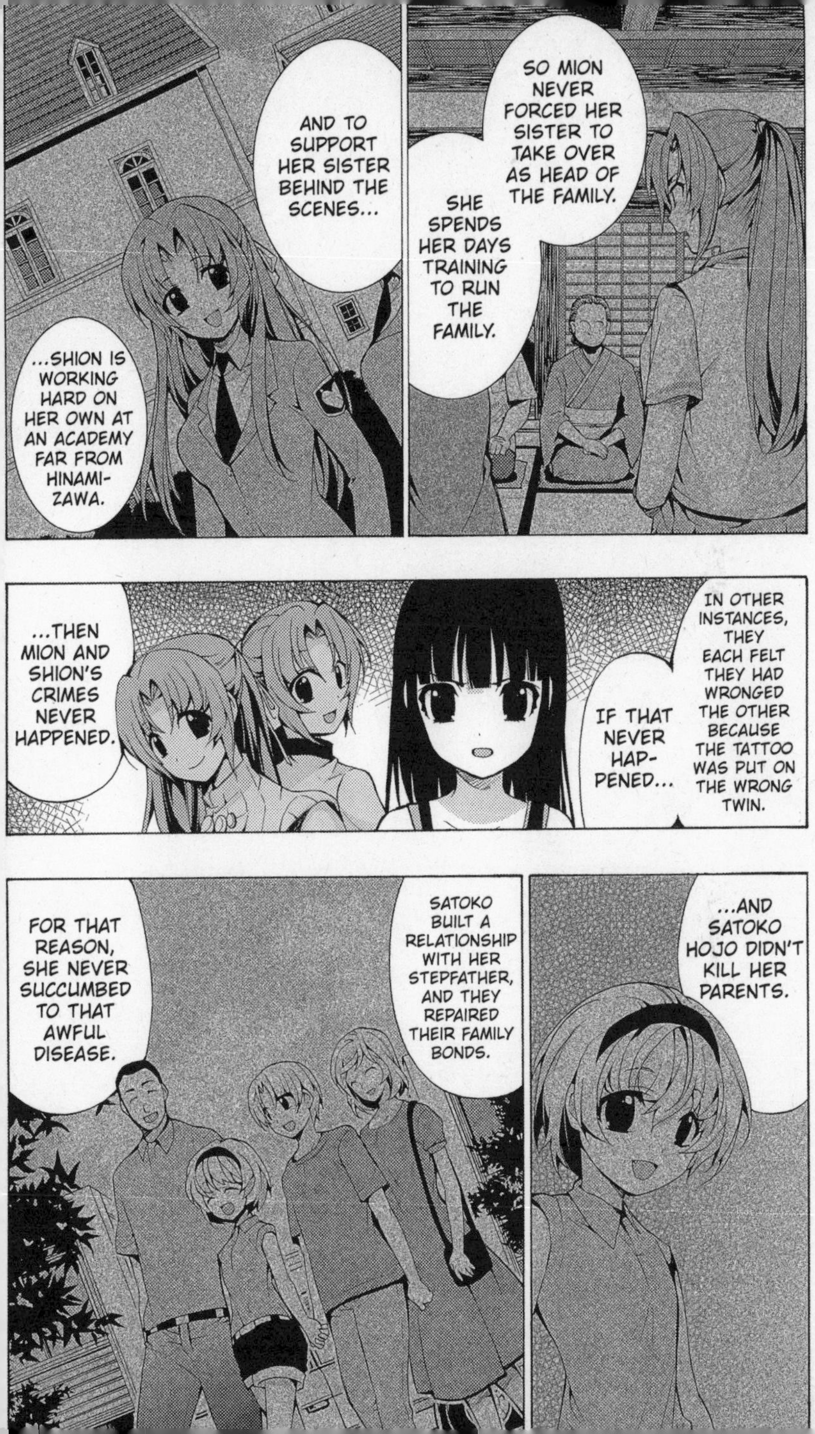
SO MION NEVER FORCED HER SISTER TO TAKE OVER AS HEAD OF THE FAMILY.
SHE SPENDS HER DAYS TRAINING TO RUN THE FAMILY.
AND TO SUPPORT HER SISTER BEHIND THE SCENES...
...SHION IS WORKING HARD ON HER OWN AT AN ACADEMY FAR FROM HINAMI-ZAWA.
IN OTHER INSTANCES, THEY EACH FELT THEY HAD WRONGED THE OTHER BECAUSE THE TATTOO WAS PUT ON THE WRONG TWIN.
IF THAT NEVER HAP-PENED...
...THEN MION AND SHION'S CRIMES NEVER HAPPENED.
...AND SATOKO HOJO DIDN'T KILL HER PARENTS.
SATOKO BUILT A RELATIONSHIP WITH HER STEPFATHER, AND THEY REPAIRED THEIR FAMILY BONDS.
FOR THAT REASON, SHE NEVER SUCCUMBED TO THAT AWFUL DISEASE.

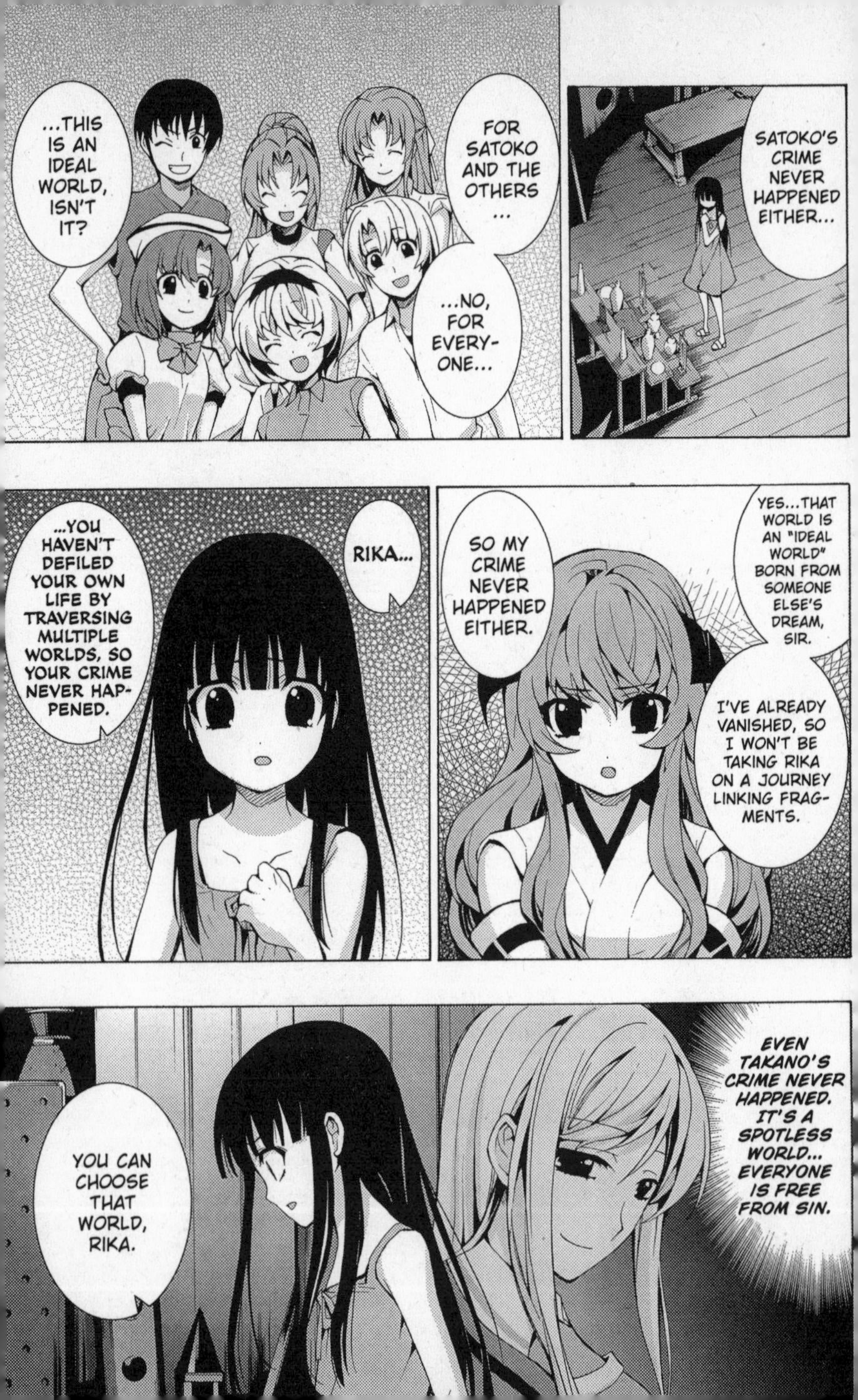
SATOKO'S CRIME NEVER HAPPENED EITHER...
FOR SATOKO AND THE OTHERS ...
...NO, FOR EVERY-ONE...
...THIS IS AN IDEAL WORLD, ISN'T IT?
YES...THAT WORLD IS AN "IDEAL WORLD" BORN FROM SOMEONE ELSE'S DREAM, SIR.
SO MY CRIME NEVER HAPPENED EITHER.
I'VE ALREADY VANISHED, SO I WON'T BE TAKING RIKA ON A JOURNEY LINKING FRAG-MENTS.
RIKA...
...YOU HAVEN'T DEFILED YOUR OWN LIFE BY TRAVERSING MULTIPLE WORLDS, SO YOUR CRIME NEVER HAP-PENED.
EVEN TAKANO'S CRIME NEVER HAPPENED. IT'S A SPOTLESS WORLD... EVERYONE IS FREE FROM SIN.
YOU CAN CHOOSE THAT WORLD, RIKA.

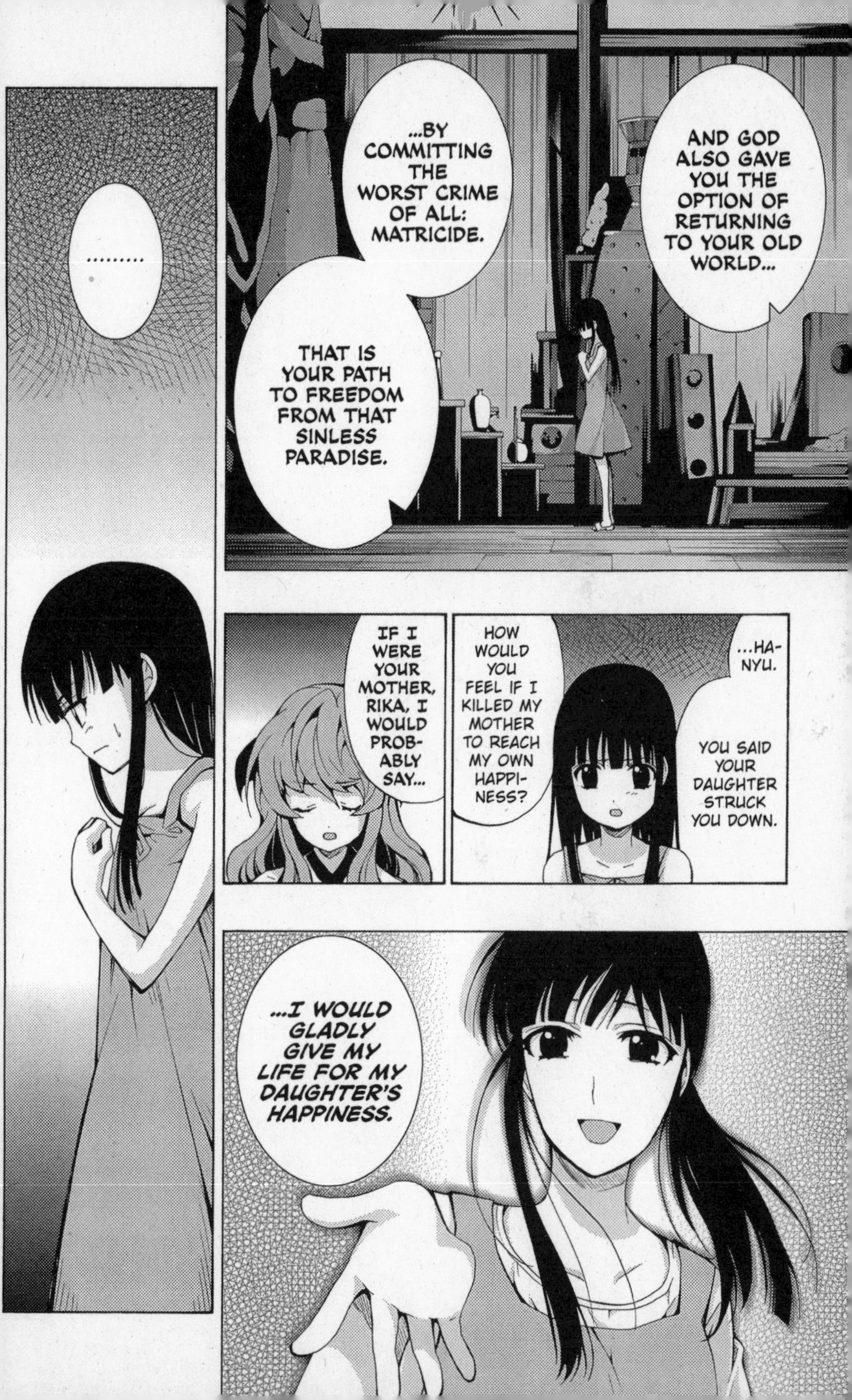
AND GOD ALSO GAVE YOU THE OPTION OF RETURNING TO YOUR OLD WORLD...
...BY COMMITTING THE WORST CRIME OF ALL: MATRICIDE.
THAT IS YOUR PATH TO FREEDOM FROM THAT SINLESS PARADISE.
...HA-NYU.
YOU SAID YOUR DAUGHTER STRUCK YOU DOWN.
HOW WOULD YOU FEEL IF I KILLED MY MOTHER TO REACH MY OWN HAPPI-NESS?
IF I WERE YOUR MOTHER, RIKA, I WOULD PROB-ABLY SAY...
...I WOULD GLADLY GIVE MY LIFE FOR MY DAUGHTER'S HAPPINESS.
....

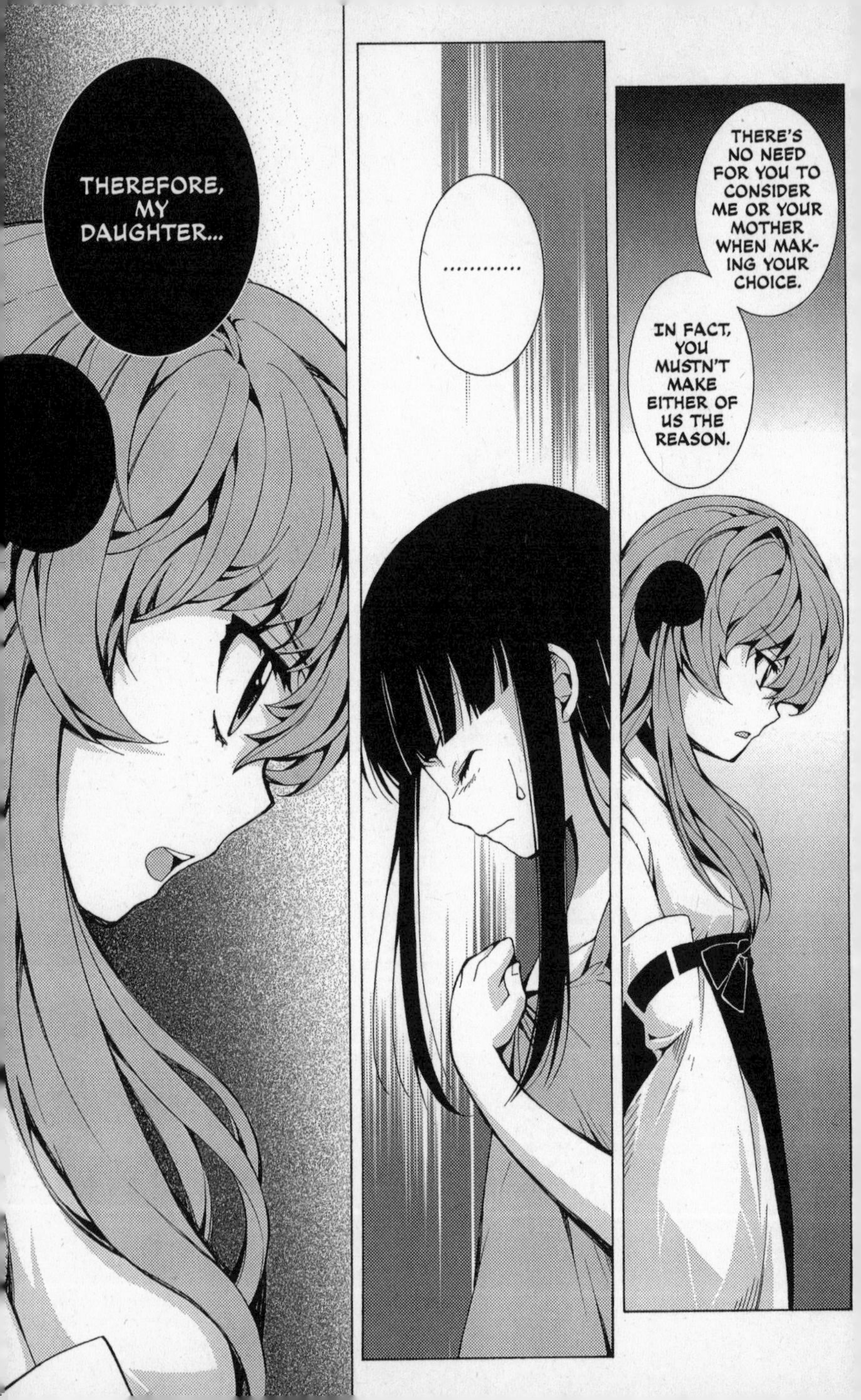
THERE'S NO NEED FOR YOU TO CONSIDER ME OR YOUR MOTHER WHEN MAKING YOUR CHOICE.
IN FACT, YOU MUSTN'T MAKE EITHER OF US THE REASON.
....
THEREFORE, MY DAUGHTER...

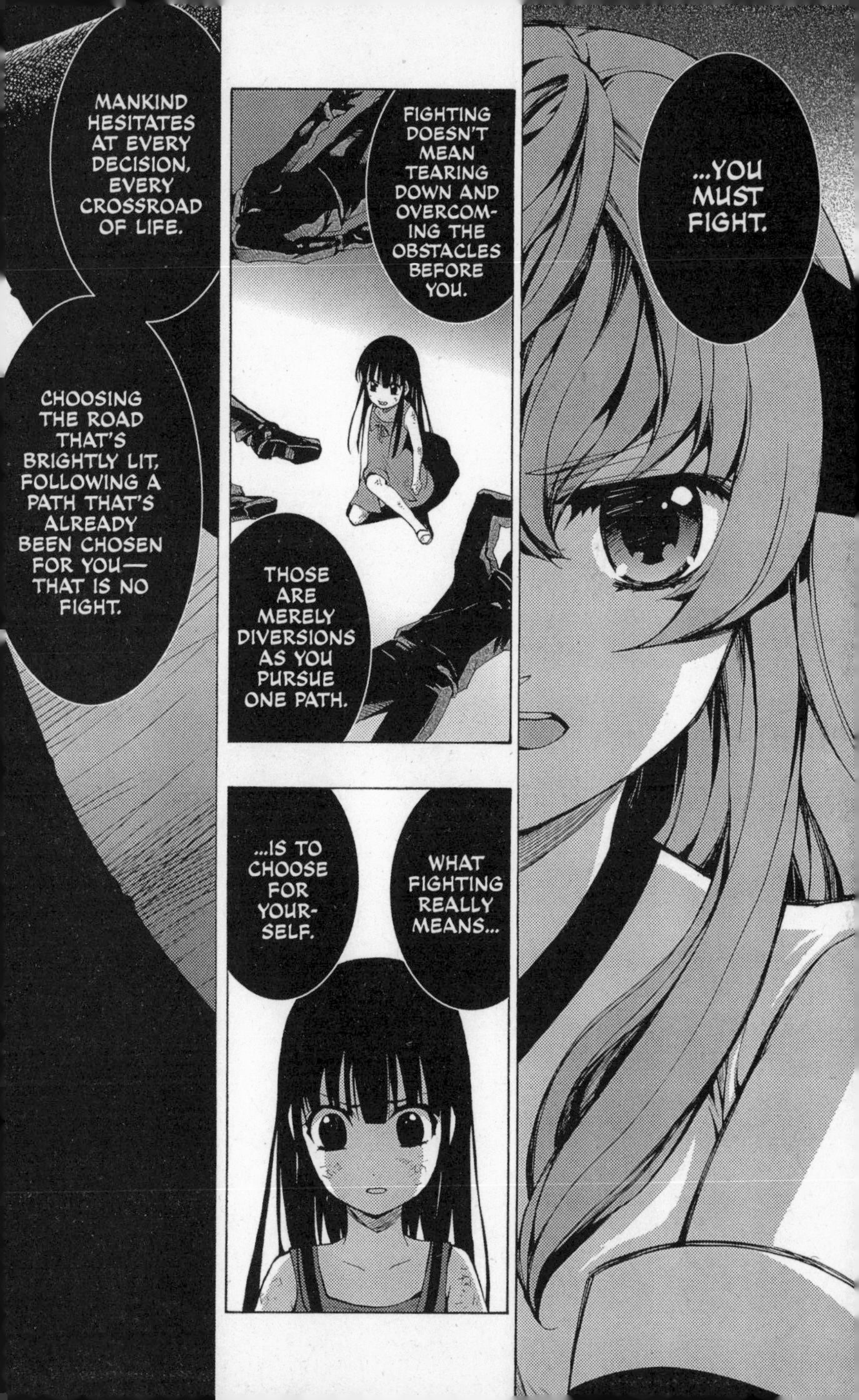

...YOU MUST FIGHT.
FIGHTING DOESN'T MEAN TEARING DOWN AND OVERCOMING THE OBSTACLES BEFORE YOU.
THOSE ARE MERELY DIVERSIONS AS YOU PURSUE ONE PATH.
WHAT FIGHTING REALLY MEANS...
...IS TO CHOOSE FOR YOURSELF.
MANKIND HESITATES AT EVERY DECISION, EVERY CROSSROAD OF LIFE.
CHOOSING THE ROAD THAT'S BRIGHTLY LIT, FOLLOWING A PATH THAT'S ALREADY BEEN CHOSEN FOR YOU—THAT IS NO FIGHT.

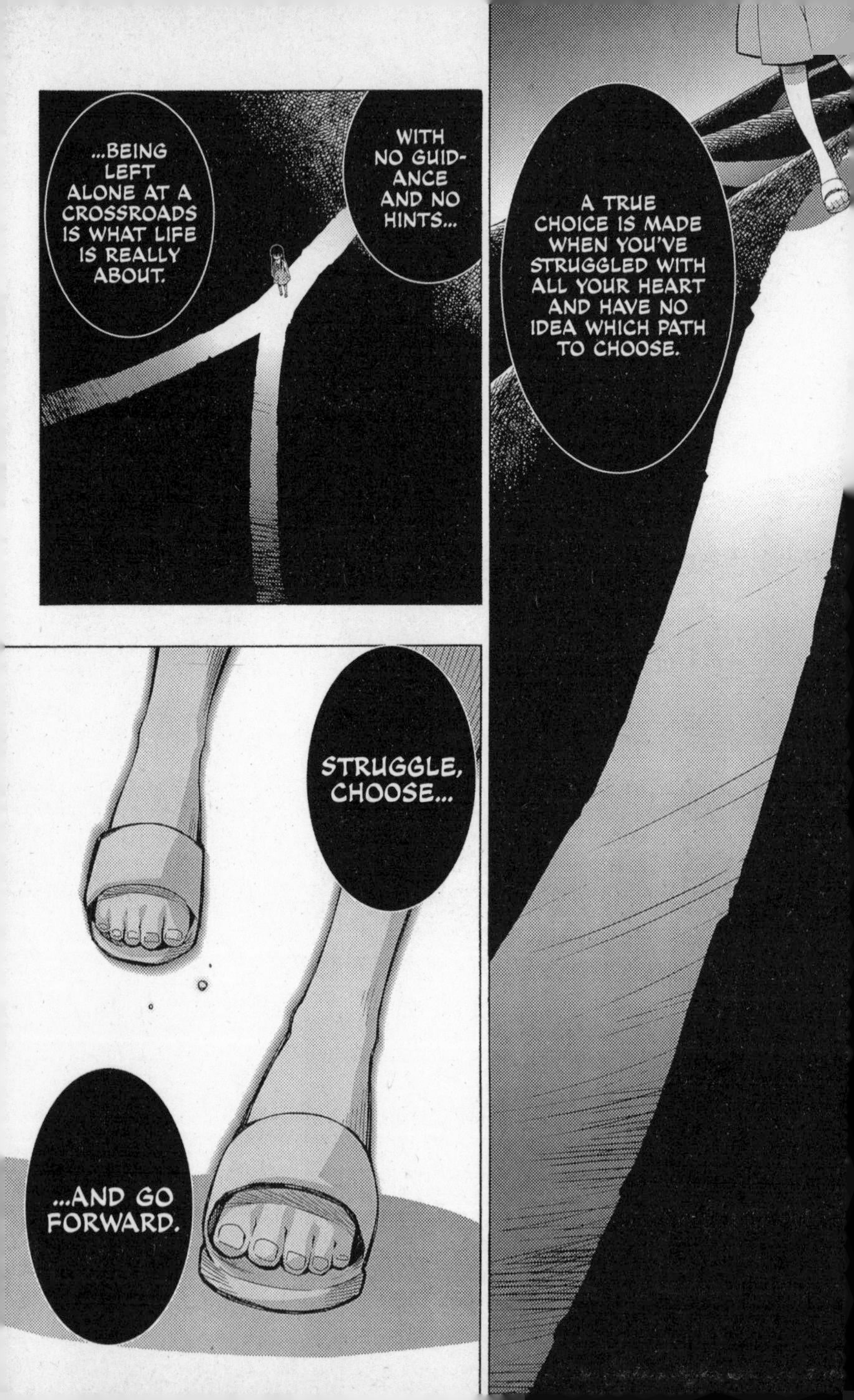
A TRUE CHOICE IS MADE WHEN YOU'VE STRUGGLED WITH ALL YOUR HEART AND HAVE NO IDEA WHICH PATH TO CHOOSE.
WITH NO GUID-ANCE AND NO HINTS...
...BEING LEFT ALONE AT A CROSSROADS IS WHAT LIFE IS REALLY ABOUT.
STRUGGLE, CHOOSE...
...AND GO FORWARD.

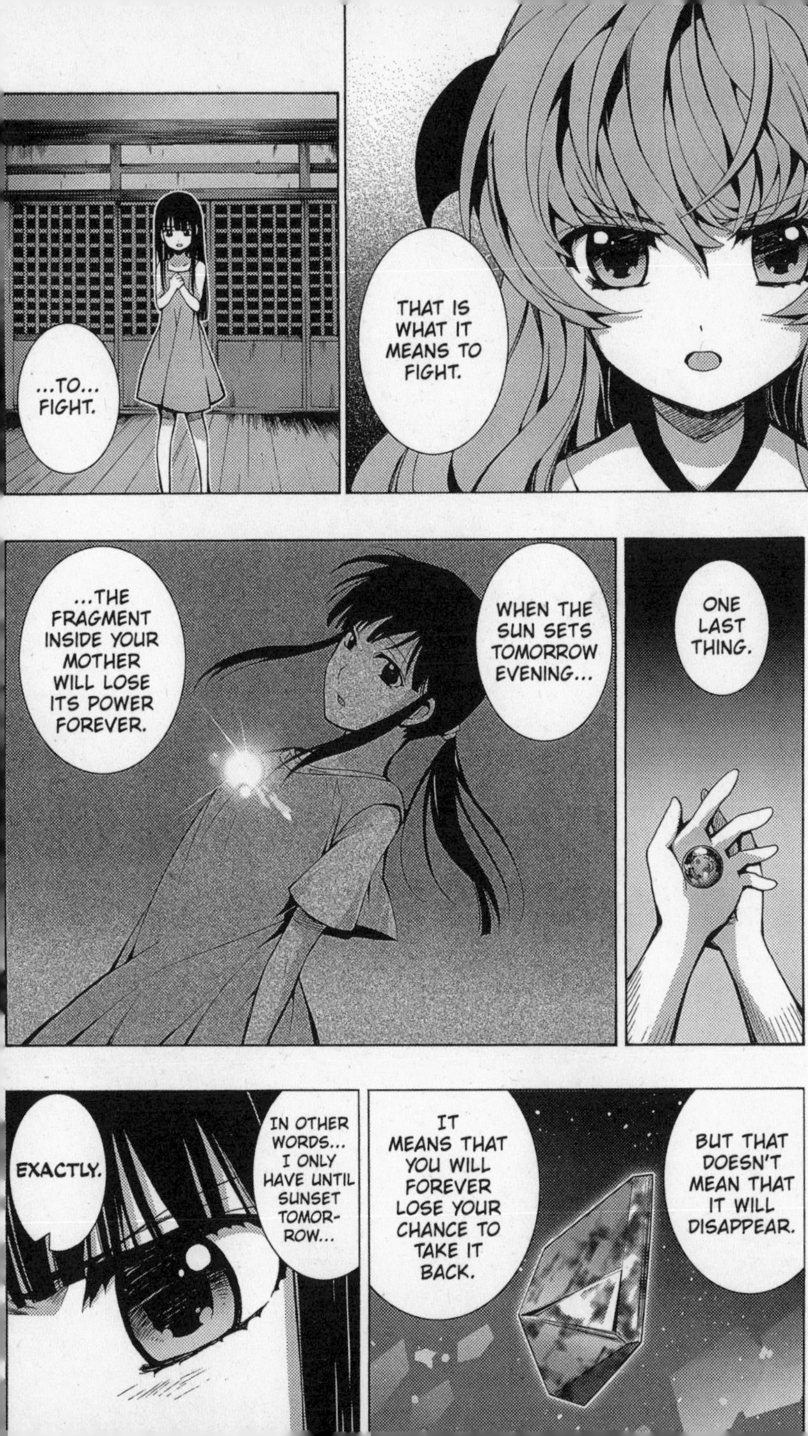
THAT IS WHAT IT MEANS TO FIGHT.
...TO... FIGHT.
ONE LAST THING.
WHEN THE SUN SETS TOMORROW EVENING...
...THE FRAGMENT INSIDE YOUR MOTHER WILL LOSE ITS POWER FOREVER.
BUT THAT DOESN'T MEAN THAT IT WILL DISAPPEAR.
IT MEANS THAT YOU WILL FOREVER LOSE YOUR CHANCE TO TAKE IT BACK.
IN OTHER WORDS... I ONLY HAVE UNTIL SUNSET TOMOR-ROW...
EXACTLY.

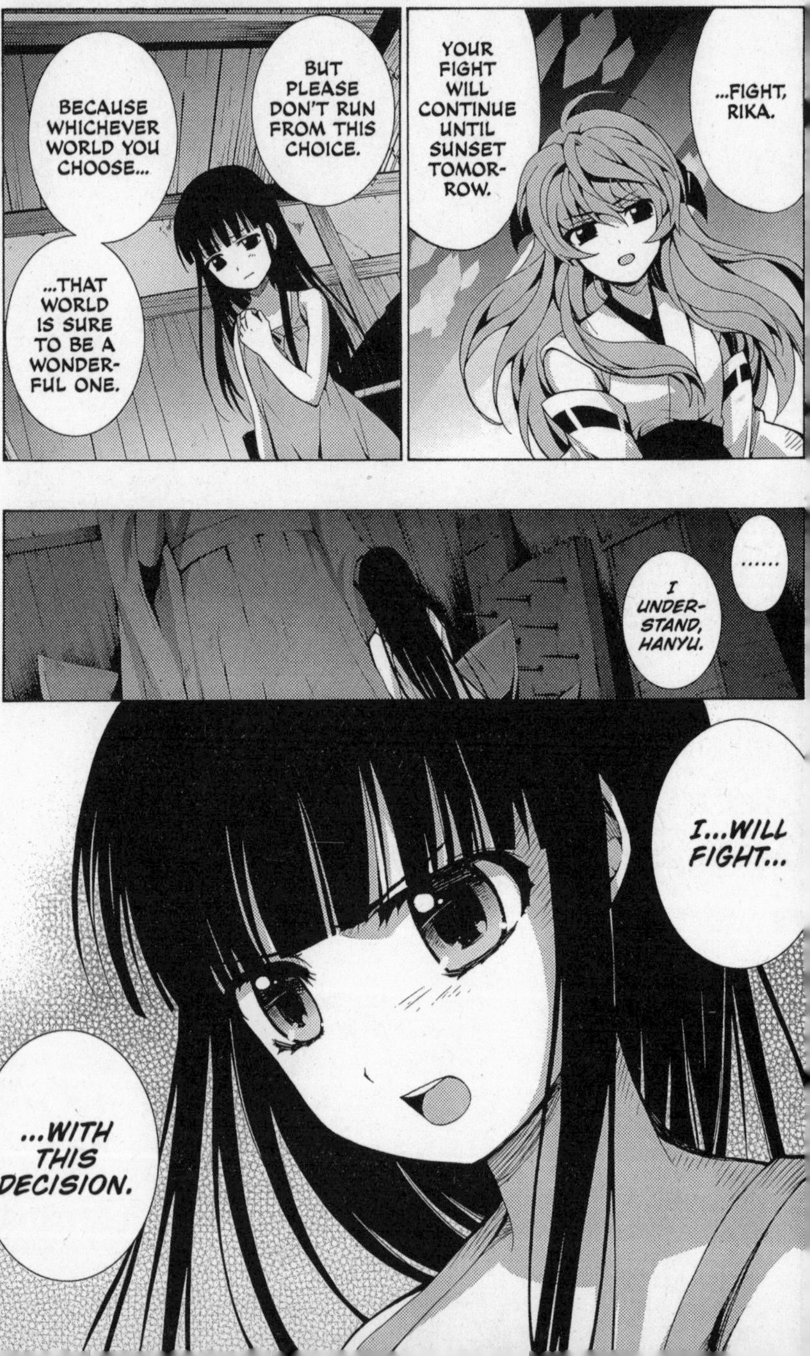
...FIGHT, RIKA.
YOUR FIGHT WILL CONTINUE UNTIL SUNSET TOMOR-ROW.
BUT PLEASE DON'T RUN FROM THIS CHOICE.
BECAUSE WHICHEVER WORLD YOU CHOOSE...
...THAT WORLD IS SURE TO BE A WONDER-FUL ONE.
......
I UNDER-STAND, HANYU.
I...WILL FIGHT...
...WITH THIS DECISION.

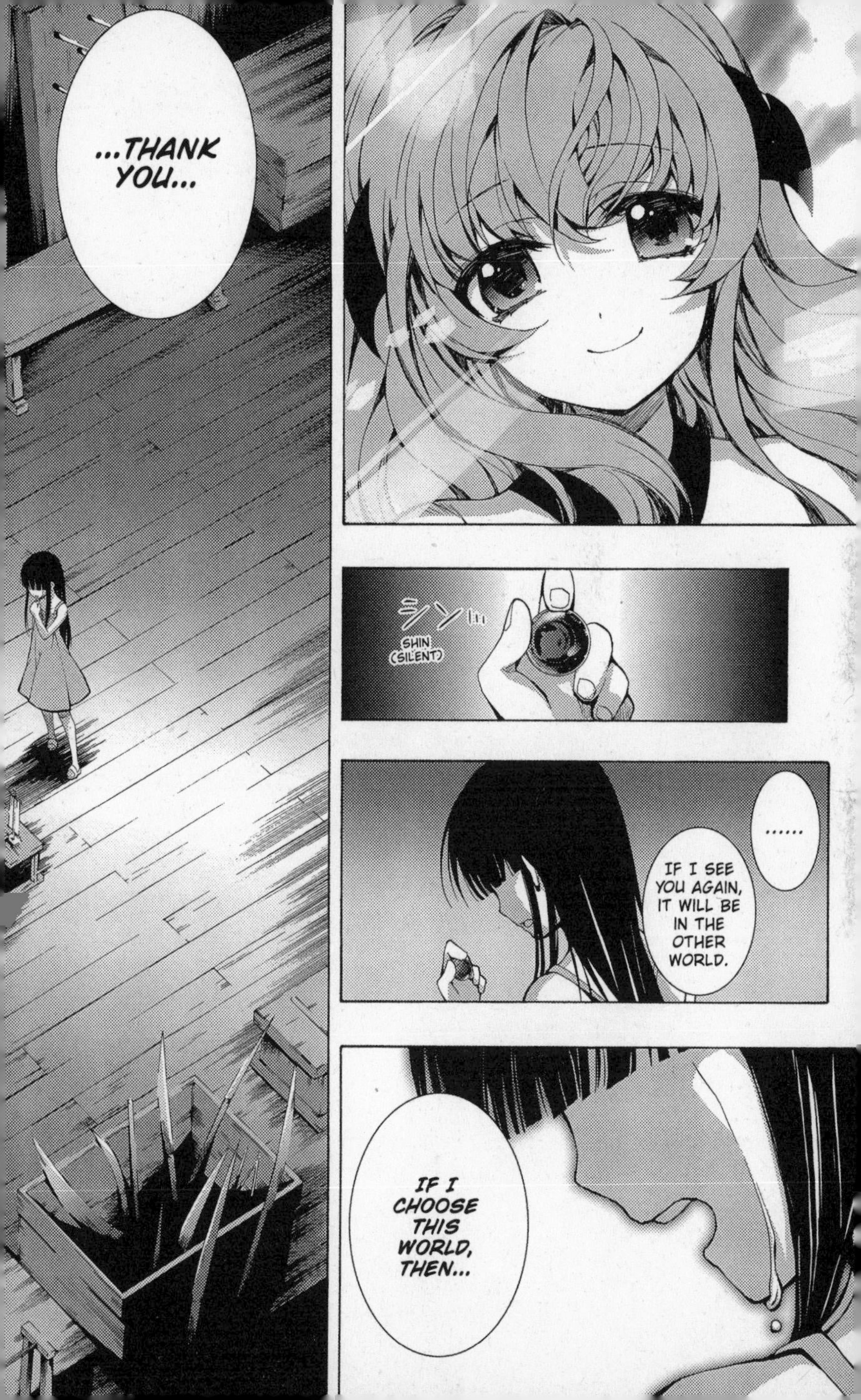
シン
SHIN (SILENT)
......
IF I SEE YOU AGAIN, IT WILL BE IN THE OTHER WORLD.
IF I CHOOSE THIS WORLD, THEN...
...THANK YOU...

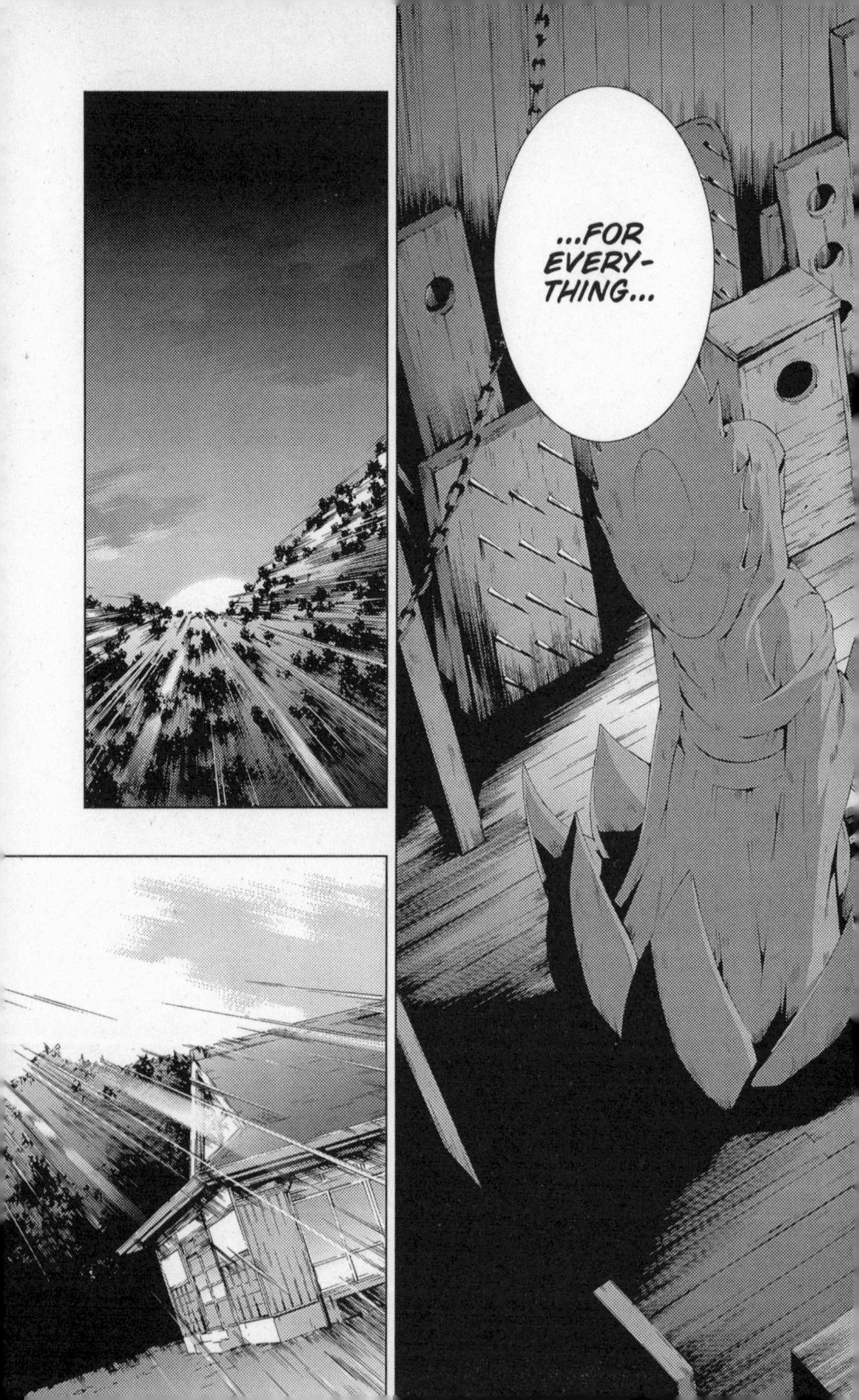
...FOR EVERY-THING...

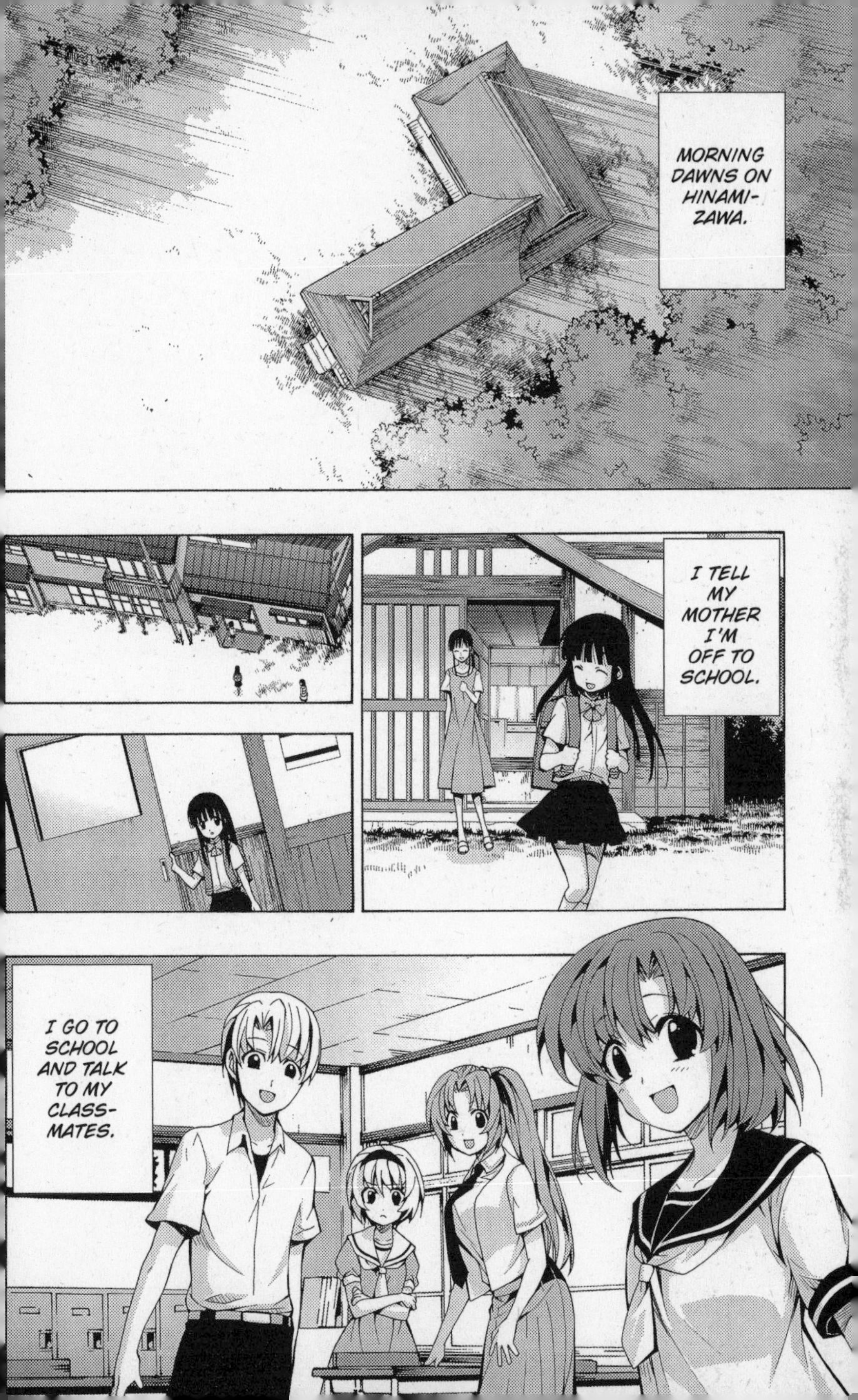
MORNING DAWNS ON HINAMI-ZAWA.
I TELL MY MOTHER I'M OFF TO SCHOOL.
I GO TO SCHOOL AND TALK TO MY CLASS-MATES.

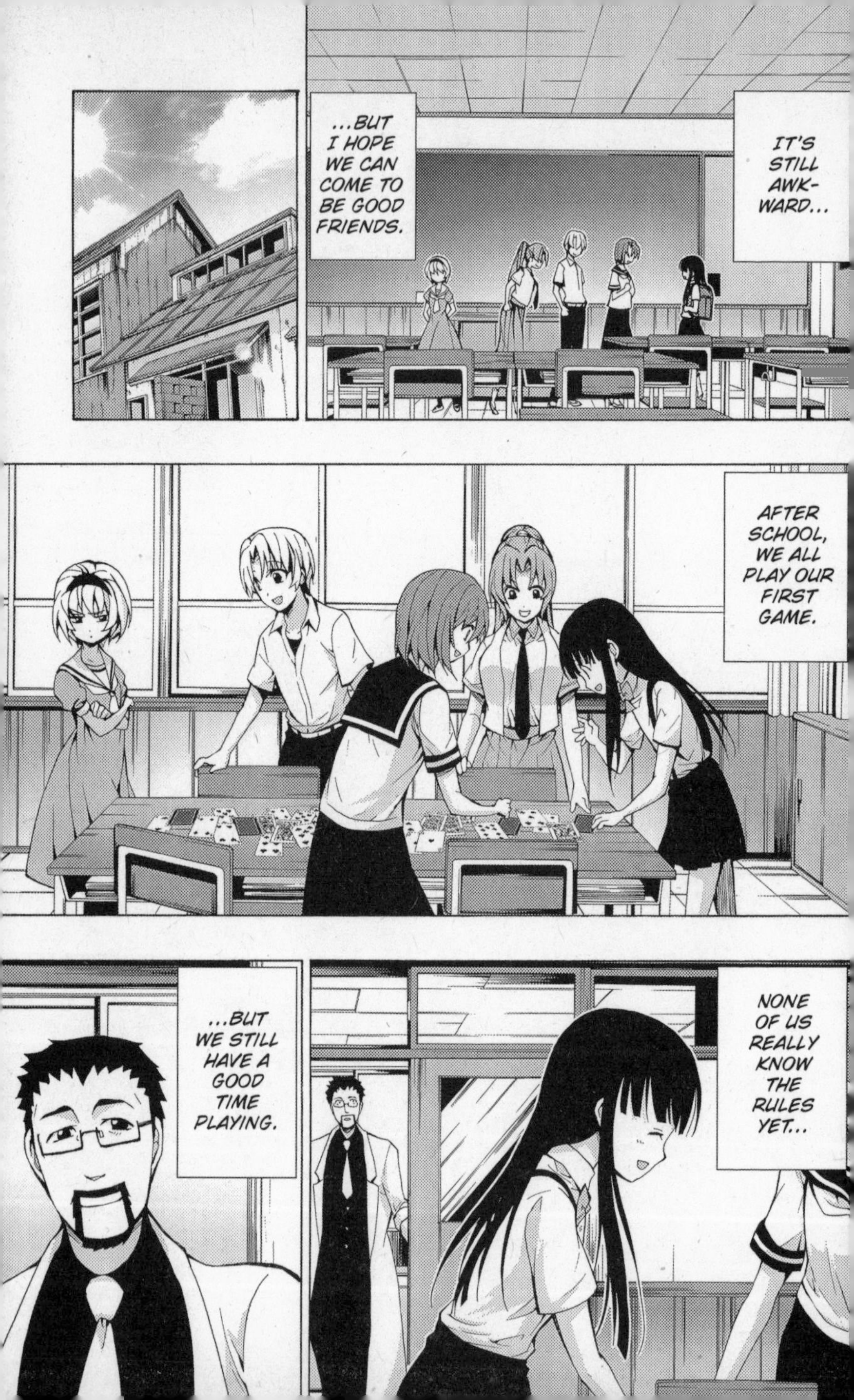
IT'S STILL AWK-WARD...
...BUT I HOPE WE CAN COME TO BE GOOD FRIENDS.
AFTER SCHOOL, WE ALL PLAY OUR FIRST GAME.
NONE OF US REALLY KNOW THE RULES YET...
...BUT WE STILL HAVE A GOOD TIME PLAYING.

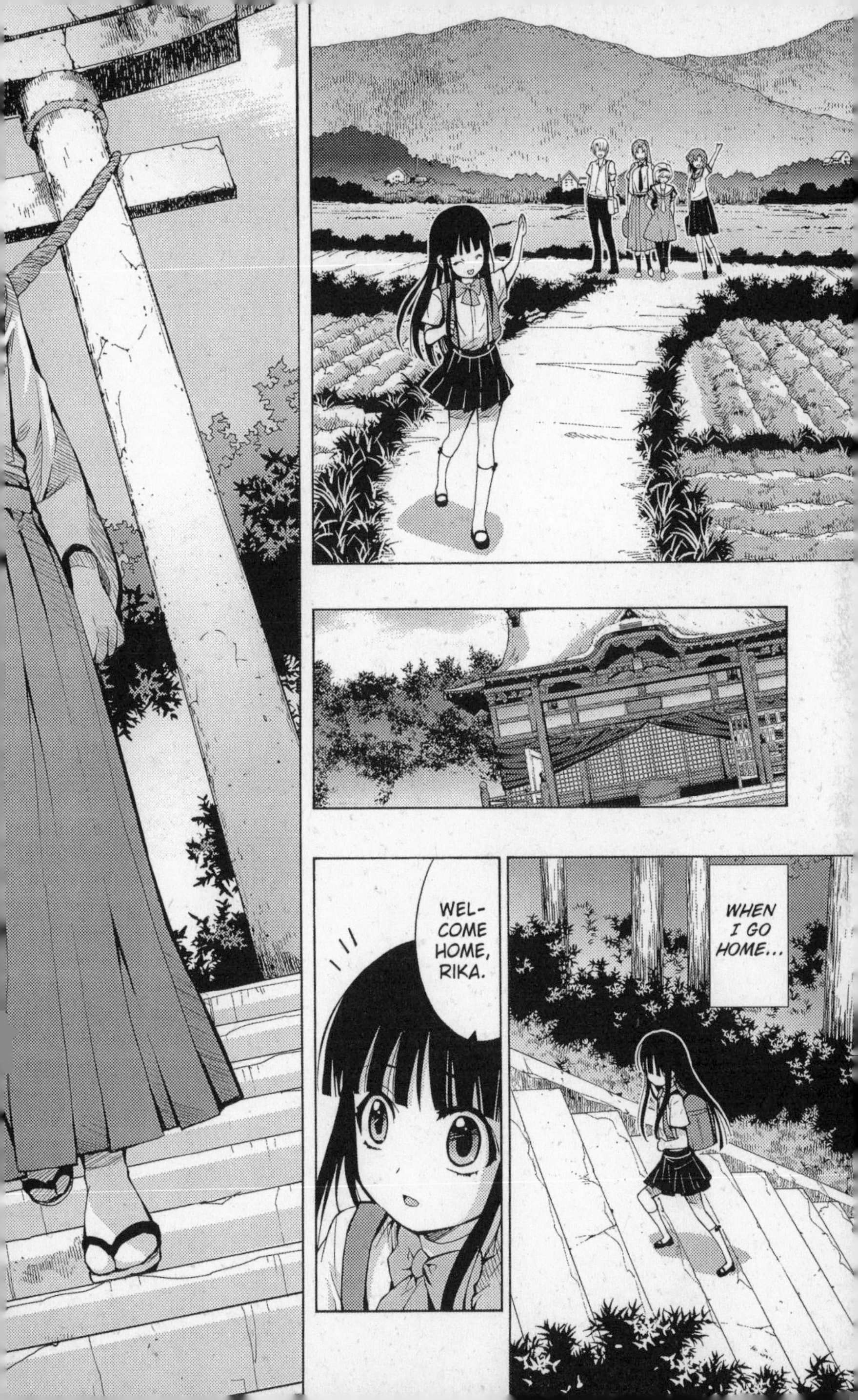
WHEN I GO HOME...
WEL-COME HOME, RIKA.

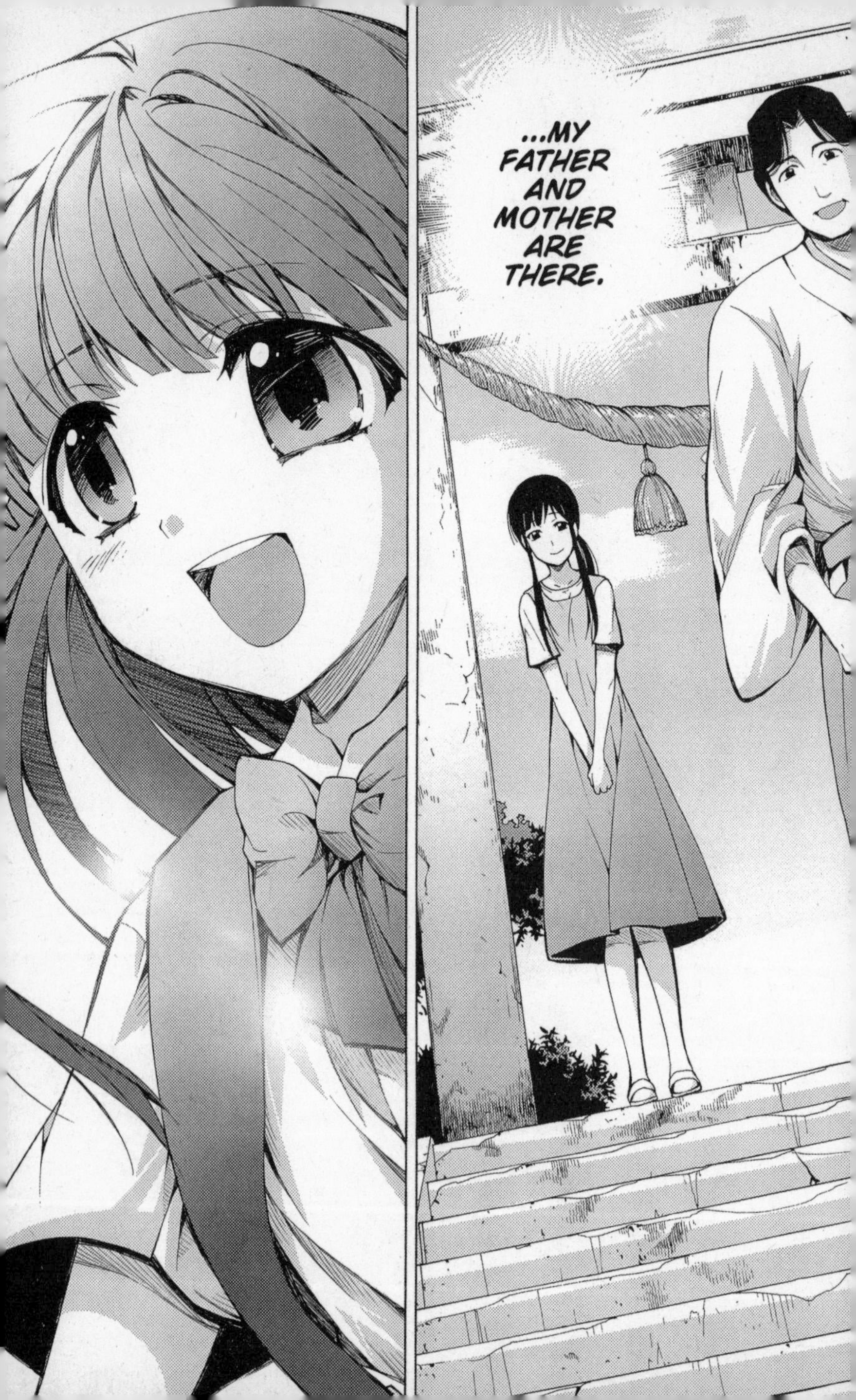
...MY FATHER AND MOTHER ARE THERE.

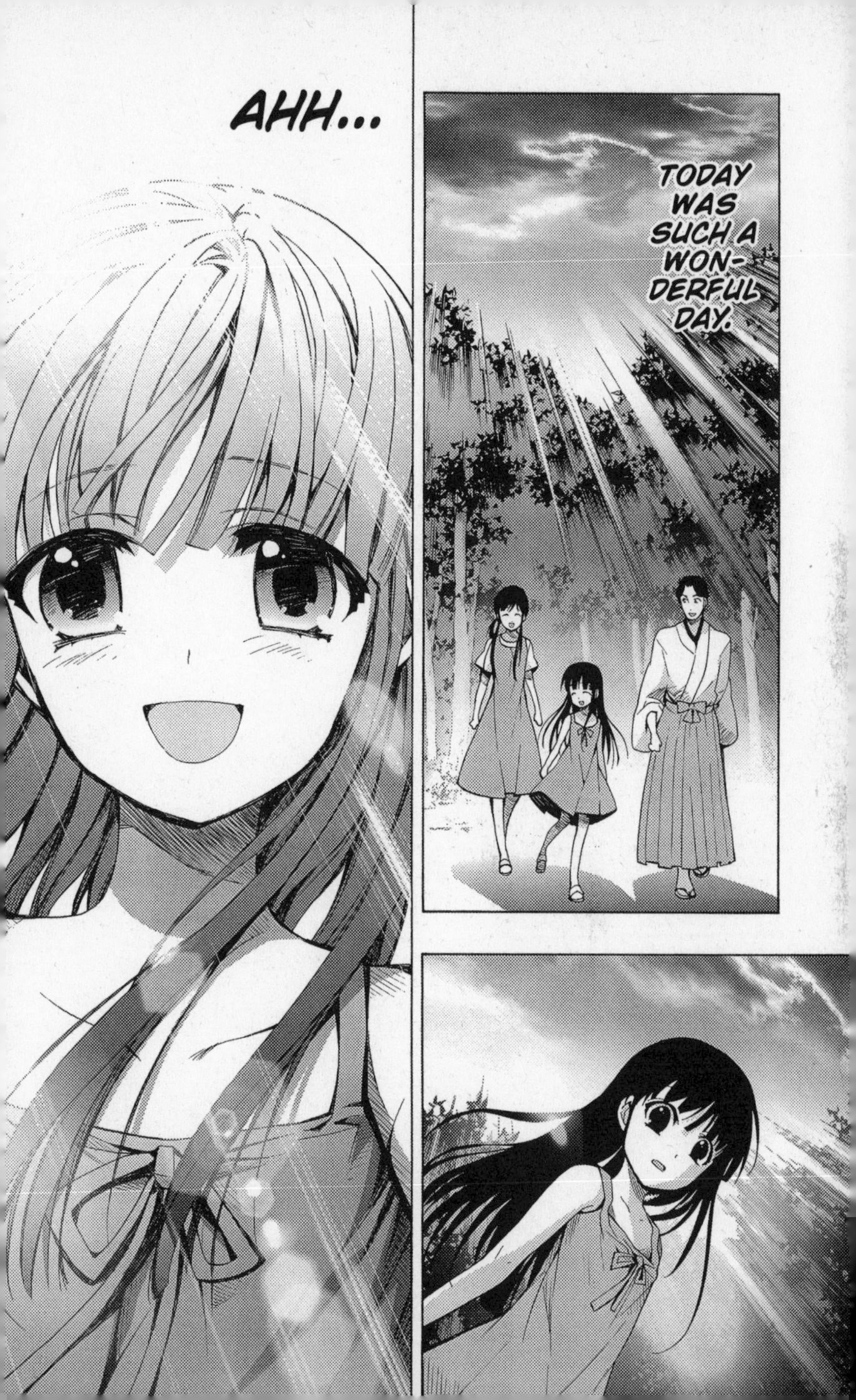
TODAY WAS SUCH A WON-DERFUL DAY.
AHH...

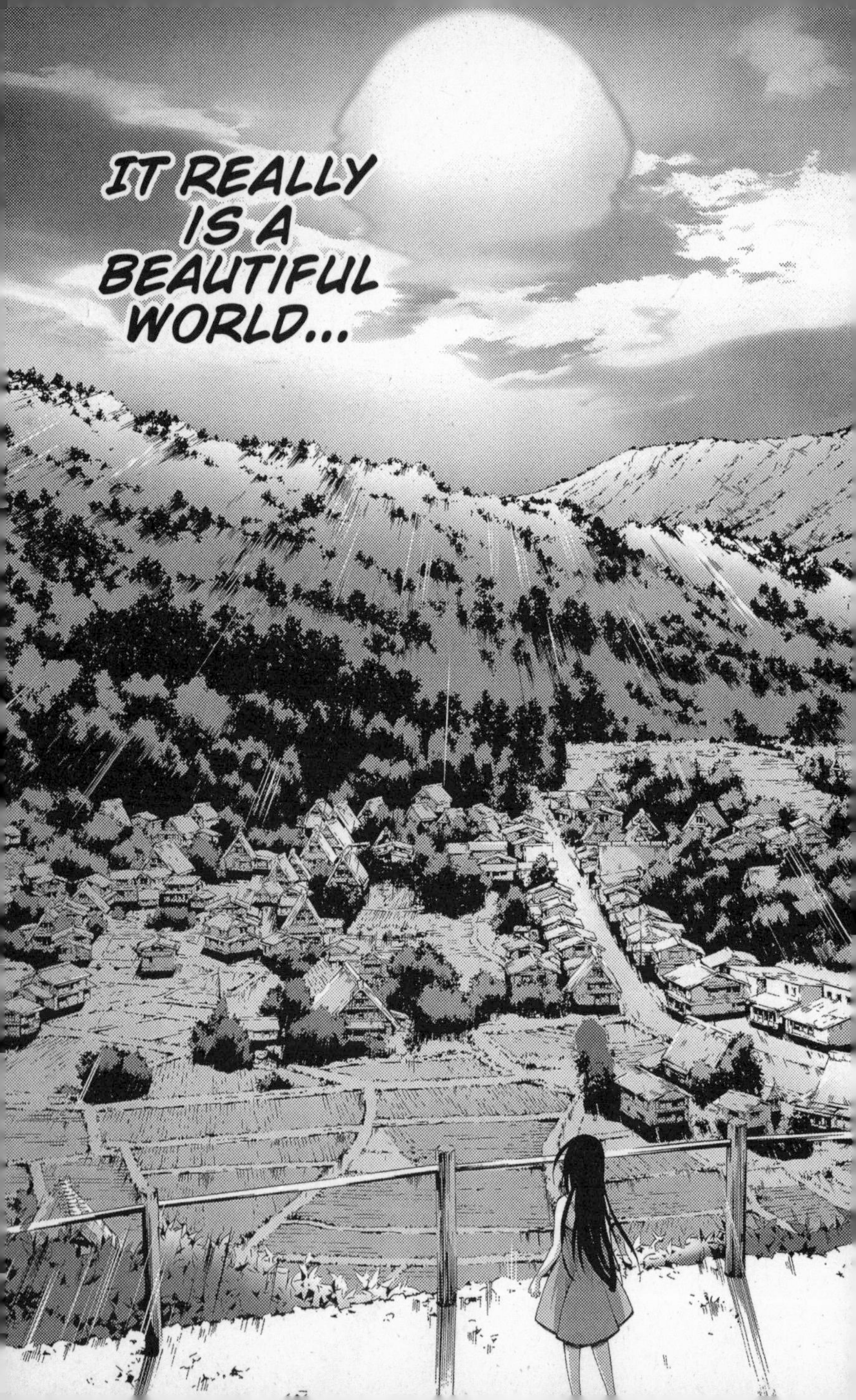
IT REALLY IS A BEAUTIFUL WORLD...

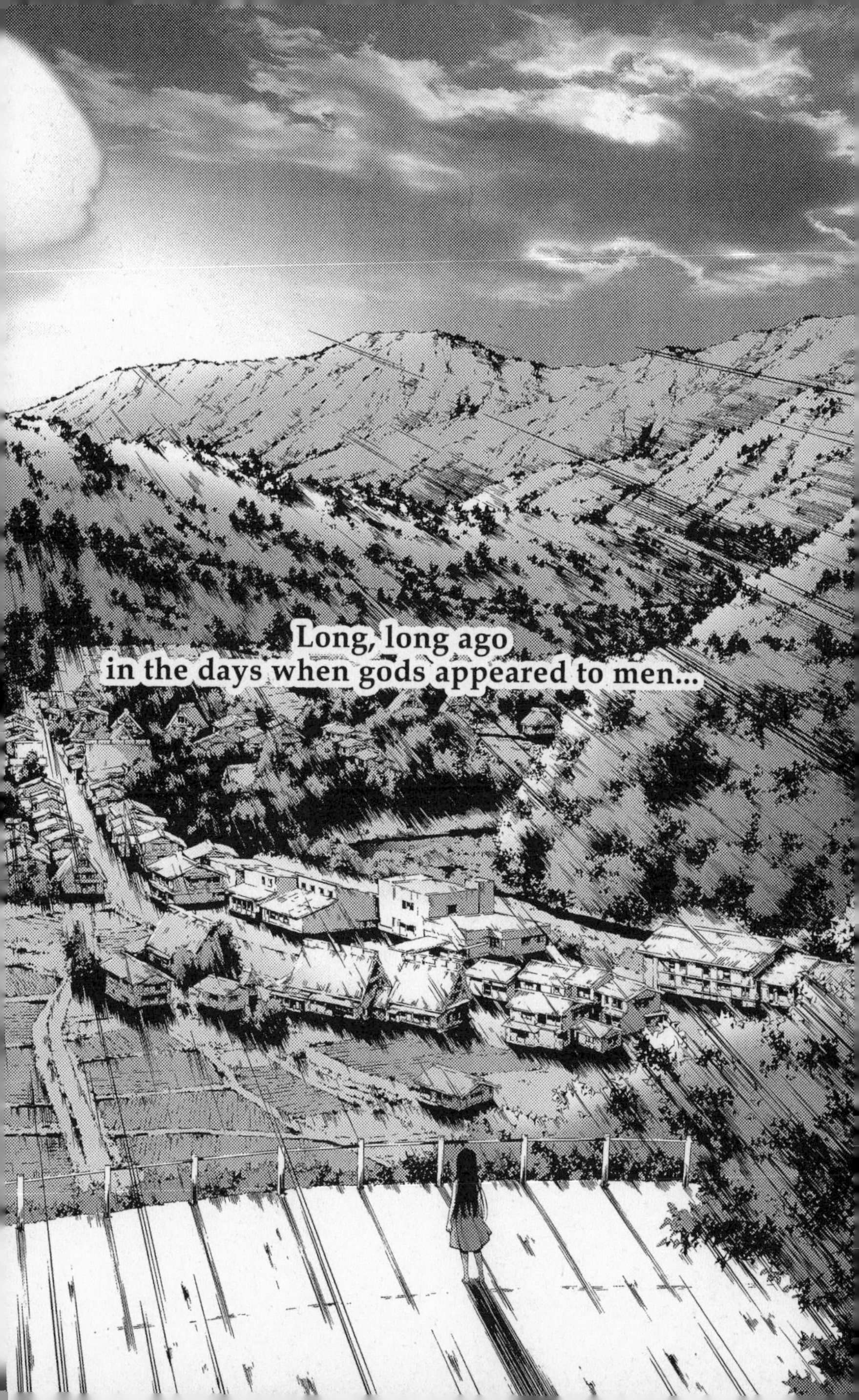
Long, long ago
in the days when gods appeared to men...

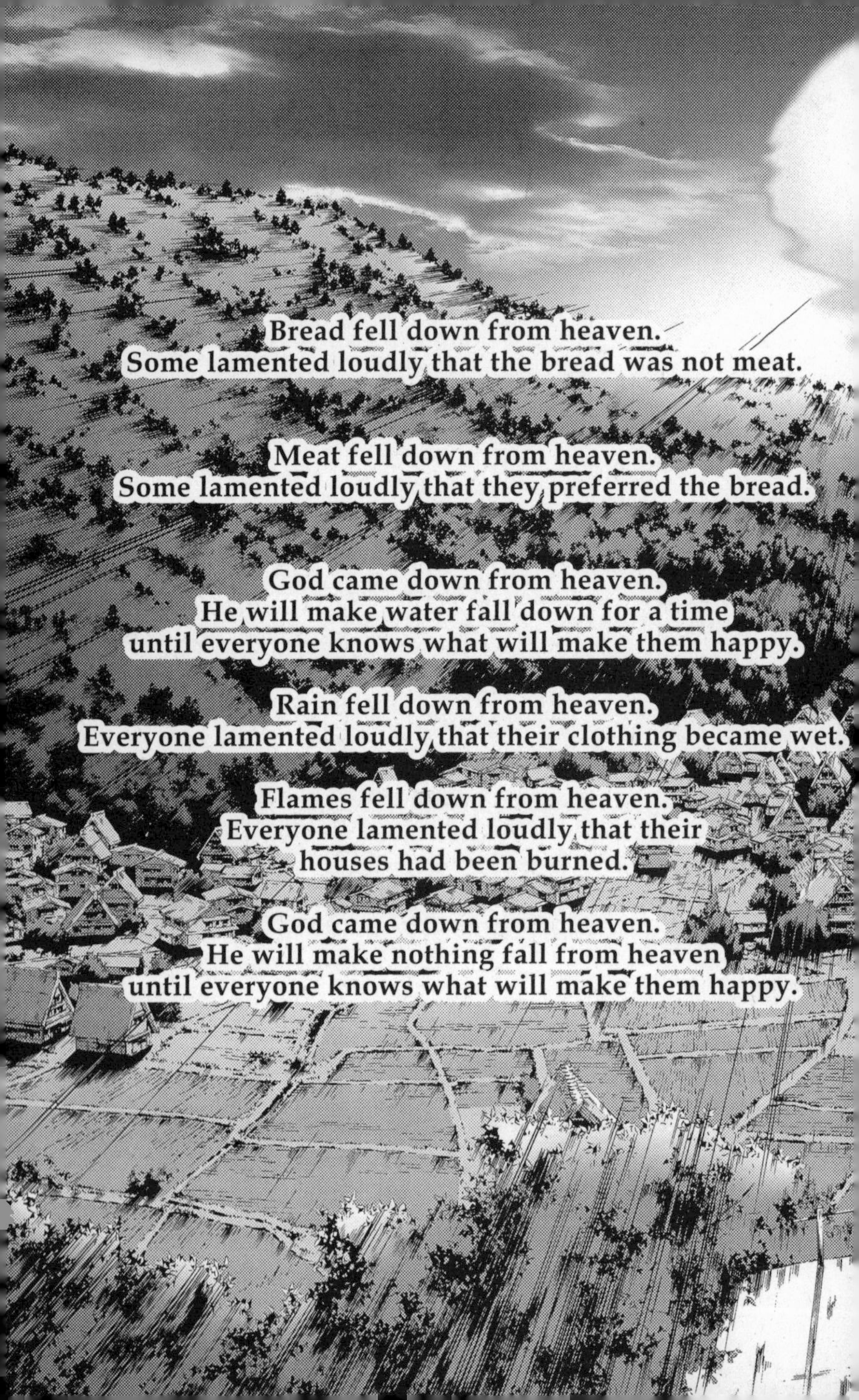
Bread fell down from heaven.
Some lamented loudly that the bread was not meat.
Meat fell down from heaven.
Some lamented loudly that they preferred the bread.
God came down from heaven.
He will make water fall down for a time
until everyone knows what will make them happy.
Rain fell down from heaven.
Everyone lamented loudly that their clothing became wet.
Flames fell down from heaven.
Everyone lamented loudly that their
houses had been burned.
God came down from heaven.
He will make nothing fall from heaven
until everyone knows what will make them happy.

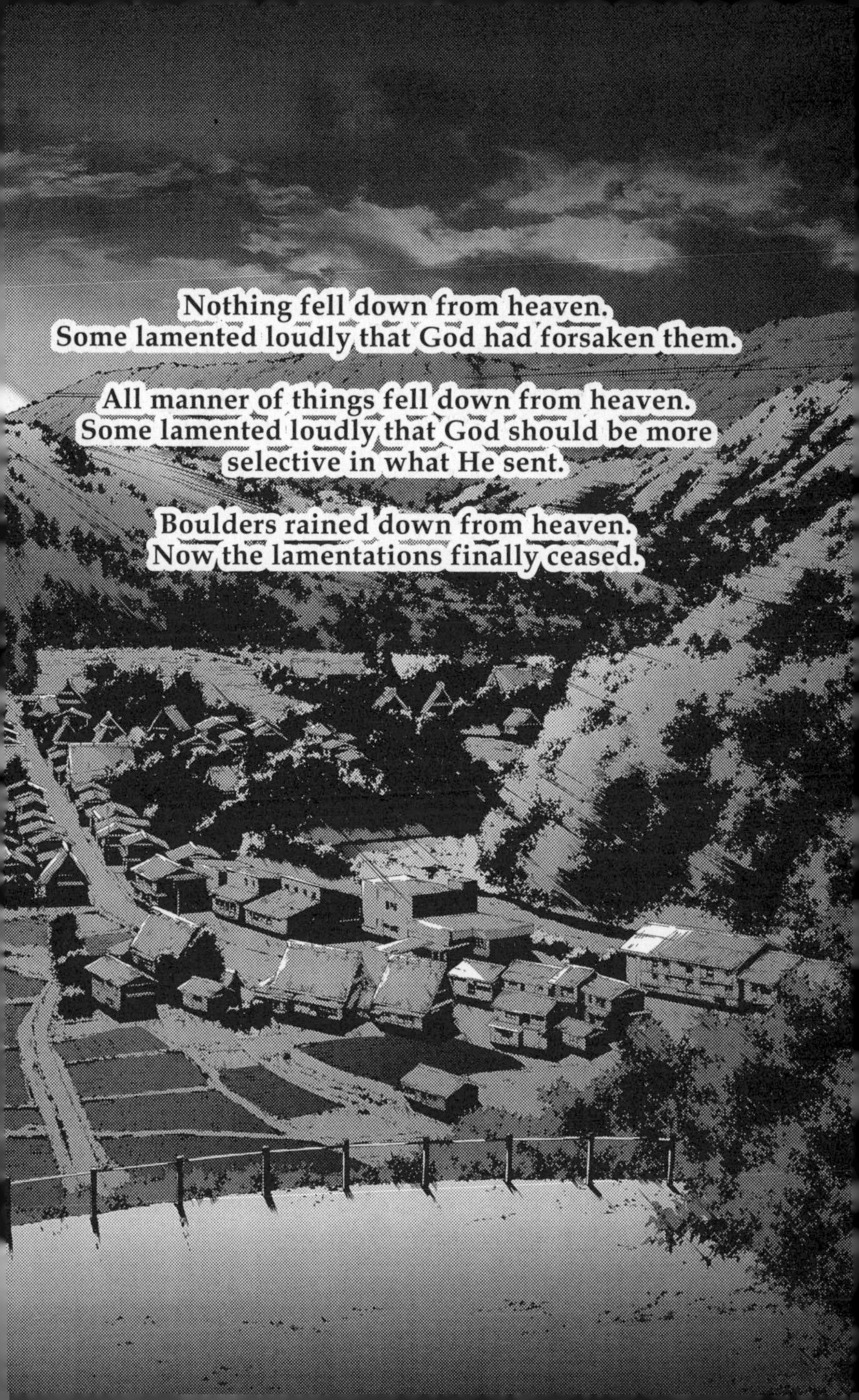
Nothing fell down from heaven.
Some lamented loudly that God had forsaken them.
All manner of things fell down from heaven.
Some lamented loudly that God should be more selective in what He sent.
Boulders rained down from heaven.
Now the lamentations finally ceased.

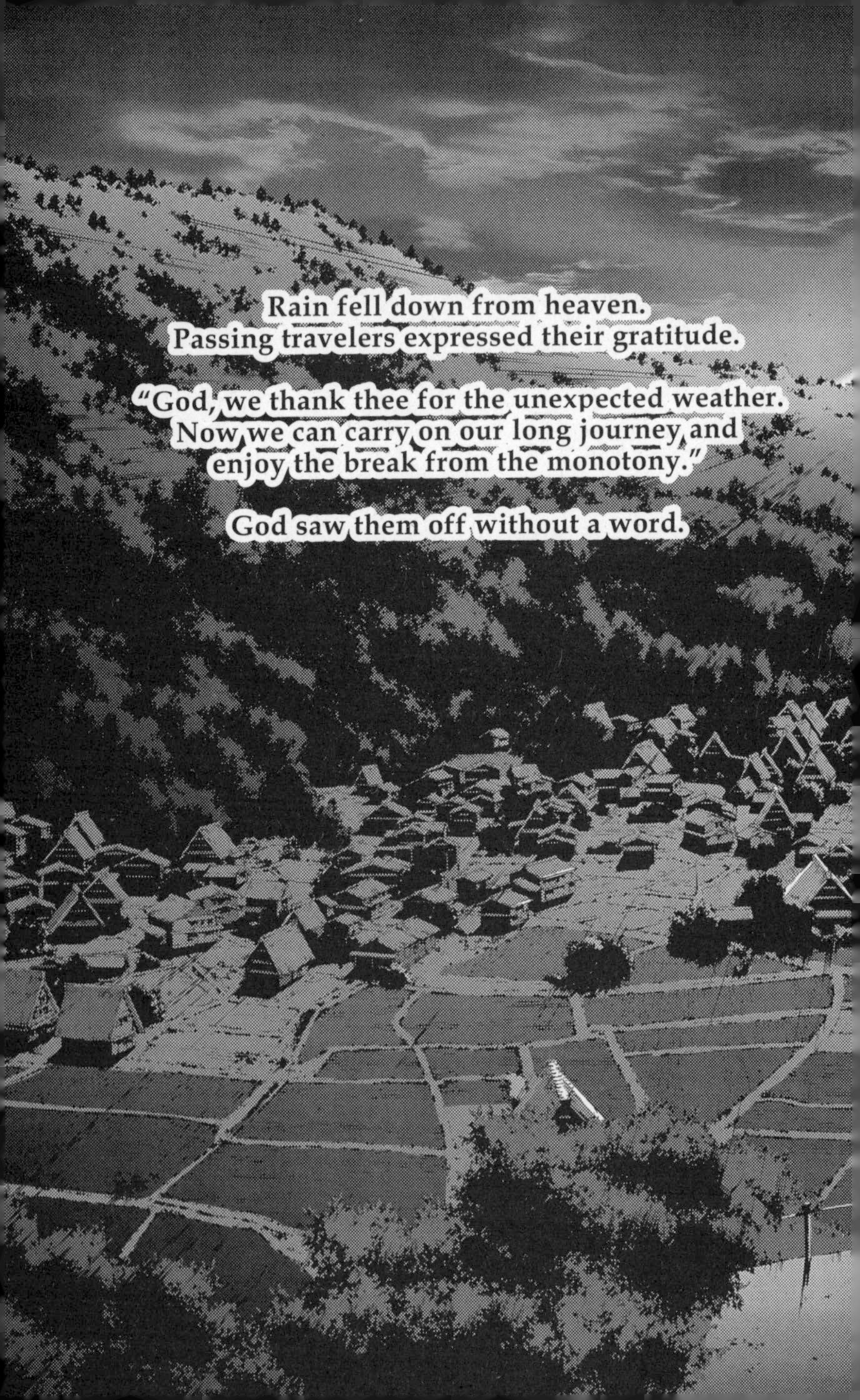
Rain fell down from heaven.
Passing travelers expressed their gratitude.
"God, we thank thee for the unexpected weather. Now we can carry on our long journey and enjoy the break from the monotony."
God saw them off without a word.

As it should be. Gods and dice are best when silent.

Frederica Bernkastel

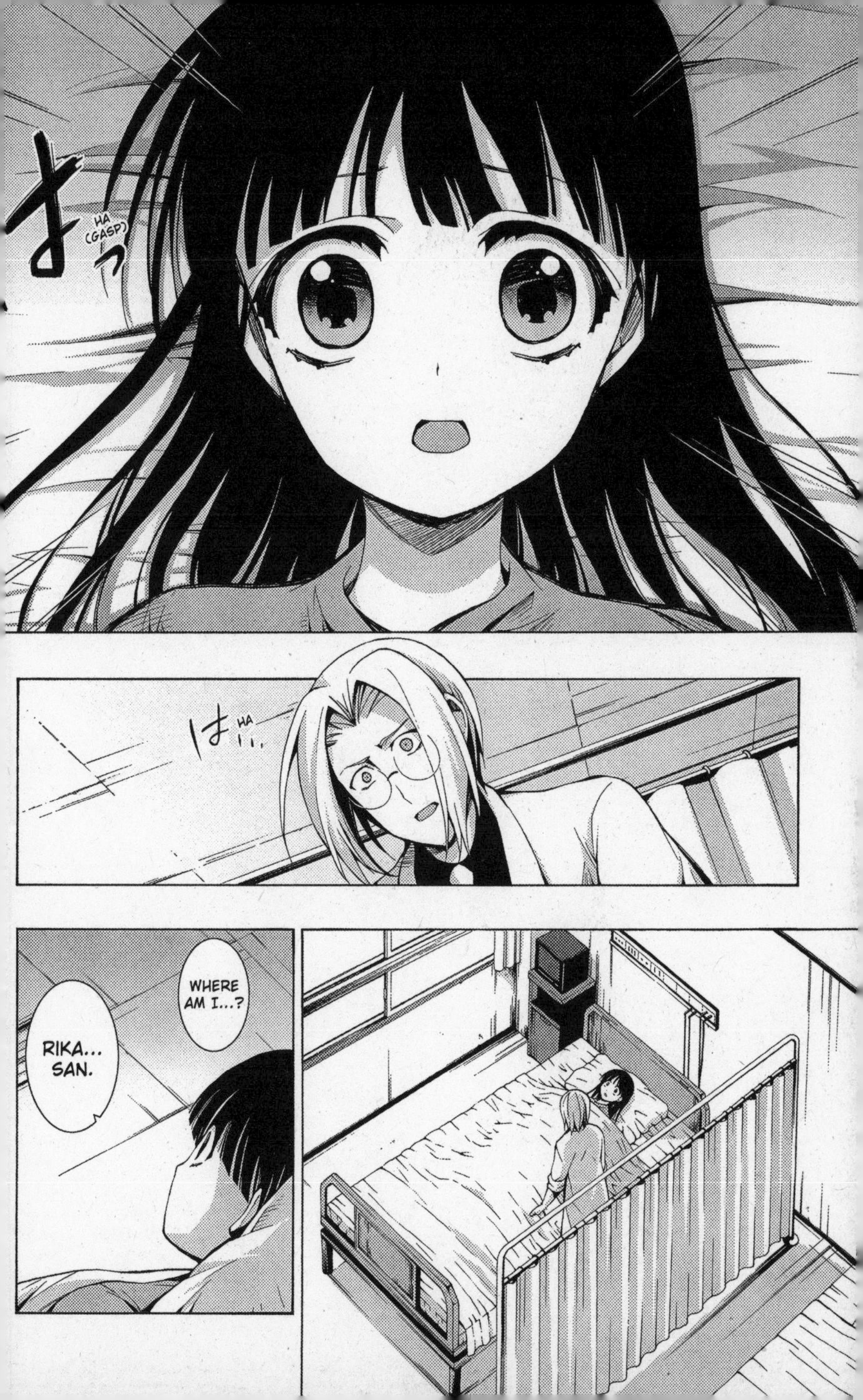
はっ
HA (GASP)
は…
HA…
WHERE AM I...?
RIKA... SAN.

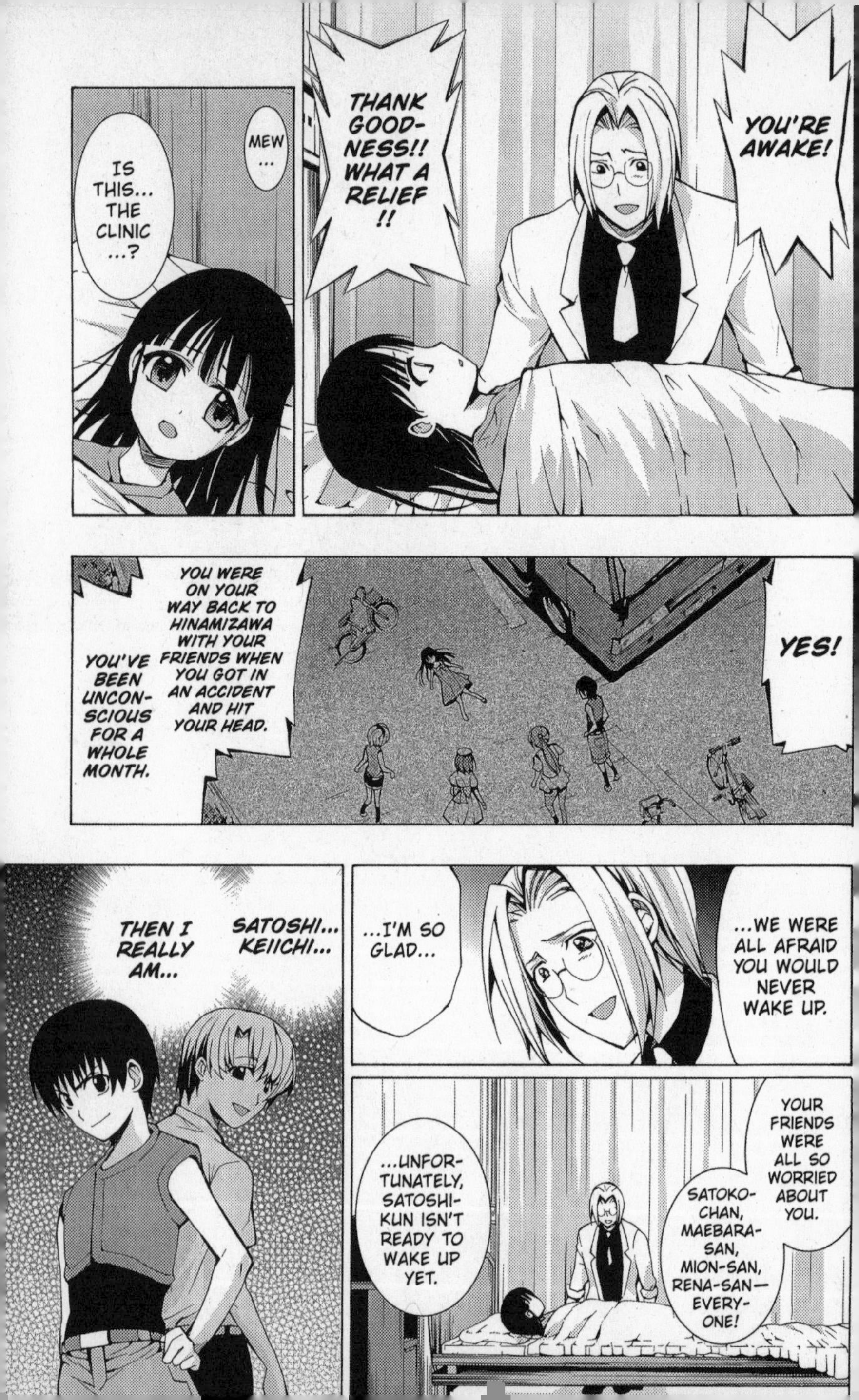
YOU'RE AWAKE!
THANK GOODNESS!! WHAT A RELIEF!!
MEW...
IS THIS... THE CLINIC...?
YES!
YOU WERE ON YOUR WAY BACK TO HINAMIZAWA WITH YOUR FRIENDS WHEN YOU GOT IN AN ACCIDENT AND HIT YOUR HEAD.
YOU'VE BEEN UNCONSCIOUS FOR A WHOLE MONTH.
...WE WERE ALL AFRAID YOU WOULD NEVER WAKE UP.
...I'M SO GLAD...
YOUR FRIENDS WERE ALL SO WORRIED ABOUT YOU.
SATOKO-CHAN, MAEBARA-SAN, MION-SAN, RENA-SAN—EVERYONE!
...UNFORTUNATELY, SATOSHI-KUN ISN'T READY TO WAKE UP YET.
SATOSHI... KEIICHI...
THEN I REALLY AM...

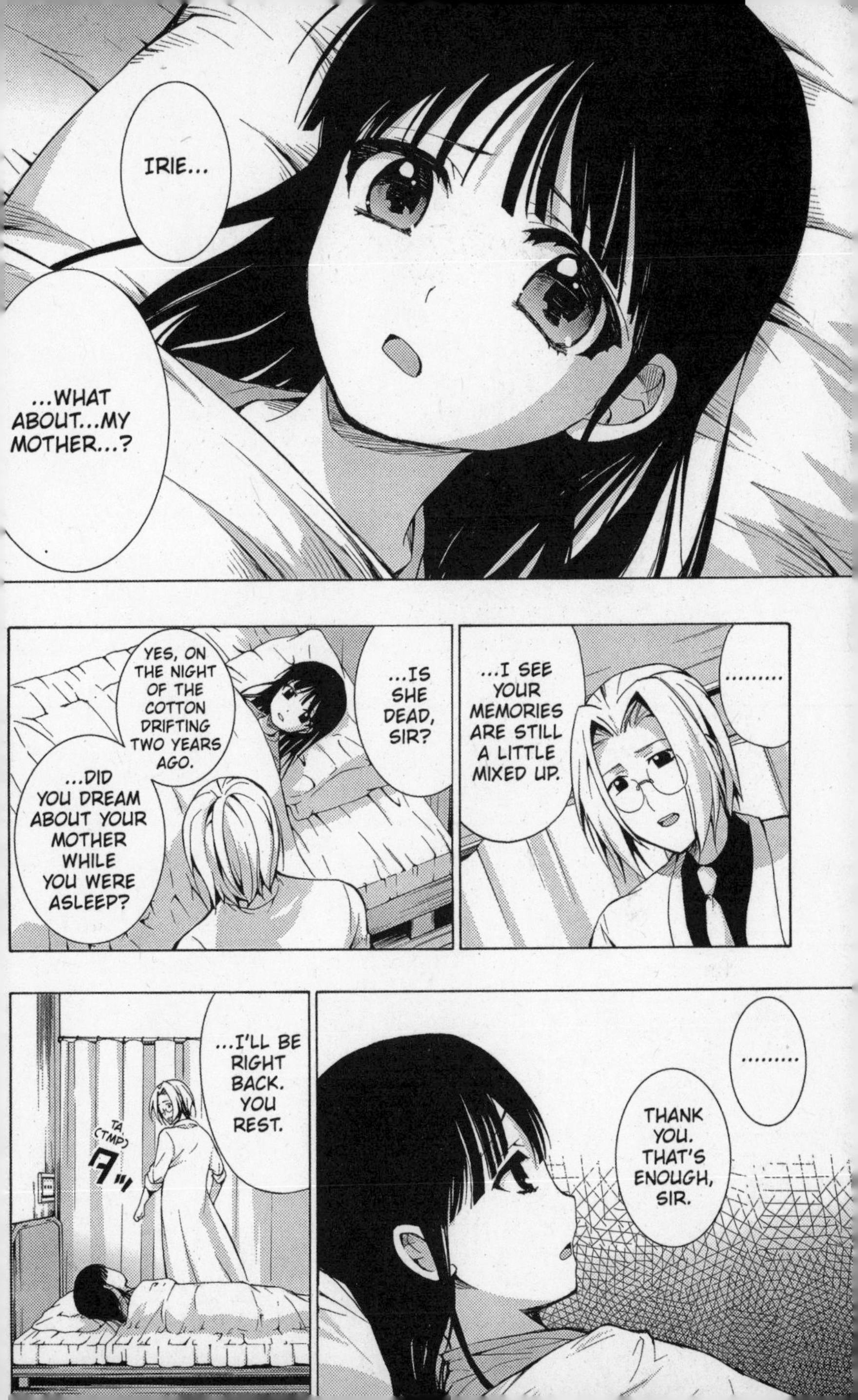
IRIE...
...WHAT ABOUT...MY MOTHER...?
....
...I SEE YOUR MEMORIES ARE STILL A LITTLE MIXED UP.
...IS SHE DEAD, SIR?
YES, ON THE NIGHT OF THE COTTON DRIFTING TWO YEARS AGO.
...DID YOU DREAM ABOUT YOUR MOTHER WHILE YOU WERE ASLEEP?
....
THANK YOU. THAT'S ENOUGH, SIR.
...I'LL BE RIGHT BACK. YOU REST.
TA (TMP)

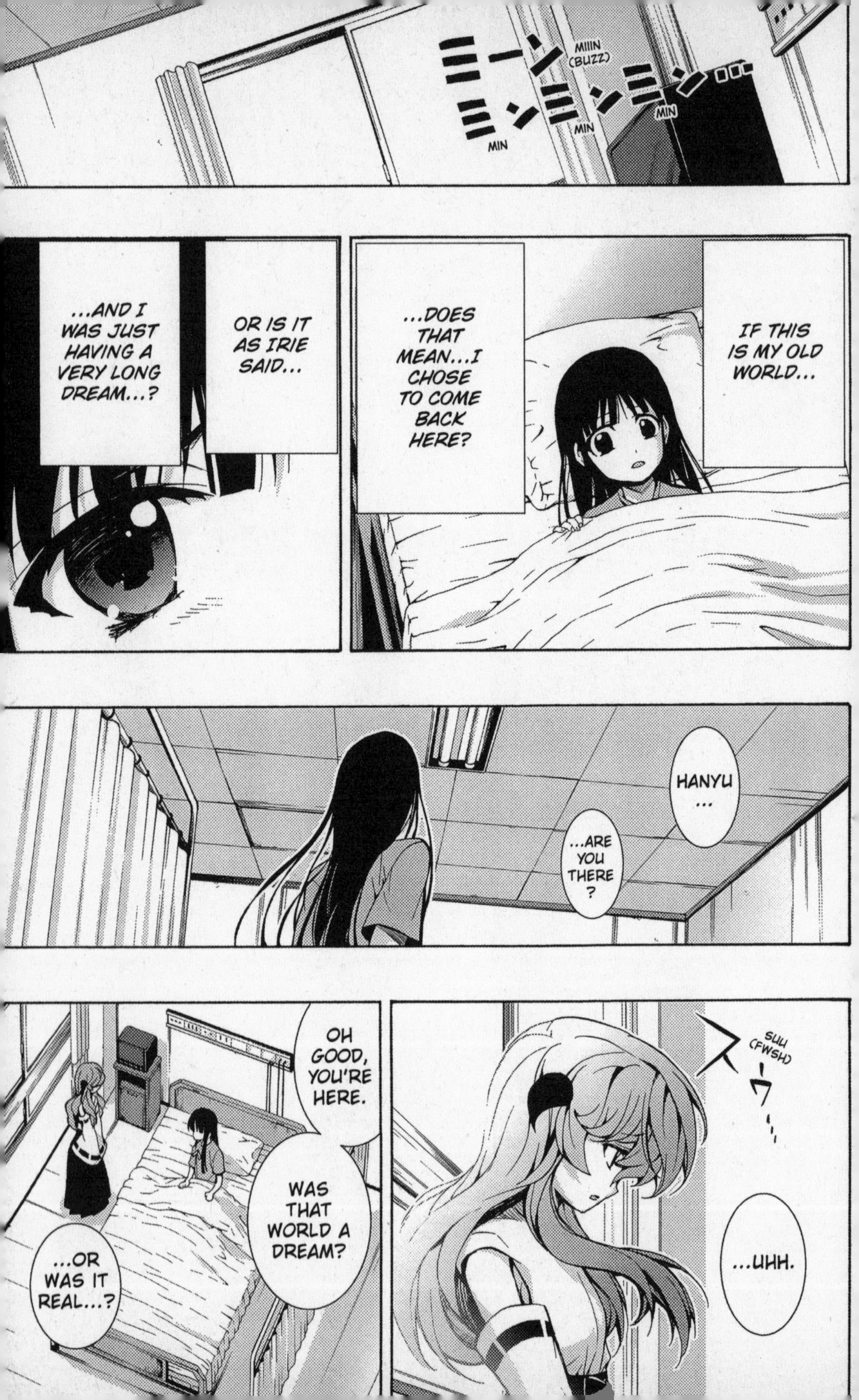
ミーン
MIIIN (BUZZ)
ミン
MIN
ミン
MIN
ミン
MIN
IF THIS IS MY OLD WORLD...
...DOES THAT MEAN...I CHOSE TO COME BACK HERE?
OR IS IT AS IRIE SAID...
...AND I WAS JUST HAVING A VERY LONG DREAM...?
HANYU ...
...ARE YOU THERE ?
スゥ
SUU (FWSH)
...UHH.
OH GOOD, YOU'RE HERE.
WAS THAT WORLD A DREAM?
...OR WAS IT REAL...?

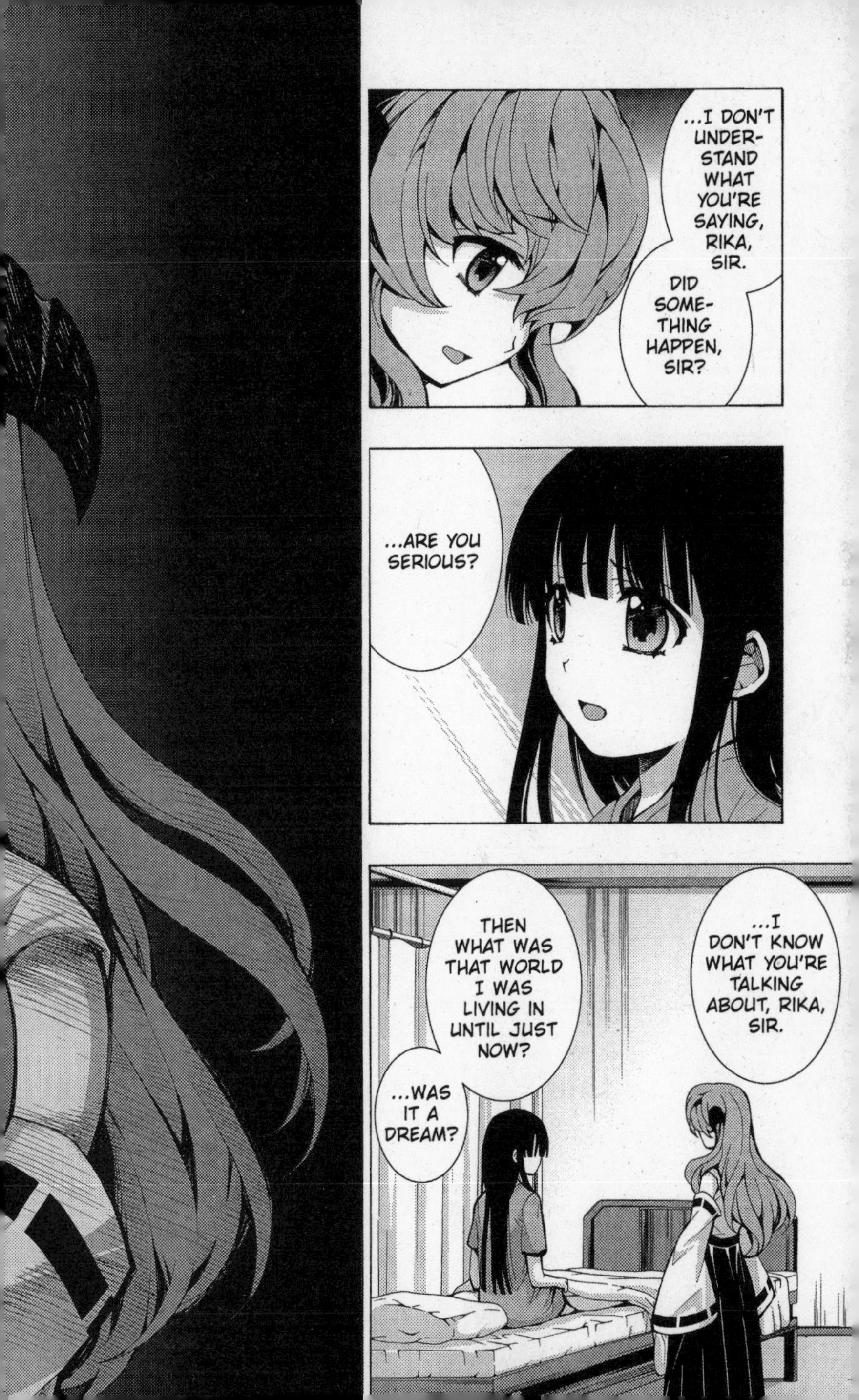
...I DON'T UNDER-STAND WHAT YOU'RE SAYING, RIKA, SIR.
DID SOME-THING HAPPEN, SIR?
...ARE YOU SERIOUS?
...I DON'T KNOW WHAT YOU'RE TALKING ABOUT, RIKA, SIR.
THEN WHAT WAS THAT WORLD I WAS LIVING IN UNTIL JUST NOW?
...WAS IT A DREAM?

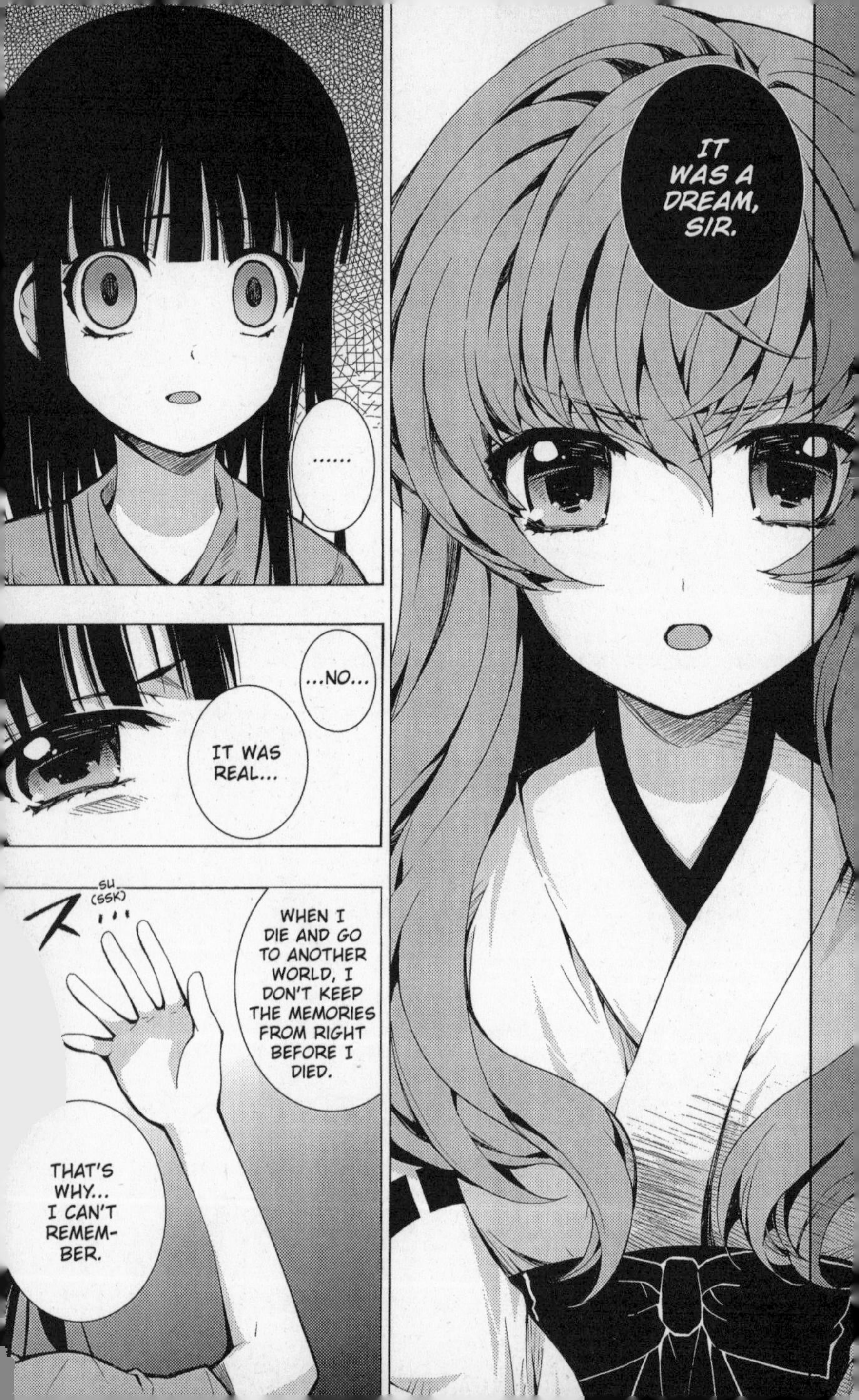
IT WAS A DREAM, SIR.
......
...NO...
IT WAS REAL...
ス
SU (SSK)
WHEN I DIE AND GO TO ANOTHER WORLD, I DON'T KEEP THE MEMORIES FROM RIGHT BEFORE I DIED.
THAT'S WHY... I CAN'T REMEMBER.

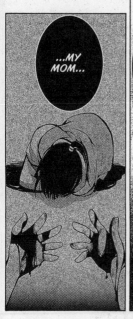

...MY MOM...

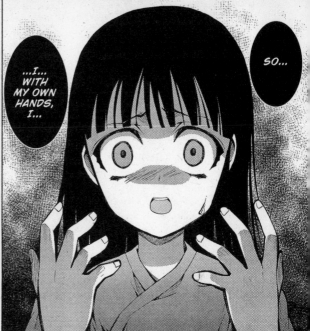

SO...

...I... WITH MY OWN HANDS, I...

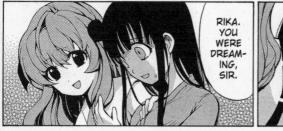

RIKA. YOU WERE DREAM-ING, SIR.

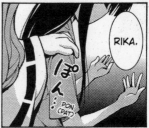

RIKA.

ぽん
PON (PAT)

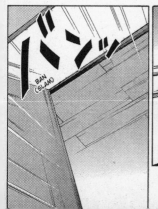

バン
BAN (SLAM)

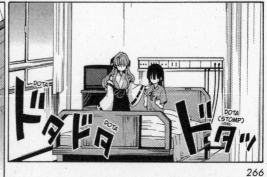

ドタ
DOTA

ドタ
DOTA

ドタッ
DOTA (STOMP)

266

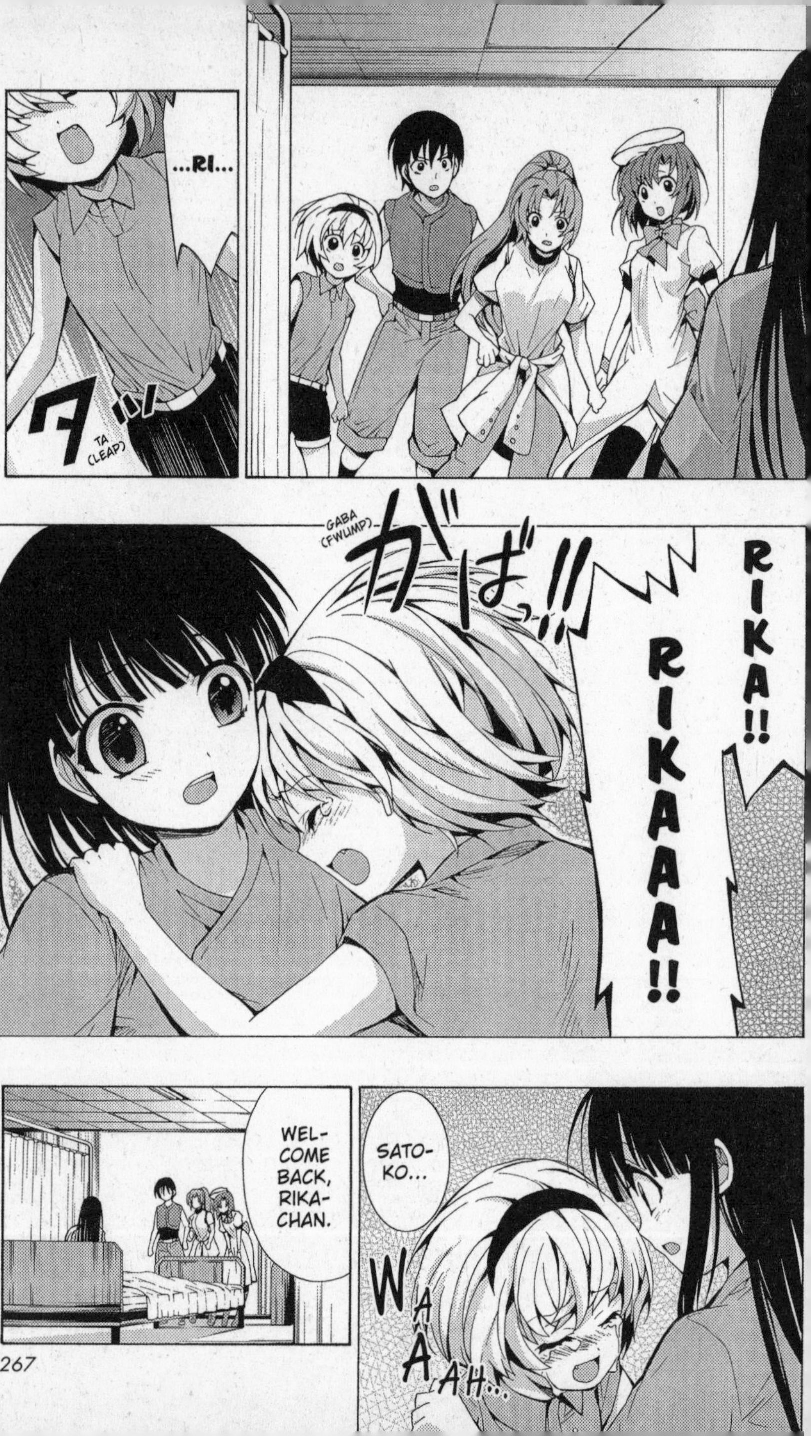

...RI...
タッ
TA (LEAP)
がばっ!!
GABA (FWUMP)
RIKA!!
RIKAAA!!
SATO-KO...
WAAAH...
WEL-COME BACK, RIKA-CHAN.

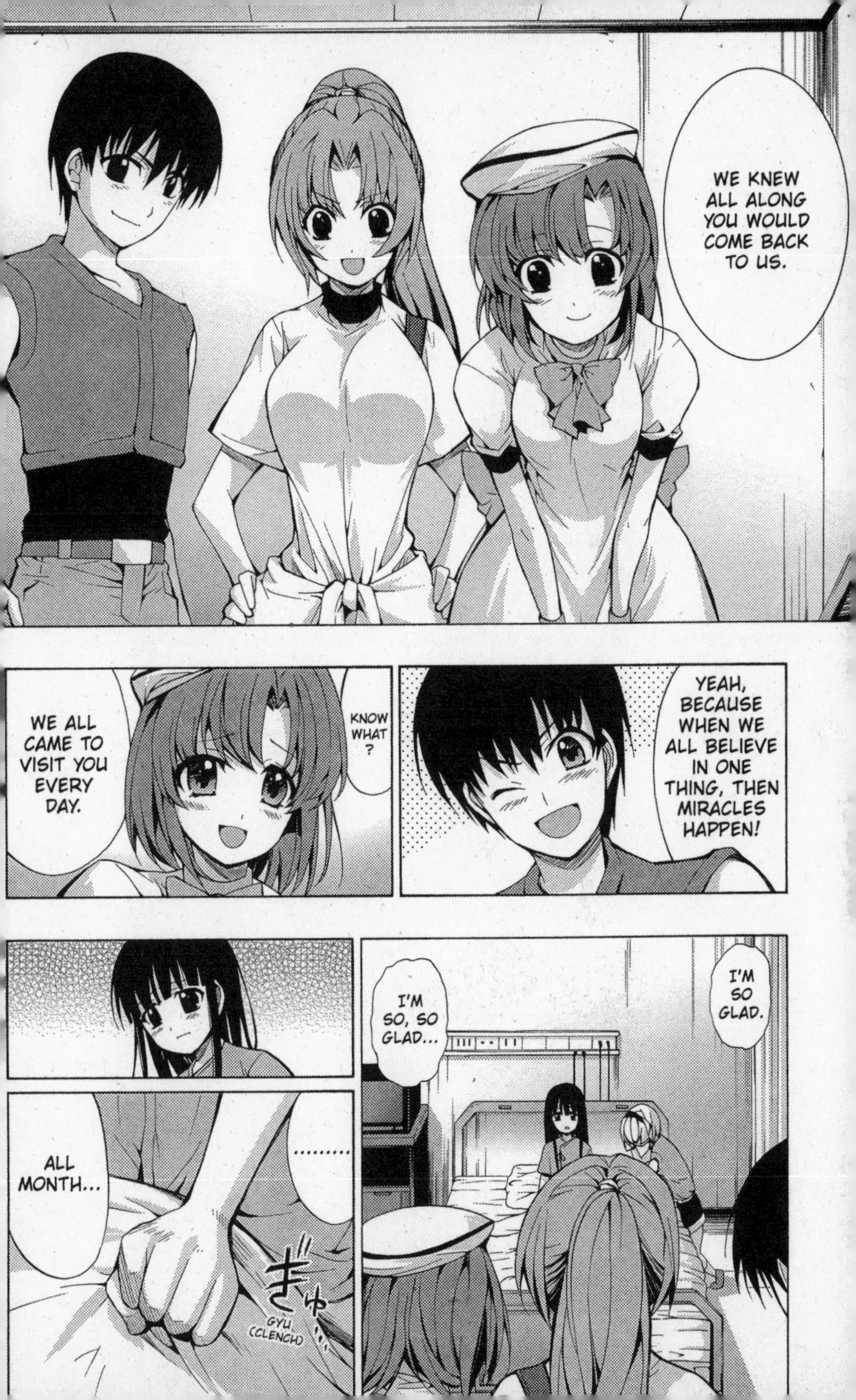
WE KNEW ALL ALONG YOU WOULD COME BACK TO US.
YEAH, BECAUSE WHEN WE ALL BELIEVE IN ONE THING, THEN MIRACLES HAPPEN!
KNOW WHAT?
WE ALL CAME TO VISIT YOU EVERY DAY.
I'M SO GLAD.
I'M SO, SO GLAD...
....
ALL MONTH...
GYU (CLENCH)

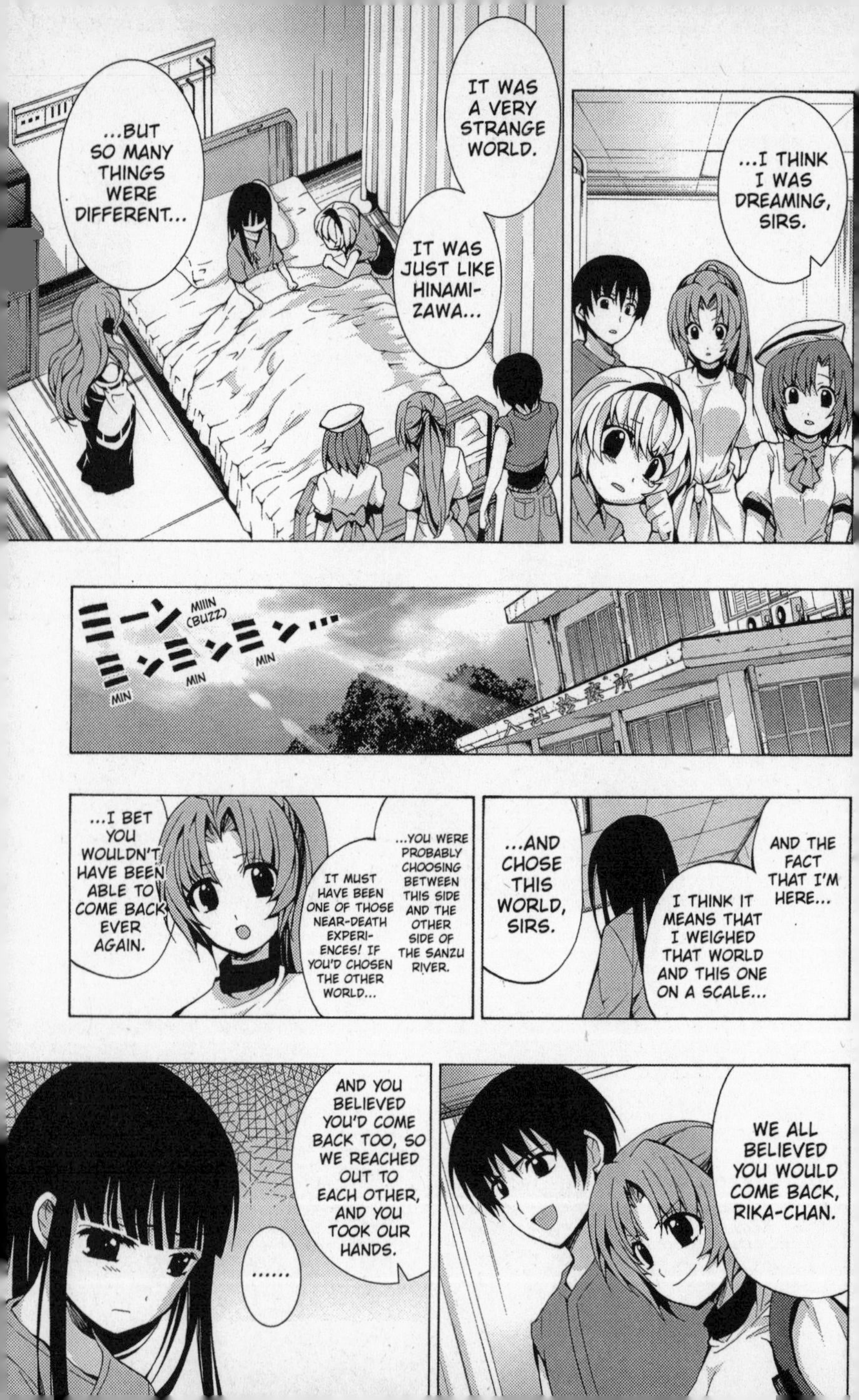
...I THINK I WAS DREAMING, SIRS.
IT WAS A VERY STRANGE WORLD.
IT WAS JUST LIKE HINAMI-ZAWA...
...BUT SO MANY THINGS WERE DIFFERENT...
ミーン
MIIIN (BUZZ)
ミンミンミン…
MIN MIN MIN
入江診療所
AND THE FACT THAT I'M HERE...
I THINK IT MEANS THAT I WEIGHED THAT WORLD AND THIS ONE ON A SCALE...
...AND CHOSE THIS WORLD, SIRS.
...YOU WERE PROBABLY CHOOSING BETWEEN THIS SIDE AND THE OTHER SIDE OF THE SANZU RIVER.
IT MUST HAVE BEEN ONE OF THOSE NEAR-DEATH EXPERI-ENCES! IF YOU'D CHOSEN THE OTHER WORLD...
...I BET YOU WOULDN'T HAVE BEEN ABLE TO COME BACK EVER AGAIN.
WE ALL BELIEVED YOU WOULD COME BACK, RIKA-CHAN.
AND YOU BELIEVED YOU'D COME BACK TOO, SO WE REACHED OUT TO EACH OTHER, AND YOU TOOK OUR HANDS.
......

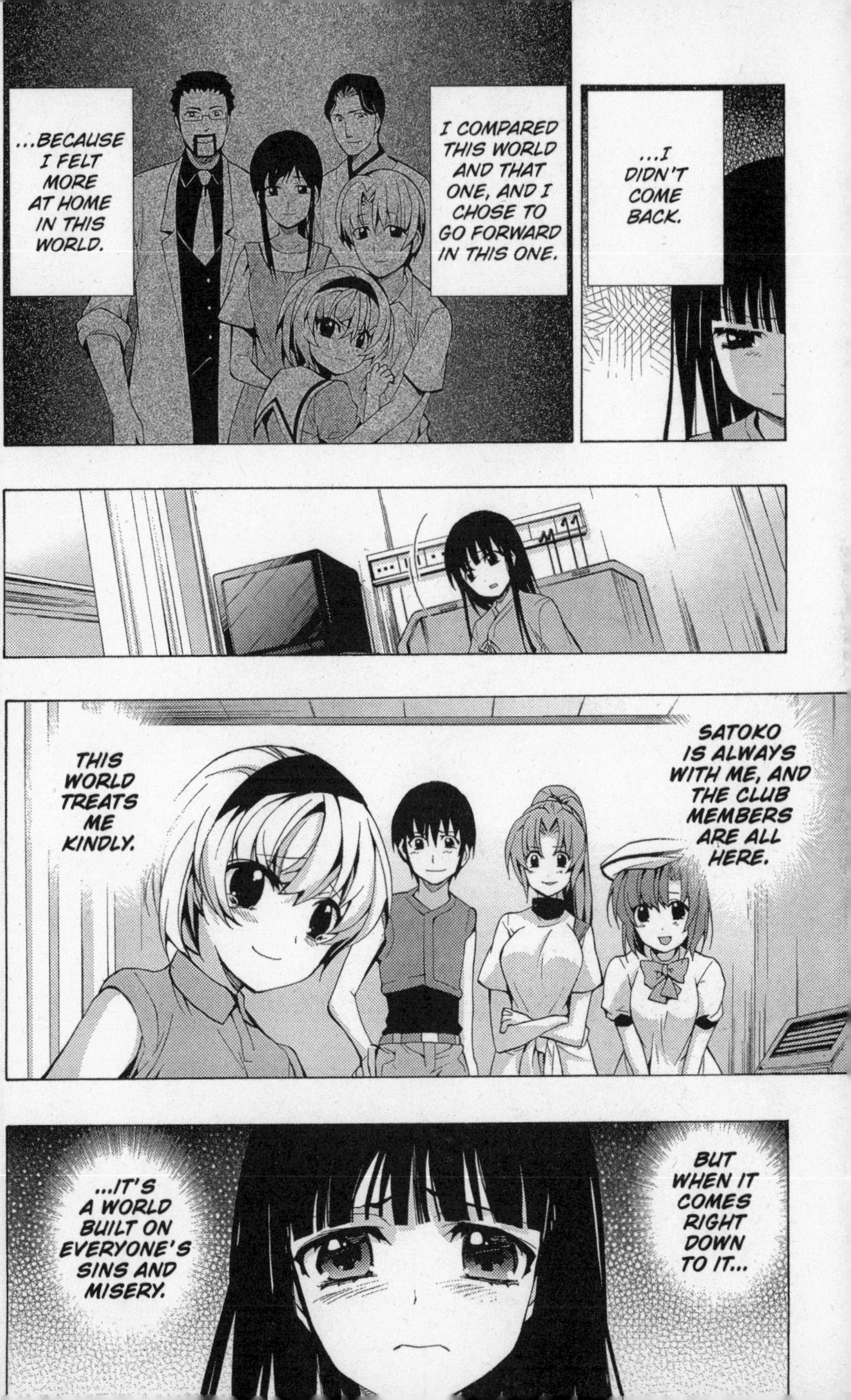
...I DIDN'T COME BACK.
I COMPARED THIS WORLD AND THAT ONE, AND I CHOSE TO GO FORWARD IN THIS ONE.
...BECAUSE I FELT MORE AT HOME IN THIS WORLD.
SATOKO IS ALWAYS WITH ME, AND THE CLUB MEMBERS ARE ALL HERE.
THIS WORLD TREATS ME KINDLY.
BUT WHEN IT COMES RIGHT DOWN TO IT...
...IT'S A WORLD BUILT ON EVERYONE'S SINS AND MISERY.

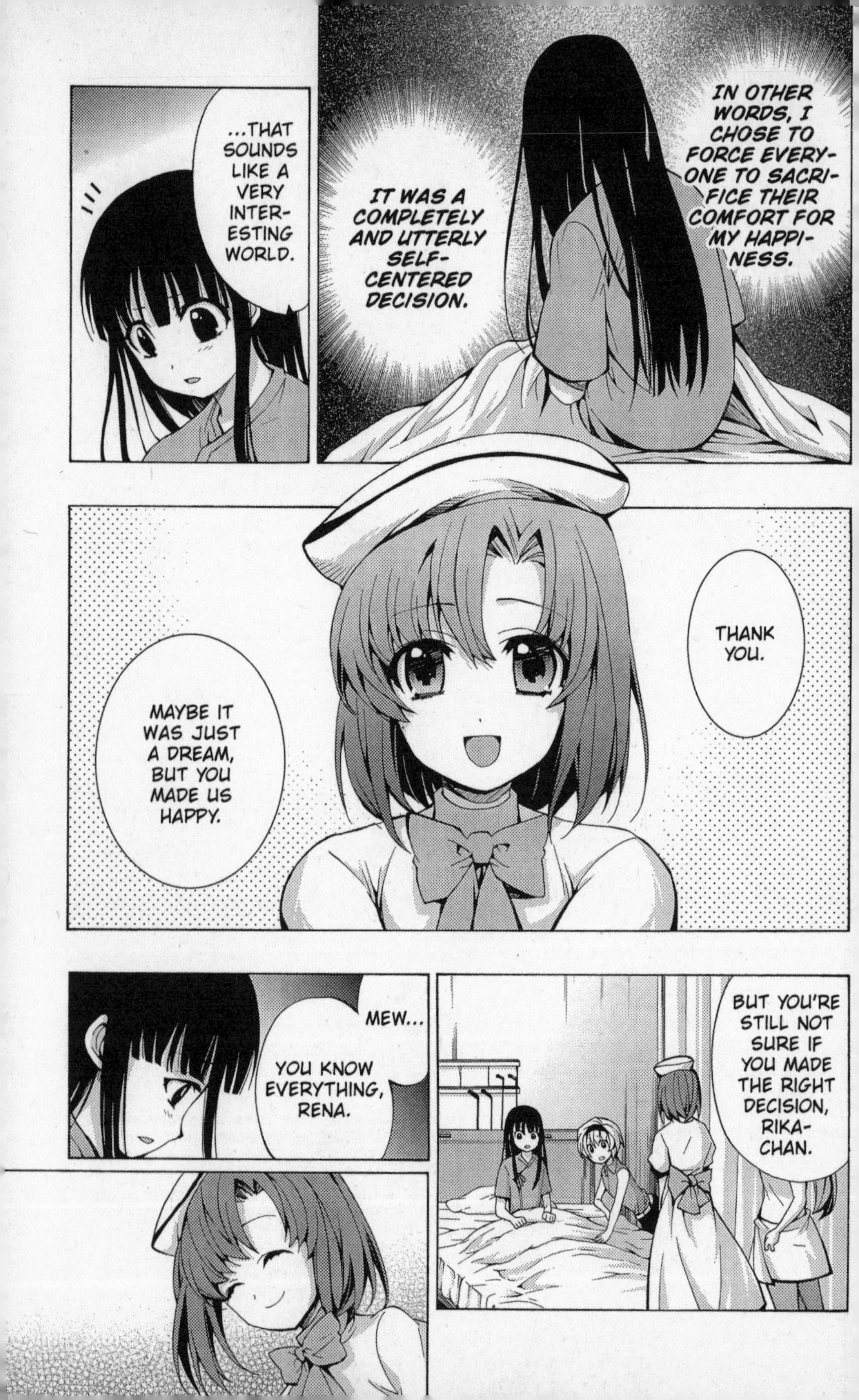
IN OTHER WORDS, I CHOSE TO FORCE EVERYONE TO SACRIFICE THEIR COMFORT FOR MY HAPPINESS.
IT WAS A COMPLETELY AND UTTERLY SELF-CENTERED DECISION.
...THAT SOUNDS LIKE A VERY INTERESTING WORLD.
THANK YOU.
MAYBE IT WAS JUST A DREAM, BUT YOU MADE US HAPPY.
BUT YOU'RE STILL NOT SURE IF YOU MADE THE RIGHT DECISION, RIKA-CHAN.
MEW...
YOU KNOW EVERYTHING, RENA.

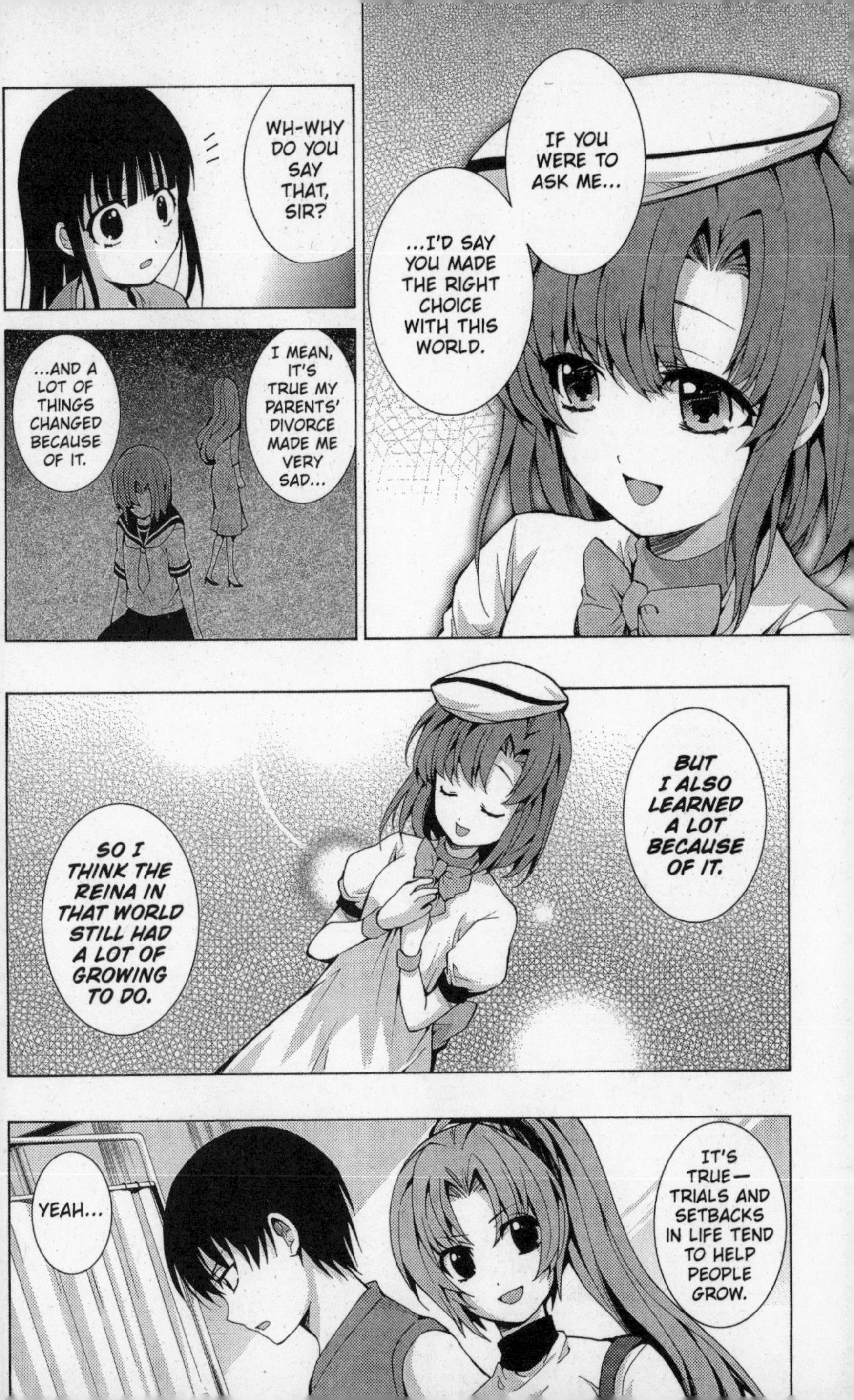
IF YOU WERE TO ASK ME...
...I'D SAY YOU MADE THE RIGHT CHOICE WITH THIS WORLD.
WH-WHY DO YOU SAY THAT, SIR?
I MEAN, IT'S TRUE MY PARENTS' DIVORCE MADE ME VERY SAD...
...AND A LOT OF THINGS CHANGED BECAUSE OF IT.
BUT I ALSO LEARNED A LOT BECAUSE OF IT.
SO I THINK THE REINA IN THAT WORLD STILL HAD A LOT OF GROWING TO DO.
IT'S TRUE— TRIALS AND SETBACKS IN LIFE TEND TO HELP PEOPLE GROW.
YEAH...

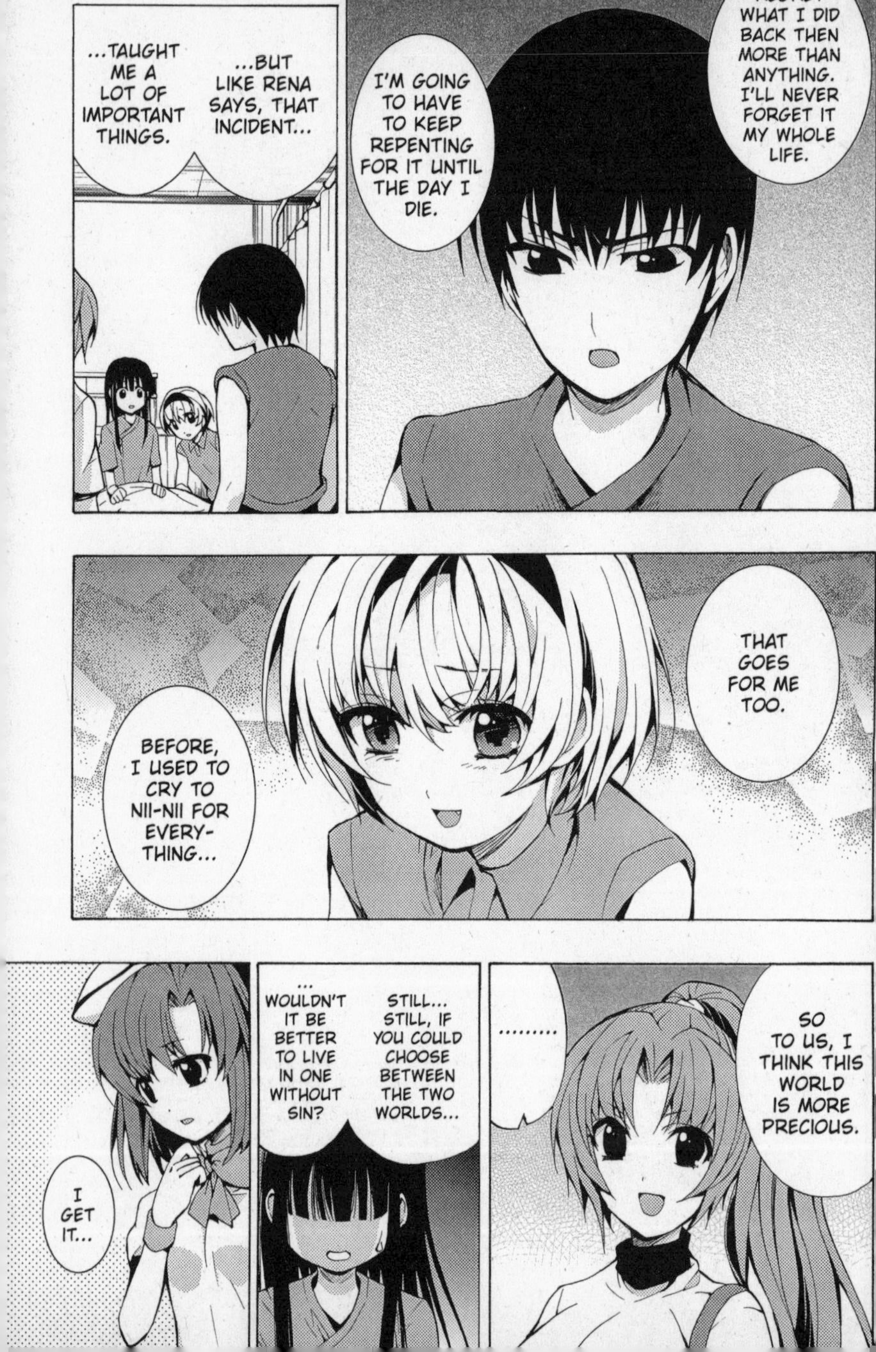
...I REGRET WHAT I DID BACK THEN MORE THAN ANYTHING. I'LL NEVER FORGET IT MY WHOLE LIFE.
I'M GOING TO HAVE TO KEEP REPENTING FOR IT UNTIL THE DAY I DIE.
...BUT LIKE RENA SAYS, THAT INCIDENT...
...TAUGHT ME A LOT OF IMPORTANT THINGS.
THAT GOES FOR ME TOO.
BEFORE, I USED TO CRY TO NII-NII FOR EVERY-THING...
SO TO US, I THINK THIS WORLD IS MORE PRECIOUS.
....
STILL... STILL, IF YOU COULD CHOOSE BETWEEN THE TWO WORLDS...
...WOULDN'T IT BE BETTER TO LIVE IN ONE WITHOUT SIN?
I GET IT...

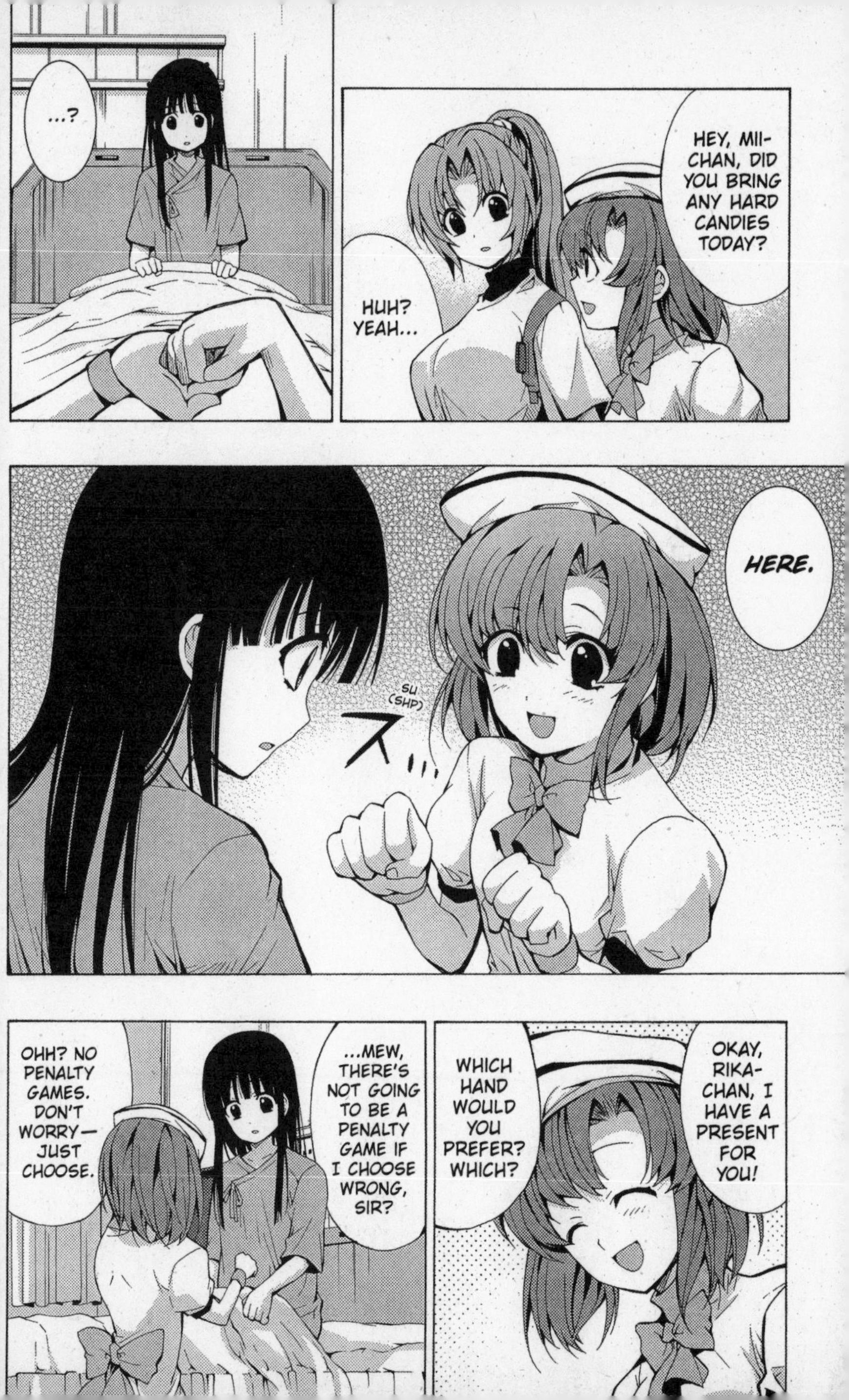
HEY, MII-CHAN, DID YOU BRING ANY HARD CANDIES TODAY?
HUH? YEAH...
...?
HERE.
SU (SHP)
OKAY, RIKA-CHAN, I HAVE A PRESENT FOR YOU!
WHICH HAND WOULD YOU PREFER? WHICH?
...MEW, THERE'S NOT GOING TO BE A PENALTY GAME IF I CHOOSE WRONG, SIR?
OHH? NO PENALTY GAMES. DON'T WORRY—JUST CHOOSE.

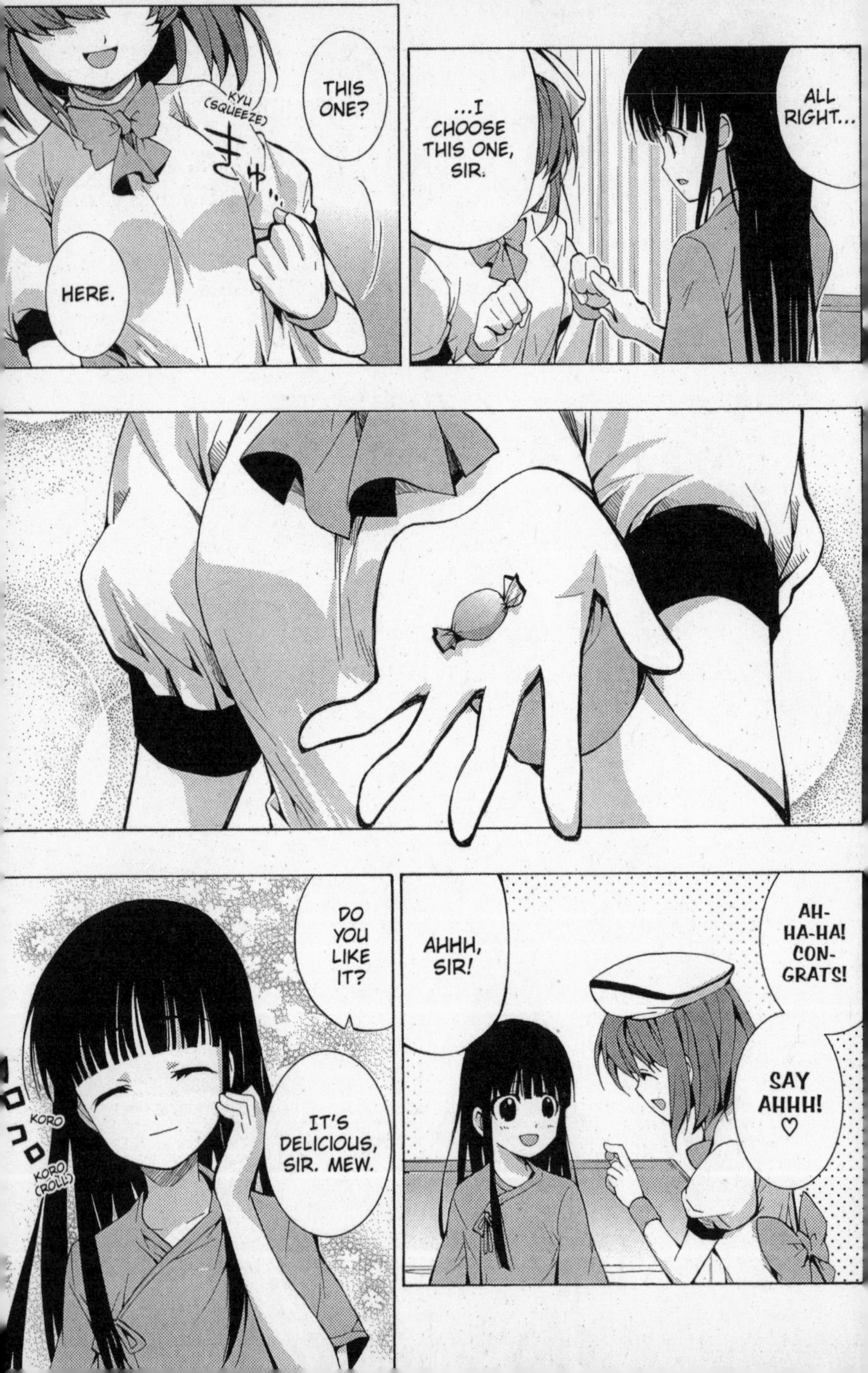
ALL RIGHT...
...I CHOOSE THIS ONE, SIR.
THIS ONE?
KYU (SQUEEZE)
HERE.
AH-HA-HA! CONGRATS!
SAY AHHH! ♡
AHHH, SIR!
DO YOU LIKE IT?
IT'S DELICIOUS, SIR. MEW.
KORO KORO (ROLL)

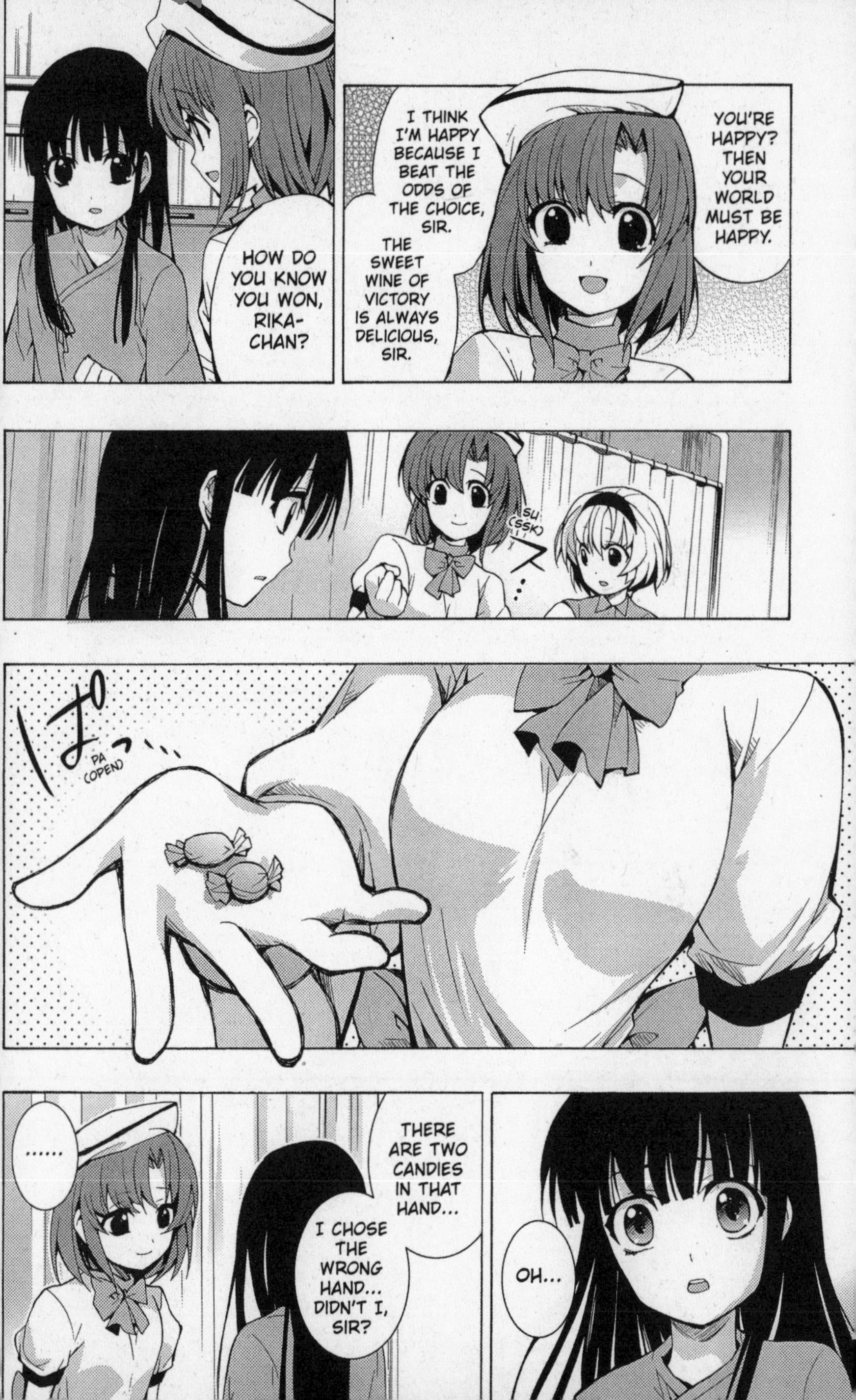
YOU'RE HAPPY? THEN YOUR WORLD MUST BE HAPPY.
I THINK I'M HAPPY BECAUSE I BEAT THE ODDS OF THE CHOICE, SIR.
THE SWEET WINE OF VICTORY IS ALWAYS DELICIOUS, SIR.
HOW DO YOU KNOW YOU WON, RIKA-CHAN?
SU (SSK)
ぱっ
PA (OPEN)
OH...
THERE ARE TWO CANDIES IN THAT HAND...
I CHOSE THE WRONG HAND... DIDN'T I, SIR?
......

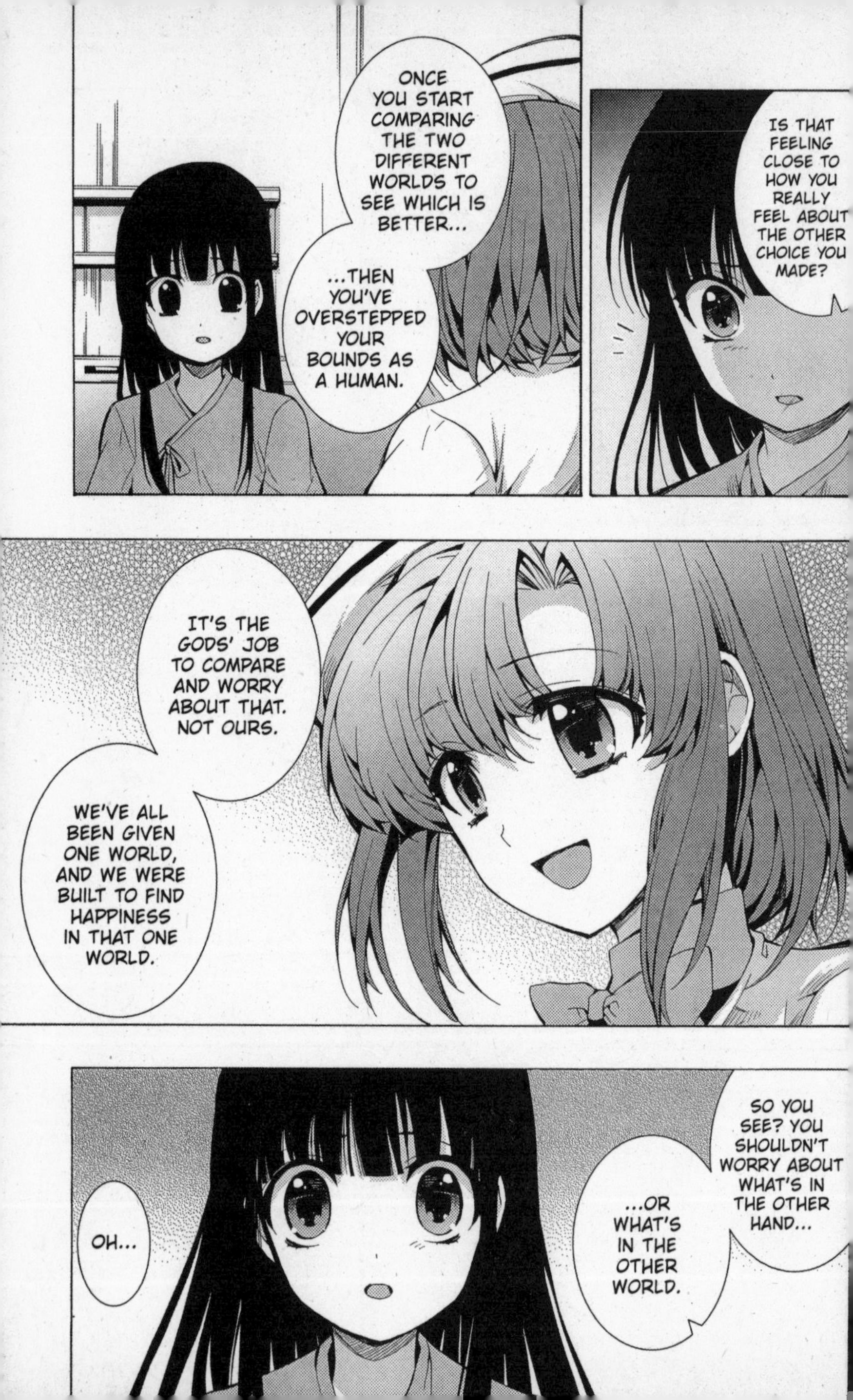
IS THAT FEELING CLOSE TO HOW YOU REALLY FEEL ABOUT THE OTHER CHOICE YOU MADE?
ONCE YOU START COMPARING THE TWO DIFFERENT WORLDS TO SEE WHICH IS BETTER...
...THEN YOU'VE OVERSTEPPED YOUR BOUNDS AS A HUMAN.
IT'S THE GODS' JOB TO COMPARE AND WORRY ABOUT THAT. NOT OURS.
WE'VE ALL BEEN GIVEN ONE WORLD, AND WE WERE BUILT TO FIND HAPPINESS IN THAT ONE WORLD.
SO YOU SEE? YOU SHOULDN'T WORRY ABOUT WHAT'S IN THE OTHER HAND...
...OR WHAT'S IN THE OTHER WORLD.
OH...

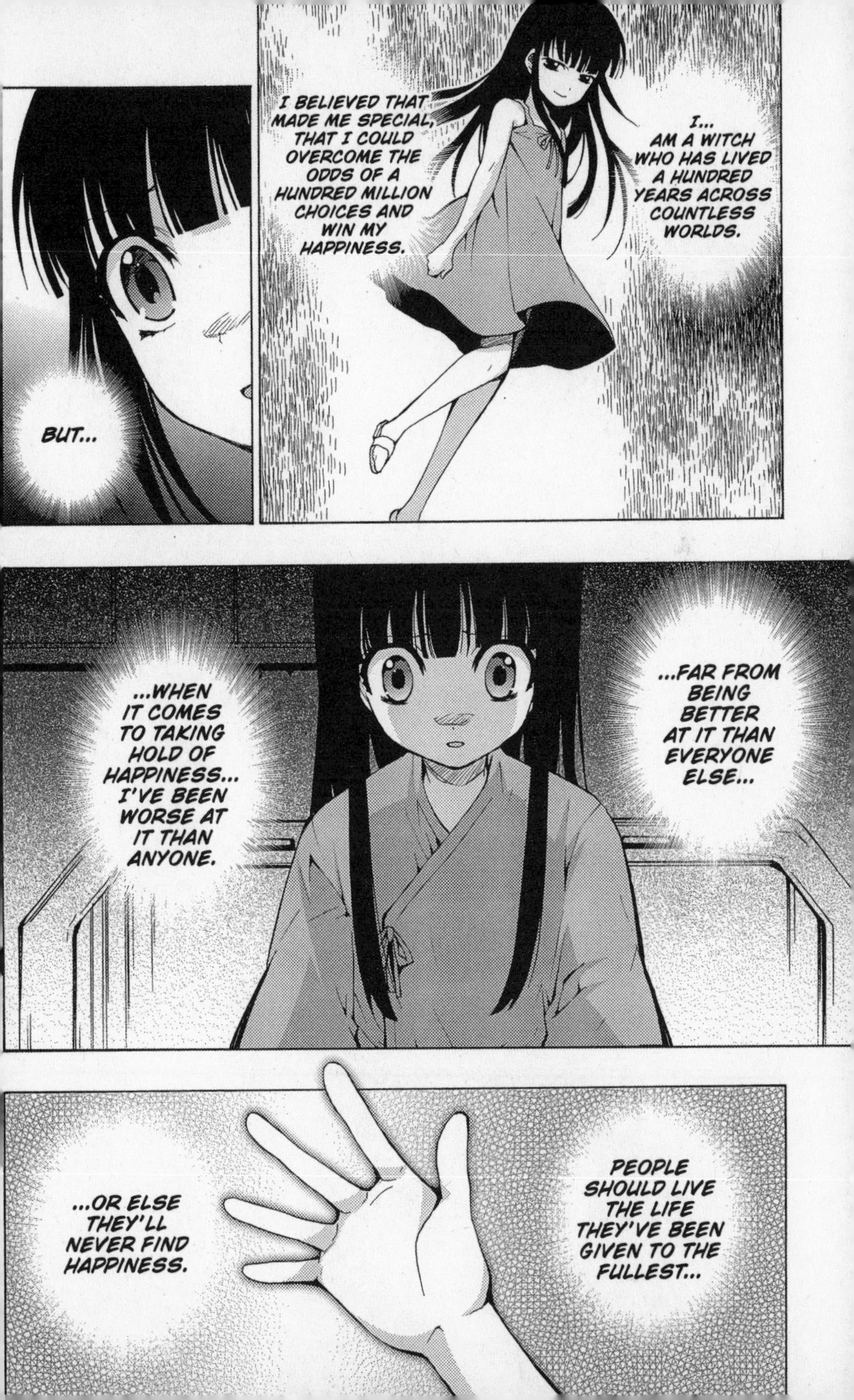
I... AM A WITCH WHO HAS LIVED A HUNDRED YEARS ACROSS COUNTLESS WORLDS.
I BELIEVED THAT MADE ME SPECIAL, THAT I COULD OVERCOME THE ODDS OF A HUNDRED MILLION CHOICES AND WIN MY HAPPINESS.
BUT...
...FAR FROM BEING BETTER AT IT THAN EVERYONE ELSE...
...WHEN IT COMES TO TAKING HOLD OF HAPPINESS... I'VE BEEN WORSE AT IT THAN ANYONE.
PEOPLE SHOULD LIVE THE LIFE THEY'VE BEEN GIVEN TO THE FULLEST...
...OR ELSE THEY'LL NEVER FIND HAPPINESS.

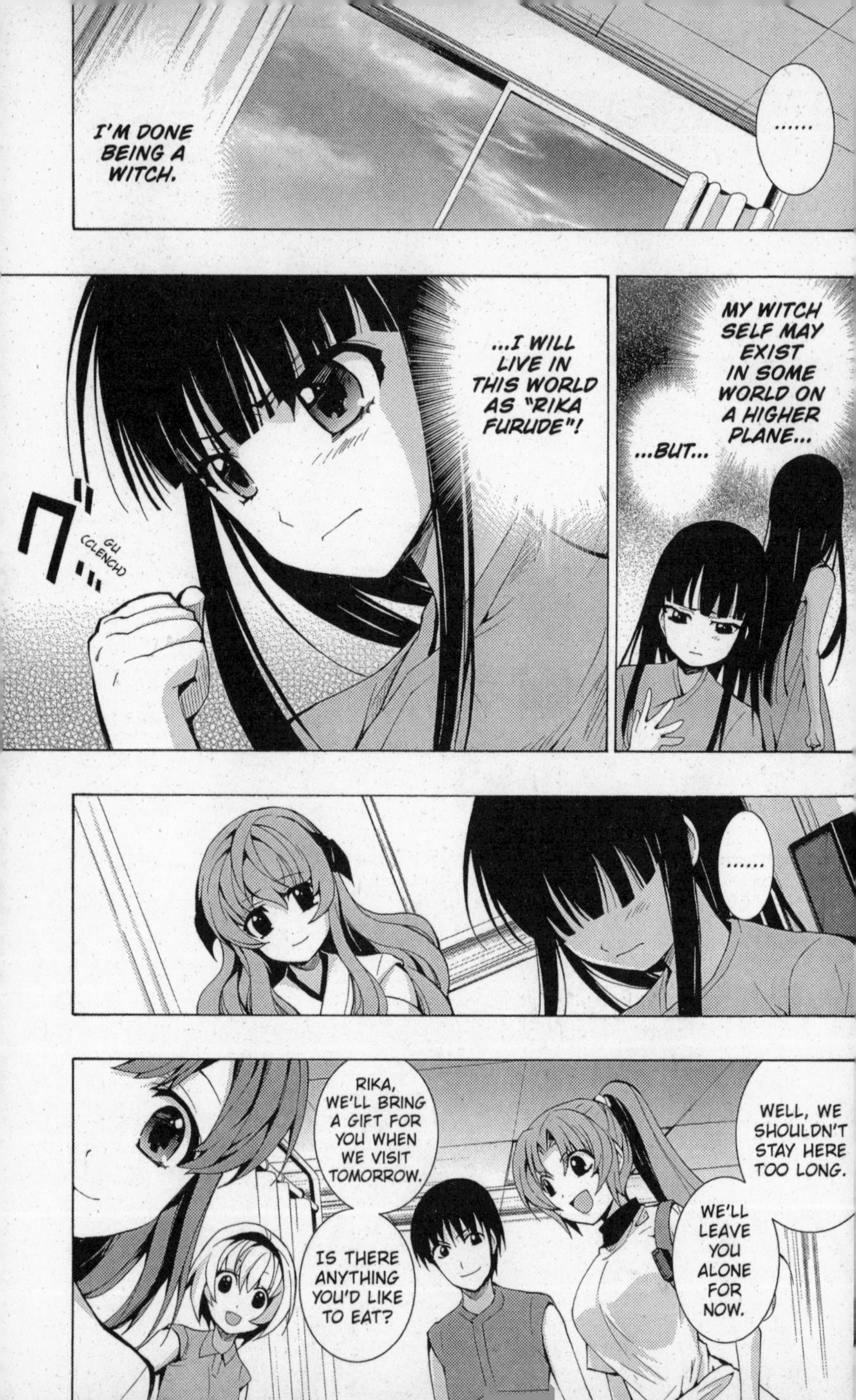
......
I'M DONE BEING A WITCH.
MY WITCH SELF MAY EXIST IN SOME WORLD ON A HIGHER PLANE...
...BUT...
...I WILL LIVE IN THIS WORLD AS "RIKA FURUDE"!
GU (CLENCH)
......
WELL, WE SHOULDN'T STAY HERE TOO LONG.
WE'LL LEAVE YOU ALONE FOR NOW.
RIKA, WE'LL BRING A GIFT FOR YOU WHEN WE VISIT TOMORROW.
IS THERE ANYTHING YOU'D LIKE TO EAT?

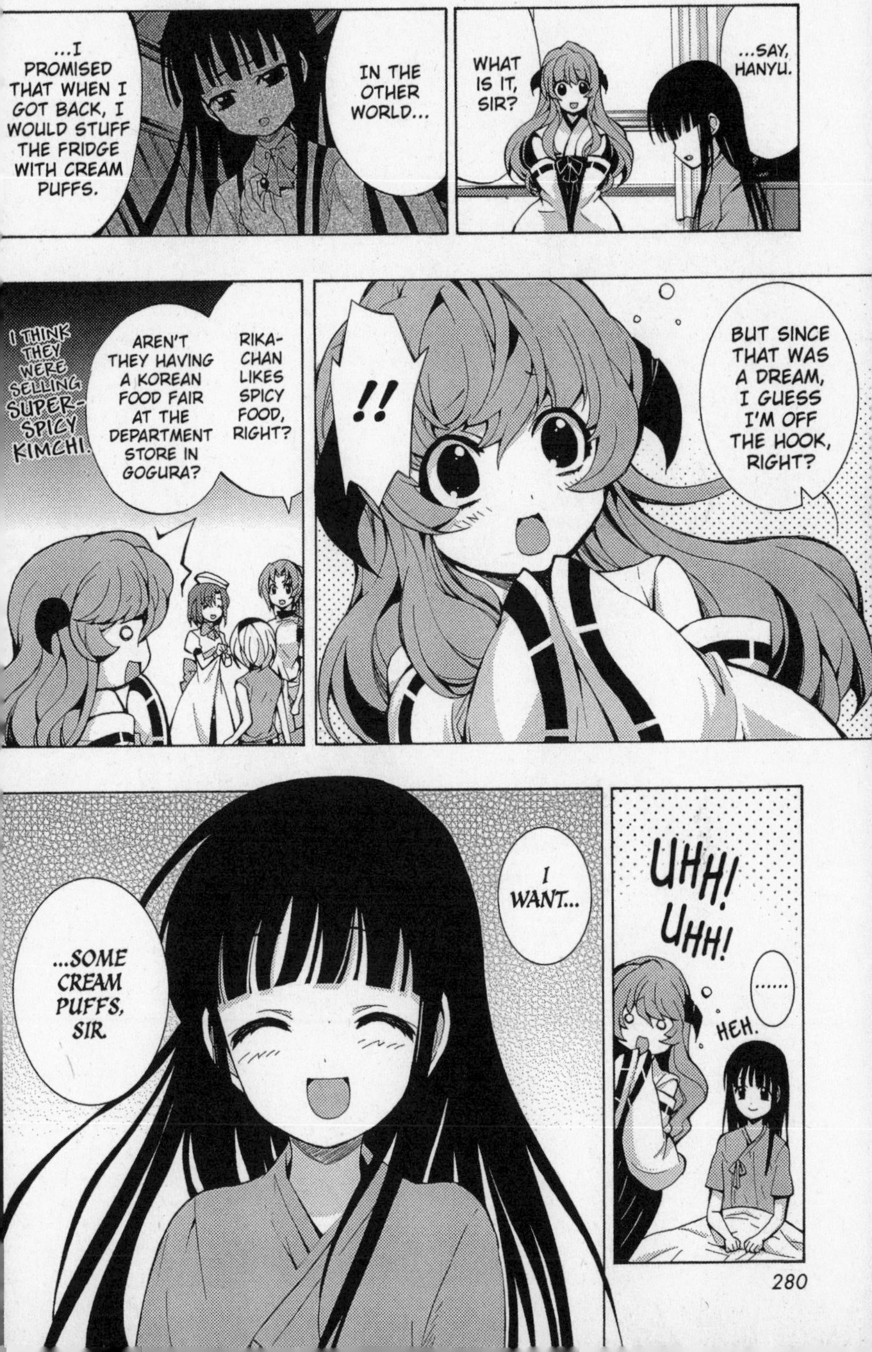
...SAY, HANYU.
WHAT IS IT, SIR?
IN THE OTHER WORLD...
...I PROMISED THAT WHEN I GOT BACK, I WOULD STUFF THE FRIDGE WITH CREAM PUFFS.
BUT SINCE THAT WAS A DREAM, I GUESS I'M OFF THE HOOK, RIGHT?
!!
RIKA-CHAN LIKES SPICY FOOD, RIGHT?
AREN'T THEY HAVING A KOREAN FOOD FAIR AT THE DEPARTMENT STORE IN GOGURA?
I THINK THEY WERE SELLING SUPER-SPICY KIMCHI.
UHH! UHH!
......
HEH.
I WANT...
...SOME CREAM PUFFS, SIR.

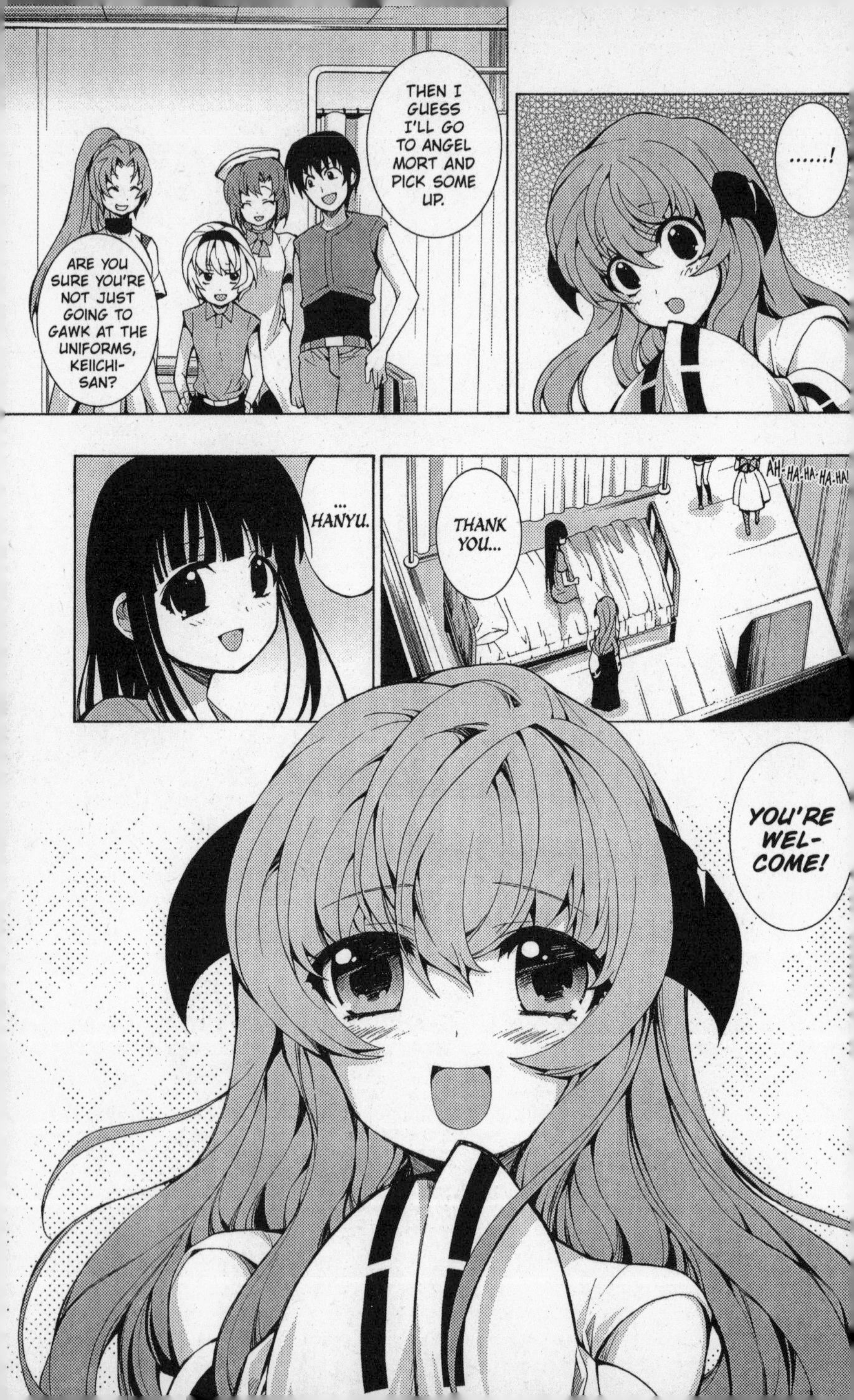
......!
THEN I GUESS I'LL GO TO ANGEL MORT AND PICK SOME UP.
ARE YOU SURE YOU'RE NOT JUST GOING TO GAWK AT THE UNIFORMS, KEIICHI-SAN?
AH-HA-HA-HA-HA!
THANK YOU...
... HANYU.
YOU'RE WEL-COME!

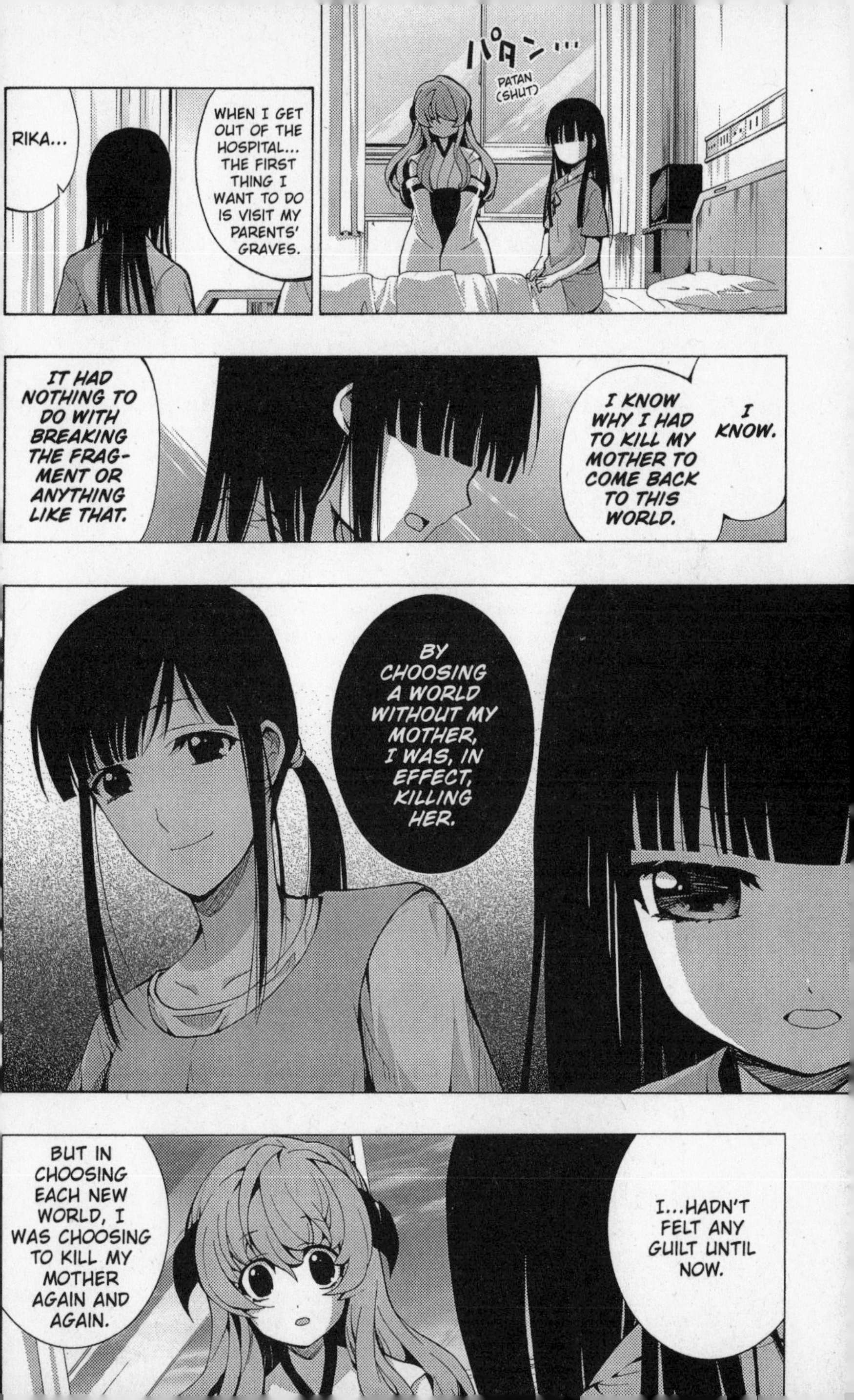
パタン…
PATAN (SHUT)
WHEN I GET OUT OF THE HOSPITAL... THE FIRST THING I WANT TO DO IS VISIT MY PARENTS' GRAVES.
RIKA...
I KNOW.
I KNOW WHY I HAD TO KILL MY MOTHER TO COME BACK TO THIS WORLD.
IT HAD NOTHING TO DO WITH BREAKING THE FRAG-MENT OR ANYTHING LIKE THAT.
BY CHOOSING A WORLD WITHOUT MY MOTHER, I WAS, IN EFFECT, KILLING HER.
I...HADN'T FELT ANY GUILT UNTIL NOW.
BUT IN CHOOSING EACH NEW WORLD, I WAS CHOOSING TO KILL MY MOTHER AGAIN AND AGAIN.

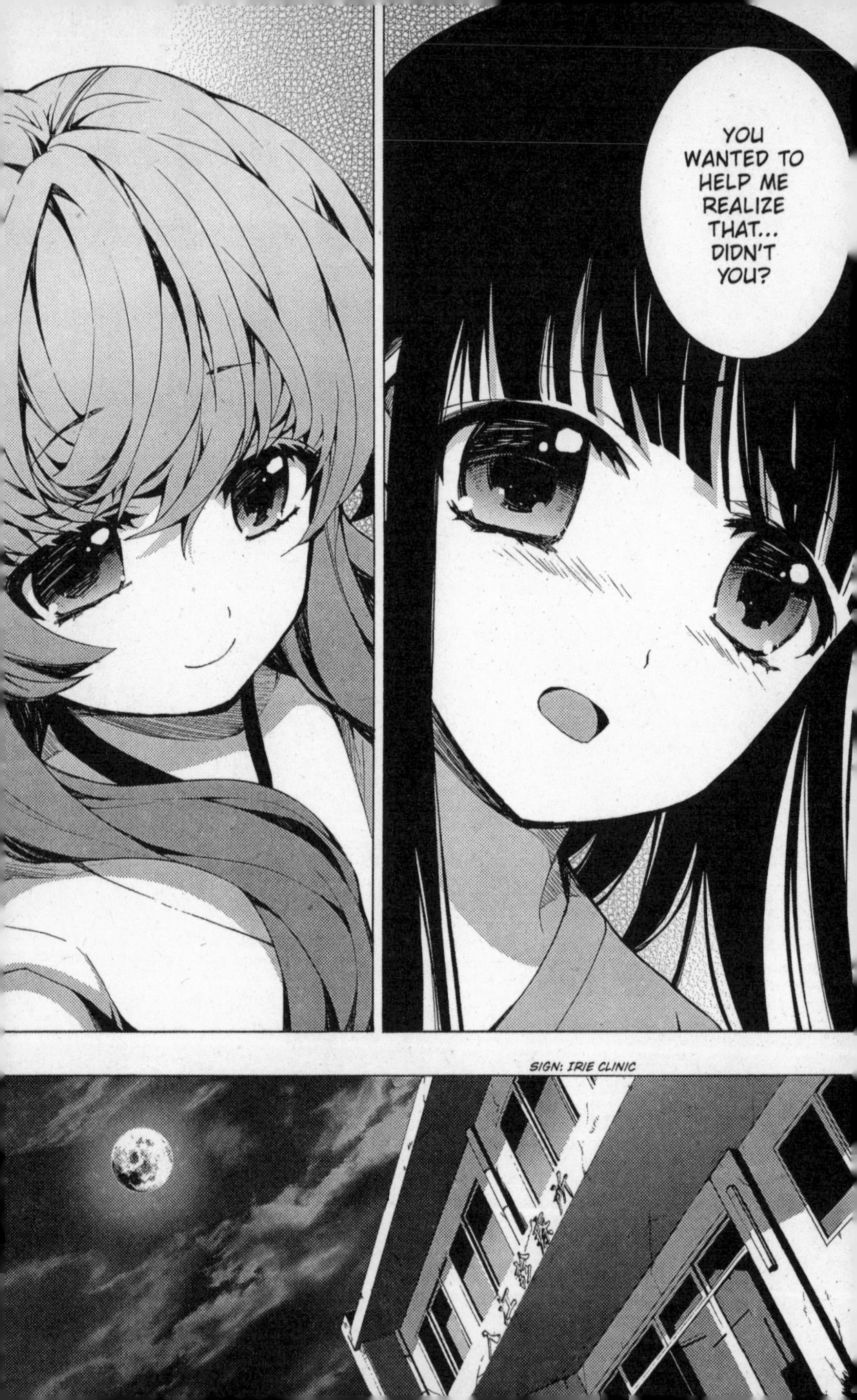
YOU WANTED TO HELP ME REALIZE THAT... DIDN'T YOU?
SIGN: IRIE CLINIC

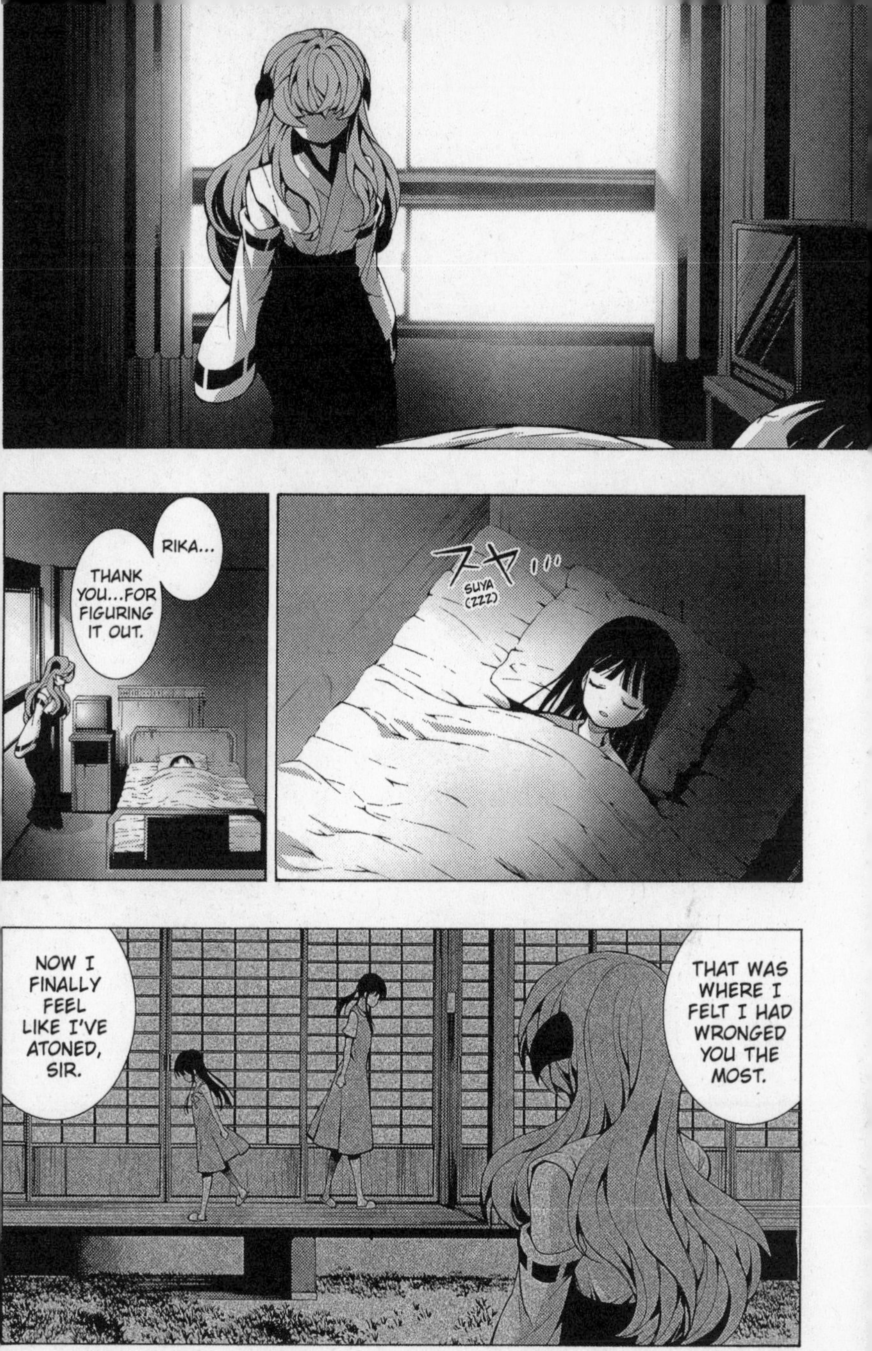
スヤ
SUYA (ZZZ)
RIKA...
THANK YOU...FOR FIGURING IT OUT.
THAT WAS WHERE I FELT I HAD WRONGED YOU THE MOST.
NOW I FINALLY FEEL LIKE I'VE ATONED, SIR.

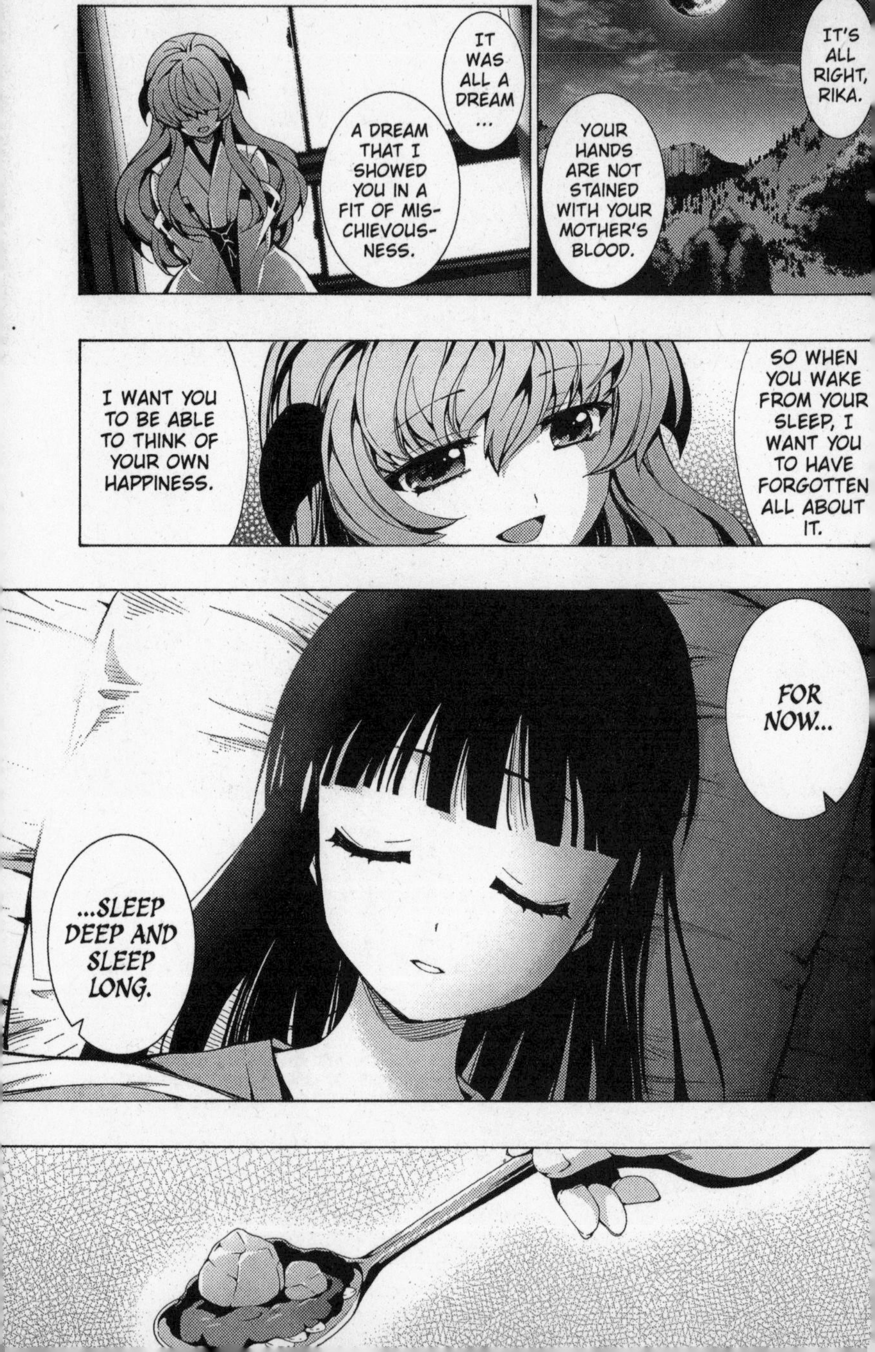
IT'S ALL RIGHT, RIKA.
YOUR HANDS ARE NOT STAINED WITH YOUR MOTHER'S BLOOD.
IT WAS ALL A DREAM...
A DREAM THAT I SHOWED YOU IN A FIT OF MIS-CHIEVOUS-NESS.
SO WHEN YOU WAKE FROM YOUR SLEEP, I WANT YOU TO HAVE FORGOTTEN ALL ABOUT IT.
I WANT YOU TO BE ABLE TO THINK OF YOUR OWN HAPPINESS.
FOR NOW...
...SLEEP DEEP AND SLEEP LONG.

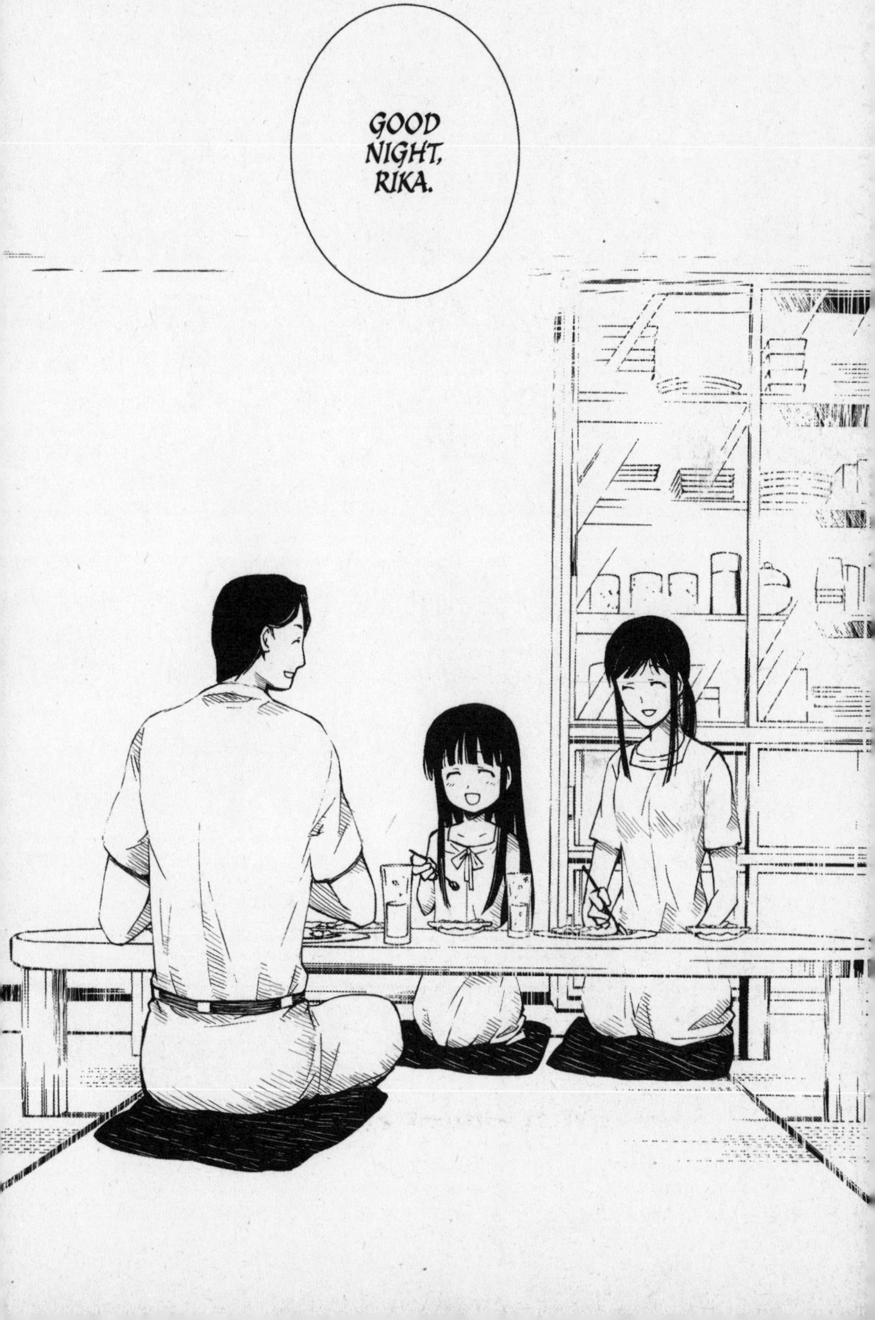
GOOD NIGHT, RIKA.

Higurashi
WHEN THEY CRY

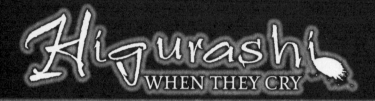

DICE KILLING ARC

FIN

HIGURASHI WHEN THEY CRY

07th Expansion presents. Welcome to Higurashi.
WHEN THEY CRY.

ABOUT THE "DICE KILLING ARC": THE POWER OF MEANINGFUL DAILY COMMUNICATION

ORIGINAL STORY, SUPERVISOR: RYUKISHI07

HELLO, I'M RYUKISHI07.

LOOKING BACK, I'M SUDDENLY STRUCK BY THE REALIZATION THAT IT'S BEEN FIVE YEARS SINCE WE BEGAN—THIS HAS BEEN A VERY LONG STORY. FOR THE TIME BEING, *HIGURASHI WHEN THEY CRY* REACHES ITS CONCLUSION IN THE "DICE KILLING ARC." FIRST, TO ALL OF YOU WHO READ THE MANGA, TO EVERYONE INVOLVED IN THIS PROJECT, AND SUZURAGI-SENSEI—THANK YOU VERY, VERY MUCH.

BACK WHEN I WAS WRITING THE SCRIPT FOR THE ORIGINAL, I DIDN'T HAVE ANY EXPERIENCE WRITING NOVELS. I CAME UP AGAINST MANY CHALLENGES, AND AT ONE POINT, I EVEN HAD TO STOP WRITING ALTOGETHER. NEVERTHELESS, THOUGH IMPERFECT, THE SERIES MADE IT FAR ENOUGH TO BE TURNED INTO A MANGA. I OWE IT ALL TO EVERYONE WHO SUPPORTED ME AND THE HELP OF MY FRIENDS. AS FOR THE "DICE KILLING ARC," ITS THEME IS DAILY COMMUNICATION.

I PRAY WITH ALL MY HEART THAT WE ALL RECOGNIZE THE OVERWHELMING SUPPORT WE GET FROM THE PEOPLE AROUND US AND THAT WE WILL TREASURE AND CULTIVATE THE POWER THAT COMES FROM THAT.

THANK YOU FOR STAYING WITH US ALL THIS TIME. I BELIEVE THE FUTURE THAT RIKA CHOSE FOR HERSELF WILL SURELY BE A HAPPY ONE. I THINK THAT WE ONLY LIVE ONCE, AND WE FACE LOTS OF BIG CHOICES AND DIFFICULT DECISIONS ON THE WAY. IF WE DON'T ALLOW OURSELVES TO BE CARRIED AWAY BY OUR SURROUNDINGS AND CHOOSE OUR OWN PATH—ONE THAT SUITS OUR NEEDS—THEN THAT IS THE RIGHT ANSWER. WE'VE EACH BEEN GIVEN OUR OWN LIFE, AND I WANT TO LIVE MINE TO THE FULLEST.

I AM TRULY GRATEFUL FOR THE BLESSING OF BEING ALLOWED TO WORK ON *HIGURASHI* FROM THE "ABDUCTED BY DEMONS ARC" TO THE "DICE KILLING ARC." IT WAS A LOT OF FUN DRAWING ALL THE *HIGURASHI* CHARACTERS AND THEIR MYRIAD EMOTIONS. THANK YOU TO EVERYONE WHO SUPPORTED ME, TO MY EDITOR WHO HELPED ME WITH THE WRITING, AND TO MY STAFF. WITH ALL OF YOUR HELP, WE MADE IT TO THE END. I HOPE THAT THIS ARC, WHERE RIKA-CHAN FIGHTS HER OWN BATTLE, WILL REACH BT-SAN TOO.

BT-SAN ONCE SAID TO ME THAT IT'S IMPORTANT TO KEEP RUNNING AT 70 PERCENT POWER. I DON'T THINK I'LL EVER FORGET THAT. ALTHOUGH SOMETIMES YOU HAVE TO GO AT 120 PERCENT TO TAKE HOLD OF AN OPPORTUNITY, AND YOU CAN CHOOSE TO KEEP UP THAT PACE. THERE ARE MANY DIFFERENT PATHS AND MANY DIFFERENT CHOICES.

I'M ROOTING FOR ALL OF YOU, THAT YOU WILL CREATE GREAT FUTURES. AND I'M LOOKING FORWARD TO 07TH EXPANSIONS'S FUTURE WORKS. I EXPECT BRILLIANT STORIES FILLED WITH EMOTION, SUSPENSE, AND TERROR—ALL KINDS OF THINGS TO SHAKE UP PEOPLE'S HEARTS.
IT'S A BLESSING THAT I CAN LOOK FORWARD TO SOMETHING TWICE A YEAR, EVERY YEAR. BUT PLEASE TAKE CARE OF YOUR HEALTH.

THANK YOU FOR EVERYTHING. IF WE GET A CHANCE TO MEET AGAIN, I LOOK FORWARD TO IT!

KARIN SUZURAGI.

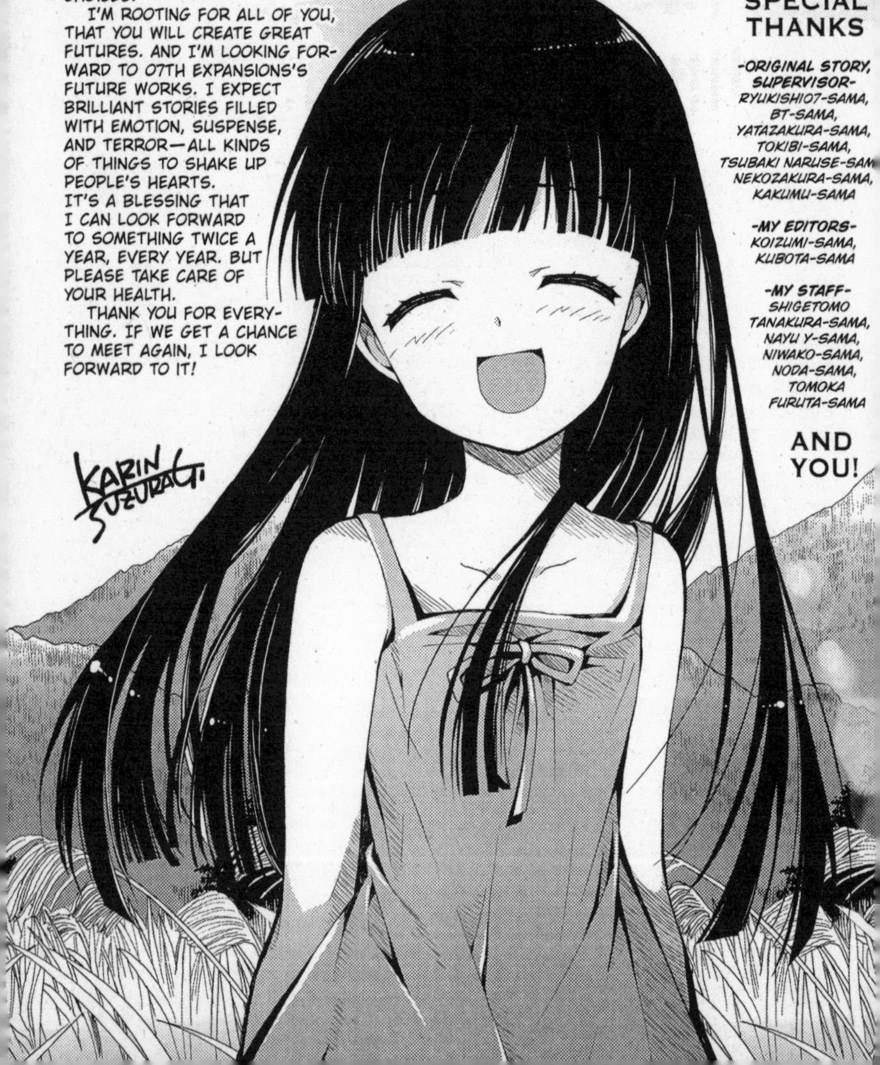

SPECIAL THANKS

-ORIGINAL STORY, SUPERVISOR-
RYUKISHI07-SAMA,
BT-SAMA,
YATAZAKURA-SAMA,
TOKIBI-SAMA,
TSUBAKI NARUSE-SAMA
NEKOZAKURA-SAMA,
KAKUMU-SAMA

-MY EDITORS-
KOIZUMI-SAMA,
KUBOTA-SAMA

-MY STAFF-
SHIGETOMO TANAKURA-SAMA,
NAYU Y-SAMA,
NIWAKO-SAMA,
NODA-SAMA,
TOMOKA FURUTA-SAMA

AND YOU!

HIGURASHI
WHEN THEY CRY

DICE KILLING ARC

RYUKISHI07
KARIN SUZURAGI

Translation: Alethea Nibley and Athena Nibley

Lettering: Abigail Blackman and Stephanie Lee

Higurashi WHEN THEY CRY Dice Killing Arc
© RYUKISHI07 / 07th Expansion © 2011 Karin Suzuragi / SQUARE ENIX CO., LTD. First published in Japan in 2011 by SQUARE ENIX CO., LTD. English translation rights arranged with SQUARE ENIX CO., LTD. and Hachette Book Group through Tuttle-Mori Agency, Inc.

Translation © 2014 by SQUARE ENIX CO., LTD.

Yen Press
Hachette Book Group
1290 Avenue of the Americas
New York, NY 10104

www.hachettebookgroup.com
www.yenpress.com

Yen Press is an imprint of Hachette Book Group, Inc. The Yen Press name and logo are trademarks of Hachette Book Group, Inc.

First Yen Press Edition: November 2014

ISBN: 978-0-316-33649-9

10 9 8 7 6 5 4 3 2 1

BVG

Printed in the United States of America